OXFORD INTERNATIONAL ARBITR᷉ᵗ

Series Editor: LOUKAS MISTE

Professor of Transnational Commercial Law anₐ
Queen Mary, University of London

INTERNATIONAL INVESTMENT ARBITRATION

Substantive Principles

OXFORD INTERNATIONAL ARBITRATION SERIES

Series Editor: Loukas Mistelis

The aim of this new series is to publish works of quality and originality on
specific issues in international commercial and investment arbitration.
The series aims to provide a forum for the exploration of important emerging
issues and those issues not adequately dealt with in leading works. It should
be of interest to both practitioners and scholarly lawyers.

Forthcoming Titles

Chinese Investment Treaties
Wenhua Shan and Norah Gallagher

Compensation and Damages in International Investment Law
Irmgard Marboe

INTERNATIONAL INVESTMENT ARBITRATION

Substantive Principles

Campbell McLachlan QC

LL.B. (Well.), Ph.D. (London),
Dip.(c. l.) (Hag. Acad. Int'l. Law)
Professor of Law, Victoria University of Wellington
Barrister (N.Z.), Bankside Chambers (Auckland), Essex Court Chambers (London)

Laurence Shore

B.A. (North Carolina), M.A., Ph.D. (Johns Hopkins), J.D. (Emory)
Attorney (Wash., D.C., Virginia), Solicitor (England and Wales),
Partner, Gibson, Dunn & Crutcher LLP
Visiting Professor, School of International Arbitration,
Queen Mary, University of London

Matthew Weiniger

M.A. (Cantab)
Solicitor, Partner, Herbert Smith LLP
Visiting Professorial Fellow, Centre for Commercial
Law Studies, Queen Mary, University of London

OXFORD
UNIVERSITY PRESS

OXFORD
UNIVERSITY PRESS

Great Clarendon Street, Oxford OX2 6DP

Oxford University Press is a department of the University of Oxford.
It furthers the University's objective of excellence in research, scholarship,
and education by publishing worldwide in

Oxford New York

Auckland Cape Town Dar es Salaam Hong Kong Karachi
Kuala Lumpur Madrid Melbourne Mexico City Nairobi
New Delhi Shanghai Taipei Toronto

With offices in

Argentina Austria Brazil Chile Czech Republic France Greece
Guatemala Hungary Italy Japan Poland Portugal Singapore
South Korea Switzerland Thailand Turkey Ukraine Vietnam

Oxford is a registered trade mark of Oxford University Press
in the UK and in certain other countries

Published in the United States
by Oxford University Press Inc., New York

British Library Cataloguing in Publication Data

Data available

Library of Congress Cataloging in Publication Data

Data available

Typeset by Newgen Imaging Systems (P) Ltd, Chennai, India
Printed in Great Britain
on acid-free paper by
CPI Antony Rowe, Chippenham, Wiltshire

ISBN 978–0–19–928664–5 (Hbk.)
ISBN 978–0–19–955751–6 (Pbk.)

3 5 7 9 10 8 6 4 2

PREFACE TO THE PAPERBACK EDITION

> . . . doth it not appear to be base, and a great sign of want of education, to be obliged to observe justice pronounced upon us by others, as our masters and judges, and to have no sense of it in ourselves?

Plato *The Republic* Book III[1]

Delivering its recent judgment in the *Diallo Case*, the International Court of Justice observed that:

> . . . in contemporary international law, the protection of the rights of companies and the rights of their shareholders, and the settlement of the associated disputes, are essentially governed by bilateral or multilateral agreements . . .[2]

In writing this book, we set out to restate the general principles of international law found in the numerous investment treaties in force around the world today in light of the jurisprudence of arbitral tribunals. The field of foreign investment has always attracted considerable political controversy, and continues to do so. The hope of the authors was that a careful analysis of the law in this field would assist the many persons who have the responsibility to consider and apply it: whether as legal advisors to sovereign states and corporations; arbitrators; scholars; or legal policy-makers.

We are most grateful for the exceptionally warm reception which greeted the publication of the first hard-bound edition of the book in July 2007, and for the many kind comments from scholars and practitioners received since then. We thank in particular Jan Paulsson, Professor Christopher Greenwood CMG QC, and Professor Martin Hunter, all eminent experts in international law and arbitration, for lending their names in support of the work. We understand that the book has been cited in many briefs, and arbitral tribunals also appear to have found the work useful in their deliberations.[3]

But there is another equally important group, which has found the book indispensable, but for whom the handsomely-produced hard-bound edition proved

---

[1] Plato *The Republic* trans H Spens (1763) Book III, 115.

[2] *Case concerning Ahmadou Sadio Diallo (Guinea v Congo)* Preliminary Objections, ICJ General List No 103, 24 May 2007, para 88 (a diplomatic protection claim).

[3] See eg *Sempra Energy Int'l v Argentina* (Award) ICSID Case No ARB/02/16 (ICSID, 2007, Orrego Vicuña P, Lalonde & Rico) para 284; *Desert Line Projects LLC v Yemen* (Award) ICSID Case No ARB/05/17 (ICSID, 2008, Tercier P, Paulsson & El-Kosheri) para 113.

out of reach. We refer of course to the many students, especially at Masters and Post-graduate level, who are now studying international investment arbitration.

We were each conscious of this as a result of teaching courses, and supervising research, in this field. But we also received considerable support for the publication of a student edition from many other academics teaching in this field. We would like to thank in particular Professor Loukas Mistelis (Queen Mary, University of London) and General Editor of the Oxford International Arbitration Series, who, together with the other eminent members of the Editorial Board for the series, supported this idea. We also warmly thank Professor Susan Karamanian (George Washington University Law School), who graciously hosted a Symposium at her law school in October 2007 which addressed the topic 'Is there a new Common Law of Investment Arbitration?' We also acknowledge Professor Ko-Yung Tung (Yale) and Professor Robert Howse (Michigan & NYU), who kindly added their support to the proposal for a student edition. Finally, we thank our publishers, Oxford University Press, and especially our editor, Catherine Redmond, for their continuing support for the book and for the idea of a paperback edition.

Since the book was first published in July 2007, each of our careers has continued to develop in different ways. Campbell McLachlan was nominated by New Zealand to replace the late Lord Cooke of Thorndon on the ICSID Panel of Arbitrators, and has accepted his first appointment to an annulment committee. Laurence Shore has returned to his native America, and has joined the partnership of Gibson, Dunn & Crutcher, practising international arbitration from the firm's New York office. Matthew Weiniger continues to flourish in the practice of international arbitration at Herbert Smith in London—the firm where we first met, and to which we all owe so much.

But irrespective of our dispersal across the globe, our friendship and our collaboration in this work continues to bring us together. The rich harvest of arbitral awards, which has carried on unabated since our book was first published, brings with it the prospect that a second edition will be necessary at some stage.

In the meantime, we are delighted that the Press has agreed to make our work available to a wider audience, and in particular to the students of today, who will become the scholars and practitioners of tomorrow.

Professor Campbell McLachlan QC
Wellington

Laurence Shore
New York

Matthew Weiniger
London

1 May 2008

GENERAL EDITOR'S PREFACE

Only about twenty-five years ago, most lawyers saw international arbitration as a branch of another legal discipline. Arbitration was either connected with civil procedure, a subject tied to and regulated by national procedural codes and mainly taught and practised by proceduralists, or seen as a subject associated with private international law and the so-called *droit des affaires internationales* (international business law). There was also public international arbitration, which was somehow a different beast. An additional problem related to the fact that arbitration was treated as an esoteric subject, practised by a few eccentric and cosmopolitan legal practitioners with an international flair (which often meant that they were fluent in a second language or that they had studied abroad). While arbitration was practised by bigger law firms with strong international litigation practices, there were hardly any specialist arbitration practice groups or departments in most major law firms.

In the last twenty years there has been greater acceptance of, and resort to, arbitration for international disputes of all kinds and under all systems. While it remains difficult or even impossible to determine exact numbers, the figures given by the major institutions suggest continuous growth in numbers. International arbitration is nowadays well established at the junction of national, international and conflicts laws, public and private law and substantive and procedural law. Arbitration has become a more prominent area of legal practice and a distinct academic subject in many universities, typically at post-graduate level.

This new monograph series is dedicated to specific issues in international arbitration law and practice. It gives authors the opportunity and the challenge of a more in-depth treatment than is possible in leading generalist works. It also provides an international forum for the profound exploration of important practical and theoretical matters. It is hoped that it will thereby further the development of arbitration as an academic discipline and as an area of international legal practice.

This first volume in the series addresses the investment treaty arbitration phenomenon.

While there have been disputes between investors and States for centuries, modern international investment arbitration, based on treaty rather than on diplomatic protection, is a relatively new phenomenon. In 1970, the International Court of Justice noted, in delivering its judgment in *Barcelona Traction*, the surprisingly slow evolution of investment law.[1] Since 1970 we have had the firm establishment of the International Centre for the Settlement of Investment Disputes (ICSID), one of the outcomes of the 1965 Washington Convention. Between 1965 and 1995, ICSID handled on average one case per year. Since 1995 up to 30 cases per year have been registered, with a trend in recent years of about two new cases per month. Since 1959, when we witnessed the birth of new Bilateral Investment Treaties (BITs), we have some 2,500 BITs involving some 180 countries. The main characteristic of modern BITs is the widespread provision for the direct invocation of claims by investors against the host State in (ad hoc, ICSID, or other institutional) arbitration. The first BIT arbitration was registered with ICSID in 1987 and since then the growth has been exponential, with more than 200 registered cases so far.

This development stimulated a great deal of interest in investment arbitration both as an academic subject (half-sister of public international law and international commercial arbitration) and as an area of practice. However, the rapid evolution of the field over the last ten years has led to a situation in which significant parts of the literature are designed to be informative rather than analytical, and seek to cover both practical matters, eg procedure or remedies, and substantive issues, eg scope of expropriation, fair and equitable treatment and the like.

The authors of this book assumed a very difficult task and succeeded in its delivery. In short, the authors aim to provide an analysis of those common features of multilateral and bilateral investment treaties which may form the legal basis of an arbitration claim, in the light of reported jurisprudence. To achieve this aim, the book explores both the fields of arbitration and public international law. In this respect the book has three parts: (I) Overview—highlighting the basic features of investment treaties, and an insightful appraisal of four fundamental issues in the settlement of investment disputes via arbitration, ie dispute settlement provisions, transparency, the legal nature of the rights at issue, and interpretation of BITs; (II) Ambit of Protection, which addresses three main theoretical and practical problems: parallel proceedings, the nationality condition, and the notion of investment; and (III) Substantive Rights, ie treatment of investors, expropriation and compensation.

The book succeeds in distilling substantive principles pertaining to investment treaty arbitration. This is the result of profound critical analysis of the awards and treaties themselves, which in turn demonstrates the relevance of general public international law. The authors argue for the emergence of, and contribute to the creation of, a common law of investment protection. In so doing, they seek to strike a balance between the rights of investors and host States.

---

[1] *Case concerning the Barcelona Traction, Light & Power Co Ltd (Belgium v Spain) Second Phase* [1970] ICJ Rep 3, 46–7.

One of the main assets of the book is the authors themselves. All three are academically well versed in both international commercial and investment arbitration as well as public international law. They also have an enviable practical experience putting them at the forefront of the area. Their book is a measured balance of both the academic and the practical. It is informed but not guided by practice, and its conclusions are of the highest academic merit.

I am personally delighted with this book, the first one of the new Oxford International Arbitration Series.

Loukas Mistelis
New York, 16 February 2007

ACKNOWLEDGEMENTS

The genesis of the idea for this book grew out of our shared experiences, practising together in the fields of International Arbitration and Public International Law, and teaching and researching the law applicable in investment arbitration. It became apparent to us that there was no modern attempt to state the substantive principles enshrined in investment treaties, which have been the subject of so much consideration in recent arbitral awards, in the light of the general principles of international law. This book is our attempt to fill that gap.

Special thanks go to the partners in Herbert Smith (and particularly Charles Plant and Julian D M Lew) for their early encouragement to pursue the project, and for huge support in so many ways in completing it. Thanks go also to our publishers (and particularly our editors Chris Rycroft and Catherine Redmond), who saw the potential of our vision, and provided highly professional assistance in seeing it through. We received superb assistance in referencing and checking from Christopher Reeves in London and Joanna Campbell (and Elizabeth-Jane Ryan) in Wellington, and many helpful comments from Norah Gallagher. Our thanks go also to our external reviewers for their many invaluable insights. Many of them are anonymous, but we are able to mention especially and thank Professor Jack Coe, who took much time and trouble in commenting on earlier drafts of chapters, demonstrating his own deep knowledge of the field. Any errors are of course the sole responsibility of the authors.

We, and Oxford University Press, also express our thanks to the NAFTA Secretariat, the Energy Charter Treaty Secretariat, the ASEAN Secretariat, the Foreign and Commonwealth Office of the Government of the United Kingdom, the Office of the United States Trade Representative, the German Federal Foreign Office, The Netherlands Ministry of Foreign Affairs, the French Ministry of Foreign Affairs, ICSID and the World Bank for granting permission to reproduce the documents used as appendices. All efforts were made to contact the Government of Sri Lanka to gain permission.

This book has been a collaborative exercise in planning and execution, and the three authors take joint responsibility for the whole. Research and writing of the chapters was distributed as follows: Chapters 1, 4 & 7, McLachlan; Chapters 5 & 8, Shore; Chapters 2, 3, 6 & 9, Weiniger. If, in the process of writing this book, we have succeeded in some small measure in mapping out the terrain of investment treaty law, the game will have been worth the candle.

The law is stated as at 1 September 2006.

Campbell McLachlan
Laurence Shore
Matthew Weiniger
5 February 2007

CONTENTS—SUMMARY

CONTENTS

II AMBIT OF PROTECTION

4. Parallel Proceedings

TABLE OF CASES

This Table contains an alphabetical listing of all arbitral awards and other arbitral and judicial decisions cited in the text. Investment arbitral awards are cited to a print source, where this was available when the book went to press. The principal print sources for such awards are: *ICSID Reports* (ICSID Rep), *ICSID Review – Foreign Investment Law Journal* (ICSID Rev-FILJ) and *International Legal Materials* (ILM). Unreported awards are cited by neutral citation (giving a docket number, where one has been used). The majority of such awards can be accessed electronically on one or more of the following websites: <http://www.worldbank.org/icsid> (the official ICSID website); <http://ita.law.uvic.ca> and, in the case of claims under NAFTA, <http://www.naftaclaims.com>.

TABLE OF TREATIES

This table lists all treaties, together with draft and model form treaties, ILC draft articles and other international instruments, cited in the text. It includes references to where these treaties may be found in the official treaty series or in *International Legal Materials*. Many investment treaties are collected by UNCTAD (the United Nations Commission on Trade and Development) and published in print form in *International Investment Instruments: A Compendium (III Compendium)*, and online at <http://www.unctad.org>. The *III Compendium* (available in print and online) provides the best source for Model BITs.

*References in **bold** are to material reproduced in the text.*

MULTILATERAL TREATIES AND OTHER INTERNATIONAL INSTRUMENTS

BILATERAL TREATIES

LIST OF ABBREVIATIONS

General

ACP	African, Caribbean and Pacific Group of States
ASEAN	Association of South East Asian Nations
BITs	bilateral investment treaties
DCF	discounted cash flow
ECJ	European Court of Justice
ECT	Energy Charter Treaty
FCN treaties	bilateral treaties of Friendship, Commerce and Navigation
FTC	Free Trade Commission (NAFTA)
GATT	General Agreement on Tariffs and Trade
ICCA	International Council for Commercial Arbitration
ICJ	International Court of Justice
ICSID	International Centre for Settlement of Investment Disputes
ICSID Convention	Convention on the Settlement of Investment Disputes between States and Nationals of Other States 1965
ILA	International Law Association
ILC	International Law Commission
ITLOS	International Tribunal for the Law of the Sea
LCIA	London Court of International Arbitration
MAI	Draft Multilateral Agreement on Investment
MFN	most-favoured-nation
MITs	multilateral investment treaties
NAFTA	North American Free Trade Agreement
OECD	Organisation for Economic Co-operation and Development
PCIJ	Permanent Court of International Justice
SCC	Stockholm Chamber of Commerce
TRIMS	Agreement on Trade-Related Investment Measures
UNCITRAL	United Nations Commission on International Trade Law
UNCTAD	United Nations Commission on Trade and Development
UNCTC	United Nations Centre on Transnational Corporations
UNGA Res	United Nations General Assembly Resolution
VCLT	Vienna Convention on the Law of Treaties 1969
WTO	World Trade Organization

Journals, Reports, and Treaty Series

AJIL	American Journal of International Law
Arb Int'l	Arbitration International

ATS	Australian Treaties Series
BGBl	Bundesgesetzblatt
BYIL	British Yearbook of International Law
CTS	Canadian Treaty Series
Can-USLJ	Canada-United States Law Journal
Con TS	Consolidated Treaty Series
DSR	WTO Dispute Settlement Reports
ICLQ	International and Comparative Law Quarterly
ICSID Rep	ICSID Reports
ICSID Rev-FILJ	ICSID Review—Foreign Investment Law Journal
ILM	International Legal Materials
ILR	International Law Reports
Iran-USCTR	Iran-United States Claims Tribunal Reports
J Int'l Arb	Journal of International Arbitration
J Pub L	Journal of Public Law
Law & Cont Prob	Law and Contemporary Problems
Lloyd's Rep	Lloyd's Law Reports
LNTS	League of Nations Treaty Series
Mich LR	Michigan Law Review
Minn LR	Minnesota Law Review
NYLJ	New York Law Journal
NYU JIL	New York University Journal of International Law
RIAA	Reports of International Arbitral Awards (UN)
RO	Recueil Officiel du Droit Fédéral (Switzerland)
Sb	Sbírka Zákonu (Czech Republic Collection of Laws)
Stat	Statutes at Large (United States)
TDM	Transnational Dispute Management
UKTS	United Kingdom Treaty Series
UNTS	United Nations Treaty Series
UST	United States Treaties
Yale JIL	Yale Journal of International Law
YB ILC	Yearbook of the International Law Commission

PART I

OVERVIEW

1

INTRODUCTION

> Owing to the binding character of express promises and agreements, a wise
> and prudent Nation will carefully examine and maturely consider a treaty of
> commerce before concluding it, and will take care not to bind itself to any-
> thing contrary to its duties to itself and to others.
>
> Vattel, *Le Droit des Gens* (1758) Book II Chapter VIII para 28[1]

A. Objective

The investment treaty arbitration phenomenon

The great accumulation of capital in the money centers of the world, far in excess of **1.01**
the opportunities for home investment, has led to a great increase of international
investment extending over the entire surface of the earth ... All these forms of peace-
ful interpenetration among the nations of the earth naturally contribute their

---

[1] M de Vattel, *Le Droit des Gens ou Principes de la Loi Naturelle* (1758) trans C Fenwick (1916)
Vol III, 122.

3

instances of citizens justly or unjustly dissatisfied with the treatment they receive in foreign countries . . .[2]

1.02 These comments could be a description of the contemporary investment scene. In fact, they were delivered by Elihu Root, President of the American Society of International Law, in 1910. The issue of the appropriate means of achieving investment protection has not evaporated in the intervening century. But a development in legal technique in the latter part of the twentieth century has fundamentally altered the context in which disputes between foreign investors and host States fall to be resolved.

1.03 For Root, the only available solution for the foreigner aggrieved at the treatment which he had received in the host State was to seek diplomatic protection from his home State. Of course, the result of such protection might be an agreement of the host State to submit to the arbitration of the dispute by a claims commission. But the prior intervention of the home State was always required.

1.04 This did not of course mean that the protection of foreign investment was solely the province of customary international law, with all the uncertainty and dissension about basic principles with which this area of custom has been bedevilled. As the passage from Vattel cited at the outset of this work illustrates, States had been concluding treaties of commerce between themselves for centuries. Guarantees of investment treatment have long been a subject of specific agreement by treaty.[3] However, treaty provision alone would not justify the claim made by a distinguished arbitration expert of the emergence of a field 'dramatically different from anything previously known in the international sphere'.[4]

1.05 Nor did the development in 1965 of a dedicated framework for the arbitration of investor-State disputes on its own provoke a revolutionary new form of jurisprudence. The Convention on the Settlement of Investment Disputes between States and Nationals of other States 1965 (the ICSID Convention)[5] undoubtedly marks a considerable improvement in the procedures available for the settlement of such disputes. Its uniquely self-contained process avoids many of the pitfalls which may otherwise attend the pursuit of such a claim before a national court or commercial arbitration body. But the ICSID Convention found widespread consensus on procedure by deliberately eschewing any provisions on the substance of investment law, and enshrining the consent of the host State as the sole basis for the jurisdiction of the International Centre for Settlement of Investment

---

[2] E Root, 'The Basis of Protection to Citizens Residing Abroad' (1910) 4 AJIL 517, 518–519.
[3] See eg the references cited in Chap 7 fns 69 & 70 below.
[4] J Paulsson, 'Arbitration without Privity' (1995) 10 ICSID Rev-FILJ 232, 256.
[5] Convention on the Settlement of Investment Disputes between States and Nationals of other States (signed 18 March 1965, entered into force 14 October 1966) 575 UNTS 159 ('ICSID Convention').

Disputes (ICSID).[6] Its early modest case-load was predominantly concerned with contract claims, where the parties had nominated the Centre in their arbitration clause.

Rather, the development in legal technique which has transformed the landscape **1.06** of modern investment protection has been the emergence of widespread provision, within investment treaties, for the direct invocation of arbitration claims by investors themselves against the host State. Suggestively described as 'arbitration without privity',[7] this new form of dispute resolution does not require the intervention of the home State in the prosecution of a claim. Nor does it require any prior contractual relationship between host State and investor. Previously, the concession contract, complete with arbitration agreement, had been the essential predicate for investor-State arbitrations. But successful recourse to arbitration on the basis of the standing and general consent of the host State to all nationals of the other contracting State requires no such privity of contract. The result is dispute resolution which is arbitration in procedural terms, but which in substance has been said to share more of the characteristics of the direct right of action before human rights courts.[8] The State will always be the respondent, never a claimant. Its conduct vis-à-vis the investor falls to be judged according to general standards imposed by international law and not by reference to any national system of law.

Since the potential of this form of dispute resolution was realized, the results have **1.07** been dramatic. The first arbitration under a bilateral investment treaty (BIT) was registered in 1987.[9] The growth in this form of dispute resolution in the two decades since then has been exponential, with the number of registered cases now totalling over 200.[10] If this level of activity seems daunting enough, it is dwarfed by the scale of the underlying network of BITs, with over 2,500 such agreements having been concluded since the first such treaty in 1959.[11]

Exposition of common principles of investment protection

Yet, this patchwork quilt of interlocking but separate bilateral treaties—each the **1.08** product of its own negotiation—in fact betrays a surprising pattern of common features. No doubt part of the ready success of the investment treaty phenomenon has been the willingness of negotiators to confine their texts, for the most part, to

---

[6] ibid (Appendix 11 below) Art 25.   [7] Paulsson (n 4 above).
[8] G Burdeau, 'Nouvelles Perspectives pour l'Arbitrage dans le Contentieux Economique intéressant l'Etat' [1995] Revue de l'Arbitrage 3, 16.
[9] *Asian Agricultural Products Ltd v Republic of Sri Lanka* (Award) 4 ICSID Rep 245 (ICSID, 1990, El-Kosheri P, Goldman & Asante).
[10] UNCTAD, 'IIA Monitor No 4 (2005) Latest Developments in Investor-State Dispute Settlement' UNCTAD/WEB/ITE/IIT/2005/2.
[11] UNCTAD, 'IIA Monitor No 3 (2006) The Entry into Force of Bilateral Investment Treaties (BITs)' UNCTAD/WEB/ITE/IIA/2006/9.

a limited number of rather general guarantees, each expressed in conventional form. The form of the modern BIT may be traced to a series of initiatives shortly after World War II, which produced draft conventions.[12] In turn, State practice in this area has been characterized by an ongoing sharing and borrowing of concepts, which one of the authors has described elsewhere as 'akin to a continuous dialogue within an open-plan office'.[13] Moreover, the inclusion of most favoured nation (MFN) clauses in most BITs drives convergence in treaty drafting, as each State strives to ensure that the benefits which it is extending to the nationals of one State are consistent with obligations already undertaken in prior treaties—the very point made by Vattel, cited at the outset of this chapter. This means that it is possible to speak of a common lexicon of investment treaty law.

1.09   In earlier decades, these common features might simply have provided food for thought for the dedicated observer of treaty-making practice. However, the inclusion of provision for direct investor-State arbitration in so many modern investment treaties has ensured that the general treaty guarantees would be tested in the crucible of the arbitration process. The result, even after what may be regarded as simply the first wave of awards, is the emergence of a jurisprudence of investment treaty law, which interprets the key common provisions of the treaties, and applies them to the myriad of contexts in which relations between host State and foreign investor are played out.

1.10   To date, however, this jurisprudence has not been the subject of critical analysis within the compass of a monograph. For reasons which will be shortly explained, this is perhaps unsurprising. The *procedural framework* of investment arbitration has been the subject of elaborate attention by scholars and practitioners.[14] But the *substantive meaning* of the central tenets of investment treaties lies, at times uncomfortably, between two different fields of legal scholarship.

1.11   To the arbitration specialist, the law applicable to the merits is a matter of secondary importance to the procedure, since it may vary from one case to the next, depending upon the expressed wishes of the parties and the discretion of the arbitrators.[15] Even where the arbitration involves a sovereign State, public international law is only one potentially applicable source of law.[16] However, the conventional

---

[12]   H Abs & H Shawcross, 'Draft Convention on Investments Abroad' (1960) 9 J Pub L 115, 116 and OECD, *Draft Convention on the Protection of Foreign Property and Resolution of the Council of the OECD on the Draft Convention* (1967). On the historical evolution see further 7.38–7.59 below.

[13]   C McLachlan, 'The Principle of Systemic Integration and Article 31(3)(c) of the Vienna Convention' (2005) 54 ICLQ 279, 284.

[14]   See, notably, CH Schreuer, *The ICSID Convention: A Commentary* (2001); and also L Reed, J Paulsson & N Blackaby, *Guide to ICSID Arbitration* (2004).

[15]   For further discussion see: L Collins et al (eds), *Dicey, Morris and Collins on the Conflict of Laws* (14th edn, 2006) 712 (Chap 16 Rule 57(3)) and commentary at 730–734; and A Redfern & M Hunter, *Law and Practice of International Commercial Arbitration* (4th edn, 2004) Chap 2.

[16]   See ICSID Convention (n 5 above) Art 42; and commentary in Schreuer (n 14 above) 549–631.

approach to applicable law in commercial arbitration is displaced in the context of a claim founded upon an investment treaty. In that case, the treaty itself forms the basis for the parties' applicable rights and duties. The treaty is itself 'governed by international law'.[17] As such it must be 'applied and interpreted against the background of the general principles of international law'.[18]

To the public international lawyer, however, the BIT sits at the margins of the mainstream. Being *lex specialis*, the traditional assumption is that its provisions cannot be said necessarily either to state, influence, or be derived from, principles of customary international law. As discussed below, recent practice may be calling that assumption into question. But, for the moment at least, the field receives only brief attention in the classic general texts.[19] The considerable repository of scholarship on the treatment of aliens, which accumulated in the first half of the twentieth century,[20] casts an uncertain light on the modern treaties. To what extent does this old law, which evolved in an era of Western expansionism, and before the independence of much of the developing world, still hold sway in interpreting subsequent compacts? **1.12**

The post-war era has been marked by continuing and fundamental disagreement between States on the basic rules of international investment law, precluding any possibility of multilateral agreement. No doubt wisely, therefore, the International Law Commission has studiously avoided tackling the *primary* rules on the treatment of aliens in its work on State responsibility and diplomatic protection. In the process, it has made clear that its codification of the customary international law rules of diplomatic protection does not apply to BITs, to the extent of any inconsistency.[21] Meanwhile, and by contrast, the process of conclusion of BITs has proceeded apace. As FA Mann wryly observed: 'The cold print of these treaties is a more reliable source of law than rhetorics in the United Nations.'[22] It is these treaties, rather than the direct application of customary international law, which have dominated the investment field in modern times. **1.13**

Yet detailed studies of the substantive rights protected in investment treaties are not abundant. Writing in 1997, Sacerdoti observed that State practice on the content **1.14**

---

[17] Vienna Convention on the Law of Treaties (signed 23 May 1969, entered into force 27 January 1980) 1155 UNTS 331 ('VCLT') Art 2(1)(a).

[18] A McNair, *The Law of Treaties* (1961) 466.

[19] See eg R Jennings & A Watts (eds), *Oppenheim's International Law* (9th edn, 1996) 925–926; M Shaw, *International Law* (5th edn, 2003) 747–749.

[20] Notably E Borchard, *The Diplomatic Protection of Citizens Abroad or The Law of International Claims* (1916); A Freeman, *The International Responsibility of States for Denial of Justice* (1938); Harvard Research Draft, 'Responsibility of States for Damage done in their Territory to the Person or Property of Foreigners' (1929) 23 AJIL 133 (Special Supplement).

[21] ILC (Dugard, Special Rapporteur), 'Draft Articles on Diplomatic Protection with Commentaries' in *Report of the International Law Commission on the Work of Its Fifty-Eighth Session* (1 May–9 June; 3 July–11 August 2006) UN Doc A/61/10, 89–90, Art 17.

[22] FA Mann, 'British Treaties for the Promotion and Protection of Investments' (1981) 52 BYIL 241, 250 reprinted in FA Mann, *Further Studies in International Law* (1990) 234, 246.

of the applicable standards of treatment is rare outside the area of the deprivation of property.[23] Both this important study, and the invaluable 1995 work by Dolzer and Stevens on *Bilateral Investment Treaties*,[24] were written before the protections embodied in BITs had been tested to any significant degree in arbitration.[25] Sacerdoti's conclusion that 'major conflicts between host States and foreign investors tend to be rare',[26] undoubtedly justified by the evidence in 1997, has been dramatically disproved in the decade since then.

1.15 In the result, therefore, this book aims to address what has become a substantial gap in the literature. Its simple (but nevertheless demanding) aim is to provide an analysis of those common features of investment treaties which may form the basis of an arbitration claim, in the light of the reported jurisprudence. In so doing, it seeks to marry the twin influences in this field of both arbitration and public international law. It brings together guidance derived from the applicable general international law with the specific consideration of the concepts in arbitral awards in order, by close analysis, to elucidate the meaning and application of those key common terms.

1.16 Others have sought to describe the emergence of the modern investment treaties within the broad lines of development of international economic law in the twentieth century.[27] This book's objective is modest in comparison. Yet the very novelty and variety of the problems being constantly thrown up in investment arbitrations has made its ambit challenging enough.

B. Structure

1.17 In addressing this task, the authors have adopted a structure which seeks to address the main *substantive* principles of investment treaty law in an order in which they are likely to be addressed in arbitration. Accordingly, the work is divided into three parts: Overview; Ambit of Protection; and Substantive Rights. Each Part contains three chapters.

Part I: Overview

1.18 Following this Introduction, Chapter 2 sets out the basic features of investment treaties. It is designed to provide a route map to the book as a whole.

---

[23] G Sacerdoti, 'Bilateral Treaties and Multilateral Instruments on Investment Protection' (1997) 269 *Recueil des Cours* 269, 339.

[24] R Dolzer and M Stevens, *Bilateral Investment Treaties* (1995).

[25] Sacerdoti (n 23 above) 453.   [26] ibid 454.

[27] eg AF Lowenfeld, *International Economic Law* (2002); M Sornarajah, *The International Law on Foreign Investment* (2nd edn, 2004); P Muchlinski, *Multinational Enterprises and the Law* (1995).

Chapter 3: Dispute Settlement then looks in more detail at four fundamental **1.19** issues in the settlement of investment disputes through arbitration—issues which may be said to frame the rest of the debate:

(1) *Dispute Settlement Provisions.* In the first place, Chapter 3 analyses the clauses in investment treaties which provide for investor-State arbitration. Although dispute resolution provisions are commonly found towards the conclusion of an investment treaty, it is these provisions, and the array of options which they provide to the investor, which provide the key to the rest of the process. They are therefore dealt with at the outset.

(2) *Transparency.* A feature of investment arbitration, which distinguishes it from commercial arbitration, and which reflects its mixed public/private character, is the extent to which the process, and the resulting award, is exposed to public scrutiny. An important element of this is the extent to which non-parties may be heard in the process, whether as *amici curiae* or otherwise.

(3) *Legal Nature of the Rights at Issue.* The rights contained in investment treaties have been rightly described as having a mixed or hybrid character,[28] entered into on the plane of public international law between States, but vindicated directly through claims brought by private investors. This section explores the relative emphasis to be put on the respective roles of the contracting State and the claimant investor in determining the basis of the rights asserted.

(4) *Interpretation of BITs.* The final section examines the overall approach to be taken to the interpretation of investment treaties, and discusses in particular whether a doctrine of precedent is emerging in investment arbitration.

Part II: Ambit of protection

Part II is concerned with three major sets of issues related to the ambit of the pro- **1.20** tections afforded by investment treaties. In turn, these provisions contribute to the determination of whether the arbitral tribunal may, or should, assume jurisdiction to hear the claim. It is divided into three chapters: Parallel Proceedings; Nationality; and Investment.

Parallel proceedings

Chapter 4 is concerned with a complex set of problems which have arisen in deter- **1.21** mining the relationship between parallel claims in investment arbitration, and other forms of dispute resolution, notably proceedings in host State courts. These issues typically arise at the preliminary jurisdictional phase of investment arbitration. The response of tribunals has been shaped by a combination of the specific treaty provisions dealing with conflicts of jurisdiction, and consideration of more

---

[28] Z Douglas, 'The Hybrid Foundations of Investment Treaty Arbitration' (2003) 74 BYIL 151.

general principles of *lis pendens* and *res judicata*. The chapter addresses four issues in particular:

(1) *Breach of contract and breach of treaty.* What is the essential basis of the distinction between those claims which may properly be characterized as treaty claims, which are therefore amenable to arbitration under the provisions of an investment treaty, and claims which instead are founded upon contractual or other rights? This distinction provides the starting-point for the analysis of the problems in this area, since it provides a tool to delimit the respective provinces of investment treaty arbitration and host State litigation or commercial arbitration.

(2) *Election, waiver, and 'fork in the road'.* May the parties resolve some of the conflict between jurisdictions by requiring the claimant to make a choice between available fora? The techniques which insist that the claimant *electa una via*, comprise both election (the suggestively entitled 'fork in the road'), as well as waiver upon the commencement of an arbitration proceeding.

(3) *Internationalized contract claims and 'umbrella clauses'.* Conversely, to what extent can specific provisions in an investment treaty extend the scope of disputes amenable to investment arbitration to contract claims by way of an 'umbrella clause'?

(4) *Parallel treaty arbitration.* Finally, what restrictions, if any, does international law impose upon parallel treaty arbitrations brought under different investment treaties, but concerning the same underlying dispute?

These issues are not only of fundamental practical importance to the successful invocation of an investment arbitration claim. They also shed light on the underlying role of treaty arbitration vis-à-vis other methods of resolving investment disputes.

Nationality and investment

1.22 Chapter 5: Nationality and Chapter 6: Investment address the two principal respects in which investment treaties define the ambit of their protection. Since these provisions are the critical, if not exclusive, determinant of the jurisdiction of an arbitral tribunal in an investment claim, they have not unnaturally attracted a considerable number of preliminary objections by States.

1.23 The authors have deliberately resisted the temptation, now fashionable in some awards,[29] to impose an *a priori* distinction between jurisdiction *ratione personae* and jurisdiction *ratione materiae*. For many purposes, the treaty provisions on nationality may be said to deal with arbitral jurisdiction over persons (*ratione*

---

[29] eg *Impregilo SpA v Islamic Republic of Pakistan* (Jurisdiction) ICSID Case No ARB/03/3 (ICSID, 2005, Guillaume P, Cremades & Landau).

personae); while the treaty provisions on investment prescribe the extent of arbitral jurisdiction over subject-matter (*ratione materiae*). But the treaties themselves proceed simply on the basis of nationality and investment, and the dividing line between persons and things is not exact. Indeed, the definition of 'investment' may well extend the reach of a treaty's protection to many classes of persons (such as minority shareholders) who would have no basis for a claim under customary international law. The temporal application of investment treaties (*ratione temporis*) is dealt with as part of the consideration of covered investments.

Part III: Substantive rights

The third Part of the book deals with the core substantive rights accorded to investors under an investment treaty. It is divided into three chapters: Treatment of Investors, Expropriation, and Compensation. **1.24**

Chapter 7: Treatment of investors

In general, investment treaties seek to protect investors by assuring them of two types of treatment. The standards of fair and equitable treatment and full protection and security have been described as 'non-contingent' in the sense that the protections which they extend are absolute.[30] They are not dependent upon the extent of protection afforded to others. By contrast, the provisions for national treatment and MFN treatment and the guarantee of non-discrimination are contingent standards. The extent of the protection which they afford is dependent upon that which the host State metes out to others, who stand in the requisite legal relationship to the protected investor. **1.25**

The concepts of national treatment and MFN treatment have long been widely used in international economic law. Such protections are only obtained by way of express provision by treaty. The non-contingent standards, on the other hand, while employing language which is distinctive to the treaty context, perform in substance a task which has long been an important part of the minimum standard of treatment of aliens expected by customary international law. **1.26**

Non-contingent standards The assurance of 'fair and equitable treatment' provides the most basic protection for foreign investment. Yet the expression has proved stubbornly resistant to precise definition. This section therefore puts the evolution of the standard in historical context, in order to provide a framework for analysis of its present application by arbitral tribunals in relation to: **1.27**

(1) *Denial of justice*, or the breach of the standard in the course of the host State's judicial process; and,

---

[30] H Walker Jr, 'Modern Treaties of Friendship, Commerce and Navigation' (1957–1958) 42 Minn LR 805, 810–811.

(2) *Review of administrative action*, or the breach of the standard in the investor's treatment by the executive.

1.28   As will be seen, in both contexts, the standard is concerned with the process of decision-making in the host State, rather than with the prescription of substantive outcomes. Analysis of arbitral awards enables a distillation of the factors which are likely to indicate that the standard has been breached, and a comparison with those factors which have been successfully relied upon by host States to show that the standard has been met.

1.29   **Contingent standards**   The discussion of the contingent standards draws together the common threads of national treatment and MFN treatment with the more general right of non-discrimination. It does so by examining the techniques for the identification of a difference in treatment, and then considering whether any such difference in fact breaches the standard.

Chapter 8: Expropriation

1.30   By contrast with the rights discussed in Chapter 7, the protection of property rights in investments from expropriation has long been the subject of close consideration by arbitral tribunals. However, the factual matrix in which the modern expropriation claim arises may well be very different to the context of outright nationalization of foreign property, which characterized many of the earlier causes célèbres. Giving her lectures at The Hague Academy of International Law in 1982 on 'The Taking of Property by the State',[31] Rosalyn Higgins commented on the relative paucity of literature dealing with the concept of 'indirect expropriation', which addressed many of the more difficult questions in which the law of State takings had to be applied in modern times.[32] The observation proved prescient. Many of the modern arbitral awards have been concerned with the determination of the appropriate boundary between two potentially conflicting values: a legitimate sphere for State regulation in the pursuit of public goods on the one hand (even if it may result in a loss of economic benefits to those subject to the regulation); and the protection of private property from State interference on the other.

Chapter 9: Compensation

1.31   The final chapter is concerned with the approach to be taken to the determination of the appropriate level of compensation for breach of treaty rights. The law on this topic is an amalgam of the provisions of general international law with the specific provisions of the treaties themselves. Compensation is a potential form of reparation for any internationally wrongful act of a State.[33] This part of the work

---

[31] (1982) 176 *Recueil des Cours* 259.   [32] ibid 322.

[33] ILC (J Crawford, Special Rapporteur), 'Draft Articles on Responsibility of States for Internationally Wrongful Acts with Commentaries' in *Report of the International Law Commission*

is therefore closely linked to the international law of State responsibility. But the specific provisions of investment treaties, as *lex specialis*, have resolved a number of contentious issues as to the appropriate approach to be taken to the calculation of the amount of compensation. Nevertheless, the detailed principles to be applied when determining the amount of compensation, both for expropriation claims, as for other claims for breach of treaty, have continued to raise difficulties for arbitral tribunals. This chapter discusses the range of options adopted in actual practice by tribunals, dealing in addition with interest and costs.

C. Approach

With this syllabus in mind, it is now possible to make three points about the overall approach which the authors have sought to adopt throughout the work. **1.32**

The principles of investment treaty law

The overall purpose of the book is to distil the principles which apply in the application of the general standards found in investment treaties. This is not a matter of mere description. On the contrary, it is the authors' view that what has been most needed in this area is to subject the awards to critical analysis. Where possible, the authors have also sought to assist the reader by providing a principled approach to problem-solving, setting out guidance by way of specific conclusions. **1.33**

Awards

The authors consider that this critical analysis is best fostered through a selective approach to reference to both awards and to treaties. In contrast to commercial arbitration, where the reporting of awards is often restricted or fragmentary, the practice in investment arbitration, described in more detail in Chapter 3, has come to be that the majority of awards are made public. They are widely available in full text, both in published law reports, such as *ICSID Reports, ICSID Review—Foreign Investment Law Journal* and *International Legal Materials*, as well as in electronic form, in particular on the ICSID website.[34] As the volume of awards has continued to grow, it has become more and more important to be discriminating. This work does not purport to be an exhaustive digest. Rather, it aims to select and discuss in depth the significant investment arbitration awards in terms of doctrinal development or the exposition of original perspectives. **1.34**

---

of the Work of Its Fifty-Third Session (23 April–1 June; 2 July–10 August 2001) UN Doc A/56/10, 243–263.

[34] <http://www.worldbank.org\icsid>. Also useful are <http://ita.law.uvic.ca> and <http://www.naftaclaims.com>.

Treaties

1.35 How should a work on the principles of investment treaties cope with the sheer multiplicity of texts? With over 2,500 agreements in force, an attempt to be encyclopedic would quickly bury the reader under the weight of detail, and obscure the lines of principle. In addition to the official treaty series (which the authors have cited wherever possible), investment treaties have also been usefully collected by the United Nations Commission on Trade and Development (UNCTAD), both in a multi-volume compendium and in electronic form.[35] Of course, any process of interpretation of the rights arising from an investment treaty must start from the specific provisions of the treaty in force between the relevant States. However, the striking degree of commonality of language between treaties does facilitate a general work of this kind. This is particularly so as many States, capital-importing as well as capital-exporting, have adopted model form BITs. These are of more general significance, since they are a statement of the provisions which that State considers acceptable in its international relations.

1.36 Nevertheless, a choice has had to be made for the purpose of this volume. In the result, the authors have selected the model bilateral investment treaties of Sri Lanka (as a representative example of a capital-importing State), the United Kingdom, France, Germany, the Netherlands, and the United States. Each of these is reproduced in full in the Appendices, and the clauses relevant to the particular topic are analysed chapter by chapter. These prototypes have also had considerable influence on the treaty-making practice of other States. The United States 2004 model BIT[36] is of particular current significance, and reflects the formulation of investment protection provisions in new-model free trade agreements.[37] Other bilateral treaties are referred to in the text where they offer particular solutions which are germane to the topic or award under discussion.

1.37 In addition to the bilateral treaties, there are two important multilateral instruments in this field: Chapter XI of the North American Free Trade Agreement (NAFTA)[38] and the Energy Charter Treaty (ECT),[39] whose provisions are reproduced in the Appendix and are analysed in detail in the text. Both of these treaties have a restricted scope: NAFTA is restricted *ratione personae* to its three contracting States (Canada, Mexico, and the United States). The ECT is restricted *ratione materiae* to the energy sector. Further, in important respects they adopt legal solutions which differ from the bilateral treaties. But both treaties represent significant

---

[35] <http://www.unctadxi.org/templates/Startpage____718.aspx>.

[36] 2004 US model BIT (Appendix 6 below).

[37] See eg United States-Singapore Free Trade Agreement (signed 6 May 2003) Chap 15.

[38] North American Free Trade Agreement (adopted 17 December 1992, entered into force 1 January 1994) CTS 1994 No 2, (1993) 32 ILM 612 ('NAFTA') (Chapter 11, Appendix 1 below).

[39] Energy Charter Treaty (signed 17 December 1994, entered into force 16 April 1998) 2080 UNTS 100 ('ECT') (Part III, Appendix 2 below).

State practice in the investment field, and both have given rise to a number of significant arbitration awards. Reference has also been made to the ASEAN Agreement for the Promotion and Protection of Investments of 15 December 1987, as another important regional investment treaty providing for investor-State arbitration.[40]

Relevance of general public international law

Custom in treaty interpretation

The book starts from the proposition that investment treaties are not self-contained **1.38** regimes.[41] The meaning of their operative terms must therefore be informed by reference to the 'relevant rules of international law applicable in the relations between the parties'.[42] On one level, this requirement states little more than a truism—no treaty can exist in isolation from general international law.[43] But it is nevertheless indispensable in reminding the treaty interpreter of the potential guidance in interpretation which may be obtained beyond the four corners of the treaty. This may be expressed in terms of a presumption with both positive and negative aspects:

(1) *negatively* that, in entering into treaty obligations, the parties intend not to act inconsistently with generally recognized principles of international law or with previous treaty obligations towards third States;[44] and

(2) *positively* that the parties are taken 'to refer to general principles of international law for all questions which [the treaty] does not itself resolve in express terms and in a different way'.[45]

This approach was specifically approved as part of a general approach to interpre- **1.39** tation of investment treaties by the Tribunal in the first ICSID treaty arbitration: *Asian Agricultural Products Ltd v Republic of Sri Lanka*.[46] Indeed, in this context, there may be particularly compelling reasons to refer to general international law in interpretation. In the first place, there is evidence that the treaty framers often consciously sought not to go beyond obligations which were thought to reflect the

---

[40] (1988) 27 ILM 612 (Appendix 3 below).

[41] See generally ILC, 'Fragmentation of International Law: Difficulties arising from the Diversification and Expansion of International Law, Report of the Study Group of the International Law Commission' (Koskenniemi C) UN Doc A/CN4/L682, 4 April 2006; UN Doc A/CN.4/L.702, 18 July 2006; C McLachlan, 'The Principle of Systemic Integration and Article 31(3)(c) of the Vienna Convention' (2005) 54 ICLQ 279. [42] VCLT (n 17 above) Art 31(3)(c).

[43] See the comments of R Higgins, 'A Babel of Judicial Voices? Ruminations from the Bench' (2006) 55 ICLQ 791.

[44] *Case Concerning Right of Passage over Indian Territory (Portugal v India)* (Preliminary Objections) [1957] ICJ Rep 125, 142; R Jennings & A Watts (eds), *Oppenheim's International Law* (9th edn, 1996) 1275.

[45] *Georges Pinson Case* (1927–1928) AD Case no 292, 426 per Verzijl P.

[46] *Asian Agricultural Products Ltd v Republic of Sri Lanka* (Award) (ICSID, 1990, El-Kosheri P, Goldman & Asante) 4 ICSID Rep 245, 265–266, Rule (D).

current state of international law.[47] Their purpose was to enhance the mechanisms for the protection of the rights, rather than to extend the rights themselves.

1.40 In some treaties, this is made express. Thus, for example, the French prototype guarantees: 'traitement juste et équitable, conformément aux principes du Droit international'.[48] The 2004 US model BIT goes even further, enshrining 'the customary international law minimum standard of treatment of aliens',[49] and recites a shared understanding of the parties that the expropriation and compensation clause 'is intended to reflect customary international law'.[50] For good measure, the US model even offers a definition of customary international law as resulting from 'a general and consistent practice of States that they follow from a sense of legal obligation'.[51] Even the most determined classicist could not object.

1.41 Article 1105 of NAFTA requires that: 'Each Party shall accord to investments of investors of another Party treatment in accordance with international law, including fair and equitable treatment and full protection and security.' Controversy among arbitral tribunals as to whether that form of words left room for a more expansive reading of 'fair and equitable treatment'[52] was settled by the NAFTA Free Trade Commission, which issued an Interpretation of the Article providing that it 'prescribes the customary international law minimum standard of treatment of aliens' and not more.[53]

1.42 But, even where the matter is not dealt with expressly, there is much room for reference to custom. In the case of expropriation, for example, the definition commonly found in investment treaties has been so patently adopted from a formulation widely employed in customary international law that it invites reference to the general authorities on its meaning. Similarly, the standard of full protection and security is on all fours with that expected in customary international law.[54] In the case of compensation, the concept fits within a larger framework of reparation in the law of State responsibility.

1.43 Moreover, practical considerations may impel the interpreter to seek guidance from general international law. Investment treaties typically enshrine guarantees of investor treatment in general, open-textured language. As discussed further below,[55] the standard extrinsic aids to treaty interpretation may yield only limited guidance—there is rarely much in the way of *travaux préparatoires*. The

---

[47] See eg E Denza & S Brooks 'Investment Protection Treaties: United Kingdom Experience' (1987) 36 ICLQ 908, 912.   [48] France model BIT (Appendix 10 below) Art 4.
[49] US model BIT (Appendix 6 below) Art 5.   [50] ibid Annex B.   [51] ibid Annex A.
[52] *Pope & Talbot Inc v Government of Canada* (Award on the Merits of Phase 2) 7 ICSID Rep 43 (NAFTA/UNICTRAL, 2001, Dervaird P, Greenberg & Belman).
[53] NAFTA Free Trade Commission (FTC), Interpretation of NAFTA Chapter 11 (31 July 2001) 6 ICSID Rep 567, 568. The full text is set out at 7.26 below.
[54] *Asian Agricultural Products Ltd v Republic of Sri Lanka* (Award) 4 ICSID Rep 245 (ICSID, 1990, El-Kosheri P, Goldman & Asante).   [55] See 3.66–3.77 and 7.64–7.72 below.

bilateral treaties normally lack any formal mechanism for the contracting States to agree subsequently on troublesome matters of interpretation.[56] In contrast, then, to a complex multilateral treaty in other spheres of international law, the bilateral investment treaties appear more than usually dependant upon their wider context.

Limitations in custom as a source of law

Yet the relationship between investment treaties and general international law **1.44** remains deeply problematic for at least three reasons.

In the first place, it is evident that on many issues, States have entered into invest- **1.45** ment treaties precisely in order to remedy perceived gaps or limitations in the protections afforded by customary international law in the field of the treatment of aliens. The law of diplomatic protection imposes a number of strict pre-conditions upon the exercise of an international claim. Conditions such as the requirement to exhaust local remedies, or the strict rule on nationality of claims, make good sense in the context of a remedy of last resort between sovereign States. But, as will be seen, it was part of the very object and purpose of investment treaties, with their provision for direct investor-State arbitration, to remedy the perceived shortcomings in diplomatic protection. This objective would be fundamentally undermined if restrictions of this kind were to be re-imported into investment treaties by the back-door of interpretation—a point developed in Chapters 5 and 7, for example, in relation to the *Loewen* award.[57] In any event, many of the rights found in investment treaties require the express agreement of States. National treatment and MFN treatment, for example, must always be creatures of convention, not custom. The same is true for dispute settlement provisions, and for many of the more detailed clauses summarized in Chapter 2. In short, where the treaty itself resolves the matter in a different way, it must prevail as *lex specialis*.

Secondly, the invocation of customary international law is apt to neglect the **1.46** essentially contested nature of so many of the rights in customary international law. Even in the inter-war years, when the development of this branch of the law reached its zenith in terms of both regular application and codification, the very existence of many of the rights was denied by many key capital-importing States.[58] The fate, since World War II, of any attempt to frame a multilateral treaty on investment; the development in the General Assembly of the doctrine

---

[56] cf the procedure of the Free Trade Commission under NAFTA Art 2001(2), referred to at 7.26 below.

[57] *Loewen Group Inc & anor v United States of America* (Award) 7 ICSID Rep 421 (NAFTA/ICSID (AF), 2003, Mason P, Mikva & Mustill) discussed at 5.64–5.71 and 7.87–7.98 below.

[58] eg Montevideo Convention on the Rights and Duties of States (signed 26 December 1933) 165 LNTS 19 Art 9; E Borchard, 'The "Minimum Standard" of the Treatment of Aliens' (1940) 38 Mich LR 445.

of permanent sovereignty over natural resources; the early exclusion by the International Law Commission of primary rules on the treatment of aliens from its codification of the law of State responsibility and diplomatic protection; the paucity of post-war jurisprudence applying these customary rights—all of these speak volumes as to the difficulties of stating the rules of custom in this field with any confidence. Of course, one purpose of the proliferation of treaties has been to remedy this uncertainty. The investor, who has the benefit of an applicable investment treaty, at least need not ask whether the right exists. But the wide extent of treaty protections may also be said to limit the possibility of the further development of custom outside the treaty context. In the result, one is still left with a treaty provision of an open-textured character which requires interpretation.

1.47 Thirdly, the overwhelming majority of State practice in this field in the last few decades has been through the medium of the very treaties which are the subject of this book. Is all of this to be ignored in treaty interpretation on the grounds that 'the application of international law rules on interpretation of treaties to identical or similar provisions of different treaties may not yield the same results, having regard to, *inter alia*, differences in the respective contexts, objects and purposes, subsequent practice of parties and *travaux préparatoires*'?[59] Undoubtedly, the bilateral character of most investment treaties precludes the adoption of binding rules of general application across the whole field. But the practice of international arbitrators, documented in this book, demonstrates an extensive exchange of ideas on the interpretation of similar provisions.

The emergence of a common law of investment protection

1.48 What explanation is to be given to this phenomenon? In paras 3.83 to 3.103 below, it is submitted that, while no *de jure* doctrine of precedent exists in investment arbitration, a *de facto* doctrine has in fact been building for some time. This was well put by the Tribunal in *AES v Argentina*:

> Each tribunal remains sovereign and may retain, as it is confirmed by ICSID practice, a different solution for resolving the same problem; but decisions on jurisdiction dealing with the same or very similar issues may at least indicate some lines of reasoning of real interest; this Tribunal may consider them in order to compare its own position with those already adopted by its predecessors and, if it shares the views already expressed by one or more of these tribunals on a specific point of law, it is free to adopt the same solution ... precedents may also be rightly considered, at least as a matter of comparison and, if so considered by the Tribunal, of inspiration.[60]

---

[59] *The MOX Plant Case (Ireland v United Kingdom)* (ITLOS, Provisional Measures, Order of 3 December 2001) (2002) 41 ILM 405, 413.

[60] *AES Corp v Argentine Republic* (Jurisdiction) ICSID Case No ARB/02/17 (ICSID, 2005, Dupuy P, Böckstiegel & Janeiro) paras 30–31.

The extensive exchange of ideas between tribunals has been facilitated by the **1.49** wide publication of awards, as well as by scholarly journals[61] and committees.[62] Further, it is no accident that this new jurisprudence has developed in the era of the internet, which has rapidly built a global community of scholars, practitioners, and arbitrators exchanging ideas about current developments in the field as they arise.[63]

Does this ongoing conversation between arbitrators, in which findings arrived at **1.50** in prior awards on particular provisions are cited and relied upon as authorities in the interpretation of different investment treaties, have any broader significance for the development of international law in the field? It is the thesis of this book that what is emerging is a common law of investment protection, with a substantially shared understanding of its general tenets. This still depends for the most part on the existence of a treaty forming the basis for the enforceable rights. It will always yield to particular provisions of a treaty which diverge from the general rule, or to other contrary indications resulting from the application of the rules of treaty interpretation. But the differences between treaties, and indeed between treaty and the substantive rights in custom, may be less than the common elements. As one recent award put it, 'the difference between the Treaty standard … and the customary minimum standard, when applied to the specific facts of a case, may well be more apparent than real'.[64]

This process may share more with the way in which 'general principles of law **1.51** common to civilized nations' are used as a source of law in international law.[65] Chapter 4 explores the way in which the general principles of *res judicata* and *lis pendens*, common to civilized nations, may be applied in investment arbitration, where the parallel claims meet the conditions for the application of the doctrines. In Chapter 7 it is submitted that the content of the principle of 'fair and equitable treatment' is to be derived by reference to such general principles, and reference is also made to general principles as a basis for the approach to causation in determining damages in Chapter 9.[66]

---

[61] Notably ICSID Review—Foreign Investment Law Journal (ICSID Rev-FILJ), and Journal of World Investment and Trade.

[62] Notably, the International Law Association Committee on International Law on Foreign Investment (est 2003), and the British Institute of International & Comparative Law Investment Treaty Forum (est 2004), as to which see: F Ortino, A Sheppard & H Warner, *Investment Treaty Law: Current Issues Volume 1* (2006).

[63] Notably the OGEMID Discussion List established by the Centre for Energy Petroleum and Mineral Law and Policy at the University of Dundee, together with its online subscription service <http://www.transnational-dispute-management.com>.

[64] *Saluka Investments BV (The Netherlands) v Czech Republic* (Partial Award) (UNCITRAL, 2006, Watts C, Fortier & Behrens) para 291.

[65] Statute of the International Court of Justice (26 June 1945 annexed to the Charter of the United Nations) Art 38(1)(c).   [66] See especially 7.176–7.188 and 9.86–9.94 below.

1.52 The point here is a related, but broader one. It is that the very iterative process of the formulation and conclusion of investment treaties, and the vindication of the rights contained in those treaties in arbitration, is producing a set of general international principles about the meaning of the common substantive clauses, and indeed the larger operation of the system of investment arbitration.

1.53 To what extent can it be said that this common treaty practice itself contributes to the development of customary international law? FA Mann gave an initial answer to this question in 1981. While accepting the general point made by the International Court of Justice in the *North Sea Continental Shelf Cases*,[67] that it is difficult to deduce a rule of international law from a treaty, he continued that the significance of that decision should not be overrated, at least in the context of investment treaties:

> There is, in the first place, the very large number of treaties the scope of which is increased by the operation of the most-favoured-nation clause. There is, secondly, the fact that many States which have purported to reject the traditional conceptions and standards included in these treaties have accepted them, when (if the colloquial phrase may be permitted) it came to the crunch. There is, thirdly, the most important fact that these treaties establish and accept and thus enlarge the force of traditional conceptions. Is it possible for a State to reject the rule according to which alien property may be expropriated only on certain terms long believed to be required by customary international law, yet to accept it for the purpose of these treaties? The paramount duty of States imposed by international law is to observe and act in accordance with the requirements of good faith. From this point of view it follows that, where these treaties express a duty which customary international law imposes or is widely believed to impose, they give very strong support to the existence of such a duty and preclude the Contracting States from denying its existence.[68]

1.54 This last point merits careful consideration, especially in the light of the practice adopted in many States of promulgating model investment treaties, which indicate the standards which those States find acceptable; and the adoption, express or implied, in many such treaties of standards which are based upon customary international law, especially in relation to the non-contingent treatment standards and expropriation. The result is a convergence, on these issues, between treaty practice and custom, in which the modern understanding of the content of the customary right is being elaborated primarily through the treaty jurisprudence. As the Tribunal put it in *CMS v Argentina*, 'the fact is that *lex specialis* in this respect is so prevalent that it can now be considered the general rule'.[69]

1.55 This process of cross-fertilization in the development of the customary standards through the treaty jurisprudence saves general international law from being cast

---

[67] *North Sea Continental Shelf Cases (Federal Republic of Germany v Denmark; Federal Republic of Germany v The Netherlands)* [1969] ICJ Rep 3.

[68] FA Mann, *Further Studies in International Law* (n 22 above) 245.

[69] *CMS Gas Transmission Co v Republic of Argentina* (Jurisdiction) 7 ICSID Rep 492, 504 (ICSID, 2003, Orrego Vicuña P, Lalonde & Rezek).

in aspic at some earlier point in time; and saves treaty tribunals from isolation and inconsistency. It reflects the fact that the general standards are of their nature evolutionary.[70] The Tribunal in *Mondev*[71] described this process in the following way. It was responding to a submission advanced by Canada that the customary international law standard incorporated into Article 1105 of NAFTA was to be determined by reference to Claims Commission awards of the inter-war years, in particular the *Neer* case.[72] It held:

> Secondly, *Neer* and like arbitral awards were decided in the 1920s, when the status of the individual in international law, and the international protection of foreign investments, were far less developed than they have since come to be ...
>
> Thirdly, the vast number of bilateral and regional investment treaties ... almost uniformly provide for fair and equitable treatment of foreign investments, and largely provide for full security and protection of investments. Investment treaties run between North and South, and East and West, and between States in these spheres *inter se*. On a remarkably widespread basis, States have repeatedly obliged themselves to accord foreign investment such treatment. In the Tribunal's view, such a body of concordant practice will necessarily have influenced the content of rules governing the treatment of foreign investment in current international law.[73]

1.56 It is this 'body of concordant practice' which serves as the central, and defining, feature of modern investment law, and which may in the end provide the most satisfactory explanation for the extensive application of precedent in the recent treaty jurisprudence.

A balance between the rights of investors and host States

1.57 The final element of the overall approach has been a conscious effort to discern an appropriate balance between protection of the rights of foreign investors on the one hand, and recognition of the legitimate sphere of operation of the host State on the other. After all, host States have a responsibility to govern in the interests of all of those within their jurisdiction, and to promote many other public objectives as well as investment. As the editors of *Oppenheim* put it: 'The requirements of international law in this field ... represent an attempt at accommodation between the conflicting interests involved.'[74] The need to chart such a balance was recognized by the Tribunal in *CMS v Argentina*, which held: 'The right of the host State to adopt its economic policies together with the rights of investors under a system

---

[70] McLachlan (n 41 above) 317; ILC (n 41 above) 16–17; *Case concerning the Gabčíkovo-Nagymaros Project (Hungary v Slovakia)* [1997] ICJ Rep 7, 67–68.
[71] *Mondev International Ltd v United States of America* (Award) 6 ICSID Rep 181 (NAFTA/ICSID(AF), 2002, Stephen P, Crawford & Schwebel).
[72] *LFH Neer & Pauline Neer (USA) v United Mexican States* (1926) IV RIAA 60.
[73] *Mondev* (n 71 above) 222.
[74] R Jennings & A Watts (eds), *Oppenheim's International Law* (9th edn, 1996) 933.

of guarantees and protection are at the very heart of this difficult balance, a balance which the [ICSID] Convention was careful to preserve'.[75]

1.58 Investment arbitration wears a very public face. A number of recent arbitrations have aroused considerable controversy amid claims that the process gives insufficient weight to other social goods, or to social and economic rights, or that it infringes national sovereignty. These objections have not been limited to traditional capital-importing States. On the contrary, arbitration under NAFTA has provoked considerable public dissent within North America.[76] Some have concluded that the existing law is 'shockingly unsuited to the task of balancing private rights against public goods'.[77] The International Institute for Sustainable Development (IISD) has developed a wholly new Model International Agreement on Investment for Sustainable Development.[78] This seeks to balance the rights of investors and duties of host States, with concomitant duties of investors and of their home States. The approach is innovative and constructive. It acknowledges the value of promoting foreign investment, but seeks to place it within the broader legal framework of host and home State regulation, as well as other international law obligations which undoubtedly apply. To date, however, there is little evidence of the direct application of this model in the investment treaty-making practice of States. Nevertheless, it has been rightly observed that: 'If investment arbitration is to fulfill its promise, however, some mechanism must be found to promote greater sensitivity to vital host state interests.'[79]

1.59 There is some recent evidence that these concerns are impacting on drafting practice. Notably, the 2004 US model BIT[80] incorporates numerous innovations designed to reflect the public interests of States, and to achieve its investment objectives 'in a manner consistent with the protection of health, safety, and the environment, and the promotion of internationally recognized labor rights'.[81] There are specific articles which are designed to ensure that investment measures will not conflict with environmental and labour standards.[82] The model treaty's extended definition of expropriation expressly provides: 'Except in rare circumstances, non-discriminatory regulatory actions by a Party that are designed and applied to protect legitimate public welfare objectives, such as public health, safety, and the environment, do not constitute indirect expropriations'.[83]

---

[75] *CMS* (n 69 above) 499.

[76] GA Alvarez & WW Park, 'The New Face of Investment Arbitration: NAFTA Chapter 11' (2003) 28 Yale JIL 365.

[77] H Mann, *International Institute for Sustainable Development and World Wildlife Fund, 'Private Rights, Public Problems: A Guide to NAFTA's Controversial Chapter on Investor Rights'* (2001) 46.

[78] H Mann, K von Moltke, L Peterson & A Cosbey, 'IISD Model International Agreement on Investment for Sustainable Development' (2005) <http://www.iisd.org> accessed 20 September 2006.

[79] Alvarez & Park (n 76 above) 399.   [80] 2004 US model BIT (Appendix 6 below).

[81] ibid Preamble.   [82] ibid Arts 12–13.

[83] ibid Annex B, discussed at 8.36 below.

Both NAFTA and the ECT similarly make provision for environmental and other **1.60**
measures. Article 1114 of NAFTA provides that nothing in its investment chapter
is to prevent a State party from adopting environmental measures and that investment should not be encouraged by relaxing domestic health, safety, or environmental measures. Article 19 of the ECT commits State parties to taking account of
environmental considerations in the formulation of energy policy.[84]

Where, however, disputes arise under treaties already in force, these issues will have **1.61**
to be worked out by arbitrators in the course of applying the general, unqualified
treaty language. In so doing, arbitrators must still adopt a balanced approach
between the rights of investors, and those of host States. As was rightly observed in
one recent important award:

> The protection of foreign investments is not the sole aim of the Treaty, but rather a
> necessary element alongside the overall aim of encouraging foreign investment and
> extending and intensifying the parties' economic relations. That in turn calls for a bal-
> anced approach to the interpretation of the Treaty's substantive provisions for the pro-
> tection of investments, since an interpretation which exaggerates the protection to be
> accorded to foreign investments may serve to dissuade host States from admitting for-
> eign investments and so undermine the overall aim of extending and intensifying the
> parties' mutual economic relations.[85]

On the present state of the law, it cannot be said that this dictum has always been **1.62**
observed. Where the authors have found instances of the balance having swung too
far against States, or where tribunals appear to have accorded more weight to the
interests of powerful States than to developing States, they have said so. However,
a close analysis of the jurisprudence developed through the recent awards demonstrates that the general concepts do in fact contain within them considerable flexibility. This enables arbitrators to balance the public and the private interest, and to
ensure that the treaty protections retain their role as a safety-net, leaving a considerable margin of appreciation for the exercise of State sovereignty. Indeed, the
open-textured nature of tests such as fairness and equity invites such an exercise.
This work seeks to facilitate such a balancing exercise, by isolating the factors which
tribunals have regarded as significant in deciding which side of the line particular
conduct may fall.

---

[84] See further T Wälde & A Kolo, 'Environmental Regulation, Investment Protection and
"Regulatory Taking" in International Law' (2001) 50 ICLQ 811.
[85] *Saluka Investments BV (The Netherlands) v Czech Republic* (Partial Award) (UNCITRAL,
2006, Watts C, Fortier & Behrens) para 300.

2

THE BASIC FEATURES OF
INVESTMENT TREATIES

A. Introduction

This chapter is an introduction to the basic features of investment treaties. It sets **2.01** out their common provisions, making reference where necessary to other parts of the book.

The treaties under which investment arbitrations have arisen have either been **2.02** bilateral investment treaties (treaties between two States containing reciprocal undertakings) or multilateral investment treaties. The multilateral investment treaties under which arbitrations have arisen are the North American Free Trade Agreement (NAFTA)[1] and the Association of South East Asian Nations (ASEAN) Agreement,[2] which are organized on a regional basis, and the Energy Charter

---

[1] North American Free Trade Agreement (adopted 17 December 1992, entered into force 1 January 1994) CTS 1994 No 2; (1993) 32 ILM 612 ('NAFTA') (Appendix 1 below).
[2] ASEAN Agreement for the Promotion and Protection of Investments (15 December 1987) (1988) 27 ILM 612 (Appendix 3 below).

Treaty (ECT),[3] a treaty focused on a particular economic activity. Bilateral investment treaties (BITs) and the principal multilateral investment treaties are considered below.

2.03 In addition to entering into investment treaties, many States have enacted foreign investment laws which can provide a basis for investment arbitrations. While arbitration under a foreign investment law will, by definition, not be a treaty arbitration, such arbitrations share a number of factors in common with treaty arbitrations, which will be noted in the final section of this Chapter.

B. Bilateral Investment Treaties

2.04 The large number of treaty arbitrations in recent years has been a product of an exponential growth in the number of BITs. The first BIT was signed in 1959 between Germany and Pakistan.[4] By 1970 there were 72 BITs, by 1980 165, and by 1990 385.[5] The numbers have grown even faster since 1990 and the global total at the end of 2005 was put at 2,495.[6]

2.05 BITs tend to resemble each other in their purpose and content. This similarity is due to their being derived from a limited number of common sources. Among these sources are drafts prepared in 1959 by a private group (led by Abs and Shawcross) and in 1967 by the Organisation for Economic Co-operation and Development (OECD).[7] BITs also have their origins in bilateral treaties of Friendship, Commerce and Navigation (FCN treaties). While FCN treaties commonly contained investment protection provisions, their chief weakness as compared to BITs was the absence of an investor/State dispute resolution provision. FCNs covered a far wider variety of matters than the protection of investments and as a new type of State began to emerge in the 1950s and onwards, they were perceived as unsuitable for agreements between States of differing economic stature. BITs became viewed as a preferred type of international instrument to regulate the bilateral treatment of foreign investments.[8] Two foreign office lawyers

---

[3] Energy Charter Treaty (signed 17 December 1994, entered into force 16 April 1998) 2080 UNTS 100 (Appendix 2 below).

[4] Vertrag zwischen der Bundesrepublik Deutschland und Pakistan zur Förderung und zum Schutz von Kapitalanlagen ('Treaty for the Promotion and Protection of Investments, with Protocol and exchange of notes') (Germany-Pakistan) (signed 25 November 1959, entered into force 28 April 1962) 457 UNTS 23; 1961 BGBl II 793.

[5] UNCTAD, *Bilateral Investment Treaties 1959–1999* (2000) 1.

[6] UNCTAD, *World Investment Report 2006—FDI from Developing and Transition Economies: Implications for Development* (2006) 26.

[7] FA Mann, 'British Treaties for the Promotion and Protection of Investments' (1981) 52 BYIL 241, 241; H Abs & H Shawcross, 'Draft Convention on Investments Abroad' (1960) 9 J Pub L 115; OECD, '1967 Draft Convention on the Protection of Foreign Property' reprinted (1968) 7 ILM 117.

[8] R Dolzer & M Stevens, *Bilateral Investment Treaties* (1995) 10–11.

involved in developing the United Kingdom's BIT network have ascribed the developed world's push for wide BIT coverage as a reaction to the proposals formulated by newly industrialized States in the 1970s to severely reduce the protections afforded to the property of foreign nationals in international law.[9]

Many Western States have adopted model form BITs which they use as a starting **2.06** point in their treaty negotiations. The current model form BITs of France, Germany, the Netherlands, Sri Lanka, the United Kingdom, and the United States appear as appendices to this book in order to allow the reader to consult their provisions as the text considers their key points. Other model forms can be found online at <http://www.unctadxi.org/templates/Startpage____718.aspx>.

Lawyers drafting agreements governed by common law systems usually evolve **2.07** their drafts and models in line with shifting case law to accept explicitly or to reject interpretations of standard wording handed down by judges. With the tendency of BIT tribunals to have regard to each others' rulings in interpreting standard BIT provisions, one could expect a similar process to take place in the development of BITs. However, of the recent model BITs, only the United States has revised its model's provisions to take direct notice of tribunal rulings. Examples of these changes, such as the more descriptive definition of investment (see paras 6.28–6.29 below) or the mechanism, contained in Article 28(4) mandating a tribunal to dismiss claim without legal merit (see para 3.15 below) are discussed in later chapters of this book.

In advising on a particular situation, the first step is to ascertain whether a relevant **2.08** BIT applies. The most accessible lists of BITs are the compilations appearing on the UNCTAD website[10] and the ICSID website.[11] Neither listing is complete, as can be seen from the fact that each refers to BITs absent from the other list. Other good sources include the nine volume loose-leaf compendium of investment treaties published by Oceana Publications[12] and the United Nations Treaty Collection[13] (UN member States parties to BITs are obliged to deposit them with the United Nations Secretariat pursuant to Article 102 of the Charter of the United Nations). If these sources do not show that a BIT exists between two States, that should not mean the end of a search. One should also check with the relevant Ministry of Foreign Affairs (usually the Treaty Records Department) or local embassy staff.

---

[9] E Denza & S Brooks, 'Investment Protection Treaties: United Kingdom Experience' (1987) 36 ICLQ 908, 908–917.
[10] <http://www.unctadxi.org/templates/DocSearch____779.aspx>.
[11] <http://www.worldbank.org/icsid/treaties/treaties.htm>.
[12] International Centre for the Settlement of Investment Disputes (ICSID), *Investment Promotion and Protection Treaties* (1983—last updated June 2006).
[13] Available online at <http://untreaty.un.org>.

Structure of BITs

2.09   The following paragraphs discuss provisions common to almost all BITs.

Preamble

2.10   The preamble to a BIT usually mentions both the desire to intensify economic cooperation between the contracting States and a recognition that encouraging and protecting investments will stimulate such economic cooperation. Thus the preamble to the Germany model BIT provides:

> desiring to intensify economic co-operation between both States,
>
> intending to create favourable conditions for investments by investors of either State in the territory of the other State,
>
> recognizing that the encouragement and contractual protection of such investments are apt to stimulate private business initiative and to increase the prosperity of both nations . . .[14]

2.11   Treaty tribunals often have regard to treaty preambles in interpreting BITs. For example, the Tribunal in *Saluka v Czech Republic* drew upon the preamble to state:

> This is a more subtle and balanced statement of the Treaty's aims than is sometimes appreciated. The protection of foreign investments is not the sole aim of the Treaty, but rather a necessary element alongside the overall aim of encouraging foreign investment and extending and intensifying the parties' economic relations. That in turn calls for a balanced approach to the interpretation of the Treaty's substantive provisions for the protection of investments, since an interpretation which exaggerates the protection to be accorded to foreign investments may serve to dissuade host States from admitting foreign investments and so undermine the overall aim of extending and intensifying the parties' mutual economic relations.[15]

2.12   Brownlie, in his Separate Opinion following the quantum stage of the *CME v Czech Republic* arbitration, had regard to the preamble of the BIT in question in asking whether it was reasonable to suppose that when a State accepted foreign investment it was accepting the risk of national economic disaster.[16]

2.13   A recurring theme of recent criticisms of investment treaties is their failure to take the wider interests of civil society into account.[17] Similarly, certain critics[18] point to the need for the advantages created by foreign investment to be shared among

---

[14]   Germany model BIT (Appendix 7 below).
[15]   *Saluka Investments BV (The Netherlands) v Czech Republic* (Partial Award) (UNCITRAL, 2006, Watts C, Fortier & Behrens) para 300.
[16]   *CME Czech Republic BV (The Netherlands) v Czech Republic* (Separate Opinion of Brownlie) 9 ICSID Rep 412, 431 (UNCITRAL, 2003, Brownlie).
[17]   eg L Peterson, 'Bilateral Investment Treaties and Development Policy-Making' <http://www.iisd.org/pdf/2004/trade_bits.pdf> accessed 20 September 2006.
[18]   United States, Subcommittee on Investment, 'Report of the Subcommittee on Investment Regarding the Draft Model Bilateral Investment Treaty' (Presented to the Advisory Committee on International Economic Policy, 30 January 2004) <http://www.ciel.org/Publications/BIT_Subcmte_Jan3004.pdf> accessed 20 September 2006.

all sectors of society. In the light of such criticisms the 2004 model US BIT refers in its preamble to improving living standards. It also speaks of a desire to achieve its objectives 'in a manner consistent with the protection of health, safety, and the environment, and the promotion of internationally recognized labor rights'.[19]

Definitions

The two most important definitions in a BIT are the definitions of 'national' **2.14** (which determines the jurisdiction *ratione personae* of the treaty) and the definition of 'investment' (which determines the subject matter jurisdiction, or jurisdiction *ratione materiae*). These definitions set the limits to the rights protected as BITs only cover qualifying investments belonging to qualifying investors. These issues are examined in depth in Chapters 5 and 6.

Another important definition relates to territory. Many developed States admin- **2.15** ister or oversee the foreign relations of territories which play an important role in the world economy.

In general, BITs of the Netherlands apply to the Netherlands Antilles and to Aruba.[20] **2.16** The United Kingdom's treaties do not generally extend to overseas territories such as the Cayman Islands without a separate Exchange of Notes. The claimant in *AAPL v Sri Lanka*[21] was a Hong Kong company claiming under the UK-Sri Lanka BIT,[22] which had been extended to Hong Kong by virtue of an Exchange of Notes.[23] (The United Kingdom has extended its accession to the ICSID Convention to many of its overseas territories.)[24]

Admission

BITs usually contain a provision pursuant to which investments are encouraged, **2.17** but within the legal framework prevailing in the host State. For example, the

---

[19] 2004 US model BIT (Appendix 6 below).
[20] Netherlands model BIT (Appendix 8 below) Art 13; see also Agreement on Encouragement and Reciprocal Protection of Investments (Netherlands-Bolivia) (signed 10 March 1992, entered into force 1 November 1994) Tractatenblad 1992, 081 Art 11.
[21] *Asian Agricultural Products Ltd v Republic of Sri Lanka* (Award) 4 ICSID Rep 245 (ICSID, 1990, El-Kosheri P, Goldman & Asante).
[22] Agreement for the Promotion and Protection of Investments (UK-Sri Lanka) (signed 13 February 1980, entered into force 18 December 1980) 1227 UNTS 391.
[23] Application to Hong Kong by an agreement in the form of an exchange of notes dated 14 January 1981 (UK-Sri Lanka-Hong Kong) 1249 UNTS 453.
[24] The Arbitration (International Investment Disputes) Act 1966 (Application to Colonies etc) Order 1967, SI 1967/159 as amended by SI 1967/249 extended the Convention to (of those that remain under British jurisdiction) Bermuda, British Virgin Islands, Cayman Islands, Falkland Islands (Malvinas), Falkland Islands (Malvinas) Dependencies, Gibraltar, Montserrat, Anguilla, St Helena, St Helena Dependencies, Turks & Caicos Islands; and to the Bailiwick of Guernsey, by Order 1968, SI 1968/1199 and the Bailiwick of Jersey, by Order 1979, SI 1979/572. The application of the Convention was also extended to the Isle of Man. Those territories still excluded include the British Indian Ocean Territory, Pitcairn Islands, British Antarctic Territory and the Sovereign Base Areas of Cyprus. ICSID, *Contracting States and Measures Taken by Them for the Purpose of the Convention* (2003) Part B.

Netherlands model BIT provides: 'Either Contracting Party shall, within the framework of its laws and regulations, promote economic cooperation through the protection in its territory of investments of nationals of the other Contracting Party. Subject to its right to exercise powers conferred by its laws or regulations, each Contracting Party shall admit such investments.'[25]

2.18 The meaning of the phrase 'within the framework of its laws and regulations' is considered further at paras 6.63 to 6.66 below. The distinction between pre- and post-admission protection is set out at paras 7.33 to 7.36 below.

2.19 The US model BIT (Article 8) and the NAFTA Agreement (Article 1106) contain provisions relating to performance requirements. These are extremely broad obligations which apply as early as the establishment and acquisition stages of the development of an investment. They impose prohibitions upon the imposition of any commitment to export a given level of goods, achieve a given level of domestic content, purchase goods in the territory, relate the value of imports to the value of exports, transfer a particular technology or proprietary knowledge to a person within the territory, or supply exclusively from the territory. Similar prohibitions are imposed upon a party conditioning the receipt of an advantage upon specific performance requirements.

Substantive rights

2.20 The substantive rights protected under BITs generally include the following:

- Fair and equitable treatment. This is discussed in detail at paras 7.76 to 7.140.
- National treatment. This is discussed in detail at paras 7.152 to 7.160.
- Most favoured nation (MFN) treatment. This is discussed in detail at paras 7.161 to 7.169.
- Full protection and security. This is discussed in detail at paras 7.141 to 7.151.
- Protection from expropriation. This is discussed in detail in Chapter 8.
- A significant proportion of BITs contain clauses whereby States promise to observe obligations entered into in respect of investments. These so-called 'umbrella clauses' are discussed in detail at paras 4.93 to 4.116.

Compensation for losses (war clause)

2.21 Most BITs contain provisions regulating the host State's liability in the event that the investor's property is damaged due to war or civil unrest. For example, the UK-Sri Lanka BIT provides:

(1) Nationals or companies of one Contracting Party whose investments in the territory of the other Contracting Party suffer losses owing to war or other armed

---

[25] Netherlands model BIT (Appendix 8 below) Art 2.

conflict, revolution, a state of national emergency, revolt, insurrection or riot, in the territory of the latter Contracting Party shall be accorded by the latter Contracting Party treatment, as regards restitution, indemnification, compensation or other settlement, no less favourable than that which the latter Contracting Party accords to its own nationals or companies or to nationals or companies of any third State.

(2) Without prejudice to paragraph (1) of this article, nationals and companies of one Contracting Party who in any of the situations referred to in that paragraph suffer losses in the territory of the other Contracting Party resulting from

> (a) Requisitioning of their property by its forces or authorities, or
> (b) Destruction of their property by its forces or authorities which was not caused in combat action or was not required by the necessity of the situation,

shall be accorded restitution or adequate compensation. Resulting payments shall be freely transferable.[26]

This provision was examined in *AAPL v Sri Lanka*.[27] The Tribunal noted that **2.22** Article 4(2) is tailored specifically to more serious wrongful action by the host State and provides for a higher level of compensation. If the investor's property is damaged in circumstances not falling within Article 4(2), a sort of *renvoi* takes place to find the appropriate solution. The search is first directed towards finding rules more favourable than those existing under Article 4(1) or the treaty's standard of full protection and security. If no more favourable system can be found, the applicable rules become those governing the host State's liability under Article 4(1) or the full protection and security provisions. If the investor can establish that the State failed in its obligation to protect the investment, responsibility will be engaged and compensation will be due in accordance with applicable standards of international law.[28]

The compensation for losses provision was also invoked by the Tribunal in *AMT v* **2.23** *Zaire* to assist in establishing Zaire's responsibility for acts of looting perpetrated by members of Zaire's armed forces. As a result of the application of the clause it was of 'little or no consequence whether [damages be caused by] a member of the Zairian armed forces or any burglar whatsoever'.[29]

Free transfer of payments

Most BITs contain provisions by which States guarantee the free transfer of pay- **2.24** ments in connection with an investment. The type of funds falling within this

---

[26] UK-Sri Lanka BIT (n 22 above) Art 4.   [27] *AAPL v Sri Lanka* (n 21 above).
[28] *AAPL v Sri Lanka* (n 21 above) 257, 272–274.
[29] *American Manufacturing & Trading Inc [AMT] v Republic of Zaire* (Award) 5 ICSID Rep 11, 31 (ICSID, 1997, Sucharitkul P, Golsong & Mbaye).

definition are often specified together with the obligation to permit transfer in a freely convertible currency. For example, the Germany model BIT provides:

Article 5
Each Contracting State shall guarantee to investors of the other Contracting State the free transfer of payments in connection with an investment, in particular

(a) the principal and additional amounts to maintain or increase the investment;
(b) the returns;
(c) the repayment of loans;
(d) the proceeds from the liquidation or the sale of the whole or any part of the investment;
(e) . . .

Article 7

(1) Transfers . . . shall be made without delay at the market rate of exchange applicable on the day of the transfer.
(2) Should there be no foreign exchange market the cross rate obtained from those rates which would be applied by the International Monetary Fund on the date of payment for conversions of the currencies concerned into Special Drawing Rights shall apply.[30]

2.25 Some BITs permit States to suspend this requirement in crisis situations. For example, Article 7 of the French model BIT provides:

Lorsque, dans des circonstances exceptionnelles, les mouvements de capitaux en provenance ou à destination de pays tiers causent ou menacent de causer un déséquilibre grave pour la balance des paiements, chacune des Parties contractantes peut temporairement appliquer des mesures de sauvegarde relatives aux transferts, pour autant que ces mesures soient strictement nécessaires, appliquées sur une base équitable, non-discriminatoire et de bonne foi et qu'elles n'excèdent pas une période de six mois.[31]

Settlement of disputes

2.26 The dispute resolution provisions of BITs are considered in Chapter 3 below.

Subrogation

2.27 Most BITs deal with the question of subrogated claims. This is necessary because of the possibility for investors to arrange political risk insurance at the time of making their initial investment. Subrogation provisions are usually expressed in a stand-alone article, such as Article 8 of the Netherlands model BIT. This provides:

If the investments of a national of the one Contracting Party are insured against non-commercial risks or otherwise give rise to payment of indemnification in respect of such investments under a system established by law, regulation or government contract, any subrogation of the insurer or re-insurer or Agency designated by the one Contracting Party to the rights of the said national pursuant to the terms of such

---

[30] Germany model BIT (Appendix 7 below).   [31] France model BIT (Appendix 10 below).

insurance or under any other indemnity given shall be recognised by the other Contracting Party.[32]

Alternatively, subrogation rights can be included as part of the dispute resolution **2.28** clause. This is the approach adopted in the Germany model BIT where Article 11(4) of Model I provides: 'During arbitration proceedings or the enforcement of an award, the Contracting State involved in the dispute shall not raise the objection that the investor of the other Contracting State has received compensation under an insurance contract in respect of all or part of the damage.'[33]

State to State disputes

Almost all BITs provide for an arbitration mechanism in the event of a dispute **2.29** arising between the contracting States. There is a possibility that a State to State dispute could be used to impede an investor-State arbitration. This could be done by a State commencing an arbitration against an investor's home State seeking to have a dispute about treaty interpretation clarified and seeking a stay of the investor-State arbitration until the State to State dispute has been finally determined. This happened in *Lucchetti v Peru*[34] but the ICSID Tribunal rejected Peru's application to have the arbitration stayed.

Article 9 of the Czech/Netherlands BIT provides for consultations between the **2.30** State parties 'on any matter concerning the interpretation or application of the Agreement'.[35] This was brought into operation by the Czech Republic following the liability award in *CME v Czech Republic*.[36] A series of meetings were held between the two Governments which resulted in a document entitled 'Agreed Minutes'.[37] The Czech Republic contended that the Agreed Minutes constituted binding statements on the meaning and interpretation of the treaty. The Tribunal did not confirm this expressly but it made reference to the minutes in formulating its award.

The role of the NAFTA Free Trade Commission should also be mentioned in any **2.31** consideration of the role played by State parties in the interpretation of concluded treaties. This is addressed at para 2.40 below, and later at paras 7.07 to 7.08 below.

Duration

BITs generally provide for a fixed duration of at least ten years. At the end of **2.32** the period, the treaties usually continue in force until specific notice is given for

---

[32] Netherlands model BIT (Appendix 8 below).

[33] Germany model BIT (Appendix 7 below).

[34] *Empresas Lucchetti SA and Lucchetti Peru SA v Peru* (Award) (2005) 20 ICSID Rev-FILJ 359 (ICSID, 2005, Buergenthal P, Cremades & Paulsson).

[35] Agreement on Encouragement and Reciprocal Protection of Investments (Netherlands-Czech and Slovak Republic) (signed 29 April 1991, entered into force 1 October 1992) 2242 UNTS 206.

[36] *CME Czech Republic BV (The Netherlands) v Czech Republic* (Final Award) 9 ICSID Rep 264 (UNCITRAL, 2003, Kühn C, Schwebel & Brownlie).   [37] ibid 291–292.

termination. There is also usually a further period following termination during which investments originally covered retain the protection provided in the BIT.

C. Multilateral Investment Treaties

2.33 This section outlines the key features of the three multilateral investment treaties under which investment arbitrations have arisen.

NAFTA Chapter 11

2.34 Canada, Mexico, and the United States signed NAFTA in 1992. It came into force on 1 January 1994.[38] The goals set out in its Preamble include creating an expanded and secure market for the goods and services produced in the contracting parties' territories, reducing distortions to trade and ensuring a predictable commercial framework for business planning and investment. NAFTA differs from typical BITs in that it deals with trade issues as well as investment protection.

2.35 For present purposes the most pertinent features of NAFTA are the dispute resolution provisions contained at Chapter 11. These create a functioning arbitration regime to settle disputes between NAFTA investors and NAFTA States. Twenty-seven investment disputes have arisen under NAFTA. Thus more arbitrations have arisen under NAFTA than under any other modern investment treaty. Details of NAFTA claims can be found at <http://www.naftaclaims.com> which contains links to all publicly available materials. This includes awards and often the submissions and supporting documents filed by disputing parties. The NAFTA Secretariat also maintains a website, <http://www.nafta-sec-alena.org>.

2.36 The following discussion of the key features of Chapter 11 of NAFTA will follow the same format as the previous discussion about BITs and indicate certain differences between NAFTA and typical BITs.

Definitions

2.37 The NAFTA definition of investment follows a similar structure to that contained in BITs.[39] It sets out a detailed list of qualifying assets. It also goes a step further than BITs and contains a brief list of assets that do not fall within this definition. These are commercial contracts for the sale of goods or services, the extension of credit in connection with commercial transactions, and claims to money that do not involve the kinds of interests defined as investments.

2.38 NAFTA's definition of an enterprise specifically excludes corporations with no substantial existence on the territory. To qualify, an enterprise must be 'carrying

---

[38] NAFTA (Chapter 11, Appendix 1 below).
[39] NAFTA (Chapter 11, Appendix 1 below) Art 1139.

out business activities' in the territory of a party.[40] NAFTA further restricts the range of qualifying enterprises by allowing parties to deny benefits to enterprises that would otherwise qualify if investors of a non-party which does not maintain diplomatic relations with the denying party own or control the enterprise. A party may also deny the benefits of Chapter 11 of NAFTA to enterprises owned by investors of a non-party if the denying party has adopted measures prohibiting transactions with respect to the non-party State.[41]

Substantive rights

NAFTA protects the following substantive rights: **2.39**

- National treatment.[42]
- MFN treatment.[43]
- Minimum standard of treatment, including fair and equitable treatment and full protection and security.[44]
- NAFTA prohibits the imposition or enforcement of a long list of performance requirements which could act as trade barriers. This protection goes beyond the type of protection found in BITs.[45]
- Parties are prohibited from requiring locally incorporated entities from appointing individuals of any particular nationality to senior management positions. While parties may require that a majority of the board of directors be of a particular nationality or residency, such a requirement must not materially impair the ability of the investor to exercise control over the investment.[46]
- Currency transfers.[47]
- Protection from expropriation.[48]

NAFTA Free Trade Commission

Pursuant to Article 1131(2) of NAFTA, the NAFTA parties are entitled to issue, in   **2.40** the name of the NAFTA Free Trade Commission, binding interpretations of NAFTA provisions. The use of this power generated controversy when the Free Trade Commission issued a Statement on 31 July 2001 declaring that Article 1105(1) of NAFTA prescribes the customary international law minimum standard of treatment and that the concepts of 'fair and equitable treatment' and 'full protection and security' do not require treatment in addition to the customary

---

[40] NAFTA (Chapter 11, Appendix 1 below) Art 1139.
[41] NAFTA (Chapter 11, Appendix 1 below) Art 1113.
[42] NAFTA (Chapter 11, Appendix 1 below) Art 1102.
[43] NAFTA (Chapter 11, Appendix 1 below) Art 1103.
[44] NAFTA (Chapter 11, Appendix 1 below) Art 1105.
[45] NAFTA (Chapter 11, Appendix 1 below) Art 1106.
[46] NAFTA (Chapter 11, Appendix 1 below) Art 1107.
[47] NAFTA (Chapter 11, Appendix 1 below) Art 1109.
[48] NAFTA (Chapter 11, Appendix 1 below) Art 1110.

international law minimum standard.[49] This controversy arose over the question of whether the Free Trade Commission could use its powers to amend, rather than merely interpret. The issue is further addressed at paras 7.07 to 7.08 below. Subsequent statements have been limited to procedural issues.

Settlement of disputes

2.41 NAFTA allows investors to bring two categories of claims. The first is a claim by an investor of a party arising out of loss or damage suffered as a result of another NAFTA party breaching an obligation.[50] The second category is a claim by an investor of a party on behalf of an enterprise. In this situation the investor brings a claim on behalf of an enterprise with a different NAFTA nationality that the investor owns or controls directly or indirectly where the enterprise has incurred loss or damage by reason of, or arising out of, a breach by a NAFTA party. See paras 6.71 to 6.98 below, for a discussion of indirect claims and claims on behalf of corporations.[51]

2.42 Claims cannot be brought if more than three years have elapsed from the date on which the investor or the enterprise respectively acquired or should have acquired knowledge of the alleged breach and knowledge of loss or damage.

2.43 NAFTA arbitrations can be brought under the ICSID Convention, the ICSID Additional Facility, and the UNCITRAL arbitration rules.[52] In practice, however, NAFTA arbitrations have only arisen under the ICSID Additional Facility or the UNCITRAL arbitration rules as only one of the NAFTA parties (the United States) is an ICSID party.[53] As a result, NAFTA awards can only be enforced under the New York Convention and are amenable to review by the courts at the seat.

2.44 Other features of the NAFTA dispute resolution provisions are:

(1) Consolidation.[54] Article 1126 of NAFTA permits a disputing party to request the Secretary General of ICSID to establish a tribunal to order consolidation of one or more claims that have a question of law or fact in common. Once such a tribunal has assumed jurisdiction, other tribunals lose their jurisdiction to decide claims. This consolidation provision allows multiple claims arising from a single measure taken by a NAFTA party to be decided consistently in a way that relieves States from the administrative difficulties and potential legal perils of facing a multiplicity of actions arising out of the same underlying facts. This provision is considered further at para 4.146 below.

---

[49] NAFTA Free Trade Commission (FTC), Interpretation of NAFTA Chap 11 (31 July 2001) 6 ICSID Rep 567, 568.
[50] NAFTA (Chapter 11, Appendix 1 below) Art 1116.
[51] NAFTA (Chapter 11, Appendix 1 below) Art 1117.
[52] NAFTA (Chapter 11, Appendix 1 below) Art 1120.
[53] Canada became a signatory to the ICSID Convention on 15 December 2006.
[54] NAFTA (Chapter 11, Appendix 1 below) Art 1126.

(2) Once an investor or enterprise has commenced arbitration proceedings, it must waive its right to initiate or continue proceedings before any domestic administrative tribunal or court seeking relief in respect of the measure alleged to be a breach. However, proceedings for injunctive, declaratory, or other extraordinary relief not involving the payment of damages may be brought.[55] Alternatively, a tribunal may order interim measures of protection.[56]

(3) The only relief a tribunal may award is monetary damages or restitution of property. Thus NAFTA tribunals cannot grant injunctions or make declarations.[57]

ASEAN Investment Agreement

The ten ASEAN nations, Brunei, Cambodia, Indonesia, Malaysia, Myanmar, the **2.45** Philippines, Singapore, Thailand, Laos, and Vietnam are parties to the ASEAN Agreement for the Promotion and Protection of Investments of 15 December 1987.[58] This Agreement is intended to further the ASEAN goals of increasing investment among the member States and creating favourable conditions for investment. A Protocol to amend the ASEAN Agreement was signed in Jakarta on 12 September 1996[59] but is not yet in force.

In its length and coverage the ASEAN Agreement resembles a bilateral investment **2.46** treaty. Its notable difference to standard BITs is its requirement, in Article II, for investments to be specifically approved in writing and registered by the host country in order to be covered. Another restrictive requirement is the necessity for a corporation to have its place of effective management in the territory of a contracting party in order to qualify as a '"company" of a Contracting Party'.[60] As a result of this provision, the ASEAN Agreement will not protect assets owned by shell companies incorporated in ASEAN States. These provisions were analysed by the Tribunal in the first ASEAN Agreement arbitration, *Yaung Chi Oo Trading Pte Ltd v Government of the Union of Myanmar*.[61] They are discussed at paras 6.99 to 6.102 below.

The Tribunal in *Yaung Chi Oo* had to consider the relationship between the **2.47** ASEAN Agreement and the Framework Agreement on the ASEAN Investment Area of 7 October 1998.[62] The Framework Agreement contains, among other

---

[55] NAFTA (Appendix 1 below) Art 1121.   [56] NAFTA (Appendix 1 below) Art 1134.
[57] NAFTA (Appendix 1 below) Art 1135.
[58] ASEAN Agreement (Appendix 3 below). Brunei Darussalem, Indonesia, Malaysia, the Philippines, Singapore and Thailand were the original signatories; by Protocols of Accession, Vietnam acceded on 16 August 1996, Myanmar and Laos acceded on 23 July 1997 and Cambodia acceded on 30 April 1999.
[59] ASEAN Protocol to Amend the Agreement for the Promotion and Protection of Investments (12 September 1996) available at <http://www.aseansec.org/6465.htm> accessed 20 September 2006.   [60] ASEAN Agreement (Appendix 3 below) Art I(2).
[61] *Yaung Chi Oo Trading Pte Ltd v Government of the Union of Myanmar* (Award) 8 ICSID Rep 452 (ASEAN, 2003, Sucharitkul P, Crawford & Delon).
[62] Framework Agreement on the ASEAN Investment Area (signed 7 October 1998) available at <http://www.aseansec.org/6466.htm> accessed 20 September 2006.

matters, further investment protection provisions. It is possible that both agreements can cover the same investment, leading the *Yaung Chi Oo* Tribunal to conclude that 'the system of investment protection established by the 1987 ASEAN Agreement and enhanced by the parallel provisions of the 1998 Framework Agreement raises difficult questions'.[63]

2.48   The Tribunal noted that the ASEAN tradition was progressively to introduce improvements or revisions to existing Agreements or Framework Agreements and that it was not the practice for early agreements to be impliedly amended by the conclusion of later agreements.[64] The claimant had attempted to use the Framework Agreement's more liberal definition of investor in order to allow it the benefits of the Investment Agreement without satisfying the latter's strict requirements as to registration. The Tribunal rejected this approach, concluding that the two agreements are intended to operate separately. While any investments covered by both agreements will enjoy the most beneficial treatment afforded by either, the Framework Agreement would not give a claimant any new rights in relation to investments not covered by the Investment Agreement.

Energy Charter Treaty

2.49   The Energy Charter Treaty (ECT) was opened for signature in December 1994. It followed the earlier non-binding European Energy Charter of 1991. Signatories include all countries of the Former Soviet Union, Central and Eastern European States, Japan, Australia, and the European Union with its Member States. The United States is not a signatory although it did participate in the drafting of the Treaty. There are no signatory States from the Middle East or South America.

2.50   Some States have signed but not ratified the Treaty. They include Russia, Australia, Belarus, Iceland, and Norway.

2.51   As specified in its Article 2, the ECT 'establishes a legal framework in order to promote long-term co-operation in the energy field'. The intention is to create a stable and reliable legal framework for energy investments. Its provisions go beyond investment protection and extend to competition, transit, and trade. It is described by a commentator as 'a diluted version of Western (mainly European, but also NAFTA) economic integration law'.[65]

Definitions

2.52   The ECT definition of 'investment' follows the familiar form of providing for 'every kind of asset' and then setting out a comprehensive list of specific asset types. At one of its broadest points it includes 'returns' which are defined as 'the

---

[63] *Yaung Chi Oo* (n 61 above) 488.   [64] *Yaung Chi Oo* (n 61 above) 468–469.
[65] TW Wälde, 'Investment Arbitration under the Energy Charter Treaty—From Dispute Settlement to Treaty Implementation' (1996) 12 Arb Int'l 429, 430.

amounts derived from or associated with an Investment, irrespective of the form in which they are paid, including profits, dividends, interest, capital gains, royalty payments, management, technical assistance or other fees and payments in kind'.[66]

'Investment' is also stated to refer to any investment associated with an economic   **2.53** activity in the energy sector.[67]

Investors can include natural persons having citizenship of or residency in a con-   **2.54** tracting party or companies organized according to the law of a contracting party. However, pursuant to Article 17 contracting parties reserve the right to deny the benefit of investment promotion and protection to legal entities owned by citizens or nationals of a third State if the legal entity has no substantial business activities in a contracting party. A contracting party can also deny benefits to investments of third State investors if the denying contracting party does not maintain diplomatic relations, or has prohibited transactions, with investors of that third State.

Article 17 of the ECT was considered by the Tribunal in *Plama v Bulgaria*.[68] The   **2.55** respondent State relied upon Article 17 to claim that it could refuse to arbitrate with the claimant, a Cypriot investment vehicle. The Tribunal rejected the juris-dictional objection, making three key findings:

(1) Article 17 did not automatically deny benefits to companies falling within its terms. It merely provided the State with an option to deny. Among the rea-sons for this finding was the permissive language of Article 17. This language reserves 'the right to deny' as compared with mandatory language 'shall be denied' found in other treaties, such as the ASEAN Framework Agreement on Services Article VI.[69]

(2) The option to deny could only be exercised with prospective, not retrospect-ive effect. To find otherwise would counter the ECT's stated aim of promot-ing 'long-term co-operation'.[70]

(3) Any denial of benefits would only apply to benefits contained in Part III 'Investment Promotion and Protection' in accordance with the wording of Article 17 'Each Contracting Party reserves the right to deny the advantages of this Part . . . '. Thus a right to arbitrate disputes under the dispute reso-lutions provisions at Part V cannot be denied.[71]

---

[66] Energy Charter Treaty (signed 17 December 1994, entered into force 16 April 1998) 2080 UNTS 100 art 1(6)(e) and 1(9) (Appendix 2 below).   [67] ibid Art 1(6).
[68] *Plama Consortium Ltd v Republic of Bulgaria* (Jurisdiction) 20 ICSID Rev-FILJ 262 (ICSID, 2005, Salans P, van den Berg & Veeder). Art 17 was also considered in *Petrobart Ltd v Kyrgyz Republic* (Award) SCC Case No 126/2003 (SCC, 2005, Danelius C, Bring & Smets). The Tribunal rejected the respondent State's Art 17 objection because it accepted information presented by the claimant showing that it was either owned or controlled by UK nationals or had substantial business there.
[69] ibid 309–312.
[70] ibid 312–314. Quotation taken from Energy Charter Treaty (Appendix 2 below) Art 2.
[71] ibid 306–309.

Substantive rights

2.56 The substantive rights protected under the ECT include:

- Fair and equitable treatment, the most constant protection and security, the minimum standard of protection under international law together with the observance of any obligations entered into with an investor or an investment of an investor.[72]
- National treatment and MFN treatment.[73]
- Rights in relation to key personnel.[74]
- Protection from expropriation.[75]
- The right to transfer capital.[76]

Settlement of disputes

2.57 Disputes which cannot be settled within a three-month cooling off period can be referred by the investor to any one of a number of dispute resolution fora.[77] These are:

(1) the courts or administrative tribunals of the host State;
(2) any applicable, previously agreed dispute settlement procedure;
(3) ICSID or if that is not available, the ICSID Additional Facility;
(4) a sole arbitrator or three-person tribunal established under UNCITRAL; or
(5) the Arbitration Institute of the Stockholm Chamber of Commerce.

2.58 Article 23 specifically provides that contracting parties are responsible for the observance of all provisions of the Treaty and shall take such reasonable measures as may be available to ensure its observance by regional or local governments and authorities. The Treaty's dispute settlement provisions may be invoked in respect of measures taken by regional or local governments or authorities. A tribunal determining a claim arising out of a measure of a provincial or local governmental authority may only award monetary damages. Thus a tribunal cannot make an award requiring central government to ensure that local government carries out any specific action.

2.59 The Energy Charter Treaty's contracting parties have created a mutually applicable system of rules binding on themselves which can be enforced by private economic actors. The States are thus encouraging a situation whereby the policing and enforcement of these rules is to be carried out by private attorneys general in

---

[72] Energy Charter Treaty (Appendix 2 below) Art 10(1).
[73] Energy Charter Treaty (Appendix 2 below) Art 10(7).
[74] Energy Charter Treaty (Appendix 2 below) Art 11.
[75] Energy Charter Treaty (Appendix 2 below) Art 13.
[76] Energy Charter Treaty (Appendix 2 below) Art 14.
[77] Energy Charter Treaty (Appendix 2 below) Art 26.

a manner familiar to certain domestic legal systems, particularly in the United States.[78]

D. Foreign Investment Laws

Many capital importing countries have enacted foreign investment laws. These set out standards that will be applied to protect investors. The goals of foreign investment laws are to promote and control investment. They seek to present in one piece of legislation the basic provisions on investment in the country concerned. Foreign investment laws define the desired investment, specify incentives and guarantees, provide for investment controls, and set out the administration of the foreign investment process. They often contain protections which are similar to protections found in BITs, including the right for investors to take disputes to international arbitration. **2.60**

Foreign investment laws are not the subject of this work, although they have provided some of the awards commonly relied upon in interpreting BITs. For that reason they are briefly noted in this section but extensive treatment is beyond the scope of this book. **2.61**

Reference is made below to the basis upon which an ICSID Tribunal asserted jurisdiction in *SPP v Egypt*,[79] a decision decided under the 1974 Egyptian Law No 43 Concerning the Investment of Arab and Foreign Funds and the Free Zone. The ICSID Tribunal in a subsequent case based upon a foreign investment law, *Tradex v Albania*,[80] referred to *SPP v Egypt* in arriving at its conclusion on jurisdiction. It noted that Albania did not contest the principle by which the investor asserted jurisdiction on the basis of an offer contained in the foreign investment law. It stated that: **2.62**

> . . . it can now be considered as established and not requiring further reasoning that such consent can also be effected unilaterally by a Contracting State in its national laws, the consent becoming effective at the latest if and when the foreign investor files its claim with ICSID making use of the respective national law. Therefore, the 1993 Law together with Tradex's Request for Arbitration must be considered as sufficient consent . . .[81]

One practical difference between consent in a foreign investment law and consent in a BIT is that in the former case the State will find it easier to revoke its offer by **2.63**

---

[78] TW Wälde, 'Investment Arbitration under the Energy Charter Treaty—From Dispute Settlement to Treaty Implementation' (1996) 12 Arb Int'l 429, 445.

[79] *Southern Pacific Properties (Middle East) Ltd [SPP] v Arab Republic of Egypt* (Jurisdiction No 2) 3 ICSID Rep 101 (ICSID, 1988, Jiménez de Aréchaga P, El Mahdi & Pietrowski).

[80] *Tradex Hellas SA v Republic of Albania* (Jurisdiction) 5 ICSID Rep 43 (ICSID, 1996, Böckstiegel P, Fielding & Giardina). [81] ibid 63.

repealing its legislation. For example, in 2003 Kazakhstan revised its foreign investment law eliminating its standing offer of consent to arbitration. Thus a potential claimant will be well advised to accept the offer in writing by filing an official notice or by sending a suitable letter if the wording of the foreign investment law allows a claimant to perfect the consent at an early stage before the dispute is ripe for arbitration.

2.64 The Tribunal in *SPP v Egypt* had to rule upon the law to be applied in determining its jurisdiction. The relevant piece of Egyptian legislation was not a treaty which could be interpreted by applying international law rules of treaty interpretation. However, one of the questions at issue was whether the parties' acts under the legislation amounted to consent within the meaning of Article 25 of the ICSID Convention, which is a public international law instrument. The Tribunal applied both Egyptian law and international law: 'Thus, in deciding whether in the circumstances of the present case Law No. 43 constitutes consent to the Centre's jurisdiction, the Tribunal will apply general principles of statutory interpretation taking into consideration, where appropriate, relevant rules of treaty interpretation and principles of international law applicable to unilateral declarations.'[82]

2.65 Many foreign investment laws will contain references to subjects such as 'investors' and 'investment' that are similar to those found in BITs.[83] They may also refer to substantive matters, such as expropriation or fair and equitable treatment. In interpreting such phrases tribunals are likely to make reference to public international law sources and other arbitral awards. This was the approach of the *Tradex* Tribunal:

> Although court and arbitral decisions and legal writings dealing with such other sources may be of relevance in interpreting the 1993 Law, it is this 1993 Law which the Tribunal will examine as to whether Tradex' claim is justified on the merits. This is in conformity with Art. 42(1) of the ICSID Convention according to which 'the Tribunal shall apply the law of the Contracting State party to the dispute (including its rules on the conflict of laws) and such rules of international law as may be applicable'. Accordingly, the Tribunal will make use of sources of international law insofar as that seems appropriate for the interpretation of terms used in the 1993 Law, such as 'expropriation'.[84]

2.66 The same approach had been adopted at the jurisdictional phase. In considering the question of whether the relevant Albanian law had retroactive effect Albania

---

[82] *SPP v Egypt* (n 79 above) 142–143.

[83] *Petrobart v Kyrgyz Republic* (n 68 above) is a case where the claimant succeeded in an Energy Charter Treaty arbitration having regard to the wide definition of investment contained therein. See Chap 6 below. The investor had previously been unsuccessful in a UNCITRAL arbitration arising out of the same facts brought pursuant to the Law of the Kyrgyz Republic on Foreign Investments in the Kyrgyz Republic, 24 September 1997. The UNCITRAL Tribunal had found that the asset out of which the dispute arose did not constitute an investment under the relevant provisions of the Foreign Investment Law (noted *Petrobart v Kyrgyz Republic* (n 68 above) 8–10.

[84] *Tradex Hellas SA v Republic of Albania* (Award) 5 ICSID Rep 43, 82 (ICSID, 1999, Böckstiegel P, Fielding & Giardina).

relied upon international jurisprudence, the protection of investment property rights in human rights law, and other transnational sources of law.[85] Of course, a reference to international law is expressly mandated by Article 42 of the ICSID Convention but it is likely that a tribunal would likewise refer to international law sources in deciding foreign investment law arbitrations under other arbitration regimes.

---

[85] *Tradex v Albania* (n 80 above) 68.

3

DISPUTE RESOLUTION PROVISIONS

A. Introduction

This chapter covers the following topics: **3.01**

(1) Typical dispute settlement provisions contained in BITs.
(2) Transparency in investment treaty arbitrations.
(3) The nature of the legal rights at issue in investment treaty arbitrations.
(4) Interpreting BITs.

It addresses the aspects of dispute resolution provisions commonly found in bilateral investment treaties (BITs), to the extent that they are not addressed elsewhere in this book. The protection offered to investors by the dispute resolution provisions of treaties is sufficiently important to rise to the level of a substantive principle in its own right. In addition, the number of arbitral decisions interpreting these provisions makes necessary their inclusion in a text dealing with investment treaties. However, this chapter will not deal with the internal procedure of investment treaty arbitrations.[1] In this regard, such arbitrations resemble closely international commercial arbitrations. No book yet exists dealing with the internal procedural rules and processes of investment treaty arbitrations but the standard commercial arbitration textbooks provide guidance.[2]

B. Typical Dispute Settlement Provisions Contained in BITs

Standard BITs

3.02 The following paragraphs consider the typical dispute resolution provisions contained in BITs.

3.03 The majority of BITs contain no specific provisions which either indicate the precise nature of disputes between investors and States amenable to arbitration, or prescribe a priority between alternative means of dispute settlement. Thus, for example, the Sri Lanka model BIT simply provides:

> 1. Any dispute between a Contracting Party and an investor of the other Contracting Party shall be notified in writing including a detailed information by the investor to the host party of the investment, and shall, if possible, be settled amicably.
>
> 2. If the dispute cannot be settled in this way within six months from the date of the written notification mentioned in paragraph 1 above, it may be submitted upon request of the investor either to:
>
> (a) the competent tribunal of the Contracting Party in whose territory the investment was made; or
> (b) the International Centre for the Settlement of Investment Disputes (ICSID) established by the convention [on] the settlement of investment disputes between States and Nationals of the other states opened for signature in Washington D.C. on 18th March 1965; or
> (c) the Regional Centre for International Commercial Arbitration in Cairo;
> (d) the Regional Centre for Arbitration—Kuala Lumpur;
> (e) the International Arbitration Institute of Stockholm Chamber of Commerce; or

---

[1] C Schreuer, *The ICSID Convention: A Commentary* (2001), deals with that part of ICSID arbitration procedure which is regulated by the ICSID Convention, in particular in Chap IV, 443–1141. L Reed, J Paulsson & N Blackaby, *Guide to ICSID Arbitration* (2004) deals with ICSID arbitration procedure at 73–94.

[2] See eg A Redfern & M Hunter, *Law and Practice of International Commercial Arbitration* (4th edn, 2004); JDM Lew, LA Mistelis & SM Kröll *Comparative International Commercial Arbitration* (2003); MJ Mustill & SC Boyd, *Commercial Arbitration* (2nd edn, 1989) and Companion Volume 2001; WL Craig, WW Park & J Paulsson, *International Chamber of Commerce Arbitration* (3rd edn, 2000); E Gaillard & J Savage (eds), *Fouchard, Gaillard, Goldman on International Commercial Arbitration* (1999); M Rubino-Sammartano, *International Arbitration Law* (2nd edn, 2001); GB Born, *International Commercial Arbitration: Commentary and Materials* (2nd edn, 2001); R Merkin, *Arbitration Law* (2004); G Petrochilos, *Procedural Law in International Arbitration* (2004).

(f) the Ad-hoc Court of Arbitration established under the arbitration rules of procedures of the United Nations Commission for International Trade Law.[3]

This type of dispute settlement clause may thus be described as a 'cafeteria style' **3.04** approach. It gives the investor a choice between a range of different dispute settlement fora, including the courts of the host state, and a number of arbitral tribunals. Such a clause does not deal expressly with either:

(1) whether the expression 'any dispute' is narrowly confined to the vindication of rights under the treaty, or whether it operates as a general dispute settlement clause, which may be applied in addition to the vindication of rights founded on some other legal basis. Examples would include a breach of contract or breach of local law. This issue is considered further at para 4.34 below; or

(2) what the consequences may be should elements of the same dispute have been submitted to another forum (whether one of those provided for under the treaty, or otherwise). The provision merely contemplates that the listed fora are alternatives ('may be submitted upon request of the investor *either to:*' (emphasis added)). This issue is considered further at paras 4.75 to 4.83 below.

UK model form

The UK prototype[4] does not contain a menu of different dispute settlement **3.05** options. Rather, it provides for a wide clause submitting 'any legal dispute . . . concerning an investment of the [investor] in the territory of the [host State]' to ICSID arbitration. It provides a window of three months within which the parties may reach agreement 'through pursuit of local remedies or otherwise', failing which the dispute may be submitted to arbitration. Thus, what is described as the 'preferred' option for the dispute settlement article provides, in relevant part:

> (1) Each Contracting Party hereby consents to submit to the International Centre for the Settlement of Investment Disputes (hereinafter referred to as 'the Centre') for settlement by conciliation or arbitration under the Convention on the Settlement of Investment Disputes between States and Nationals of Other States opened for signature at Washington on 18 March 1965 any legal dispute arising between that Contracting Party and a national or company of the other Contracting Party concerning an investment of the latter in the territory of the former.
>
> . . .
>
> (3) If any such dispute should arise and agreement cannot be reached within three months between the parties to this dispute through pursuit of local remedies or otherwise, then, if the national or company affected also consents in writing to submit the dispute to the Centre for settlement by conciliation or arbitration under the Convention, either party may institute proceedings by addressing a request to

---

[3] Sri Lanka model BIT (Appendix 9 below) Art 8.
[4] UK model BIT (Appendix 4 below) Art 8 [preferred].

that effect to the Secretary-General of the Centre as provided in Articles 28 and 36 of the Convention. In the event of disagreement as to whether conciliation or arbitration is the more appropriate procedure the national or company affected shall have the right to choose. The Contracting Party which is a party to the dispute shall not raise as an objection at any stage of the proceedings or enforcement of an award the fact that the national or company which is the other party to the dispute has received in pursuance of an insurance contract an indemnity in respect of some or all of his or its losses.

France model form

3.06 The French prototype also provides only for ICSID arbitration:

> Si un tel différend n'a pas pu être réglé dans un délai de six mois à partir du moment où il a été soulevé par l'une ou l'autre des parties au différend, il est soumis à la demande de l'une ou l'autre de ces parties à l'arbitrage du Centre international pour le règlement des différends relatifs aux investissements (C.I.R.D.I.), créé par la Convention pour le règlement des différends relatifs aux investissements entre Etats et ressortissants d'autres Etats, signée à Washington le 18 mars 1965.[5]

NAFTA

3.07 Chapter 11 of NAFTA expressly limits the scope of the claims amenable to arbitration under its provisions to the breach of the obligations specifically protected by the substantive provisions of that Chapter.[6] It offers, then, a choice to the investor of arbitration under either ICSID, the ICSID Additional Facility, or the UNCITRAL Arbitration Rules.[7] As the United States is the only NAFTA party that is a signatory to the ICSID Convention, in practice only the latter two options are feasible.

3.08 NAFTA goes on to make specific provision for waiver of alternative claims, which is discussed at para 4.86 below.[8] It also provides for the consolidation of related claims upon application by a party to a special ad hoc tribunal established to decide the issue of consolidation. (See further at para 4.146 below.)[9]

Energy Charter Treaty

3.09 Article 26 of the Energy Charter Treaty also expressly limits the scope of its dispute settlement provisions to investment disputes 'which concern an alleged breach of an obligation of the [host State] under Part III', which contains the Treaty's specific substantive investment protections.[10] It adopts a 'cafeteria style' approach

---

[5] France model BIT (Appendix 10 below) Art 8.
[6] North American Free Trade Agreement (adopted 17 December 1992, entered into force 1 January 1994) (Appendix 1 below) CTS 1994 No 2; (1993) 32 ILM 612 ('NAFTA') Art 1116.
[7] ibid Art 1120.   [8] ibid Art 1121.   [9] ibid Art 1126.
[10] Energy Charter Treaty (signed 17 December 1994, entered into force 16 April 1998) 2080 UNTS 100 ('ECT') (Appendix 2 below) Art 26(1). But the last sentence of Art 10(1) contains an umbrella clause, as to which see para 4.50 below.

and permits the investor to choose between (a) host state courts; (b) previous contractually agreed methods of dispute settlement; or (c) arbitration under ICSID, the ICSID Additional Facility, the UNCITRAL Rules, or the Arbitration Institute of the Stockholm Chamber of Commerce.[11] The Treaty contains complex provisions (together with permitted reservations) contemplating successive claims, and also permits an opt-out in relation to its umbrella clause provisions.[12]

ASEAN Agreement

The dispute resolution provisions of the 1987 ASEAN Agreement for the **3.10** Promotion and Protection of Investments apply to '[a]ny legal dispute arising directly out of an investment'.[13] The parties to the dispute may mutually agree to arbitration under (a) ICSID; (b) UNCITRAL Rules; (c) the Regional Centre for Arbitration at Kuala Lumpur; or (d) any other regional centre in ASEAN.[14] Failing such an agreement, the parties are to form a three-person tribunal. Each party appoints one tribunal member and the two arbitrators thus appointed select a third to act as chairman, subject to the approval of the disputing parties. If a tribunal cannot be formed the parties may ask the President of the International Court of Justice to make the relevant appointments.[15]

US model form

The 2004 US model BIT has a whole section (Section B) which makes elaborate **3.11** provision for investor-State arbitration. Article 24 makes clear that the investor's claim to arbitration may be based on the host State's breach of either: (a) the substantive obligations of the BIT; (b) an investment authorization;[16] or, critically, (c) an investment agreement. The term 'investment agreement' is in turn defined as a written agreement, binding on both parties under its governing law (and not a unilateral permit or licence) which is made after the date of the BIT between a national authority of a host State and the investor, granting the investor rights over natural resources or other assets, upon which the investor relies.[17]

Any such claims may, after a lapse of six months, be submitted to arbitration **3.12** under ICSID, its Additional Facility, UNCITRAL Rules, or any other form of

---

[11] ibid Art 26(2).   [12] ibid Art 26(3).
[13] ASEAN Agreement for the Promotion and Protection of Investments (signed 15 December 1987) (1988) 27 ILM 612 ('ASEAN Agreement') (Appendix 3 below) Art X(1).
[14] ibid Art X(2).   [15] ibid Art X(3) and (4).
[16] 2004 US model BIT (Appendix 6 below) Art 1 defines this as an authorization granted by a State's foreign investment authority.   [17] ibid.

arbitration agreed between the parties.[18] The model form then provides for a waiver of any other form of dispute resolution as a condition of a valid submission to arbitration, which will be discussed at para 4.56 below.[19] It also contains a consolidation clause, similar to that found in NAFTA.[20]

3.13 As is the case with its substantive provisions, the dispute resolution provisions in the 2004 US model BIT contain a number of provisions which are not generally found in other BITs. They represent a deliberate attempt by the United States to provide drafting solutions to difficulties perceived in treaty arbitration practice.

3.14 One of the innovations is a three-year limitation provision.[21] The model also contains provisions relating to interim measures. Article 26(3) permits the claimant to seek interim injunctive relief that does not involve the payment of monetary damages before a judicial or administrative tribunal of the respondent, provided that the application is brought for the sole purpose of preserving the claimant's rights and interests during the arbitration. Article 28(8) permits the tribunal to order interim measures of protection, including orders to preserve evidence.

3.15 A tribunal is also provided with a mechanism whereby claims without legal merit can be dismissed on a preliminary basis. Article 28(4) mandates a tribunal to address and decide as a preliminary question any objection that, as a matter of law, a claim submitted is not a claim for which an award in favour of the claimant may be made. The amended ICSID Arbitration Rules contain a similar provision. Pursuant to Rule 41(5) a party may file an objection that a claim is 'manifestly without legal merit'.[22] The tribunal shall rule on the objection at its first session or promptly thereafter.[23]

Specific issues

Cooling off period

3.16 Most BITs prescribe a period within which claims cannot be brought pending settlement attempts. For example, the France model BIT provides, at Article 8, that: 'Si un tel différend n'a pas pu être réglé dans un délai de six mois à partir du moment où il a été soulevé par l'une ou l'autre des parties au différend, il est soumis à la demande de l'une ou l'autre de ces parties à l'arbitrage' . . .

---

[18] ibid Art 24(3).   [19] ibid Art 26(2).

[20] ibid Art 33, cf NAFTA (Appendix 1 below) Art 1126.

[21] 2004 US model BIT (Appendix 6 below) Art 26(1).

[22] ICSID, *Rules of Procedure for Arbitration Proceedings (Arbitration Rules)* (2006) <http://www.worldbank.org/icsid/basicdoc/partF.htm> accessed 20 September 2006.

[23] Such provisions are well-known to domestic litigation systems (eg motion to dismiss for failure to present a claim upon which relief can be granted pursuant to US Federal Rules of Civil Procedure, Rule 12(b)(6) or summary judgment on the grounds that the claimant has no real prospect of success pursuant to Part 24.2 of the English Civil Procedure Rules). Such provisions are, however, not generally found in international arbitration rules.

The cooling off period varies from treaty to treaty. For example the UK model **3.17** BIT provides for a three-month cooling off period,[24] the German model has six months,[25] and the Spain-Indonesia BIT provides for a twelve-month period.[26]

In practice, however, the majority of tribunals have not penalized claimants for **3.18** failing to observe these cooling off periods. In *Bayindir v Pakistan*[27] one of Pakistan's objections to the Tribunal's jurisdiction was that Bayindir had failed to give any notice of its claim and was thus not entitled to submit a dispute to arbitration. It contended that Bayindir had failed to fulfil the provisions of Article VII of the Turkey-Pakistan BIT,[28] which requires investors to provide six months' notification of a dispute prior to commencing arbitration and to endeavour to settle disputes in good faith. The Tribunal rejected Pakistan's arguments. It agreed with the view expressed by many previous tribunals that the need to give notice was not a jurisdictional requirement: 'Contrary to Pakistan's position, the non-fulfilment of this requirement is not "fatal to the case of the claimant". As Bayindir pointed out, to require a formal notice would simply mean that Bayindir would have to file a new request for arbitration and restart the whole proceeding, which would be to no-one's advantage.'[29]

Two cases which decided the point differently are *Goetz v Burundi* [30] and *Enron* **3.19** *and Ponderosa Assets v Argentine Republic*.[31] Here, the Tribunals found that the cooling off period was a jurisdictional, and not merely a procedural, requirement. In both cases the claimant had given notice in respect of parts of its claim but later sought to expand the scope. However, even though the Tribunal in *Enron* found the observance of the six-month cooling off period was a jurisdictional require-ment, it held that satisfaction of the period in respect of the original claim would also be sufficient for ancillary or additional claims.

---

[24] UK model BIT (Appendix 4 below) Art 8(1) [alternative]; Art 8(3) [preferred].

[25] Germany model BIT (Appendix 7 below) Art 11(2).

[26] Agreement on the Reciprocal Promotion and Protection of Investments (Spain-Indonesia) (signed 30 May 1995, entered into force 18 December 1996) 1965 UNTS 103, Art X(2).

[27] *Bayindir Insaat Turizm Ticaret Ve Sanayi AS v Islamic Republic of Pakistan* (Jurisdiction) ICSID Case No ARB/03/29 (ICSID, 2005, Kaufmann-Kohler P, Berman & Böckstiegel). Similar rulings were reached by the Tribunals in *Ethyl Corp v Government of Canada* (Jurisdiction) 7 ICSID Rep 3, 36–40; (1999) 38 ILM 708, 727–729 (NAFTA/UNCITRAL, 1998, Böckstiegel C, Brower & Lalonde); *Lauder v Czech Republic* (Final Award) 9 ICSID Rep 62, 89 (UNCITRAL, 2001, Briner C, Cutler & Klein); *SGS Société Générale de Surveillance SA v Islamic Republic of Pakistan* (Jurisdiction) 8 ICSID Rep 383, 448–449; (2003) 42 ILM 1290, 1322 (ICSID, 2003, Feliciano P, Faurès & Thomas).

[28] Agreement Concerning the Reciprocal Promotion and Protection of Investments (Turkey-Pakistan) (16 March 1995).   [29] *Bayindir v Pakistan* (n 27 above) para 100.

[30] *Goetz & ors v Republic of Burundi* (Award: First Part) 6 ICSID Rep 3, 32 (ICSID, 1999, Weil P, Bedjaoui & Bredin).

[31] *Enron Corp and Ponderosa Assets LP v Argentine Republic* (Jurisdiction) ICSID Case No ARB/01/3 (ICSID, 2004, Orrego Vicuña P, Espiell & Tschanz) paras 82–88.

3.20 In circumstances where a claimant fails entirely to give advance warning of its intention to commence proceedings, it is possible that a respondent State could argue that the tribunal lacks jurisdiction because of the non-existence of a dispute as required by the BITs arbitration provisions. Such arguments have been made by States in the International Court of Justice (ICJ) and are generally rejected. For example, in *Case Concerning the Genocide Convention (Bosnia-Herzegovina v Yugoslavia)*[32] the ICJ held that it was sufficient that the rejection of complaints by Yugoslavia, necessary to constitute its dispute with Bosnia-Herzegovina, had emerged in the course of proceedings.[33]

Offer to arbitrate

3.21 In the event that the dispute is not resolved within the cooling off period, the BIT will provide that the investor may submit the dispute to one of a number of dispute resolution options. These most commonly include ICSID, with a reference to the ICSID Additional Facility if one of the State parties to the BIT is not an ICSID signatory. Other common options are ad hoc arbitration, often under the UNCITRAL rules. References to the International Chamber of Commerce or the Arbitration Institute of the Stockholm Chamber of Commerce are also often used. In addition, some BITs[34] provide for the competent courts of the territory in which the investment has been made.

3.22 The drafters of the ICSID Convention envisaged the possibility of a State giving its consent in advance to ICSID arbitrations, albeit they envisaged this happening through investment legislation rather than BITs: 'Nor does the Convention require that the consent of both parties be expressed in a single Instrument. Thus a host State might in its investment promotion legislation offer to submit disputes arising out of certain classes of investments to the jurisdiction of the Centre, and the investor might give his consent by accepting the offer in writing.'[35]

3.23 In the first ICSID case where an advance offer of jurisdiction was invoked, *SPP v Egypt*,[36] the respondent State argued that the 'offer' contained in its investment

---

[32] *Case Concerning Application of the Convention on the Prevention and Punishment of the Crime of Genocide (Bosnia and Herzegovina v Yugoslavia)* (Preliminary Objections) [1996] ICJ Rep 595, 614–615; (1996) 115 ILR 1, 27–28.

[33] Similar rulings were made by the Permanent Court of International Justice (PCIJ) in *Interpretation of Judgments Nos 7 and 8 (The Chorzów Factory) (Germany-Poland)* PCIJ Rep Series A No 13, 10–12 and *Application for Revision and Interpretation of the Judgment of 24 February 1982 in the Case Concerning the Continental Shelf* (Tunisia/Libyan Arab Jamahiriya) *(Tunisia v Libya)* [1985] ICJ Rep 192, 217–218.

[34] eg Agreement Regarding the Promotion and Mutual Protection of Investments (Cyprus-Russian Federation) (signed 11 April 1997) Art 7(2).

[35] ICSID, *Documents Concerning the Origin and the Formulation of the Convention on the Settlement of Investment Disputes between States and Nationals of Other States* (1969) Vol II(2) 1069. 1 ICSID Rep, 28.

[36] *Southern Pacific Properties (Middle East) Limited [SPP] v Arab Republic of Egypt* (Jurisdiction No 1) 3 ICSID Rep 112 (ICSID, 1985, Jiménez de Aréchaga P, El Mahdi & Pietrowski); *Southern*

legislation could not amount to consent in writing for the purposes of Article 25 of the ICSID Convention. The Tribunal analysed the issue at length before concluding that the relevant article of the Egyptian Foreign Investment Law constituted an express consent in writing to ICSID's jurisdiction and that no further ad hoc expression of consent on the part of the State was required.

The point remained controversial prior to the birth of BIT arbitration. In his oft-cited 1995 article, 'Arbitration Without Privity',[37] Paulsson expended some effort in refuting the proposition that the right to arbitrate contained in a BIT would exist only in the presence of a specific agreement to arbitrate concluded between the disputing parties. **3.24**

Yet Sri Lanka did not seek to take this point on receiving the first BIT request for arbitration in 1987. Zaire, however, did in the second BIT claim, commenced in 1993.[38] In response to Zaire's objection, the Tribunal rejected the contention that specific consent was required between Zaire and the investor to submit the dispute to the Centre: **3.25**

> In other words, does the consent of the United States create an obligation for its national? Should there not be, in addition to that consent, also the consent by AMT itself relating to a specific dispute? . . . The Tribunal holds that this question must be answered in the negative . . . In the present case, it happens that AMT . . . has opted for a proceeding before ICSID. AMT has expressed its choice without any equivocation; this willingness together with that of Zaire expressed in the Treaty, creates the consent necessary to validate the assumption of jurisdiction by the Centre.[39]

The point was also disputed in another early case, *CSOB v Slovak Republic*.[40] The Slovak Republic sought to rely on the wording of Article 8(2) of the Czech Republic/Slovak Republic BIT which provided that 'the investor and the Party shall have the right to submit the dispute to [arbitration]'[41] to contend that a joint submission was required. One of the grounds upon which the Tribunal rejected the submission was that the respondent State's suggested interpretation 'would **3.26**

Pacific Properties (Middle East) Ltd [SPP] v Arab Republic of Egypt (Jurisdiction No 2) 3 ICSID Rep 131 (ICSID, 1988, Jiménez de Aréchaga P, El Mahdi & Pietrowski).

[37] J Paulsson, 'Arbitration Without Privity' (1995) 10 ICSID Rev-FILJ 232, 240–241.

[38] *American Manufacturing and Trading Inc v Republic of Zaire* (Award) 5 ICSID Rep 11 (ICSID, 1997, Sucharitkul P, Golsong & Mbaye).

[39] ibid 25–26. CH Schreuer in *The ICSID Convention: A Commentary* (2001) 212–213, states that the claimants' reliance on the ICSID clause in the BIT was not called into question in *AMT v Zaire* (ibid). Although the Tribunal's award is not entirely clear, we respectfully disagree with him on this point.

[40] *Ceskoslovenska Obchodni Banka AS v Slovak Republic* (Jurisdiction) 5 ICSID Rep 330, 343–350 (ICSID, 1999, Buergenthal P, Bernardini & Bucher).

[41] Dahoda medzi vládou Slovenskej republiky a vládou Českej republiky o podpore a vzájomnej ochrane investicii ('Agreement Regarding the Promotion and Protection of Reciprocal Investments') (signed 23 November 1992, entered into force 1 January 1993) Zbierka zákonov č 231/1993.

leave investors without the protection afforded by international arbitration, contrary to the main objective of bilateral investment treaties'.[42]

3.27 The point is no longer controversial. Thus, when Professor Lauterpacht provided his foreword to Schreuer's *The ICSID Convention: A Commentary*[43] he noted research carried out by Professor Brigitte Stern in 2000 to the effect that of the twenty-nine cases pending at ICSID, twenty-one were based on multilateral or bilateral treaties. Professor Stern's conclusion was that 'we are walking with giant steps towards a general system of compulsory arbitration against States for all matters relating to international investments, at the initiative of the private actors of international economic relations'.[44]

3.28 The fact that the State's written consent (in the treaty) and the investor's written consent (in the request for arbitration) are not contained in the same document has not given rise to difficulties either under the requirement of Article 25 of the ICSID Convention for 'consent in writing' or the requirement in Article II of the New York Convention for an 'agreement in writing'.[45]

3.29 The 2004 US model BIT[46] specifically provides that the State's consent and the investor's submission of a claim to arbitration shall satisfy the requirements of the ICSID Convention for written consent and (where the claim is not brought under ICSID) the requirements of the New York Convention for an agreement in writing.[47] The parties to the English litigation arising out of the *Occidental v Ecuador* arbitration both accepted that the award could, if not challenged, be recognized and enforced under the New York Convention.[48] In that case, the arbitration had been brought under the provisions of the US-Ecuador BIT and the parties had elected ad hoc arbitration under UNCITRAL Rules in London. Thus, even where an investment treaty award is not rendered under the ICSID Convention, it will still be enforceable under the New York Convention as having been rendered pursuant to an agreement in writing.

Fork in the road

3.30 Many BITs contain provisions stating that a choice of a particular dispute resolution procedure, once taken, forecloses the possibility of electing any other

---

[42] *CSOB v Slovak Republic* (n 40 above) 349.   [43] Schreuer (n 39 above).

[44] Schreuer (n 39 above) xii.

[45] International Bank for Reconstruction and Development, *Report of the Executive Directors on the Convention on the Settlement of Investment Disputes between States and Nationals of Other States* [published with the text of the Convention] (1965) 43. Although the Report refers to 'investment promotion legislation', the reasoning would apply equally to consent contained in a BIT.

[46] 2004 US model BIT (Appendix 6 below) art 25(2).

[47] Convention on the Recognition and Enforcement of Foreign Arbitral Awards (adopted 10 June 1958, entered into force 7 June 1959) 330 UNTS 38 ('New York Convention') Art II.

[48] *Republic of Ecuador v Occidental Exploration and Production Co* [2005] EWHC 774 (Comm); [2005] 2 Lloyd's Rep 240, 249.

dispute resolution procedures potentially available. Such provisions are commonly known as 'fork in the road' provisions. They represent a marked distinction from the position under diplomatic protection procedures whereby an investor is forced to exhaust all available alternative remedies before having his State assert the claim on his behalf. If a fork in the road provision applies, seeking a remedy before a domestic court would cause a claimant to lose its right to arbitrate under a BIT.

3.31 An example of a fork in the road provision is Article VI(3) of the US-Czech Republic BIT:

> . . . either party to the dispute may institute [an arbitration] provided:
>
> (i) the dispute has not bee[n] submitted by the national or company for resolution in accordance with any applicable previously agreed dispute-settlement procedures; and
> (ii) the national or company concerned has not brought the dispute before the courts of justice or administrative tribunals or agencies of competent jurisdiction of the Party that is a party to the dispute.[49]

3.32 Such provisions are considered in detail at paras 4.75 to 4.83 below.

C. Treaty Arbitration under the ICSID Convention

3.33 At paras 3.04 and 3.09 above, mention was made of the 'cafeteria style' approach adopted in many investment treaties whereby a range of dispute resolution options are offered. In respect of any of the choices other than ICSID arbitration, the *lex arbitri* will be selected by application of the methods used in commercial arbitration.[50] The *lex arbitri* will be a municipal system of law. Arbitration under the ICSID Additional Facility would also be treated in this manner. However, the combination of ICSID arbitration and investment treaties raises particular issues. These are the subjects of this section.

3.34 The *lex arbitri* of an ICSID arbitration is the ICSID Convention itself. Thus, the rules of law pursuant to which the arbitration is conducted are supplied by the Convention as interpreted under principles of public international law. The laws of the physical place of arbitration have no bearing whatsoever on the arbitration procedure. ICSID arbitration only intersects with domestic law for the purposes of (a) seeking a stay of domestic court proceedings brought in breach of an agreement to arbitrate under ICSID and (b) enforcement.

---

[49] Treaty Concerning the Reciprocal Encouragement and Protection of Investment (Czech Republic-US) (signed 22 October 1991, entered into force 19 December 1992) 187/1993 Sb.
[50] Lew, Mistelis & Kröll (n 2 above) 523–527; Redfern & Hunter (n 2 above) 78–93; Gaillard & Savage (eds) *Fouchard, Gaillard, Goldman* (n 2 above) 633ff.

3.35 The provision of the ICSID Convention that regulates jurisdiction is Article 25. It is commonly interpreted[51] as requiring the fulfilment of five criteria. These are:

(1) a legal dispute;
(2) arising directly out of an investment;
(3) between a contracting State; and
(4) the national of another contracting State; and
(5) which the parties to the dispute consent in writing to submit to ICSID.

3.36 Some of these criteria are addressed elsewhere in this book. Criterion (2) (investment) is considered in Chapter 6 and criterion (4) (nationality) is discussed in Chapter 5. The manner in which the requirement for consent in writing is fulfilled by the joining of the State's offer of arbitration to qualifying investors under the treaty to the investor's written acceptance of the offer is addressed at paras 3.21 to 3.29 above.

3.37 Pursuant to Article 26 of the ICSID Convention a choice of ICSID arbitration will exclude any other dispute resolution remedy. It would also exclude diplomatic protection.[52] These other dispute resolution options will not necessarily be excluded by the choice of a non-ICSID arbitration remedy under an investment treaty.

3.38 The ICSID Convention will also supply the choice of law rule pursuant to which the law governing the substantive rights in the arbitration will be selected. ICSID Convention Article 42 provides:

(1) The Tribunal shall decide a dispute in accordance with such rules of law as may be agreed by the parties. In the absence of such agreement, the Tribunal shall apply the law of the Contracting State party to the dispute (including its rules on the conflict of laws) and such rules of international law as may be applicable.

(2) The Tribunal may not bring in a finding of *non-liquet* on the ground of silence or obscurity of the law.

(3) The provisions of paragraphs (1) and (2) shall not prejudice the power of the Tribunal to decide a dispute *ex aequo et bono* if the parties so agree.

3.39 As stated above, the substantive provisions of BITs are interpreted in accordance with public international law, although some role for the law of the host State remains (see further at paras 3.74 to 3.82 below). This would be the effect of Article 42 of the ICSID Convention irrespective of whether the parties to the BIT have expressly agreed that the tribunal shall determine the dispute in accordance with principles of international law.

---

[51] Schreuer (n 125 above) 89. *Continental Casualty Co v Argentine Republic* (Jurisdiction) ICSID Case No ARB/03/9 (ICSID, 2006, Sacerdoti P, Veeder & Nader) para 58.

[52] Convention on the Settlement of Investment Disputes between States and Nationals of Other States (signed 18 March 1965, entered into force 14 October 1966) 575 UNTS 159 ('ICSID Convention') Art 27.

D. Transparency

In international commercial arbitration, only parties to a dispute may participate **3.40** in the arbitral proceedings. A third party may not do so without the arbitrating parties' consent. In investment dispute arbitration, however, the presence of States and State entities as well as issues of a public nature mean that transparency and accountability are beginning to outweigh privacy and confidentiality in importance.

For example, in June 2005 the OECD Investment Committee released a state- **3.41** ment supporting additional transparency in international investment arbitration in the following terms:

> There is a general understanding among the Members of the Investment Committee that additional transparency, in particular in relation to the publication of arbitral awards, subject to necessary safeguards for the protection of confidential business and governmental information, is desirable to enhance effectiveness and public acceptance of international investment arbitration, as well as contributing to the further development of a public body of jurisprudence. Members of the Investment Committee generally share the view that, especially insofar as proceedings raise important issues of public interest, it may also be desirable to allow third party participation, subject however to clear and specific guidelines.[53]

In investment disputes under ICSID, it is routine for the basic details of the **3.42** arbitration to be in the public domain. These details include matters such as the existence of the arbitration, the parties, the tribunal, and the nature of the dispute.[54] The greatest degree of transparency is evident after the arbitration is concluded, through the publication of the award. The parties are usually encouraged to allow the award to be published. Under the new ICSID arbitration rules, ICSID is obliged to publish excerpts of the legal reasoning of the tribunal even if the parties do not consent to publication.[55] In NAFTA cases, submissions, orders, and awards are available on the internet.[56]

The new ICSID rules have also provided a boost for non-disputing parties seek- **3.43** ing to participate in arbitrations. Pursuant to Rule 37(2) after consulting with the parties (but without seeking their consent) the tribunal may allow a non-disputing party to file a written submission. In deciding whether to allow such a filing the tribunal is to consider, among other things, the extent to which the non-disputing party submission would assist the tribunal by bringing a perspective, particular

---

[53] OECD, *Transparency and Third Party Participation in Investor-State Dispute Settlement Procedures: Statement by the OECD Investment Committee* (2005) 1. <http://www.oecd.org> accessed 20 September 2006. [54] See <http://www.worldbank.org/icsid/cases/cases.htm>.
[55] ICSID, *Rules of Procedure* (n 22 above) Rule 48(4).
[56] An excellent resource is <http://www.naftaclaims.com> which contains links to all publicly available legal documents.

knowledge, or insight that is different from that of the disputing parties, whether the non-disputing party submission would address a matter within the scope of the dispute and whether the non-disputing party has a significant interest in the proceedings. The tribunal is obliged to ensure that the non-disputing party submission does not disrupt the proceedings or unduly burden or unfairly prejudice either party. Both parties must be given an opportunity to present observations on the non-disputing party submission.

3.44 Even before the change in the rules, ICSID tribunals had begun to allow for the possibility of non-disputing party submissions. The Tribunal in *Vivendi Universal v Argentine Republic*[57] set out three basic criteria for determining whether to exercise the power to admit such submissions: the appropriateness of the subject-matter of the case; the suitability of a given non-party to play a role in the case; and the procedure by which the non-disputing party submission was made and considered.[58]

3.45 The Tribunal noted that State courts have traditionally accepted so-called *amicus curiae* submissions from suitable non-parties in cases featuring matters of public interest of an appropriate nature. Nonetheless, the Tribunal considered that the aspect of public interest, on its own, was insufficient to satisfy the requirements. There must be something more—a 'particular public interest'. The particular public interest in the *Vivendi* case arose because the dispute revolved around the water distribution and sewerage systems of the City of Buenos Aires and surrounding municipalities. The outcome of the case could affect the operation of these systems, thus providing a legitimate public interest in the subject-matter before the Tribunal.

3.46 On suitability to make a non-disputing party submission, the Tribunal stated that it would 'only accept *amicus* submissions from persons who establish to [its] satisfaction that they have the expertise, experience, and independence to be of assistance in this case'.[59] To enable a tribunal to make such a determination, a non-disputing party must first apply to the tribunal for permission to make a submission explaining in its petition: the petitioner's identity and background, including the nature of its relationships (if any) with the parties to the dispute; the nature of the petitioner's interest in the case; whether the petitioner has received financial or other material support from any of the parties or from any person connected with the parties in the case; and the reasons why the tribunal should accept the petitioner's submission.[60]

---

[57] *Aguas Argentinas SA, Suez Sociedad General de Aguas de Barcelona SA and Vivendi Universal SA v Argentine Republic* (Order in Response to a Petition for Transparency and Participation as *Amicus Curiae*) ICSID Case No ARB/03/19 (ICSID, 2005, Salacuse P, Kaufmann-Kohler & Nikken).
[58] ibid para 17.   [59] ibid para 24.   [60] ibid para 25.

In a subsequent case[61] the same Tribunal considered near-identical issues and **3.47**
produced a near-identical order. In this second order, the Tribunal elaborated on
its requirements. In particular, it emphasized that the petitioners must provide
detailed and specific information. Although the petitioners failed to meet the
burden, the Tribunal said it would be prepared to consider whether the petitioners could qualify if they presented a new application with appropriate and
sufficient information and granted them an opportunity to do so.

Non-disputing party submissions were allowed by NAFTA Tribunals applying **3.48**
the UNCITRAL rules in *Methanex v USA*[62] and *UPS v Canada*.[63] The NAFTA
Free Trade Commission issued a statement on 7 October 2004 recommending
procedures to be followed by NAFTA tribunals with respect to non-disputing
party participation.[64] The ICSID Tribunal in *Aguas del Tunari v Bolivia* refused to
accept non-disputing party submissions during the jurisdictional phase[65] but this
could be attributed to the fact that jurisdictional proceedings generally focus more
on pure legal questions rather than questions of public legitimacy that arise in
considering issues of expropriation or fair and equitable treatment.

The US model BIT specifically provides for the tribunal to have the authority to **3.49**
accept and consider submissions from non-disputing parties.[66] It goes further
than the new ICSID rules by providing also for documents to be made available
to the public and for open hearings.[67]

It could be argued that non-disputing parties have no place in investor-State **3.50**
arbitration, as States should be fully competent to deal with all matters arising in
their territory. Yet, in reality, there are many reasons why States will not, or cannot,
bring all relevant matters to the tribunal's attention. For example, a State might
omit matters for reason of litigation strategy, because it cannot obtain evidence
outside its territory or because it lacks litigation resources or expertise. There may be

---

[61] *Aguas Provinciales de Santa Fe SA, Suez, Sociedad General de Aguas de Barcelona SA and InterAguas Servicios Integrales de Agua SA v Argentine Republic* (Order in Response to a Petition for Participation as *Amicus Curiae*) ICSID Case No ARB/03/17 (ICSID, 2006, Salacuse P, Kaufmann-Kohler & Nikken).

[62] *Methanex Corp v United States of America* (Decision on Petitions from Third Persons to Intervene as *Amici Curiae*) 7 ICSID Rep 208 (NAFTA/UNCITRAL, 2001, Veeder P, Rowley & Christopher).

[63] *United Parcel Service of America Inc v Government of Canada* (Decision of the Tribunal on Petitions for Intervention and Participation as *Amici Curiae*) (NAFTA/UNCITRAL, 2001, Keith C, Fortier & Cass).

[64] NAFTA Free Trade Commission (FTC), *Statement of the Free Trade Commission on Non-Disputing Party Participation* (2004) <http://www.naftaclaims.com/Papers/Nondisputing-en.pdf> accessed 20 September 2006.

[65] *Aguas del Tunari SA v Republic of Bolivia* (Letter, 29 January 2003 by Caron P) 20 ICSID Rev-FILJ 450, 574–576; ICSID Case No ARB/02/3 (ICSID, 2003, Caron P, Alberro-Semerena & Alvarez).   [66] 2004 US model BIT (Appendix 6 below) Art 28(3).

[67] ibid Art 29.

domestic political reasons for a State failing to emphasize certain environmental or human rights issues.[68] Non-disputing parties have the potential to fill all these gaps and ensure that the tribunal has the benefit of a wider spectrum of relevant views. This in turn will increase the political legitimacy of the process.

E. The Nature of the Legal Rights at Issue in Investment Treaty Arbitrations

Legal rights arising under investment treaties

3.51 In any consideration of the legal relations arising between investors and host States under a bilateral investment treaty it is important to distinguish three principal situations in which rights can arise. These are:

(1) *Law applicable to the substance of the dispute (*lex causae*).* These are the primary obligations (the substantive rights provided by the treaty) that the investor is seeking to enforce. These rights arise under the treaty and are interpreted according to public international law.

(2) *Law applicable to the agreement to arbitrate between the investor and the State.* This agreement is created by the BIT and is closely linked to it. As such, while the agreement is not contained in the BIT itself, it should be seen as governed by public international law. If one were instead to determine the proper law of the agreement by looking for the jurisdiction with closest connection to the dispute, one would be drawn to the law of the host State. This would be the jurisdiction of one of the two disputing parties and the physical place where the subject-matter of the dispute, the investment, is located. However, such a conclusion would be at odds with the policy of protection of investments which the BIT is supposed to promote.[69]

(3) *The law applicable to the arbitration procedure itself (*lex arbitri*).* If the parties have started an ICSID arbitration the arbitration procedure will be governed by the ICSID Convention and thus take place under public international law. If they have chosen any other system the law governing the arbitration procedure would be municipal law and it is on this basis that national courts have reviewed the actions of BIT tribunals.[70]

---

[68] D Shelton, 'The Participation of Non-Governmental Organizations in International Judicial Proceedings' (1994) 88 AJIL 611, 615. The article is an excellent introduction to the issue generally in international law.

[69] This is the conclusion reached in *Republic of Ecuador v Occidental Exploration and Production Co* [2005] EWCA Civ 1116; [2006] QB 432, 458–459.

[70] See eg L Collins et al, *Dicey, Morris & Collins on the Conflict of Laws* (14th edn, 2006) 778–784.

Direct rights or derivative rights?

This book is primarily concerned with the first category of rights listed above, **3.52**
those applicable to the substance of the dispute.

Do those substantive rights asserted in investment treaty arbitrations belong to the **3.53**
claimant investor itself or to that investor's home State, asserted on behalf of the
State by the investor? This question is addressed by Douglas in his article 'The
Hybrid Foundations of Investment Treaty Arbitration'.[71] Douglas describes these
two theories as the direct rights theory and the derivative rights theory respectively.[72]

The direct rights theory would at first sight seem an unusual position in public **3.54**
international law as the treaty would be creating rights in favour of non-State
actors. Nonetheless, there is precedent for this, in particular in the field of human
rights. For example, the ICJ in the *LaGrand case*[73] held that a provision of the
Vienna Convention on Consular Relations, requiring prison authorities to
'inform the person concerned without delay of his rights under this sub-paragraph'
creates rights for individuals. Similarly, it is well understood that individuals can
bring direct claims before the European Court of Human Rights as a result of a
State's breach of the European Convention on Human Rights.

The derivative rights theory is based upon the international law concept of **3.55**
diplomatic protection. Under international law, a State is responsible for injuries
caused to foreign nationals by its wrongful acts or omissions. The State of the
injured national may use the procedure of diplomatic protection to obtain
reparation for the wrong.[74] In so doing, the State of the wronged national will be
seen as seeking redress for an injury caused to itself. In the words of the Permanent
Court of International Justice (PCIJ), 'By taking up the case of one of its subjects
and by resorting to diplomatic action or international judicial proceedings on his
behalf, a State is in reality asserting its own rights—its right to ensure, in the
person of its subjects, respect for the rules of international law.'[75]

The weakness of this system, from the injured national's point of view, is that he has **3.56**
no way of compelling his State to act in protection of his interests in this regard:

> . . . within the limits prescribed by international law, a State may exercise diplomatic
> protection by whatever means and to whatever extent it thinks fit, for it is its own
> right that the State is asserting. Should the natural or legal persons on whose behalf
> it is acting consider that their rights are not adequately protected, they have no

---

[71] Z Douglas, 'The Hybrid Foundations of Investment Treaty Arbitration' (2003) 74 BYIL 151.
[72] ibid especially 162–164.
[73] *LaGrande Case (Germany v United States of America)* [2001] ICJ Rep 466.
[74] 'Diplomatic Protection: Text of the Draft Articles with Commentaries thereto' (Dugard,
Special Rapporteur) in *Report of the International Law Commission on its Fifty-eighth Session
(1 May–9 June, 3 July–11 August 2006), Official Records of the General Assembly Sixty-first Session,*
Supplement No. 10, UN Doc A/61/10, 24.
[75] *The Mavrommatis Palestine Concessions (Greece v United Kingdom)* PCIJ Rep Series A, No 2, 12.

remedy in international law. All they can do is to resort to municipal law, if means are available, with a view to furthering their cause or obtaining redress . . . The State must be viewed as the sole judge to decide whether its protection will be granted, to what extent it is granted, and when it will cease. It retains in this respect a discretionary power the exercise of which may be determined by considerations of a political or other nature, unrelated to the particular case.[76]

3.57 Bilateral investment treaties are a way of filling the gap between the rights offered (through the fiction[77] of diplomatic protection) to individuals and the remedies available. The derivative rights theory thus directly places investment treaties as a supplement to the traditional concept of diplomatic protection.

3.58 The derivative rights theory does, however, cause some theoretical difficulties. For example, if the rights belong to the State and not to the investor, it is difficult to see how the investor could ever waive them by contract.[78] It is also difficult to explain how compensation can be calculated with no reference to the injury suffered by the State. If the direct rights theory is adopted, there will be no difficulties in investors waiving their rights to arbitration and in tribunals applying an arbitration model closer to that of international commercial arbitration, where parties exercise their own rights. This may also emphasize to tribunals the novelty of this area of law and free them from any perceived need to look to precedents from the field of diplomatic protection for guidance.

3.59 The ILC Draft Articles on State Responsibility take no position on the direct/derivative rights question. Article 33 provides that the obligations of a responsible State may be owed to another State, to several States, or to the international community as a whole but goes on to add that this 'is without prejudice to any right, arising from the international responsibility of a State, which may accrue directly to any person or entity other than a State'.[79]

3.60 Crawford's Commentary on this Article makes reference to bilateral investment agreements,[80] and elsewhere he emphasizes that the Articles take no position on the question of whether the rights are those of the State or the investor.[81] Article 33 is thus not referring to the question of who owns the primary rights and obligations (this phrase is used in public international law to refer to substantive rights and

---

[76] *Case concerning the Barcelona Traction, Light and Power Co Ltd (New Application: 1962) (Belgium v Spain)* [1970] ICJ Rep 3, 44.

[77] ILC, *Draft Articles on Diplomatic Protection* (n 74 above) 25.

[78] On this subject see O Spiermann, 'Individual Rights, State Interests and the Power to Waive ICSID Jurisdiction under Bilateral Investment Treaties' (2004) 20 Arb Int'l 179.

[79] 'Responsibilities of States for Internationally Wrongful Acts: Text of the Draft Articles with Commentaries thereto' (Crawford, Special Rapporteur) in *Report of the International Law Commission on its Fifty-third Session (23 April–1 June and 2 July–10 August 2001) Official Records of the General Assembly Fifty-sixth Session*, Supplement UN Doc A/56/10, 25.

[80] n 79 above, 210.

[81] J Crawford, 'The ILC's Articles on Responsibility of States for Internationally Wrongful Acts: A Retrospect' (2002) 96 AJIL 874, 888.

obligations). Instead, Article 33 is explaining that the non-State actor may be owed the secondary obligations (the secondary rules of international law provide the framework within which substantive rights and obligations are addressed and include matters such as the general rules on State responsibility including the consequence of a breach of the primary obligation).[82] In the words of Professor Crawford:

> . . . what Article 33 clearly shows is that the secondary obligations arising from a breach may be owed directly to the beneficiary of the obligation, in this case the investor, who effectively opts in to the situation as a secondary right holder by commencing arbitral proceedings under the treaty. A new legal relation, directly between the investor and the responsible state, is thereby formed, if it did not already exist. Thus, at some level a modern bilateral investment treaty disaggregates the legal interests that were clumped together under the *Mavrommatis* formula.[83]

Those advocating the derivative rights formula often point to the dicta of the **3.61** Tribunal in *Loewen v USA*.[84] The Tribunal specifically stated that the NAFTA treaty (and for these purposes there would be no difference between the NAFTA treaty and a BIT) worked on a derivative rights basis:

> Rights of action under private law arise from personal obligations (albeit they may be owed by or to a State) brought into existence by domestic law and enforceable through domestic tribunals and courts. NAFTA claims have a quite different character, stemming from a corner of public international law in which, by treaty, the power of States under that law to take international measures for the correction of wrongs done to its nationals has been replaced by an ad hoc definition of certain kinds of wrong, coupled with specialist means of compensation. These means are both distinct from and exclusive of the remedies for wrongful acts under private law . . . It is true that some aspects of the resolution of disputes arising in relation to private international commerce are imported into the NAFTA system via Article 1120.1(c), and that the handling of disputes within that system by professionals experienced in the handling of major international arbitrations has tended in practice to make a NAFTA arbitration look like the more familiar kind of process. But, this apparent resemblance is misleading. The two forms of process, and the rights which they enforce, have nothing in common. There is no warrant for transferring rules derived from private law into a field of international law where claimants are permitted for convenience to enforce what are in origin the rights of Party States.[85]

The *Loewen* Tribunal was correct to note the often substantial differences between **3.62** the theoretical underpinnings of commercial arbitration and investment arbitration.[86] Nonetheless, the direct rights theory is better able to explain the concepts

---

[82] ILC, 'Draft Articles on State Responsibility' (n 79 above) 233–235; J Crawford, *The International Law Commission's Articles on State Responsibility: Introduction, Text and Commentaries* (2002) 14–16. [83] Crawford (n 81 above) 888.

[84] *The Loewen Group Inc and Raymond L Loewen v United States of America* (Award) 7 ICSID Rep 421 (NAFTA/ICSID (AF), 2003, Mason P, Mikva & Mustill). [85] ibid 488.

[86] These are well summarized by Blackaby 'Investment Arbitration and Commercial Arbitration (or the tale of the dolphin and the shark)' in LA Mistelis and J Lew (eds), *Pervasive Problems in International Arbitration* (2006).

that are created by investment treaty arbitrations. Douglas points out a number of features of the system that cannot be reconciled with the derivative rights theory.[87] These include:

- In cases such as *GAMI Inc v United Mexican States*[88] and *Mondev International Ltd v USA*[89] the investor's home State actively opposed the claims before the Tribunal.

- It is possible for investors to waive their rights to bring claims, either in investment agreements, by choosing to litigate in a municipal court and thereby triggering a fork in the road provision, or by settling a dispute once proceedings are initiated. While there is some dispute as to the scope of the investor's ability to waive this right to arbitrate, the maximalist position to the effect that an investor cannot in any way renounce any of its rights under a treaty because they are the rights of its home State is not sustainable.[90] The question of the relationship between choice of forum clauses and investment arbitration is addressed further at paras 4.68 to 4.72 below.

- In the absence of a specific provision, investment treaties do not require the investor to exhaust available local remedies before asserting a claim.

- Compensation awards consider only the interests of an investor without taking into account any independent interests of the national State which may have been prejudiced by the breach.

3.63   The direct rights analysis was adopted by the English Court of Appeal when it considered the issue in *Occidental v Ecuador*.[91] The English hearing arose out of Ecuador's challenge to an award made against it under the US-Ecuador BIT. Occidental brought a preliminary objection to the challenge based on the English law concept of non-justiciability. Under this doctrine, English courts will not adjudicate upon the transactions of foreign sovereign States. Occidental argued that the BIT between the United States and Ecuador was such a transaction. Thus, the English courts should not hear the challenge to the arbitration award as, by doing so, it would have to opine on the rights existing between the United States and Ecuador arising out of their BIT. In considering the question, the Court of

---

[87] Z Douglas, 'The Hybrid Foundations of Investment Treaty Arbitration' (2003) 74 BYIL 151, 169–181.

[88] *GAMI Investments Inc v United Mexican States* (Final Award) (2005) 44 ILM 545 (NAFTA/UNCITRAL, 2004, Paulsson P, Reisman & Muró).

[89] *Mondev International Ltd v United States of America* (Award) 6 ICSID Rep 181 (NAFTA/ICSID (AF), 2002, Stephen P, Crawford & Schwebel).

[90] See further O Spiermann, 'Individual Rights, State Interests and the Power to Waive ICSID Jurisdiction under Bilateral Investment Treaties' (2004) 20 Arb Int'l 179.

[91] *Republic of Ecuador v Occidental Exploration and Production Co* [2005] EWCA Civ 1116; [2006] QB 432 (CA).

Appeal addressed the issue of whether the rights Occidental was enforcing under the BIT belonged to it or to the United States. It adopted Douglas' comment that: 'The functional assumption underlying the investment treaty regime is clearly that the investor is bringing a cause of action based upon the vindication of its own rights rather than those of its national State.'[92]

The Court of Appeal also cited a number of ICSID jurisdiction decisions involv- **3.64** ing claims brought against Argentina where tribunals had permitted shareholders to bring claims arising out of breaches allegedly committed by Argentina towards companies in which they held shares. These decisions[93] all distinguish the investment treaty situation, whereby the foreign investor acquires rights directly, from the diplomatic protection position as addressed by the ICJ in the *Barcelona Traction*[94] case.

Treaty arbitrations are commercial disputes

Notwithstanding the debate about the extent to which an analogy can be main- **3.65** tained between BIT arbitrations and commercial arbitrations, domestic courts have consistently held that non-ICSID BIT arbitrations are reviewable as 'commercial' for the purposes of Article 1(3) of the New York Convention and the UNCITRAL Model Law. Before the Supreme Court of British Columbia in the proceedings arising out of the *Metalclad* award,[95] Mexico argued that the NAFTA award would not fall within the Canadian definition of a commercial arbitration because it arose out of a regulatory rather than a commercial relationship.[96] This argument was rejected by the Court on the basis that the arbitration had arisen out of an investment relationship and this was a commercial matter. Similarly, the Svea Court of Appeal hearing the challenge to the *CME v Czech Republic*[97] award found that the arbitration was 'an international commercial dispute which has been handled within the scope of the bilateral investment treaty'.

---

[92] *Occidental* (ibid) [2006] QB 432, 450; Douglas (n 71 above) 182.

[93] *Enron Corp v Argentine Republic* (n 31 above); *LG&E Energy Corp, LG&E Capital Corp, and LG&E International Inc v Argentine Republic* (Jurisdiction) ICSID Case No ARB/02/1 (ICSID, 2004, de Maekelt P, Rezek & van den Berg); *GAMI v Mexico* (n 88 above); *Camuzzi International SA v Argentine Republic* (Jurisdiction) ICSID Case No ARB/03/2 (ICSID, 2005, Orrego Vicuña P, Lalonde & Rico); *Gas Natural SDG SA v Argentine Republic* (Jurisdiction) ICSID Case No ARB/03/10 (ICSID, 2005, Lowenfeld P, Alvarez & Nikken).

[94] *Case Concerning the Barcelona Traction, Light and Power Co Ltd (New Application: 1962) (Belgium v Spain)* [1970] ICJ Rep 3.

[95] *United Mexican States v Metalclad Corp* [2001] BCSC 664; 5 ICSID 236 (Supreme Court of British Colombia). [96] ibid 5 ICSID Rep 246–247.

[97] *Czech Republic v CME Czech Republic BV (Case No T8735–01)* 9 ICSID Rep 439 (Sweden, Svea Court of Appeal).

F. Interpreting BITs

3.66 BITs, as treaties, 'must be interpreted according to the Law of Nations, and not according to any municipal code'.[98] The substantive law applied in a treaty arbitration is the treaty itself. The applicable law for the interpretation of the treaty is international law. In interpreting treaties, tribunals consistently apply the 1969 Vienna Convention on the Law of Treaties (VCLT), either because both State parties are signatories to the VCLT or because the rules of interpretation it provides represent customary international law.[99]

3.67 The general rule of interpretation contained in the VCLT is found at Article 31:

1. A treaty shall be interpreted in good faith in accordance with the ordinary meaning to be given to the terms of the treaty in their context and in the light of its object and purpose.
2. The context for the purpose of the interpretation of a treaty shall comprise, in addition to the text, including its preamble and annexes:
   (a) Any agreement relating to the treaty which was made between all the parties in connexion with the conclusion of the treaty;
   (b) Any instrument which was made by one or more parties in connexion with the conclusion of the treaty and accepted by the other parties as an instrument related to the treaty.
3. There shall be taken into account, together with the context:
   (a) Any subsequent agreement between the parties regarding the interpretation of the treaty or the application of its provisions;
   (b) Any subsequent practice in the application of the treaty which establishes the agreement of the parties regarding its interpretation;
   (c) Any relevant rules of international law applicable in the relations between the parties.
4. A special meaning shall be given to a term if it is established that the parties so intended.

3.68 The VCLT's approach to interpretation was summarized by the Tribunal in *AdT v Bolivia*[100] as follows: 'Interpretation under Article 31 of the Vienna Convention is a process of progressive encirclement where the interpreter starts under the general rule with (1) the ordinary meaning of the terms of the treaty, (2) in their context and (3) in light of the treaty's object and purpose, and by

---

[98] *Asian Agricultural Products Ltd [AAPL] v Republic of Sri Lanka* (Award) 4 ICSID Rep 245, 264 (ICSID, 1990, El-Kosheri P, Goldman & Asante).

[99] eg *Eureko BV v Republic of Poland* (Partial Award) (Ad Hoc Arb Trib, 2005, Fortier P, Schwebel & Rajski) para 247; *Tokios Tokelés v Ukraine* (Jurisdiction) (2005) 20 ICSID Rev-FILJ 205, 216 (ICSID, 2004, Weil P, Price & Bernardini); *Siemens AG v Argentine Republic* (Jurisdiction) ICSID Case No ARB/02/8 (ICSID, 2004, Sureda P, Brower & Bello Janeiro) para 80.

[100] *Aguas del Tunari SA v Republic of Bolivia* (Jurisdiction) (2005) ICSID Rev-FILJ 450 (ICSID, 2005, Caron P, Alberro-Semerena & Alvarez).

cycling through this three step inquiry iteratively closes in upon the proper interpretation.'[101]

The potential importance of Article 31(3)(c) of the VCLT and its requirement to **3.69** pay regard to other rules of international law binding between the parties should not be overlooked. It will require tribunals to interpret BITs in the light of potentially competing standards (for example relating to environmental obligations) contained in other treaties binding among the State parties.[102] A reference in the BIT to its need to be interpreted in accordance with principles of international law will have the same effect.[103]

Article 32 of the VCLT provides (supplementary means of interpretation): **3.70**

> Recourse may be had to supplementary means of interpretation, including the preparatory work of the treaty and the circumstances of its conclusion, in order to confirm the meaning resulting from the application of article 31, or to determine the meaning when the interpretation according to article 31:
>
> (a) leaves the meaning ambiguous or obscure; or
> (b) leads to a result which is manifestly absurd or unreasonable.

However, references to *travaux préparatoires* in investment arbitrations have not proved fruitful. The *AdT v Bolivia* Tribunal requested evidence of the negotiation history of the Netherlands/Bolivia BIT. It received very limited information of little use.[104] In *Pope & Talbot v Canada* the Tribunal received a substantial amount of information but it did little to illuminate the matters in dispute.[105]

In practice, the VCLT is only of limited use in giving guidance to a tribunal in its **3.71** interpretive task. Problems arise because the VCLT's rules of construction are capable of supporting a wide range of potential interpretations. The fact that both parties to a dispute usually rely on its provisions is a good indication of its inherent flexibility. The Tribunal in *Plama v Bulgaria*[106] honestly appraised the difficulty of its interpretative task, notwithstanding the guidance offered by the VCLT. It had to decide whether Article 17(1) of the Energy Charter Treaty (denial of benefits) had retrospective or prospective effect. It considered the tools of interpretation available to it before describing the question as 'a short point of almost first impression'.[107]

---

[101] ibid para 91.
[102] See C McLachlan, 'The Principle of Systemic Integration and Article 31(3)(c) of the Vienna Convention' (2005) 54 ICLQ 279.
[103] eg 'Agreement for the Promotion and Protection of Investments' (UK-Lebanon) (signed 16 February 1999, entered into force 16 September 2001) UKTS 3 (2002) Art 8(3); 'Agreement on the Reciprocal Promotion and Protection of Investments' (Portugal-Mexico) Art 15(1).
[104] *AdT v Bolivia* (n 100 above) 534–535.
[105] *Pope & Talbot Inc v Government of Canada* (Award on Damages) 7 ICSID Rep 148, 157–159 (NAFTA/UNICTRAL, 2002, Dervaird P, Greenberg & Belman).
[106] *Plama Consortium Ltd v Republic of Bulgaria* (Jurisdiction) (2005) 20 ICSID Rev-FILJ 262 (ICSID, 2005, Salans P, van den Berg & Veeder).   [107] ibid 312.

3.72 Thus the principles contained in the VCLT are not wholly useful in resolving difficult questions of BIT interpretation. The guidance they provide is insufficiently concrete.

3.73 When tribunals themselves have attempted to establish canons of construction for interpreting BITs, the principles that they have established are contradictory. Accordingly, dicta from previous tribunal practice in this respect are unhelpful as a guide for future tribunals. For example, one tribunal established a pro-State principle that far-reaching effects arising out of the text of BITs must be confirmed by clear and convincing evidence of the State parties' intent.[108] Another tribunal established the opposite in finding that it is legitimate to resolve uncertainties in the interpretation of a BIT so as to favour the protection of covered investments.[109] The dissenting President of the Tribunal in *Tokios Tokelės v Ukraine* perhaps established a middle ground in stating that BITs must be applied and interpreted having regard to the object and purpose of the ICSID system.[110] At the extreme of the pro-investor position is perhaps the dissent of Professor Crivellaro in *SGS v Philippines*[111] where he stated that provisions granting rights to investors should be read in the way that is most favourable to the investor. An extreme in the other direction can perhaps be taken from Professor Brownlie's Separate Opinion in *CME v Czech Republic*.[112] He reintroduced subjectivity into the calculation of 'just compensation' by remarking that 'the host State is not accepting a risk which will have the consequence of paying compensation at a level which would cause catastrophic economic consequences'.[113]

3.74 It is tempting to try to categorize the array of often contradictory 'principles' of interpretation by reference to whether they are pro-State or pro-investor and it is not possible to discount the effect of arbitrators' personal perspectives in formulating the canons of construction they have individually developed. Indeed, Dolzer and Stevens offer guidance as to the interpretation of BITs depending on whether such treaties should be viewed as either evidence of the parties' intentions to enhance the protection of the foreign investor or as providing a fair and balanced protective regime.[114]

---

[108] *SGS Société Générale de Surveillance SA v Islamic Republic of Pakistan* (Jurisdiction) 8 ICSID Rep 383, 442–443 (ICSID, 2003, Feliciano P, Faurès & Thomas).

[109] *SGS Société Générale de Surveillance SA v Republic of the Philippines* (Jurisdiction) 8 ICSID Rep 515, 550 (ICSID, 2004, El-Kosheri P, Crawford & Crivellaro).

[110] *Tokios Tokeles v Ukraine* (n 99 above) (Dissenting Opinion of Weil) (2005) 20 ICSID Rev-FILJ 245, 252, 254 & 258.

[111] *SGS Société Générale de Surveillance SA v Republic of the Philippines* (Declaration of Crivellaro) 8 ICSID Rep 515, 570 (ICSID, 2004, Crivellaro).

[112] *CME Czech Republic BV (The Netherlands) v Czech Republic* (Final Award) 9 ICSID Rep 264 (ICSID, 2003, Kühn C, Schwebel & Brownlie); (Separate Opinion of Brownlie) 9 ICSID Rep 412.

[113] ibid 424.

[114] R Dolzer & M Stevens, *Bilateral Investment Treaties* (1995) 15–16. See also M Weiniger, 'Jurisdiction Challenges in BITs Arbitrations—Do You Read a BIT by Reading a BIT or by Reading

Tribunals have not derived much assistance when searching for the meaning of a **3.75** treaty in sources other than the treaty itself. For example, the *AdT v Bolivia* Tribunal asked the parties to submit such evidence as was available on the interpretation and practice of the Netherlands/Bolivia BIT. The parties, however, only came up with 'little evidence of the negotiating history of the BIT'[115] leading the Tribunal to conclude: 'This sparse negotiating history thus offers little additional insight into the meaning of the aspects of the BIT at issue, neither particularly confirming nor contradicting the Tribunal's interpretation.'[116]

The *AdT* Tribunal also carried out an extensive review of the BIT practice of both **3.76** the Netherlands and Bolivia. Despite the relatively large number of BITs entered into by the State parties they concluded that their BIT practice was 'necessarily of limited probative value to the task of interpreting the BIT between the Netherlands and Bolivia'.[117]

In a further quest for external assistance, the *AdT* Tribunal wrote to the Legal **3.77** Advisor of the Foreign Ministry of the Netherlands, posing several specific questions. This is the only time that a BIT tribunal has made an enquiry of the non-disputing state party to a BIT. The Tribunal analysed the response received and concluded that it could 'find no "subsequent practice . . . which establishes an agreement of the parties" regarding the interpretation of the BIT. In addition, the response from the Netherlands provides no additional information of the type suggested by Article 31 of the Vienna Convention on the Law of Treaties as being possibly relevant and upon which a general interpretative position might be based'.[118]

Paragraphs 7.64 to 7.72 below, further address the question of interpretation of **3.78** investment treaties in the specific context of finding the meaning of investment treatment provisions.

The role played by domestic law in treaty arbitrations

The fact that the interpretation of BITs is governed by public international law **3.79** does not exclude domestic law from consideration by investment treaty tribunals. The main role of domestic law is in defining the scope of the investment protected. This is discussed in more detail at paras 6.67 to 6.70 below.

Douglas emphasizes the role of domestic law in describing the substantive law **3.80** governing investment disputes as 'necessarily a hybrid of international and

---

into a BIT?' in LA Mistelis and J Lew (eds), *Pervasive Problems in International Arbitration* (2006) 235–256.

[115] *AdT v Bolivia* (n 100 above) 534.
[116] *AdT v Bolivia* (n 100 above) 535. See also *Methanex Corp v United States of America* (Award) (2005) 44 ILM 1345, 1354 (NAFTA/UNCITRAL, 2005, Veeder P, Rowley & Reisman).
[117] *AdT v Bolivia* (n 100 above) 547.   [118] *AdT v Bolivia* (n 100 above) 532.

municipal law due to the private or commercial interests at the heart of this jurisdiction'.[119] The investments of non-State actors are creatures of private law and tribunals cannot avoid addressing issues arising under the law pursuant to which investments owe their existence in adjudicating treaty questions. It is only once a right has been created and recognized by domestic law that standards of investment protection under the treaty take over in regulating a State's behaviour towards those rights.[120]

3.81 At times tribunals will have to consider findings of domestic law by national courts, tribunals, or regulatory bodies on the status of investments in domestic legal systems. Often the tribunals making these findings will be part of the regulatory or judicial machinery of the host State. However, in the absence of any evidence that the findings are tainted by some lack of due process, deference should be shown to decisions of domestic courts or tribunals.[121] At times, in investigating whether any breach of due process has occurred, investment tribunals will have to shed their public international law clothes to consider carefully the correctness of rulings made by domestic tribunals on issues of domestic law. The Tribunal in *Occidental v Ecuador*[122] took such a step in analysing applicable Ecuadorian tax provisions:

> The Tribunal agrees with the [Internal Revenue Service of Ecuador] that Article 69A [of the Tax Law Regulations] grants the right to a tax refund to exporters of goods involved in activities such as mining, fishing, lumber, bananas and African palm oil. The Tribunal does not, however, agree that the oil industry is excluded from the application of Article 69A . . .
>
> As has been explained above, the Tribunal has concluded that VAT reimbursement was not included in [Occidental]'s Contract. It follows that under Ecuadorian tax legislation the Claimant is entitled to such a refund . . . [123]

3.82 Of course, if the State itself uses the tools available to it in municipal law to mistreat the investment, investors will be able to rely upon the principle of international law that a State cannot invoke provisions of its own law to justify a breach of an international obligation.[124]

Precedent

3.83 This book represents an attempt to state the legal principles applied by investment treaty tribunals, in part, by analysing the awards of those tribunals. The assumption

---

[119] Z Douglas, 'The Hybrid Foundations of Investment Treaty Arbitration' (2003) 74 BYIL 151, 195. [120] ibid 199.

[121] Douglas (n 119 above) 273–274.

[122] *Occidental Exploration and Production Co v Republic of Ecuador* (Award) LCIA Case No UN3467 (UNCITRAL, 2004, Orrego Vicuña P, Brower & Sweeney).

[123] ibid paras 136, 143; see also Z Douglas, 'Nothing if not Critical for Investment Treaty Arbitration: *Occidental, Eureko and Methanex*' (2006) 22 Arb Int'l 27, 29–38.

[124] ILC, *Draft Articles on State Responsibility* (n 79 above) Art 3.

is, and past performance probably constitutes a good guide for the future in this respect, that tribunals will continue to render awards having carefully considered previous awards and by incrementally building a common case law.

It is a truism to say that there is no system of binding precedent in international **3.84** law. Each State is sovereign and it is not possible for one to be bound by an interpretation of the law offered by a tribunal deciding a different dispute brought against a different State under a different treaty. Even when the same treaty or State is involved, decisions have no precedential value. A concrete example of this position is Article 53(1) of the ICSID Convention which provides that: 'The award shall be binding on the parties . . . '

Schreuer interprets this to exclude a doctrine of precedent within the ICSID **3.85** system, that is to say, the award is binding on the parties and on no-one else.[125] This point has also been made by treaty tribunals.[126]

Under common law systems, a doctrine of precedent exists to provide 'guidance, **3.86** predictability, efficiency, uniformity and impersonality'.[127] Within a unified legal system a consistent application of precedent provides fairness and equality as like cases are treated alike. These concepts are difficult to apply to a series of unconnected arbitrations governed by public international law. The system, if it can even be called a system, of investment treaty arbitration is not unitary in the sense of each tribunal sitting under the same source of jurisdiction. More fundamentally, it is not a common law system. The common law system of precedent, with judges inching step by step towards a current exposition of the law is at odds with the code-based approach where the law is set out, in a fully developed form, for all to know in advance.[128] It would be inappropriate for investment treaty tribunals to be preferring a common law approach over that of the civil law.

The Statute of the ICJ is even more explicit than the ICSID Convention in reject- **3.87** ing the precedent value of its decisions. Article 59 provides that: 'The decision of the Court has no binding force except between the parties and in respect of that particular case.'

---

[125] CH Schreuer, *The ICSID Convention: A Commentary* (2001) 1082.

[126] *AES Corp v Argentine Republic* (Jurisdiction) ICSID Case No ARB/02/17 (ICSID, 2005, Dupuy P, Böckstiegel & Janeiro) para 23(d); *Amco Asia Corp v Republic of Indonesia* (Decision on Annulment) 1 ICSID Rep 509, 521 (ICSID, 1986, Seidl-Hohenveldern P, Feliciano & Giardina); *Liberian Eastern Timber Corp [LETCO] v Republic of Liberia* (Award) 2 ICSID Rep 343, 352 (ICSID, 1986, Cremades P, Conçalves Pereira & Redfern).

[127] J Hardisty, 'Reflections on *Stare Decisis*' (1979–1980) 55 Ind LJ 41, 55; see also Prime & Scanlon, '*Stare Decisis* in the Court of Appeal Judicial Confusion and Judicial Reform' [2004] Civil Justice Quarterly 212, 215 where these English authors describe the doctrine of precedent 'as a mechanism for promoting certainty and predictability in the law'.

[128] R Bhala, 'The Power of the Past: Towards *De Jure Stare Decisis* in WTO Adjudication *(Part Three of a Trilogy)*' (2000–2001) 33 George Washington International Law Review 873, 941.

3.88 In practice, this does not prevent parties to litigation before the ICJ from making reference to, and seeking to rely upon, findings and dissenting opinions made in earlier cases.

3.89 Article 38 of the ICJ Statute, in listing the four sources of law to be applied by the Court, mentions 'judicial decisions' in fourth place. Even then, they are only 'subsidiary means for the determination of rules of law'. This can be contrasted with the first three listed, which are primary means for establishing, rather than merely determining, rules of law. There is no doubt that 'the role of precedent in international law is a matter of considerable delicacy. Just as jealous sovereign States are averse to any suggestion that compacts other than those to which they have consented may be invoked against them, so too are they unwilling to submit to the elaboration of international law by anything resembling the accretion of binding precedents known as common law'.[129]

3.90 Notwithstanding the purity of the doctrinal position, a *de facto* doctrine of precedent for investment treaty arbitration has been building up for some time. Investment tribunals approach their task in the same way as other international judicial bodies, namely by carefully considering the work of other tribunals. This may not be a *de jure* system of precedent, but, as has been observed in relation to the WTO adjudication system, it is important to be 'honest about the "disconnect" between the myth and the true role of prior holdings in affecting adjudicatory outcomes'.[130]

3.91 There is nothing unusual about international law developing in this manner. Crawford has observed this common law-style process having begun long before the present system of treaty arbitration developed:

> . . . the content of the law of state responsibility, at least in the important field of injury to the persons and property of aliens, was not based on any codified approach, or even on any general principle of law. It was dependent largely on diplomatic correspondence or decisions of arbitral commissions in relation to particular fact situations. In some respects at least, it resembled the evolution of the common law of torts before *Donoghue v. Stevenson*. For example, we are still working out the content of the 'international minimum standard' on a case-by-case basis—as witness current developments in the application of Articles 1105 and 1110 of the North American Free Trade Agreement and their equivalents in bilateral investment treaties.[131]

3.92 One of the members of the US negotiating team for NAFTA has written that a purpose behind the incorporation of the customary international law standard of treatment in Article 1105 of NAFTA was to allow NAFTA practice to develop in

---

[129] J Paulsson, 'International Arbitration and the Generation of Legal Norms: Treaty Arbitration and International Law', TDM (Sept 2006) <http://transnational-dispute-management.com> accessed 20 September 2006. [130] Bhala (n 128 above) 877.

[131] J Crawford, 'The ILC's Articles on Responsibility of States for Internationally Wrongful Acts: A Retrospect' (2002) 96 AJIL 874, 886.

line with decisions of other tribunals in spite of the formal absence of a *stare decisis* effect.[132] Yet NAFTA contains a specific article providing that a decision from one panel has no precedent effect on any other panel.[133]

The fact that tribunals are aware of the role they play in developing legal princi- **3.93** ples should be welcomed. Part of the responsibility of a tribunal is to work out the applicable principles of international law to be applied to the dispute before it. A tribunal should be seeking to set out the principles it finds as clearly as possible as part of its professional duty to render the best award possible. If this is achieved, it is understandable and positive that the award should be perceived as a contribution to the field of international legal scholarship. Investment treaty awards can thus play a role in slowing down the increasing fragmentation of international law.

The Tribunal in *AES Corp v Argentine Republic*[134] has made the most detailed **3.94** examination of the role of precedent in investment arbitration to date. The claimant pointed out that Argentina's five objections to jurisdiction were similar or identical to arguments that Argentina had presented unsuccessfully in a number of previous arbitrations. The claimant sought to persuade the Tribunal to treat the objections as 'moot if not even useless'[135] on the basis that previous tribunals had consistently rejected the objections.

The Tribunal was not willing to accept the extremities of the claimant's position. **3.95** It agreed with Argentina that every BIT has its own identity. Its terms should thus be carefully analysed for determining the exact scope of the consent expressed by the two parties. Here the *AES* Tribunal is following the position taken by the International Tribunal for the Law of the Sea in the *MOX Plant* and *OSPAR* cases where it was stated that identical or similar provisions of different treaties may not necessarily yield the same interpretive results once differences in the respective context, objects and purposes, subsequent practice of parties, and *travaux préparatoires* have been taken into account.[136]

Argentina could thus not be prevented from raising its objections again. However, **3.96** the Tribunal was not prepared to ignore decisions reached by other tribunals:

> Each tribunal remains sovereign and may retain, as it is confirmed by ICSID practice, a different solution for resolving the same problem; but decisions on jurisdiction dealing with the same or very similar issues may at least indicate some

---

[132] DM Price, 'Chapter 11—Private Party vs. Government, Investor-State Dispute Settlement: Frankenstein or Safety Valve?' (2000) 26 Can-USLJ 107, 111.
[133] North American Free Trade Agreement (adopted 17 December 1992, entered into force 1 January 1994) CTS 1994 No 2; (1993) 32 ILM 612 ('NAFTA') (Appendix 1 below) Art 1136(1). See Price (ibid) 111.   [134] *AES Corp v Argentine Republic* (n 126 above).
[135] *AES Corp v Argentine Republic* (n 126 above) para 18.
[136] *The MOX Plant Case (Ireland v United Kingdom)* (Provisional Measure, Order of 3 December 2001) (2005) 126 ILR 260, 273–274; *Dispute Concerning Access to Information Under Article 9 of the OSPAR Convention (Ireland v United Kingdom)* (2005) 126 ILR 334.

lines of reasoning of real interest; this Tribunal may consider them in order to compare its own position with those already adopted by its predecessors and, if it shares the views already expressed by one or more of these tribunals on a specific point of law, it is free to adopt the same solution . . . precedents may also be rightly considered, at least as a matter of comparison and, if so considered by the Tribunal, of inspiration.[137]

3.97   In a similar manner the Tribunal in *Bayindir v Pakistan*[138] considered the issue of precedents and concluded that it was 'not bound by earlier decisions, but will certainly carefully consider such decisions whenever appropriate'.[139]

3.98   Thus a *de facto* doctrine of precedent certainly exists. However, it is not identical to that prevailing within domestic common law systems. For example, there is no doctrine of hierarchy whereby certain courts are obliged to defer to judgments rendered by higher courts. Instead, individual tribunal decisions have persuasive force and compel the respectful attention of tribunals confronted with similar cases. But parties are entitled to have the tribunals that they have appointed exercising their own independent judgment. Tribunals must accordingly examine critically the precedents cited to them. To date, every indication is that tribunals have taken the appropriate path when presented with precedents. Those that are compelling are adopted. (For example, the fact that early investment tribunals rejected respondents' objections has led to a situation where it is no longer seriously doubted that arbitrations can take place under bilateral investment treaties without a separate submission to arbitration—see the discussion at paras 3.21 to 3.27 below). Others are not, in a manner that generates a useful inter-tribunal debate on critical issues. Thus when the Tribunal in *SGS v Philippines*[140] differed in its interpretation of key provisions with the conclusions reached by the Tribunal in *SGS v Pakistan*,[141] it stated that:

> . . . although different tribunals constituted under the ICSID system should in general seek to act consistently with each other, in the end it must be for each tribunal to exercise its competence in accordance with the applicable law, which will by definition be different for each BIT and each Respondent State. Moreover there is no doctrine of precedent in international law, if by precedent is meant a rule of the binding effect of a single decision. There is no hierarchy of international tribunals, and even if there were, there is no good reason for allowing the first tribunal in time to resolve issues for all later tribunals.[142]

---

[137] *AES Corp v Argentine Republic* (n 126 above) paras 30–31.
[138] *Bayindir Insaat Turizm Ticaret Ve Sanayi AS v Islamic Republic of Pakistan* (Jurisdiction) ICSID Case No ARB/03/29 (ICSID, 2005, Kaufmann-Kohler P, Berman & Böckstiegel).
[139] ibid para 76.
[140] *SGS Société Générale de Surveillance SA v Republic of the Philippines* (Jurisdiction) 8 ICSID Rep 515 (ICSID, 2004, El-Kosheri P, Crawford & Crivellaro).
[141] *SGS Société Générale de Surveillance SA v Islamic Republic of Pakistan* (Jurisdiction) 8 ICSID Rep 383 (ICSID, 2003, Feliciano P, Faurès & Thomas).
[142] *SGS v Philippines* (n 140 above) 545.

The academic community has played its part in developing the debate around **3.99** difficult awards.[143] A number of cases which could as easily have been resolved in the other direction have received detailed critiques in scholarly journals. Examples are the awards reached in *Loewen v USA*,[144] *Tokios Tokelės v Ukraine*,[145] and the two *SGS* cases.[146]

In working with dicta from other awards, counsel and arbitrators must take care **3.100** to use judicial precedent in a proper manner. To be of assistance to a tribunal, counsel must take care to explain the relevant factual background, the precise nature of the legal principles identified, and the reasons contended for those legal principles applying to the factual matrix of the present case.

In general, it is true to say that the decisions of previous tribunals influence later **3.101** decisions, but the influence of individual awards is variable. A Darwinian reality exists in which, over time, the unfit will perish.[147]

Those involved in investment treaty arbitrations should take care not to allow the **3.102** use of other awards to transgress the appropriate boundaries. Their citation should not overwhelm a tribunal's consideration of the case before it. At the same time, awards should be focused on deciding the issues raised by the parties rather than providing a detailed discussion of all interesting legal issues that could potentially arise with an eye for posterity. It is not clear why the parties to one dispute should pay their lawyers and the tribunal for the time taken to analyse and state legal principles in a manner that exceeds the need of a particular case. Arbitrators should not fall into the trap of becoming:

> . . . *ad hoc* judges whose decisions are scrutinised and commented as if they were decisions of a domestic Supreme Court. The arbitration community has rarely basked in such publicity as lawyers attempt to define the frontiers of abstract concepts such as 'fair and equitable treatment' or 'full protection and security'. Quite naturally, recognising this broader role, arbitrators have begun to act like judges— often commenting on issues not strictly necessary for the resolution of the dispute in *obiter dicta*. The award also becomes a showcase for legal erudition.[148]

---

[143] The role played by the OGEMID Electronic Discussion List is particularly important <http://www.dundee.ac.uk/cepmlp/journal/html/ogemidannounce.html> accessed 20 September 2006. Many leading scholars and practitioners participate in its debates which often focus on the merits or otherwise of individual awards.

[144] *The Loewen Group Inc and Raymond L Loewen v United States of America* (Award) 7 ICSID Rep 421 (NAFTA/ICSID (AF), 2001, Mason P, Mikva & Mustill).

[145] *Tokios Tokelės v Ukraine* (Jurisdiction) 20 ICSID Rev-FILJ 205 (ICSID, 2004, Weil P, Bernardini & Price).

[146] *SGS v Philippines* (n 140 above); *SGS v Pakistan* (n 141 above).

[147] J Paulsson, 'International Arbitration and the Generation of Legal Norms: Treaty Arbitration and International Law', TDM draft paper submitted at ICCA 2006, 4.

[148] N Blackaby, 'Investment Arbitration and Commercial Arbitration' in LA Mistelis and J Lew (eds), *Pervasive Problems in International Arbitration* (2006) 217, 228.

3.103 The precedent value of the system of investment arbitration awards is enhanced by the readiness of tribunal members to dissent from the decisions of their co-arbitrators. Dissenting opinions vary in quality[149] but well-written and tightly argued dissents have contributed greatly to the ability of those involved in successive arbitrations to engage critically in the debate at the point at which the previous tribunal left off.

---

[149] A Redfern, 'The 2003 Freshfields—Lecture Dissenting Opinions in International Commercial Arbitration: The Good, the Bad and the Ugly' (2004) 20 Arb Int'l 223. The reasons for Redfern terming certain Dissenting Opinions as either 'bad' or 'ugly' could be applied to certain investment arbitration dissents.

Part II

AMBIT OF PROTECTION

4

PARALLEL PROCEEDINGS

1. Basis and Nature of Jurisdictional Conflicts in Investment Arbitration

A. The Nature of the Problem

4.01 This work is devoted to a study of the substantive rights which form the subject of claims made before international arbitral tribunals under investment treaties. Nevertheless, it will be appreciated that the underlying dispute between an investor and its host State may give rise to multiple claims. If there is a contract between State and investor, that contract will create its own justiciable rights and duties, the breach of which may give rise either to litigation before host State courts or to arbitration before a tribunal to whose jurisdiction the parties have submitted. Even if there is no such contract, the underlying property rights of the investor, which form the subject-matter of the investment, may have been the subject of adjudication by the host State courts. Further, the investor may have sought vindication of its rights in the host State courts. In this context, the very nature of investment arbitration gives rise to the possibility of parallel proceedings, or of determinations in another forum which may be said to affect the issue to be determined by the investment tribunal. Moreover, it is possible that more than one investment tribunal, each constituted by a different investment treaty, may be asked to rule upon the same underlying factual dispute.

4.02 In any one of these situations, the tribunal may have to consider the impact of the proceedings in the other court or tribunal upon its own work. Should it stay its own proceedings in deference to the alternative tribunal? Should it, on the contrary, insist on the priority of its own process? Should it put the parties to their election as to which mode of adjudication they wish to choose for the resolution of their dispute? What effect, if any, should it accord to the judgments or awards of other courts or tribunals? This part of the law is often described by reference to the techniques applied to deal with multiple claims between the same parties and on the same subject-matter in domestic law: the principles of *lis alibi pendens* (dispute pending elsewhere), *res judicata*, and *electa una via*. There are useful analogies to be drawn from domestic law. But, as will be seen, the peculiar characteristics of international investment arbitration fundamentally alter the way in which the issues arising from parallel litigation fall to be dealt with.

In one sense, the issues raised may be said to be procedural. They arise incidentally **4.03** in the course of a treaty arbitration, which must be based upon the rights created or recognized as a basis for a substantive claim under the treaty. They are often raised at the jurisdictional phase, as part of the submission that the tribunal either has no jurisdiction over the claim, or should decline or stay the exercise of its jurisdiction. Yet the issues raised by parallel proceedings do require treatment within a work on the substantive principles of investment arbitration law. These problems are not concerned with the internal procedure of the arbitral tribunal, whether operating under ICSID or under some other arbitral institution or set of procedural rules. Rather, they relate to the relationship between the rights created under investment treaties, which it is the responsibility of an investment tribunal to apply, and rights existing under other systems of law. From the perspective of the tribunal, such issues have to be resolved by reference to the treaty rules, interpreted by reference to such other rules of public international law as may be applicable between the parties.[1]

Although, therefore, these issues do bear some comparison to a set of problems **4.04** encountered in the related areas of private international law, international commercial arbitration, and in other parts of public international law, in important respects the ways in which the issues arise (and thus the techniques required to resolve them) differ from these fields, as a result of the *sui generis* character of investment arbitration.

B. Comparison with Related Fields

Private international law

Relation between lis pendens *and* res judicata

Private international law is intimately familiar with the problems created by **4.05** parallel proceedings. When the two claims are being pursued at the same time, the issue is categorized as one of *lis pendens*. When they are pursued sequentially, there already being a judgment from the first court, the matter is treated as a question of *res judicata*. Both sets of rules are really concerned with answering the same set of questions as to whether there is sufficient identity of parties, subject-matter, and cause of action to grant preclusive effect to another set of proceedings or judgment. However, the existence of a rule of *res judicata* applying to foreign judgments is more widely and firmly established than a *lis pendens* provision. It is possible to operate an international litigation system on the basis that parallel litigation is tolerated, but inconsistent judgments are not.[2] The effect is to shift a

---

[1] Vienna Convention on the Law of Treaties (signed 23 May 1969, entered into force 27 January 1980) 1155 UNTS 331 ('VCLT') Art 31(3)(c), as to which see 1.38–1.43 and 3.69 above.

[2] See eg the position in the United States: G Born, *International Civil Litigation in United States Courts* (4th edn, 2006) Chap 6.

possible race to the courthouse to issue proceedings into a race to judgment. The *lis pendens* rule, on the other hand, cannot exist independently from a provision for *res judicata*, and it can operate either as a mandatory rule or in the exercise of discretion—to stay rather than dismiss an action.

Lis pendens

4.06 Many legal systems, but not all, have adopted rules to ensure that two national courts do not proceed to determine the same claim at the same time.[3] A common technique is for the court second seised to decline jurisdiction in favour of the court first seised. Within Europe this rule is embodied in Article 27(1) of the Brussels Regulation,[4] which provides: 'Where proceedings involving the same cause of action and between the same parties are brought in the courts of different Member States, any court other than the court first seised shall of its own motion stay its proceedings until such time as the jurisdiction of the court first seised is established.'

4.07 The requirement of identity of cause of action is rendered in the French version as 'la même objet et la même cause', and has been authoritatively determined by the European Court to require that the two actions (a) have the same ends in view, and (b) involve the same facts and rule of law relied upon as the basis of the action.[5] Thus, provided, for example, that the two actions involve the same contract, it matters not that the two claims seek different forms of relief.[6]

4.08 The Brussels Regulation also endows the court second seised with a broader discretion to stay its proceedings if there is a related action already pending which is so closely connected that it is expedient to hear and determine them together to avoid the risk of irreconcilable judgments.[7] Even in legal systems which do not enforce a strict *lis pendens* rule of priority, the court may still retain a discretion to

---

[3] See London/Leuven Principles on Declining and Referring Jurisdiction in Civil and Commercial Matters, Principle 4.1 and International Law Association Committee on International Civil and Commercial Litigation (C McLachlan, Rapporteur), 'Third Interim Report: Declining and Referring Jurisdiction in International Litigation' in International Law Association (ILA), *Report of the Sixty-ninth Conference* (2000) 137; J Fawcett, 'General Report' in J Fawcett (ed), *Declining Jurisdiction in Private International Law* (1995) 27–43; P Schlosser, 'Jurisdiction and International Judicial and Administrative Co-operation' (2000) 284 *Recueil des Cours* 13, 76–87; A von Mehren, 'Theory and Practice of Adjudicatory Authority in Private International Law: a Comparative Study of the Doctrine, Policies and Practices of Common- and Civil-Law Systems' (2002) 295 *Recueil des Cours* 13, 341–369.

[4] Council Regulation (EC) 44/2001 of 22 December 2000 on Jurisdiction and the Recognition and Enforcement of Judgments in Civil and Commercial Matters [2001] OJ L12/1. The rule was formerly embodied in the Brussels Convention on Jurisdiction and the Recognition and Enforcement of Judgments in Civil and Commercial Matters (signed 27 September 1968, entered into force 1 February 1973) 1262 UNTS 153 Art 21.

[5] Case C-406/92 *The Tatry* [1994] ECR I–5439; [1999] QB 515.

[6] Case 144/86 *Gubisch Maschinenfabrik KG v Giulio Palumbo* [1987] ECR 4861.

[7] Brussels Regulation (n 4 above) Art 28. In addition, a court at first instance may also decline its jurisdiction on such a ground, provided the court first seised has jurisdiction and its law permits the two actions to be consolidated: Art 28(2).

decline or stay the exercise of its jurisdiction, or even to enjoin a party from pursuing his claim simultaneously in two fora, if he is doing so vexatiously or oppressively.[8]

Res judicata

Irrespective of whether the court is empowered to cede jurisdiction to another **4.09** court, it will generally be bound as a result of the application of the doctrine of *res judicata* to foreign judgments, to recognize and give effect to foreign judgments which determine the matter in issue before it.[9] In this situation, the legal issue arising in *lis pendens*, namely whether there is sufficient identity of parties and cause of action, will also be likely to apply.

While the experience of private international law has therefore produced much in **4.10** the way of legal technique which may be helpful, it should be remembered that it deals with judicial decisions of parallel legal orders, ie national legal systems. It does not deal with the parallel pursuit of claims in fora of different types, such as is entailed in the resolution of a conflict of jurisdiction between, for example, a national court and an investment arbitral tribunal. For reasons which are developed below, this may fundamentally alter the equation.

International commercial arbitration

International commercial arbitration is very familiar with the issues raised by **4.11** conflicts between national courts and international arbitral tribunals.[10] But the problems there arise against a policy framework in which the tribunal's jurisdiction is always derived from an express contractual submission clause concluded between the parties. As a result of Article II of the New York Convention on the Recognition and Enforcement of Arbitral Awards 1958,[11] which is supported by other international instruments,[12] a national court is bound to stay its proceedings in favour of arbitration in the face of a valid arbitration agreement. This creates an automatic priority for arbitration over national court litigation, and ensures that the merits of the dispute are submitted to only one tribunal. This fundamental rule has provided the essential starting-point in the treatment of conflicting domestic court proceedings by arbitral tribunals.

---

[8] For the position in the Common Law see L Collins et al (eds), *Dicey, Morris & Collins on the Conflict of Laws* (14th edn, 2006) 482–484, paras 12-035–12-037 (on *lis alibi pendens*); 500–511, paras 12-067–12-081 (on anti-suit injunctions).

[9] See P Barnett, *Res Judicata, Estoppel and Foreign Judgments: The Preclusive Effects of Foreign Judgments in Private International Law* (2001). Recognition of the preclusive effect of foreign judgments within Europe is provided for by Chap III Sect 1 of the Brussels Regulation.

[10] See generally B Cremades & J Lew (eds), *Parallel State and Arbitral Procedures in International Arbitration* (2005).

[11] Convention on the Recognition and Enforcement of Foreign Arbitral Awards 1958 (signed 10 June 1958, entered into force 7 June 1959) 330 UNTS 3.

[12] See UNCITRAL, 'Model Law on International and Commercial Arbitration' (1985) 24 ILM 1302.

4.12 That said, international commercial arbitration has begun to recognize that it may encounter issues of *litispendence* and *res judicata* as between arbitral tribunals.[13] In such cases, however, the response of the tribunal, and that of any reviewing court, may be dictated by the *lex arbitri* governing the proceedings, which will generally be the national law of the seat of the arbitration.

Public international law

4.13 In public international law, outside the sphere of investment arbitration, the principle of *res judicata* has long been accepted as a general principle of law common to civilized nations applicable to international courts and tribunals in accordance with Article 38(1)(c) of the Statute of the International Court of Justice.[14] However, the doctrine only applies to decisions within the same legal order, namely those of other international tribunals applying public international law. It has no application to the decisions of national courts.[15] From the perspective of public international law, however eminent the national tribunal, its decision is still simply the practice of an organ of the State. As such, it is open to evaluation on the international plane.

4.14 The importance of this distinction between the national and international planes is underlined by the fundamental rule enshrined in both the law of treaties and the law of State responsibility that lawfulness under national law is no defence to a claim of breach of international law. Thus, Article 27 of the Vienna Convention on the Law of Treaties provides: 'A party may not invoke the provisions of its internal law as justification for its failure to perform a treaty.'[16]

4.15 Similarly, Article 3 of the International Law Commission's Draft Articles on the Responsibility of States for Internationally Wrongful Acts (2001) provides: 'The characterization of an act of a State as internationally wrongful is governed by international law. Such characterization is not affected by the characterization of the same act as lawful by internal law.'

4.16 In the *ELSI* case, a Chamber of the International Court emphasized the significance of this rule in the context of the international law of investment protection,

---

[13] See Committee on International Commercial Arbitration, 'Final Report on *Res Judicata* and Arbitration' in *International Law Association Report of the ILA Seventy-Second Conference* (Toronto, 2006); Committee on International Commercial Arbitration, 'Final Report on *Lis Pendens* and Arbitration' in *International Law Association Report of the ILA Seventy-Second Conference* (Toronto, 2006).

[14] The classic dictum is that of Judge Anzilotti (dissenting) in *Interpretation of Judgments Nos 7 and 8 (The Chorzów Factory) (Germany v Poland)* PCIJ Rep Series A No 13, 27. See Y Shany, *The Competing Jurisdictions of International Courts and Tribunals* (2003); V Lowe, '*Res Judicata* and the Rule of Law in International Arbitration' (1996) 8 RADIC 38; I Scobbie, '*Res Judicata*, Precedent and the International Court: A Preliminary Sketch' (1999) 20 Australian Yearbook of International Law 299; A Reinisch, 'The Use and Limits of *Res Judicata* and *Lis Pendens* as Procedural Tools to avoid Conflicting Dispute Settlement Outcomes' (2004) 3 Law and Practice of International Courts and Tribunals 37.

[15] *Certain German Interests in Polish Upper Silesia (Germany v Poland)* (Jurisdiction) PCIJ Rep Series A No 6, 20.   [16] VCLT (n 1 above).

stating that: 'Compliance with municipal law and compliance with the provisions of a treaty are different questions. What is a breach of treaty may be lawful in the municipal law and what is unlawful in the municipal law may be wholly innocent of violation of a treaty provision.'[17] As the Chamber further explained:

> . . . the fact that an act of a public authority may have been unlawful in municipal law does not necessarily mean that that act was unlawful in international law, as a breach of treaty or otherwise. A finding of the local courts that an act was unlawful may well be relevant to an argument that it was also arbitrary; but by itself, and without more, unlawfulness cannot be said to amount to arbitrariness . . . Nor does it follow from a finding by a municipal court that an act was unjustified, or unreasonable, or arbitrary, that that act is necessarily to be classed as arbitrary in international law, though the qualification given to the impugned act by a municipal authority may be a valuable indication.[18]

The separation between the spheres of national and international law is reinforced **4.17** by an equally important rule of customary international law, namely the exhaustion of local remedies rule.[19] This rule precludes a State from bringing an international claim in respect of an injury to one of its nationals before the injured person has exhausted all legal remedies open to him before the judicial or administrative bodies of the State alleged to be responsible for the injury. The effect of this rule is to preclude the possibility of parallel proceedings between national and international courts. The national court proceedings must be exhausted before the claim can be espoused by the injured person's home State on the international plane. In that event, it is the very treatment meted out to the injured person by the national courts which will fall under the scrutiny of the international claim.

Turning to the relations between international tribunals, the evidence in public **4.18** international law for a developed doctrine of *lis pendens* is much weaker. In his detailed review of the matter in 2003, Shany concluded: 'In sum, it looks as if existing case-law on the question of *lis alibi pendens* is also too scarce and non-definitive to establish the existence of such a general rule or principle in international law, in the relations between two international courts and tribunals.'[20]

Of course, it should not be forgotten that the proliferation of international tribunals **4.19** has been a very recent phenomenon.[21] Only if multiple fora are potentially available to litigants can issues of their interrelation arise. In the few cases where the principle

---

[17] *Case Concerning Elettronica Sicula SpA (ELSI) (United States of America v Italy)* [1989] ICJ Rep 15, 51.   [18] ibid 74.

[19] *Interhandel Case (Switzerland v United States of America)* [1959] ICJ Rep 6, 27. See generally ILC (Dugard, Rapporteur), 'Second Report on Diplomatic Protection' (23 April–1June, 2 July–18 August 2001) UN Doc A/CN 4/514; CF Amerasinghe, *Local Remedies in International Law* (2nd edn, 2004); J Paulsson, *Denial of Justice in International Law* (2005) Chap 5.

[20] Shany (n 14 above) 244. See also V Lowe, 'Overlapping Jurisdiction in International Tribunals' (1999) 20 Australian Yearbook of International Law 191.

[21] See CPR Romano 'The Proliferation of International Judicial Bodies: The Pieces of the Puzzle' (1998–1999) 31 NYU Journal of International Law and Politics 709.

has been mentioned, the tribunal has generally been able to exclude its operation in view of the fact that the other proceedings were taking place in a different legal order.[22] However, one recent important decision approached the application of the principle in a way which is of some significance to the present study. That is the decision of the International Tribunal for the Law of the Sea (ITLOS) in the *MOX Plant* litigation.[23] In that case, Ireland had sought provisional measures against the United Kingdom, before the Tribunal, in support of its claim for redress against radioactive pollution in the Irish Sea arising from the operation of a nuclear reprocessing plant at Sellafield. It proposed to bring substantive proceedings before an arbitral tribunal under the Law of the Sea Convention, and also under the OSPAR Convention. There were further possibilities of proceedings under the EC Treaty and the EURATOM Treaty. The United Kingdom argued that, in the light of those actual or threatened parallel proceedings, the jurisdiction of the arbitral tribunal under UNCLOS was excluded, and, as a consequence, ITLOS was precluded from ordering interim relief in support. The Tribunal rejected this argument. Instead, it adopted a highly fragmented approach to parallel international litigation. It found:

> 50. *Considering* that, even if the OSPAR Convention, the EC Treaty and the Euratom Treaty contain rights or obligations similar to or identical with the rights or obligations set out in the Convention, the rights and obligations under those agreements have a separate existence from those under the Convention;
>
> 51. *Considering* also that the application of international law rules on interpretation of treaties to identical or similar provisions of different treaties may not yield the same results, having regard to, *inter alia*, differences in the respective contexts, objects and purposes, subsequent practice of parties and *travaux préparatoires*;
>
> 52. *Considering* that the Tribunal is of the opinion that, since the dispute before the Annex VII arbitral tribunal concerns the interpretation or application of the Convention and no other agreement, only the dispute settlement procedures under the Convention are relevant to that dispute;
>
> 53. *Considering* that, for the reasons given above, the Tribunal considers that, for the purpose of determining whether the Annex VII arbitral tribunal would have *prima facie* jurisdiction, article 282 of the Convention is not applicable to the dispute submitted to the Annex VII arbitral tribunal;

4.20 The reasoning of the Tribunal was thus that the separate treaty basis for the jurisdiction of, and law applicable to, each of the fora was sufficient to defeat an argument of *litispendence*.

4.21 While it may well have been the case that other disputes were founded upon different causes of action, it is submitted that the mere fact that each tribunal was created under a separate treaty regime should not be dispositive of itself. If that

---

[22] eg *Certain German Interests* (n 15 above) 20.
[23] *The MOX Plant Case (Ireland v United Kingdom)* (ITLOS, Provisional Measures, Order of 3 December 2001) (2002) 41 ILM 405.

approach were followed, it would mean that neither the rule of *res judicata* nor that of *lis pendens* could ever apply as between international tribunals. Yet, whatever their distinct treaty origin, all international tribunals may be said to belong to the same legal order of public international law. In the private international law context, the rules of *litispendence* are always concerned with the effect of proceedings in courts of separate legal systems. Indeed, the rules are crafted so as to require application in such situations, and the applicable tests (such as same parties and same cause or object) are designed to enable comparison between parallel courts in different legal systems.

As it transpired, a subsequent phase of the same *MOX Plant* litigation produced a **4.22** result more receptive to the significance of parallel adjudication. The Arbitral Tribunal established under the Law of the Sea Convention decided to stay the exercise of its jurisdiction. It did so in view of the fact that the European Court of Justice was to consider a fundamental question affecting the Tribunal's jurisdiction, namely whether competence to pursue the claim had been transferred from Ireland to the European Union.[24]

What, then, is the relevance of these points of departure in related fields for the **4.23** resolution of parallel proceedings in investment arbitration? There are important comparisons to be drawn. But, in a number of respects, the particular characteristics of investment arbitration conspire to increase both the likely incidence of conflicts of jurisdiction, and their likely complexity.

C. The Potential for Conflicts of Jurisdiction in Investment Arbitration

Four features of the mixed character of investment arbitration may be singled out **4.24** as provoking both more, and more complex, possibilities of parallel litigation:[25]

Bilateralism. The first feature is the very nature of the basis for such arbitration, in **4.25** bilateral treaties. The consequence of this is that every dispute comes before a tribunal which has been separately constituted to determine a dispute based upon the adjudication of rights arising from that treaty. Even where the tribunal is constituted according to ICSID rules, it enjoys a wholly separate identity.

Non-exclusivity. Investment arbitration was created in order to provide an alterna- **4.26** tive avenue for redress to the courts of the host State. But investment treaties rarely

---

[24] *The MOX Plant Case (Ireland v United Kingdom)* (PCA, Order No 3, 24 June 2003) (2003) 42 ILM 1187. The European Court of Justice subsequently ruled that Ireland was not competent to bring the claim, and had violated European law in so doing; *Commission of the European Communities v Ireland* (Case C–459/03) [2006] ECR I–4635.

[25] See generally Z Douglas, 'The Hybrid Foundations of Investment Treaty Arbitration' (2003) 74 BYIL 151, 236–281.

exclude all recourse to state courts. Much more commonly, the treaty leaves it equally open to the claimant to seek its remedy in those courts. The dividing line is especially difficult to draw in those cases where the investor has a concession contract with the State. In such cases, it may be necessary to distinguish between contract claims and treaty claims arising out of the same factual matrix.[26] But even then, the treaty may treat breaches of contract as breaches of treaty. The implications of these options will be discussed further below. Alternatively, the contract itself may contain a clause submitting contractual disputes to investor-State arbitration.

4.27 *Exclusion of local remedies rule.* Investment treaties typically exclude the operation of the exhaustion of local remedies rule, so that the investor is not required to complete all recourse to host State courts before instituting a claim before an international arbitral tribunal. On the contrary, it may elect to proceed directly to the international forum. Whatever may be its impact on the substantive rights of the parties,[27] the local remedies rule has no application as a procedural bar to recourse to investment arbitration, unless the host State has expressly imposed such a condition by treaty.[28] Despite some academic commentary to the contrary, it is not the case that, where investment arbitration is provided for, the local remedies rule will nevertheless survive unless expressly excluded.[29] On the contrary, an unqualified clause enabling an investor to submit its dispute with a host State to arbitration will operate in the same way as any other arbitration clause: as a prorogation of litigation.

4.28 *Multiple investor claims.* The extended definition of what constitutes an investment for the purpose of many bilateral investment treaties has opened up the possibility for different companies in a chain of investment each to pursue their own treaty claims.[30] Thus, in the dispute arising out of the operation of the TV Nova television channel in the Czech Republic, the ultimate American investor, Ron Lauder, brought arbitration proceedings against the Czech Republic under the US-Czech bilateral treaty of 1991.[31] At the same time, the Dutch investment vehicle, through which Mr Lauder's investment was held, brought its own arbitration claim under the Dutch-Czech investment treaty.[32] Both claims were held admissible under the respective treaties.

---

[26] The issue which proved of particular difficulty in *Compañia de Aguas del Aconquija SA and Vivendi Universal v Argentine Republic* (Decision on Annulment) 6 ICSID Rep 327 (ICSID, 2002, Fortier P, Crawford & Fernández Rozas). [27] As to which see 7.92–7.98 below.

[28] Thus, Art 26 of the Convention on the Settlement of Investment Disputes between States and Nationals of Other States (signed 18 March 1965, entered into force 14 October 1966) 575 UNTS 159 ('ICSID Convention') permits a State to reserve the right to require the exhaustion of local remedies as a condition of its consent to arbitration (Appendix 11 below).

[29] eg Amerasinghe (n 19 above) 269–276. [30] See further Chap 6 below.

[31] *Lauder v Czech Republic* (Award) 9 ICSID Rep 62 (UNCITRAL, 2001, Briner C, Cutler & Klein), discussed further at 4.119–4.126 below.

[32] *CME Czech Republic BV (The Netherlands) v Czech Republic* (Partial Award) 9 ICSID Rep 121 (UNCITRAL, 2001, Kühn C, Schwebel & Hándl).

D. Available Techniques for Conflict Resolution

What techniques, then, are potentially available for the resolution of conflicts of **4.29** jurisdiction in investment arbitration? Rules determining the priority and effect to be accorded to other means of dispute resolution may conveniently be divided between those which are found within the text of the treaty itself; and those which are external to the treaty, and find their origin in general principles of law.

Internal rules: express provisions within an investment treaty

In the first category, there are a group of rules which are jurisdiction-conferring, **4.30** in the sense that they indicate an intention on the part of the treaty parties to extend the jurisdiction of the tribunal to cover disputes which might otherwise be subject to adjudication in other fora. The second group of rules are jurisdiction declining. Their function is to enable or require the tribunal to decline jurisdiction, or to stay its exercise on the ground that another court or tribunal has been chosen by the parties or is otherwise competent to resolve the matter. In each case, these rules relating to jurisdiction may be relevant to the resolution of a conflict of jurisdictions between parallel proceedings.

Jurisdiction-conferring rules

Where an arbitral tribunal enjoys jurisdiction pursuant to an investment treaty, **4.31** the extent of that jurisdiction will be primarily determined by the rules discussed in Chapters 5 and 6 below. These rules will determine whether the claimant meets the basic hurdles of nationality and investment to come within the jurisdictional provisions of the treaty. The treaty may go further and require, as a condition of submission to the tribunal's jurisdiction, that the parties expressly waive any right of recourse to other means of dispute resolution.[33] Failure to meet such a waiver requirement through continued pursuit, for example, of host State court remedies may preclude a party from resort to treaty arbitration.[34]

The claimant must then satisfy the tribunal that its claims fall within the substan- **4.32** tive protections of the Treaty, by constituting either a breach of one of the protected investors' rights, discussed in Chapter 7 below, or an expropriation of property, discussed in Chapter 8 below. The scope of substantive protection afforded by an investment treaty will typically fall short of covering the full range of disputes which may arise between an investor and the host State. A number of the cases discussed in Chapter 7 below are thus concerned with the question of

---

[33] eg North American Free Trade Agreement (adopted 17 December 1992, entered into force 1 January 1994) CTS 1994 No 2, (1993) 32 ILM 612 ('NAFTA') Art 1121, discussed at 4.55 and 4.86–4.92 below.

[34] *Waste Management Inc v United Mexican States (Waste Management I)* (Award) 5 ICSID Rep 443 (NAFTA/ICSID (AF), 2000, Cremades P, Highet & Siqueiros).

whether the particular claim rises to the level of a breach of the treaty. They establish that neither a simple breach of contract on the part of the State,[35] nor a breach by State officials of an internal provision of the State's own law[36] will necessarily amount to a breach of treaty.

Relation between breach of contract and breach of treaty

4.33   The need to make such a distinction arises in a particularly acute form where the parties are also in contractual relations with each other— typically by means of a concession contract. Where this contract itself contains a dispute resolution clause, it will be essential to distinguish between disputes covered by that clause, and those amenable to treaty arbitration. This issue has arisen in a number of the most controversial awards, and applications for annulment.

4.34   However, a bright line between treaty claims and contract claims may potentially be affected by three types of clause within an investment treaty:

(1) *Investment disputes clause.* It has been argued that a broad form of jurisdiction clause submitting any investment dispute to arbitration may include disputes between an investor and the host State irrespective of whether the dispute is founded on the breach of a specific treaty provision.[37]

(2) *Investment agreements clause.* The treaty may include a clause expressly submitting disputes under an investment agreement to arbitration.[38]

(3) *Umbrella clause.* The treaty may include a so-called 'umbrella' clause, by which a State confirms its commitment to honour its obligations to investors of the other State.

Jurisdiction-declining rules

4.35   **The fork in the road/*electa una via***   Where the tribunal would otherwise have jurisdiction pursuant to a treaty, a party may lose the ability to avail itself of such jurisdiction by choosing another forum for the resolution of its dispute. Many investment treaties offer the parties a 'cafeteria-style' choice of alternative fora. That choice typically includes the courts of the host State, along with various forms of arbitration. The choice of one such form of dispute resolution may expressly preclude resort to another under the principle of *electa una via*.[39] This

---

[35]   *Waste Management Inc v United Mexican States (Waste Management II)* (Award) (2004) 43 ILM 967 (NAFTA/ICSID (AF), 2004, Crawford P, Civiletti & Gómez).

[36]   *ADF Group Inc v United States of America* (Award) 6 ICSID Rep 449, 532 (NAFTA/ICSID (AF), 2003, Feliciano P, de Mestral & Lamm).

[37]   On this issue see E Gaillard, 'Treaty-Based Jurisdiction: Broad Dispute Resolution Clauses' (6 October 2005) 234 (68) NYLJ 3.

[38]   eg US model BIT 2004 (Appendix 6 below) Art 24.

[39]   *Electa una via, non datur recursus ad alteram* ('When one way has been chosen, no recourse is given to another.') BA Garner & HC Black, *Black's Law Dictionary* (8th edn, 2004) 1716. For discussion see Shany (n 14 above) 23; 212–217.

approach in the drafting of dispute resolution clauses in treaties gives effect to a notion of estoppel by election. It has become known in the recent jurisprudence as 'the fork in the road', since, by making the choice, the investor may be held to have irrevocably chosen the forum in which its disputes are to be resolved.

The operation of such clauses has posed particular difficulties. These may arise as **4.36** a result of the interrelation with the treaty/contract divide. Has the choice by the investor of a forum to litigate another part of the same factual dispute really precluded it from treaty arbitration, if, on analysis, the other claim was founded on contract rather than treaty? But, even where there is no contract, the investor may have sought recourse before the national courts of the host State. Does this prevent it from pursuing a subsequent claim in international arbitration?

External rules: application of general principles of law

The techniques available to resolve conflicts between rival fora in investment **4.37** disputes are not, however, limited to those contained within the express terms of the treaty itself. It would be surprising if they were, since, by definition, the tribunal is being asked to recognize and give effect to proceedings and decisions emanating from other sources. Not even the most hermetically sealed vision of the task of an investment arbitral tribunal could exclude all impacts of other decisions relating to the same factual matrix. The basis for their potential application is as general principles of law, applied as a source for the interpretation of the treaty pursuant to Article 31(3)(c) of the VCLT.[40] As discussed above, the two techniques which are likely to apply most directly are:

(1) *Res judicata*. The requirement to recognize the preclusive effect of other international arbitral awards has been considered and approved in principle in several recent cases.[41] The critical question for tribunals has been the conditions for the application of the doctrine: the legally-binding extent of what was adjudicated by the prior tribunal; and the requisite extent of identity between the parties and the cause in the prior action, and that of the second action brought before the tribunal.

(2) *Lis pendens*. Tribunals have also recently heard arguments on the application of a doctrine of *lis alibi pendens* in investment arbitration. In many ways, this principle reflects the same underlying concerns for the reduction in the multiplicity of litigation as that of *res judicata*. Similar techniques as to identity of parties and claims are deployed to determine its application. The differences between the two techniques are of timing and effect. *Lis pendens* applies only while the dispute is actually pending in two competing fora. Its effect is spent

---

[40] VCLT (n 1 above). As to which see C McLachlan, 'The Principle of Systemic Integration and Article 31(3)(c) of the Vienna Convention' (2005) 54 ICLQ 279.
[41] See, notably, *CME* (n 32 above); *Waste Management II* (n 35 above).

once one tribunal reaches a decision on the merits. It may operate as a discretion to decline jurisdiction, rather than a binding rule. *Res judicata*, on the other hand, applies only once such a decision has been rendered. Where it applies, it has a mandatory preclusive effect on subsequent claims.

2. Treatment of Jurisdictional Conflicts in Investment Treaties

4.38 For the reasons discussed above, the express terms of investment treaties themselves will provide only limited guidance on the problems of parallel proceedings. It is proposed to examine, first, the ways in which their jurisdiction-conferring clauses may condition the approach of the tribunal to such a problem, especially by the use of umbrella clauses. Secondly, techniques for the limitation of jurisdiction will be treated. These include two ways of giving effect to the principle of *electa una via*: fork in the road provisions, and waiver upon submission. In each case, this will be done by reference to a number of model form bilateral investment treaties (BITs), as well as NAFTA, and the Energy Charter Treaty. Finally, the impact of the jurisdiction provisions of the ICSID Convention itself will be considered.

A. Jurisdiction-Conferring Provisions

Standard forms

4.39 The standard forms of general jurisdiction-conferring provisions in investment treaties are set out in paras 3.02–3.15 above.

Umbrella clauses

Origins

4.40 Another technique found in investment treaties, which may extend the scope of their protection, is the so-called 'umbrella clause'. By this technique, the host State guarantees by treaty the specific undertakings which it has entered into by contract or otherwise with investors of the other contracting State, bringing those undertakings under the umbrella of protection of the treaty.[42]

4.41 The underlying concept may be linked to the (contested) proposition in customary international law that contracts entered into between States and foreign investors

---

[42] I Seidl-Hohenveldern, 'The Abs-Shawcross Draft Convention to Protect Private Foreign Investment: Comments on the Round-table' (1961) 10 J Pub Law 100, 104. One account of the history of such clauses is A Sinclair, 'The Origins of the Umbrella Clause in the International Law of Investment Protection' (2004) 20 Arb Int, 411.

are entitled to special protection, especially in the light of the host State's municipal law-making competence, which can subsequently affect the parties' contractual bargain.[43] This concept is supported by the jurisprudence of a number of international arbitral tribunals, adjudicating upon long-term concession contracts, which have found that:

(1) international law rules are applicable to such contracts, even where host State law is otherwise considered to be applicable to the contract;[44] and

(2) there is a rule in international law that a State is bound by its contracts with foreign parties notwithstanding the power of its legislature under municipal law to alter the contract.[45]

But these propositions were always strongly contested by those, usually non-Western, States which contended that the foreign investment contract was in the same position as an ordinary municipal contract.   **4.42**

The idea of using investment treaties to give effect to this principle has been traced   **4.43**
from negotiations on Iranian oil nationalization disputes into the Abs-Shawcross draft of 1959.[46] A centre-piece of the substantive provisions of that draft was Article II, which provided: 'Each Party shall at all times ensure the observance of any undertakings which it may have given in relation to investments made by nationals of any other Party.'

This provision was regarded as of fundamental importance by its drafters, who   **4.44**
saw it as an application of the principle of *pacta sunt servanda* to agreements concluded between a State and foreigners.[47] The provision was subsequently incorporated into the OECD Draft Convention as well.[48] From there, it may be traced into the BIT practice of a number of States.

---

[43] See TW Wälde, 'The "Umbrella" (or Sanctity of Contract/Pacta sunt servanda) Clause in Investment Arbitration: A Comment on Original Intentions and Recent Cases' (2004) 1(4) TDM 1.

[44] *Lena Goldfields Ltd v Soviet Union*, The Times, 3 September 1930, reprinted in (1950–1951) 36 Cornell Law Quarterley 42. For a full account based on historical research and appraisal of its significance see VV Veeder, 'The *Lena Goldfields* Arbitration: The Historical Roots of Three Ideas' (1998) 47 ICLQ 747.

[45] *Revere Copper and Brass Inc v Overseas Private Investment Corp* (Award) (1978) 17 ILM 1321, 1331–1343 applying *Saudi Arabia v Arabian American Oil Co* (ARAMCO) (1958) 27 ILR 117 (Arb Trib, 1958, Sauser-Hall R, Badawi/Hassan & Habachy); *Shufeldt Claim* (US v Guatemala) II RIAA 1079 (Sisnett, 1930); *Sapphire International Petroleums Ltd v National Iranian Oil Co* (Award) (1963) 35 ILR 136 (Cavin). This rule was already well established before *Revere Copper*: see T Meron, 'Repudiation of Ultra Vires State Contracts and the International Responsibility of States' (1957) 6 ICLQ 273. See now also: *Sandline International Inc v Independent State of Papua New Guinea* (Interim Award) (1998) 117 ILR 552 (UNCITRAL, 1998, Somers P, Kerr & Dawson).

[46] H Abs & H Shawcross, 'The Proposed Convention to Protect Private Foreign Investment' (1960) 9 J Pub Law 115. For the evidence in support of this historical origin see Sinclair (n 42 above).   [47] ibid 120.

[48] OECD, *Draft Convention on the Protection of Foreign Property and Resolution of the Council of the OECD on the Draft Convention* (1967) Art 2.

Current practice

4.45 Unlike many of the other protected rights discussed in this work, however, the protection of contractual rights by treaty under an umbrella clause does not find universal application in modern investment treaties. On the contrary, it is notably absent from the model forms of many, in particular non-Western, States. It does not appear, for example, in the Sri Lankan model form, which is otherwise in conventional form,[49] nor does it figure in China's model BIT,[50] nor that of Chile.[51] In each case, the definition of 'investment' includes concession agreements, so that the other substantive protections of the treaty are extended to this class of property. But the treaties do not separately confirm the enforceability of undertakings.

4.46 By contrast, the practice of Western States has been to seek to include such a protection as a distinct obligation. Thus, the UK model form adds to its general clause protecting investments a final sentence providing: 'Each contracting Party shall observe any obligation it may have entered into with regard to investments of nationals or companies of the other Contracting Party.'[52]

4.47 The French model accords priority to the more favourable of a contract between host State and investor, but at the same time ensures that the treaty submission to arbitration will apply irrespective of contrary provision in such agreements:

> Les investissements ayant fait l'objet d'un engagement particulier de l'une des Parties contractantes à l'égard des investisseurs de l'autre Partie contractante sont régis, sans préjudice des dispositions du présent accord, par les termes de cet engagement dans la mesure où celui-ci comporte des dispositions plus favorables que celles qui sont prévues par le présent accord. Les dispositions de l'article 8 du présent Accord s'appliquent même en cas d'engagement spécifique prévoyant la renonciation à l'arbitrage international ou désignant une instance arbitrale différente de celle mentionnée à l'article 8 du présent Accord.[53]

4.48 The US model deals with the direct enforceability of contractual claims under the treaty arbitration mechanisms simply by bringing such claims expressly within the scope of the disputes stated to be amenable to arbitration.[54]

4.49 There is no express undertaking in relation to contractual obligations in NAFTA.

4.50 Article 10(1) of the Energy Charter Treaty provides, in its final sentence, that: 'Each Contracting Party shall observe any obligations it has entered into with an Investor or an Investment of an Investor of any other Contracting Party.'

---

[49] Sri Lanka model BIT (Appendix 9 below).
[50] China model BIT reprinted in UNCTAD, *International Investment Instruments: A Compendium* Vol III (1996) 151.
[51] Chile model BIT reprinted in UNCTAD, *International Investment Instruments: A Compendium* Vol III (1996) 143.   [52] UK model BIT (Appendix 4 below) Art 2.
[53] French model BIT (Appendix 10 below) Art 10.   [54] See 3.11 above.

However, this provision is one to which a State may enter a reservation, an option **4.51** utilized by a small number of the negotiating States.[55]

B. Jurisdiction-Limiting Provisions: *Electa una Via*

Investment treaties are often silent as to the preclusive effect to be accorded to the **4.52** different modes of dispute resolution afforded to the investor. However, two techniques in particular have been employed in order to limit the investor's choice, by utilizing the concepts of estoppel and waiver. The first technique requires the investor to choose a method of dispute resolution *ab initio*, and estops him from subsequently re-litigating the dispute in other fora. The choice thus made has been described in the literature and in the awards as the 'fork in the road'. The second does not require an early election. Rather, the investor may pursue any and all domestic remedies available to him in the courts of the host State. However, once the investor has elected to pursue investment arbitration, he must waive his rights to pursue any other form of dispute resolution.

'Fork in the road' provisions

The typical form which an election of the first type takes is that found in the Chile **4.53** model BIT. Article 8 provides two alternative forms of dispute resolution open to an investor under the Treaty; either international arbitration under ICSID or litigation before host State courts. Article 8(3) then provides: 'Once the investor has submitted the dispute to the competent tribunal of the Contracting Party in whose territory the investment was made or to international arbitration, that election shall be final.'[56] Clauses in similar form to this were those found in the France/Argentina BIT, which was at issue in the *Vivendi* affair,[57] and in the US-Argentina BIT,[58] which was discussed by the Tribunal in *CMS Gas Transmission Co v Argentina*.[59]

The Energy Charter Treaty (ECT) permits member States to choose to make an **4.54** investor's prior election of a domestic remedy preclusive of the submission to

---

[55] Energy Charter Treaty (Appendix 2 below) pursuant to Art 26(3)(c). The States withholding their consent to arbitration under this clause are: Australia, Canada, Hungary and Norway (Annex IA). Of those, Canada did not in the event sign the ECT, and ratification of it is still pending in Australia and Norway.   [56] See n [51] above.

[57] *Compañia de Aguas del Aconquija SA and Compagnie Générale des Eaux v Argentine Republic* (Award) 5 ICSID Rep 296 (ICSID, 2000, Rezek P, Buergenthal & Trooboff); *Compañia de Aguas del Aconquija SA and Vivendi Universal v Argentine Republic* (Decision on Annulment) 6 ICSID Rep 327 (ICSID, 2002, Fortier P, Crawford & Fernández Rozas).

[58] Treaty Concerning the Reciprocal Encouragement and Protection of Investment (US-Argentina) (signed 14 November 1991, entered into force 20 October 1994) Senate Treaty Doc 103–02, Art VII (3)(a).

[59] *CMS Gas Transmission Co v Republic of Argentina* (Jurisdiction) 7 ICSID Rep 492, 510–512 (ICSID, 2003, Orrego Vicuña P, Lalonde & Rezek).

international arbitration. This is done by the rather curious mechanism of scheduling a list of State parties who 'do not give such unconditional consent' to the submission of the dispute to international arbitration 'where the Investor has previously submitted the dispute' to local courts or to any contractually agreed dispute resolution.[60] There are twenty-two State parties which have made this election.[61]

Waiver of alternative options

4.55 The second approach ensures the exclusivity of the arbitral process, but only once it has been commenced. In the interim, the investor may take his chances in the local courts. This type of clause is exemplified by Article 1121(1)(b) of NAFTA, which provides:

> Article 1121: Conditions Precedent to Submission of a Claim to Arbitration
>
> 1. A disputing investor may submit a claim . . . to arbitration only if:
>
> . . . .
>
> (b) the investor and . . . the enterprise, waive their right to initiate or continue before any administrative tribunal or court under the law of any Party, or other dispute settlement procedures, any proceedings *with respect to the measure of the disputing Party that is alleged to be a breach* . . . except for proceedings for injunctive, declaratory or other extraordinary relief, not involving the payment of damages . . . [emphasis added].

4.56 This approach is also adopted in Article 26(2) of the 2004 US model form, which provides that:

> No claim may be submitted to arbitration under this Section unless:
>
> . . .
>
> (b) the notice of arbitration is accompanied . . . by the claimant's written waiver . . . of any right to initiate or continue before any administrative tribunal or court under the law of either Party, or other dispute settlement procedures, any proceeding with respect to any measure alleged to constitute a breach referred to in Article 24.

C. Effect of the ICSID Convention

4.57 Thus far, the consideration has been limited to the provisions of investment treaties themselves. However, despite the distinction generally drawn in this work between substantive principles and procedural matters, it is not possible to conclude consideration of this topic without an examination of Article 26 of the ICSID Convention itself.[62] This provides: 'Consent of the parties to arbitration under this Convention shall, unless otherwise stated, be deemed consent to such

---

[60] Energy Charter Treaty (Appendix 2 below) Art 26(3)(b)(i).
[61] These are listed in Annex ID.
[62] See C Schreuer, *The ICSID Convention: A Commentary* (2001) 345–396.

arbitration *to the exclusion of any other remedy*. A Contracting State may require the exhaustion of local administrative or judicial remedies as a condition of its consent to arbitration under this Convention' (emphasis added).[63]

First case: exceptional specific requirement to exhaust local remedies

The second sentence of Article 26 has had very limited application in practice. **4.58** Although it was much debated during the drafting process,[64] at present only Guatemala has made a declaration to this effect. Of course, it is still open to a State to include such a requirement in the bilateral investment treaty itself (or in an investment agreement or any other instrument by which the State gives its consent to the jurisdiction of the Centre).[65] But reported examples of this are rare. This is perhaps unsurprising, given that avoidance of the expense and delay of meeting the requirements of the exhaustion of local remedies rule under the customary international law rules of diplomatic protection is seen as one of the main benefits of the conclusion of an investment treaty. Clauses which merely permit the pursuit of local remedies within a specified time frame prior to the institution of arbitral proceedings do not import a requirement to exhaust local remedies. Indeed, given the time limits often specified, it is impossible to see how they could be treated otherwise.

Second case: specific provision for alternative remedies

If no such requirement has been imposed by the host State, the parties may still **4.59** nevertheless validly provide for alternative options to ICSID arbitration—hence the parenthetical 'unless otherwise stated'. It is by virtue of this exception that 'cafeteria-style' clauses giving the investor a choice between different forms of dispute resolution are nevertheless still valid under the Convention.[66]Article 26 is merely a deeming provision—a rule of construction or interpretation which can be displaced should the contrary intention be clear.

Third case: ICSID as an exclusive remedy

Nevertheless, if neither of these options has been exercised, the question remains **4.60** as to the effect of the operative provision of Article 26 where other dispute resolution methods have been pursued prior to the institution of ICSID arbitration. Does the investor forfeit his right to pursue arbitration under ICSID by his prior pursuit of other remedies? The answer to this question may partly be provided by

---

[63] Convention on the Settlement of Investment Disputes between States and Nationals of Other States (signed 18 March 1965, entered into force 14 October 1966) 575 UNTS 159 (Appendix 11 below).

[64] Schreuer (n 62 above) 389.

[65] See ICSID, 'Revised Model Clauses' (1993) 4 ICSID Rep 357, 365 Clause 13.

[66] See ibid Clause 12.

an analysis of the nature of consent to ICSID arbitration under investment treaties. Tribunal jurisprudence has established that the ICSID Convention's requirement of consent in writing is met, in the case of investment treaties, by the State's consent given in the treaty, combined with the investor's consent signified by his submission of the claim to arbitration.[67] This being so, the exclusion of other remedies under Article 26 will not apply vis-à-vis the investor until such time as he files his request for arbitration.

4.61 There are, in that event, three consequences for ICSID arbitration of treaty disputes:

(1) The choice of ICSID arbitration is only to be treated as exclusive once it has been commenced. Any prior proceedings in national courts, or pursuit of other alternative remedies, will then simply form part of the sub-stratum of fact which the tribunal must consider in order to decide whether the State has met or failed in its substantive obligations under the Treaty. This could include, for example, whether the State has committed a denial of justice through the decisions of its national courts such as to amount to a breach of the obligation to accord fair and equitable treatment.[68]

(2) The right to pursue ICSID arbitration for breach of Treaty is not waived under Article 26 by the investor's prior invocation of domestic or contractual remedies. In this respect, the invocation of a Treaty claim is fundamentally unlike a request for arbitration under ICSID based upon a contractual submission clause. In the case of contractual submission, the investor's consent is given at the time of contracting, with the consequence that both parties are from that point precluded from seeking remedies elsewhere.[69] By the same token, however, the right to invoke the arbitration clause by seeking a mandatory stay of judicial proceedings may be waived by steps taken in the domestic proceedings.

(3) The exclusivity of ICSID arbitration in the case of treaty claims will, however, only relate to the investment dispute which forms the subject of such a claim. Thus it will not operate so as to preclude pursuit of claims by the investor against the host state which are not founded upon treaty rights, and which can thus only be the subject of other forms of dispute resolution.

4.62 It is to the significance of this fundamental distinction between treaty and other forms of disputes, in particular contractual disputes, that this chapter must now turn. However difficult and controversial the jurisprudence on this issue may have been, a proper analysis of the treaty/contract divide forms the foundation for subsequent consideration of many of the other issues relating to parallel proceedings.

---

[67] See 3.21–3.29 above.   [68] See 7.80–7.98 below.
[69] *Attorney-General v Mobil Oil NZ Ltd* 4 ICSID Rep 117 (New Zealand High Court, 1987, Heron J).

3. Modern Application in Investment Arbitral Awards

The first wave of jurisprudence developed by international investment tribunals **4.63** on the issues of parallel proceedings needs to be seen in context. For the reasons explained in Part 1 above, investor-State arbitration raises problems in its relation to other forms of dispute resolution, which are unprecedented in international dispute resolution. Tribunals have quickly developed an approach to these issues. But there have been significant shifts in approach, whether as a result of the annulment of awards;[70] or as a result of their reconsideration in subsequent closely-related cases.[71] The law is in a state of rapid development, and it is not to be expected that the current awards represent the last word on the topic. Moreover, as the analysis in Part 2 above shows, this is an area where States have experimented with a wide range of different solutions in the language which they have employed in their treaties. The awards are naturally shaped by these specific solutions, and one must be careful to read the dicta of arbitral tribunals in the context of the particular claim and treaty basis.

A. Breach of Contract and Breach of Treaty

The first issue which arbitral tribunals have had to confront in considering the **4.64** impact of other forms of dispute resolution upon their jurisdiction has been how to distinguish the proper sphere of the treaty dispute from other disputes arising from the factual matrix of the same investment, which either have been, or are in the course of being, litigated in other fora; or are subjected by contractual submission to other forms of dispute resolution.

National law and international law remedies distinguished

The starting-point in analysing this distinction is to recall the basic principle that **4.65** rights created by treaty exist on the plane of international law. Consequently, no provision of national law may constitute a defence to such a claim.[72] The importance of

---

[70] eg *Compañía de Aguas del Aconquija SA and Compagnie Générale des Eaux v Argentine Republic* (Award) 5 ICSID Rep 296 (ICSID, 2000, Rezek P, Buergenthal & Trooboff); *Compañía de Aguas del Aconquija SA and Vivendi Universal v Argentine Republic* (Decision on Annulment) 6 ICSID Rep 327 (ICSID, 2002, Fortier P, Crawford & Fernández Rozas).

[71] eg *SGS Société Générale de Surveillance SA v Republic of the Philippines* (Jurisdiction) 8 ICSID Rep 515 (ICSID, 2004, El-Kosheri P, Crawford & Crivellaro). cf the earlier decision on very similar facts in *SGS Société Générale de Surveillance SA v Islamic Republic of Pakistan* (Jurisdiction) 8 ICSID Rep 383 (ICSID, 2003, Feliciano P, Faurès & Thomas).

[72] See 4.14–4.15 above, citing VCLT Art 27 and the ILC Draft Articles on State Responsibility Art 3.

this distinction was well explained by the Tribunal in *GAMI Investments Inc v Mexico*.[73] Mexico had raised an objection to the jurisdiction of the NAFTA Tribunal. It claimed that GAMI, an American minority shareholder in a Mexican company, GAM, was precluded from bringing its claim because GAM had already challenged the measure which GAMI claimed was expropriatory before the Mexican courts. In an important passage, the Tribunal rejected this submission on the basis of the separate role of international law.[74] It cited *Selwyn*, in which the umpire had held: 'International arbitration is not affected jurisdictionally by the fact that the same question is in the courts of one of the nations. Such international tribunal has power to act without reference thereto, and if judgment has been pronounced by such court, to disregard the same so far as it affects the indemnity to the individual . . . '[75]

4.66 This ruling was in turn based upon the venerable authority of *The Betsey* (1796), in which the American members of the Claims Commission established under the Jay Treaty had opined that even decisions of the British Lords Commissioners of Appeal in Prize Cases were not binding upon the international tribunal.[76]

4.67 The *GAMI* Tribunal continued:

> . . . ultimately each jurisdiction is responsible for the application of the law under which it exercises its mandate. It was for the Mexican courts to determine whether the expropriation was legitimate under Mexican law. It is for the present Tribunal to judge whether there have been breaches of international law by any agency of the Mexican government. A fundamental postulate in applying NAFTA is that enshrined in Article 27 of the Vienna Convention on the Law of Treaties: 'A party may not invoke the provisions of its own internal law as justification for its failure to perform a treaty.' Whether such national laws have been upheld by national courts is ultimately of no moment in this regard.[77]

Effect of contractual jurisdiction clause

4.68 If, then, a claim to breach of treaty is in principle a claim governed exclusively by international law which is separate and distinct from a claim of breach of national law, what is the effect of an investor's contractual submission to the jurisdiction of the host State courts? This question was answered decisively by the Tribunal (as to jurisdiction) and the Annulment Committee (as to the merits) in the *Vivendi* affair.[78]

---

[73] *GAMI Investments Inc v United Mexican States* (Award) (2005) 44 ILM 545 (NAFTA/UNCITRAL, 2004, Paulsson P, Muró & Reisman).   [74] ibid 552.

[75] JH Ralston, *Venezuelan Arbitrations of 1903* (1904) 322, 327.

[76] *The Betsey* (1796), J Moore, *International Adjudications* Modern Series, Vol IV (1931) 182. For an account of the controversy which these Opinions provoked, and its eventual resolution in favour of the jurisdiction of the Claims Commission see ibid 81–87.

[77] *GAMI* (n 73 above) 552.

[78] *Compañia de Aguas del Aconquija SA and Compagnie Générale des Eaux v Argentine Republic* (Award) 5 ICSID Rep 296 (ICSID, 2000, Rezek P, Buergenthal & Trooboff) *(CGE)*; *Compañía de*

The result was a clear affirmation that the investor was entitled to pursue his claim for breach of treaty irrespective of such a clause, since the nature and basis of the cause of action before the international tribunal was entirely different.

In that case, the claimants (a French company and its Argentine affiliate, **4.69** together 'CGE') had entered into a concession contract with the Argentine province of Tucumán, pursuant to which they had assumed responsibility for the operation of the provincial sewage and water system. The contract contained an exclusive jurisdiction clause (clause 16.4) in favour of the administrative courts of the Province of Tucumán. From an early stage in the performance of the contract, disputes arose between CGE and the Province. Ultimately, the Province terminated the contract, whereupon CGE brought a claim against Argentina under the French-Argentine BIT.[79] The gravamen of the claim was that Argentina had breached its treaty obligations by failing to ensure that the Province properly performed the contract. Alternatively, it claimed that the actions of the Province were attributed to Argentina as a matter of international law, and that those actions themselves constituted a breach of the treaty. Argentina submitted that the Tribunal had no jurisdiction to hear the claim in the light of the contractual jurisdiction clause.

The Tribunal held that it had jurisdiction, but denied the claim on the merits. In **4.70** both cases, the decisive factor was the Tribunal's view of the impact of the jurisdiction clause choosing local courts. As to jurisdiction, the Tribunal held that the claim was properly brought against Argentina itself, whether on the basis of its own defaults, or on the basis of the attribution to it, as a matter of State responsibility, of the defaults of its Province.[80] It also held that the contractual jurisdiction clause did not deprive it of jurisdiction:

> . . . Article 16.4 of the Concession Contract does not divest this Tribunal of jurisdiction to hear this case because that provision did not and could not constitute a waiver by CGE of its rights under Article 8 of the BIT to file the pending claims against the Argentine Republic . . . In this case the claims filed by CGE against Respondent are based on violation by the Argentine Republic of the BIT through acts or omissions of that government and acts of the Tucumán authorities that Claimants assert should be attributed to the central government. As formulated, these claims . . . are not based on the Concession Contract but allege a cause of action under the BIT. [81]

Aguas del Aconquija SA and Vivendi Universal v Argentine Republic (Decision on Annulment) 6 ICSID Rep 327 (ICSID, 2002, Fortier P, Crawford & Fernández Rozas) *(CAA and Vivendi).*

[79] Accord sur l'Encouragement et la Protection Réciproques des Investissements ('Agreement on the Reciprocal Promotion and Protection of Investments') (France-Argentina) (signed 3 July 1991, entered into force 3 March 1993) 1728 UNTS 281.　　　　　　　[80] *CGE* (n 78 above) 313–314.

[81] *CGE* (n 78 above) 315, applying *Lanco International Inc v Argentine Republic* (Jurisdiction) 5 ICSID Rep 367 (ICSID, 1998, Cremades P, Alvarez & Baptista).

4.71 However, the Tribunal found against CGE on the merits, holding that the jurisdiction clause precluded any claim under the Treaty unless and until an action in the local courts had been pursued. The Tribunal reasoned:

> ... because of the crucial connection in this case between the terms of the Concession Contract and these alleged violations of the BIT, the Argentine Republic cannot be held liable unless and until Claimants have, as Article 16.4 of the Concession Contract requires, asserted their rights in proceedings before the contentious administrative courts of Tucumán and have been denied their rights, either procedurally or substantively. [82]

4.72 The award was challenged by CGE by way of annulment proceedings. The Annulment Committee agreed with the Tribunal's analysis as to jurisdiction.[83] However, it annulled its decision on the merits insofar as it applied to the claims based on Argentina's responsibility for the actions of the provincial authorities.[84] The Committee's reasoning merits close study, and has been widely adopted and followed in subsequent awards.[85] It was as follows:

(1) A State may breach a treaty without breaching a contract and vice versa, since the treaty sets an independent standard: Article 3 of the International Law Commission Draft Articles on State Responsibility.[86]

(2) Each claim is to be determined by its own proper law: in the case of the treaty claim—international law; in the case of the contract claim—the proper law of the contract, in this case the law of Tucumán. Different legal consequences may well flow from the application of the different applicable law.[87]

(3) In a case where the essential basis of a claim brought before an international tribunal is a breach of contract, the tribunal will give effect to any valid choice of forum clause in the contract: citing *Woodruff*[88] in which the American-Venezuelan Mixed Commission of 1903 had dismissed a claim under a contract with an exclusive jurisdiction clause in favour of the Venezuelan

---

[82] *CGE* (n 78 above) 321.   [83] *CAA and Vivendi* (n 78 above) 360–362.

[84] *CAA and Vivendi* (n 78 above) 364–371.

[85] *CMS Gas Transmission Co v Argentine Republic* (Jurisdiction) 7 ICSID Rep 492 (ICSID, 2003, Orrego Vicuña P, Lalonde & Rezek); *Azurix Corp v Argentine Republic* (Jurisdiction) (2004) 43 ILM 262 (ICSID, 2003, Sureda P, Lauterpacht & Martens); *SGS Société de Surveillance SA v Islamic Republic of Pakistan* (n 71 above); *PSEG Global Inc et al v Republic of Turkey* (Jurisdiction) ICSID Case No ARB/02/5 (ICSID, 2004, Orrego Vicuña P, Fortier & Kaufmann-Kohler); *Enron Corp & anor v Argentine Republic* (Jurisdiction) ICSID Case No ARB/01/3 (ICSID, 2004, Orrego Vicuña P, Gros Espiell & Tschanz); *AES Corp v Argentine Republic* (Jurisdiction) ICSID Case No ARB/02/17 (ICSID, 2005, Dupuy P, Böckstiegel & Janiero); *Impregilo SpA v Islamic Republic of Pakistan* (Jurisdiction) ICSID Case No ARB/03/3 (ICSID, 2005, Guillaume P, Cremades & Landau); *Eureko BV v Republic of Poland* (Partial Award) (Ad hoc, 2005, Fortier P, Schwebel & Rajski); *Bayindir Insaat Turizm Ticaret Ve Sanayi AS v Islamic Republic of Pakistan* (Jurisdiction) ICSID Case No ARB/03/29 (ICSID, 2005, Kaufmann-Kohler P, Bermann & Böckstiegel).

[86] *CAA and Vivendi* (n 78 above) 365.   [87] *CAA and Vivendi* (n 78 above) 365.

[88] *Woodruff Case* IX RIAA 213.

courts on the ground that 'by the very agreement that is the fundamental basis of the claim, it was withdrawn from the jurisdiction of the Commission'.[89]

(4) 'On the other hand, where "the fundamental basis of the claim" is a treaty laying down an independent standard by which the conduct of the parties is to be judged, the existence of an exclusive jurisdiction clause in a contract between the claimant and the respondent state or one of its subdivisions cannot operate as a bar to the application of the treaty standard.'[90]

Breach of treaty involves an exercise of sovereign authority

Whether particular conduct involves a breach of a treaty is not determined **4.73** by asking whether the conduct involves a breach of contract, since a breach of contract is not per se a breach of the international treaty obligation.[91] It will only be where the host State acts in the exercise of its governmental or sovereign authority, rather than merely as a commercial party, that it can be liable for breach of treaty. As it was put in *Impregilo SpA v Pakistan*:

> In fact, the State or its emanation, may have behaved as an ordinary contracting party having a difference of approach, in fact or law, with the investor. In order that the alleged breach of contract may constitute a violation of the BIT, it must be the result of behaviour going beyond that which an ordinary contracting party could adopt. Only the State in the exercise of its sovereign authority ('puissance publique'), and not as a contracting party, may breach the obligations assumed under the BIT.[92]

The Tribunal went on to emphasize that this meant that a treaty and a contract **4.74** claim may overlap or coincide, but that, even if they did so, they would remain analytically distinct. This was important because different rules, for example on issues such as attribution, would apply to each.[93]

B. Election, Waiver, and the 'Fork in the Road'

Fork in the road provisions

To what extent, then, are these basic distinctions between national law and inter- **4.75** national law, and between contract claims and treaty claims discussed in paras 4.64–4.74 above, affected by an express treaty provision requiring an irrevocable

---

[89] ibid 223.   [90] *CAA and Vivendi* (n 78 above) 367.
[91] ibid 369 and fn 78. This is subject to the effect of umbrella clauses, discussed at 4.93–4.116 below.
[92] *Impregilo SpA v Islamic Republic of Pakistan* (Jurisdiction) ICSID Case No ARB/03/3 (ICSID, 2005, Guillaume P, Cremades & Landau) para 260. See also *Joy Mining Machinery Ltd v Arab Republic of Egypt* (Jurisdiction) (2004) 19 ICSID Rev-FILJ 486 (ICSID, 2004, Orrego Vicuña P, Weeramantry & Craig).   [93] ibid para 262.

election in remedies to be made? As has been seen,[94] provisions of this kind, known as 'fork in the road' provisions, abound in BITs.[95]

4.76 It is submitted that, where the parties to an investment treaty agree that the choice of any particular dispute settlement option will preclude resort to any other option, the operation of the clause will be affected by the juridical nature of the claims asserted:

(1) *Different applicable law.* If the claims asserted in the host State courts or other arbitral tribunal are contractual and not treaty-based, the existence of a fork in the road clause will have no effect upon the subsequent invocation of a treaty claim before an investment tribunal, since the fundamental basis of the claim is different. The same reasoning applies to attempts on the part of the investor to obtain relief from the host State measure in the local courts, which fall short of seeking substantially the same relief as that claimed in the treaty arbitration.

(2) *Parallel applicable law.* On the other hand, if the claims asserted before the investment tribunal are substantially the same as those already asserted before host State courts (or another arbitral tribunal contemplated in the relevant clause), the investor will be held to his election. Thus:

    (a) *Contract claim.* If a contract claim has already been submitted to a national court or other arbitral tribunal, then the investor will be precluded from subsequently re-litigating that dispute before an investment tribunal.

    (b) *Treaty claim.* Similarly, where the investor chooses to assert in substance the same cause of action as found in the treaty before a host State's administrative courts he may forfeit the right to sue before an investment tribunal. In the latter case, it will not be every resort to the host State courts which has such preclusive effect. It must be such as to put in issue in substance the same claim for relief from a State measure which would otherwise be sought in international arbitration (as, for example, by claiming that the loss of his property without adequate compensation, which may constitute an expropriation at international law, is an unjustified State taking of property under national administrative law).

4.77 The jurisprudence discussed below demonstrates that most attempts by States to invoke fork in the road provisions in bilateral investment treaties have failed because the fundamental basis of the claims asserted in the other proceedings has been found to be different. An effective interpretation must be given to such clauses where the claims are properly parallel. That said, there has not yet been a

---

[94] See 4.53–4.54 above.
[95] See C Schreuer, 'Travelling the BIT Route: Of Waiting Periods, Umbrella Clauses and Forks in the Road' (2004) 5 Journal of World Investment and Trade 231.

case in which the tribunal has found itself deprived of jurisdiction by virtue of such a clause.

Different applicable law

In a number of cases, tribunals have rejected the State's attempted invocation of a **4.78** fork in the road clause on the grounds that there is insufficient identity either of cause of action or parties. The rationale for this was well explained in *Genin v Estonia*,[96] in which the respondent State had challenged ICSID jurisdiction on the grounds that, under the terms of the US-Estonia BIT,[97] such jurisdiction was precluded if the investor had previously submitted the dispute to the Estonian courts. The local bank, which was the subject of the investment, had taken proceedings in Estonia to seek to overturn the decision of the Bank of Estonia to revoke its banking licence. The Tribunal held that this could not disqualify Genin from its ICSID claim. First, the parties to the two claims were different. In the Estonian proceedings, the local bank sued in its own name, and the outcome affected all shareholders, and other stakeholders, in the bank.[98] The ICSID proceedings were concerned with Genin's investment alone. Secondly, the cause of action was different. It was obvious, the Tribunal considered, that the claim for restoration of the banking licence had to be pursued in Estonia. The ICSID claim was, however, concerned only with whether the losses suffered by Genin were attributable to breaches of the Treaty.[99] Thus, it concluded that: 'Although certain aspects of the facts that gave rise to this dispute were also at issue in the Estonian litigation, the "investment dispute" itself was not, and the Claimants should not therefore be barred from using the ICSID arbitration mechanism.'[100]

Similar reasoning has been applied by tribunals to find that such a clause was not **4.79** applicable when the claim pursued locally was for breach of contract, not breach of treaty. Thus, for example, in *CMS v Argentina*[101] the Tribunal observed: 'Decisions of several ICSID tribunals have held that as contractual claims are different from treaty claims, even if there had been or there currently was a recourse to the local courts for breach of contract, this would not have prevented submission of the treaty claims to arbitration.'

Parallel applicable law

Where, however, the claims are in fact between the same parties, have the same **4.80** object, and are founded upon the same cause of action, in principle a fork in the

---

[96] *Genin, Eastern Credit Ltd Inc and AS Baltoil v Republic of Estonia* (Award) 6 ICSID Rep 236 (ICSID, 2001, Fortier P, Heth & van den Berg).
[97] Treaty Concerning the Encouragement and Reciprocal Protection of Investment (US-Estonia) (signed 19 April 1994, entered into force 16 February 1997) Senate Treaty Doc 103-38.
[98] *Genin* (n 96 above) 291–292.   [99] ibid 292.   [100] ibid 292.
[101] *CMS* (n 85 above) 511, applied in *Azurix Corp v Argentine Republic* (Jurisdiction) (2004) 43 ILM 262, 280 (ICSID, 2003, Sureda P, Lauterpacht & Martins).

road clause ought to be effective. This was recognized in *CMS*, where the Tribunal accepted that the investor could renounce recourse to arbitration by bringing his claim before the local courts.[102] Where the claim sought to be brought is founded upon contract in both tribunals, determination of sufficient identity of parties, cause of action, and object should in most cases be relatively straightforward.

4.81 However, even taking account of the various possibilities for the pursuit of contract claims before an investment tribunal discussed in paras 4.93 to 4.116 below, this type of parallelism can hardly be said to be the primary focus of the fork in the road provisions.

4.82 The remaining question, therefore, is how such a clause may operate in relation to the causes of action, which are the primary subject of this work. It is, of course, possible to take the view that treaty claims exist only on the plane of international law, and thus that no claim brought before a municipal court could ever invoke such a clause. To some extent, the reasoning applied in those cases which have considered the breach of treaty/breach of contract distinction, discussed in paras 4.64 to 4.74 above, would support such an analysis. The problem with it in the present context is that it would give no effective scope of operation to the fork in the road clause in the context of the rights which are the principal subject of investment treaties. It is a basic principle of treaty interpretation that treaties should be interpreted, so far as possible, to give an effective meaning to their provisions.[103] The choice which such clauses offer to the investor must be construed as being between real alternatives.

4.83 Of course, it cannot be every administrative appeal from a decision of a State agency, even if brought by the investor himself, rather than the local investment company, which provokes the operation of the clause. Many such proceedings could be seen as an inevitable by-product of doing business in the relevant country. They would not be apt to seek damages from the State for its substantive default—being expropriation, failure to provide fair and equitable treatment, etc. But nor is it necessary to go as far as Schreuer and conclude that the disputes have to be identical, so that, if the dispute before the international tribunal concerns breach of the BIT 'the dispute before the domestic courts or administrative tribunals would also have to concern an alleged breach of a right conferred or created by the BIT'.[104] In jurisdictions which apply a dualist approach to the reception of

---

[102] *CMS* (n 85 above) 511.

[103] See eg the principle of effectiveness enunciated by Fitzmaurice on the basis of the jurisprudence of the International Court of Justice; GG Fitzmaurice, 'The Law and Procedure of the International Court of Justice: Treaty Interpretation and Certain Other Treaty Points' (1951) 28 BYIL 1; GG Fitzmaurice, 'The Law and Procedure of the International Court of Justice 1951–4: Treaty Interpretation and Other Treaty Points' (1957) 33 BYIL 203.

[104] C Schreuer 'Travelling the BIT Route: Of Waiting Periods, Umbrella Clauses and Forks in the Road' (2004) 5 Journal of World Investment and Trade 231, 248.

conventional international law,[105] the rights created by the BIT will not be capable of direct vindication as such before national courts. However, as Waelde and Kolo have shown,[106] such jurisdictions may well have remedies against the State which are substantively equivalent to those protected under the Treaty. Thus, for example, there are close parallels between the protection afforded by international law against regulatory taking as expropriation, and the protection against regulatory taking under the US Constitution or the First Protocol of the European Convention on Human Rights.[107] In the absence as yet of direct authority, it is submitted that the fork in the road clause ought to operate should the investor choose to pursue *a claim equivalent in substance* to that created by the BIT against the host State.

Waiver

Election at the time of institution of the first proceedings, which is discussed **4.84** in the previous section, is one method of seeking to limit an investor's claims to a single forum. As has been seen, such an election, in order to operate, requires identity of cause of action between the two proceedings. This will normally not be present where the actions taken in the local courts are founded upon breach of contract, or seek limited domestic administrative law remedies.

However, an alternative method to that of election is to require the claimant to **4.85** waive all other claims at the time when he brings his claim before an investment tribunal. This route presents an advantage for both the investor and the host State, in that the investor may choose to seek to resolve his dispute in the local courts of the host State, without prejudice to subsequent resort to an investment tribunal should the investor still consider that the treaty standards have not been met. Once treaty arbitration has been invoked, the tribunal will be able to view the host State's conduct in the round, including the treatment accorded to the investor in the State's courts or administrative tribunals. As set out in Chapter 7 below, this can be an important element of an investor's claim to fair and equitable treatment. But neither the tribunal nor the host State will, at that stage, have to contend with parallel proceedings.

The main example in practice of the adoption of such a method is Article 1121 of **4.86** NAFTA.[108] A similar approach has now been adopted in Article 26(2) of the 2004 US model BIT.[109]

---

[105] MN Shaw *International Law* (5th edn, 2003) 121–122.
[106] T Waelde & A Kolo, 'Environmental Regulation, Investment Protection and "Regulatory Taking" in International Law' (2001) 50 ICLQ 811.   [107] ibid 826–835.
[108] Appendix 1 below.   [109] Appendix 6 below.

4.87 The operative part of Article 1121 requires that the investor may submit a claim to arbitration only if:

> Both the investor and an enterprise of another Party that is a juridical person that the investor owns or controls directly or indirectly, waive their right to initiate or continue before any administrative tribunal or court under the domestic law of any Party *any proceedings with respect to the measure of the disputing Party* that is alleged to be a breach of Subchapter A of this Chapter, Article 1502(3)(a) (Monopolies and State Enterprises) or Article 1503(2) (State Enterprises), except for proceedings for injunctive, declaratory or other extraordinary relief, not involving the payment of damages, before an administrative tribunal or court under the domestic law of the disputing Party [emphasis added].

4.88 The test therefore focuses not on the juridical nature of the cause of action, but rather on whether the local proceedings were brought 'with respect to the measure of the disputing Party' that was alleged to be a breach of treaty. Moreover, Article 1121 requires the investor to procure a waiver both on its own behalf and on behalf of any enterprise which it owned or controlled, directly or indirectly—thus catching the complete economic investment unit within its purview *ratione personae*. Its focus is on avoiding any risk of double recovery through awards of damages. The Article makes a useful distinction between claims for damages and other forms of relief, respecting the power of the local courts to grant injunctions and the like.

4.89 In *Waste Management I*[110] the investor had not given an unequivocal waiver. Rather it had sought to preserve the right of its local investment vehicle in Mexico to continue to pursue local court and arbitration proceedings there, claiming that Article 1121 did not require a waiver which extended to proceedings which relied upon other sources of law, such as the municipal law of Mexico.[111] The Tribunal held that this reservation to the waiver rendered it ineffective. It held that Article 1121 was not limited to a waiver of claims equivalent to, or based upon, breaches of NAFTA. Rather, it extended to any claims, whatever their legal basis, which were derived from or concerned the same measures adopted by the host State, which were to be the subject of the investment arbitration claim.[112]

4.90 Highet dissented on the ground that a 'measure . . . that is alleged to be a breach' must be interpreted to mean only the full extent of measures necessary to constitute a breach of the international obligation created by NAFTA, and thus local proceedings to enforce contractual rights were not caught by the provision.[113]

4.91 It is submitted that the approach of the majority is to be preferred on the language of Article 1121. Indeed, in contrast to the formulations in 'fork in the road'

---

[110] *Waste Management I* (n 34 above).   [111] *Waste Management I* (n 34 above) 448.
[112] *Waste Management I* (n 34 above) 457–460.
[113] *Waste Management I* (n 34 above) Dissenting Opinion (Highet) 462, 465–470.

clauses, or in Article 26 of ICSID[114] the formulation in Article 1121 focuses on the State measure—the governmental act—which has given rise to the dispute, and not on the claims to which such a measure may give rise. This language is apt to include both municipal law claims and international law claims. Such an approach also seems consonant with the policy of Article 1121: to prevent any other court or tribunal from considering the investor's complaint at the same time as the NAFTA tribunal; and to ensure no double recovery of damages. The adoption of this broad interpretation may be justified by the fact that it will only come into operation at the time the investment claim is filed. Thus, in contrast to a 'fork in the road' provision, the investor will not be prejudiced unintentionally by pursuing local court claims when the dispute first arises—often a natural response—before elevating the claim to the level of an international tribunal.

The fact, however, that a claimant may have failed to give an unequivocal **4.92** waiver will not prevent him from subsequently issuing fresh proceedings once he is in a position to comply with the requirements of the rule. Thus, in *Waste Management II*[115] the claimants filed fresh proceedings before ICSID accompanied by an unequivocal waiver. A newly-constituted Tribunal held that the previous dismissal of the claim on jurisdictional grounds for failure to provide the requisite form of waiver in no way precluded the issue of fresh proceedings.[116] Further, although the Tribunal accepted the application of the doctrine of *res judicata* to investment arbitration, it found that the doctrine did not apply here. All that the Tribunal had decided was that it lacked jurisdiction in view of the defective form of waiver. That in no way precluded a subsequent tribunal, which did have jurisdiction, from proceeding to adjudicate on the merits.[117]

C. Internationalized Contract Claims under 'Umbrella Clauses'

Thus far, the problems of parallel proceedings which have potentially been raised **4.93** by the existence of litigation in host State courts, or the existence of a contractual jurisdiction clause in a contract between host State and investor, have proved capable of resolution mainly on the grounds of a lack of true parallelism. Since the claims open to an investor by treaty are founded upon a different cause of action to those created by contract, there is no inconsistency in the pursuit of both

---

[114] cf Schreuer (n 62 above) 368.

[115] *Waste Management Inc v United Mexican States (No 2)* (Preliminary Objections) 6 ICSID Rep 538 (NAFTA/ICSID (AF), 2002, Crawford P, Civiletti & Magallón Gómez) *(Waste Management II (Preliminary Objections))*.

[116] ibid 558. Citing, *inter alia*, *Case concerning the Barcelona Traction, Light and Power Co Ltd (New Application: 1962) (Belgium v Spain)* (Preliminary Objections) [1964] ICJ Rep 6, 26.

[117] ibid 559–562. Citing, *inter alia*, the *Trail Smelter Arbitration* (1941) 35 AJIL 684, 702.

claims. Similarly, where the investor has sued in the host State courts, a 'fork in the road' clause will not operate as an election of that remedy to the exclusion of international arbitration unless there is identity of cause of action. Thus, the pursuit of contractual or local remedies will not bring the clause into operation. What is required is in substance the pursuit of the same claim, founded upon the rights under treaty.

4.94 However, the clarity of this distinction between breach of treaty (under international law) and breach of contract (under the contract's applicable law) is potentially disturbed by the inclusion in some investment treaties of an 'umbrella clause', whereby the parties commit to honouring obligations which they have entered into vis-à-vis investors of the other party. Does such a clause operate, as some commentators have suggested, so as to elevate all contract claims to the level of international law? What is the effect of such a clause upon an exclusive jurisdiction clause in the contract, conferring jurisdiction upon the host State courts or another arbitral tribunal?

ICSID jurisdiction over contract claims

4.95 There is of course nothing unusual about an arbitral tribunal established under ICSID determining claims founded upon breach of a concession contract, and based primarily upon host State law. After all, the most direct route by which ICSID may receive jurisdiction is where the host State and investor have specifically agreed by contract to confer such jurisdiction upon it. Indeed, for much of the first three decades of the life of the ICSID Convention, the claims entertained by ICSID tribunals were primarily founded on such a basis. The applicable law for such claims was, pursuant to Article 42 of the Convention, and in the absence of express provision, 'the law of the Contracting State party to the dispute (including its rules on the conflict of laws) and such rules of international law as may be applicable'.

4.96 Thus, where the parties to an investment treaty agree that any dispute arising between an investor and a host State may be submitted to arbitration under the provisions of that treaty, it is submitted that there is no reason in principle to exclude contract claims from the operation of the clause. The consent of the parties will be provided by the combination of the State's standing consent by treaty and the investor's consent given when it initiates the claim. It is now conventional in ICSID jurisprudence that the mutual consent necessary for ICSID jurisdiction may be established in this way.[118] In such a case, however, the treaty provision does no more than confer jurisdiction upon the tribunal. The cause of action would have to be found elsewhere: in the provisions of the contract itself, interpreted in

---

[118] See 3.21–3.29 above.

accordance with its applicable law. The claim thus entertained would remain a contract claim irrespective of whether it was adjudicated by a treaty tribunal.

Effect of umbrella clauses upon applicable law and jurisdiction

The issue raised by umbrella clauses is therefore a different, and substantive, one. **4.97** It is whether the inclusion of such a clause in the treaty transforms the nature of the obligation being enforced, so that it may be said that the tribunal is now concerned with a breach of treaty and not a breach of contract *simpliciter*. This question of the proper construction to apply to an 'umbrella clause' has been considered in two awards arising on substantially similar facts: *SGS v Pakistan*[119] and *SGS v Philippines*.[120] In these cases, the arbitrators came to diametrically opposed views on the key issues. This clash of views has provoked a spirited further debate in subsequent arbitral awards.[121]

SGS v Pakistan

In *SGS v Pakistan* the Swiss company SGS provided services in Pakistan under **4.98** the terms of a concession contract providing for local arbitration in Pakistan. When disputes arose between the parties, SGS sued in the Swiss courts. The Swiss courts held the contractual arbitration clause to be enforceable, and SGS then commenced arbitration of its contract claims in Pakistan. Only subsequently did it bring a claim before a treaty tribunal under the Swiss/Pakistan BIT.[122] The Treaty contained a clause (Article 11) by which: 'Either Contracting Party shall constantly guarantee the observance of the commitments it has entered into with respect to the investments of the investors of the other Contracting Party.'

The claim made in the treaty arbitration alleged both breaches of contract, on the **4.99** basis of the umbrella clause, and breaches of other independent standards enshrined in the Treaty.

---

[119] *SGS v Pakistan* (n 71 above).   [120] *SGS v Philippines* (n 71 above).

[121] Decisions in essence following the *SGS v Pakistan* approach include: *Salini Costruttori SpA v Hachemite Kingdom of Jordan* (Jurisdiction) ICSID Case No ARB/02/13 (ICSID, 2004, Guillaume P, Cremades & Sinclair); *Joy Mining Machinery Ltd v Arab Republic of Egypt* (Jurisdiction) (n 92 above); *El Paso Energy International Co v Argentine Republic* (Jurisdiction) ICSID Case No ARB/03/15 (ICSID, 2006, Caflisch P, Stern & Bernadini). Decisions in essence following the *SGS v Philippines* approach include: *Eureko BV v Republic of Poland* (n 85 above) and *Noble Ventures Inc v Romania* (Award) ICSIC Case No ARB/01/11(ICSID, 2005, Böckstiegel P, Lever & Dupuy).

[122] Accord concernant la Promotion et la Protection Réciproque des Investissements ('Agreement Concerning the Promotion and Reciprocal Protection of Investments') (Switzerland-Pakistan) (signed 11 July 1995, entered into force 6 May 1996) RO 1998 2601. The Supreme Court of Pakistan held that SGS had waived its right to do so by commencing the local arbitration, and issued an injunction restraining SGS from proceeding with the treaty arbitration: *Société Générale de Surveillance SA v Pakistan* (Judgment) 8 ICSID Rep 352 (Supreme Court of Pakistan, Appellate Jurisdiction, 2002, Sheikh, Farooq & Dogar JJ).

4.100 The Tribunal decided that it had jurisdiction to entertain the independent treaty claims. But it held that the umbrella clause did not operate so as to make the contract claims justiciable before it. Indeed its approach served to emphasize the distinction between treaty and contract claims irrespective of those provisions of the Treaty which might have indicated that the State parties had had a more expansive intention. Thus, the Tribunal construed the reference in the dispute settlement clause in the BIT conferring jurisdiction in relation to 'disputes with respect to investments' as merely denoting the factual subject-matter of the claims, and not their legal basis. Such a reference was insufficient, concluded the Tribunal, to convey an implication that the parties had intended to subject contract claims to ICSID arbitration.[123] Rather, the Tribunal maintained a strict delineation between breaches of the treaty and contract claims, and found that the arbitration clause in the contract 'is a valid forum selection clause *so far as concerns the Claimant's contract claims which do not also amount to BIT claims* . . . (original emphasis).'[124] Equally, the prior assertion of those claims in other fora could not preclude the investor from pursuing its treaty claims before the ICSID Tribunal.[125]

4.101 The Tribunal then decided that the umbrella clause did not have the effect of elevating the contract claims to treaty claims. It reasoned that, under general international law, a violation of a contract entered into by a State with an investor of another State was not by itself a violation of international law.[126] The Tribunal was concerned that, if construed so as to extend to all commitments of the host State, such a clause might be capable of infinite expansion, and render all other commitments in the treaty superfluous.[127] It would also negate the effect of the contractual submission clause. In consequence, therefore, the clause was to be interpreted merely as a commitment to enact implementing rules to give effect to the host State's contractual commitments. The Tribunal also speculated that if a host State, for example, deprived the investor of a contractually agreed right to submit his contract claim to international arbitration, that might itself constitute a breach of the clause.[128] But this did not mean that the clause mandated the 'instant transubstantiation of contract claims into BIT claims'.[129] Accordingly, the Tribunal concluded that it had jurisdiction over the treaty claims, but not over the contract claims.

SGS v Philippines

4.102 The subsequent award of a differently-constituted Tribunal in *SGS v Philippines*[130] was concerned with a very similar claim. Just as in the *Pakistan* case, SGS had a concession contract with the Philippines. It contained its own jurisdiction

---

[123] *SGS v Pakistan* (n 71 above) 441.   [124] *SGS v Pakistan* (n 71 above) 441.
[125] *SGS v Pakistan* (n 71 above) 447.   [126] *SGS v Pakistan* (n 71 above) 443.
[127] *SGS v Pakistan* (n 71 above) 443–444.   [128] *SGS v Pakistan* (n 71 above) 445–446.
[129] *SGS v Pakistan* (n 71 above) 446.   [130] *SGS v Philippines* (n 71 above).

clause,[131] which in this case submitted disputes to the Philippine courts. The Swiss-Philippines BIT also contained an umbrella clause.[132] The claim brought before the ICSID Tribunal also concerned allegations of both direct breach of treaty and breach of contract. The latter were alleged by SGS to be justiciable by virtue of the umbrella clause.

The Tribunal agreed with the Tribunal in *SGS v Pakistan* as to the law applicable **4.103** to the contractual claims. It held that the extent of the parties' contractual obligation 'is still governed by the contract, and it can only be determined by reference to the terms of the contract'.[133] The validity of a contractual obligation was 'a matter for determination under the applicable law, normally the law of the host State'.[134] However, it differed fundamentally as to the consequences of that upon the jurisdiction of the ICSID Tribunal in view of the umbrella clause. The Tribunal held that such a clause could bring specific obligations of a host State vis-à-vis a particular investor within the framework of the BIT;[135] and that the general reference in the dispute settlement clause to 'disputes with respect to investments' was apt to confer jurisdiction upon the tribunal to adjudicate the contract claims.[136] In both cases, the tribunal found that, applying ordinary techniques of treaty interpretation, the Treaty provisions had to be given an effective interpretation, and there was no reason to read them more restrictively.

However, that did not mean that the parties' express and exclusive choice of forum **4.104** by contract was overridden by the Treaty clauses. The Tribunal held that: 'The basic principle in each case is that a binding exclusive jurisdiction clause in a contract should be respected, unless overridden by another valid provision.'[137]

A majority of the Tribunal took the view that the general provisions of the BIT did **4.105** not override the contractual jurisdiction clause. They did so first by applying the *lex specialis* rule of treaty interpretation, so that: 'It is not to be presumed that such a general provision has the effect of overriding specific provisions of particular contracts, freely negotiated between the parties.'[138] Secondly, they reasoned that a BIT should be seen as a framework treaty 'to support and supplement, not to override or replace, the actually negotiated investment arrangements made between the investor and the host State'.[139]

---

[131] Clause 12.

[132] Art X(2) Accord Concernant la Promotion et la Protection Réciproque des Investissements ('Agreement Concerning the Promotion and Reciprocal Protection of Investments') (Switzerland-Philippines) (signed 31 March 1997, entered into force 23 April 1999) RO 2001 438.

[133] *SGS v Philippines* (n 71 above) 553.   [134] *SGS v Philippines* (n 71 above) 550.

[135] *SGS v Philippines* (n 71 above) 550–551.   [136] *SGS v Philippines* (n 71 above) 554–556.

[137] *SGS v Philippines* (n 71 above) 557, doubting *Lanco v Argentina* (n 81 above) 378 insofar as it suggests that a contractual choice of the jurisdiction of a host State's administrative courts is to be disregarded, as such courts would have jurisdiction in any event, and the choice cannot be treated as an exercise of free will.   [138] *SGS v Philippines* (n 71 above) 557–558.

[139] *SGS v Philippines* (n 71 above) 558.

4.106 Article 26 of the ICSID Convention did not, they decided, have the effect of creating a subsequent agreement between the parties in favour of ICSID as the exclusive remedy for the simple reason that Article 26 itself was subject to contrary provision by the parties. Such contrary provision could include a contractual choice of forum nominating local host State courts.[140] The Tribunal found support for this deference to local courts in relation to contract claims in the *Woodruff* case,[141] which had also been cited with approval by the annulment committee in Vivendi; and in other jurisprudence of the early twentieth-century claims commissions, which had held such clauses enforceable in relation to contract claims.[142]

4.107 In the end, therefore, the Tribunal found that it had jurisdiction over the contract claim, but that it was not *admissible* in the light of the jurisdiction clause: 'SGS should not be able to approbate and reprobate in respect of the same contract: if it claims under the contract, it should comply with the contract in respect of the very matter which is the foundation of its claim.'[143]

4.108 The Request for Arbitration did not clearly disclose breaches of treaty, since in substance the only claim made by SGS against the Philippines was its failure to pay the alleged sum due under the contract. An unjustified refusal to pay sums payable under a contract might potentially amount to a breach of the fair and equitable treatment standard, but it would be premature so to hold in view of the fact that there was undoubtedly a dispute between the parties as to what sum was contractually due.[144] In the circumstances, and citing the precedent of the decision of the arbitral tribunal in *MOX Plant*,[145] the Tribunal decided to stay the case pending the outcome of proceedings in the host State courts.

4.109 Crivellaro dissented from this last finding of the majority.[146] He considered that the dispute resolution clause in the BIT, which had entered into force some years after the contract, extended to all Swiss investors a singularly important advantage. Thenceforward, they were to have the liberty to choose between different forms of dispute resolution in their disputes with the Philippines Government, which would include ICSID arbitration. He declared that the BIT should be construed so that this important benefit was not cut down or lost. By comparison, the jurisdiction clause in the contract, which had on the evidence been inserted by the Philippines, represented no real choice by the investor.

---

[140] Accord C Schreuer (n 62 above) 363.   [141] *Woodruff* (n 88 above).
[142] *North American Dredging Co of Texas v United Mexican States* (1926) 20 AJIL 800, 808.
[143] *SGS v Philippines* (n 71 above) 561–562.   [144] *SGS v Philippines* (n 71 above) 563.
[145] *The MOX Plant Case (Ireland v United Kingdom)* (Order No 3) (2003) 42 ILM 1187, 1199.
[146] *SGS v Philippines* (n 71 above) Dissenting Opinion (Crivellaro) 568.

Analysis

Neither of the *SGS* decisions has found favour with those who would wish to **4.110**
extend the greatest possible freedom to investors to bring their claims against host
States, even if founded on contract, before an investment arbitral tribunal. In both
cases, the result was to remit the contract claims to adjudication within the host
State, and to exclude those claims, at least initially, from the purview of the ICSID
Tribunal. This was so despite the existence of broad jurisdiction and umbrella
clauses in the relevant treaties. Yet the need to distinguish between the proper
province of treaty arbitration and contract dispute resolution, where the parties have already chosen an exclusive forum for the latter, represents a powerful
imperative, both as a matter of principle and policy.

In articulating the balance to be struck, it is submitted that the approach taken in **4.111**
SGS v Philippines is to be preferred. There is no reason to give a construction to
either the dispute resolution or the umbrella clauses of an investment treaty which
would exclude claims in contract per se from the purview of an investment arbitral tribunal. After all, ICSID arbitration is specifically designed to provide an
available forum where the host State has entered into direct contractual relations
with a foreign investor. States are at liberty to extend the benefit of such arbitration to their respective investors. They may do so by giving their consent by treaty,
with the investor giving its own consent when bringing its claim. None of this
should occasion surprise or difficulty. The result, as the Tribunal in the *Philippines*
case found, is simply to give the ICSID Tribunal jurisdiction over a contract
claim, which is subject to its governing law. Neither the formulation nor the background to umbrella clauses (insofar as it is known) indicates a contrary intention.

However, it is equally right that if the investor wishes to enforce its contract, it must **4.112**
do so in accordance with its terms. In the absence of evidence to the contrary, these
represent a *consensus ad idem* between State and investor as to the arrangements for
the resolution of any disputes. A valid choice of arbitration will be enforceable to
exclude the jurisdiction of the courts under Article II of the New York Convention
1958. Similarly, under most systems of private international law, a valid exclusive
jurisdiction clause will be effective to oust the jurisdiction of otherwise competent
courts.[147] The binding nature of such clauses in relation to contractual claims
within their scope is not to be undermined by a general provision in a treaty extending a number of dispute resolution options to investors of two States generally.

Does the umbrella clause also import a substantive treaty standard?

The issue to which the award in *SGS v Philippines* did not advert, however, is this: **4.113**
Does the umbrella clause nevertheless provide a substantive guarantee of the

---

[147] eg Brussels Regulation (n 4 above) Art 23.

observance of undertakings by the host State given on the making of the investment, where the host State's own law may not?[148] This is not purely a question of denial of justice. As will be seen, denial of justice, as part of the guarantee of fair and equitable treatment, provides a procedural protection only. But the issue raised here is one of substantive legal protection. Lying behind many of the measures introduced in relation to State contracts has been a concern to protect investors from subsequent changes in host State law, especially where they may have been introduced specifically to excuse the State from liability under the concession contract in question. Of course, if the governing law of the contract chosen by the parties is international law, such changes would have no effect. Similarly, a prime function of that part of Article 42 of the ICSID Convention which requires the tribunal, in the absence of express choice of law by the parties, to apply 'the law of the Contracting State party to the dispute (including its rules on the conflict of laws) *and such rules of international law as may be applicable*' (emphasis added) has been to permit the tribunal to disregard provisions of host State law which infringe international law.[149] But, where the parties have expressly chosen host State law as the applicable law, subsequent changes in that law will be prima facie applicable as part of the *lex causae* of the contract.

4.114 In such a case, it is submitted that the existence of an umbrella clause provides an independent treaty standard pursuant to which the investor could require the host State to honour its original bargain irrespective of subsequent changes in its law. It would thus fulfil a similar purpose to that sought to be achieved through a contractual stabilization clause, but without the artificial attempt to exclude all changes in host State law. This construction would give the clause an independent and additional sphere of operation on the plane of international law. It would link the operation of the clause with the general requirement emerging in the jurisprudence on the contract/treaty divide, requiring the breach of treaty to involve the exercise of sovereign authority.[150]

4.115 For the Tribunal in *El Paso Energy*[151] this distinction was fundamental. The umbrella clause would only operate where the State acted as a sovereign rather than as a merchant. Thus, it would not cover ordinary contract claims, but would cover 'additional investment protections contractually agreed by the State as a sovereign—such as a stabilization clause—inserted in an investment agreement'.[152] For the reasons just outlined, this conclusion does not appear to be warranted by the language of the treaties or by any necessary restriction on the jurisdiction of an investment arbitral tribunal. This is particularly so of the notion that, in order to gain the benefit of the clause, an investor would have to have persuaded the host

---

148 cf the argument advanced by Wälde (n 43 above).
149 See C Schreuer (n 62 above) 612ff, especially at 631.   150 See 4.73–4.74 above.
151 *El Paso Energy* (n 121 above) para 81.   152 ibid.

State to grant a contractual stabilization clause. Investment treaties are designed to provide a predictable framework for all investors as a result of mutual guarantees exchanged between the contracting States. The operation of those guarantees should not be dependant upon the happenstance of individual contractual bargaining for a type of clause, which was never popular with States, and was in any event a blunt, and at times unpredictable, instrument for stability of contract. However, the underlying concept that the clause might protect from the abuse of State power is a valuable one.

If, then, there were a clear basis for contending that the State had made subse- **4.116** quent changes in its law which undermined its undertakings to the investor, that would constitute an exercise of sovereign authority, and would found a basis for a treaty claim, irrespective of any contractual jurisdiction clause. It is submitted that it is possible for the umbrella clause to operate on both levels at once. In the case of an ordinary contract claim, it would operate in the manner proposed in *SGS v Philippines*, conferring jurisdiction upon the treaty tribunal, but only to the extent that the parties have not by contract selected a more specific mode of dispute resolution. Where, however, there had been State interference in the contract, for example by subsequent changes in host State law which had the effect of defeating the specific undertakings which the State had given to the investor, the umbrella clause would also operate. The clause would apply in that bulwark role if, and to the extent that, the alternative contractual forum could not (as a matter of applicable law), or did not, uphold the undertaking of the State regardless of any such exercises of sovereign authority.

D. Parallel Treaty Arbitrations

Introduction

Thus far, the parallel proceedings issues considered by treaty tribunals have been **4.117** concerned with the relationship between treaty arbitration, and claims made between the same parties in national courts or in commercial arbitration. In those cases, as has been seen, there are often difficult questions of overlap in applicable law. But the rival fora are indisputably each operating within a different legal order. A different, but no less difficult, set of issues is raised by the incidence of parallel treaty arbitrations, each of which is concerned with the same underlying factual dispute. This is a by-product of the fragmented nature of modern investment protection by treaty, made up, as it is, of a huge network of bilateral arrangements.

As may be seen from the discussion of investment in Chapter 6 below, it is possible **4.118** for one or more indirect investors, who hold their investments by way of share-holding in the investment company, to bring a claim against the host State.

Equally, the investment company itself may have a claim. If, applying the rules of nationality discussed in Chapter 5 below, each of these potential claimants is to be treated as the national of a different home State, each such investor may be entitled to invoke the provisions of a different BIT with the host State. In this situation, the consolidation provisions now included in NAFTA and some new-model US investment treaties[153] will be of little assistance. These provisions assume that the parallel arbitrations are brought within the same treaty regime. There is some ICSID practice in making provision, with the consent of the parties, for related claims to be heard by the same tribunal, which will be noted below. But, for the moment at least, consolidation provisions remain a rarity in investment treaties, and it is therefore necessary to analyse the position in the absence of express provision.

The *Lauder* litigation

4.119 This issue arose directly in the *Lauder* affair.[154] In those cases, the American entrepreneur, Ron Lauder brought a claim against the Czech Republic alleging expropriation of his investment in the Czech television channel, TV Nova, under the provisions of the US-Czech BIT.[155] Mr Lauder's investment was exercised through a Dutch investment company, CME Czech Republic BV ('CME'), over which he had control.[156] CME brought its own claim for expropriation under the provisions of the Dutch-Czech BIT.[157] In both cases, the investor elected for UNCITRAL arbitration, which was one of the options available under the dispute resolution clauses of the respective treaties. The tribunals were constituted of different arbitrators in each case. Significantly, the Czech Republic did not agree to a *de facto* consolidation of the two proceedings, by insisting on a different arbitral tribunal to hear the CME claim.[158] The evidence presented to the two tribunals was substantially the same. The allegations made against the Republic in each case were substantially the same.

4.120 The two tribunals delivered their awards within ten days of each other. The *Lauder* Tribunal did so on 3 September 2001 in London. It decided that, save on one aspect, the Czech Republic had committed no breach of treaty. Rather, the

---

[153] The practice is discussed at 4.146 below.

[154] *Lauder v Czech Republic* (Award) 9 ICSID Rep 62 (UNCITRAL, 2001, Briner C, Cutler & Klein); *CME Czech Republic BV (The Netherlands) v Czech Republic* (Partial Award) 9 ICSID Rep 121 (UNCITRAL, 2001, Kühn C, Schwebel & Hándl) (*CME I*); (Final Award) 9 ICSID 264 (UNCITRAL, 2003, Kühn C, Schwebel & Brownlie) (*CME II*); Svea Court of Appeals, Sweden (2003) 42 ILM 919.

[155] Treaty Concerning the Reciprocal Encouragement and Protection of Investment (US-Czech Republic) (signed 22 October 1991, entered into force 19 December 1992) Senate Treaty Doc 102-31.   [156] *Lauder* (n 154 above) 76.

[157] Agreement on Encouragement and Reciprocal Protection of Investments (Netherlands-Czech Republic) (signed 29 April 1991, entered into force 1 October 1992) 2242 UNTS 206, Tractatenblad 1992, 146; 569/1992 Sb.   [158] *Lauder* (n 154 above) 87; *CME I* (n 154 above) 195.

whole matter was to be seen as a private commercial dispute between Mr Lauder and his Czech investment partner: 'The investment treaty created no duty of due diligence on the part of the Czech Republic to intervene in the dispute between the two companies over the nature of their legal relationships.'[159] The *CME* Tribunal delivered its award ten days later on 13 September 2001 in Stockholm. By majority,[160] it decided that the Czech Republic had committed multiple violations of the treaty, and was liable to remedy its injury to the claimant by paying the fair market value of the investment as it was prior to the Republic's breach.

There were thus diametrically opposed decisions of two tribunals hearing in substance the same facts. Mr Lauder, having lost his claim in the *Lauder* arbitration would be a substantial beneficiary of the award of damages in *CME*. The claims thus raised important questions about the scope of the principles of *lis pendens* and *res judicata* in investment treaty arbitration. The Czech Republic raised submissions as to the application of these principles, and as to an alleged broader notion of abuse of process, before both tribunals, and before the Svea Court of Appeals, when it challenged the award in Sweden. In each case, the Republic's submissions were rejected. **4.121**

In *Lauder*, the only question which arose was one of *litispendence*, since this Tribunal delivered its decision first. The Tribunal rejected the application of the doctrine of *lis pendens* holding: **4.122**

> The Arbitral Tribunal considers that the Respondent's recourse to the principle of *lis alibi pendens* to be of no use, since all the other court and arbitration proceedings involve different parties and different causes of action . . . Therefore, no possibility exists that any other court or arbitral tribunal can render a decision similar to or inconsistent with the award which will be issued by this Arbitral Tribunal, i.e. that the Czech Republic breached or did not breach the Treaty, and is or is not liable for damages towards Mr Lauder. [161]

For similar reasons, it rejected the argument of abuse of process, finding that 'the Arbitral Tribunal is the only forum with jurisdiction to hear Mr Lauder's claims based on the Treaty'.[162] The most the Tribunal was prepared to accept was that there should be no double recovery,[163] a matter which it considered should be taken into account by the second seised arbitral tribunal in assessing any award of damages which it might decide to make. **4.123**

In *CME* the Tribunal also rejected an abuse of process argument on similar grounds. Emphasizing that the Czech Republic had not sought consolidation, it observed: 'Should two different Treaties grant remedies to the respective claimants **4.124**

---

[159] *Lauder* (n 154 above) 111.
[160] One of the arbitrators, Hándl, refused to sign the award and delivered a Dissenting Opinion.
[161] *Lauder* (n 154 above) 87.   [162] *Lauder* (n 154 above) 87.
[163] *Lauder* (n 154 above) 87.

deriving from the same facts and circumstances, this does not deprive one of the claimants of jurisdiction.'[164] In its Final Award, delivered in March 2003, the *CME* Tribunal also considered whether the *Lauder* award amounted to *res judicata*. It rejected this submission as well for the following reasons:

> The parties in the London arbitration differ from the parties in this arbitration. Mr Lauder is the controlling shareholder of CME Media Ltd, whereas in this arbitration a Dutch holding company being part of the CME Media Ltd Group is the Claimant. The two arbitrations are based on differing bilateral investment treaties, which grant comparable investment protection, which, however, is not identical. Both arbitrations deal with the Media Council's interference with the same investment in the Czech Republic. However, the Tribunal cannot judge whether the facts submitted to the two tribunals for decision are identical . . .[165]

4.125 The Svea Court of Appeals also rejected the proposition that the principles of *lis pendens* and *res judicata* applied to this case.[166] There was no identity of parties, as Mr Lauder had a controlling interest in CME, but did not hold a majority of the share capital. Thus, to deny effect to the CME claim would be to deny a remedy to the other investors. Moreover, there was no identity of claim, as the arbitral proceedings had been brought under two different bilateral treaties, which were not identical.

4.126 The *Lauder* litigation provides the most sustained examination yet undertaken in investment arbitration jurisprudence as to the manner in which the issues of parallel treaty arbitrations are to be resolved. But the result there expressed needs to be put into context. The following observations may be made.

Applicability of *res judicata* and *lis pendens* in principle

4.127 Neither the *Lauder* Tribunal nor the *CME* Tribunal, nor the Swedish court expressly rejected the proposition that the principles of *lis pendens* and *res judicata* might have an application in this field.[167] In part this may have been because the case was argued on the broader ground of abuse of process. However, the reasoning of the Tribunals and the Court in each case essentially rejected the submission by applying elements of the legal test applicable to the formal legal doctrines, requiring identity of parties, object, and cause of action.

4.128 In consequence, it is submitted that the doctrines may in principle be applied in investment treaty arbitration, provided that the conditions for their application are made out. Indeed, in one of the earliest ICSID cases, a plea of *lis pendens* arising from a related contract claim had been rejected, the Tribunal requiring 'identity of the parties, object and cause of action in the proceedings pending

---

[164] *CME I* (n 154 above) 195.   [165] *CME II* (n 154 above) 355.
[166] *CME* (Svea Court of Appeal) (n 154 above) 953.
[167] eg the implicit acceptance of the doctrine of *res judicata* in *CME II* (n 154 above) 356.

before both tribunals'.[168] The legal basis for applying the doctrines, as submitted above,[169] is that these principles may be regarded as general principles of law, which are applicable in the interpretation and application of investment treaties since: 'Every international convention must be deemed tacitly to refer to general principles of international law for all questions which it does not itself resolve in express terms and in a different way.'[170]

Res judicata

The rules of *res judicata* are long accepted to meet this criterion in international law **4.129** generally.[171] They have been specifically upheld in the context of investment arbitration. Thus, in *Waste Management II*[172] the Tribunal found that *res judicata* was in principle applicable to its proceedings, so as to give preclusive effect to an earlier decision of another investment tribunal between the same parties and on the same matter, as a general principle of law.[173] However, such effect could only relate to an issue actually decided by the earlier tribunal. Since the findings of the earlier tribunal were limited to a denial of jurisdiction on grounds that an inadequate waiver of claims had been filed, this could not constitute a *res judicata* on the merits.

Lis pendens

International tribunals have also accepted that they have a *discretion* to stay their **4.130** proceedings, if there is another tribunal seised of the matter, and it is more appropriate in the interests of both parties and the ends of justice to defer to that tribunal. In this way, *lis pendens* has been viewed by tribunals not as a mandatory rule, but rather as the basis for the exercise of a discretion. The discussion in paras 4.05 to 4.08 above showed that, in private international law, *lis pendens* has variously found application as either a strict rule or a discretion. A preference for the latter approach was clearly expressed by the Tribunal in *SPP v Egypt*:

> When the jurisdictions of two unrelated and independent tribunals extend to the same dispute, there is no rule of international law which prevents either tribunal from exercising its jurisdiction. *However, in the interest of international judicial order, either of the tribunals may, in its discretion and as a matter of comity, decide to stay the exercise of its jurisdiction pending a decision by the other tribunal* [emphasis added].[174]

---

[168] *Benvenuti & Bonfant Srl v People's Republic of the Congo* (Award) 1 ICSID Rep 330, 340 (ICSID, 1980, Trolle P, Bystricky & Razafindralambo).   [169] See 4.37 above.

[170] *Georges Pinson Case* (1927–8) AD Case no 292, 426, 427 per Verzijl P.

[171] See 4.13 above and the authorities there cited.

[172] *Waste Management II (Preliminary Objections)* (n 115 above) 559–562.

[173] Citing, *inter alia*, the earlier practice of the mixed claims commissions in *Compagnie Générale de l'Orénoque* (1905) Ralston's Report 244, 355–357 and *In the Matter of the SS Newchwang, Claim No 21* (1922) 16 AJIL 323, 324.

[174] *Southern Pacific Properties (Middle East) Ltd [SPP] v Arab Republic of Egypt* (First Jurisdiction) 3 ICSID Rep 101, 129 (ICSID, 1985, Jiménez de Aréchaga P, El Mahdi & Pietrowski).

4.131 The Tribunal in *SPP* did in fact decide to stay the exercise of its jurisdiction pending a decision by the courts at the seat of a parallel ICC arbitration as to the scope of the ICC arbitration clause.

4.132 However, if the view taken by the tribunals on the application of the tests of identity of parties and cause of action to the context of investment arbitration prevails, the doctrines will have a very limited application, since they will be confined to concurrent arbitrations brought by the identical claimant under the same investment treaty. In these circumstances, it is necessary to examine in a little more detail the reasoning applied to the two elements of the test, which were said not to have been met in the *Lauder* case.

Identity of cause of action and parties

Identity of cause of action

4.133 The principal basis adopted by each of the tribunals and the Svea Court for finding a lack of identity of cause of action was that each of the claims had been brought under different investment treaties. The *CME* Tribunal expressly relied upon the approach taken by the International Tribunal for the Law of the Sea in *MOX Plant*.[175] ITLOS had reasoned that the rights and obligations of the parties under each treaty, even if framed identically, had a separate existence. Moreover, the application of the ordinary rules of treaty interpretation could lead to apparently identical language in fact being interpreted differently in each of the treaties. There was thus no identity of claims sufficient to exclude the jurisdiction of any one tribunal.

4.134 The *CME* Tribunal applied this approach to investment treaties, deciding that: 'Because the two bilateral investment treaties create rights that are not in all respects exactly the same, different claims are necessarily formulated.'[176]

4.135 Even if another court or tribunal were seised of the identical dispute, opined the Tribunal, this would not deprive it of jurisdiction.[177]

4.136 It is plainly right that there may be important differences between the substantive obligations created by different investment treaties. Thus, to return to the formulation of private international law, claims under two different investment treaties may involve the application of different rules of law, even if to the same facts, and with the same end in view.[178] But it is submitted that the mere fact that the rules appear in different treaties should not per se result in the same forms of legal

---

[175] *The MOX Plant Case* (ITLOS, Provisional Measures, Order of 3 December 2001) (n 23 above) 413. [176] *CME II* (n 154 above) 355.

[177] Citing, *inter alia*, *SPP v Egypt* (n 174 above).

[178] See 4.07 above, applying Case C–406/92 *The Tatry* [1994] ECR I–5439; [1999] QB 515.

protection being treated as different. Although each may owe its binding force to a different legal obligation, both obligations operate upon the same plane of public international law. In the same way, a claim in delict made in a French court has its origin within French law from which it derives its obligatory force. But this does not of itself deprive a defendant from raising a plea of *litispendence* or *res judicata* should in substance the same claim be raised in tort before an English court, even though the basis for the legal obligation might in that case be English, rather than French, law. Both claims are made on a symmetrical basis,[179] since they are both made before national courts. The experience of private international law shows that these doctrines cannot be confined within a single legal order. Rather, they may also apply across borders to resolve problems of identical claims asserted within different legal systems.

This is not a question of the *jurisdiction* of the tribunal. Rather, as the Tribunal **4.137** correctly observed in *SPP*, it is a question of whether the tribunal should stay the exercise of its jurisdiction. Whilst the Tribunal in *CME* was content to rely upon *SPP* for the proposition that it was not deprived of jurisdiction, it did not refer to this second part of the Tribunal's reasoning, which in fact formed the ratio of the decision. Similarly, in *MOX Plant* the arbitral tribunal constituted under UNCLOS decided to stay the exercise of its jurisdiction pending a decision by the European Court of Justice on the question of whether the provisions of UNCLOS on which Ireland (the claimant) relied, were matters on which competence had been transferred to the exclusive competence of the ECJ.[180] In neither case, therefore, was the fact that the two tribunals were constituted under different legal arrangements ultimately dispositive of the question of whether there was sufficient identity of claims to justify a stay.

Identity of parties

The requirement that there must be identity of parties is a common element for **4.138** rules of *litispendence* or *res judicata*. The question is whether the test is confined to identical legal persons, or whether it may also apply to investors with an identity of legal interest in the claim. The tribunals in the *Lauder* litigation all took a strict view of this requirement. On the fact pattern as it arose in those cases, this is perhaps unsurprising. The *Lauder* Tribunal was first seised, and applying normal principles of *litispendence*, one might therefore have expected the *CME* Tribunal to be the one which deferred as to process and result. However, the benefit of any damages award in *CME* would have extended to other shareholders in the company in addition to Mr Lauder. Yet, can it really be said that the limit of a tribunal's obligations is to ensure that the same parties do not secure a double recovery? The

---

179 The term utilized by Douglas (n 25 above) 238.
180 *The MOX Plant Case* (PCA) (n 24 above) 1190–1191.

doctrine of *res judicata* also exists in order to prevent re-litigation by a claimant who has failed in his first claim, and not merely to prevent double recovery.

4.139 The *CME* Tribunal specifically rejected an argument based on the economic identity of the parties. It held that the single economic entity theory had only been accepted by courts or tribunals in exceptional cases, such as competition law. Moreover, the company group theory had not gained acceptance in international arbitration. The Tribunal held that its conclusion accorded with established international law, citing *Barcelona Traction*[181] and *Holiday Inns*.[182]

4.140 However, it is submitted that there must at least be doubt about whether these authorities provide a sound basis for decision in the case of a claim made in investment arbitration. The International Court of Justice rejected the economic entity theory in *Barcelona Traction* in the context of a claim to diplomatic protection made by the State of nationality of the shareholders in a company. It found that a claim on diplomatic protection for expropriation of shares in a company could only be pursued by the State of nationality of the company itself. Despite its distinguished opponents,[183] this rule is probably still part of the customary international law of diplomatic protection, and has been recently upheld by the International Law Commission.[184] But this very restriction in the customary law is one of the matters addressed by the broad definition of investment in investment treaties, as discussed in Chapter 6 below. This very point was made in *CMS v Argentina*.[185] In that case, Argentina had contended, relying on *Barcelona Traction*, that a minority shareholder, with a different nationality to that of the investment company, could not pursue his own claim against it under a BIT. The Tribunal distinguished *Barcelona Traction* on the basis that it was concerned solely with diplomatic protection, which had become a 'residual mechanism to be resorted to in the absence of other arrangements recognizing the direct right of action by individuals'.[186] The Tribunal went on: 'It is precisely this kind of arrangement that has come to prevail under international law, particularly in respect of foreign investments, the paramount example being that of the [ICSID] 1965 Convention.'[187]

---

[181] *Case Concerning the Barcelona Traction, Light and Power Co (New Application: 1962) (Belgium v Spain) Second Phase* (Judgment) [1970] ICJ Rep 3, 48–50.

[182] *Holiday Inns SA et al v Kingdom of Morocco*, discussed in P Lalive, 'The First "World Bank" Arbitration (*Holiday Inns v Morocco*): Some Legal Problems' 1 ICSID Rep 645, 664.

[183] eg FA Mann, 'The Protection of Shareholders' Interests in the Light of the *Barcelona Traction* Case' (1973) 67 AJIL 259, reprinted in FA Mann, *Further Studies in International Law* (1990) 217.

[184] ILC 'Diplomatic Protection: Text of the Draft Articles with Commentaries thereto' (Dugard, Special Rapporteur) in *Report of the International Law Commission as its Fifty-eighth Session (1 May–9 June, 3 July–11 August 2006), Official Records of the General Assembly, Sixty-first Session*, Supplement No. 10, UN Doc A/61/10, 22–100. On the distinction see 6.72–6.78 below.

[185] *CMS* (n 85 above) 502–506.   [186] *CMS* (n 85 above) 503.

[187] *CMS* (n 85 above) 503.

If, then, the definition of investment preferred in the majority of investment   **4.141**
treaties permits a minority shareholder with different nationality from that of the
investment company to have the benefit of pursuing his own direct claim against
the host State, it must be questioned whether a consistent approach should not
also be taken to the definition of identity of parties for the purpose of the rule of
res judicata; otherwise the investor would be able to approbate and reprobate from
the same investment treaty. He would take the benefit of an extended right of
direct action—looking through the investment company at the economic effect
of the host State's actions directly upon his shareholding—which would not
found the basis of a claim under customary international law. But he would
not bear the burden of being bound by any finding arising out of a claim by the
investment company itself on the same facts.

The doctrine of *res judicata*, at least in some legal systems, applies not simply to   **4.142**
the parties themselves, but also to those who are in privity of interest with them.
As Megarry V-C put it, 'there must be a sufficient degree of identification between
the two to make it just to hold that the decision to which one was party should be
binding in proceedings to which the other is party. It is in that sense that I would
regard the phrase "privity of interest" '.[188]

It is submitted that parallel treaty arbitration claims by company and shareholder   **4.143**
relating to the same underlying facts could well meet this criterion.[189]

Consolidation

Consolidation of related investment arbitral proceedings will only be available if   **4.144**
either:

(1) all parties consent;[190] or
(2) there is express provision in the treaty for the consolidation of claims.

If there is no such provision, but related claims are submitted to arbitration under   **4.145**
the supervision of the same arbitral institution (such as ICSID), then it may be
possible to reduce duplicative litigation by appointing the same tribunal to hear
all of the claims, either together or *seriatim*.[191]

---

[188] *Gleeson v J Wippell & Co Ltd* [1977] 1 WLR 510, 515.
[189] cf its application in a European context to overlapping claims by a parent and subsidiary in
Berkeley Administration Inc v McClelland & ors [1995] IL Pr 201 (CA).
[190] The fact that the Czech Republic did not consent to consolidation in the *Lauder* affair was
considered by all tribunals which considered its submissions on *litispendence* and *res judicata* to be a
fundamental problem: see 4.122–4.125 above.
[191] For an example see *Sempra Energy International v Argentine Republic* (Jurisdiction) ICSID
Case No ARB/02/16 (ICSID, 2005, Orrego Vicuña P, Lalonde & Rico); *Camuzzi International SA
v Argentine Republic* (Jurisdiction) ICSID Case No ARB/03/2 (ICSID, 2005, Orrego Vicuña P,
Lalonde & Rico).

4.146　As has been seen,[192] the most detailed provisions for consolidation are to be found in Article 1126 of NAFTA. These provisions have now been considered by two Consolidation Tribunals established under the distinctive provisions of that article.[193] In one case, *Corn Products*,[194] the Consolidation Tribunal found against consolidation of two claims brought in relation to the same excise tax measure against Mexico. In the second case, *Canfor*, the Consolidation Tribunal decided to consolidate and hear a series of cases on antidumping duty in the softwood lumber industry against the United States.[195] The order in *Canfor* represents a particularly elaborate consideration of the requirements of Article 1126. The Tribunal found the overriding object and purpose of the procedure to be that of 'procedural economy'.[196] It treated this as an objective test, to be judged against the position which would obtain were no consolidation to be ordered. The Tribunal identified three factors which would bear on that question: time, costs, and the avoidance of conflicting decisions.[197] Deprecating the result in the *Lauder* and *CME* cases, it observed: 'The desirability of avoiding conflicting results is not limited to cases where the parties are the same. Cases with different parties may present the same legal issues arising out of the same event or related to the same measure. Conflicting results then may take place if the findings with respect to those issues differ in two or more cases.'[198]

4. Conclusions

4.147　In the light of the above analysis, it is submitted that the following points may be advanced by way of conclusion:

4.148　*Jurisdiction and applicable law.* Analysis of issues in the overlap between proceedings between the host State and investor relating to the same investment requires first a careful distinction between jurisdiction (the kinds of claims which a particular tribunal has power to hear and determine) and the law which it must apply to those claims. The two are not necessarily coextensive. Thus, an investment

---

[192]　See 2.44 above.　　[193]　Appendix 1 below.

[194]　*Corn Products International Inc v United Mexican States* ICSID Case No ARB(AF)/04/1 and *Archer Daniels Midland Co and Tate & Lyle Ingredients Americas Inc v United Mexican States* ICSID Case No ARB(AF)/04/5 (Consolidation) (NAFTA/ICSID (AF), 2005, Cremades P, Rovine & Siqueiros).

[195]　*Canfor Corp v United States of America, Tembec et al v United States of America, Terminal Forest Products Ltd v United States of America* (Consolidation) (NAFTA, 2005, van den Berg P, de Mestral & Robinson).

[196]　ibid para 73; accord: H Alvarez, 'Arbitration under the North American Free Trade Agreement' (2000) 16 Arb Int'l 393, 414.　　[197]　ibid para 126.

[198]　ibid para 133.

tribunal, though established pursuant to treaty, may either be limited jurisdictionally to determining claims of breach of treaty, or it may have had conferred upon it by the parties power to determine contractual rights, even where those rights owe their origin to national law. In each case it is a matter of construing separately the basis for jurisdiction, and the nature of the rights which form the subject-matter of the claim.

Breach of treaty and breach of contract. Claims of breach of rights which were **4.149** created by treaty are to be distinguished from breach of contract claims. Treaty claims exist on the plane of international law. Their scope of application falls to be determined on their own terms, and accordance with the principles of international law (enunciated and discussed in other chapters of this work). Contract claims, on the other hand, flow from the parties' express agreement. They fall to be determined in accordance with the law applicable to the contract, which, even in the case of a concession contract with a State, will often be national law.

Consequences for overlapping claims. This distinction between treaty and contract **4.150** claims has the consequences that:

(1) The pursuit of a claim for breach of contract does not of itself preclude a claim of breach of treaty, since the legal basis for each claim is different. This conclusion is unaffected even if the investment is founded on an investment contract with the host State, since the question of law is still fundamentally different: it is whether the actions of the host State constitute a breach of the treaty. Contract rights, on the other hand, will respond according to the terms of the contract to breaches of many different kinds arising in the course of the contract's performance. There must be something more than a mere breach of contract to constitute a breach of treaty. Of their nature, treaty rights will only respond where there has been an exercise of sovereign authority by the host State affecting the investment.

(2) The existence of an exclusive jurisdiction or arbitration clause in a contract between host State and investor will be valid and enforceable as regards contract claims, and should be upheld by investment tribunals. But it will not affect claims based upon breach of treaty.

Drawing the line between treaty and contract. The test which tribunals will apply to **4.151** distinguish between claims which involve breach of treaty and those which involve a breach of contract is to ask: what is the fundamental basis of the claim? As the question will normally arise at the preliminary jurisdiction stage, it will be primarily for the claimant to formulate his claim so as to constitute a breach of treaty. However, the tribunal is entitled to, and must, examine the pleaded case in order to decide whether it does in fact disclose a treaty cause of action. The fact that the claim must be founded upon a breach of treaty does not prevent the claimant, or the tribunal, from referring to the contract in considering whether such a breach of treaty has been made out.

4.152 *Prior pursuit of local remedies.* Unless the treaty parties have expressly provided to the contrary, the effect of the prior pursuit of remedies before a national court in respect of a measure taken by the host State affecting the investment upon a subsequent treaty claim is as follows:

(1) *No exhaustion.* Save in the case of express provision to the contrary, there is no requirement to exhaust local remedies as a condition precedent to the invocation of the tribunal's jurisdiction. This is because one of the purposes of investment arbitration is to provide a neutral forum for dispute resolution of investor-State disputes, which does not carry the strict concomitants of the diplomatic espousal of claims by home States.

(2) *No estoppel.* The pursuit of local remedies will not preclude or estop the investor from subsequent invocation of a treaty claim, assuming that the breach of treaty was not thereby cured. Indeed, any other rule would be contrary to common sense. Treaty rights such as fair and equitable treatment are concerned with an assessment of systemic failures in the due process accorded to the investor by the administrative and judicial decision-makers of the host State. Such rights can only be invoked by reference to the experience of the investor in resorting to local remedies. By the same token, the invocation of a breach of treaty which depends upon such treatment could not be precluded by it.

4.153 Electa una via/*Fork in the road.* However, this principle may be fundamentally affected by an express treaty provision requiring an election in remedies to be made. Where the parties to an investment treaty agree that the choice of any particular dispute settlement option will preclude resort to any other option, the operation of the clause will be affected by the juridical nature of the claims asserted:

(1) *Parallel applicable law.* If a contract claim has already been submitted to a national court or other arbitral tribunal, then the investor will be precluded from subsequently re-litigating that dispute before an investment tribunal. Similarly, where the investor chooses to assert in substance the treaty cause of action before a host State's administrative courts (for example by claiming that the loss of his property without adequate compensation, which may constitute an expropriation at international law, is an unjustified State taking of property under national constitutional law), he may forfeit the right to pursue his claim before an investment tribunal. In the latter case, it will not be every resort to the host State courts which has such preclusive effect. It must be such as to put in issue in substance the same cause of action and object which would otherwise be sought in international arbitration.

(2) *Different applicable law.* If, however, the claims asserted in the host State courts or other arbitral tribunal are contractual and not treaty-based, the

existence of a fork in the road clause will have no effect upon the subsequent invocation of a treaty claim before an investment tribunal.

Waiver. The investor's pursuit of its claim in other fora may also be affected by a **4.154** treaty provision as to waiver, which may be express or implied:

(1) *Express.* Where the investment treaty requires the waiver of all claims, with respect to the measure of the host State which is alleged to be a breach of treaty, as a condition for the valid invocation of treaty arbitration (as, for example, does Article 1121 of NAFTA), such waiver will operate as at the date of filing the investment arbitration (but not before) to preclude the pursuit of all other claims arising out of the act of the host State which is complained of, even if such claims are founded upon municipal law.

(2) *Implied.* Where, however, as in Article 26 of the ICSID Convention itself, the waiver is merely implied, exclusivity being deemed by virtue of the investor's submission of the claim to ICSID, unless the parties have otherwise expressly provided, it will only operate so as to preclude the subsequent pursuit of other claims which are in substance the same as those to be pursued in ICSID arbitration. Thus, the submission of a claim to ICSID founded upon treaty rights will not preclude a concurrent claim for breach of contract.

Investment tribunal jurisdiction over contract claims. An international tribunal **4.155** constituted to hear investment disputes by treaty may nevertheless have jurisdiction over investment contract claims between investor and host State by one of three routes:

(1) express choice of the parties by contract;
(2) standing consent given by the host State by treaty to submit to arbitration all disputes relating to investments, or specifically disputes relating to investment agreements;
(3) an umbrella clause in the treaty, pursuant to which the host State agrees to observe any undertakings which it has entered into with regard to investments.

Priority of contractual choices of jurisdiction. Where the parties to an investment **4.156** contract have specifically chosen the court or tribunal to resolve their *contractual* dispute, that choice will take priority. Therefore:

(a) The parties' choice of an investment tribunal by contract will, unless otherwise stated, confer exclusive jurisdiction upon that tribunal to determine the dispute;
(b) The availability of investment arbitration for contractual disputes under options (2) or (3) above, however, may be precluded by a contractual clause submitting such disputes to another forum. In such cases, the investment tribunal is bound to enforce the clause and decline or stay the exercise of its own jurisdiction over such claims. This is because the parties' more specific

choice should take priority over the general provisions of a treaty relating to all investments, an application of the *lex specialis* rule.

4.157 *Effect of umbrella clause.* In the case of an umbrella clause, this approach may also be justified on the basis that the enforcement of an obligation to observe undertakings actually *requires* the tribunal to hold both parties to their contractual bargain, which includes the choice of jurisdiction agreement. However, the resulting determination of a contractual entitlement (for example by way of a judgment or award of damages) thereafter becomes itself enforceable through investment arbitration by virtue of the clause. Further, a subsequent change in municipal law by the host State in the exercise of its sovereign authority, which fundamentally affects the nature of the contractual bargain, may constitute a free-standing breach of an umbrella clause, enforceable as a breach of treaty irrespective of a contractual jurisdiction clause.

4.158 *Parallel treaty arbitrations.* Where the same underlying dispute gives rise to claims under two different investment treaties, each tribunal is faced with a potential problem of parallel proceedings within the same legal order:

(1) *Res judicata.* The doctrine of *res judicata* applies to the decisions of international arbitral tribunals, as a general principle of law common to civilized nations. In applying the doctrine to another arbitral award, the tribunal must consider whether there is sufficient identity of:
  (a) parties;
  (b) subject-matter; and
  (c) cause of action.
To date, tribunals have taken a narrow view of these tests, requiring strict identity of parties, and finding that each treaty creates separate causes of action. It is submitted that in principle a wider approach should be adopted by tribunals, in which:
  (a) parties would include those in privity of interest with them (such as the shareholders of a company); and
  (b) the cause of action is assessed substantively, by reference to the nature of the right asserted, and not its source.

(2) *Lis Pendens.* In investment arbitration, the existence of proceedings before another international tribunal in which substantially the same matter is raised for determination, entitles the tribunal, in the exercise of its discretion, to stay its proceedings if it is satisfied that it would be in the interests of justice to do so.

5

NATIONALITY

1. Introduction

A. The Nationality Controversy

The investment protection regime is based on the principle that its protections **5.01** extend to investors who are nationals of a contracting State other than the host State in which the investment is made. Thus, it is the nationality of the claimant that determines whether it is entitled to take the benefit of the treaty protections, and which, in turn, determines the jurisdiction *ratione personae* of the tribunal. This principle is clear. However, the variety of circumstances of its application has raised difficulties. In particular, the wide range of commercial arrangements to structure investments and the desire of investors to gain the benefits of certain protections in bilateral investment treaties (BITs) have led to a number of cases in which boundaries have been stretched. This stretching has chiefly occurred in two directions: characterizing an investor corporation as a national of the contracting home State when it arguably has only a tenuous relationship with that state; and characterizing an investor corporation as foreign when it arguably has a close relationship with the host contracting State.

5.02 In considering the leading cases on nationality issues (and the commentary on them), it appears that the predominant approach has been a formal one, in which international law places few, if any, controls upon a claim of nationality determined by reference to formal incorporation under the law of the home State. That is, unless qualified by the relevant treaty, a claimant corporation's State of incorporation will serve as the claimant's nationality.[1] Formal nationality defined by incorporation has not, to date, been significantly qualified by the application of an 'effective control' test, unless the treaty has done so expressly.

5.03 The point of contention regarding nationality usually arises in relation to corporate investors, and whether there is a basis for applying a controlling interests test, and if so, how to apply that test. For natural persons, the matter is generally less complex and less problematic. Many if not most BITs simply provide for the contracting States' citizenship laws to govern the issue of the nationality of natural persons. Moreover, Article 25(2) of the ICSID Convention,[2] does not define the concept of nationality. In the case of natural persons, it is primarily concerned with the matter of timing and dual nationality; Article 25(2)(a) provides that nationality for natural persons must exist on the date on which the parties consented to ICSID arbitration, as well as on the date that ICSID registers the request for arbitration. The ICSID Convention further clarifies—by denying—arbitral jurisdiction in the case of natural persons who also hold the nationality on either date of the contracting State party to the arbitration.[3]

5.04 Issues of some intricacy and contentiousness may nonetheless arise in establishing whether a natural person qualifies as a national of the home contracting State or whether a natural person is a dual national (ie is a national of both the home and host contracting States).[4] Certain of these are considered below. However, the nationality of corporations is likely to remain a matter of greater debate in

---

[1] eg *Ceskoslovenska Obchodni Banka AS [CSOB] v Slovak Republic* (Jurisdiction) 5 ICSID Rep 330 (ICSID, 1999/2000, Buergenthal P, Bernardini & Bucher), in which more than 65% of the claimant's shares were owned by the Czech Republic, the Tribunal ruled that the claimant was a 'national of another Contracting State'.

[2] Convention on the Settlement of Investment Disputes between States and Nationals of Other States (signed 18 March 1965, entered into force 14 October 1966) 575 UNTS 159 ('ICSID Convention') (Appendix 11 below) Art 25(2).

[3] ibid Art 25(2)(a). See discussion in 5.43–5.44 of Art 25(2)(b) regarding 'juridical' persons.

[4] eg *Hussein Nuaman Soufraki v United Arab Emirates* (Award) ICSID Case No ARB/02/7 (ICSID, 2004, Fortier P, Schwebel & El Kholy); *Champion Trading Co and Ameritrade International Inc v Arab Republic of Egypt* (Jurisdiction) (2004) 19 ICSID Rev-FILJ 275 (ICSID, 2003, Briner P, Fortier & Aynès).

international investment arbitration. The key principles and debates (including those involving individuals) are best approached through an examination of three highly controversial cases: *Tokios Tokelės v Ukraine*[5] (on corporate nationality and the host State) *Loewen Group v USA*[6] (on continuous nationality) and *Aguas del Tunari SA v Republic of Bolivia*[7] (on corporate reorganization). These awards are analysed in Part 3 below. However, in order to place these awards in context, this chapter first discusses briefly the role which nationality has played in the general international law of international claims (see paras 5.05 to 5.15 below), and the specific treatment of nationality in key investment treaties (see Part 2 below).

B. The Function of Nationality in the Law of International Claims

Diplomatic protection

The nature of the nationality debate has been transformed by the mechanism for **5.05** direct claims by private parties that is a central feature of modern investment treaties. Before this development, the issue of nationality arose primarily in the context of whether a State wished to espouse the claim of an injured alien by way of diplomatic protection.[8] In this context, the rules of nationality exist in order to define the circumstances when the *State* may espouse a claim. In *Barcelona Traction*[9] the International Court of Justice (ICJ) emphasized the discretionary nature, as an initial matter, of the State's decision: 'within the limits prescribed by international law, a State may exercise diplomatic protection by whatever means and to whatever extent it thinks fit, for it is its own right that the State is asserting. Should the natural or legal persons on whose behalf it is acting consider that their rights are not adequately protected, they have no remedy in international law'.[10]

A State's decision on whether to invoke diplomatic protection and espouse a claim **5.06** on behalf of a national of the State was only the commencement of the international claims process. The jurisdictional question that remained was whether

---

[5] *Tokios Tokelės v Ukraine* (Jurisdiction) (2005) 20 ICSID Rev-FILJ 205 (ICSID, 2004, Weil P, Bernardini & Price).

[6] *The Loewen Group Inc and Raymond L Loewen v United States of America* (Award) 7 ICSID Rep 421 (NAFTA/ICSID (AF), 2003, Mason P, Mikva & Mustill); (Decision on Request for a Supplementary Decision) (2005) 44 ILM 836.

[7] *Aguas del Tunari SA [AdT] v Republic of Bolivia* (Jurisdiction) (2005) 20 ICSID Rev-FILJ 450 (ICSID, 2005, Caron P, Alvarez & Alberro-Semerena).

[8] ILC (Dugard, Special Rapporteur), 'Draft Articles on Diplomatic Protection with Commentaries' in *Report of the International Law Commission on the Work of its Fifty-eighth Session* (1 May–9 June; 3 July–11 August 2006) UN Doc A/61/10, 22–100.

[9] *Case Concerning the Barcelona Traction, Light and Power Co Ltd (Belgium v Spain)* (New Application: 1962) (Second Phase) [1970] ICJ Rep 3.　　　　　　　　　　　　[10] ibid 44.

the State was entitled, as a matter of international law, to espouse the claim on behalf of the particular natural or juridical person.[11] That is, as a matter of international law, was the natural or juridical person a national of the espousing State? Even in the non-BIT (and largely pre-BIT) realm of diplomatic protection, there was no firm consensus in international law on some of the more complex issues concerning the nationality of claims. Despite this lack of consensus, a relatively high threshold for the espousing State to establish nationality (in the already unusual circumstances when a State decided to invoke diplomatic protection) can be seen in the decisions of international courts and tribunals.

5.07 In the *Nottebohm Case*,[12] the ICJ stated international law regarding nationality (of natural persons) in the context of diplomatic protection as follows:

> According to the practice of States, to arbitral and judicial decisions and to the opinions of writers, nationality is a legal bond having as its basis a social fact of attachment, a genuine connection of existence, interests and sentiments, together with the existence of reciprocal rights and duties. It may be said to constitute the juridical expression of the fact that the individual upon whom it is conferred . . . is in fact more closely connected with the population of the State conferring nationality than with that of any other State. Conferred by a State, it only entitles that State to exercise protection vis-à-vis another State, if it constitutes a translation into juridical terms of the individual's connection with the State which has made him its national.[13]

5.08 Soon after the *Nottebohm* judgment, the Italian-US Conciliation Commission Tribunal[14] interpreted the 'genuine connection' test not as a general rule, but as a consideration that was limited to the facts of the particular case, such that only a State in the somewhat unusual position of Liechtenstein (where Mr Nottebohm had spent only a very short period of time and had very tenuous ties, compared to Guatemala, where he had lived for some thirty years and carried out business) was required to show the existence of a 'genuine connection' between itself and the individual claimant. This is the position adopted by the International Law Commission (ILC) in its 'Draft Articles on Diplomatic Protection with Commentaries', in which the 'genuine connection' rule has been rejected in draft Article 4.[15]

5.09 However, it should be noted that some thirty years after the *Nottebohm* case, the Iran-US Claims Tribunal addressed the question of nationality of claims in the context of dual nationality, and relied heavily on *Nottebohm*.

---

[11] See Hague Convention on Certain Questions Relating to the Conflict of Nationality Laws (signed 12 April 1930, entered into force 1 July 1937) 179 LNTS 89 ('1930 Hague Convention'), Art 1: 'It is for each State to determine under its own law who are its nationals. This law shall be recognised by other States in so far as it is consistent with international conventions, international custom, and the principles of law generally recognised with regard to nationality.'

[12] *Nottebohm Case (Liechtenstein v Guatemala)* (Second Phase) [1955] ICJ Rep 4.

[13] ibid 23.

[14] *Flegenheimer Claim* (1958) 25 ILR 91, 148 (Italian-US Conciliation Commission, 1958, Sauser-Hall, Matturri & Sorrentino).

[15] ILC, 'Draft Articles on Diplomatic Protection with Commentaries' (n 8 above) 32–33.

The specific context of claims between foreign investors and a State, and the need **5.10** to interpret the terms of the Claims Settlement Declaration, may have been thought to distance the Iran-US Claims Tribunal's decision-making both from customary international law and diplomatic protection.[16] Nonetheless, the Iran-US Claims Tribunal did rely on its understanding of customary international law. In *Iran-United States, Case No A/18* (6 April 1984)[17] the Claims Tribunal considered the issue of dual nationality—ie whether claims filed by persons who were both nationals of the United States and Iran were admissible. In a hotly contested award, which did not adopt the formulation of either the US or Iranian party disputants and which featured a Dissenting Opinion by Iranian Tribunal members and a concurring opinion by certain US Tribunal members, it was held that the text of the Claims Settlement Declaration did not permit an unequivocal answer, and recourse was had to general rules of international law.[18] The 1930 Hague Convention[19] and a number of judicial decisions and early twentieth-century arbitral awards were referred to by the Tribunal majority. But particular significance was also accorded to the *Nottebohm Case*,[20] from which the Tribunal extracted the importance of the search for 'real and effective nationality', as opposed to an approach relying on more formalistic criteria. Accordingly, the Tribunal concluded that the international law rule was 'real and effective nationality', entailing a search for 'stronger factual ties between the person concerned and one of the States whose nationality is involved'.[21] When determining 'dominant and effective' nationality, the Tribunal stated that all relevant factors would be considered including 'habitual residence, center of interests, family ties, participation in public life and other evidence of attachment'.[22]

The rule on dual nationality of natural persons expounded in *Case No A/18* remains **5.11** a substantive principle of international law (one that is now expressly accepted in treaty drafting practice).[23] Of particular interest is the Tribunal's determination, in

---

[16] See *Case Concerning Elettronica Sicula SpA (ELSI) (United States of America v Italy)* [1989] ICJ Rep 15, 64 & 79 where the ICJ, in interpreting the bilateral Treaty of Friendship, Commerce and Navigation between the US and Italy (and therefore not concerned with the evaluation of customary international law), accepted that the narrower approaches in diplomatic protection will not necessarily apply for a treaty-based claim. See also ILC, 'Draft Articles on Diplomatic Protection with Commentaries' (n 8 above) 64–65.

[17] *Iran-United States, Case No A/18* (1984) 5 Iran-USCTR 251. GH Aldrich, *The Jurisprudence of the Iran-United States Claims Tribunal* (1996) 492ff. See also, to like effect, the Tribunal's earlier decision in *Nasser Esphahanian v Bank Tejarat* (1983) 2 Iran-USCTR 157.

[18] *Iran-United States, Case No A/18* (n 17 above) 259–260. Pursuant to Art 31(3)(c) of the Vienna Convention on the Law of Treaties (signed 23 May 1969, entered into force 27 January 1980) 1155 UNTS 331.

[19] 1930 Hague Convention (n 11 above).

[20] *Nottebohm Case (Liechtenstein v Guatemala)* (Second Phase) (n 12 above).

[21] *Iran-United States, Case No A/18* (n 17 above) 265.

[22] ibid 265.

[23] eg 2004 US model BIT Art 1 (definition of 'investor of party') (Appendix 6 below) (discussed at 5.26 below); ILC, 'Draft Articles on Diplomatic Protection with Commentaries' (n 8 above) Art 7: 'A State of nationality

the case of natural persons, that an investigation of the factual background to establish actual relationships is necessary. When the Iran-US Claims Tribunal addressed the issue of corporate nationality, however, there was substantial uncertainty on whether to prefer a formalistic test of incorporation or, as in the case of individuals, at least for the purposes of dual nationality, an investigation into actual relationships. Here the diplomatic protection background was again significant, and is helpfully set out in the ILC's August 2006 Report. The ILC Draft Articles on Diplomatic Protection address the question of a corporation's nationality in Articles 9 to 12; the commentary discusses at some length the *Barcelona Traction Case* and the controversies that have attended the judgment of the ICJ and the various opinions of the judges. Among the swirl of opinions, the ICJ's judgment appears to establish certain principles, a non-exhaustive summary of which may be extracted from FA Mann's famous critique of the case:

(1) Diplomatic protection cannot in general 'be exercised by the state of the shareholders who possess mere interests in the property of the corporation'.[24]

(2) However, an 'exception may arise if the corporation has suffered a "legal demise"':
  (a) the law of the State of the company's nationality determines whether such a demise has occurred;
  (b) a company that is a mere shell but has legal existence by such law would not qualify for the exception;
  (c) this remains the case even if the company is declared bankrupt and is incapacitated by the host (respondent) State.[25]

(3) 'A second exception may arise where the company's national state lacks capacity to act on its behalf, *i.e.* fails to have some "genuine connection" with it.'[26]

(4) A lack of capacity is not created by a failure to afford protection [for 18 years].[27]

(5) 'No rule of customary international law has yet come into existence which would confer a right of diplomatic protection on a state merely by reason of the fact that the value of its nationals' shareholdings and thus its own economic resources suffer damage.'[28]

(6) 'It is likely that the shareholders' state has a right of diplomatic protection if the company is a national of the Respondent state'[29] (though such nationality does not arise from the fact that the respondent State has exercised bankruptcy jurisdiction).

---

may not exercise diplomatic protection in respect of a person against a State of which that person is also a national unless the nationality of the former State is predominant, both at the date of injury and at the date of the official presentation of the claim.'

[24] FA Mann, 'The Protection of Shareholders' Interests in the Light of the *Barcelona Traction Case*' (1973) 67 AJIL 259, 272–273.　　　　　　　　　　　　　　　　[25] ibid 273.
[26] ibid 273.　　　　　[27] ibid.　　　　　[28] ibid.　　　　　[29] ibid.

For FA Mann, the ICJ's judgment amounted to a proclamation that 'the legal **5.12** structure of the formal (national) law must prevail, however much the company as a living entity may have been distorted or undermined by realities or by factual disorganization'.[30] The ILC has explained that *Barcelona Traction* required, for the purposes of diplomatic protection, 'incorporation and the presence of the registered office of the company in the State of incorporation', with incorporation being the most important criterion since most States require a registered office in the State if a company wishes to be incorporated in the State.[31] However, the ILC added that the ICJ also suggested that there was a further need for some 'permanent and close connection' between the State exercising diplomatic protection and the corporation. Thus, although *Barcelona Traction* did not confront the situation where a company had only a tenuous link with the State of incorporation but a close link with another State, draft Article 9 provides for an exception to the 'formal' corporate nationality rule in these circumstances. This, the ILC notes, acknowledges the reality that a State will in practice be unwilling to exercise diplomatic protection for a corporation with only a tenuous connection to the State.[32] But it is an 'either/or' rule: either the State of incorporation or, if the required links are met, the State of control will be entitled to exercise diplomatic protection (but not both).[33]

As for the other aspects of corporate nationality addressed (to some degree) in **5.13** *Barcelona Traction*, the ILC's Draft Articles devote substantial attention (Articles 11 and 12) to the principle that diplomatic protection is accorded to a company based on the company's nationality, and not the nationality of the shareholders. *Barcelona Traction* reaffirmed this principle.[34] However, as FA Mann and the ILC have observed, there were some exceptions to this principle. For the ILC, the exceptions can be logically extended to the points set out at draft Article 11(a) and (b), in which case the nationality of shareholders may be relevant. The ILC makes its case not only on logic,[35] but on State practice, arbitral awards, and doctrine,[36] particularly in circumstances where the corporation has been injured by the State of incorporation itself. Similarly, draft Article 12 extends another *Barcelona Traction* point not fully discussed in that case to the status of a rule: 'direct injury' to shareholders entitles the State of nationality of such shareholders to exercise diplomatic protection.[37]

---

[30] ibid 273–274.
[31] ILC, 'Draft Articles on Diplomatic Protection with Commentaries' (n 8 above) 53.
[32] ibid 54.
[33] ibid 55.
[34] ibid 58. *Case Concerning the Barcelona Traction, Light and Power Co, Limited (Belgium v Spain)* (New Application: 1962) (Second Phase) (n 9 above) 42; 48–50.
[35] ILC, 'Draft Articles on Diplomatic Protection with Commentaries' (n 8 above) 61.
[36] ibid 62.
[37] ibid 66.

5.14 The ILC was careful to note that the *ELSI* case, on which it relied for certain matters, did not expound on rules of customary international law and was instead concerned with the interpretation of a treaty.[38] As noted above, the Iran-US Claims Tribunal was also requried to interpret a treaty, and was not bound by the rules of diplomatic protection. Nonetheless, the Iran-US Claims Tribunal's struggle with 'formalism' is instructive.

5.15 For example, in *The Management of Alcan Aluminium Ltd v Ircable Corp*[39] the Tribunal stated that it 'may be shown that, at the appropriate time, such [US nationals] shareholders controlled the corporation in fact, regardless of the total proportion of their shares'.[40] Judge Charles N Brower later commented (with JD Brueschke) that while 'this proposition suggests that factual control is relevant to the inquiry, it is not clear whether the "interests sufficient to control" test requires a showing of factual control or whether instead a showing of ultimate legal control is necessary'.[41] Other decisions (for example *Sedco v National Iranian Oil Co*)[42] pointed towards the existence of 'ownership interests sufficient to control'.[43] However, as Brower and Brueschke observe, the *Sedco* comments were obiter dicta and under *Alcan*[44] and *Sedco*[45] there remained many unresolved questions, such as whether control can be exercised by more than one owner.[46]

The new context of investment treaties

5.16 The landscape has shifted with the advent and proliferation of investment treaties. The ILC Draft Articles provide in Article 17 that they 'do not apply to the extent that they are inconsistent with special rules of international law, such as treaty provisions for the protection of investments'. The Commentary on Article 17 notes that the field of foreign investment is today largely regulated by BITs, which may abandon or relax certain requirements of diplomatic protection. In the investment arbitration context, the claimants are private, and the dispute resolution provisions 'offer greater advantages to the foreign investor than the customary international law system of diplomatic protection'.[47] Thus, nationality no longer serves the function of defining when a home State may espouse a claim, though the threshold jurisdictional question of nationality—like the threshold question of 'investment'—looms large as the basis for potential objections to jurisdiction on the part of respondent States.

---

[38] ILC, 'Draft Articles on Diplomatic Protection with Commentaries' (n 8 above) 66–67.
[39] *The Management of Alcan Aluminium & ors v Ircable Corp* (1983) 2 Iran-USCTR 294.
[40] ibid 297.
[41] CN Brower & JD Brueschke, *The Iran-United States Claims Tribunal* (1998) 108.
[42] *Sedco Inc v National Iranian Oil Co & anor* (Interlocutory Award) (1985) 9 Iran-USCTR 248; (Interlocutory Award) (1986) 10 Iran-USCTR 180; (Award) (1987) 15 Iran-USCTR 23.
[43] *Sedco* (Interlocutory Order) (ibid) 259.   [44] *Alcan* (n 39 above).
[45] *Sedco* (n 42 above).   [46] Brower & Brueschke (n 41 above) 108–109.
[47] ILC, 'Draft Articles on Diplomatic Protection with Commentaries' (n 8 above) 90.

Such States have evinced a threefold concern: (a) seeking to ensure that pursuant **5.17** to a specific request for arbitration the tribunal is jurisdictionally competent to hear the claim (ie seeking to ensure that the putative claimant has the right to invoke the protections of a particular treaty); (b) seeking to ensure that any compensation that may ultimately be paid is to a *foreign* investor; and (c) seeking to ensure that, as a matter of international law and future interpretation of the nationality requirement, States will not have previously acceded to the blurring of remaining boundaries, despite the proliferation of investment vehicles and the increasingly complex cross-border structure of investments.

Among the cluster of related nationality questions that have driven the current **5.18** jurisdictional challenges before many international investment tribunals are the following:

(1) Is 'nationality'—however it is to be determined—a relevant test in a particular case or generally for delimiting the class of valid claimants (*ratione personae*)?

(2) If so, which law defines the designation of nationality? Is it the municipal law of the home or host State, the specific provisions of the relevant treaties, customary international law, or a combination of these (and if a combination, what hierarchy is to be applied between them)? How many nationality tests must be satisfied, and in what order—BIT plus ICSID, or ICSID plus BIT? What if the ICSID Convention does not govern because the arbitration proceeds under, for example the UNCITRAL Rules?

(3) Which substantive test for nationality governs—place of incorporation versus place of effective control—and when does the test apply?

(4) When must nationality be determined? Is it the time at which the claim arises or the time of lodging the claim? After the commencement of the proceedings, must nationality be maintained continuously through to the date of the tribunal's award?

Underlying the consideration by tribunals of these issues has been an ongoing **5.19** controversy over the relevance and application of the rules of nationality developed in the context of the customary international law of diplomatic protection. As will be seen below, tribunals have variously applied principles developed in this field to the specific problems of investment treaties or rejected them. Thus, a determination of the guidance which can properly be taken from the law of diplomatic protection provides an important element of the doctrinal context for the broader policy debate as to whether nationality can be treated as a purely formal matter determined by reference to home State law, or whether it is to be controlled by substantive criteria imposed by tribunals.

In considering the impact of general international law on the construction of the **5.20** investment treaty criteria, the complex interplay between the definition of 'investment' and that of 'nationality' in such treaties should not be forgotten. As discussed above, the customary international law of diplomatic protection gives priority to the State of incorporation in determining the nationality of a corporation in most cases.[48] It also strictly limits the extent to which a shareholder may pursue a claim against the host State for injuries done to the company in which he has invested.[49] Taken together, these two rules strictly limit the potential claims to nationality which may be made. By contrast, as explained in Chapter 6 below, the much broader notion of 'investment' in investment treaties permits claims by shareholders against the host State for losses occasioned by the (indirect) reduction in the value of the shareholding caused by damage to the company. One consequence of the treaty-based approach to investment is to widen the range of potential claimants, and thus the number of potentially relevant claims to nationality. In turn, as the awards discussed in paras 5.47 to 5.87 below demonstrate, nationality has been relied upon by respondent States to perform a limiting function: to exclude claims where it is said that the claim to nationality is formal and not substantive.

5.21 In the first instance, it is of course crucial, both in examining an individual case and in attempting to extract substantive principles, to consider the provision controlling nationality in a particular BIT or multilateral investment treaty (MIT) (such as NAFTA[50] or the ECT[51]) that may be applicable, as well as the language in Article 25 of the ICSID Convention (in cases where that Convention applies). Accordingly, it is to a consideration of the treatment of nationality requirements in the texts of investment treaties that this chapter now turns.

2. Definition of Nationality in Investment Treaties

A. Bilateral Investment Treaties

Individuals

5.22 The definition of a 'national', or an individual 'investor', for the purpose of the BIT may be the same overarching definition for both contracting States, or may include a more specific definition for one or both States.

---

[48] *Case Concerning the Barcelona Traction, Light and Power Co, Ltd (Belgium v Spain)* (New Application: 1962) (Second Phase) (n 9 above) 42; ILC, 'Draft Articles on Diplomatic Protection with Commentaries' (n 8 above) Art 9.

[49] *Barcelona Traction Case* (n 9 above) 48–50. ILC, 'Draft Articles on Diplomatic Protection with Commentaries' (n 8 above) Arts 11 & 12.

[50] North American Free Trade Agreement (adopted 17 December 1992, entered into force 1 January 1994) CTS 1994 No 2; (1993) 32 ILM 612 ('NAFTA') (Appendix 1 below).

[51] Energy Charter Treaty (signed 17 December 1994, entered into force 16 April 1998) 2080 UNTS 100 ('ECT') (Appendix 2 below).

The France model BIT offers an example of a single definition: 'Les nationaux, **5.23** c'est-à-dire les personnes physiques possédant la nationalité de l'une des parties contractantes.'[52]

This approach is similar to that of the 1994 US model BIT, which defines a **5.24** 'national' of a party as 'a natural person who is a national of that Party under its applicable law'.[53]

The China model BIT defines investor 'in respect of the People's Republic of **5.25** China' as 'natural persons who have nationality of the People's Republic of China in accordance with its laws'.[54] The UK and Germany model BITs also define 'nationals' specifically by reference to the law in force in their respective countries.[55]

The 2004 US model BIT has been developed to include two separate definitions of **5.26** 'national', specifically incorporating the Iran-United States Claims Tribunal's test for dual nationality. Therefore, while a 'national' is defined by 'Title III of the Immigration and Nationality Act' (ie by reference to the domestic law), the definition in Article 1 of an 'investor of a party' specifically determines that 'a natural person who is a dual national shall be deemed to be exclusively a national of the State of his or her dominant and effective nationality'.

The Sri Lanka model BIT sets forth only the single definition of 'national', but **5.27** qualifies this to exclude those who share dual nationality with the other contracting party: 'natural persons who, having the nationality of one Contracting Party, in accordance with its laws and are not nationals of the other Contracting Party'.[56]

Some BITs require the additional criterion of residence; Israel requires that Israeli **5.28** 'nationals' be 'permanent residents of the State of Israel' under the Germany-Israel BIT,[57] and similar requirements are set out in the Denmark-Indonesia BIT.[58]

It was once common for socialist States to exclude natural persons, and limit the **5.29** protection afforded in the treaty to, for instance 'Romanian economic units having

---

[52] France model BIT (Appendix 10 below) Art 1(2)(a).
[53] 1994 US model BIT (Appendix 5 below) Art 1(c).
[54] China model BIT reprinted in UNCTAD, *International Investment Instruments: A Compendium* Vol III (1996) 151, 152 Art 1(2).
[55] UK model BIT (Appendix 4 below) Art 1(c)(i); Germany model BIT (Appendix 7 below) Art 1(3)(a).
[56] Sri Lanka model BIT (Appendix 9 below) Art 1(2)(a); Agreement for the Promotion and Reciprocal Protection of Investments (Israel-Romania) (signed 2 September 1991, entered into force 26 August 1992) invokes the same qualification.
[57] Treaty concerning the Encouragement and Reciprocal Protection of Investments (Germany-Israel) (signed 24 June 1976, prov. in force) 1978 BGBl II 209 Art 1(3)(b).
[58] Agreement Concerning the Encouragement and the Reciprocal Protection of Investments (Denmark-Indonesia) 720 UNTS 223 (signed 30 January 1968, entered into force 2 July 1968) Art 1(a): 'domiciled in the territory of their nationality'.

legal personality and which, under the law of Romania, are entitled to trade abroad or undertake international economic cooperation activities'.[59]

5.30 However, with the transition to market economies, such treaties have been reconsidered and include 'natural persons who, according to the law in force in Romania, are considered to be its citizens'.[60]

Companies

5.31 The nationality of companies in the model BITs may comprise three criteria, referring to the nation of incorporation, control, or management (seat) of the company.

5.32 The incorporation approach is adopted by the UK model BIT, whereby UK companies are 'corporations, firms and associations incorporated or constituted under the law in force in any part of the United Kingdom'.[61]

5.33 This conception is invoked by the 2004 US model BIT, with the additional criterion that 'a branch [is] located in the territory of a Party and carrying out business activities there'.[62]

5.34 The Germany model BIT, however, determines the nationality of the company according to the actual management, or seat: 'any juridical person as well as any commercial or other company or association with or without legal personality having its seat in the territory of the Federal Republic of Germany, irrespective of whether or not its activities are directed at profit'.[63]

5.35 The Sri Lanka model BIT requires both that the legal entity be 'formed and incorporated under the laws of one Contracting Party and have their seat together with their substantial economic activities in the territory of that same Contracting Party'.[64]

5.36 The Netherlands requires either incorporation or control, affording protection to both those 'legal persons constituted under the law of that Contracting Party' (ie incorporated) and those 'legal persons not constituted under the law of that Contracting Party but controlled, directly or indirectly, by natural persons as defined in (i) or by legal persons as defined in (ii)'.[65]

---

[59] Agreement on the Mutual Promotion and Protection of Investments of Capital (UK-Romania) 1049 UNTS 215 (signed 19 March 1976, entered into force 22 November 1976) Art 2(3)(a).

[60] Agreement for the Promotion and Reciprocal Protection of Investments (Romania-UK) 1957 UNTS 99 (signed 13 July 1995, entered into force 10 January 1996) Art 1(c)(ii).

[61] UK model BIT (Appendix 4 below) Art 1(d)(i).

[62] 2004 US model BIT (Appendix 6 below) Art 1 (definition of 'enterprise of a Party').

[63] Germany model BIT (Appendix 7 below) Art 1(3)(a).

[64] Sri Lanka model BIT (Appendix 9 below) Art 1(2)(b).

[65] Netherlands model BIT (Appendix 8 below) Art 1(b)(iii).

The nationality of a company with respect to the Swiss Confederation is expanded **5.37** to any entity that can demonstrate any of the above criteria.[66]

B. Multilateral Investment Treaties

NAFTA

The nationality requirements under NAFTA are as follows for the individual: **5.38** 'a natural person who is a citizen or permanent resident of a Party and any other natural person referred to in Annex 201.1'.[67]

Annex 201.1 offers specific definitions, for the purpose of the treaty, by reference **5.39** to the domestic Mexican and US laws on citizenship; respectively Articles 30 and 34 of the Mexican Constitution and the 'existing provisions of the [United States] *Immigration and Nationality Act*'.[68]

The nationality of a company is conferred upon an enterprise constituted or organ- **5.40** ized under the law of, or principally carrying on its business in the territory of, a party.[69]

Energy Charter Treaty

The Energy Charter Treaty (ECT) defines as an 'investor' both 'a natural person' **5.41** by reference to the contracting party's 'applicable' domestic law, and 'a company or other organization organized in accordance with the law applicable in that Contracting Party'.[70]

ASEAN

Under the ASEAN Agreement, 'nationals' are again defined by the 'respective **5.42** Constitutions and laws' of the individual State, while a company requires that both the incorporation and seat are within the territory of the specific State, 'a corporation, partnership or other business association, incorporated or constituted under the laws in force in the territory of any Contracting Party wherein the place of effective management is situated'.[71]

---

[66] Switzerland model BIT reprinted in UNCTAD *International Investment Instruments: A Compendium* (1996) Vol III 177, 177–178 Art 1(b) & (c).
[67] NAFTA (Appendix 1 below) Art 201.   [68] ibid Annex 201.1.
[69] ibid Art 201, 1139.
[70] ECT (Appendix 2 below) Art 1(7). This is qualified by Art 17(1) for corporate investors; see AC Sinclair, 'The Substance of Nationality Requirements in Investment Treaty Arbitration' (2005) 20 ICSID Rev-FILJ 357, 378–387.
[71] ASEAN Agreement for the Promotion and Protection of Investments (signed 15 December 1987) (1988) 27 ILM 612 ('ASEAN Agreement') (Appendix 3 below) Art I.

ICSID Article 25

5.43 The ICSID Convention's definition of natural persons or individuals is discussed at para 5.03 above.[72] For juridical persons, such as corporations, nationality is defined under the ICSID Convention at Article 25(2)(b):

> any juridical person which had the nationality of a Contracting State other than the State party to the dispute on the date on which the parties consented to submit such dispute to conciliation or arbitration and any juridical person which had the nation-ality of the Contracting State party to the dispute on that date and which, because of foreign control, the parties have agreed should be treated as a national of another Contracting State for the purposes of this Convention.

5.44 With the Convention silent on the method to be employed, early ICSID awards such as *Amco v Indonesia*, applied the requirements for nationality of the 'place of incorporation' and the 'place of its registered seat'.[73] As Schreuer rightly asserts: 'The overwhelming weight of the authority ... points towards the traditional cri-teria of incorporation or seat for the determination of corporate nationality under Art. 25(2)(b). The situation may be otherwise if the parties have entered into an agreement on the investor's nationality'.[74]

3. Treatment of Nationality in Investment Arbitration Awards

5.45 Three main issues in the application of the nationality test have emerged in the recent jurisprudence of investment arbitral tribunals:

(1) *Corporate nationality.* May a company which is registered in one State pursue a claim against the host State in a case where it is controlled by shareholders in the host State?

(2) *Continuous nationality.* Does it matter if the corporate claimant ceases to be registered in the home State between the date when the claim is brought and the date when it is resolved?

(3) *Control by foreign nationals.* Where the claim is brought on the basis that a host State company is 'controlled' by a national of another State party, is it

---

[72] ICSID Convention (Appendix 11 below). See C Schreuer, 'Commentary on the ICSID Convention: Article 25' (1997) ICSID Rev-FILJ 59, 68–78 for a detailed analysis.

[73] *Amco Asia Corp & ors v Republic of Indonesia* (Jurisdiction: Original Proceedings) 1 ICSID Rep 376, 394 (ICSID, 1983, Goldman P, Foighel & Rubin).

[74] See C Schreuer, 'Commentary on the ICSID Convention: Article 25' (n 72 above) 84. For fur-ther analysis see CH Schreuer, *The ICSID Convention: A Commentary* (2001) 275–286.

sufficient that the foreign national has legal control (as a shareholder), or must it also exercise factual control?

These issues have been considered in three awards of pivotal importance, which **5.46** are discussed below. In each case, an affirmative answer given by the tribunal has preferred form over substance. But two of the awards were accompanied by strong and erudite Dissenting Opinions and one has been the subject of extensive critical commentary, so that the opposing arguments are well developed.

A. Corporate Nationality, 'Veil Piercing', and ICSID

Tokios: the context and issues

The *Tokios*[75] arbitration places in stark relief the relative weight of substantive con- **5.47** trol versus corporate form of the investment vehicle. In the absence of an express 'control' provision in the relevant BIT,[76] and interpreting the ICSID Convention on jurisdictional requirements, the Tribunal found that corporate form was the correct focus, and accordingly rejected Ukraine's jurisdictional objection.

This important majority decision, in which the dissenting arbitrator was actually **5.48** the President of the Tribunal (Professor Prosper Weil), was based on the following background facts. The claimant, Tokios, was a Lithuanian corporation. It created a wholly-owned subsidiary under Ukrainian law. The claimant alleged that Ukraine took actions regarding the subsidiary that constituted a breach of the Ukraine-Lithuania BIT. Tokios therefore filed a request for arbitration with ICSID in 2002, together with its Ukrainian subsidiary.[77] Tokios removed the subsidiary as a claimant after Ukraine and Lithuania did not agree that the subsidiary should be considered a national of Lithuania under the BIT and Article 25(2)(b) of the ICSID Convention.[78]

The Ukraine-Lithuania BIT defined 'investors' in respect of Ukraine as natural **5.49** persons who are nationals of Ukraine under Ukrainian law, and entities established in Ukraine. In respect of Lithuania, the same natural person, entity definitions used for Ukraine (of course substituting Lithuania for Ukraine) were

---

[75] *Tokios* (n 5 above).
[76] The Ukraine-Lithuania BIT contained a control provision, but it only related to nationals of any third State, not to the two contracting States; Agreement for the Promotion and Reciprocal Protection of Investments (Ukraine-Lithuania) (signed 8 February 1994, entered into force 27 February 1995).
[77] *Tokios* (n 5 above) 208–209: the request for arbitration was withdrawn and resubmitted to satisfy the BIT's six-month negotiation requirement.
[78] ibid 209–210; ICSID Convention (Appendix 11 below) Art 25(2)(b).

included. There was also an additional category of nationals in respect of either Ukraine or Lithuania—any entity established in any third State that is controlled, directly or indirectly, by nationals of either Ukraine or Lithuania or by entities with their seat in the contracting party. 'Control' was defined as requiring 'a substantial part in the ownership'.[79] This 'third state' control test, it should be noted, had no impact on the question of nationality as between corporations and owners which were themselves nationals of the two contracting States. This was what the case turned on.

5.50 Tokios, although a Lithuanian corporation, was 99 per cent owned by nationals of Ukraine. Ukrainian nationals also made up two-thirds of the management of Tokios.[80] Relying on the principle that the purpose of the ICSID Convention is to 'facilitate the settlement of investment disputes between States and nationals of other States', and 'is not meant for disputes between States and their own nationals',[81] Ukraine argued that the Tribunal should 'pierce the corporate veil' and find that despite the claimant's having Lithuania as its State of incorporation, the claimant's nationality should be determined on the basis of the nationality of its predominant ownership and management, and the site of its headquarters. This, Ukraine contended, would lead to a determination of Ukrainian nationality and would therefore disqualify Tokios from maintaining an ICSID arbitration against Ukraine.[82]

5.51 The particular arguments assessed by the Tribunal included the following. First, does the ICSID Convention prescribe any method for assessing nationality of juridical entities? As noted above, the Convention does not—which led the Tribunal to consider the definitions supplied in the BIT.[83] The BIT did not prescribe any test other than establishment under Lithuanian law. Tokios met that test. Moreover, if the contracting States had wanted to impose a 'control' requirement, they would have done so and in fact did so in the case of third States. Thus, the absence of a control requirement vis-à-vis nationals of the two contracting States gave even greater reason not to impose such a test. Other provisions of the BIT supported the notion of a broad scope of investment protection.[84]

5.52 Other BITs and MITs to which Ukraine is a party expressly denied protection benefits to corporations owned or controlled by nationals of a third state if such entities have no substantial business activities in the contracting State in which they are

---

[79] *Tokios* (n 5 above) 211–213.

[80] ibid 213. It was disputed whether Tokios had any substantial business activities in Lithuania and whether it maintained its administrative headquarters in Ukraine (*Tokios* (n 5 above) 214).

[81] CH Schreuer, *The ICSID Convention: A Commentary* (2001) 290 cited in *Tokios* (n 5 above) 214 fn 6.   [82] *Tokios* (n 5 above) 214.

[83] *Tokios* (n 5 above) 215.   [84] *Tokios* (n 5 above) 216–218.

organized. Article 17(1) of the Energy Charter Treaty[85] was considered in this regard by the Tribunal. Again, the control provisions in these treaties were further evidence that if a limitation on nationality based on ownership or control were to be applied, the contracting States were free to include it. They did not do so. The Tribunal majority emphasized that it was simply interpreting the BIT according to the ordinary meaning of its words, consistent with its context, and consistent with the concept of corporate nationality in the ICSID Convention, which, accordingly to *Amco Asia Corp v Indonesia*,[86] was the 'classical' concept by which nationality is determined on the basis of the law and place of incorporation.[87]

Stepping back from a review of the *Tokios* decision at this stage, it is necessary to consider whether a substantive control test may not accord more closely with the object and purpose of investment treaties, and of the ICSID Convention, in the protection of *foreign* investment and investors. This may be seen as stemming in large part from the economic rationale underlying the dispute resolution provisions in such treaties, which is to enable capital importing countries to attract foreign investment. The question, then, is whether such a 'control' or 'piercing' test may not be read into the treaty requirement of a foreign national.   **5.53**

The majority decision on jurisdiction: formal corporate nationality

The *Tokios* majority firmly answered that in no respect did international law permit it to impose a control test. And in this, the *Tokios* majority, despite the vigorous dissent of the president, Professor Weil, appears to be firmly within the majority of international tribunals and scholars that have addressed the corporate nationality issue. To be sure, the bulk of the *Tokios* decision concerns a discussion of what can or cannot be construed from Article 25 of the ICSID Convention. Still, the *Tokios* majority also explained that the international law direction was to favour the expansion of arbitral jurisdiction when the issue was whether the claimant was incorporated in the home contracting State but owned by nationals of the host contracting State.[88] The decision on jurisdiction in *Wena Hotels Ltd v Arab Republic of Egypt* is important in this regard, as the Tribunal in that case also found that expanding jurisdiction was the modern tendency.[89] Beyond the confines of   **5.54**

---

[85] ECT (Appendix 2 below) Art 17(1). On the interpretation of ECT Art 17 see *Plama Consortium Ltd v Republic of Bulgaria* (Jurisdiction) (2005) 20 ICSID Rev-FILJ 262; (2005) 44 ILM 721 (ICSID, 2005, Salans P, van den Berg & Veeder).

[86] *Amco Asia Corp & ors v Republic of Indonesia* (Jurisdiction: Original Proceedings) 1 ICSID Rep 376, (n 73 above) 396.

[87] *Tokios* (n 5 above) 218–221.

[88] ibid 221–225. If Tokios had not opted for ICSID arbitration and instead had pursued UNCITRAL arbitration, the object of the ICSID Convention would clearly not have been such a substantial issue, and Professor Weil's dissent would have necessarily been different. There would still have been the issue of interpreting the BIT in the light of customary international law.

[89] ibid 223–224; *Wena Hotels Ltd v Arab Republic of Egypt* (Jurisdiction) 6 ICSID Rep 67, 81–82; (2002) 41 ILM 881, 888 (ICSID, 1999, Leigh P, Fadlallah & Haddad).

Article 25 of the ICSID Convention, the *Tokios* majority also found support from the classic *Barcelona Traction* decision of the ICJ.[90] The ICJ commented on the use of piercing under municipal law, but did not define the conduct that would support piercing by an international tribunal—although Tokios' conduct, according to the Tribunal majority, did not approach the municipal law standards that were discussed in *Barcelona Traction*.[91]

5.55 The *Tokios* Decision also referred to the 'predominant approach in international law', whereby the Tribunal observed, it is usual to attribute corporate nationality to the State where the corporation has been incorporated, together with the need for the head or registered office or *siège social* to be in the same State. For this 'predominant approach' the Tribunal relied on *Barcelona Traction* and *Oppenheim's International Law*.[92] This does not appear wholly satisfactory as an exegesis of the customary international law position. It relies on statements in two sources that themselves referred to what is 'usual' or to the 'traditional rule', without exploring other sources since *Barcelona Traction* and, specifically, whether what is 'traditional' should carry weight in the investment protection context. In view of the *Tokios* majority's research, its conclusion that the 'Ukraine-Lithuania BIT uses the same well established method for determining corporate nationality as does customary international law',[93] is perhaps less reliable than other aspects of its decision.

5.56 Nonetheless, given the importance of certain international investment tribunal decisions and awards in themselves developing or at least clarifying commonly used treaty provisions as well as customary international law, the *Tokios* decision is of crucial significance in giving added life to the traditional rule by clearly extending its applicability to the investment protection field in general and to the ICSID Convention in particular. Indeed, the dissenting opinion of Weil (discussed below), whereby under the ICSID Convention one must take into account the origins of capital in assessing whether ICSID's jurisdictional requirements have been met, has become emblematic of a minority position that, although forcibly and in many respects persuasively presented, shows no signs of becoming the foundation of an emerging majority.[94]

5.57 Two final points regarding the majority decision should be noted. First, the *Tokios* tribunal had to address *Loewen v USA*,[95] a case relied upon by Ukraine. This case,

---

[90] *Tokios* (n 5 above) 225–226; *Case Concerning the Barcelona Traction, Light and Power Co Ltd (Belgium v Spain)* (New Application: 1962) (Second Phase) (n 9 above) 39.

[91] *Tokios* (n 5 above) 226.

[92] R Jennings and A Watts (eds), *Oppenheim's International Law* (9th edn, 1996) 859–60.

[93] *Tokios* (n 5 above) 231.

[94] Of course, crystal-ball gazing in a developing field of law where awards do not carry precedential authority is an especially uncertain activity. If two adherents of Weil's views were to sit on an ICSID tribunal that had to resolve a *Tokios*-type corporate nationality jurisdictional challenge, it is conceivable that one would not readily ascribe minority status to the *Tokios* dissent.

[95] *The Loewen Group Inc and Raymond L Loewen v United States of America* (Award) 7 ICSID Rep 421 (n 6 above).

discussed below, raises the issue of 'continuous nationality': that is, must the claimant's nationality be 'continuous' from the date of the events underlying the claim until the date of the resolution of the claim (or some other shorter period)? The *Loewen* Tribunal deemed continuous nationality until the date of the resolution of the claim to be required (both under NAFTA[96] and customary international law).[97] The *Tokios* majority contended that although the *Loewen* Tribunal denied that it pierced the corporate veil in order to find no continuous nationality in the claim before it, the Tribunal had in fact done so (though it need not have done so in order to reach the same finding).[98] The *Tokios* majority was thus interested in using the *Loewen* Tribunal's comment that it had not pierced to support its position on international law regarding piercing, discussed above.[99] However, the *Loewen* Tribunal was grappling with the meaning of a different treaty, NAFTA rather than ICSID, and was expressly interpreting public international law as distinct from private law rules.[100] It is of crucial importance to appreciate *why* the *Loewen* Tribunal denied that it was engaged in piercing the corporate veil: under the terms of NAFTA, the Tribunal understood its task as being to consider the effects of change of ownership 'not by inapt analogies with private law rules, but from the words of Chapter 11, read in the context of the Treaty as a whole, and of the purpose which it sets out to achieve'.[101] Thus, as the *Loewen* Tribunal put it, because NAFTA looks to substance over form, and the substance was that the original claimant's 'assets and business ... have been reorganized under the mantle of an American corporation',[102] the exercise was not piercing but applying the treaty to the facts.

The *Tokios* majority also briefly addressed Ukraine's argument that the origin of the **5.58** capital used was Ukrainian.[103] As noted above, this argument is the centrepiece of Weil's Dissenting Opinion. It would undoubtedly have been useful to the further development of the law on interpreting the ICSID Convention had the *Tokios* majority directly considered (and rebutted) the origin-of-capital points made by Weil. Instead, the *Tokios* decision simply reports that the ICSID Convention contains no jurisdictional requirement that the origin of capital be non-domestic.

Weil's Dissenting Opinion: the origin of capital approach

Weil's Dissenting Opinion identifies no express ICSID requirement in relation to **5.59** the origin of capital. However, Weil's position was that the object and purpose of

---

[96] NAFTA (Appendix 1 below).
[97] The *Tokios* decision fails to note the significance placed by the *Loewen* Tribunal on interpreting NAFTA to reach its decision on continuous nationality (*Tokios* (n 5 above) 229). See *Loewen* (n 6 above) 485–489.   [98] *Tokios* (n 5 above) 229.
[99] *Tokios* (n 5 above) 229.   [100] *Loewen* (n 6 above) 485–488.
[101] *Loewen* (n 6 above) 488.   [102] *Loewen* (n 6 above) 489.
[103] *Tokios* (n 5 above) 235–236.

the ICSID Convention—as explicitly set out in the Preamble to the Convention and the Report of the Executive Directors[104]—made the origin of capital a highly relevant issue:

> The ICSID mechanism and remedy are not meant for investments made in a State by its own citizens with domestic capital through the channel of a foreign entity, whether pre-existent or created for that purpose. To maintain, as the Decision does, that 'the origin of capital is not relevant' and that 'the only relevant consideration is whether the Claimant is established under the laws of Lithuania' [footnotes omitted] runs counter to the object and purpose of the whole ICSID system.[105]

5.60 The dissent further observed that the *Tokios* majority had been unsystematic in its analysis of jurisdiction as between the Convention and the BIT.[106] In particular, the *Tokios* decision reversed the proper order of analysis: the majority should first have considered whether the Tribunal had jurisdiction under Article 25 of the Convention, and only after that assessed jurisdiction under the BIT, in keeping with the ICSID principle that parties to a BIT can narrow but not expand the jurisdiction provided by the Convention. The majority, however, worked from the opposite direction, emphasizing its deference to the parties' treatment of corporate nationality in the BIT.[107] Again, it would have been useful had the majority actually engaged this critique of Weil, which appears persuasive on its face. The absence of dialogue between the majority and the dissent is unsatisfactory and contrary to the approach of other tribunals and, of course, many national courts. The absence is particularly unfortunate in a field in which each tribunal award or decision is treated as being worthy of consideration as a source of public international law, even though it carries no precedential authority.

5.61 Weil also identifies the majority's unfortunate excursion into the realm of 'piercing'. Weil opines that 'piercing' is wholly irrelevant to the jurisdictional assessment that needs to be made. The issue is not whether Tokios, the claimant, has somehow acted improperly or unfairly taken advantage of the corporate form. Rather, the issue is whether, as a matter of substance, the original capital is domestic. If it is, then, in Weil's view, as a matter of public international law and the ICSID Convention the claimant is not entitled to investment protection under the BIT.[108]

5.62 The concluding section of the Dissenting Opinion raises a policy point: are tribunals meant to scrutinize the claimant's legal structure and determine whether there is a hidden 'reality' carrying jurisdictional consequences? The answer is not

---

[104] World Bank, 'Report of the Executive Directors on the Convention on the Settlement of Investment Disputes between States and Nationals of Other States, 1965' 1 ICSID Rep 23.
[105] *Tokios Tokelės v Ukraine* (Dissenting Opinion of Weil P) (2005) 20 ICSID Rev-FILJ 205, 246; 252–253 (ICSID, 2004, Weil P, Bernardini & Price).   [106] ibid 250.
[107] ibid 249–250.   [108] ibid 253–256.

clear. Weil appears to endorse a 'flexible approach' while observing that the task of determining the origin of capital may be clear cut, as in the present case, and even if not, is no more complex than other jurisdictional issues such as the identification of the relevant corporation within a group of corporations for ICSID jurisdiction.[109]

One potential risk of the Dissenting Opinion's support for a 'flexible approach' is   **5.63** that it might encourage States to insist on investigatory opportunities at the jurisdictional stage which could also threaten the efficient workings of the ICSID arbitration system. There is a reason why public international lawyers as well as private international lawyers prefer bright-line tests such as that applied by the *Tokios* majority: such tests provide predictability and therefore stability. In this, investors are of course in accord: they are more likely to contribute capital to a venture if they are confident of a reasonable level of protection. Weil's origin of capital test is more likely to place protection at risk than would the bright-line place of incorporation test. Indeed, the flexible approach could well lead to the need for the tribunal to make difficult assessments regarding the nationality status of the claimant corporation. For example, the shareholders could, by nationality, be widely dispersed, or the shares could be held by legal entities incorporated in turn in one or more third States with the majority of shares being held by nationals of the respondent State. Alternatively, the shareholders of the respondent State could exert certain aspects of control over the claimant corporation even though they are not majority owners.

B. *Loewen* and 'Continuous Nationality'

Is it a principle of international investment law—either as a matter of customary   **5.64** international law or pursuant to interpretation of a particular treaty—that a claimant's nationality must remain unchanged 'from the date of the events giving rise to the claim, which date is known as the *dies a quo*, through the date of the resolution of the claim, which date is known as the *dies ad quem*'?[110] The *Loewen* Tribunal answered this question in the affirmative, and therefore determined, as discussed above, that the jurisdictional objection of the State was accepted. Leaving aside the issue of 'piercing' or whether, as a factual matter, the *Loewen* Tribunal was correct in determining that the claimant's nationality was not continuous, one needs to assess whether the Tribunal was nonetheless right to apply

---

[109] ibid 256–257.
[110] *The Loewen Group Inc and Raymond L Loewen v United States of America* (Award) 7 ICSID Rep 421, 485 (n 6 above).

its version of the 'continuous nationality' principle. On what basis did the *Loewen* Tribunal discern the existence of this version of the principle?

5.65 The *Loewen* Tribunal stated that continuous nationality was a requirement both as a matter of 'historical and current international precedent'.[111] It noted that the NAFTA Treaty provided for nationality requirements at the beginning date of the claim, but was silent on 'the question of whether nationality must continue to the time of resolution of the claim'. That silence required the application of customary international law to resolve the matter. As a historical matter, the Tribunal explained, there was only limited dispute as to the requirement of continuous nationality. When governments dealt directly with each other on investment claims, it was clear that nationality had to be continuous; if there were a break in the chain, then the home government no longer had a citizen to protect. However, as private claimants began to pursue their own claims under investment treaties, 'provision has been made for amelioration of the strict requirement of continuous nationality'. The Tribunal emphasized that because such provisions were 'specifically spelled out' in various treaties (including, for example, the Iran-US claims settlement agreement pursuant to the Algiers Accords and many BITs), NAFTA's silence on the point spoke volumes. The contracting states were content to rely on the customary international law rule.[112]

5.66 The *Loewen* Tribunal then sought to explain at some length, as discussed above, that under domestic law it might be highly unusual for a vested claim to cease to exist because of, for example, insolvency or the change of a claimant's identity. However, private law is not international law: 'NAFTA claims have a quite different character, stemming from a corner of public international law in which, by treaty, the power of States under that law to take international measures for the correction of wrongs done to its nationals has been replaced by an ad hoc definition of certain kinds of wrong, coupled with specialist means of compensation.'[113]

5.67 Because rules derived from private law cannot simply be transferred into the international law of investment protection, the tribunal sought to consider NAFTA's purpose and language as a whole. In doing so, the ICSID Convention's nationality provisions were not relevant, nor was the ILC's report proposing to eliminate the continuous nationality rule (a report that was 'met with criticism in many quarters and from many points of view').[114] What was relevant was NAFTA's purpose to protect a foreign (in this case a Canadian) investor. As a substantive matter, the claim, following the bankruptcy of the Canadian claimant, would only inure to the

---

[111] ibid 485.   [112] ibid 485–487.   [113] ibid 488.   [114] ibid 488–489.

benefit of a US corporation. Accordingly, the continuous nationality rule applied and the claim therefore failed.[115]

Many aspects of the *Loewen* award have been subject to intense scrutiny and crit-   **5.68**
icism by the community of international law scholars and investment arbitration practitioners.[116] But one might immediately note the troublingly cursory treatment of customary international law provided by the *Loewen* Tribunal on the continuous nationality rule. The *Loewen* Tribunal may not have deserved the criticism by the *Tokios* majority of its 'piercing' approach, discussed above. However, one may well have concerns about the application of a customary international law rule that the Tribunal appears to acknowledge has little relevance to circumstances where private claimants, under investment protection treaties, directly pursue private claims. In this, there is a curious linkage between the *Loewen* and *Tokios* tribunals: they both refuse to import language into a treaty; they both purport to rely on a customary international law rule that has not been adopted in many other treaties; and they both remark on the significance of the silence of the respective treaties that they interpret in permitting them—or requiring them—to find that the hoary international law rule shall be applied. It is an irony that, in the case of *Loewen*, this approach leads to a restriction on jurisdiction whereas in the case of *Tokios* the approach led to an expansion of jurisdiction. In neither case did the Tribunal appear particularly interested in considering whether the customary international law rule that it decided to apply had been rendered ineffective because of the many investment protection treaties that expressly pointed to a different approach to the nationality question. In short, in certain respects that are fundamental to the interpretation of principles of international investment arbitration, the reasoning of the two tribunals is dismayingly similar, whatever one's view may be of the outcomes of the jurisdictional challenges.

Under the ICSID Convention and the US and Canada model BITs, continuous   **5.69**
nationality through to the date of resolution of the claim does not appear to be a requirement, at least in the strict sense as described by the *Loewen* Tribunal.[117] NAFTA itself should not be regarded as silent on the matter of the dates relevant to nationality, since nationality at the date of submission of the claim is expressly

---

[115] ibid 489.
[116] See, notably, M Mendelson, 'The Runaway Train: the "Continuous Nationality Rule" From the *Panevezys-saldutiskis Railway* case to *Loewen*' in T Weiler (ed), *International Investment Law and Arbitration; Leading Cases from the ICSID, NAFTA, Bilateral Treaties and Customary International Law* (2005). See also J Paulsson, *Denial of Justice in International Law* (2005) 183–184, and his 'Continuous Nationality in *Loewen*' (2004) 20 Arb Int'l 213, and E Gaillard, 'Centre International pour le Reglement des Differends relatifs aux Investissements (CIRDI): Chronique des Sentences Arbitrales' [2004] Journal du Droit International 213, 230–233.
[117] A point made by Mendelson (ibid) 134.

provided for.[118] Mendelson further criticizes the tribunal's treatment of customary international law as follows:

> The Tribunal's attempt to use these and other treaties as the basis for an *a contrario* argument to the effect that, because the NAFTA does not contain specific provisions modifying the continuous nationality rule, the (supposed) customary rule must apply, might have been more convincing if it had satisfactorily established that the extended version of the rule *was* an established principle of customary law—which, for the reasons provided above, it could not and in any event did not convincingly do. Nor did it explain why a rule developed in one context (diplomatic protection) necessarily carried over into another area (investor claims). It did not even cite a single authority in support of any of its propositions.[119]

5.70 Thus, the *Loewen* Tribunal's explication of the customary international law principle of continuous nationality must be regarded as too strict and unsupported. Further, the Tribunal's approach to the interpretation of NAFTA must, at least in this respect, be considered questionable, although as the tribunal in *EnCana v Ecuador*[120] commented, there is in NAFTA at least an 'apparent co-mingling of diplomatic protection concepts with investor-State claims (see, for example, Article 1136(5))'.[121] In international investment arbitration, continuous nationality, if not specifically defined by the relevant treaty, probably should not be taken to mean anything more than continuous nationality from the date of injury to the date of submission of the claim.

5.71 A further revealing perspective on *Loewen*'s approach to customary international law and diplomatic protection is provided by the ILC's draft Articles 5 and 10, and Commentary, on Diplomatic Protection. The ILC firmly stated that it was not prepared to follow the *Loewen* Tribunal 'in adopting a blanket rule that nationality must be maintained to the date of resolution of the claim'[122] (regarding draft Article 5, natural persons). Instead, the ILC preferred 'the date of the official presentation of the claim as the *dies ad quem*'.[123] The same principle is applied to corporations by the ILC.[124] The draft articles on Diplomatic Protection, combined with the point on interpretation of NAFTA made in *EnCana* (see para 5.70 above), thus provide a complete answer to—and rejection of—the *Loewen* Tribunal's position on continuous nationality.

---

[118] NAFTA (Appendix 1 below) Arts 1116, 1117.

[119] Mendelson (n 116 above) 141.

[120] *EnCana Corp v Republic of Ecuador* (Award) LCIA Case No UN3481 (LCIA/UNCITRAL, 2006, Crawford P, Grigera Naón & Thomas).

[121] ibid para 128. In fn 84, the Tribunal observed that 'According to the ILC's Draft Articles on Diplomatic Protection (as adopted on first reading), art 5, the critical date in relation to the espousal of a claim by way of diplomatic protection by the national State is the "date of the official presentation of the claim".'

[122] ILC, 'Draft Articles on Diplomatic Protection with Commentaries' (n 8 above) 37–38.

[123] ibid 38.

[124] ibid 56.

C. *AdT* and the Issue of 'Control'

Restructured corporate holdings: 'legal' or 'factual' control?

In *AdT*[125] the jurisdictional point before the ICSID Tribunal was whether, in the **5.72**
context of the respondent State's contention that it had structured a concession
agreement to preclude ICSID jurisdiction, changes to the control structure of the
claimant company at the time of the dispute, leading to the claimant's assertion of
jurisdiction under the Netherlands-Bolivia BIT,[126] would be recognized as valid
for the purposes of maintaining the claim. The Tribunal held that it had jurisdiction under the Netherlands-Bolivia BIT invoked by the claimant. This was, however, another split tribunal.[127]

The claimant company, Aguas del Tunari SA (AdT), was incorporated in Bolivia. **5.73**
It had entered into a concession agreement in September 1999, and claimed that
through Bolivia's acts and omissions regarding this concession, which had ceased
to be effective in 2000, Bolivia had breached the Netherlands-Bolivia BIT.

At the time the concession agreement was entered into, AdT's shares were owned **5.74**
by a combination of Bolivian companies (20 per cent), a Uruguayan company (25
per cent), and a Cayman Islands company, International Water (55 per cent),
which itself was 100 per cent owned by Bechtel, a US company. Some months
later (the factual background was disputed by the parties), but prior to the termination of the concession, it was at least clear that the Cayman Islands company
had 'migrated' to Luxembourg, and it became 100 per cent owned by a Dutch
company, though Bolivia contended that the Dutch companies (more than one
was involved in the complex restructuring) were mere shells.[128]

Both Bolivia and the Netherlands are parties to the ICSID Convention. The **5.75**
claimant asserted jurisdiction under Article 9(6) of the Netherlands-Bolivia BIT,
which provides that if both contracting parties have acceded to ICSID, 'any disputes that may arise from investment between one of the Contracting Parties and
a national of the other Contracting Party' shall be submitted to ICSID for resolution.[129] The claimant asserted that it was a national of the Netherlands under

---

[125] *Aguas del Tunari SA [AdT] v Republic of Bolivia* (Jurisdiction) (2005) (n 7 above).
[126] Agreement on Encouragement and Reciprocal Protection of Investments (Netherlands-
Bolivia) (signed 10 March 1992, entered into force 1 November 1994) Tractatenblad 1992, 081.
[127] Caron, P, Alberro-Semerena & Alvarez; Alberro-Semerena filed a Dissenting Declaration.
[128] *AdT* (n 7 above) 470–475.
[129] Netherlands-Bolivia BIT (n 126 above). *AdT* (n 7 above) 476–477. As the Tribunal commented: 'The Netherlands-Bolivia BIT, like the ICSID Convention and the majority of BITs, recognizes that the investor of one of the State Parties may incorporate an entity in the other State Party
as a vehicle for its investment activity. Indeed, it is by no means uncommon practice that foreign
investors may be required to incorporate locally by the host State' (*AdT* (n 7 above) 515).

Article 1(b) of the BIT: '(iii) legal persons controlled directly or indirectly, by nationals of that Contracting Party, but constituted in accordance with the law of the other Contracting Party'.[130]

5.76 In particular, AdT identified itself as a national of Bolivia, 'controlled directly or indirectly' by nationals of the Netherlands. Bolivia countered, *inter alia*, with the argument (Bolivia's 'Second Objection') that AdT was not a national of the Netherlands under the BIT, as it was not 'controlled directly or indirectly' by nationals of the Netherlands.[131]

5.77 This jurisdictional dispute required the Tribunal to choose between two competing approaches to the BIT term 'controlled'. On the one hand, the Tribunal could equate control with ownership (or the legal potential to control)—the claimant's position, as the Dutch companies, through their ownership of the Luxembourg company and its majority shareholding in the claimant, could be said to control the claimant. Alternatively, the tribunal could assess the matter more contextually, requiring real or ultimate control—the State's position, as it suggested that if the Dutch companies were mere shells of other corporate owners, they could not be considered to control the claimant.[132] In short, as the Tribunal put it: 'the difference in view between the Parties is not between 'control' and 'ownership', but rather between 'control' as requiring the legal potential to control [claimant] and 'control' as requiring the actual exercise of control [state]'.[133]

The majority approach: legal control

5.78 The Tribunal proceeded to address applicable substantive law, and in this viewed the BIT as determinative, with jurisdiction under the BIT being limited by the jurisdictional provisions of the ICSID Convention.[134] The applicable law for interpreting the BIT was to be found in customary international law, as codified in Articles 31 to 32 of the Vienna Convention on the Law of Treaties (VCLT).[135] Accordingly, the Tribunal determined that it would start with the ordinary meaning of the terms of the BIT, in their context and in light of the treaty's object and purpose. The Tribunal specifically noted that the BIT was not to be construed narrowly. Rather, the task was instead to find the intent of the parties in the specific instrument, taking into account the fact that the parties had used the BIT to address 'issues of mutual concern in innovative ways', and not to seek to tie the specific aims of the BIT to 'general assumptions about the intent of States, assumptions which necessarily are based on assessments of past practice'.[136] The Tribunal

---

[130] *AdT* (n 7 above) 477.　　[131] ibid 478.
[132] ibid 517–518.　　[133] ibid 518.
[134] ibid 478.
[135] ibid 478–479. Vienna Convention on the Law of Treaties (signed 23 May 1969, entered into force 27 January 1980) 1155 UNTS 331 ('VCLT') discussed at 3.66–3.78 above.
[136] *AdT* (n 7 above) 480–481.

thus proceeded to engage in an extensive and intensive examination of 'controlled directly or indirectly', considering first the meaning of the words of the text (Article 31 of the VCLT), secondly confirming the resulting interpretation in accordance with Article 32 of the VCLT (looking to background circumstances when the meaning of the words themselves are ambiguous or would lead to an absurd or unreasonable result), and thirdly applying the interpretation to the specific case at hand.[137]

The Tribunal majority concluded that the phrase 'controlled directly or indirectly' **5.79** referred to legal capacity rather than fact.[138] The Tribunal started from the ordinary meaning of the phrase. This included considering the grammatical point that ' "controlled" is the past participle of the transitive verb "control" ',[139] and research-ing standard desk dictionaries for definitions.[140] The respondent had raised what it contended were four tests under international law for defining corporate national-ity and advanced the idea that the 'control' test (as opposed to, for example, the cor-porate seat test or the predominant interest test) was favoured by States in order to 'focus on the reality behind the corporate personality' and to 'avoid inequitable results'.[141] However, the Tribunal determined that the record disclosed no special meaning for control as used by the contracting parties: 'Nor should such intent be assumed since the Tribunal finds the contexts of foreign investment protection and the regulation of corporate activity to be sufficiently distinct.'[142]

The tribunal majority's textual analysis led it to agree with the claimant that the **5.80** phrase 'creates the possibility of there simultaneously being a direct controller and one or more indirect controllers. The BIT does not limit the scope of eligible claimants to only the "ultimate controller" '.[143] However, that still left the question of whether any controller, indirect or direct, had to exercise actual control. To assess this point, the Tribunal focused on the object and purpose of the BIT, as stated in the preamble to be to 'stimulate the flow of capital and technology', based on 'agreement upon the treatment' to be accorded to investments by nationals of one contracting party in the territory of the other contracting party.[144] The Tribunal majority further observed that the nationality definition in the BIT was intended in part to define 'the scope of eligible claimants' (and not just the persons and entities to be accorded substantive rights under the BIT).[145] Given this background, 'controlled' indicated a quality of ownership interest (control in the absence of an ownership interest might not qualify jurisdictionally), and the question then became how 'controlled' was meant to qualify 'ownership'.[146] Again, the majority accepted the claimant's view, in this instance that 'control' 'is a quality that accompanies ownership'.[147] The majority

---

[137] ibid 481.   [138] ibid 533.
[139] ibid 519.   [140] ibid 519–520.
[141] ibid 522–523.   [142] ibid 523 (fn omitted).
[143] ibid 523.
[144] Netherlands-Bolivia BIT (n 126 above) Preamble; *AdT* (n 7 above) 524–525.
[145] *AdT* (n 7 above) 525.   [146] ibid 525.
[147] ibid 525–526.

was not troubled by the elevation of corporate formality in this respect (in the same way as the majority in *Tokios* was untroubled by the reliance on corporate formality). The majority approvingly quoted the *Aucoven* Tribunal (albeit in the different context of interpreting Article 25 of the ICSID Convention) as saying: 'this formality is the fundamental building block of the global economy'.[148] These determinations, it should be noted, were not principally or even apparently driven by any clear concepts of international law, apart from following the very broad precepts of interpretation laid down in the VCLT. The majority found that the negotiating history of the BIT, jurisprudence regarding Article 25(2) of the ICSID Convention,[149] the holdings of other arbitral awards concerning 'control', and the BIT practice generally of the Netherlands and Bolivia did not alter its conclusions—and actually provided little assistance in any respect.[150]

5.81 The commercial implications of the tribunal majority's decision are highly significant. In effect, corporations or rather corporate chains can be restructured[151] so as to claim direct or indirect control by companies in several jurisdictions that may have favourable (for investors) BITs with a host State. Is this a desirable consequence? That is a question of policy, as well as international law and treaty drafters may well be attentive to it when BITs are negotiated (or renegotiated when the initial termination period is reached).

5.82 Even if some States have reacted with undue alarm to a few awards requiring the payment of significant sums to investors, there can be little doubt that the very real possibility of 'treaty forum shopping' by investors, as permitted by international law, will cause more than a few States—and not merely those which are commonly thought of as capital-importing States—to reconsider the renewal (at least in current form) of their network of BITs. In this regard it should be noted that under Article 24(1)(b) of the 2004 US model BIT,[152] the class of potential claimants includes 'the claimant, on behalf of an enterprise of the respondent that is a juridical person that the claimant owns or controls directly or indirectly',[153] suggesting that control will have to be actual or functional, on which see the dissenting declaration in *AdT* (discussed at 5.83 to 5.87 below).

---

[148] *AdT* (n 7 above) 526 fn 218; *Autopista Concesionada de Venezuela CA v Bolivarian Republic of Venezuela* (Jurisdiction) 6 ICSID 417, 432 (ICSID, 2001, Kaufmann-Kohler P, Böckstiegel & Cremades) ('*Aucoven*').   [149] ICSID Convention (Appendix 11 below).

[150] *AdT* (n 7 above) 533–547.

[151] However, the timing of the restructuring may be an issue to be taken into account, depending on whether nationality must be established at the date of injury or the date of submission of the claim—and whether it must be maintained continuously through to the issuance of the award. See the discussion of the *Loewen* award at 5.64–5.71, above.

[152] 2004 US model BIT (Appendix 6 below).

[153] On the question of dual nationality, the 2004 US model BIT (Appendix 6 below) Art 1 specifies that 'a natural person who is a dual national shall be deemed to be exclusively a national of the State of his or her dominant and effective nationality'.

Alberro-Semerena's dissent: a functional definition of control

As in the case of *Tokios*, the Dissenting Declaration in *AdT* is of substantial inter- **5.83**
est and importance both in clarifying the international law points of difference
between eminent arbitrators and scholars and in indicating, again, the minority
position of those who favour a 'flexible' jurisdictional approach (at least on the
issue of nationality) as opposed to more formal or bright-line tests. The context
for the dissent of Alberro-Semerena was his concern that if AdT could restructure
itself while the State engaged in a course of action that breached AdT's rights, 'the
balance between the benefits and obligation of the host State is broken since the
latter become unpredictable'.[154]

Further, on the particular issue of the meaning of 'controlled', the Dissenting **5.84**
Declaration found, as a matter of grammar, that for jurisdiction to exist, 'Claimant
has to prove that AdT received the effect of actions by Dutch companies'.[155]
Considered in the context of the object and purpose of the BIT, 'the access mechanism to the privileges concomitant to Article 1(b)(iii) [providing for investment
protection] should be an actual event, an action (controlled) and not a possibility'.[156] The Dissenting Declaration agreed with the majority that ICSID jurisprudence and other arbitral awards and the BIT practices of the parties could not assist
in interpreting Article 1(b)(iii).[157] However, Alberro-Semerena commented:
'Many cases underline the importance of the Tribunal's authority to interpret
access provisions past formal interpretations to actual relationships.'[158] The dissent
found support for this proposition in international law, pursuant to which a corporate nationality test had been difficult to fashion over the past century; accordingly, a 'mechanistic interpretation' should be rejected, and an 'interpretation that
favors an action is in keeping with the search for a functional definition'.[159]

The Dissenting Declaration made the point that previous tribunal awards in **5.85**
which an investor with minority share ownership was found to control a company
cast doubt on the proposition that majority share ownership was sufficient to
establish control, and the majority's position was therefore 'logically inconsistent'.[160] Without evidence to demonstrate that AdT received the effects of actions
of control from Dutch nationals, the dissent's position was that the dispute had
not been shown to be within the jurisdictional reach of the BIT.[161]

---

[154] *Aguas del Tunari SA v Republic of Bolivia* (Dissenting Declaration of Alberro-Semerena)
(2005) 20 ICSID Rev-FILJ 450, 556 (ICSID, 2005, Alberro-Semerena).

[155] ibid 559–560.   [156] ibid 561.   [157] ibid 561.

[158] ibid 561. The dissent relied in particular on *Banro American Resources Inc and Société Aurifère
du Kivu et du Maniema SARL v Democratic Republic of the Congo* (Award) ICSID Case No ARB/98/7
(ICSID, 2000, Weil P, Geach & Diagne) from which it quoted as follows: 'ICSID Tribunals do not
accept the view that their competence is limited by formalities, and rather they rule on their competence based on a review of the circumstances surrounding the case, and, in particular, the actual relationships among the companies involved.'   [159] ibid 561–562.

[160] ibid 562–563.   [161] ibid 564.

5.86 Many aspects of the Dissenting Declaration in *AdT* are familiar in view of the above discussion of *Tokios*. Like Weil, Alberro-Semerena sought to examine actual relationships rather than formal structures, in an effort to preserve the integrity of investment arbitration in general and ICSID arbitration in particular. Like Weil, he was able to adduce support for this approach from certain other scholars and awards, and to refer to an international law history that was at best uncertain and did not preclude a flexible approach designed to reveal actual relationships. Moreover, it is a matter of some frustration that the majority in *AdT* like the majority in *Tokios* did not directly engage and reply to the points raised in the dissenting opinion. It would have been useful to have had a reply to the dissent's invocation of *Banro*[162] and to its assertion of a logical inconsistency in the conclusion that majority shareholding and majority voting rights per se constitute control when minority share ownership has also been found to constitute control. The majority would undoubtedly have pointed to its position that there can be many 'controllers', and jurisdiction is not limited to the 'ultimate' controller, but this still leaves some analysis to be completed and might well have led—ideally—to a more systematic formulation of a claimant's burden in proving control.

5.87 Perhaps the most striking similarity between the *AdT* and *Tokios* dissents is that while they clearly do not at present form part of the development of substantive principles of international investment arbitration, they nonetheless stand as a plausible source of international law scholarship. Such scholarship, in the absence of a system of precedent, may be relied on by future tribunals and could contribute to the reshaping of the international law landscape even as the contours of that landscape are being drawn. The 'flexible approach' to piercing and to 'indirect control' has by no means been consigned to the dustbin of international law.

4. Conclusion

5.88 To assess the nationality prerequisite to an investment claim, the following series of short propositions should be considered as the framework for analysis, in view of recent cases, treaties, and the 2006 ILC draft Articles (and commentary) on Diplomatic Protection:

  (1) The starting point for analysis is the express provision (if any) on nationality in the BIT (or MIT) that is the foundation of the foreign investor's claim:
   • Paragraphs 5.22 to 5.42 above provide examples of such express provisions.

---

[162] *Banro* (n 158 above).

(2) In instances where the ICSID Convention is applicable to the claim, (paras 5.43 to 5.44 above) Article 25(2)(b):

- pursuant to *Tokios*, serves as a further jurisdictional test, by which the classical 'formal' requirement (ie attributing corporate nationality to the State of incorporation) is the preferred approach, as opposed to an 'origin of capital' approach.

(3) In determining a claimant's nationality, the claimant's putative home State provides the legal determination that is to be accepted (pursuant to the 1930 Hague Convention), 'in so far as it is consistent with international conventions, international custom, and the principles of law generally recognised with regard to nationality':

- thus, in the context of an investment treaty claim, the home State's law may be said to provide a powerful, though rebuttable, presumption regarding the claimant's nationality.

(4) The nationality of a natural person-claimant is generally conclusively determined by the home State's citizenship laws:

- it is usually the case that the natural person must possess home State citizenship continuously from the date of injury to the date of official commencement of the arbitration request;
- dual nationality (ie the natural person is a national of both the home and host States) may preclude the maintenance of a claim (see Article 25(2)(b) of the ICSID Convention); in the event that it does not, it is generally the case that a 'predominant' connection test will be applied:

(5) In the case of corporate nationality, a 'formal' State of incorporation test (the *Tokios* majority) usually applies, unless the relevant BIT or MIT provides otherwise:

- in limited and extreme instances where the corporation is controlled by nationals of another State and the corporation has no substantial business activities and no management seat in the State of incorporation, the corporation may be regarded as the national of the State where control and management are located;
- it is usually the case that the corporation must possess home State nationality continuously from the date of injury to the date of official commencement of the arbitration request;
- the nationality of the corporation's shareholders will not be regarded as the nationality of the corporation unless the corporation has ceased to exist pursuant to the law of the State of incorporation or the corporation had the nationality of the host State at the date of injury and (a) the host State is alleged to be responsible for the injury, and (b) incorporation in the host State was required by it as a precondition for doing business there (Article 11, ILC draft Articles on Diplomatic Protection);

- the nationality of the shareholders will further be relevant in the event that they claim direct injury to their rights as opposed to injury to the corporation itself.

(6) Where an investment treaty extends its protections to legal persons controlled directly or indirectly by nationals of one Contracting Party but constituted in accordance with the law of the other Contracting Party, it is necessary to determine whether 'control' is sufficiently established by formal ownership or whether ultimate substantive control is required. The current majority view is that formal ownership is sufficient, so that any corporate vehicle that owns directly or indirectly the investment company may qualify, if it is a national of a Contracting Party (*AdT* majority). But this view cannot be regarded as settled in view of the cogent arguments advanced *a contrario* (*AdT* minority).

6

INVESTMENT

A. Introduction

In recent years, the question of what constitutes an investment has become increas- **6.01** ingly important as a threshold jurisdictional question in treaty arbitration.[1] Tribunals often need to consider the definition of 'investment' under two instruments:

(1) the investment treaty; and
(2) Article 25 of the ICSID Convention.[2]

---

[1] For a thorough treatment of this subject, see N Rubins, 'The Notion of "Investment" in International Investment Arbitrations' in N Horn (ed), *Arbitrating Foreign Investment Disputes* (2003) 292.
[2] Convention on the Settlement of Investment Disputes between States and Nationals of Other States (signed 18 March 1965, entered into force 14 October 1966) 575 UNTS 159 ('ICSID Convention') (Appendix 11 below) Art 25.

6.02   While the ICSID definition is of course only relevant in ICSID arbitrations, many of the awards and writings dealing with Article 25 of the ICSID Convention are relevant for a consideration of the definition of investment under other investment treaties. Similarly, the approaches taken by tribunals considering the issue under bilateral investment treaties (BITs) have relevance for the consideration of investment in the ICSID context.

6.03   In this chapter, the issue is analysed in two sections:

(1) the definition of 'investment' in treaties; and
(2) the role played by arbitral tribunals in building upon treaty definitions in relation to specific property interests.

B. Definition of 'Investment' under Treaties

Under the ICSID Convention

6.04   Article 25 of the ICSID Convention[3] limits the Centre's jurisdiction to legal disputes arising 'directly out of an investment'. No definition of this central term is offered. The Report of the Executive Directors explains this lack of further clarification by saying: 'No attempt was made to define the term "investment" given the essential requirements of consent by the parties, and the mechanisms through which Contracting States can make known in advance, if they so desire, the classes of disputes which they would or would not consider submitting to the Centre (Article 25(4)).'[4]

6.05   As Schreuer points out, this statement of the position is historically inaccurate. Schreuer explains how a number of differing views relating to the definition of 'investment' were discussed, but no resolution was reached.[5] The absence of any clarification in the ICSID Convention means that, within a wide area of discretion, the parameters of what constitutes an investment fall to be supplied by the parties' consent and ultimately by tribunals.

6.06   The importance of Article 25 of the ICSID Convention in ICSID arbitrations is that it places a limit upon the parties' ability to consent to ICSID jurisdiction, whether that consent be expressed in a concession agreement or in a treaty. While the word 'investment' in Article 25 has been construed widely, it is not without limits, as the discussion in this chapter will show. Schreuer helpfully lists the

---

[3] Appendix 11 below.
[4] World Bank, 'Report of the Executive Directors on the Convention on the Settlement of Investment Disputes between States and Nationals of Other States, 1965' 1 ICSID Rep 23, 28.
[5] C Schreuer, *The ICSID Convention: A Commentary* (2001), 121–125, especially at 124.

various areas of economic activity that have come before ICSID tribunals as including:

> ... the building and operation of hotels, the production of fibres and textiles, the mining of minerals, the construction of a hospital ward, the exploration, exploitation and distribution of petroleum products, the manufacture of plastic bottles, the construction and operation of a fertilizer factory, the construction of housing units, the operation of a cotton mill, aluminium smelter, forestry, the conversion, equipping and operation of fishing vessels, the production of weapons, tourism resort projects, maritime transport of minerals, a synthetic fuels project, shrimp farming, banking, agricultural activities, the construction of a cable TV system and the provision of loans.[6]

Schreuer drew up this list in 2001. Since then, the categories of covered economic **6.07** activities have continued to increase. Yet certain activities which would as easily fall into these categories have also been excluded, such as the provision of guarantees,[7] power generation,[8] telecommunications licensing,[9] and consumer banking.[10] This indicates that the key issue is not the area of economic activity covered, but the form and nature of that activity. Certain criteria have been developed in the case law, and applied consistently thereafter.

The earliest award to consider the meaning of 'investment' in depth is *Fedax NV v* **6.08** *Republic of Venezuela*.[11] Fedax, a company claiming under the Netherlands-Venezuela BIT,[12] was the beneficiary, by way of endorsement, of debt instruments issued by Venezuela. Thus Fedax had not come into possession of the promissory notes as a result of any relationship with Venezuela, or any direct investment made in its territory. Venezuela argued that Fedax's holding of the promissory notes in question did not qualify as an investment because Fedax had not made a direct foreign investment involving a long-term transfer of financial resources. The Tribunal rejected this position. It adopted an approach based upon an article written by Schreuer to the effect that: 'The basic features of an investment have been described as involving a certain duration, a certain regularity of profit and return, assumption of risk, a substantial commitment and a significance for the host State's development.'[13]

---

[6] ibid 138.

[7] *Joy Mining Machinery Ltd v Arab Republic of Egypt* (Jurisdiction) (2004) 19 ICSID Rev-FILJ 486 (ICSID, 2004, Orrego Vicuña P, Weeramantry & Craig).

[8] *Mihaly International Corp v Republic of Sri Lanka* (Award) 6 ICSID Rep 308 (ICSID, 2002, Sucharitkul P, Rogers & Suratgar).

[9] *William Nagel v Czech Republic* (Award) SCC Case 49/2002 (SCC, 2003).

[10] *Genin, Eastern Credit Ltd Inc and AS Baltoil v Republic of Estonia* (Award) 6 ICSID Rep 236 (ICSID, 2001, Fortier P, Heth & van den Berg).

[11] *Fedax NV v Republic of Venezuela* (Jurisdiction) 5 ICSID Rep 183 (ICSID, 1997, Orrego Vicuña P, Heth & Owen).

[12] Agreement on Encouragement and Reciprocal Protection of Investments (Netherlands-Venezuela) (signed 22 October 1991, entered into force 1 November 1993) Tractatenblad 1993, 154.

[13] *Fedax* (n 11 above) 199; C Schreuer, 'Commentary on the ICSID Convention' (1996) 11 ICSID Rev-FILJ 316, 372.

6.09 The Tribunal considered the status of the promissory notes under Venezuelan law and concluded that they met the basic features of an investment. In particular, they pointed out the 'significant relationship' between the transaction and the host State's development.[14]

6.10 Another objection raised by Venezuela was that the dispute did not arise 'directly out of an investment' because the disputed transaction was not a direct foreign investment. However, the Tribunal found that the term 'directly' relates to the 'dispute' and not to the 'investment'. Accordingly, jurisdiction can exist even in respect of investments that are not made directly into the host State's economy, so long as the dispute arises directly from the transaction.[15]

6.11 A similar approach was adopted by the Tribunal in *CSOB v Slovakia*.[16] This ICSID case, brought under the Czechoslovakia-Slovakia BIT,[17] arose after the separation of the Slovak and Czech Republics. The claimant bank was privatized and its portfolio of certain non-performing loan receivables was assigned to a so-called 'Collection Company'. The Collection Company was to pay CSOB for the assigned receivables. This payment was guaranteed by an obligation of the Ministry of Finance of the Slovak Republic.

6.12 When a dispute arose, Slovakia contended that it did not arise out of an investment, as CSOB had not undertaken any spending, outlays, or expenditure in the Slovak Republic. As with *Fedax*, the Tribunal rejected this argument. It expressly adopted the *Fedax* approach.[18] Rather than look at the single transaction underlying the dispute, the Tribunal looked at the question more broadly:

> ... the basic and ultimate goal of the Consolidation Agreement was to ensure a continuing and expanding activity of CSOB in both Republics. This undertaking involved a significant contribution by CSOB to the economic development of the Slovak Republic; it qualified CSOB as an investor and the entire process as an investment in the Slovak Republic within the meaning of the [ICSID] Convention ... CSOB's claim and the related loan facility made available to the Slovak Collection Company are closely connected to the development of CSOB's banking activity in the Slovak Republic ...[19]

---

[14] *Fedax* (n 11 above) 199.

[15] *Fedax* (n 11 above) 192. Almost all of the jurisdiction decisions made in the Argentine cases come to the same conclusion on this point, eg *Siemens AG v Argentine Republic* (Jurisdiction) ICSID Case No ARB/02/8 (ICSID, 2004, Sureda P, Brower & Bello Janeiro) para 150; *Metalpar SA & Buen Aire SA v Argentine Republic* (Jurisdiction) ICSID Case No ARB/03/5 (ICSID, 2006, Blanco P, Cameron & Chabaneix) paras 84–93.

[16] *Ceskoslovenska Obchodni Banka AS [CSOB] v Slovak Republic* (Jurisdiction) 5 ICSID Rep 330 (ICSID, 1999, Buergenthal P, Bernardini & Bucher).

[17] Dahoda medzi vládou Slovenskej republiky a vládou Českej republiky o podpore a vzájomnej ochrane investicii ('Agreement Regarding the Promotion and Reciprocal Investments') (signed 23 November 1992, entered into force 1 January 1993) Zbierka zákonov č 231/1993.

[18] *CSOB* (n 16 above) 350–353.   [19] *CSOB* (n 16 above) 356–357.

The Tribunal was thus again looking at the entire concept of what should consti- **6.13** tute an 'investment' rather than narrowly focusing on the particular economic activity giving rise to the dispute.[20]

Similarly, in *Eureko BV v Republic of Poland*[21] the Tribunal had regard to the over- **6.14** all nature of the underlying transaction in concluding that contractual corporate governance rights could constitute an investment under the Netherlands-Poland BIT. While this is not an ICSID case, the reasoning for the Tribunal's conclusion, that 'those rights, critical as they were to the conclusion of the SPA and hence to the making of Eureko's very large investment, do so qualify' would apply equally to a consideration of the issue under Article 25 of the ICSID Convention.

An indication of the consistency on this issue between ICSID tribunals is the **6.15** award in *Joy Mining Machinery Ltd v The Arab Republic of Egypt*.[22] Here the Tribunal denied jurisdiction while adopting a similar approach to the *Fedax* and *CSOB* Tribunals. The claim, brought under the UK-Egypt BIT,[23] related to performance guarantees given by the claimant to an Egyptian State-controlled enterprise. The underlying contract related to the supply (and related activities) of mining equipment. The Tribunal considered the criteria first adopted in *Fedax* and, as the Tribunal had done in *CSOB*, looked at the transaction in its broader context: 'a given element of a complex operation should not be examined in isolation because what matters is to assess the operation globally or as a whole'.[24]

On the basis of this examination, by reference to the *Fedax* criteria, the Tribunal **6.16** found that no investment had been made and thus denied jurisdiction. The Tribunal considered the contract as a whole and listed with some particularity the specific obligations the claimant had undertaken to perform. However, it concluded that the contract amounted to no more than a sales contract on 'normal commercial terms'[25] and this had to be distinguished from investment activity.[26]

There is no inconsistency in one tribunal holding, as in *CSOB v Slovakia*, that a **6.17** guarantee amounts to an investment, where the underlying transaction meets the

---

[20] In *Link-Trading v Department for Customs Control of Republic of Moldova* (Jurisdiction) (UNCITRAL, 2001, Hertzfeld P, Buruiana & Zykin) 8, the tribunal concluded, based only on the broad definition of 'investment' in the USA-Moldova BIT, that debt financing qualified as an 'investment'.

[21] *Eureko BV v Republic of Poland* (Partial Award) (Ad Hoc Arb Trib, 2005, Fortier P, Schwebel & Rajski) para 144.   [22] *Joy Mining* (n 7 above).

[23] Agreement for the Promotion and Protection of Investments (UK-Egypt) (signed 11 June 1975, entered into force 24 February 1976) 1032 UNTS 31.   [24] *Joy Mining* (n 7 above) 500.

[25] *Joy Mining* (n 7 above) 501.

[26] See also *Middle East Cement Shipping and Handling Co SA v Arab Republic of Egypt* (Award) 7 ICSID Rep 173, 204 (ICSID, 2002, Böckstiegel P, Bernardini & Wallace Jr) where the Tribunal concluded that a claim based upon the liquidation of a letter of guarantee fell outside the Greece-Egypt BIT as it was 'a commercial matter'.

criteria, and another tribunal holding, as in *Joy Mining v Egypt*, that it does not. In the latter case the guarantee supported a mere contract of sale.

6.18 In another non-ICSID case, *Franz Sedelmayer v The Russian Federation*,[27] a tribunal constituted under the Germany-Russia BIT[28] found that the project as a whole constituted an investment but rejected those parts of the claim based on premises and belongings used by the investor personally. Mr Sedelmayer had lived in part of a building from which he ran his expropriated business. The building and its contents had been seized by the Russian authorities. The Tribunal concluded that items used by Mr Sedelmayer in his personal capacity 'cannot be considered as being so closely related to [the investment] that they shall be regarded as investments under the Treaty'.[29]

6.19 The duration aspect of the *Fedax* criteria was specifically considered in *Jan de Nul v Egypt*.[30] The investment consisted of a dredging operation in the Suez Canal. While the parties agreed that the magnitude, complexity, and risk profile of the project met the definition of investment, there was a dispute over the significance of the project's duration. Both parties agreed that a two-year duration would be sufficient but Egypt pointed out that a timescale measured from the date of the contract to the date of completion would fall short of two years. The claimant contended that the time it had spent on pre-contractual activities should be taken into consideration. The Tribunal did not decide this point as it held that the 23-month period starting from the contract's signature would suffice.[31]

6.20 The *Fedax* criteria have also been applied in *Consortium RFCC v Kingdom of Morocco*[32] and *Salini Costruttori SPA v Kingdom of Morocco*[33] in support of the idea that large-scale construction contracts can be investments. In *Autopista Concesionada de Venezuela CA v Bolivarian Republic of Venezuela*[34] the respondent State appears not even to have challenged the idea that a contract to design, construct, and maintain two roads was an investment. Yet it is not at all obvious that all civil engineering contracts would amount to an 'investment' being made by the

---

[27] *Franz Sedelmayer v Russian Federation* (Award) (Ad Hoc Arb Trib, 1998, Magnusson P, Wachler & Zykin).

[28] Vertrag über die Förderung und den Gegenseitigen Schutz von Kapitalanlagen ('Agreement concerning the Promotion and Reciprocal Protection of Investments') (Germany-Russia) (signed 13 June 1989, entered into force 5 August 1991) 1707 UNTS 171; 1990 BGBl II 342.

[29] *Sedelmayer* (n 27 above) pt V para 3.4.3.

[30] *Jan de Nul NV & Dredging International NV v Arab Republic of Egypt* (Jurisdiction) ICSID Case No ARB/04/13 (ICSID, 2006, Kaufmann-Kohler P, Mayer & Stern).

[31] ibid paras 90–95.

[32] *Consortium RFCC v Kingdom of Morocco* (Award) 20 ICSID Rev-FILJ 391 (ICSID, 2003, Briner P, Cremades & Fadlallah).

[33] *Salini Costruttori SpA and Italstrade SpA v Kingdom of Morocco* (Jurisdiction) 6 ICSID Rep 398 (ICSID, 2001, Briner P, Cremades & Fadlallah).

[34] *Autopista Concesionada de Venezuela CA v Bolivarian Republic of Venezuela* (Jurisdiction) 6 ICSID Rep 417 (ICSID, 2001, Kaufmann-Kohler P, Böckstiegel & Cremades).

contractor. As pointed out by Nathan, the contractor is providing materials and services for a fixed sum, including profit.[35] When the works are complete the contractor returns home with its plant, personnel, and profit. This point has also been taken up by Yala,[36] who distinguishes contracts in which the State has a 'vendor-client' relationship with investors from those where there exists a relationship of partnership.[37] In this vein he criticizes the award made in *Salini* on the basis that the Tribunal applied the correct (ie *Fedax*) criteria but in an insufficiently rigorous manner.[38]

Those defending the inclusion of construction contracts within the definition of **6.21** investment would point to the often large sums advanced by the contractor and the long-term contribution such projects make to the host State's development. These factors were cited expressly by the Tribunal in *Bayindir Insaat Turizm Ticaret Ve Sanayi, AS v Islamic Republic of Pakistan*.[39] It found that a project to construct a major motorway in Pakistan constituted an investment: 'Considering Bayindir's contribution both in terms of know how, equipment and personnel and in terms of injection of funds . . .'[40]

There is no doubt that the issue of what constitutes an 'investment' within the **6.22** terms of the ICSID Convention has come under increased scrutiny in recent cases. In the 1975 cases of *Kaiser Bauxite Co v Government of Jamaica*[41] and *Alcoa Minerals of Jamaica Inc v Jamaica*[42] the Tribunal found, with little investigation, that a situation where a mining company had invested substantial amounts in a foreign State was an investment. The Tribunal found no need to consider by what criteria this question should be assessed. In another older case, *Atlantic Triton Co v People's Revolutionary Republic of Guinea*,[43] the Tribunal accepted, without even considering the question, that a dispute arising out of an agreement for the

---

[35] KV Nathan, 'Submissions to the International Centre for Settlement of Investment Disputes in Breach of the Convention' (1995) 12(1) J Int'l Arb 27, 44.

[36] F Yala, 'The Notion of "Investment" in ICSID Case Law: A Drifting Jurisdictional Requirement? Some "Un-Conventional" Thoughts on *Salini, SGS* and *Mihaly*' (2005) 22 J Int'l Arb 105.

[37] ibid 107.

[38] Yala denies the existence of an investment on the facts of *Salini* because: 'The mere presence of equipment or a plant, which do contain some elements of technology, or the commitment of a highly specialized workforce in the territory of a host country, even for several years, is hardly sufficient to permit the efficient transfer of technology considering the learning process involved for the host state authorities or local personnel' (ibid 110).

[39] *Bayindir Insaat Turizm Ticaret Ve Sanayi AS v Islamic Republic of Pakistan* (Jurisdiction) ICSID Case No ARB/03/29 (ICSID, 2005, Kaufmann-Kohler P, Berman & Böckstiegel).

[40] ibid para 121.

[41] *Kaiser Bauxite Co v Government of Jamaica* 1 ICSID Rep 296 (ICSID, 1975, Trolle P, Kerr & Rouhani).

[42] *Alcoa Minerals of Jamaica Inc v Jamaica* (Jurisdiction) 4 Yearbook of Commerical Arbitration 206 (ICSID, 1975, Trolle P, Kerr & Rouhani).

[43] *Atlantic Triton Co Ltd v People's Revolutionary Republic of Guinea* (Award) 3 ICSID Rep 13 (ICSID, 1986, Sanders P, Prat & van den Berg).

conversion, equipping, and operation of three fishing vessels was a suitable agreement for resolution at ICSID. The dispute in *Colt Industries v Korea* (a case that settled six years after registration) arose out of technical and licensing agreements for the production of weapons.[44] It is unlikely that these cases would be decided today without a detailed assessment of whether the underlying transaction met the *Fedax* criteria of what constitutes an investment.

6.23　It is possible for a particular asset to constitute an investment under an investment treaty but not under Article 25 of the ICSID Convention. Schreuer observes that the ICSID Convention 'does not imply unlimited freedom for the parties . . . the term "investment" has an objective meaning independent of the parties' disposition'.[45] As a result, it is necessary to check carefully the context in which dicta from awards have been made before applying them in considering the status of an investment under the ICSID Convention or under some other instrument.

6.24　*Petrobart v Kyrgyz Republic*,[46] a Stockholm Chamber of Commerce arbitration arising out of the Energy Charter Treaty (ECT), is a case where an investment was found to exist under an investment treaty but where none would have existed under the ICSID Convention had the Tribunal applied the criteria set out in *Fedax* and *Salini*.

6.25　The dispute in *Petrobart* arose out of a contract to sell 200,000 tons of gas condensate over a period of twelve months. As part of its reasoning, the Tribunal made reference to the *Fedax* line of authority to support the proposition that 'investment' can have a wide meaning. However, it did not consider the criteria for defining 'investment' laid down in those awards. Instead it based its finding that an investment existed upon the definition contained in the ECT. The ECT's wide definition of investment includes 'Economic Activity in the Energy Sector' which in turn refers to a further defined term: 'economic activity concerning the exploration, extraction, refining, production, storage, land transport, transmission, distribution, trade, marketing, or sale of Energy Materials and Products'. Thus marketing and sale are explicitly covered by the ECT's definition of 'investment' with no exclusion based upon concepts such as duration or importance for the development of the host State's economy.[47]

---

[44] Nathan (n 35 above) 33, 51; *Colt Industries Operating Corp v Republic of Korea* ICSID Case No ARB/84/2. *Société Ouest Africaine des Bétons Industriels [SOABI] v State of Senegal* (Award) 2 ICSID Rep 164, 215 (ICSID, 1988, Broches P, Mbaye & Schultsz) would also fall within this category of cases. The Tribunal rejected the respondent State's submission that no investment had been made as the contract related only to building a house.

[45] C Schreuer, *The ICSID Convention: A Commentary* (2001) 125.

[46] *Petrobart Ltd v Kyrgyz Republic* (Award) SCC Case 126/2003 (SCC, 2005, Danelius C, Bring & Smets).

[47] See Observations by G Petrochalos and N Rubins on the award in 2005:3 Stockholm International Arbitration Review 100, 107–115. The award is criticized by B Poulain, '*Petrobart v The Kyrgyz*

Under bilateral investment treaties

Almost all BITs adopt a similar formula to define 'investment'. The formula com- **6.26**
mences with a wide inclusive phrase and then lists approximately five specific categories of rights. These categories generally include property, shares, contracts,
intellectual property rights, and rights conferred by law. For example, the UK
model BIT provides that:

> For the purposes of this Agreement:
> (a) 'investment' means every kind of asset and in particular, though not exclusively,
>   includes:
>   (i)   movable and immovable property and any other property rights such as
>   mortgages, liens or pledges;
>   (ii) shares in and stock and debentures of a company and any other form of
>   participation in a company;
>   (iii) claims to money or to any performance under contract having a financial
>   value;
>   (iv) intellectual property rights, goodwill, technical processes and know-how;
>   (v)   business concessions conferred by law or under contract, including conces-
>   sions to search for, cultivate, extract or exploit natural resources.[48]

Similar provisions are found in, for example, the Germany, France, and Netherlands **6.27**
model BITs.[49]

The US model BIT adopts a different approach to other models currently used. **6.28**
Its definition of 'investment' (footnotes included) is as follows:

> 'investment' means every asset that an investor owns or controls, directly or indir-
> ectly, that has the characteristics of an investment, including such characteristics as
> the commitment of capital or other resources, the expectation of gain or profit, or the
> assumption of risk. Forms that an investment may take include:
> (a) an enterprise;
> (b) shares, stock, and other forms of equity participation in an enterprise;
> (c) bonds, debentures, other debt instruments, and loans;[1]
> (d) futures, options, and other derivatives;
> (e) turnkey, construction, management, production, concession, revenue-sharing,
>   and other similar contracts;
> (f) intellectual property rights;
>
> [1] Some forms of debt, such as bonds, debentures, and long-term notes, are
> more likely to have the characteristics of an investment, while other forms of
> debt, such as claims to payment that are immediately due and result from the sale
> of goods or services, are less likely to have such characteristics.

Republic—a few reservations regarding the Tribunal's constructions of the material, temporal and
spatial application of the Treaty' (2005) 2(5) TDM. Poulain states that the Tribunal should have confined itself to a traditional view of investment before seeking reasons and justifications to extend the
definition (at 5).

[48] UK model BIT (Appendix 4 below) Art 1.   [49] See Appendices 7, 8, and 10 below.

(g) licenses, authorizations, permits, and similar rights conferred pursuant to applicable domestic law;[2, 3] and

(h) other tangible or intangible, movable or immovable property, and related property rights, such as leases, mortgages, liens and pledges.

> [2]   Whether a particular type of license, authorization, permit, or similar instrument
> (including a concession, to the extent that it has the nature of such an instrument) has the
> characteristics of an investment depends on such factors as the nature and extent of the rights
> that the holder has under the domestic law of the Party. Among the licenses, authorizations,
> permits, and similar instruments that do not have the characteristics of an investment are
> those that do not create any rights protected under domestic law. For greater certainty, the
> foregoing is without prejudice to whether any asset associated with the license, authorization,
> permit, or similar instrument has the characteristics of an investment.
>
> [3]   The term 'investment' does not include an order or judgment entered in a judicial or
> administrative action.[50]

6.29   It is noteworthy that the preamble to this definition takes up the *Fedax* criteria,
albeit without referring to the cases directly. This more specific definition is likely
to lead to more certainty by crystallizing issues that have been developed in the
case law into the wording of the BITs.

6.30   Tribunals have been reluctant to base decisions solely on the wide inclusive phrase
commonly found at the beginning of definitions of 'investment'. *Petrobart v
Kyrgyz Republic*[51] and *Jan de Nul v Egypt*[52] are two cases where tribunals have
found an investment to exist by reference to the detailed criteria contained in the
ECT and Belgo-Luxemburg Economic Union-Egypt BIT respectively. It is, however, noteworthy that in neither case did the Tribunals base their decisions on the
wide opening phrases in the treaty definitions, 'every kind of asset'[53] and 'any kind
of assets'[54] respectively. Before deciding that the asset in dispute was an 'investment', the Tribunals sought confirmation from the non-exhaustive list following
the introductory phrase. This is perhaps particularly surprising in *Petrobart*
because the Tribunal ultimately found an investment to exist where the usual criteria for investment under the ICSID Convention were not met. If the Tribunal
was not going to be bound by any considerations of the usual meaning of investment in international investment arbitration it is difficult to see why it could not
have rested its finding on the wide phrase 'every kind of asset' above.

6.31   In any event, the very fact that the Tribunal found an investment to exist demonstrates an intention, similar to that shown by the Tribunal dealing with nationality
in *Tokios Tokelės v Ukraine*,[55] not to read limiting phrases into treaties where none

---

[50]   US model BIT (Appendix 5 below) Art 1.   [51]   *Petrobart* (n 46 above).
[52]   *Jan de Nul v Egypt* (n 30 above).
[53]   Energy Charter Treaty (signed 17 December 1994, entered into force 16 April 1998) 2080
UNTS 100 ('ECT') (Appendix 2 below) Art 1(6).
[54]   Agreement on the Reciprocal Promotion and Protection of Investments (Belgo-Luxembourg
Economic Union-Egypt) (signed 28 February 1999, entered into force 24 May 2002) 2218 UNTS
4 Art 1(1).
[55]   *Tokios Tokelės v Ukraine* (Jurisdiction) (2005) 20 ICSID Rev-FILJ 205 (ICSID, 2004, Weil P,
Bernardini & Price).

exist in the text.[56] The requirement in the US model BIT that an 'investment' should have 'the characteristics of an investment' is precisely such a limiting phrase.

Under multilateral investment treaties

NAFTA

The definition of 'investment' in the North American Free Trade Agreement **6.32** (NAFTA) follows the conventional format of listing types of investment. However, claims that arise solely from 'commercial contracts for the sale of goods' or 'the extension of credit in connection with a commercial transaction' are expressly excluded.[57]

Energy Charter Treaty

The ECT definition of 'investment' follows the familiar form of providing for **6.33** 'every kind of asset' and then setting out a comprehensive list of specific asset types. At one of its broadest points it includes 'returns', which are defined as 'the amounts derived from or associated with an Investment, irrespective of the form in which they are paid, including profits, dividends, interest, capital gains, royalty payments, management, technical assistance or other fees and payment in kind'.[58]

'Investment' is also stated to refer to any investment associated with 'an Economic **6.34** Activity in the Energy Sector'. This phrase is itself widely defined in Article 1(5) as 'an economic activity concerning the exploration, extraction, refining, production, storage, land transport, transmission, distribution, trade, marketing, or sale of Energy Materials and Products except those included in Annex NI, or concerning the distribution of heat to multiple premises'.[59]

ASEAN Agreement of 15 December 1987

The definition of 'investment' in the 1987 ASEAN Agreement is in the usual form. **6.35** However, pursuant to Article 2, investments need to be specifically approved in writing and registered by the host country. Similarly, investments made prior to the ASEAN Agreement coming into force are only covered in the event that they are specifically approved in writing subsequent to entry into force.[60]

---

[56] ibid 219.
[57] North American Free Trade Agreement (adopted 17 December 1992, entered into force 1 January 1994) CTS 1994 No 2; (1993) 32 ILM 612 ('NAFTA') (Appendix 1 below) Art 1139.
[58] Energy Charter Treaty (Appendix 2 below) Art 1(9).
[59] Energy Charter Treaty (Appendix 2 below) Art 1(5).
[60] ASEAN Agreement for the Promotion and Protection of Investments (15 December 1987) (1988) 27 ILM 612, 613 (Appendix 3 below) Art II(3) and see discussion of *Yaung Chi Oo* (6.100–6.102 below).

C. Role Played by Arbitral Tribunals in Building upon Treaty Definitions in Relation to Specific Property Interests

6.36 In this section various issues addressed by investment treaty tribunals relating to the definition of 'investment' are considered. A number of awards have looked at these issues. For the purposes of this section they are grouped into the following categories:

(1) timing issues—when is an investment made?
(2) pre-contract investment;
(3) territorial issues—where must the investment be made?
(4) the role played by the law of the host State in determining the nature of the investor's property rights;
(5) requirements for investments to be specifically approved; and
(6) individual corporate identity and direct/indirect investment.

Timing issues—when is an investment made?

Timing issues before a treaty comes into force

6.37 It is not usually necessary for an investment to be made after the BIT has come into force in order to be protected. Many investment treaties contain a 'scope of application' provision which expressly states that the treaties apply to investments made both prior and subsequent to the coming into force of the treaty.[61] One of the jurisdictional challenges raised by the respondent State in *Nykomb v Latvia*[62] was that the ECT did not cover contracts entered into before the Treaty came into force. The Tribunal disposed of this objection in a single paragraph, pointing to the fact that: 'Both the changes in the law and the breach of contract occurred after the entry into force of the Treaty. There is therefore no question of retroactive effects of the Treaty in this situation.'[63] The Tribunal did not even refer to the specific provision of the ECT which, by specifying that the Treaty covers investments existing at the time the Treaty enters into force,[64] would have provided a complete answer.

6.38 In considering the temporal definition of an investment, the first matter to consider would always be the wording of the instrument upon which the dispute is based. In *Tradex v Albania* the Tribunal relied upon the wording of the foreign investment law under which the claim was brought. The foreign investment law

---

[61] Netherlands model BIT (Appendix 8 below) Art 10; NAFTA (Appendix 1 below) Note 39, *Mondev International Ltd v United States of America* (Award) 6 ICSID Rep 181, 208 (NAFTA/ICSID (AF), 2002, Stephen P, Crawford & Schwebel).

[62] *Nykomb Synergetics Technology Holding AB v Republic of Latvia* (Award) SCC Case 118/2001 (SCC, 2003, Haug C, Schütze & Gernandt).   [63] ibid para 4.3.3(a).

[64] Energy Charter Treaty (Appendix 2 below) Art 1(6)(f).

came into force on 1 January 1994 and the underlying claim related to a business that had been liquidated on 16 December 1993. However, the Tribunal held that the investor was protected, not least because the foreign investment law specifically stated that it covered investments made after 31 July 1990.[65]

Another issue of timing which arises by reference to the date treaties enter into **6.39** force is the question of whether a dispute has arisen before the treaty took effect. This is not strictly a question of the definition of 'investment' under a treaty, but since it is also a matter of jurisdiction *ratione temporis*, it is appropriate to consider the matter here.

A number of BITs contain provisions which specifically provide that their protec- **6.40** tions do not apply to disputes arising before their entry into force. For example, Article II(2) of the Argentina-Spain BIT provides: 'This agreement shall not, however, apply to disputes or claims arising before its entry into force'.[66]

This provision was considered in *Maffezini v Spain*.[67] The Argentina-Spain BIT **6.41** came into force in September 1992 but the claimant was relying on acts that took place 'as early as 1989 and throughout 1990, 1991 and the first part of 1992'.[68] The Tribunal considered the issue by seeking to clarify what constituted a 'dispute' within the meaning of the BIT. It referred to jurisprudence of the ICJ to the effect that 'it is "a disagreement on a point of law or fact, a conflict of legal views or interests between parties" '.[69]

Other frequently cited ICJ dicta in this regard are that a dispute is a 'situation in **6.42** which the two sides hold clearly opposite views concerning the question of the performance or non-performance' of a legal obligation[70] or when 'the claim of one party is positively opposed by the other'.[71]

The *Maffezini* Tribunal upheld jurisdiction. While it recognized that the criteria **6.43** of a 'dispute' should not be as formal as those of a 'claim', it held that Article II(2) would not bite until 'the conflict of legal views and interests came to be clearly

---

[65] *Tradex Hellas SA v Republic of Albania* (Jurisdiction) 5 ICSID Rep 43, 59 (ICSID, 1996, Böckstiegel P, Fielding & Giardina).

[66] Acuerdo para la Promoción y la Protección Recíprocas de Inversiones ('Agreement on the Reciprocal Promotion and Protection of Investments') (Argentina-Spain) (signed 3 October 1991, entered into force 28 September 1992) 1699 UNTS 187.

[67] *Emilio Agustín Maffezini v Kingdom of Spain* (Jurisdiction) 5 ICSID Rep 387 (ICSID, 2000, Orrego Vicuña P, Buergenthal & Wolf).

[68] ibid 417.

[69] ibid 417 quoting *Case Concerning East Timor (Portugal v Australia)* [1995] ICJ Rep 90, 99–100.

[70] *Interpretation of Peace Treaties with Bulgaria, Hungary and Romania* (Advisory Opinion) [1950] ICJ Rep 65, 74.

[71] *South West Africa Cases (Ethiopia v South Africa; Liberia v South Africa)* (Preliminary Objections) [1962] ICJ Rep 319, 328.

established'.[72] This only happened at the point of the dispute spectrum when 'events acquire a precise legal meaning through the formulation of legal claims, their discussion and eventual rejection or lack of response by the other party'.[73]

6.44 While the *Maffezini* Tribunal upheld jurisdiction, another BIT tribunal used a similar provision to deny jurisdiction. In *Lucchetti v Peru*,[74] a dispute arising under the Chile-Peru BIT, the Tribunal distinguished *Maffezini* on the basis that the dispute in the *Lucchetti* case had 'crystallized'[75] before the treaty came into force by the investor (who was the second claimant) having commenced proceedings to have certain administrative steps annulled before the local court. The Tribunal rejected the argument that the treaty reference to 'disputes' in its provisions dealing with the scope of its coverage should relate only to proceedings between the foreign investor and the State over treaty questions. It found that the meaning of 'disputes' should be ascertained by reference to the subject-matter rather than the parties or the cause of action upon which the litigation is based.[76] The *Lucchetti* Tribunal's decision is thus open to criticism as its consideration of the phrase 'disputes' runs counter to the finding of tribunals considering the meaning of 'dispute' in other provisions in BITs. For example, in considering the impact of so-called 'fork in the road' provisions, tribunals have focused solely on the parties and the cause of action rather than the subject-matter.[77] The decision is thus open to criticism on the ground that the word 'dispute' should be given the same meaning whether in a scope of application provision or in any other provision of a BIT.

6.45 NAFTA does not contain a provision specifically excluding pre-existing disputes. Nonetheless, the Tribunal in *Feldman v Mexico*[78] decided it did not have jurisdiction to adjudicate upon measures adopted by Mexico before NAFTA came into force. Its reason for so finding was that: 'Since NAFTA, and a particular part of NAFTA at that, delivers the only normative framework within which the Tribunal may exercise its jurisdictional authority, the scope of application of NAFTA in terms of time defines also the jurisdiction of the Tribunal *ratione temporis*.'[79]

6.46 However, the Tribunal did accept jurisdiction to consider measures adopted after the date NAFTA came into force even though they formed part of a permanent cause of action commencing before that date.

Timing issues once the investment has come to an end

6.47 An investment will not cease to be covered under a treaty merely because it has ceased to exist. In the NAFTA case of *Mondev v USA* the respondent State sought

---

[72] *Maffezini* (n 67 above) 418.   [73] *Maffezini* (n 67 above) 418.
[74] *Empresas Lucchetti SA and Lucchetti Peru SA v Peru* (Award) (2005) 20 ICSID Rev-FILJ 359 (ICSID, 2005, Buergenthal P, Cremades & Paulsson).   [75] ibid 385–386.
[76] ibid 387.   [77] See 4.77 above.
[78] *Feldman v United Mexican States* (Jurisdiction) 7 ICSID Rep 318 (NAFTA/ICSID (AF), 2000, Kerameus P, Covarrubias Bravo & Gantz).   [79] ibid 340.

to exclude the Tribunal's jurisdiction on the basis that the failure of the investment project meant that there was no underlying investment which could be the subject of a dispute. Not surprisingly, the Tribunal rejected this assertion, as it would have undermined the whole principle of investment treaty arbitration:

> ... once an investment exists, it remains protected by NAFTA even after the enterprise in question may have failed ... a person remains an investor for the purposes of [NAFTA] Articles 1116 and 1117 even if the whole investment has been definitively expropriated, so that all that remains is a claim for compensation. The point is underlined by the definition of an 'investor' as someone who 'seeks to make, is making or has made an investment.' Even if an investment is expropriated, it remains true that the investor 'has made' the investment.[80]

The point was also addressed by a BIT tribunal in *Jan de Nul v Egypt*.[81] The investment consisted of a contract which had come to an end long before the claimant commenced treaty arbitration proceedings. The respondent State argued that at the time the dispute arose the investment no longer existed. Both the BIT and the ICSID Convention would prevent an investment claim being brought in such circumstances. The Tribunal rejected this argument, recognizing that accepting it would defeat the entire logic of investment protection treaties. It quoted from an expert report made by Schreuer which had been submitted by the claimant: **6.48**

> Providing an effective remedy is part of the duties of fair and equitable treatment and of continuous protection and security for investments. A violation of that duty after the investment has come to an end does not change its nature. The duty to provide redress for a violation of rights persists even if the rights as such have come to an end. Otherwise an expropriating State might argue that it owes no compensation since the investment no longer belongs to the previous owner.[82]

These principles were also considered, in slightly different circumstances, in *National Grid v Argentina*.[83] The claimant had commenced the arbitration in April 2003. In August 2004 it sold the shares that constituted its investment. It asserted that this share sale was done by way of mitigation. The alternative would have been 'to continue pumping money into a ruinous enterprise'.[84] One of the bases upon which Argentina challenged jurisdiction was that the claimant was no longer an investor under the BIT. Argentina sought to distinguish *Mondev* and similar authorities on the basis that none covered cases where assets had been relinquished voluntarily. Yet the Tribunal supported the claimant, stating that the key factor under *Mondev* 'is to have been an investor and to have suffered a wrong before the sale or disposition of [the] assets, without the need to remain an investor for [the] purposes of the arbitration proceedings'.[85] **6.49**

---

[80] *Mondev* (n 61 above) 211–212.   [81] *Jan de Nul* (n 30 above).
[82] *Jan de Nul* (n 30 above) paras 134–136.
[83] *National Grid Plc v Argentine Republic* (Jurisdiction) (UNCITRAL, 2006, Sureda P, Debevoise & Garro).   [84] ibid para 110.
[85] ibid para 120.

Pre-contract investment

6.50 Notwithstanding the wide definition of 'investment' in investment treaties, tribunals addressing the question of pre-contract expenditure have consistently developed the idea that, in the absence of the specific consent of the State, such costs are not covered.

6.51 The earliest case addressing the issue is *Mihaly International Corp v Republic of Sri Lanka*.[86] This was an ICSID arbitration brought under the US-Sri Lanka BIT.[87] The claimant was seeking reimbursement of expenses incurred pursuing a proposed power project in Sri Lanka that never happened. The Tribunal found that no investment, under the terms of Article 25 of the ICSID Convention, had taken place. Its main reason for so finding was that: 'The Respondent clearly signalled, in the various documents which are relied upon by the Claimant, that it was not until the execution of a contract that it was willing to accept that contractual relations had been entered into and that an investment had been made.'[88]

6.52 *Mihaly* was closely considered in *PSEG v Turkey*.[89] In this ICSID arbitration, brought under the US-Turkey BIT, the Turkish Government had cancelled a concession contract before any works commenced. At the time of its cancellation, the concession contract still had a number of incomplete clauses and Turkey argued that no investment had been made because the project had not 'moved off the drawing board'.[90] Yet the Tribunal distinguished *Mihaly* on the basis that the contract in this case had become effective. The contract was valid as the remaining gaps to be negotiated would not have prevented the claimant executing it.[91] Thus a distinction can be drawn between disputes arising out of situations where expenses have been incurred before a contract has become effective and those arising after the contract has come into existence.

6.53 The *PSEG* Tribunal also discussed the unpublished award in *Zhinvali Development Limited v Republic of Georgia*,[92] another case where a pre-investment expenditure claim was rejected on jurisdictional grounds. Although the *Zhinvali* award is not published, it was made available to the *PSEG* Tribunal.[93] The award is described by

---

[86] *Mihaly International Corp v Republic of Sri Lanka* (Award) 6 ICSID Rep 308 (ICSID, 2002, Sucharitkul P, Rogers & Suratgar).

[87] Treaty Concerning the Encouragement and Reciprocal Protection of Investment (US-Sri Lanka) (signed 20 September 1991, entered into force 1 May 1993) Senate Treaty Doc 102-25.

[88] *Mihaly* (n 86 above) 320.

[89] *PSEG Global Inc & ors v Republic of Turkey* (Jurisdiction) (2005) 44 ILM 465 (ICSID, 2004, Orrego Vicuña P, Fortier & Kaufmann-Kohler).   [90] ibid 475.

[91] ibid 479.

[92] *Zhinvali Development Ltd v Republic of Georgia* (Award) ICSID Case No ARB/00/1 (ICSID, 2003, Robinson P, Jacovides & Rubin).   [93] *PSEG* (n 89 above) 478 fn 12.

Ben Hamida[94] as arising out of the Georgian Investment Law No 473–1S of 12 November 1996 which contains a general offer of ICSID arbitration. Zhinvali was excluded from a project to rehabilitate a hydro-electricity plant after three years of negotiations. Ben Hamida states that the Tribunal denied jurisdiction on the ground that the pre-investment expenditure did not qualify as an investment under the 1996 Georgian Investment Law.[95] The *PSEG* Tribunal describes *Zhinvali* as a case where the parties expressly acknowledged that the claimant did not have an investment.[96]

The claim in *Petrobart v Kyrgyzstan*[97] comprised two elements. The first was a con-   **6.54**
tract for delivery of 200,000 tons of gas concentrate over twelve months and the second was an agreement to agree additional supplies at a later stage. The Tribunal upheld the first part of the claim as constituting an investment but rejected the second on the grounds that 'whatever discussions may have taken place between the parties about further business relations, they did not result in any binding undertakings in the Contract'.[98]

While the awards of tribunals dealing with this issue are consistent with each   **6.55**
other, the point has generated some controversy among those commenting on the awards. The *Mihaly* award features a separate concurring opinion on the grounds that: 'Expenditure[s] incurred by successful bidders do indeed produce "economic value" … and the protection mechanism developed under the aegis of the World Bank in the form of the ICSID Convention should be available to those who are encouraged to embark on such expensive exercises'.[99]

This observation has some persuasive value, in particular given the recognition in   **6.56**
other awards that investment treaty claims arise out of abusive governmental acts and are not related to claims existing under domestic law contracts.[100] It is thus somewhat inconsistent for the existence of a contract to be the central question in circumstances where investments, in an economic sense, have been made. In addition, the absence of a contract may not have been an issue had Mihaly incorporated a specific company in Sri Lanka through which it pursued the project, a point specifically not considered by the Tribunal.[101]

---

[94] W Ben Hamida, 'The *Mihaly v. Sri Lanka* case: Some Thoughts Relating to the Status of Pre-Investment Expenditures' in T Weiler (ed), *International Investment Law and Arbitration; Leading Cases from the ICSID, NAFTA, Bilateral Treaties and Customary International Law* (2005).

[95] ibid 68.   [96] *PSEG* (n 89 above) 479.

[97] *Petrobart Ltd v Kyrgyz Republic* (Award) SCC Case 126/2003 (SCC, 2005, Danelius C, Bring & Smets).   [98] ibid 69.

[99] *Mihaly* (n 86 above) (Concurring Opinion Suratgar) 326.

[100] See *Compañía de Aguas del Aconquija SA and Vivendi Universal ('Vivendi') v Argentine Republic* (Decision on Annulment) 6 ICSID Rep 327, 360–361 discussed at 4.72 above.

[101] *Mihaly* (n 86 above) 321.

6.57 Ben Hamida points out that the result in *Mihaly* may well have been different had the investor relied to a greater extent on the detailed definition of investment contained in the BIT.[102] There is little doubt that if *Mihaly* was being argued today, its counsel would follow the practice adopted by claimants in many of the cases considered in this chapter, of focusing in detail upon the BIT definition. Nonetheless, it must be recalled that the *Mihaly* Tribunal not only found that Mihaly's expenditure did not amount to an investment under the BIT, but also under the ICSID Convention itself.

6.58 The Tribunal's decision in *Mihaly* is defended strongly by Hornick.[103] Hornick points out that any pre-investment process would involve a large number of bidders, only one of whom can be successful.[104] If treaty claims could be brought in respect of pre-investment disputes, a wide category of claimants would be created. In addition, the issues which may be covered by such claims, namely bribery and corruption, would be more appropriately reviewed by a national court applying domestic criminal law than by an arbitral tribunal applying principles of public international law. These contentions would of course have no relevance if jurisdiction could be found to exist under the wording of a BIT.

Place of investment

6.59 Most investment treaties contain provisions explicitly limiting their application to investments territorially made within a host State. For example, Article 2 of the Swiss-Pakistan BIT provides that: 'Le présent Accord est applicable aux investissements effectués sur le territoire d'une Partie Contractante par des investisseurs de l'autre Partie Contractante . . .'[105]

6.60 As with other investment treaties, the Swiss-Pakistan BIT contains many other references to the territory of the host State.

6.61 The question of which investments are to be considered as being made on the territory of the host State was considered in the jurisdiction awards in *SGS v Pakistan*[106] and *SGS v Philippines*.[107] Both cases concern agreements by which

---

[102] Ben Hamida (n 94 above) 64–67. A similar point is made by C Chatterjee, 'When Pre-Investment or Development Costs May or May Not be Regarded as Part of "Investment" under Article 25(1) of the ICSID Convention; The *Mihaly* Case' (2003) 4(5) Journal of World Investment and Trade 918, 923. Chatterjee states that had it not been for the Government of Sri Lanka explicitly exempting its liability, the claim would have been admissible under the BIT (924).

[103] RN Hornick, 'The *Mihaly* Arbitration Pre-Investment Expenditure as a Basis for ICSID Jurisdiction' (2003) 20 J Int'l Arb 189.   [104] ibid 192–193.

[105] Accord Concernant la Promotion et la Protection Réciproques des Investissements (Switzerland-Pakistan) (signed 11 July 1995, entered into force 6 May 1996) RO 1998, 2601.

[106] *SGS Société Générale de Surveillance SA v Islamic Republic of Pakistan* (Jurisdiction) 8 ICSID Rep 384 (ICSID, 2003, Feliciano P, Faurès & Thomas).

[107] *SGS Société Générale de Surveillance SA v Republic of the Philippines* (Jurisdiction) 8 ICSID Rep 515 (ICSID, 2004, El-Kosheri P, Crawford & Crivellaro).

SGS was to provide pre-shipment customs inspection services. These services would be carried out outside the host State. Following an inspection, SGS would provide an inspection certificate to the customs authorities in Pakistan and the Philippines respectively. In both cases the respondent States contested jurisdiction by arguing that the large majority of SGS's expense, and thus its investment, took place outside the host State in the many places where the inspections physically took place.

Both tribunals rejected this narrow contention. The reasoning of the *SGS v* **6.62** *Philippines* Tribunal is fuller. It relied on the fact that the focal point of SGS's services was the provision of a reliable inspection certificate in the host State itself. It also took into account that a proportion of SGS's expenditure took place in the Philippines. Ultimately the Tribunal considered the matter 'as a whole',[108] adopting the approach taken by the tribunals in *Fedax v Venezuela* and *CSOB v Slovakia* to the question as to whether an investment had been made at all (see paras 6.08 to 6.14 above). The important aspect was ' "the entire process" of economic activity, even though particular aspects of it were not locally performed'.[109] The *SGS v Philippines* Tribunal also agreed with the reasoning applied by the *SGS v Pakistan* Tribunal which had characterized the transaction as involving 'the injection of funds into the territory of Pakistan for the carrying out of SGS's engagements under the PSI Agreement.'[110]

The role played by the law of the host State in defining 'investment'

Investment according to law

In many investment treaties the definition of 'investment' includes a requirement **6.63** that the categories of assets admitted as 'investments' must be made 'in accordance with the laws and regulations of the said party'.[111] The plain meaning of this phrase is that investments which would be illegal upon the territory of the host State are disqualified from the protection of the BIT. Attempts by respondent States to broaden the matters encompassed by this phrase have failed.

In *Salini Costruttori SpA and Italstrade SpA v Kingdom of Morocco*[112] Morocco **6.64** argued that the Tribunal lacked jurisdiction as the transaction in question would be regarded by Moroccan law as a business contract rather than investment. As a result, an investment had not taken place 'in accordance with the laws and regulations' of Morocco as required by Article 1(1) of the Italy-Morocco BIT. The

---

[108] *SGS v Philippines* (n 107 above) 549. [109] *SGS v Philippines* (n 107 above) 549.
[110] *SGS v Pakistan* (n 106 above) 433 cited ibid 549.
[111] Tra sulla Promozione e Protezione Degli Investimenti ('Treaty for the Promotion and Protection of Investments') (Italy/Morocco) (signed 18 July 1990, entered into force 26 April 2000) Art 1(1).
[112] *Salini Costruttori SpA and Italstrade SpA v Kingdom of Morocco* (Jurisdiction) 6 ICSID Rep 398 (ICSID, 2001, Briner P, Cremades & Fadlallah).

Tribunal rejected this argument, confirming that the phrase should be maintained within its proper scope: 'In envisaging "the categories of invested assets ... in accordance with the laws and regulations of the said party", the provision in question refers to the legality of the investment and not to its definition. It aims in particular to ensure that the bilateral Agreement does not protect investments which it should not, generally because they are illegal.'[113]

6.65 The role played by the phrase was also restricted by the Tribunal in *Tokios Tokelēs v Ukraine*.[114] Ukraine attempted to deny the Tribunal's jurisdiction because of various technical defects in the manner in which the investment had been registered under Ukrainian law. The Tribunal was unwilling to withdraw the protection of the BIT on the basis of such defects saying that 'to exclude an investment on the basis of such minor errors would be inconsistent with the objects and purpose of the Treaty'.[115]

6.66 According to a report on the ITA website,[116] the Tribunal in *Inceysa Vallisoletana v El Salvador* used the 'accordance with law' provision contained in the Spain-El Salvador BIT to deny jurisdiction in circumstances where the investor was found to have misled Salvadoran officials and to have made misrepresentations at the initial tender stage. The Tribunal also noted that a finding in favour of the offending investor on this point would run counter to the general principle that a party should not be able to benefit from its own wrongdoing.

The role played by the law of the host State in determining the nature of the investor's property rights

6.67 In 'The Hybrid Foundations of Investment Treaty Arbitration',[117] Douglas has highlighted the importance of the role played by the municipal law of the host State in determining whether an investment has taken place. He states that the typical definition of an investment found in a BIT requires that the status of the asset claimed to be an investment must be considered under the host State's domestic property law. At the same time, of course, international law must prevent a State from using its own laws wrongfully to deny the investment's status as an investment.[118] The respective roles of international law and domestic law are

---

[113] ibid 411. See also *Consortium RFCC v Kingdom of Morocco* (Award) ICSID Case No ARB/00/6 (ICSID, 2003, Briner P, Cremades & Fadlallah); *Bayindir Insaat Turizm Ticaret Ve Sanayi AS v Islamic Republic of Pakistan* (Jurisdiction) ICSID Case No ARB/03/29 (ICSID, 2005, Kaufmann-Kohler P, Berman & Böckstiegel) para 109.   [114] *Tokios* (n 55 above).

[115] *Tokios* (n 55 above) 237.

[116] *Inceysa Vallisoletana SL v Republic of El Salvador* ICSID Case No ARB/03/26 (Summary of Decision on Jurisdiction by Counsel for El Salvador) <http://ita.law.uvic.ca/documents/InceysaDescription.pdf> accessed 20 September 2006.

[117] Z Douglas, 'The Hybrid Foundations of Investment Treaty Arbitration' (2003) 74 BYIL 151.

[118] ibid 198–199.

well set out in a statement taken from a decision of the American-Mexican Claims Commission:

> When questions are raised before an international tribunal ... with respect to the application of the proper law in the determination of rights grounded on contractual obligations, it is necessary to have clearly in mind the particular law applicable to the different aspects of the case. The nature of such contractual rights or rights with respect to tangible property, real or personal, which a claimant asserts have been invaded in a given case is determined by the local law that governs the legal effects of the contract or other form of instrument creating such rights. But the responsibility of a respondent Government is determined solely by international law ...[119]

Douglas himself defines different roles to be played by domestic and international **6.68** law in the following terms:

> At the first stage, the treaty tribunal must decide, if it is a matter of contention, whether particular rights *in rem* constituting the alleged investment exist, the scope of those rights, and in whom they vest. [Douglas states that this is a question of municipal law.] At the first stage of the analysis, the treaty tribunal must also determine whether or not the rights *in rem* that have been identified in accordance with the municipal law of the host state constitute an investment as defined by the investment treaty itself. This is a question of treaty interpretation that is ultimately governed by principles of international law.[120]

An example of this two-headed approach being adopted in practice is *Generation* **6.69** *Ukraine Inc v Ukraine*.[121] In this claim, brought under the US-Ukraine BIT, the claimant asserted claims both under the treaty and under Ukrainian law. The Tribunal was only willing to hear the treaty claims[122] and thus took pains to ensure that the disputes it was asked to adjudicate related to 'investments' as defined under the BIT.[123] The Tribunal carried out this exercise by considering in detail the content of various rights, permits, protocols, and agreements existing under Ukrainian law. Once it had used domestic law to determine the precise nature of these rights, it considered whether they fell within the definition of 'investment' set out in the BIT.[124]

This analysis was also used by the Tribunal in *Nagel v Czech Republic*.[125] The **6.70** Tribunal cited the need to look to the treaty itself but also stated the need to have regard to domestic law when considering the words 'asset' and 'investment' in the UK-Czech Republic BIT. These terms 'refer to rights and claims which have a financial value for the holder. This creates a link with domestic law, since it is to a

---

[119] *George W Cook (USA) v United Mexican States* (1927) IV RIAA 213, 215. The passage is quoted by Douglas at page 196 where he points out that this statement was made by one Commissioner and the other members of the Commission did not endorse these remarks.

[120] Douglas (n 117 above) 211.

[121] *Generation Ukraine Inc v Ukraine* (Award) (2005) 44 ILM 404 (ICSID, 2003, Paulsson P, Salpius & Voss). [122] ibid 425–426.

[123] ibid 435. [124] ibid 436–449. [125] *Nagel* (n 9 above).

large extent the rules of domestic law that determine whether or not there is a financial value'.[126]

Indirect investment

Introduction—claiming for losses suffered by a direct subsidiary

6.71 Investments are often made through subsidiary companies incorporated under the law of the host State. There are different reasons for this—sometimes States require a participant in a local industry to be a locally incorporated entity. Alternatively, the investor may find it more convenient to trade through a local company. If the State commits a breach, the wrong will be done to the local subsidiary or investment vehicle. Without a specific agreement to the contrary,[127] the subsidiary will not be able to bring a treaty claim as any dispute it may have with the government will be a domestic dispute. The shareholder investor may be able to qualify as a claimant under an investment treaty but it will need to show that it has standing to recover damages for a wrong committed to a separate corporate entity. The question is thus whether investment treaty jurisprudence allows an investor to look through the corporate structure (or pierce the corporate veil) to claim losses suffered by a separate juridical entity.

6.72 Prior to the development of investment treaty arbitration, the classic statement of public international law in this scenario was to be found in the judgment of the ICJ in *Barcelona Traction*.[128] The case concerned bonds issued by a Canadian company operating in Spain. The company was majority owned by Belgian nationals. It became bankrupt as a result of actions taken by the Spanish Government. The ICJ denied standing to Belgium to assert a claim on behalf of the shareholders against Spain stating that 'where it is a question of an unlawful act committed against a company representing foreign capital, the general rule of international law authorizes the national State of the company alone to make a claim'.[129]

6.73 The ICJ decision thus established that public international law would not in general allow the veil of separate corporate identity to be pierced. The shareholders (or their government) could not establish a right to bring an action in their own name.[130]

---

[126] ibid 158.

[127] Convention on the Settlement of Investment Disputes between States and Nationals of Other States (signed 18 March 1965, entered into force 14 October 1966) 575 UNTS 159 ('ICSID Convention') (Appendix 11 below) Art 25(2)(b); Schreuer (n 45 above) 290–334.

[128] *Case Concerning the Barcelona Traction, Light and Power Co Ltd (New Application: 1962) (Belgium v Spain)* [1970] ICJ Rep 3.   [129] ibid 46.

[130] For an interesting summary of the development of international law since *Barcelona Traction* see FA Mann, 'The Protection of Shareholders' Interests in the Light of the *Barcelona Traction* Case' (1973) 67 AJIL 259; I Laird, 'A community of destiny—the *Barcelona Traction case*

The decision remains in good standing in customary international law and has **6.74** been codified into Article 11 of the International Law Commission's *Draft Articles on Diplomatic Protection*.[131]

The ICJ's restrictive ruling in *Barcelona Traction* has never been followed in treaty **6.75** arbitrations. The issue arose in the first BIT arbitration, *Asian Agricultural Products Lt v Republic of Sri Lanka*.[132] In this claim, brought under the UK-Sri Lanka BIT, a Hong Kong corporation held 48 per cent of the shares in a Sri Lankan company that had suffered the loss. It is not clear from the award whether Sri Lanka sought to argue that the claimant was precluded from seeking recovery in circumstances where the loss had been suffered by a subsidiary. However, the Tribunal had no difficulties with allowing the claimant to recover. It stated that: 'The undisputed "investments" effected since 1985 by AAPL in Sri Lanka are in the form of acquiring shares in Serendib Company, which has been incorporated in Sri Lanka under the domestic Companies Law ... The scope of the international law protection granted to the foreign investor in the present case is limited to a single item: The value of his share-holding in the joint-venture entity (Serendib Company).'[133]

In another early case, *American Manufacturing and Trading Inc v The Republic of* **6.76** *Zaire*,[134] the Tribunal considered the definition of investment provided by the USA-Zaire BIT. This provided, in Article 1(c), that the term 'investment' included 'every kind of investment, owned or controlled directly or indirectly, including equity' as well as 'a company or shares of stock or other interests in a company or interests in the assets thereof'.[135] When Zaire contested the claimant's right to recover for losses suffered by a local subsidiary, the Tribunal concluded that the point was 'perfectly clear'.[136]

Neither the *AAPL* nor the *AMT* tribunals made reference to *Barcelona Traction*. **6.77** It is of course possible that the point was not raised before them, but it is also possible that they believed that as the claims arose out of BITs they were dealing with

---

and the development of shareholder rights to bring investment claims' in T Weiler (ed), *International Investment Law and Arbitration; Leading Cases from the ICSID, NAFTA, Bilateral Treaties and Customary International Law* (2005). For a discussion of the principle and its exceptions see 5.05 above.

[131] 'Diplomatic Protection: Text of the Draft Articles with Commentaries thereto' (Dugard, Special Rapporteur) in *Report of the International Law Commission on its Fifty-eighth Session (1 May–9 June; 3 July–11 August 2006) Official Records of the General Assembly Sixty-first Session,* Supplement No. 10 UN Doc A/61/10, 22–100.

[132] *Asian Agricultural Products Ltd v Republic of Sri Lanka* (Award) 4 ICSID Rep 245 (ICSID, 1990, El-Kosheri P, Goldman & Asante). [133] ibid 290.

[134] *American Manufacturing and Trading Inc (AMT) v Republic of Zaire* (Award) 5 ICSID Rep 11 (ICSID, 1997, Sucharitkul P, Golsong & Mbaye).

[135] Treaty Concerning the Reciprocal Encouragement and Protection of Investment (US-Democratic Republic of Congo (Kinshasa) formerly Zaire) (signed 3 August 1984, entered into force 28 July 1989) Senate Treaty Doc 99-17.

[136] *AMT* (n 134 above) 25. Almost all of the jurisdiction decisions in the Argentine cases came to the same conclusion on this point.

a *lex specialis* rather than customary international law. Given the wide definition of investment contained in most bilateral investment treaties, if an 'investment' can include shares in a company there is no conceptual reason to prevent an investor recovering for damage caused to those shares which has resulted in a diminution in their value. Tribunals have been so consistent in applying the *lex specialis* in this regard that it is arguable that the special rule has become the general rule. This was the conclusion of the Tribunal in *CMS Gas Transmission Co v The Republic of Argentina*[137] where the Tribunal permitted a claim by the US shareholder company on the basis that:

> ... *lex specialis* in this respect is so prevalent that it can now be considered the general rule, certainly in respect of foreign investments and international claims and increasingly in respect of other matters. To the extent that customary international law or generally the traditional law of international claims might have followed a different approach—a proposition that is open to debate—then that approach can be considered the exception.[138]

6.78 For the purposes of investment treaty jurisprudence, it is not necessary to find that *Barcelona Traction* has been wrongly decided. It suffices to limit its effect to the field of diplomatic protection and to posit a different rule for treaty claims. Such an approach would be consistent with the ICJ decision in *ELSI*[139] and the numerous arbitration awards considered in this section.

Alternative approaches to justify indirect claims

6.79 The simplest approach to justify indirect claims is that taken by the tribunals in the cases cited above, based upon the wording of the treaty. However, other tribunals have adopted different approaches to grant shareholders standing to assert a claim.[140] In the NAFTA case of *SD Myers Inc v Government of Canada* the claimant was a US company bringing a claim in respect of harm suffered by a Canadian subsidiary, SD Myers (Canada), Inc.[141] The claimant and the subsidiary were part of the same family group but the claimant did not directly own shares in the subsidiary. Rather, the same four members of the Myers family owned all the shares in both companies. The Tribunal was not concerned with the niceties of corporate ownership. It stated that:

> ... the Tribunal does not accept that an otherwise meritorious claim should fail solely by reason of the corporate structure adopted by a claimant in order to organise the way

---

[137] *CMS Gas Transmission Co v Republic of Argentina* (Jurisdiction) 7 ICSID Rep 492 (ICSID, 2003, Orrego Vicuña P, Lalonde & Rezek).

[138] ibid 504. See also *GAMI Investments Inc v United Mexican States* (2005) 44 ILM 545, 550 (NAFTA/UNCITRAL, 2004, Paulsson P, Reisman & Muró).

[139] *Case Concerning Elettronica Sicula SpA (ELSI) (United States of America v Italy)* [1989] ICJ Rep 15.

[140] *Pope & Talbot Inc v Government of Canada* 7 ICSID Rep 43 (NAFTA/UNCITRAL, 2002, Dervaird P, Greenberg & Belman).

[141] *SD Myers Inc v Government of Canada* (First Partial Award) 8 ICSID Rep 3 (NAFTA/UNCITRAL, 2000, Hunter P, Schwartz & Chiasson).

in which it conducts its business affairs ... there are a number of other bases on which SDMI could contend that it has standing to maintain its claim including that (a) SDMI and Myers Canada were in a joint venture, (b) Myers Canada was a branch of SDMI, (c) it had made a loan to Myers Canada, and (d) its market share in Canada constituted an investment.[142]

The Tribunal in *Azurix Corp v Argentine Republic*[143] based its analysis not only on **6.80** the USA-Argentina BIT's inclusion of 'shares of stock' in the definition of investment, but also on the contractual rights held by the subsidiary. Contractual rights were also specifically protected under the BIT. The US company Azurix had obtained a concession to provide water and waste water services to an Argentinean province. In order to implement the investment it had been required to establish a locally registered company. The Tribunal held that:

> Provided the direct or indirect ownership or control is established, rights under a contract held by a local company constitute an investment protected by the BIT
>
> ...
>
> (a) Azurix indirectly owns 90% of the shareholding in [the local subsidiary], (b) Azurix indirectly controls [the local subsidiary], and (c) [the local subsidiary] is party to the Concession Agreement and was established for the specific purpose of signing the Concession Agreement as required by the Bidding Terms.[144]

In addition, its conclusion was based on the fact that the treaty defined 'invest- **6.81** ment' in a wide, non-exhaustive manner, with the only condition being that the investment be directly or indirectly owned or controlled by a national of the investing State.

Minority shareholders' rights

In the passage quoted above, the *Azurix* Tribunal expressly included, as a step in **6.82** its reasoning, the fact that the US parent company indirectly controlled the local subsidiary. However, tribunals have consistently stated that the presence of such control is not required to bring an interest in a subsidiary within a BIT's definition of 'investment'. It is noteworthy that the first BIT case, *AAPL*, not only dealt with losses suffered by a subsidiary, but the claimant's stake in that subsidiary was a minority stake.[145] Investment tribunals have consistently held that minority shareholdings are included in the definition of investment. For example, the claimant in *CMS v Argentina*[146] was a US company with a 29.42 per cent share in an Argentinian company with a licence to transport gas. The measures taken by Argentina were directed at the gas transportation licence which was owned by the Argentinian company, not by the US claimant. The Tribunal held that

---

[142] ibid 50–51.
[143] *Azurix Corp v Argentine Republic* (Jurisdiction) ICSID Case No ARB/01/12 (ICSID, 2003, Sureda P, Lauterpacht & Martins).   [144] ibid paras 63, 65.
[145] *AAPL* (n 132 above) 290.   [146] *CMS* (n 137 above).

notwithstanding the minority shareholding there would be a direct right of action for shareholders whether under the BIT or the ICSID Convention:

> Precisely because the [ICSID] Convention does not define 'investment', it does not purport to define the requirements that an investment should meet to qualify for ICSID jurisdiction. There is indeed no requirement that an investment, in order to qualify, must necessarily be made by shareholders controlling a company or owning the majority of its shares ... The reference that [ICSID Convention] Article 25(2)(b) makes to foreign control in terms of treating a company of the nationality of the Contracting State party as a national of another Contracting State is precisely meant to facilitate agreement between the parties, so as not to have the corporate personality interfering with the protection of the real interests associated with the investment. The same result can be achieved by means of the provisions of the BIT, where the consent may include non-controlling or minority shareholders.[147]

6.83 This statement was quoted with approval in *Azurix Corp v Argentine Republic*.[148] A similar conclusion was reached in *Lanco International Inc v Argentine Republic*,[149] *Enron Corp and Ponderosa Assets LP v Argentine Republic*,[150] the NAFTA case *GAMI Investments Inc v Government of the United Mexican States*[151] as well as many other cases.

6.84 Extending the right of action to minority shareholders will create problems for respondent States. Argentina relied on four such difficulties in contesting jurisdiction in *CMS v Argentina*.[152] These were:

(1) the local subsidiary could negotiate a settlement with the government but at the same time an ICSID tribunal could grant a remedy to foreign shareholders with minority interests in that local subsidiary;

(2) allowing a foreign investor to bring a treaty claim would lead to discrimination between domestic and foreign investors as only foreign investors would have access to arbitration;

(3) allowing all minority shareholders to bring claims could lead to the multiplication of international claims by investors of different nationalities and under separate treaties; and

(4) it cannot be assumed that a minority shareholder should be entitled to claim compensation in proportion to its minority stake. This is because, if the local company owning the asset were to be compensated, there is no guarantee that the benefit would flow through to its shareholders.

---

[147] *CMS* (n 137 above) 504–505.

[148] *Azurix Corp v Argentine Republic* (Jurisdiction) ICSID Case No ARB/01/12 (ICSID, 2003, Sureda P, Lauterpacht & Martins) para 64.

[149] *Lanco International Inc v Argentine Republic* (Jurisdiction) 5 ICSID Rep 367 (ICSID, 1998, Cremades P, Alvarez & Baptista).

[150] *Enron Corp and Ponderosa Assets LP v Argentine Republic* (Jurisdiction: Ancillary Claim) ICSID Case No ARB/01/3 (ICSID, 2004, Orrego Vicuña P, Espiell & Tschanz).

[151] *GAMI* (n 138 above).   [152] *CMS* (n 137 above) 512.

These objections are all well-founded and could result in substantial prejudice for **6.85** respondent States. However, as long as tribunals proceed upon an interpretation of the wording of BITs, without regard to potential wider consequences, they will not be able to find any legal reasons for denying jurisdiction to minority share-holders. As the *CMS* Tribunal recognized: 'The Tribunal notes in this respect that [ICSID] has made every effort possible to avoid a multiplicity of tribunals and jurisdictions, but that it is not possible to foreclose rights that different investors might have under different arrangements. The Tribunal also notes that, while it might be desirable to recognize similar rights to domestic and foreign investors, this is seldom possible in the present state of international law in this field.'[153]

In *GAMI Investments Inc v Government of the United Mexican States*[154] the **6.86** Tribunal considered the issues that could arise by granting a minority share-holder standing to pursue its NAFTA claim.[155] In this case a US shareholder was bringing a claim to recover for losses allegedly caused to his minority sharehold-ing in a Mexican company. While the Tribunal ruled liberally on jurisdiction, in considering the merits of the claim it took a very strict stance in defining the substantive rights a minority shareholder could assert. Despite the fact that the minority shareholder had US nationality, the Tribunal refused to consider acts taken towards the Mexican subsidiary company as discriminatory because, by definition, they were acts taken against a Mexican company.[156] However, if a tribunal can only limit injustice to respondent States by a restrictive analysis of the claimant's substantive rights, any problems potentially thrown up by allowing minority shareholders to bring claims can only be resolved on a case-by-case basis.

Claims brought by holding companies

Similar problems to those raised by minority shareholders can be raised by the fact **6.87** that holding companies may also bring treaty claims. In this respect, a holding company can be any participant in a corporate ownership chain save for the ultim-ate beneficiary and the company directly affected. The potential for disruption created by allowing claims to be brought at various levels of the corporate chain was illustrated by the TV Nova saga. TV Nova was a very successful Czech televi-sion station which was set up by the American investor Ronald S Lauder. Upon losing control of the station, Mr Lauder brought two arbitrations. One, *Ronald S Lauder v Czech Republic*[157] was brought by Mr Lauder in his personal capacity under the USA-Czech Republic BIT. Mr Lauder was the ultimate beneficiary in the corporate chain. The other was brought by a Netherlands holding company in

---

[153] *CMS* (n 137 above) 512.   [154] *GAMI* (n 138 above).
[155] *GAMI* (n 138 above) 551–552.   [156] *GAMI* (n 138 above) 564.
[157] *Lauder v Czech Republic* 9 ICSID Rep 62 (UNCITRAL, 2001, Briner P, Cutler & Klein).

CME Czech Republic v Czech Republic.[158] Both claims arose out of same set of facts. One tribunal found that there had been an expropriation and awarded substantial damages while the other tribunal rejected the claim. This was a clear demonstration of the possibility of 'a multiplicity of tribunals and jurisdictions', as noted by the *CMS v Argentina* Tribunal.[159]

6.88 Allowing wide latitude for holding companies to bring claims is consistent with the idea that investors do not need to fund investments with their own resources,[160] and encourages claimants to structure their investments through a variety of jurisdictions to ensure maximum treaty coverage. There appears to be nothing wrong in principle with claimants taking such steps. Moreover, it may be that certain States will be encouraged to develop a wide network of bilateral treaty relationships in order to encourage investors to route investments through their legal and fiscal frameworks. This point arose in *Aguas del Tunari SA v Republic of Bolivia*[161] where the respondent State contended that it had carefully structured the concession contract to preclude ICSID jurisdiction. At the time of entering into the concession contract the claimant company was controlled through the Cayman Islands, but by the time a dispute arose the control structure had been altered and a Netherlands holding company had been inserted into the corporate chain. The Tribunal held that it had jurisdiction under the Netherlands-Bolivia BIT[162] as the changes to the corporate structure did not affect any of the undertakings given in the concession agreement.[163]

6.89 The ability of a holding company to assert a claim was taken to an extreme in *Tokios Tokelės v Ukraine.*[164] In this arbitration, brought under the Lithuania-Ukraine BIT, the Lithuanian claimant was owned and controlled by Ukrainian nationals. As a matter of economic substance, therefore, the claim was a domestic Ukrainian dispute. Nonetheless the majority of the Tribunal pointed out that the parties to the BIT could have included a 'denial of benefits' provision. Such a provision is regularly included by State parties to investment treaties to prevent holding or shell companies from asserting treaty rights. For example, the Energy Charter Treaty allows State parties to deny the benefits of the treaty to 'a legal entity if citizens or nationals of a third state own or control such entity and if that

---

[158] *CME Czech Republic BV (The Netherlands) v Czech Republic* 9 ICSID Rep 121, 238 (UNCITRAL, 2001, Kühn C, Schwebel and Hándl).

[159] *CMS* (n 137 above) 512.

[160] *Tokios Tokelės v Ukraine* (Jurisdiction) (2005) 20 ICSID Rev-FILJ 205, 235 (ICSID, 2004, Weil P, Bernardini & Price). This is an aspect of tribunals rejecting the idea that an investment needs to be made 'directly'. See further 6.10 above.

[161] *Aguas del Tunari SA (AdT) v Republic of Bolivia* (Jurisdiction) 20 ICSID Rev-FILJ 450 (ICSID, 2005, Caron P, Alberro-Semerena & Alvarez).

[162] Agreement on Encouragement and Reciprocal Protection of Investments (Netherlands-Bolivia) (signed 10 March 1992, entered into force 1 November 1994) Tractatenblad 1992, 081.

[163] *AdT* (n 161 above) paras 160–180.   [164] *Tokios* (n 160 above).

entity has no substantial business activities in the Area of the Contracting Party in which it is organized'.[165]

In the absence of such a provision, however, the Tribunal refused to read one into the BIT.   **6.90**

On the basis of the awards rendered thus far, in the absence of specific treaty pro-   **6.91**
visions denying benefits to companies lacking substantial economic activities in
the investor's home State, tribunals have not been able to prevent, even if they had
so wished, holding or shell companies from asserting jurisdiction under BITs
available in their States of incorporation. The Tribunal in *Soufraki v UAE*[166] recognized that the unsuccessful claimant in that case could have overcome the dis-
advantages of his dual nationality merely by incorporating an Italian corporate
vehicle, rather than by investing in his personal capacity. Tribunals can only deny
jurisdiction in such circumstances if they are willing to read policy considerations
into the BIT, something which they have not been willing to do in considering
questions of indirect investment.

Claims brought by ultimate beneficiaries

The relaxed attitude to piercing the corporate veil demonstrated by investment tri-   **6.92**
bunals also extends to allowing claims to be asserted by the ultimate beneficial owner
in a corporate structure. An example of this is *Franz Sedelmayer v The Russian
Federation*.[167] Mr Sedelmayer, a German citizen, brought a claim against Russia
under the Germany-Russia BIT.[168] His investment had been made through a US
corporation, Sedelmayer Group of Companies International Inc ('SGC
International'). The policy reason for denying the benefit of investment treaties to
beneficial owners of a corporate structure is that allowing them treaty protection
gives them a double advantage. The first advantage is that while making their investment they can hide behind the shield of limited corporate liability. The second
advantage is that, in the event of a dispute, they can cast away the separate corporate
personality through which they invested and bring a claim in their own right.
However, the *Sedelmayer* Tribunal had no difficulty in accepting the claimant's
standing as an investor under the treaty because the treaty's definition of 'investment' clearly covered a beneficial owner bringing a claim in his own name. In addition, the Tribunal's analysis went further than the wording of the treaty alone. It
referred to the 'control theory' of international law. As the Tribunal explained:

> This theory is based on the idea that the decisive factor is who <u>de facto</u> controls the
> entity which has, for example, made investments in a foreign country. Consequently,

---

[165] Energy Charter Treaty (Appendix 2 below) Art 17(1).
[166] *Hussein Nuaman Soufraki v United Arab Emirates* (Award) ICSID Case No ARB/02/7
(ICSID, 2004, Fortier P, El Kholy & Schwebel) para 83.
[167] *Franz Sedelmayer v Russian Federation* (Ad hoc Arb Trib, 1998, Magnusson P, Wachler &
Zykin).   [168] Germany-Russian BIT (n 28 above).

the control theory leads to the piercing of SGC International's corporate veil and to putting the <u>de facto</u> investor—<u>i.e.</u> the Claimant—in the focus

. . .

Mr. Sedelmayer shall, thus, be regarded as an investor under the Treaty, even with respect to investments formally made by SGC International or the other companies.[169]

6.93 In relying upon the 'control theory' in international law, the *Sedelmayer* Tribunal looked to the 1989 ICJ decision in *ELSI*.[170] In the *ELSI* case a chamber of the ICJ was prepared to allow the United States to bring a claim on behalf of two US corporations which owned shares in an Italian corporation in respect of actions taken by the Italian Government. The *ELSI* judgment is thus an example of a tribunal in a State-to-State case taking the same approach to the admissibility of indirect claims as the investment arbitration tribunals that are the subject of this section.

6.94 In *ELSI* the ICJ was considering claims arising under the Treaty of Friendship, Commerce and Navigation between the USA and Italy of 1948. The ICJ did not refer to *Barcelona Traction* in its main decision. However, Judge Schwebel in his Dissenting Opinion specifically noted that the Chamber had not accepted arguments that would have denied the right of the United States to bring a claim on behalf of its nationals owning shares in an Italian company.[171]

6.95 One commentator has noted that the decision of the majority in *Tokios Tokelés v Ukraine* is one example of a tribunal not applying a control test to determine a corporation's nationality.[172]

6.96 Another example of an ultimate beneficiary bringing a claim is *Waste Management Inc v United Mexican States*.[173] Here the claim was brought by a US Corporation which owned a Mexican company party to a waste disposal concession in Mexico. The Mexican subsidiary was owned through two Cayman Island Corporations. As in so many of the other awards dealing with indirect claims, the Tribunal based its decision upon the simple text of the particular instrument, in this case NAFTA. The Tribunal spelt out clearly its reasons for taking such an approach:

> Where a treaty spells out in detail and with precision the requirements for maintaining a claim, there is no room for implying into the treaty additional requirements, whether based on alleged requirements of general international law in the field of diplomatic protection or otherwise. If the NAFTA Parties had wished to limit their obligations of conduct to enterprises or investments having the nationality of one of the other Parties they could have done so. Similarly they could have restricted claims of loss or damage by reference to the nationality of the corporation which itself

---

[169] *Sedelmayer* (n 167 above) 27, 59.   [170] *ELSI* (n 139 above).

[171] *ELSI* (n 139 above) 94.

[172] EC Schlemmer, 'Investment, Investor, Nationality, Shareholders and Foreign Investment Law' <http://www.ila-hq.org> accessed 20 September 2006 at 25. See further 5.47 *et seq* above.

[173] *Waste Management Inc v United Mexican States* (2004) 43 ILM 967 (NAFTA/ICSID (AF), 2004, Crawford P, Civiletti & Gómez).

suffered direct injury. No such restrictions appear in the text. It is not disputed that at the time the actions said to amount to a breach of NAFTA occurred, [the Mexican subsidiary] was an enterprise owned or controlled indirectly by the Claimant, an investor of the United States. The nationality of any intermediate holding companies is irrelevant to the present claim.[174]

Portfolio investment

A significant potential difficulty which could be thrown up by the wide inter- **6.97** pretation of 'investment' in indirect investment cases is posed by the portfolio investor. The facts underlying many of the claims against Argentina, where the breach Argentina is alleged to have committed consists of an economic measure affecting all Argentinian companies, could potentially give rise to claims brought by investors whose only interest in a company's shares is as an investment, rather than holding a stake for management purposes. This is often referred to as 'portfolio investment'. Investment treaty tribunals have yet to rule on the question of whether portfolio investors are covered.[175]

The issue arose between the parties in *Philippe Gruslin v Malaysia*[176] but ulti- **6.98** mately the Tribunal was not asked to rule on the issue. Mr Gruslin claimed he had made an investment in securities listed on the Kuala Lumpur stock exchange through an emerging Asian markets mutual fund based in Luxembourg. The issue was also considered in *Enron v Argentina*[177] where the Tribunal admitted that while investors could claim in their own right under the treaty, there existed a need to establish a cut-off point beyond which claims would not be permissible. Such a cut-off point could be established by reference to the extent of the consent to arbitration of the host State. However, it is not clear that a tribunal would be able to deny jurisdiction over a claim brought by a portfolio investor by reference only to the remoteness of the connection to the affected company. Previous tribunals have taken a strict approach to the literal wording of treaties and if this approach is followed, remoteness per se would not be a sufficient ground on which to deny jurisdiction when such jurisdiction could be demonstrated to exist within the wide definition terms of the BIT.

Investment approval

A number of investment treaties contain a provision that goes beyond the general **6.99** requirement that for a foreign investment to enjoy protection it must be lawful

---

[174] ibid 983. See also *Lauder v Czech Republic* (n 157 above) 84–85, where the Czech Republic ultimately did not even seek to contest that Mr Lauder had standing to bring a claim in his own name.

[175] In this section, the term 'portfolio investment' is taken to refer to circumstances when an investor owns shares in an investment. Thus *Fedax NV v Republic of Venezuela* (Award) 5 ICSID Rep 183 (ICSID, 1998, Orrego Vicuña P, Heth & Owen) when the investor held promissory notes, allowing it to take a financial interest without management control, is not included.

[176] *Philippe Gruslin v Malaysia* (Award) 5 ICSID Rep 483 (ICSID, 2000, Griffith).

[177] *Enron* (n 150 above).

under the law of the host State. These provisions, which are particularly prevalent in centrally planned economies, contain an express requirement for approval in writing and registration of a foreign investment. For example, Article II of the 15 December 1987 ASEAN Agreement provides that:

> This agreement shall apply only to investments brought into, derived from or directly connected with investments brought into the territory of any Contracting Party by nationals or companies of any other Contracting Party and which are specifically approved in writing and registered by the host country and upon such conditions as it deems fit for the purposes of this Agreement.
>
> . . .
>
> This Agreement shall also apply to investments made prior to its entry into force, provided such investments are specifically approved in writing and registered by the host country and upon such conditions as it deems fit for [the] purposes of this Agreement subsequent to its entry into force.[178]

6.100   These provisions, which are similar in nature to other approval of investments provisions, were considered in detail by the Tribunal in the first ASEAN arbitration, *Yaung Chi Oo Trading Pte Ltd v Government of the Union of Myanmar*.[179] The arbitration was brought by a Singaporean company whose investment had been made prior to Myanmar's accession to the ASEAN Treaty. At the time of making the investment, the investor had fulfilled the detailed and demanding procedure necessary to obtain the required permit under the Union of Myanmar's Foreign Investment Law and Procedures. Myanmar challenged the Tribunal's jurisdiction saying that the investment did not qualify for protection under the ASEAN Treaty as approval under the Myanmar Foreign Investment Law did not constitute approval 'for the purposes of this Agreement' as required by Article II(1) of the ASEAN Treaty. It also argued that the claimant had failed to obtain specific approval in writing subsequent to the ASEAN Treaty coming into force in Myanmar as required by Article II(3).

6.101   The Tribunal rejected Myanmar's first argument. It said that registration pursuant to an internal foreign investment law would amount to approval under the ASEAN Agreement:

> No doubt a Party to the 1987 ASEAN Agreement could establish a separate register of protected investments for the purposes of that Agreement, in addition to or in lieu of approval under its internal law. But if Myanmar had wished to draw a distinction between approval for the purposes of the 1987 ASEAN Agreement and approval for the purposes of its internal law, it should have made it clear to potential investors that both procedures co-exist and, further, how an application for treaty protection could be made. At the least it would be appropriate to notify the ASEAN Secretariat of any special procedure. None of these things was done. In the Tribunal's view, if a State

---

[178]   ASEAN Agreement (Appendix 3 below).

[179]   *Yaung Chi Oo Trading Pte Ltd v Government of the Union of Myanmar* (Award) 8 ICSID Rep 452 (ASEAN, 2003, Sucharitkul P, Crawford & Delon).

Party to the 1987 ASEAN Agreement unequivocally and without reservation approves in writing a foreign investment proposal under its internal law, that investment must be taken to be registered and approved also for the purposes of the Agreement.[180]

The Tribunal did, however, accept Myanmar's second contention. It felt com- **6.102** pelled to give effect to the actual language of Article II(3). As this called for 'an express subsequent act amounting at least to a written approval'[181] the Tribunal could not consider the investment to be protected without such a subsequent act.

Philippe Gruslin v Malaysia[182] is another example of an investment being denied **6.103** protection for failure to comply with a registration requirement. The require-ment in this case was contained in an Inter-Governmental Agreement (IGA) between the Belgo-Luxembourg Economic Union and Malaysia.[183] It provided, in Article I(3)(e)(i), that assets invested in Malaysia had to be 'invested in a pro-ject classified as an "approved project" by the appropriate Ministry in Malaysia, in accordance with the legislation and the administrative practice, based thereon'. The investment consisted of an interest in shares traded on the Kuala Lumpur Stock Exchange. The investor argued that the approval obtained from the Stock Exchange's Capital Issues Committee would be sufficient for the purposes of the IGA. The Tribunal rejected this contention: 'The answer to this proposition is that proviso (i) [of the IGA] and the [Stock Exchange] requirements concern dif-ferent subject matters . . . What is required is something constituting regulatory approval of a 'project', as such, and not merely the approval at some time of the general business activities of a corporation.'[184]

The registration requirement was read restrictively, in the claimant's favour, by the **6.104** Tribunal in *Middle East Cement v Republic of Egypt*.[185] Egypt's Investment Law No 43 of 1974 required foreign interests to be registered to qualify as an invest-ment. However, the claim was brought under the Greece-Egypt BIT which, while not requiring registration, stated that investments are admitted by the host State 'in accordance with its legislation'.[186] The Tribunal proceeded on the basis that as the BIT did not require a specific registration, one could not be read in from the investment law.

In *Metalpar v Argentina*[187] the respondent State sought to rely upon the claimant's **6.105** failure to make necessary registrations as a ground to deny jurisdiction. In this case

---

[180] ibid 480.   [181] ibid 481.   [182] *Gruslin* (n 176 above).
[183] Agreement on Encouragement and Reciprocal Protection of Investments (Belgo-Luxembourg Economic Union-Malaysia) (signed 22 November 1979, entered into force 8 February 1982) 1284 UNTS 121.   [184] *Gruslin* (n 176 above) 507.
[185] *Middle East Cement Shipping and Handling Co SA v Arab Republic of Egypt* (Award) 7 ICSID Rep 173 (ICSID, 2002, Böckstiegel P, Bernardini & Wallace Jr).
[186] Agreement for the Promotion and Reciprocal Protection of Investments (Greece-Egypt) (signed 16 July 1993, entered into force 6 April 1995) 1895 UNTS 173 Art 2(1).
[187] *Metalpar SA & Buen Aire SA v Argentine Republic* (Jurisdiction) ICSID Case No ARB/03/5 (ICSID, 2006, Blanco P, Cameron & Chabaneix).

the requirement to register arose under Argentinian law, rather than under the treaty. The Tribunal rejected Argentina's submission on the basis that Argentinian law prescribed its own sanctions for a failure to register. It stated that it would be disproportionate to punish a failure to register with a denial of the ability to seek investment protection before an ICSID tribunal.[188]

6.106 In examining challenges to jurisdiction brought by respondent States in reliance upon their domestic registration requirements, it is important to bear in mind the correct choice of law, as described above. In principle, the question as to whether registration has been properly obtained will be considered under the domestic law of the State whose approval is required. However, these requirements must be exercised subject to the overriding concerns of good faith contained in international law. This was emphasized by the Tribunal in *Southern Pacific Properties (Middle East) Ltd v Arab Republic of Egypt*.[189] Here the project had been registered under Egypt's Investment Law No 43 but the approval was subsequently withdrawn. The Tribunal applied general principles of law to conclude that Egypt would not be permitted to repeal the approval or the investment law in a manner that would allow it to escape international arbitration. Cancellation of the approval would not alter the fact that an investment had been made under the investment law.[190]

---

[188] ibid paras 83–84.
[189] *Southern Pacific Properties (Middle East) Ltd v Arab Republic of Egypt* (Jurisdiction) 3 ICSID Rep 101 (ICSID, 1985, Jiménez de Aréchaga P, El Mahdi & Pietrowski).   [190] ibid 124.

Part III

SUBSTANTIVE RIGHTS

7

TREATMENT OF INVESTORS

1. Basis and Character of Treatment Obligations

A. The Rule of Law in International Investment Protection

7.01 Of all the catalogue of rights vouchsafed to investors under bilateral investment treaties (BITs), none has proved more elusive, or occasioned as much recent controversy as the guarantee of 'fair and equitable treatment'. The provision lies at the centre of a set of interlocking treatment obligations which will form the subject of this chapter: the non-contingent standards of fair and equitable treatment, full protection and security; and the contingent standards of national treatment; most favoured nation treatment (MFN), and non-discrimination.[1]

7.02 The assurance of fair and equitable treatment simply provides, with Delphic economy of language, that investments shall 'at all times be accorded fair and equitable treatment and shall enjoy full protection and security in the territory [of the reciprocating host State]'.

7.03 No doubt the beguiling simplicity of the phrase secured its easy passage into treaty practice. What State seeking to attract foreign investment could fail to agree to make such provision? Indeed, what State would concede that its legal system might fail to provide such an elementary protection? Yet, despite having been included almost universally in the modern investment treaty lexicon, this guarantee has until recently received scant attention or analysis. The extent of the neglect was such that one commentator concluded an exhaustive survey of the practice in 1999 by observing

---

[1] On the meaning of this distinction see 7.19 below; H Walker Jr, 'Modern Treaties of Friendship, Commerce and Navigation' (1957–1958) 42 Minn LR 805; S Vasciannie, 'The Fair and Equitable Treatment Standard in International Investment Law and Practice' (1999) 70 BYIL 99, 105–107.

'the paucity of jurisprudence'.[2] BITs, he observed 'are yet to generate a substantial flow of international litigation, and, even where litigation has occurred, the fair and equitable standard has not been decisive in the proceedings.'[3] The most that could be said on the meaning of the standard was the tentative conclusion that it barred 'host countries from treating foreign investors unfairly and inequitably'.[4]

The investment arbitration experience of the last five years has turned a drought **7.04** into a flood.[5] It has produced an important stream of jurisprudence, in which the fair and equitable standard is not merely considered by arbitral tribunals, but, in a number of cases, has actually emerged as the outcome-decisive right, eclipsing even the more established protection against expropriation. National treatment and MFN treatment have also figured in recent awards. But a determination of their content has, on the whole, proved less controversial,[6] even if their application has on occasion produced results which may not have been anticipated by host State or investor.[7] By contrast, fair and equitable treatment has emerged from the shadows of investment law to become a potent tool in the assessment of the adequacy of the judicial and administrative systems of host States. For that very reason, its dangers have also become apparent, perhaps especially when the legal systems placed under the microscope of the international arbitral process are those of developed Western States, such as Canada and the United States.

In the course of this process, arbitral tribunals have to determine for themselves **7.05** the content of the concept and its application to the many and various contexts of the State regulation of the modern globalized economy. Hazardous waste disposal in Mexico;[8] populist television channels in the Czech Republic;[9] the building of a

---

[2] Vasciannie (ibid) 162–163.   [3] ibid.   [4] ibid 163.

[5] For more recent studies on the jurisprudence from 2000–2005 see: OECD, *International Investment Law: A Changing Landscape* (2005) Chap 3; R Dolzer, 'Fair and Equitable Treatment: A Key Standard in Investment Treaties' (2005) 39 Int'l Law 87; C Schreuer, 'Fair and Equitable Treatment in Arbitral Practice' (2005) 6 Journal of World Investment and Trade 357.

[6] But see 7.162–7.169 below for the controversy over the application of the MFN clause to the submission to arbitration. cf *Emilio Agustín Maffezini v Kingdom of Spain* (Jurisdiction) 5 ICSID Rep 387, 404 (ICSID, 2000, Orrego Vicuña P, Buergenthal & Wolf) and *Plama Consortium Ltd v Republic of Bulgaria* (Jurisdiction) 20 ICSID Rev-FILJ 262; 44 ILM 717 (ICSID, 2005, Salans P, van den Berg & Veeder).

[7] eg the use of the MFN clause to apply protections from a BIT between Croatia and Chile for the benefit of a Malaysian investor in Chile in *MTD Equity Sdn Bhd & anor v Republic of Chile* (Award) (2005) 44 ILM 91 (ICSID, 2004, Sureda P, Lalonde & Oreamuno Blanco) request for annulment pending.

[8] The context for numerous disputes to date: *Azinian, Davitian & Baca v United Mexican States* (Award) 5 ICSID Rep 269 (NAFTA, 1998, Paulsson P, Civiletti & von Wobeser); *Metalclad Corp v United Mexican States* (Award) 5 ICSID Rep 209 (NAFTA, 2000, Lauterpacht P, Civiletti & Siqueiros); *Tecnicas Medioambientales Tecmed SA v United Mexican States* (Award) (2004) 43 ILM 133 (ICSID (AF), 2003, Grigera Naon P, Fernandez Rozas & Bernal Verea); *Waste Management Inc v United Mexican States* (Award) (2004) 43 ILM 967 (NAFTA/ICSID (AF), 2004, Crawford P, Civiletti, & Gómez).

[9] *Lauder v Czech Republic* (Award) 9 ICSID Rep 62 (UNCITRAL, 2001, Briner C, Cutler & Klein); *CME Czech Republic BV v Czech Republic* (Partial Award) 9 ICSID Rep 121 (UNCITRAL, 2001, Kühn C, Schwebel & Hándl).

new town in Chile;[10] and the conduct of a jury trial in Mississippi[11] have all provoked international investment disputes. These cases of the early twenty-first century are a far cry from the mistreatment of aliens in South American jails, or the
failures in the investigation of crimes against the person, which populate the early
twentieth-century reports of arbitral awards.

7.06 The transformation of the standard in the theatre of rights and duties which is
international arbitration has exposed the relative poverty of the interpretation
process, when applied to the open-textured language of an investment treaty.
Tribunals have turned to dictionaries for definitions of the concepts of 'fair' and
'equitable'. But, because these terms are general descriptors of the qualities of a
system of justice, it is essential first to ask: by reference to what system of law are
these concepts to derive their meaning? One can look in vain for guidance from
travaux préparatoires. The bilateral process does not typically produce informative
guidance on the public record as to the parties' intentions, and when such information does become available,[12] the results are often inconclusive.

7.07 The process of the adjudication of these rights has also exposed considerable
divergencies in approach, both between arbitrators, and between arbitrators and
contracting States. Some of these differences have had serious consequences for
litigants, as well as for the future development of the law in this area. In *Metalclad v
Mexico*, the Tribunal's finding that Mexico had failed to provide such treatment
because its administrative procedures were not transparent[13] was reversed in a
challenge to the award in the Canadian courts on the ground that the requirement of transparency was outside the arbitrators' jurisdiction.[14] The Tribunal in
Pope & Talbot Inc v Canada decided that it was not limited in its interpretation of
the standard in the North American Free Trade Agreement (NAFTA) by the minimum standard of treatment at customary international law.[15] The Free Trade
Commission of the three State Parties responded, while the arbitration was still on
foot, by issuing an Interpretation of the treaty provision in which it confirmed that
'the concepts of "fair and equitable treatment" and "full protection and security" *do
not require* treatment in addition to or beyond that which is required by the customary international law minimum standard of treatment of aliens'[16] (emphasis

---

[10] *MTD* (n 7 above).
[11] *The Loewen Group Inc and Raymond L Loewen v United States of America* 7 ICSID Rep 421
(NAFTA/ICSID (AF), 2003, Mason P, Mikva & Mustill).
[12] As it did dramatically in *Pope & Talbot Inc v Government of Canada* (Award on Damages) 7
ICSID Rep 43 (NAFTA/UNCITRAL, 2002, Dervaird P, Greenberg & Belman).
[13] *Metalclad* (n 8 above).
[14] Sub nom *United Mexican States v Metalclad Corp* 2001 BCSC 664; 5 ICSID Rep 236
(Supreme Court of British Colombia).
[15] *Pope & Talbot Inc v Government of Canada* (Award on the Merits of Phase 2) 7 ICSID Rep 43
(NAFTA/UNCITRAL, 2001, Dervaird P, Greenberg & Belman).
[16] NAFTA Free Trade Commission (FTC), Interpretation of NAFTA Chap 11 (31 July 2001) 6
ICSID Rep 567, 568.

added). In the controversy between the American investor Ron Lauder and the Czech Republic over the operation of a television channel, two separate tribunals were constituted under the US-Czech and the Dutch-Czech BITs respectively (the latter vested with a claim by the Dutch corporate vehicle for the investment). Within an interval of ten days, the two tribunals rendered awards on the basis of substantially the same evidence. One found that there was no breach of the standard.[17] The other found that there had been an unjustified interference in private contractual relations by the State which did amount to a breach of the standard.[18] An attempt to set aside that award in the Swedish courts on grounds of inconsistency failed. The Court held that the awards, having been rendered under separate BITs, and in disputes brought by different plaintiffs, were not subject to the doctrine of *res judicata*.[19]

Thus, the appearance of virtual unanimity in State practice, which is gleaned from **7.08** a comparison of the language of the multitude of treaties, masks an absence of any kind of settled agreement over content. Much of the controversy has focused on whether, as FA Mann once contended, the terms 'are to be understood and applied independently and autonomously'[20] and 'envisage conduct which goes far beyond the minimum standard'[21] of the treatment of aliens at customary international law. The alternative view, espoused not just by the NAFTA Free Trade Commission but also in the interpretation of other BITs which do not have an express reference to an external international law standard[22] is that fair and equitable treatment is synonymous with a customary concept of the minimum standard.

It is suggested that this controversy is misguided, and the dichotomy presented by **7.09** the opposing views is a false one on a number of levels. It takes an overly simplistic view of differences in formulation of the right in different treaties. It suggests that the only choice open to a tribunal is between a complete discretion to determine whether particular conduct is 'unfair and inequitable' on the one hand, and the application of a conception of customary international law 'frozen in amber'[23]

---

[17] *Lauder v Czech Republic* (n 9 above).
[18] *CME Czech Republic BV v Czech Republic* (n 9 above).
[19] *Czech Republic v CME Czech Republic BV (Case No T8735-01)* 9 ICSID Rep 439 (Sweden, Svea Court of Appeal). On the application of the doctrines of *lis pendens* and *res judicata* in these cases see 4.119–4.143 above.
[20] FA Mann, 'British Treaties for the Promotion and Protection of Investments' (1981) 52 BYIL 241, 244. But cf the considered view which he subsequently expressed in the 5th edition of *The Legal Aspect of Money* (1992) 526, referring to ' ... the overriding principle of "fair and equitable treatment", which, it must be repeated, in turn is perhaps no more than a (welcome) contractual recognition and affirmation of that principle of customary international law which requires States to act in good faith, reasonably, without abuse, arbitrariness, or discrimination'. The formulation is in substance repeated in the 6th edition, C Proctor, *Mann on the Legal Aspect of Money* (2005) para 22.53. See JC Thomas 'Reflections on Article 1105 of NAFTA: History, State Practice and the Influence of Commentators' (2002) 17 ICSID Rev-FILJ 21, 57.   [21] ibid.
[22] eg Statement by Swiss Foreign Office [1980] Annuaire Suisse de droit international 178.
[23] *ADF Group Inc v United States of America*, Second Submission of Canada pursuant to NAFTA Art 1128, 19 July 2002, para 33.

at some time in the past. Most seriously of all, it falsely presents the minimum standard of treatment of aliens in customary international law as having a well-settled content. In so doing, it ignores the level of dissent among States throughout much of the twentieth century not only over the content of such a standard, but even over whether it existed at all.[24]

7.10 Indeed, for much of the twentieth century, the international minimum standard of treatment was vigorously opposed by many States, which saw the limit of the obligation upon them as being to accord national treatment to alien investors.[25] In the current BIT practice these two standards, traditionally placed in opposition, are almost universally placed alongside one another without any attempt at reconciliation.

7.11 It is submitted that it is both possible and necessary to reconcile the particular treaty language with requirements of general international law. Indeed, as it was put in one recent award, 'the difference between the Treaty standard . . . and the customary minimum standard, when applied to the specific facts of a case, may well be more apparent than real'.[26] In any event, the legal protection afforded by the guarantee of fair and equitable treatment cannot be understood without a conception of the proper function of international law in assessing the standards of justice achieved by national systems of law and administration.

7.12 Elihu Root, speaking on the appropriate treatment to be accorded to aliens in 1910, concluded that: 'There is a standard of justice, very simple, very fundamental, and of such general acceptance by all civilized countries as to form a part of the international law of the world. The condition upon which any country is entitled to measure the justice due from it to an alien by the justice which it accords to its own citizens is that its system of law and administration shall conform to this general standard.'[27] Root here makes four points which continue to be of fundamental relevance in understanding the function of fair and equitable treatment today. First, he posits the *source* of the standard as being a principle of 'general acceptance by all civilized countries'. Secondly, he sees the *concern* of the standard as being that of justice. Thirdly, the *subject-matter* of the enquiry is a country's system of law and administration. Fourthly, he saw the *rationale* for a standard which was absolute, and not merely an assurance of national treatment, as being a means of ensuring that that basic standard of justice to which the citizens of all countries ought to be entitled is at least available to the alien, who might otherwise lack the claim of a national on his own legal system. Thus, for Root, the

---

[24] E Borchard, 'The "Minimum Standard" of the Treatment of Aliens' (1940) 38 Mich LR 445.

[25] I Brownlie, *Principles of Public International Law* (6th edn, 2003) 501–505.

[26] *Saluka Investments BV (The Netherlands) v Czech Republic* (Partial Award) (UNCITRAL, 2006, Watts C, Fortier & Behrens) para 291.

[27] E Root, 'The Basis of Protection to Citizens Residing Abroad' (1910) 4 AJIL 517, 521–522.

standard was not a matter of establishing two systems of law. Rather the action mandated by the standard 'is always action which would be equally required in case a native citizen were placed under the same circumstances of exigency'.[28]

Seen in this light, the fair and equitable standard gives modern expression to a *general principle of due process* in its application to the treatment of investors.[29] The foundation of this principle is that, by agreeing to extend such treatment to nationals of a reciprocating country, States have accepted that there is an objective standard of treatment by which their own legal and administrative system may be judged. The standard thus encapsulates the minimum requirements of the rule of law. A Chamber of the International Court of Justice (ICJ) expressed this idea by contrasting due process with arbitrariness: 'Arbitrariness is not so much something opposed to a rule of law, as something opposed to the rule of law. This idea was expressed by the Court in the *Asylum* case, when it spoke of "arbitrary action" being "substituted for the rule of law" (*Asylum Judgment, I.C.J. Reports 1950*, p. 284). It is a wilful disregard of due process of law …'[30] **7.13**

In the past, debates on minimum treatment have foundered upon the traditional hurdles of customary international law: the lack of a sufficiently uniform practice, let alone an acceptance of *opinio juris*, given the deep divergencies in the views of States exposed during the many fruitless multilateral negotiations on investment law. But the voluntary acceptance of the principle by treaty transforms the question from one of obligation to content. **7.14**

Then the issue becomes one of locating a sufficiently common consensus among civilized nations as to content. In this, reference to 'general principles of law common to civilized nations' as the third basic source of international law[31] becomes of crucial importance. In the task of finding common principles in this field, the development of modern international law presents a substantial advantage over the position in the early twentieth century as a result of the elaboration of relevant international human rights standards, and of the gradual emergence of global administrative law.[32] Reference to these sources facilitates the application of standards which may be seen as genuinely common to civilized nations. It is not, as has sometimes been suggested, that the emergence of international human rights norms would subsume and render obsolete both the international minimum **7.15**

---

[28] ibid 523.   [29] J Paulsson, *Denial of Justice in International Law* (2005) 5–6.

[30] *Case concerning Elettronica Sicula SpA (ELSI) (United States of America v Italy)* [1989] ICJ Rep 15, 76; 84 ILR 311, 382.

[31] Statute of the International Court of Justice (26 June 1945 annexed to the Charter of the United Nations) Art 38(1)(c). G Schwarzenberger, *International Law* (3rd edn 1957) vol I, 200, cited (with apparent approval) in *ADF Group Inc v United States of America* (Award) 6 ICSID Rep 449, 530 fn 176 (NAFTA/ICSID (AF), 2003, Feliciano P, de Mestral & Lamm).

[32] B Kingsbury et al (eds), 'The Emergence of Global Administrative Law' (2005) 68 Law & Cont Prob 15.

standard and the standard of national treatment.[33] Rather, some elements of human rights law may furnish a source of general principle from which the obligation of fair and equitable treatment may be given contemporary content.[34]

7.16   Importantly, however, and unlike the earlier customary international law standard, the protection is not simply concerned with 'fair' or 'just' treatment to investors. Appropriate weight and meaning must also be given to the requirement of 'equitable treatment'. Schwarzenberger observed on the first emergence of this formula, that this:

> ... presents an imaginative attempt *to combine the minimum standard with the standard of equitable treatment*. This decision is well justified on two grounds. The experiences of the last forty years suggest that whenever, in fact, an agreed settlement has been reached, the creditors have consented to temper the application of the minimum standard by the introduction of an equitable element in the form of considerable concessions on their part. Thus, it appears wise to anticipate—and limit—such contingencies. Moreover, in relations between heterogeneous communities—in varying stages of technological advancement, social structure and political organization—and in an age of rapid change, the standard of equitable treatment provides equality on a footing of commendable elasticity [emphasis added].[35]

7.17   The concept of equitable treatment provides not merely a means of doing equity as between different classes of investors, whether natives or equally favoured foreigners. That is something which the concomitant rights of national treatment and MFN treatment will secure in any event. The inclusion of the reference to equitable treatment also provides a means by which an appropriate balance may be struck between the protection of the investor and the public interest which the host State may properly seek to protect in the light of the particular circumstances then prevailing. As the editors of *Oppenheim* have observed: 'The requirements of international law in this field ... represent an attempt at accommodation between the conflicting interests involved.'[36] This process involves, as was observed in the *Saluka* award, 'a weighing of the [investor's] legitimate and reasonable expectations on the one hand and the [host State's] legitimate regulatory interests on the other'.[37]

7.18   Part 2 of this chapter will examine these propositions against the evidence in the shape of the corpus of arbitral awards which have sought to apply the provision in

---

[33] FV García-Amador, First Report on State Responsibility, UN Doc A/CN 4/96 [1956] 2 YB ILC 173, 200–203.

[34] I Brownlie, *Principles of Public International Law* (6th edn, 2003) 504–505; American Law Institute, *Restatement of the Law, Third, Foreign Relations Law of the United States* (1987) Section 711(a), 184–196.

[35] G Schwarzenberger, 'The Abs-Shawcross Draft Convention on Investments Abroad: a Critical Commentary' (1960) 9 J Public L 147, 152, repeated in his *Foreign Investments and International Law* (1969) 114.

[36] R Jennings and A Watts (eds), *Oppenheim's International Law* (9th edn, 1996) 933.

[37] *Saluka Investments BV (The Netherlands) v Czech Republic* (Partial Award) (UNCITRAL, 2006, Watts C, Fortier & Behrens) para 306.

the modern context. This will enable a distillation, in Part 3, of the measurable standards which are emerging to give content to the concept. However, it is first necessary to put the arbitral awards into context by drawing together three strands:

(1) the current structure of investor treatment provisions;
(2) some key aspects of their genesis and development; and
(3) the proper approach to interpretation.

B. The Current Structure of Investor Treatment Provisions

The standard of treatment extended to investors by investment treaties, infinitely **7.19** various in its iteration, nevertheless may be found to consist of the following two main elements: the 'non-contingent standards' of fair and equitable treatment and full protection and security; and the 'contingent standards' of national treatment, MFN treatment, and non-discrimination. The distinction drawn in the literature between contingent and non-contingent standards,[38] simply denotes the idea that the content of a contingent standard is determined, not by reference to the standard itself, but by reference to an exterior state of law or fact, namely the treatment accorded to other persons or entities, who stand in the requisite relationship to the protected investor. Non-contingent standards, on the other hand, are absolute as they apply to protect a given entity irrespective of the treatment which may be accorded to others. It is for that reason that they present a potentially more valuable tool in investor protection.

Guidance on States' views as to the appropriate formulation of both categories of **7.20** rights may best be obtained from the model form BITs adopted by many States, both capital importing and exporting. As has been rightly observed: 'A model BIT represents the set of norms that the relevant state holds out to be both reasonable and acceptable as a legal basis for the protection of foreign investment in its own economy.'[39]

Another important source of the formulation of such rights is NAFTA, not only **7.21** because it consists in an agreement between three States which have traditionally had widely different views on the protection of aliens, but also because its arbitration provisions have spawned much of the recent jurisprudence. Finally, reference will be made to the Energy Charter Treaty, as one of the most significant multilateral investment treaties—albeit one which has a limited subject-matter scope. No pretension of exhaustive treatment as to the alternative forms arrived at in bilateral negotiation will be made here, since the purpose of the enquiry is to identify the

---

[38] eg Walker (n 1 above) and Vasciannie (n 1 above).
[39] Z Douglas, 'The Hybrid Foundations of Investment Treaty Arbitration' (2003) 74 BYIL 151, 159.

common features. Of course, in the interpretation of any particular treaty, the general must yield to the particular.

Non-contingent standards

Typical model BIT

7.22 The fundamental standards of fair and equitable treatment and full protection and security are frequently grouped together with unreasonable impairment and non-discrimination in a single article which provides, without further elaboration:

> Investments of nationals or companies of either Contracting Party shall at all times be accorded fair and equitable treatment and shall enjoy full protection and security in the territory of the other Contracting Party. Neither Contracting Party shall in any way impair by unreasonable or discriminatory measures the management, maintenance, use, enjoyment or disposal of investments in its territory of nationals or companies of the other Contracting Party.[40]

7.23 This example is taken from the Sri Lankan model BIT. The concept of fair and equitable treatment finds expression in model BITs adopted in numerous States, whether capital exporting[41] or capital importing,[42] and including many States, such as those of Latin America, which had traditionally been opposed to the imposition of an international minimum standard.[43]

7.24 In the French prototype, the concept is rendered as 'juste' and is expressly linked to the general principles of international law as 'traitement juste et équitable, conformément aux principes du Droit international'.[44]

NAFTA

7.25 This link between international law and fair and equitable treatment is also made explicitly in NAFTA, but in language which suggests that the particular treatment

---

[40] Sri Lanka model BIT (Appendix 9 below) Art 2.

[41] eg Netherlands model BIT (Appendix 8 below) Art 3; Switzerland model BIT, reprinted in UNCTAD, *International Investment Instruments: A Compendium* (1996) Vol III 177, 179 Art 4(1); UK model BIT, (Appendix 4 below) Art 2(2).

[42] eg Egypt model BIT, reprinted in UNCTAD, *International Investment Instruments: A Compendium* (2000) Vol V 293, 295 Art 3; Malaysia model BIT, reprinted in UNCTAD, *International Investment Instruments: A Compendium* (2000) Vol V 325, 326 Art 2(2).

[43] eg Chile model BIT, reprinted in UNCTAD, *International Investment Instruments: A Compendium* (1996) Vol III 143, 145 Art 4(1).

[44] France model BIT, (Appendix 10 below) Art 4; see Accord sur l'encouragement et la Protection Réciproques des Investissements ('Agreement on the Reciprocal Promotion and Protection of Investments') (France-Argentina) (signed 3 July 1991, entered into force 3 March 1993) 1728 UNTS 282 Art 3, cited in *Compañía de Aguas del Aconquija and Vivendi Universal ('Vivendi') v Argentine Republic* (Decision on Annulment) 6 ICSID Rep 327, 356 (ICSID 2002, Fortier P, Crawford & Fernández Rozas): 'Each Contracting party shall undertake to accord in its territory and maritime zone *just and equitable treatment, in accordance with the principles of international law* . . .'

standards were seen by the framers as examples of a more general international law standard. Article 1105(1) provides:

Article 1105: Minimum Standard of Treatment

1. Each Party shall accord to investments of investors of another Party treatment in accordance with international law, including fair and equitable treatment and full protection and security.[45]

This provision must now be read in the light of the Interpretation issued by the **7.26** NAFTA Free Trade Commission on 31 July 2001, which provides that:

B. Minimum Standard of Treatment in Accordance with International Law

1. Article 1105(1) prescribes the customary international law minimum standard of treatment of aliens as the minimum standard of treatment to be afforded to investments of investors of another Party.

2. The concepts of 'fair and equitable treatment' and 'full protection and security' do not require treatment in addition to or beyond that which is required by the customary international law minimum standard of treatment of aliens.

3. A determination that there has been a breach of another provision of the NAFTA, or of a separate international agreement, does not establish that there has been a breach of Article 1105(1).[46]

Energy Charter Treaty

The Energy Charter Treaty (ECT), by contrast, sets international law as a mini- **7.27** mum for the standard, providing, in Article 10(1):

Each Contracting Party shall, in accordance with the provisions of this Treaty, encourage and create stable, equitable, favourable and transparent conditions for Investors of other Contracting Parties to make Investments in its Area. Such conditions shall include a commitment to accord at all times to Investments of Investors of other Contracting Parties fair and equitable treatment. Such Investments shall also enjoy the most constant protection and security and no Contracting Party shall in any way impair by unreasonable or discriminatory measures their management, maintenance, use, enjoyment or disposal. *In no case shall such Investments be accorded treatment less favourable than that required by international law, including treaty obligations.* Each Contracting Party shall observe any obligations it has entered into with an Investor or an Investment of an Investor of any other Contracting Party.' [emphasis added].

US revised model BIT

A more restrictive conception of the nature of the reference to international law is **7.28** pursued by the most recent model BIT adopted by the United States in 2004.[47]

---

[45] See generally A Bjorklund, J Hannaford & M Kinnear, *Investment Disputes under NAFTA. An Annotated Guide to NAFTA Chapter 11* (2006) paras 1105-1–1105-57.

[46] NAFTA FTC (n 16 above). The FTC is, by NAFTA Art 2001(2) empowered to, *inter alia*, 'resolve disputes that may arise regarding [the Agreement's] interpretation or application'. Pursuant to Art 1131(2) an interpretation by the FTC of a provision of the Agreement 'shall be binding on a Tribunal'.   [47] 2004 US model BIT (Appendix 6 below).

The formula adopted in this model has also begun to find its way into recent US Free Trade Agreements. Article 5 of this form provides:

> Article 5: Minimum Standard of Treatment
>
> 1. Each Party shall accord to covered investments treatment in accordance with customary international law, including fair and equitable treatment and full protection and security.
>
> 2. For greater certainty, paragraph 1 prescribes the customary international law minimum standard of treatment of aliens as the minimum standard of treatment to be afforded to covered investments. The concepts of 'fair and equitable treatment' and 'full protection and security' do not require treatment in addition to or beyond that which is required by that standard, and do not create additional substantive rights. The obligation in paragraph 1 to provide:
>
> (a) 'fair and equitable treatment' includes the obligation not to deny justice in criminal, civil, or administrative adjudicatory proceedings in accordance with the principle of due process embodied in the principal legal systems of the world; and
>
> (b) 'full protection and security' requires each Party to provide the level of police protection required under customary international law.
>
> 3. A determination that there has been a breach of another provision of this Treaty, or of a separate international agreement, does not establish that there has been a breach of this Article.

7.29 Annex A adds, for good measure, a definition of customary international law as follows:

> The Parties confirm their shared understanding that 'customary international law' generally and as specifically referenced in Article 5 ... results from a general and consistent practice of States that they follow from a sense of legal obligation. With regard to Article 5 ... the customary international law minimum standard of treatment of aliens refers to all customary international law principles that protect the economic rights and interests of aliens.

7.30 This revised formulation may be understood as a response to a perception in and by the United States that a definition of 'fair and equitable treatment' unbounded by custom had left the door open to adventurist arbitrators to exercise an unfettered discretion as to the appropriateness of State policy. Whether the faith of the drafters in the certainty of customary international law is well-founded may be debatable. But the new model form is one of the very few attempts, even if partial, at a codification of the content of the two central concepts. Importantly, the (non-exclusive) definition of 'fair and equitable treatment' draws expressly upon a principle of due process, which is described in terms consistent with it being seen as a general principle of law common to civilized nations.

Contingent standards

Typical model BIT

7.31 The other major set of treatment standards—those providing for national treatment and MFN treatment—are usually described as 'contingent standards' in that the quality of treatment which they prescribe is determined by reference to that accorded to others in the same position. In typical BIT practice, these two standards are combined in a single article. Thus, for example, the UK model provides:

Article 3

National Treatment and Most-favoured-nation Provisions

(1) Neither Contracting Party shall in its territory subject investments or returns of nationals or companies of the other Contracting Party to treatment less favourable than that which it accords to investments or returns of its own nationals or companies or to investments or returns of nationals or companies of any third State.

(2) Neither Contracting Party shall in its territory subject nationals or companies of the other Contracting Party, as regards their management, maintenance, use, enjoyment or disposal of their investments, to treatment less favourable than that which it accords to its own nationals or companies or to nationals or companies of any third State.[48]

Such provisions also normally provide for exceptions for customs unions and for taxation agreements or legislation.[49] **7.32**

Distinction between pre- and post-establishment protection

A major policy distinction in BIT practice is between those States which seek to extend the protection of national treatment to the right of establishment as well as to operation, and those that limit it to post-establishment operation.[50] The US prototype provides expressly for the pre-entry stage: 'Each party shall accord to investors of the other Party treatment no less favorable than that it accords, in like circumstances, to its own investors with respect to the *establishment, acquisition, expansion*, management, conduct, operation, and sale or other disposition of investments in its territory' (emphasis added). [51] **7.33**

On the other hand, the UK Prototype set out above provides no such extension. To the contrary, the obligation upon the host State to admit capital in Article 2(1) is made 'subject to its right to exercise powers conferred by its laws'. This difference is highly material. It is normally for the host State to determine for itself the conditions under which it will admit foreign investment, and the nature of the rights thus acquired. An extension of national treatment to the pre-entry phase fundamentally alters that balance. **7.34**

NAFTA extends both of the contingent standards, by Articles 1102 and 1103, to investors and investments of the other parties, and (subject to scheduled exceptions) extends the protections of national treatment to the pre-establishment phase. Article 1104 contains a rule of priority between the two standards. It **7.35**

---

[48] UK model BIT (Appendix 4 below).   [49] eg ibid Art 7.
[50] M Sornarajah, *The International Law on Foreign Investment* (2nd edn, 2004) 319–321.
[51] 2004 US model BIT (Appendix 6 below) Art 3(1).

provides that: 'Each Party shall accord to investors of another Party and to investments of investors of another Party the better of the treatment required by Articles 1102 and 1103.' There is an elaborate set of reservations and exceptions to Articles 1102 and 1103 set out in Article 1108. These, *inter alia*, enable parties to schedule non-conforming measures[52] and specifically exclude State procurement.[53]

7.36   The Energy Charter Treaty (ECT) distinguishes sharply between the pre-investment phase and the currency of any investment as to the extent of protection afforded by the national treatment and MFN treatment provisions of its Article 10. Paragraph 7 imposes a legal obligation to afford either such treatment (whichever is the most favourable) during the currency of the investment in all spheres save for the modalities of its application to energy technology research and development.[54] The extension of a binding obligation of national treatment to the making of an investment (ie the pre-investment phase) is, however, reserved to the negotiation of a subsequent treaty, which has not yet been concluded.[55] In the meantime, the obligation is only one of best endeavours, coupled with an obligation to notify exceptions to the principle to the ECT Secretariat.[56]

C. Evolution of the Treatment Standards

7.37   What light may be shed on the contemporary meaning to be attributed to the standards of treatment accorded to investors in modern BITs by an examination of their historical evolution? Four general themes may be drawn from the historical experience: (a) the contrast between the treaty origins of contingent standards and the customary origins of non-contingent standards; (b) the significance of the development of non-contingent standards primarily through the law of State responsibility and diplomatic protection; (c) the chill effect of international dissension on the evolution of the fair and equitable treatment standard; and (d) the implications of the revival in bilateralism for the status of the standards.

Treaty and custom in the origins of the standards

7.38   The first point is that the non-contingent standards of national treatment and MFN treatment, which are of considerable historical antiquity,[57] have always

---

[52] North American Free Trade Agreement (adopted 17 December 1992, entered into force 1 January 1994) CTS 1994 No 2; (1993) 32 ILM 612 ('NAFTA') (Appendix 1 below) Art 1108 (1)–(4).

[53] ibid Art 1108 (7).

[54] Energy Charter Treaty (signed 17 December 1994, entered into force 16 April 1998) 2080 UNTS 100 (Appendix 2 below) Art 10(8).   [55] ibid Art 10(2)–(6).

[56] ibid Art 10(9). The 2005 Annual Report of the ECT Secretariat notes some 97 such exceptions listed as notified to the Secretariat.

[57] B Nolde, 'La Clause de la Nation la plus Favorisée et les Tarifs Préférentiels' (1932) 39 *Recueil des Cours* 1, 24; JHW Verzijl, *International Law in Historical Perspective* (1972) Vol V, 429–438.

developed exclusively through express grants by treaty.[58] Customary international law does not require that States accord either form of treatment to aliens. As the editors of *Oppenheim* put it as to MFN treatment: 'Notwithstanding such force as the general principle of non-discrimination might have, a state is not normally prevented from extending to another state particularly favourable treatment which it refrains from extending to third states.'[59] And as to national treatment, 'a degree of discrimination in the treatment of aliens as compared with nationals is, generally, permissible as a matter of customary international law'.[60]

Thus, where States wish to secure for their citizens the benefits of national or **7.39** MFN treatment in a foreign State, they must do so by treaty. The negotiation of such agreements forms one of the earliest subjects of treaty-making practice, dating back at least to the seventeenth century.[61]

The lexicon of MFN and national treatment may now be said to dominate the **7.40** field of international economic law generally as a result of the adoption of these two standards as the central pillars of world trade in goods by Articles I and III respectively of the General Agreement on Tariffs and Trade 1947.[62]

By contrast, non-contingent standards have had an extensive—if controversial— **7.41** life in customary international law. Their incorporation into treaties appears almost as an incidental confirmation of the pre-existing right. As such, commerce or investment treaties have, until recently, served but little as the basis for the pursuit of international claims for the vindication of such rights.

The modern treaty-based non-contingent formula may be traced to the draft for **7.42** a multilateral convention to protect private foreign investment prepared by Hermann Abs[63] and Lord Shawcross[64] in 1959. Article I of that draft provided: 'Each Party shall at all times ensure fair and equitable treatment to the property of the nationals of the other Parties. Such property shall be accorded the most constant protection and security within the territories of the other Parties and the management, use, and enjoyment thereof shall not in any way be impaired by unreasonable or discriminatory measures.'[65]

The draft may be seen as an attempt to take forward the provisions of the **7.43** (still-born) Havana Charter for an International Trade Organization 1948, which envisaged that the Organization would make recommendations for bilateral or

---

[58] ILC, 'Draft Articles on Most-Favoured-Nation Clauses' [1978] 2(2) YB ILC 16, Arts 4, 7.
[59] *Oppenheim* (n 36 above) 1326.
[60] *Oppenheim* (n 36 above) 932.
[61] Nolde (n 57 above) 27, citing the example of the Treaty between the King of Great Britain and the King of Portugal of 1642 Art 4.
[62] World Trade Organization (WTO), *The Legal Texts: The Results of the Uruguay Round of Multilateral Trade Negotiations* (1999) 423–429.   [63] Then Chairman of Deutsche Bank.
[64] Former Attorney-General of England.
[65] H Abs & H Shawcross 'Draft Convention on Investments Abroad' (1960) 9 J Pub L 115, 116.

multilateral agreements, *inter alia*, 'to assure *just and equitable treatment* for the enterprise, skills, capital, arts and technology brought from one Member country to another ... '[66](emphasis added). Abs and Shawcross supported their formulation by reference to recent US practice in the conclusion of treaties of friendship, commerce and navigation (FCN treaties), as well as to concepts 'inherent in any system of law' and to judgments on the content of general international law.[67] In fact, the US FCN treaties had referred variously to treatment being either 'fair and equitable' or simply 'equitable', and they did so in a separate article to that which provided in more general terms for the protection and security of nationals of either Party, who were to receive 'the most constant protection and security, *in no case less than that required by international law*'[68] (emphasis added). The provision for 'full and perfect protection for their persons and property' may be traced to a much earlier period in US FCN treaty practice.[69] Indeed it was commonly included in many nineteenth century treaties of commerce and navigation concluded by other States as well.[70] The result, as Schwarzenberger observed, 'presents an imaginative attempt *to combine the minimum standard with the standard of equitable treatment*'[71] (emphasis added).

7.44 But the primary means by which the protection of the property and investments of aliens was achieved, until the advent after World War II of the modern BIT with its rights of direct recourse for investors in investor-State arbitration, was through inter-State claims of State responsibility made upon the exercise of diplomatic protection. In this, the origin of the rights claimed is found in general international law, namely in the 'general requirements of customary international law, such as those which impose on a state international responsibility for denial of justice to aliens, or which require it to observe in its treatment of aliens certain

---

[66] Havana Charter for an International Trade Organization, United Nations Conference on Trade and Employment (March 24 1948) UN Doc E/Conf 2/78 (1948) Art 11.

[67] Abs & Shawcross (n 65 above) 119–120.

[68] eg Treaty of Friendship, Commerce and Navigation between the United States of America and Ireland (signed 21 January 1950, entered into force 14 September 1950) 206 UNTS 269; 1 USTS 788, Arts II and V. See generally on the US practice: KJ Vandevelde, 'The Bilateral Investment Treaty Program of the United States' (1988) 21 Cornell International Law Journal 201 and R Wilson, *The International Law Standard in Treaties of the United States* (1953) 92–105.

[69] eg United States-Paraguay Treaty of Friendship, Commerce and Navigation 1859 Art IX in WM Malloy, *Treaties, Conventions, International Acts, Protocols and Agreements between the United States and other Powers 1776–1909* (1910) Vol II 1364, 1367.

[70] eg Treaty between Italy and Venezuela of 1861 Art 4, (in C Parry (ed) *The Consolidated Treaty Series* (1969) 199, 214) which was the subject of the *Sambiaggio Case* 10 RIAA 499, 518; and the 'Traité d'Amité, de Commerce et de Navigation' (France-Mexico) (1886) in A Ch Kiss, *Répertoire de la Pratique Française en Matière de Droit International Public* Tome III, 1965, Section 1002, 637 cited in *Asian Agricultural Products Ltd (AAPL) v Republic of Sri Lanka* (Award) 4 ICSID Rep 245, 268 (ICSID, 1990, El-Kosheri P, Goldman & Asante).

[71] Schwarzenberger (n 35 above), repeated in his *Foreign Investments and International Law* (1969) 114.

minimum international standards'.[72] Where may such requirements be found, and what continuing relevance do they have for the application of the treaty non-contingent standards?

State responsibility and the diplomatic protection of investors

In the 1926 award in *Neer v Mexico*[73] (a case which has figured prominently in **7.45** argument in a number of the recent investment arbitration awards),[74] the Mexico/United States Claims Commissioners held that 'the treatment of an alien, in order to constitute an international delinquency, should amount to an outrage, to bad faith, to wilful neglect of duty, or to an insufficiency of governmental action so far short of international standards that every reasonable and impartial man would readily recognize its insufficiency'.[75]

The case that the Commissioners had heard was one concerning whether the **7.46** Mexican authorities had done enough to apprehend and punish those guilty of the murder of an American citizen. The issue for the Tribunal was whether the failures of those authorities were enough to give rise to 'an international delinquency' so as to engage the responsibility of Mexico on the level of international law towards the United States. *Neer* is not an isolated example. On the contrary, in the latter part of the nineteenth century and the first half of the twentieth century, a very extensive body of jurisprudence and doctrine built up concerning the treatment of aliens generally, and the standard of denial of justice in particular.[76] The high water-mark of this analysis may be found in the Harvard Draft of 1929 on 'The Law of Responsibility of States for Damage done in their Territory to the Person or Property of Foreigners'[77] This provides, *inter alia*, that:

> A state is responsible if an injury to an alien results from a denial of justice. Denial of justice exists when there is a denial, unwarranted delay or obstruction of access to courts, gross deficiency in the administration of judicial or remedial process, failure to provide those guaranties which are generally considered indispensable to the proper administration of justice, or a manifestly unjust judgment. An error of a national court which does not produce manifest injustice is not a denial of justice.

---

[72] *Oppenheim* (n 36 above) 909.

[73] *LFH Neer & Pauline Neer (USA) v United Mexican States* (1926) IV RIAA 60.

[74] See eg *Pope & Talbot Inc* (n 12 above). [75] *Neer v Mexico* (n 73 above) 61–62.

[76] See E Borchard, *The Diplomatic Protection of Citizens Abroad, or, The Law of International Claims* (1916); A Freeman, *The International Responsibility of States for Denial of Justice* (1938).

[77] 'The Law of Responsibility of States for Damage done in their Territory to the Person or Property of Foreigners' (1929) 23 AJIL 133, 134 (Special Supplement). The leading post-war reformulation by American scholars was prepared in 1961 by Sohn and Baxter as part of a Harvard 'Draft Convention on the International Responsibility of States for Injuries to Aliens' in L Sohn & R Baxter, 'Responsibilities of States for Economic Injuries to Aliens' (1961) 55 AJIL 545, reprinted in F García Amador, L Sohn & R Baxter, *Draft Articles on the Responsibility of the State for Injuries caused in its Territory to the Person or Property of Aliens* (1974) 179–199 Arts 5–8.

7.47 It is submitted that the origins of the non-contingent standards of treatment in the law of State responsibility and diplomatic protection has at least five significant consequences for reference to this material in contemporary practice:

Person and property

7.48 The early twentieth century doctrine did not distinguish between the persons and the property of aliens. Yet (outside the field of expropriation) many, perhaps most, of the cases concern the mistreatment of individuals at the hands of the agencies of the State, such as by unlawful arrest, detention, and harsh treatment during imprisonment; refusal of access to a court; or unreasonable delay in administering justice. One should be cautious about an uncritical adoption of dicta pronounced in this context in the investment field. As the editors of *Oppenheim* observe, 'the basic political system and economic and social structure of the state has implications for the treatment accorded the property rights of aliens ... a principle of absolute respect for the property of aliens may not be appropriate in all circumstances'.[78]

Exhaustion of local remedies

7.49 The evolution of the standard through the medium of the law of diplomatic protection had the consequence that it could only be successfully invoked by the home State if the affected person had himself first exhausted local remedies.[79] In practice, save in cases of a refusal to investigate or prosecute, the cases on the international minimum standard and denial of justice were almost always concerned with alleged failures in the judicial system of the host State. Any failures in administrative decision-making would not give rise themselves to an international claim, since they would first have had to be tested by the investor in the local courts.

Contested status

7.50 Even at the time this standard was being developed and refined through the mixed claims commissions of the inter-war period, it was attracting increasing controversy, notably from Latin American States which opposed the imposition of a standard beyond that of national treatment,[80] and who would have limited a denial of justice to the refusal of access to a court.[81]

---

[78] n 36 above, 933; and see, to like effect, *Mondev International Ltd v United States of America* (Award) 6 ICSID Rep 181, 220 (NAFTA/ICSID (AF), 2002, Stephen P, Crawford & Schwebel).

[79] As to which see ILC, 'Second Report on Diplomatic Protection' (23 April–1 June, 2 July–18 August 2001) UN Doc A/CN 4/514; CF Amerasinghe, *Local Remedies in International Law* (2nd edn, 2004).

[80] eg Montevideo Convention on the Rights and Duties of States (signed 26 December 1933) 165 LNTS 19; USTS 881 (1935) Art 9, and generally E Borchard, 'The "Minimum Standard" of the Treatment of Aliens' (1940) 38 Mich LR 445.

[81] Guerrero Draft, cited in the Harvard Draft (n 77 above) 174.

Dissent over the primary rules of the delictual responsibility of States

Since World War II, it has proved even less possible to achieve consensus on the **7.51**
application of these principles as a matter of customary international law. In part
this is as a result of the extent of the disagreement between States which arose in
the specific context of investment law, which will be discussed further below. But
it is also a reflection of the general difficulty of reaching a consensus on the primary rules of the delictual responsibility of States. This led to their exclusion from
the work of the International Law Commission (ILC) on Draft Articles on State
Responsibility, abandoning the earlier 'enormously ambitious'[82] draft code of
Amador on the protection of aliens as unlikely to achieve a sufficient degree of
agreement by States. Similarly, the more recent work of the ILC on diplomatic
protection has been expressly limited to secondary rules.[83]

Effect of development through bilateral treaties

However, these limitations on the development of custom have always been **7.52**
expressed to be without prejudice to the right of States to accept binding standards
by treaty. Thus, for example, the ILC's draft articles on both State responsibility[84]
and diplomatic protection are expressed to be without prejudice to the right of
States to develop special rules of international law in particular areas. These
include, in the case of diplomatic protection, treaty provisions for the protection
of investments.[85] Despite, or perhaps rather because of, the huge rise in bilateral
treaty provision for investment protection, the customary international law rules
relating to the non-contingent standards of treatment have not developed in the
post-war period to the same extent through the practice of diplomatic protection.
The International Court of Justice (ICJ) has only turned to the rules of custom as
applicable to foreign investments once, and then without getting to the merits of
the claim.[86] Instead, the huge rise in the development of BITs has proceeded along
a parallel path.

But before reaching the significance of the incorporation of the non-contingent **7.53**
standards into bilateral treaties, it is necessary to say a word about the impact of
the international dissent about the standards of investment protection in the post-
war period.

---

[82] J Crawford, *The International Law Commission's Articles on State Responsibility: Introduction,
Text and Commentaries* (2002) 15.

[83] ILC, 'Diplomatic Protection: Report of the Working Group' (20 April–12 June, 27 July–14
August 1998) A/CN 4/L553 para 2.

[84] ILC, 'Draft Articles on the Responsibility of States for Internationally Wrongful Acts' (2001)
Art 55.

[85] ILC, 'Draft Articles on Diplomatic Protection' (2006) Art 17.

[86] *Case Concerning the Barcelona Traction, Light and Power Co Ltd (Belgium v Spain)* (Second
Phase) [1970] ICJ Rep 3. The decision of a Chamber of the Court in *ELSI* (n 30 above) was based
on an FCN treaty between Italy and the US.

The failure of multilateral consensus

7.54 The third general point of significance for the interpretation of the content of
investor treatment standards is the difficulty which has been encountered with
any attempt to achieve multilateral agreement by treaty on the content of such
standards.[87] As noted above, the best that could be achieved at Havana in 1948 was
a draft agreement to make recommendations for subsequent multilateral or bilateral agreements for just and equitable treatment of investments. The Havana
Charter itself never came into force. The General Agreement on Tariffs and Trade
1947 (the GATT), which then formed the cornerstone of world trade law, never
extended to investments, until the (very-limited) Agreement on Trade-Related
Investment Measures (TRIMS) was concluded some fifty years later in 1994.[88]

7.55 The formulation of fair and equitable treatment which had been proposed in the
Abs-Shawcross draft of 1959 was substantially incorporated in Article 1(a) of the
OECD Draft Convention on the Protection of Foreign Property, which was prepared in 1963. The drafters of this Convention specified that: 'The phrase "fair
and equitable treatment", customary in relevant bilateral agreements, indicates
the standard set by international law for the treatment due by each State with
regard to the property of foreign nationals … *The standard required conforms in
effect to the 'minimum standard' which forms part of customary international law.*'[89]
(emphasis added).

7.56 Although an important effort at achieving multilateral consensus, the OECD
draft offered no further elaboration on the content of the standard. The draft
Convention itself was never opened for signature, and came to be seen as embody-
ing the perspective of capital-exporting countries.

7.57 The Draft United Nations Code of Conduct on Transnational Corporations
reached no consensus on the content of the non-contingent standards, providing
in its unagreed version as of 1983:

> Transnational corporations should receive [fair and] equitable [and non-
> discriminatory] treatment [under] [in accordance with] the laws, regulations and
> administrative practices of the countries in which they operate [as well as inter-
> governmental obligations to which the Governments of these countries have freely
> subscribed] [consistent with their international obligations] [consistent with
> international law].[90]

---

[87] Detailed accounts of the failure of multilateral investment law are given in: P Muchlinski,
Multinational Enterprises and the Law (1995); AF Lowenfeld, *International Economic Law* (2002),
391–415; Sornarajah (n 50 above).

[88] WTO, *The Legal Texts: The Results of the Uruguay Round of Multilateral Trade Negotiations*
(1999) 143.

[89] OECD, *Draft Convention on the Protection of Foreign Property and Resolution of the Council of
the OECD on the Draft Convention* (1967) 13–15.

[90] Draft United Nations Code of Conduct on Transnational Corporations (1983 version), text
in UNCTC, *The United Nations Code of Conduct on Transnational Corporations*, Current Studies,

The Multilateral Agreement on Investment (MAI), proposed by the OECD in **7.58** 1995, would have provided a general protection of 'fair and equitable treatment and full and constant security. In no case shall a Contracting Party accord treatment less favourable than that required by international law.' The MAI was seen internally by the OECD as largely a harmonization exercise, and an attempt to address the fragmented nature of investment protection through BITs. However, it provoked intense opposition from NGOs on the grounds that it would weaken the regulatory capacity of host States in favour of investor protections.[91] Responding to domestic electoral pressure, a number of the States which had originally been proponents of the Agreement, including the United States and France, withdrew their support in 1998, sounding the death-knell for its successful conclusion.

This picture of the failure to reach multilateral agreement on an acceptable con- **7.59** tent of investors' rights is to some extent qualified by the emergence of significant plurilateral agreements, involving both capital-exporting and capital-importing States, which do contain such protections. Prominent among these are NAFTA and the ECT. The Lomé IV Treaty of 1990, between African, Caribbean and Pacific (ACP) and European Union States,[92] and the ASEAN Treaty of 1987[93] also contain mutual guarantees of fair and equitable treatment. The World Bank adopted such a standard in its Guidelines on the Treatment of Foreign Direct Investment of 1992.[94]

Implications for the current content of BIT treatment provisions

Against this background in general international law, what implications may be **7.60** drawn for the content of the standard to which States have voluntarily agreed in so many BITs? Three overall points may be made:

Wide acceptance of fair and equitable treatment

Despite the failure to agree upon modern multilateral standards of investor treat- **7.61** ment, and the fundamental disagreements in approach exposed by attempts to do so, there is an almost universal acceptance of a standard of fair and equitable treatment in BITs. As Mann put it: 'The cold print of these treaties is a more reliable

---

Series A (1986) UN Doc ST/CTC/SER. A/4, Annex 1, reprinted in UNCTAD, *International Investment Instruments: A Compendium* Vol I (1996) 161, 172–173.

[91] See J Salzman, 'Decentralized Administrative Law in the Organization for Economic Cooperation and Development' (2005) 68 Law & Cont Prob 189, 196–200.

[92] UNCTAD, *International Investment Instruments: A Compendium* Vol II (1996) 385, 419 Art 258(b).

[93] ASEAN Agreement for the Promotion and Protection of Investments (15 December 1987) (1988) 27 ILM 612, 613 (Appendix 3 below) Art IV.

[94] UNCTAD, *International Investment Instruments: A Compendium* Vol I (1996) 247, 249 (Appendix 12 below) Art III(2).

source of law than rhetorics in the United Nations.'[95] Further, its voluntary inclusion in the model or prototype BITs of many States, together with the ratchet effect of MFN clauses has achieved a high degree of acceptance of the standard in capital-importing, as well as capital-exporting States. This means that the standard is not to be dismissed as an imposition of Western States.[96] The content of the standard must therefore be determined on a basis which is common to all such States, and not applying the specific perspective of any particular State or legal system.

Custom in the content of treaty rights

7.62 The evidence from the drafters of BITs is that the most politically sensitive provisions were designed not 'to go beyond what was thought to reflect international law'.[97] However, this was rendered problematic by the 'argument whether the classical standards of protection still reflected the modern law'.[98] The failure to agree on the standard in multilateral fora, and the relative failure of a customary international law of investment protection to develop outside the context of BITs, has serious consequences for the determination of the *content* of the expected treatment. It means that care must be taken to ensure that guidance is not drawn from sources which have failed to receive the requisite degree of general acceptance. Similarly, the fact that these standards have been adopted through bilateral treaties, the scope of which has typically been limited to the investment field, has served to cut analysis of the content of the rights off from developments in other areas of international law.

Impact of the abrogation of the local remedies rule

7.63 The inclusion of such rights in modern BITs has fundamentally altered their character and scope of protection in at least one significant respect. Under customary international law, as has been shown, a failure to meet the international minimum standard of treatment could only constitute an international delict giving rise to an exercise of diplomatic protection if and to the extent that the individual investor had first exhausted local remedies. By contrast, tribunals determining investment arbitration claims have never considered that the local remedies rule operates so as to preclude a tribunal which otherwise has jurisdiction from entertaining a claim brought by the investor.[99] In turn, Article 26 of the ICSID Convention requires a State to make express provision if it wishes to insist on the exhaustion of local remedies. Article 27 reinforces that approach by precluding

---

[95] FA Mann, 'British Treaties for the Promotion and Protection of Investments' (1981) 52 BYIL 241, 250, reprinted in *Further Studies in International Law* (1990) 234, 246.

[96] Z Douglas (n 39 above) 159.

[97] E Denza & S Brooks, 'Investment Protection Treaties: United Kingdom Experience' (1987) 36 ICLQ 908, 912.   [98] ibid 911.

[99] See authorities cited in Douglas (n 39 above) 178–179, and at fn 195.

any exercise of a State's right of diplomatic protection for a claim which has been submitted to the Centre. Of course, the failure to pursue local remedies may still, as will be seen later, have an effect on whether the host State's *substantive* liability has been engaged. But the absence of a *jurisdictional* requirement of exhaustion of local remedies has had the consequence that an investor may bring a claim for many types of administrative treatment which could not have been the subject of a claim for diplomatic protection by the home State, whether by custom or in the exercise of its own rights under treaty. In this respect, the hybrid nature of investment arbitration has wrought a fundamental change in the classes of case which might give rise to a breach of the non-contingent standards.

D. The Process of Interpretation

The interpretation of treatment standards in investment treaties must begin, **7.64** like any other process of treaty interpretation, with the approach indicated by Articles 31 and 32 of the Vienna Convention on the Law of Treaties 1969 (VCLT).[100] These articles have been widely accepted as stating rules of customary international law on treaty interpretation.[101] They have also been repeatedly accepted by investment arbitration tribunals as constituting rules of interpretation which are binding on them in the interpretation of investment treaties, whether by virtue of being directly binding on the parties to the BIT as treaty rules, or as customary international law.[102]

The text of Article 31 is set out at para 3.67 above. Article 32 then permits refer- **7.65** ence to the *travaux préparatoires*, but only to confirm a meaning established by the approach in Article 31, or where the meaning thus established is ambiguous, obscure, or manifestly absurd or unreasonable. A number of features of these provisions deserve to be highlighted in the context of investor treatment provisions:

Article 31(1) ordinary meaning

Although the starting point of any analysis of the investor treatment provisions of an **7.66** investment treaty must be the ordinary meaning of the terms, it is unlikely that this part of the process will take the interpreter very far. It may simply result in an exchange of synonyms. Thus, the Tribunal in *MTD* began by quoting the *Concise Oxford English Dictionary* and observed: 'In their ordinary meaning, the terms "fair" and "equitable" . . . mean "just", "even-handed", "unbiased", "legitimate".'[103]

---

[100] Vienna Convention on the Law of Treaties (signed 23 May 1969, entered into force 27 January 1980) 1155 UNTS 331('VCLT'), and see generally 3.66–3.77 above.
[101] eg *Case Concerning the Territorial Dispute (Libyan Arab Jamahiriya v Chad)* [1994] ICJ Rep 6; WTO, *United States—Standards for Reformulated and Conventional Gasoline* (29 April 1996) (1 WT/DS2/AB/R) 16. [102] eg *Saluka* (n 26 above) para 296.
[103] *MTD* (n 7 above) 105.

Article 31(1) object and purpose

7.67 The reference to object and purpose may take the matter somewhat further. Investment treaties commonly contain preambular statements of purpose which are useful reference points in interpretation of the operative provisions. As the Tribunal pointed out in *Saluka*, the overall objective which is often found in such treaties of intensifying closer economic relations between the two States:

> ... is a more subtle and balanced statement of the Treaty's aims than is sometimes appreciated. The protection of foreign investments is not the sole aim of the Treaty, but rather a necessary element alongside the overall aim of encouraging foreign investment and extending and intensifying the parties' economic relations. That in turn calls for a balanced approach to the interpretation of the Treaty's substantive provisions for the protection of investments, since an interpretation which exaggerates the protection to be accorded to foreign investments may serve to dissuade host States from admitting foreign investments and so undermine the overall aim of extending and intensifying the parties' mutual economic relations.[104]

Article 31(2) subsequent agreements

7.68 Subsequent agreements between the parties may have a significant bearing on the interpretation of the treaty, especially where, as in the case of NAFTA, the parties have created a mechanism through which they may make binding interpretative decisions.

Article 31(3)(c) relevant rules of international law

7.69 The requirement in Article 31(3)(c) to take into account 'any relevant rules of international law applicable in the relations between the parties' is likely to be of particular significance in the case of investment treaties. This paragraph encapsulates a principle of systemic integration, the foundation of which is that treaties are themselves creatures of international law—predicated for their existence and operation on being part of the international legal system.[105] As such the parties are to be taken 'to refer to general principles of international law for all questions which [the treaty] does not itself resolve in express terms and in a different way'.[106] This aspect of the interpretative process is likely to be of special significance in the case of investment treaties in at least three respects. First, light may be shed on the meaning of the terms used by reference to customary international law. Of course

---

[104] *Saluka* (n 26 above) para 300. See also the more detailed provisions as to object and purpose in NAFTA (n 52 above) Preamble and Chap 1 and the Energy Charter Treaty (n 54 above) Preamble and art 2.

[105] See generally 1.38–1.43 above and C McLachlan, 'The Principle of Systemic Integration and Article 31(3)(c) of the Vienna Convention' (2005) 54 ICLQ 279.

[106] *Georges Pinson Case* (1927) AD Case no 292, 426, 427 per Verzijl P, and see the express acknowledgement of this in NAFTA (n 52 above) Art 102(2).

one must be careful not to transpose rules from custom which the parties have deliberately eschewed by the terms of their treaty. Investment treaties frequently represent an attempt by the parties to remedy some of the perceived deficiencies in protection afforded by custom, especially in the field of diplomatic protection. These are not to be re-imported into the treaty by the back-door.[107] On the other hand, there is evidence that, at least in many cases, the parties intended the substantive obligations to follow those developed in custom.[108] The use of open-textured expressions of general currency in international law also gives rise to the inference that the parties intended their meaning to be capable of evolution over time.[109] This idea has received express endorsement in the context of investor treatment.[110]

Secondly, there may be other conventional international law obligations applica- **7.70** ble in the relations between the parties which bear upon the interpretation of the investment treaty. Sometimes, this is acknowledged by them expressly. Thus, for example, the current US model Form[111] contains a recital in which the parties confirm their desire to achieve their mutual investment objectives 'in a manner consistent with the protection of health, safety, and the environment, and the promotion of *internationally recognized* labor rights' (emphasis added). But, even where there is no such express statement, the operation of Article 31(3)(c) requires consideration of other relevant treaties.[112]

Article 31(4) special meanings

Article 31(4) may also be relevant in this context. As Judge Higgins observed in **7.71** *Oil Platforms*, 'the key terms "fair and equitable treatment to nationals and companies" ... are legal terms of art well known in the field of overseas investment protection'.[113] This paragraph draws attention to a wider phenomenon in this field, which is that treaties are developed in an iterative process in which many normative elements are shared. The author has described this process of treaty-making elsewhere as 'akin to a continuous dialogue within an open-plan office.'[114] Thus, the meaning of key words in an investment treaty may well be informed by the prior practice of each of the parties in concluding such treaties, irrespective of

---

[107] Douglas (n 96 above)

[108] eg Denza and Brooks (n 97 above); the NAFTA Interpretation (7.26 above); the 2004 US model BIT (Appendix 6 below) Art 5(1); and the France model BIT (Appendix 10 below) Art 4.

[109] McLachlan (n 105 above) 316–317. For general authority see *Case concerning the Gabčíkovo-Nagymaros Project (Hungary v Slovakia)* [1997] ICJ Rep 7, 76–80.

[110] eg *Mondev* (n 78 above) 224–225.

[111] 2004 US model BIT (Appendix 6 below). See also NAFTA (n 52 above) Art 104.

[112] But in the case of NAFTA, the FTC Interpretation makes clear that the express reference to international law in Art 1105 is to customary international law only. See *Mondev* (n 78 above) 223.

[113] *Case concerning Oil Platforms (Islamic Republic of Iran v United States of America)* [1996] ICJ Rep 803, 858 (Separate Opinion of Judge Higgins).   [114] McLachlan (n 105 above) 284.

whether the norms can truly be said to have been established in customary international law. The preparation of model forms may be especially useful in this regard.

Article 32 *travaux préparatoires*

7.72 By contrast, it will be less usual for a reference to *travaux préparatoires* under Article 32 to assist greatly in this field. It is rare for bilateral negotiations to produce the kind of explanatory reports, or official records of plenary debates which are characteristic of multilateral negotiation.[115] When the confidential working papers on the negotiation of NAFTA were produced in *Pope & Talbot*, they did little to illuminate the matters in dispute. However, the transmittal statements by which domestic approval for such treaties is sought by the signatory States may well help to clarify interpretation issues—although they will inevitably carry less weight, if they are simply unilateral statements, uncorroborated by the other party. The ICJ has nevertheless referred to such material in interpreting a Treaty of Friendship, Commerce and Navigation.[116] The Tribunal in *Mondev*, despite questioning whether such statements are properly to be regarded as *travaux préparatoires*, referred to both the Canadian transmittal statement for NAFTA and US transmittal statements for BITs as confirming that the parties had intended Article 1105 of NAFTA to encapsulate a customary international law standard (and as providing evidence of *opinio juris* for such a standard, at least among the three State parties).[117]

2. Modern Application in Investment Arbitral Awards

7.73 Part 2 of this Chapter will now analyse the way in which these basic provisions, which for so long lay unlitigated, have been applied in the practice of investment arbitration since the millennium. The systemic limitations inherent in the structure of investment arbitration have a particularly acute effect in the context of the treatment provisions, where (in contrast to expropriation) there had been very little accretion of case law in the second half of the twentieth century. Each case turns in part on the specific language of the treaty under which it is conducted. As has been seen above, there may be important differences in the formulations adopted for investor protection. The claims are litigated under various fora,

---

[115] The Tribunal in *AAPL v Sri Lanka* (n 70 above) 270 referred to the difficulty of ascertaining what may have been within the parties' contemplation in including particular terms in a BIT 'in the absence of *travaux préparatoires* in the proper sense'.

[116] *Case concerning Oil Platforms (Islamic Republic of Iran v United States of America)* (Preliminary Objection) [1996] ICJ Rep 803, 814–815.   [117] *Mondev* (n 78 above) 220–221.

depending on the dispute resolution provisions of the treaty, and the election of the parties. In the case of ICSID arbitration, there is an internal system of the review of arbitral awards under the annulment procedure, the grounds for which are strictly limited.[118] Outside ICSID, the only method of recourse will be to national courts by review at the seat.[119] There is no strict doctrine of precedent which binds tribunals to apply the law as stated in prior awards.[120] Indeed, in view of the fact that such awards are confidential unless the parties otherwise agree, no other rule would be feasible. Arbitral tribunals (and courts) have even declined to apply a rule of *lis pendens* or *res judicata* as between proceedings concerning the same subject-matter and between related parties, but under different BITs.[121]

These systemic limitations have been counterbalanced by a number of aspects of **7.74** the practice to date. The majority of investment arbitral awards have been published with the consent of the parties. Arbitral tribunals deciding investor protection cases have, with some notable exceptions, shown a high degree of willingness to draw upon prior awards. The on-going conversation among arbitrators which has thus ensued is resulting in progressively more nuanced formulations of investor treatment rights. However, as was recently pointed out, these initial awards represent just the first generation of jurisprudence.[122] There are still only a small number of cases on each of the main treatment provisions. It is therefore inevitable that there will be some unevenness in the decisions, and that there will be many issues yet to be addressed. It is submitted that it is important to analyse particular cases not simply for their dicta on the formulation of the contested rights, but also to put these dicta in context: both as to their functional response to the subject-matter of the claim, and as to their consistency with the overall development of the law in this area.

This Part will review the case law on the four main rights which have been the sub- **7.75** ject of dispute: (a) fair and equitable treatment; (b) full protection and security; (c) national treatment; and (d) MFN. [123]

---

[118] Convention on the Settlement of Investment Disputes between States and Nationals of Other States (signed 18 March 1965, entered into force 14 October 1966) 575 UNTS 159 ('ICSID Convention') Art 52(1).

[119] eg *Occidental Exploration and Production Co v Republic of Ecuador* [2005] EWCA Civ 1116, [2005] 2 Lloyd's Rep 707; [2006] 2 WLR 70. This also applies to NAFTA claims since, Canada and Mexico not being parties to the ICSID Convention, these are conducted under the ICSID Additional Facility (or UNCITRAL), which does not provide for the annulment procedure. For examples of review by the courts at the seat see *United Mexican States v Metalclad Corp* 2001 BCSC 664; 5 ICSID Rep 236 (Supreme Court of British Colombia); *United Mexican States v Karpa* (2005) 248 DLR (4th) 443 (Ont. CA). [120] See the discussion at 3.83–3.103 above.

[121] eg the *Lauder/CME* litigation (n 9 above). This is the subject of detailed analysis in 4.117–4.143 above. [122] Dolzer (n 4 above) 88.

[123] The interpretation of the 'umbrella clause', providing treaty protection for contractual claims, is analysed at 4.93–4.116 above.

A. Fair and Equitable Treatment

7.76 The cases on fair and equitable treatment fall into two broad categories. The first set of cases are concerned with the treatment of investors by the courts of the host State. The second, and more numerous, set of cases deal directly with administrative decision-making.

7.77 As has been seen,[124] mistreatment by foreign courts was historically a primary focus of the minimum standard of the protection of aliens, encapsulated in the concept of denial of justice.[125] With the abrogation of the local remedies rule in investment treaty arbitration, it has been much less common for the judicial process to form the subject of a treaty claim. The investor may simply elect to by-pass the local courts altogether. If his claim concerns alleged mistreatment by the administration, he may elect to bring it directly to international arbitration.

7.78 However, where he does not do so, the treatment accorded to the investor by the local courts may well be highly relevant to the success of his claim. Thus, for example, in one of the earliest claims under this head under NAFTA, *Azinian v Mexico*,[126] the investors' claim under Article 1105 of NAFTA was brought as an adjunct to their primary claim for expropriation in the termination of their contract for waste disposal in Mexico. The contract itself was expressly governed by Mexican law and subject to the jurisdiction of the Mexican courts. It had been held invalid by three levels of Mexican courts.[127] The Tribunal accepted that in principle the host State could be liable for the decisions of its courts. The Tribunal then drew expressly upon the defined limits of the responsibility of States for the acts of judicial organs in customary international law.[128] It observed:

> A governmental authority surely cannot be faulted for acting in a manner validated by its courts *unless the courts themselves are disavowed at the international level . . .*
>
> *What must be shown is that the court decision itself constitutes a violation of the treaty.* Even if the Claimants were to convince this Arbitral Tribunal that the Mexican courts were wrong with respect to the invalidity of the Concession Contract, this would not per se be conclusive as to a violation of NAFTA. More is required; the Claimants must show either a denial of justice, or a pretence of form to achieve an internationally unlawful end [original emphasis].[129]

---

[124] Text at n 7.45–7.46 above.

[125] The classic study is AV Freeman, *The International Responsibility of States for Denial of Justice* (1938). An excellent recent evaluation of the continued relevance of the concept is J Paulsson, *Denial of Justice in International Law* (2005).

[126] *Azinian, Davitian & Baca v United Mexican States* (Award) 5 ICSID Rep 269 (NAFTA, 1998, Paulsson P, Civiletti & von Wobeser).   [127] ibid 289.

[128] ibid 290. The Tribunal cited a formulation by E Jiménez de Aréchaga, 'International Law in the Past Third of a Century' (1978) 159 *Recueil des Cours* 1.   [129] ibid 289–290.

It opined that a denial of justice might be caused (a) if the relevant courts refuse **7.79**
to entertain the suit; (b) if they subject it to undue delay; (c) if they administer
justice in a seriously inadequate way; or (d) if there is a clear and malicious misapplication of the law.[130] Since the claimants made no complaint about their
treatment by the Mexican courts, their claims had to fail: '*For if there is no complaint against a determination by a competent court that a contract governed by
Mexican law was invalid under Mexican law, there is by definition no contract to be
expropriated.*'[131]

Denial of justice

What, then, do the recent awards tell us about the way in which courts may breach **7.80**
the standard of fair and equitable treatment? For that purpose, it is necessary to
analyse two important awards which both took issue with the American judicial
system: *Mondev*[132] and *Loewen*.[133] The cases present a useful contrast. In the former, the Tribunal was concerned with the circumstances in which a State court's
substantive decision could give rise to a breach of the standard. In the latter, the
Tribunal was concerned instead with the fairness of the State court's procedures.

Mondev—*the limits of merits review*

Mondev was concerned with a claim by Canadian investors that they had been **7.81**
treated unfairly by the United States as a result of decisions of the State courts of
Massachusetts. Lafayette Place Associates (LPA), a Massachusetts limited liability
partnership owned by the claimants, had entered into a contract with the City of
Boston and the Boston Redevelopment Authority (BRA) to develop certain land
in Boston. When the project failed to secure planning consent, and the banks
foreclosed on the property, LPA sued in Massachusetts claiming breach of contract by the City and tortious interference with contract on the part of BRA. LPA
won jury verdicts against both respondents, but the trial judge ruled that BRA was
entitled to statutory immunity from suit for intentional torts. On appeal, the
Massachusetts Supreme Judicial Court (SJC) upheld the finding of immunity,
and set aside the judgment against the City. Mondev sued under NAFTA,
alleging a breach of Article 1105.[134] It questioned the decisions of the SJC on four
grounds: the dismissal of the contract claim against the City; the failure to remand
that claim to the lower courts; alleged retrospectivity in the application of a new
rule; and BRA's statutory immunity.

---

[130] ibid 290.   [131] ibid 290.   [132] *Mondev* (n 78 above).
[133] *Loewen Group Inc & anor v United States of America* 7 ICSID Rep 421 (NAFTA 2003, Mason P,
Mikva & Mustill).
[134] Its cause of action for expropriation was held inadmissible *ratione temporis*: *Mondev
International Ltd v United States of America* (Award) 6 ICSID Rep 181, 206–210 (NAFTA/ICSID
(AF), 2002, Stephen P, Crawford & Schwebel).

7.82 The claim was thus concerned not with a refusal to entertain a suit, or with the process which the courts had adopted. Rather, the Tribunal was faced with a claim which sought to impugn the correctness of the decision itself. The Tribunal referred to *Azinian*[135] in accepting that there could be a breach of the standard for clear and malicious misapplications of the law. It formulated the test, relying on *ELSI*,[136] as follows:

> The test is not whether a particular result is surprising, but whether the shock or sur-prise occasioned to an impartial tribunal leads, on reflection, to justified concerns as to the judicial propriety of the outcome, bearing in mind on the one hand that inter-national tribunals are not courts of appeal, and on the other hand that Chapter 11 of NAFTA (like other treaties for the protection of investments) is intended to provide a real measure of protection. In the end the question is whether, at an international level and having regard to generally accepted standards of the administration of just-ice, a tribunal can conclude in the light of all the available facts that the impugned decision was clearly improper and discreditable, with the result that the investment has been subjected to unfair and inequitable treatment.[137]

7.83 The Tribunal then referred for additional support to the formulation in the Harvard Draft,[138] which referred to a decision which 'unreasonably departs from the principles of justice recognized by the principal legal systems of the world.'

7.84 Applying this test, the Tribunal found that none of the aspects of the Court's deci-sion of which complaint was made breached the standard. This decision was reached relatively easily in relation to the first three allegations. The Tribunal saw these aspects of the Court's decision as being well within the margin of appreciation for the decisional responsibility of national courts. It gave fuller consideration to the Court's finding upholding BRA's statutory immunity. The Tribunal was invited to consider the jurisprudence of the European Court of Human Rights on whether immunities from suit may breach the right to a court. It took a cautious approach to the relevance of that material, finding that the European Court's decisions may provide guidance by analogy only.[139] The Tribunal then considered the rationale for the immunity. It found that there was no uniformity of practice among the major legal systems as to the existence of immunities from suit for public author-ities.[140] It held that a blanket immunity from suit, even for tortious claims against public authorities, may well breach Article 1105. But the narrow immunity from suit for tortious interference with contract served a rational purpose, which was reasonably commensurate with the authority's regulatory purpose, and did not breach the provision.

---

[135] ibid 225.

[136] *Case concerning Elettronica Sicula SpA (ELSI) (United States of America v Italy)* [1989] ICJ Rep 15; 84 ILR 311.   [137] *Mondev* (n 78 above) 225–226.

[138] Art 8(b) Final Harvard Draft Convention on the International Responsibility of States for Injuries to Aliens in L Sohn & R Baxter 'Responsibilities of States for Economic Injuries to Aliens' (1961) 55 AJIL 545, 551, reprinted in F García Amador et al above n 77, 134, 196.

[139] *Mondev* (n 78 above) 231.   [140] *Mondev* (n 78 above) 232.

Mondev was an unusual case in at least two respects. First, the conduct of the State **7.85** administrative agencies could not be impugned directly before ICSID, having been committed before NAFTA had entered into force. As a result, the claimant was forced back into a situation more closely akin to that faced in the older diplomatic protection cases, in which it was necessary to proceed less directly by attacking the court's treatment of the claim against the public authority. As the Tribunal itself pointed out, the issue as to statutory immunity before the local courts would have been academic if Mondev had been able to pursue a treaty claim directly against the BRA.[141] Secondly, the claim was framed on the basis of the fourth category of denial of justice at customary international law, ie misapplication of the law. This category had always been applied very restrictively. As the Tribunal itself pointed out in the passage cited above, the international tribunal is not a court of appeal. An attack on the substantive outcome of the national court decision can only succeed if it is clear that there has been judicial impropriety, rather than merely a mistake of law. It has been convincingly argued that the considerations which the international tribunal is weighing in a case such as *Mondev* are not directly a re-evaluation of the substance of a national court's decision under its own law at all: 'international fora have no reason to recognise a category of substantive denials of justice. In international law, denial of justice is about due process, nothing else—and that is plenty'.[142]

The relevance, then, of any such merits evaluation is simply that the incorrectness **7.86** or injustice of the judgment may afford evidence of bias, fraud, dishonesty, or lack of impartiality.[143] In other words, it may indicate a lack of due process. Of course, this type of distinction is one which must commonly be made in the enforcement of foreign judgments and awards,[144] and in domestic systems of judicial review. The next award had to confront directly the central concern of denial of justice: procedural irregularities in the judicial proceedings themselves.

Loewen—procedural failures and local remedies

By contrast with *Mondev*, the claim in *Loewen* was concerned with a very serious **7.87** breakdown in a judicial system. Raymond Loewen, and his company Loewen Group Inc (together 'Loewen') were Canadian nationals, who had become involved in a dispute with an American competitor in the funeral home business, one O'Keefe. A jury trial was held in the Mississippi State Court in which Loewen alleged that the trial judge allowed O'Keefe's lawyers to make 'extensive, irrelevant and highly prejudicial' discriminatory references to Loewen's nationality, class, and race. The jury awarded O'Keefe US$500 million in damages (of which

---

[141] *Mondev* (n 78 above) 233.   [142] Paulsson (n 125 above) 7.

[143] G Fitzmaurice, 'The Meaning of the term "Denial of Justice"' (1932) 13 BYIL 93, 112–113.

[144] See L Collins et al (eds), *Dicey, Morris & Collins on the Conflict of Laws* (14th edn 2006) para 16–133.

US$400 million were punitive damages). Loewen complained that he was unable to appeal, because local procedural rules required him to post a bond of 125 per cent of the amount of the judgment in order to secure a stay of execution pending appeal, and an application to relax that requirement was refused by the Court.

7.88 Loewen's NAFTA claim made complaint about: (a) the trial court procedure; (b) the excessive verdict; and (c) the arbitrary application of the bond requirement. He alleged a legal basis for the claim under three provisions of the investment chapter, but only the claim to fair and equitable treatment was held admissible by the Tribunal.[145] The Tribunal found on the facts that: 'By any standard of measurement, the trial involving O'Keefe and Loewen was a disgrace... By any standard of evaluation, the trial judge failed to afford Loewen the process that was due'.[146]

7.89 The Tribunal then observed that: 'we take it to be the responsibility of the State under international law ... to provide a fair trial of a case to which a foreign investor is a party. It is the responsibility of the courts of a State to ensure that litigation is free from discrimination against a foreign litigant and that the foreign litigant should not become the victim of sectional or local prejudice'.[147]

7.90 The Tribunal found that the content of the Article 1105 standard, informed by customary international law, was concerned with denials of justice in litigation. It accepted that the burden was on the claimant to make good such a claim. But it rejected the contention that bad faith or malicious intention was required. Instead the Tribunal adopted the formulation in *Mondev*[148] and opined: 'Manifest injustice *in the sense of a lack of due process* leading to an outcome which offends a sense of judicial propriety is enough ...'[149] (emphasis added).

7.91 A decision which was, however, both a violation of municipal law and discriminatory to foreigners would amount to a manifest injustice in breach of the standard.[150] The Tribunal found that, at the trial stage, this standard was clearly breached.

7.92 However, that was not an end of the matter. The Tribunal then proceeded to consider whether, in the light of the subsequent proceedings, the judicial process as a whole as applied to Loewen 'amounted to an international wrong'.[151] The Tribunal's approach was to distinguish the procedural requirement for the

---

[145] *Loewen Group Inc & anor v United States of America* (Award) 7 ICSID Rep 421 (NAFTA 2003, Mason P, Mikva & Mustill). The claim for expropriation under Art 1110 was dismissed because the Tribunal considered that it added nothing to the Art 1105 claim (469); and the claim for national treatment under Art 1102 on the ground of lack of proof as to comparable treatment (468–469) as to which see 7.156 below.　　　　　　　　　　　　　　　　　　[146] ibid 464.

[147] ibid 465.　　　[148] *Loewen* (n 145 above) 467.　　　[149] *Loewen* (n 145 above) 467.

[150] *Loewen* (n 145 above) 467, citing the Harvard Draft (n 138 above).

[151] *Loewen* (n 145 above) 469.

exhaustion of local remedies from the substantive requirement: 'The principle that a court decision which can be challenged through the judicial process does not amount to a denial of justice at the international level has been linked to the duty imposed upon a State by international law to provide a fair and efficient system of justice.[152]

Article 1121 of NAFTA, which requires the investor to waive local remedies as a **7.93** condition of proceeding to arbitration, was held not to affect the operation of this principle.[153] The Tribunal then proceeded to apply an exhaustion of local remedies standard to the content of its substantive obligation: 'It is an obligation to exhaust remedies which are effective and adequate and are reasonably available to the complainant in the circumstances in which it is situated.'[154]

Once this point had been reached in the Tribunal's reasoning, the case turned on **7.94** what steps Loewen had taken to pursue his rights to appeal. His attempt to persuade the Mississippi Supreme Court to relax the bond requirement was unsuccessful. That, on the analysis of the Tribunal, left Loewen with the option of either proceeding with his substantive appeal unprotected by a stay (with the consequent risk of immediate execution); filing for Chapter 11 bankruptcy; or filing a petition for *certiorari* with the US Supreme Court. Instead, Loewen chose to enter into a settlement agreement. The Tribunal found that, in the absence of an explanation by Loewen as to why he had settled rather than pursuing other options, such as the Supreme Court option, he had failed to discharge his burden of demonstrating that he had pursued domestic remedies.[155] The claim also failed for want of jurisdiction on the basis that the corporate claimant had failed to maintain continuous nationality.[156] Loewen made a subsequent attempt to invite the Tribunal to reconsider its decision.[157] In so doing, he waived privilege over his legal advice as to the reasons for settlement and its prospects of success in any writ of *certiorari* to the US Supreme Court. But the Tribunal declined to alter its award.

In considering the *Loewen* award, the reader may well be troubled, as the Tribunal **7.95** acknowledged,[158] that a very serious miscarriage of justice against a foreign national was dismissed as a local error, which could not be remedied by the international Tribunal. The Tribunal is of course concerned to see whether there has been a failure in the operation of the judicial system as a whole. As a general proposition, 'an aberrant decision by an official lower in the hierarchy, which is capable of being reconsidered, does not of itself amount to an unlawful act'.[159] But it is quite another

---

[152] *Loewen* (n 145 above) 471–472.   [153] *Loewen* (n 145 above) 473.
[154] *Loewen* (n 145 above) 475.   [155] *Loewen* (n 145 above) 483–484.
[156] *Loewen* (n 145 above) 484–490, as to which see paras 5.64–5.71 above.
[157] *Loewen Group Inc & anor v United States of America* (Decision on Respondent's Request for a Supplementary Decision) ICSID Case No ARB(AF)/98/3 (NAFTA, 2004, Mason P, Mustill & Mikva).   [158] *Loewen* (n 145 above) 490.
[159] ILC, 'Second Report on State Responsibility' (3 May–23 July 1999) UN Doc A/CN 4/498 34.

matter to import the full rigour of the local remedies rule into investment arbitration on the ground that, in the absence of evidence of full exhaustion, there could be no breach of the treaty standard. In this respect, one must be very careful not to borrow principles from customary international law which are inconsistent with the hybrid nature of investment arbitration. While it is doubtless correct, as the Tribunal noted, that the local remedies rule is not limited to cases of diplomatic protection,[160] it is difficult to see a convincing rationale for its place within investment treaty arbitration. Where the responsibility of a State vis-à-vis another State is engaged as a result of the treatment of an alien in the State's courts, it is only to be expected that the individual should first exhaust local remedies before the dispute is elevated to that of an international wrong between States. It was in the context of just such an inter-State claim in *ELSI* that a Chamber of the ICJ emphasized the continuing importance of the rule. But to insist on a strict application of this requirement in investor-State arbitration is simply inconsistent with the creation of a right to arbitration by investors directly. As Bennouna observed in his preliminary report to the International Law Commission on Diplomatic Protection:

> In consenting to arbitration, the parties to a dispute waive all other remedies. In this way, both the demand of the host State that local remedies be exhausted and the exercise of diplomatic protection by the State of nationality are put aside. In other words, where the right of the individual is recognized directly under international law (the bilateral agreements referred to above), and the individual himself can enforce this right at the international level, the 'fiction' [that the state is enforcing its own right on the international plane] no longer has any reason for being.[161]

7.96 Moreover, the distinction drawn by the Tribunal between the exhaustion of local remedies as a procedural bar, and a substantive requirement to pursue local remedies in order for a denial of justice to arise, is itself a matter of debate at customary international law.[162] The cases relied upon by the Tribunal were all cases which pre-date the advent of investor-State arbitration, and were therefore predicated on a system of remedies which that system was, where it applied, designed to supersede.

7.97 The problem with the Tribunal's reasoning is demonstrated by the way in which its approach would affect claims based on administrative decisions.[163] Since the State has a single legal personality at international law, there would seem to be no reason in principle to distinguish between decisions of inferior courts, and decisions of administrative officials in applying the Tribunal's test regarding local

---

[160] ILC 'Responsibilities of States for Internationally Wrongful Acts: Text of the Draft Articles with Commentaries thereto' (Crawford, Special Rapporteur) in *Report of the International Law Commission on its Fifty-third Session (23 April–1 June and 2 July–10 August 2001), Official Records of the General Assembly Fifty-sixth Session*, Supplement No. 10 UN Doc A/56/10, 59–365.

[161] ILC, 'Preliminary Report on Diplomatic Protection' (20 April–12 June 1998, 27 July–14 August 1998) UN Doc A/CN 4/484, 12.   [162] ibid.

[163] The Tribunal concedes that: 'Article 1121 may have consequences where a claimant complains of a violation of international law not constituted by a judicial act. That is not a matter which arises here.' *Loewen* (n 145 above) 473.

remedies.[164] Yet the intention, at least for cases which are subject to ICSID juris-diction, was to substitute international arbitration for domestic remedies, unless the State expressly required otherwise, or the investor elected to pursue his rem-edy in the local courts.[165] In numerous cases, which will be discussed in the next section, tribunals have rendered awards in favour of the claimants as a result of administrative decisions, in which no such application to the local courts had been made. It cannot any longer be assumed, as might have been the case in a pre-vious era, that there 'rarely exist local remedies against the acts of the authorized organs of the state'.[166] On the contrary, many national legal systems possess highly developed remedies of judicial review. Yet it would surely empty the development of investment arbitration of much of its force and effect, if, despite a clear inten-tion of State parties not to require the pursuit of local remedies as a pre-condition to arbitration, such a requirement were to be read back as part of the substantive cause of action.

Save in one recent award,[167] there has been no attempt to read in such a require-**7.98** ment in the case of administrative decisions. It is submitted that it would be anomalous if a different standard were to be applied to court decisions than to administrative ones. Of course, a claimant's prospects of success in pursuing a treaty claim based on an inferior court decision which had not been challenged through an available appeal process should be much lower, since the Tribunal must in any event be satisfied that the failure is one which displays some funda-mental breakdown in the system, justifying international intervention. But that is a very different matter from imposing a strict onus on the claimant to demon-strate that every reasonably available local remedy has been exhausted before there can be said to have been a failure to provide fair and equitable treatment. It is sub-mitted that the consequences of so doing are amply demonstrated by the outcome of the *Loewen* award itself. It is submitted that a serious failure to accord due process before national courts can form the subject of a treaty claim, as the Tribunal in *Mondev* thought, without it being necessary to demonstrate that every last domestic avenue has been exhausted.

Review of administrative action

The second major category of cases in which the standard of fair and equitable **7.99** treatment has been relied upon in investor-State claims has been in the review of

---

[164] Paulsson vigorously defends a strict application of the exhaustion requirement to cases of denial of justice (n 125 above) Chap 5. However, he also appears to consider that this is not applic-able under a treaty standard of 'fair and equitable treatment' (n 125 above) 111, fn 35.

[165] ICSID Convention (Appendix 11 below) Art 26.

[166] *Arbitration under Article 181 of the Treaty of Neuilly (Greece v Bulgaria)* 4 November 1931 (1934) 28 AJIL 760, 789, cited in Paulsson (n 125 above) 119.

[167] *Generation Ukraine Inc v Ukraine* (Award) (2005) 44 ILM 404 (ICSID, 2003, Paulsson P, Salpius & Voss).

administrative decisions. The majority of such cases have been concerned with the grant or withholding of licences for investments, or a fundamental change in the law affecting the investment climate. In giving content to the right in these cases, tribunals have been predominantly concerned to assess the treatment accorded to investors by reference to two types of factors:

(1) *Legitimate expectations.* The first has increasingly been given a label which is borrowed from national administrative law: the protection of legitimate expectations. In these cases, the tribunal's underlying concern is with the 'stability of the legal and business framework'.[168] It is concerned to assess the treatment accorded to an investor by reference to the law of the host State at the time of the investment, together with any specific assurances which the investor may have received at the time of investment in reliance upon which he decided to invest. This has been recently described as the 'dominant element' of the standard.[169]

(2) *Due Process.* The second set of situations which have arisen under this head are not adequately described by the doctrine of legitimate expectations. Rather, they are concerned with the character of the decision-making process: was the administrative decision reached through a fair process? Or did the host State use its administrative powers for improper purposes or inconsistently? These, too, are recognizable as central concerns of domestic administrative law. At the more egregious end of the spectrum are cases of coercion and harassment by State officials; bad faith; and discrimination. These latter factors are sufficient, but not necessary elements of breach of the standard. It is submitted that it is unhelpful and circular to treat these considerations as ones of 'legitimate expectation'.[170] Whether or not the conduct of the host State in the implementation of its decision-making process was 'legitimate' is a matter for international law to judge for itself, and it adds nothing to refer to the putative expectations of the investor.

Countervailing factors

7.100 The awards also help to illuminate those factors which may indicate that the standard has not been breached. A primary element in that determination is the Tribunal's evaluation of the public interest factors which may justify the State action. If the State had an objective basis for its decision, that will strongly indicate

---

[168] *Occidental Exploration and Production Co v Republic of Ecuador* (Award) (UNCITRAL, 2004, Orrego Vicuña P, Brower & Sweeney) para 183.

[169] *Saluka Investments BV (The Netherlands) v Czech Republic* (Partial Award) (UNCITRAL, 2006, Watts C, Fortier & Behrens) para 302. See also R Dolzer, 'Fair and Equitable Treatment: A Key Standard in Investment Treaties' (2005) 39 Int'l Law 87, and S Fietta 'Expropriation and the "Fair and Equitable" Standard: The Developing Role of Investors' "Expectations" in International Investment Arbitration' (2006) 23(5) J Int'l Arb 375.

[170] As the Tribunal in *Saluka* was prepared to do, (ibid) para 308.

that it did not breach the standard, especially if it cannot be said that the decision had a disproportionate impact on the particular foreign investor. In other cases, tribunals have declined to find a breach, because the alleged right for which the investor contended had no basis in international law.

Factors which may give rise to a breach of the standard

Legitimate expectations and the state of the law at the time of investment

The most far-reaching exposition of the principle underlying the developing notion **7.101** of legitimate expectations as applied to fair and equitable treatment in investment law was given by the Tribunal in *Tecmed v Mexico* in the following terms:

> The Arbitral Tribunal considers that this provision of the Agreement, in light of the good faith principle established by international law, *requires the Contracting Parties to provide to international investments treatment that does not affect the basic expectations that were taken into account by the foreign investor to make the investment.* The foreign investor expects the host State to act in a consistent manner, free from ambiguity and totally transparently in its relations with the foreign investor, so that it may know beforehand any and all rules and regulations that will govern its investments, as well as the goals of the relevant policies and administrative practices or directives, to be able to plan its investment and comply with such regulations. Any and all State actions conforming to such criteria should relate not only to the guidelines, directives or requirements issued, or the resolutions approved thereunder, but also to the goals underlying such regulations. The foreign investor also expects the host State to act consistently, i.e. without arbitrarily revoking any preexisting decisions or permits issued by the State that were relied upon by the investor to assume its commitments as well as to plan and launch its commercial and business activities. The investor also expects the State to use the legal instruments that govern the actions of the investor or the investment in conformity with the function usually assigned to such instruments, and not to deprive the investor of its investment without the required compensation. In fact, failure by the host State to comply with such pattern of conduct with respect to the foreign investor or its investments affects the investor's ability to measure the treatment and protection awarded by the host State and to determine whether the actions of the host State conform to the fair and equitable treatment principle [emphasis added]. [171]

Other recent awards have endorsed similar standards of conduct. Thus, in **7.102** *Occidental v Ecuador*[172] the Tribunal held that: 'The stability of the legal and business framework is thus an essential element of fair and equitable treatment.' In *CMS Gas Transmission Co v The Argentine Republic*[173] the Tribunal referred to the Preamble to the relevant BIT which recited that it is desirable 'to maintain a

---

[171] *Tecnicas Medioambientales Tecmed SA v United Mexican States* (Award) (2004) 43 ILM 133, 173 (ICSID (AF), 2003, Grigera Naon P, Fernandez Rozas & Bernal Verea); formulation adopted in *MTD Equity Sdn Bhd & anor v Republic of Chile* (Award) (2005) 44 ILM 91, 105–106 (ICSID, 2004, Sureda P, Lalonde & Oreamuno Blanco).   [172] *Occidental* (n 168 above) para 183.
[173] *CMS Gas Transmission Co v Argentine Republic* (Award) (2005) 44 ILM 1205, 1235 (ICSID, 2005, Orrego Vicuña P, Lalonde & Rezek).

stable framework for investments and maximum effective use of economic resources'. It held that 'fair and equitable treatment is inseparable from stability and predictability'. In *CME*[174] the Tribunal found that the host State 'breached its obligation of fair and equitable treatment by evisceration of the arrangements in reliance upon [which] the foreign investor was induced to invest'.

7.103 The enunciation of a principle of legitimate expectations based upon the legal and policy framework in place in the host State at the time of investment has had important consequences for the merits of investors' claims under this head:

(1) In *Occidental* it provided the basis for a finding that Ecuador had breached the standard when its tax agency decided that *Occidental* was not entitled to claim reimbursement for VAT on oil exports, despite the fact that it had been so entitled when it originally made its investment.

(2) The proceedings in *CMS* concerned the effect on the claimant's investment of the devaluation of the Argentinian peso. CMS claimed that the effect of the legislation and regulations, as well as its licence for gas transport, all of which were put in place when it made its original investment, entitled it to the calculation of tariffs in US dollars, conversion into pesos at the time of billing, and periodic adjustment of tariffs in accordance with the US Producer Price Index. It alleged that these arrangements had been subverted by new emergency laws and arrangements introduced following the monetary crisis in Argentina, which imposed the devaluation of the peso on the tariff arrangements. The Tribunal held that these new arrangements breached the standard:

> The measures that are complained of did in fact entirely transform and alter the legal and business environment under which the investment was decided and made. The discussion above, about the tariff regime and its relationship with a dollar standard and adjustment mechanisms unequivocally shows that these elements are no longer present in the regime governing the business operations of the Claimant. It has also been established that the guarantees given in this connection under the legal framework and its various components were crucial for the investment decision.[175]

7.104 Yet, despite its potentially far-reaching consequences, tribunals have also recognized a number of limitations on this principle.

The investor must take foreign law as he finds it

7.105 It is for the host State to decide for itself the legal framework which it will apply to foreign investments upon its territory. This principle has a more general application

---

[174] *CME Czech Republic BV (The Netherlands) v Czech Republic* (Partial Award) 9 ICSID Rep 121, 238 (UNCITRAL, 2001, Kühn C, Schwebel & Händl).
[175] *CMS Gas Transmission Co v Argentine Republic* (Award) (2005) 44 ILM 1205 (ICSID, 2005, Orrego Vicuña P, Lalonde & Rezek) 1235.

in investment law.[176] It carries with it the consequence that, in the absence of some specific representation to the contrary, the investor is bound by host State law at the date of the investment, and cannot bring a complaint of unfair treatment for a subsequent faithful application of it. Thus, in *MTD* the Tribunal held, considering a specific provision of a BIT relating to the granting of permits, that 'said provision does not entitle an investor to a change of the normative framework of the country where it invests. All that an investor may expect is that the law be applied'.[177]

In *GAMI v Mexico*[178] the Tribunal put the matter more generally: 'International **7.106** law does not appraise the content of a regulatory programme extant before an investor decides to commit. The inquiry is whether the state abided by or implemented that programme. It is in this sense that a government's failure to implement or abide by its own law in a manner adversely affecting a foreign investor may but will not necessarily lead to a violation of Article 1105.'

This may be seen as an illustration of a more general point recognized by the **7.107** Permanent Court of International Justice (PCIJ) in the *Oscar Chinn Case*,[179] which is that the investor must take the conditions of the host State as he finds them. He cannot make a subsequent complaint if his investment fails merely because of laws, policies or practices which were in place at the time of investment, and which were, or ought to have been, well known to him before making the investment.

The effect of specific representations made to the investor

On the other hand, the investor may be able to rely upon specific representations **7.108** made to him in reliance upon which he was induced to invest. The Tribunal in *Waste Management v Mexico*[180] observed that: 'In applying this standard it is relevant that the treatment is in breach of representations made by the host State which were reasonably relied on by the claimant.'

The making of specific representations has been a material factor in the decision **7.109** in favour of the investor in a number of the recent cases. Thus, in *Metalclad*[181] the Tribunal found support for its finding as to the breach of the standard in the making of representations by the federal officials, which were to the effect that the local Municipality had no legal basis for denying it a permit to operate the landfill.

---

[176] See Z Douglas, 'The Hybrid Foundations of Investment Treaty Arbitration' (2003) 74 BYIL 151, 197–211. [177] *MTD* (n 7 above) 122.
[178] *GAMI Investments Inc v United Mexican States* (Award) (2005) 44 ILM 545, 560 (NAFTA/UNCITRAL, 2004, Paulsson P, Muró & Reisman).
[179] *The Oscar Chinn Case* (1934) PCIJ Rep Series A/B No 63.
[180] *Waste Management Inc v United Mexican States* (Award) (2004) 43 ILM 967, 986 (NAFTA/ICSID (AF), 2004, Crawford P, Civiletti & Gómez).
[181] *Metalclad Corp v United Mexican States* (Award) 5 ICSID Rep 209, 228 (NAFTA/ICSID (AF), 2000, Lauterpacht P, Civiletti & Siqueiros).

7.110 *MTD v Chile*,[182] concerned an investment by Malaysian investors to build a proposed new town in Chile. The investment was approved by the Chilean Foreign
Investment Commission (FIC), despite the fact that it was against the urban policy of Chile. Subsequently, the claimants, having expended considerable sums in
acquiring the land and developing the proposal, failed to secure the necessary
permit to begin construction. The Tribunal found that 'approval of an investment
by the FIC for a project that is against the urban policy of the Government is a
breach of the obligation to treat an investor fairly and equitably'.[183]

7.111 Conversely, the absence of specific representations is a material factor in leading
to a finding that the standard has not been breached. Thus, in *International
Thunderbird Gaming Corp v United Mexican States*[184] the Tribunal held:

> Having considered recent investment case law and the good faith principle of cus-
> tomary international law, the concept of 'legitimate expectations' relates, within the
> context of the NAFTA framework, to a situation where a Contracting Party's con-
> duct creates reasonable and justifiable expectations on the part of an investor (or
> investment) to act in reliance on said conduct, such that a failure by the NAFTA
> Party to honour those expectations could cause the investor (or investment) to suffer
> damages.[185]

The official statement which the claimant had received from the relevant Mexican
State agency had not generated such an expectation. The claimant had itself provided incomplete and inaccurate information to the State agency as to the nature
of the proposed investment in gaming machines. The official statement gave no
assurance that gaming machines would be approved. On the contrary, the claimant
knew that gaming was an illegal activity in Mexico.[186]

7.112 In fact, these types of considerations have also weighed heavily with national
courts in developing a doctrine of legitimate expectations in domestic law. Thus,
for example, the English courts have consistently linked the concept of legitimate
expectations with a duty to act fairly in administrative decision-making. They
have been more concerned to provide protection for specific representations made
to individuals, rather than general policy statements.[187]

---

[182] *MTD* (n 7 above).   [183] *MTD* (n 7 above) 115.

[184] (Award) (NAFTA/UNICTRAL, 2006, van den Berg P, Ariosa & Wälde), Wälde delivered
a Separate Opinion, surveying the authorities, but dissenting in their application to the facts on
this point.   [185] ibid para 147.

[186] ibid paras 149–164.

[187] eg *Preston v Inland Revenue Commissioners* [1985] 2 All ER 327, 342 per Lord Templeman;
Council of Civil Service Unions & ors v Minister for the Civil Service [1984] 3 All ER 935, 954 per
Lord Roskill. For general accounts of the position in English administrative law see: W Wade & C
Forsyth, *Administrative Law* (9th edn, 2004) 372–376, 500–505; P Craig, *Administrative Law* (5th
edn, 2003) 639–680. The writer is indebted to Dean Knight of Victoria University of Wellington
Law School on this point. See D Knight, *Estoppel (Principles?) in Public Law: The Substantive
Protection of Legitimate Expectations* (LLM Thesis, University of British Columbia 2004).

A legitimate scope for regulatory flexibility

Finally, the protection of legitimate expectations must be qualified by the need to **7.113** maintain a reasonable degree of regulatory flexibility on the part of the host State to respond to changing circumstances in the public interest. As the Tribunal in *Saluka* observed: 'No investor may reasonably expect that the circumstances prevailing at the time the investment is made remain totally unchanged. In order to determine whether frustration of the foreign investor's expectations was justified and reasonable, the host State's legitimate right subsequently to regulate domestic matters in the public interest must be taken into consideration as well.'[188]

This may be seen as a specific application of the more general notion of balance **7.114** between the interests of the investor and the countervailing factor of the State acting in the public interest which it was earlier suggested was inherent in the concept of 'equitable treatment'. It has the consequence that the protection afforded under the rubric of fair and equitable treatment, even when applied to expectations derived from the state of host State law or specific representations made at the time of investment, is not to be equated with a vested property right.

Due process in administrative decision-making

The second category of cases has been concerned with the treatment of the **7.115** investor in the decision-making process itself. This has been a major preoccupation of the cases since the standard was first utilized in investment arbitration. The awards recognize a general duty on the part of the regulatory authorities to accord due process to the foreign investor. Without limiting the breadth of that notion, a number of interlocking concerns may be seen at play in the decisions to date: discrimination; transparency; use of powers for improper purposes; inconsistency; coercion and harassment by State officials; and bad faith. These considerations coincide with many of the classic hallmarks of the Rule of Law as a notion of formal legality.[189]

Discrimination

Thus, in one of the first decisions, *S D Myers Inc v Canada*,[190] the claim concerned **7.116** the promulgation of an export ban on the trans-boundary movement of hazardous waste. The claimant, a US company, alleged that this had been carried out in a discriminatory and unfair manner. It was particularly affected, as an important part of its business was concerned in the processing of such waste from Canada in its plant in the United States, and this was precluded while the ban was

---

[188] *Saluka* (n 26 above) para 305.
[189] eg J Raz, 'The Rule of Law and its Virtue' (1977) 93 LQR 195 (also in J Raz, *The Authority of Law* (1983) Chap 11).
[190] *SD Myers Inc v Government of Canada* 8 ICSID Rep 3 (NAFTA/UNCITRAL, 2000, Hunter P, Schwartz & Chiasson).

in force. The Tribunal agreed, essentially on the basis that, on the facts of the case, the failure to accord national treatment to Myers also amounted to a failure to accord fair and equitable treatment. In other words, the export ban was arbitrary and discriminatory against non-nationals.

7.117   Similarly, in *Saluka*[191] the Tribunal found that the Czech Government had not treated the foreign banking institution in an even-handed way vis-à-vis the local State-owned bank. It had refused to deal in a constructive manner with the foreign investor, and had instead accorded preferential treatment to the local bank. Bias of this kind against the foreign investor was held to be a breach of the standard.

7.118   However, it does not follow that, in the absence of a specific provision against discrimination, or a finding of breach of national treatment, all distinctions between nationals and foreigners made in host State law are necessarily a breach of the fair and equitable treatment standard. Thus in *Methanex*[192] the Tribunal found, construing Article 1105 of NAFTA (which contains a reference to 'treatment in accordance with international law', but no specific reference to discrimination),[193] that international law did not prohibit all distinctions between nationals and foreigners. On the contrary, the burden was on the claimant to establish a specific rule of customary international law prohibiting discrimination of the type of which complaint was made.

Transparency

7.119   Schwartz, in his Separate Opinion in *Myers*, referred to an additional consideration which had weighed with him in reaching this decision.[194] He referred to WTO authority for 'certain minimum standards for transparency and procedural fairness'.[195] While sounding a caution against too sweeping a requirement to consult individuals in the formulation of government policy, he nevertheless considered that Canada gave Myers' local competitors preferred and privileged access to key decision-makers, made no effort to consult Myers, and produced a ban that was specifically intended to minimize Myers' place in the Canadian marketplace.[196]

7.120   Failure to act in a transparent manner in administrative decision-making was a central consideration for the Tribunal in *Metalclad*.[197] The US investor had been denied a municipal construction permit to operate a hazardous waste transfer station and landfill in Mexico. The Tribunal relied in particular upon the reference

---

[191]   *Saluka* (n 26 above) paras 408–416.
[192]   *Methanex Corp v United States of America* (NAFTA/UNCITRAL, 2005, Veeder P, Rowley & Reisman).   [193]   NAFTA (Appendix 1 below).
[194]   *SD Myers Inc v Government of Canada* (Separate Opinion of Professor Schwartz) 8 ICSID Rep 3, 114ff (NAFTA/UNCITRAL, 2000, Schwartz).
[195]   ibid, citing *United States—Import Prohibition of Certain Shrimp and Shrimp Products* WT/DS58/ AB/R (12 October 1998) 75 at para 183.   [196]   *Myers* (n 194 above) 115.
[197]   *Metalclad* (n 181 above).

to transparency in NAFTA's introductory statement of principles.[198] It opined that: 'The Tribunal understands this to include the idea that all relevant legal requirements for the purpose of initiating, completing and successfully operating investments made, or intended to be made, under the Agreement should be capable of being readily known to all affected investors of another Party.'[199]

Examining the process which had in fact been adopted, the Tribunal found that **7.121** Metalclad had been led to believe that its existing Federal and State permits did allow for the construction of the landfill; that the Municipality took into account improper considerations in denying the permit; that there was no clarity about the requirement for a municipal construction permit; and that the Municipality had failed to apply an orderly and timely process in arriving at its decision to deny the permit, instead waiting until construction was nearly complete before reaching its decision. Taken together these factors breached the standard.[200]

Subsequent cases have shown that the standard of due process is not one of strict **7.122** liability. Thus, in *Genin et al v Estonia*[201] the claimant complained of the revocation of a banking licence by the Bank of Estonia. The Tribunal considered that a number of aspects of the Bank's decision-making process were contrary to generally accepted banking and regulatory practice.[202] These included the failure to give formal notice that the licence would be revoked if the Bank's demands were not met; no opportunity to be heard at the meeting of the Bank's council which decided to revoke the licence; and the fact that the revocation took effect immediately. However, the Tribunal did not consider that these failings amounted to a denial of due process rising to the level of a violation of the BIT or the international law principles enshrined therein.

Moreover, even the *Metalclad* test still leaves responsibility with the investor to **7.123** make his own investigation of the regulatory requirements in the host State before investing. The investor's failure to do so in *MTD v Chile*[203] led it to invest money

---

[198] ibid 226–227, referring to NAFTA Art 102(1). This part of the Tribunal's reasoning was annulled by the Supreme Court of British Columbia on the ground that reference to the transparency principle was outside the scope of the jurisdiction of a NAFTA Chap 11 tribunal: 5 ICSID Rep 236, 253–254. It is submitted that the Court may have gone too far in this regard. The Tribunal's reference to the statement of general principles in Art 102 is surely justified by both the general requirement of VCLT Art 31(2) to refer to the whole of a treaty text, including its preamble, in interpreting a provision, and the specific terms of NAFTA Art 1131 directing a Chapter tribunal to decide the dispute 'in accordance with this Agreement and applicable rules of international law'.

[199] ibid. Accord: *Tecmed v Mexico* (n 171 above) 173–174.

[200] Lack of transparency was also a factor indicating breach of the standard in *Saluka* (n 26 above) paras 420–425; and in the decision in *Emilio Augustín Maffezini v Kingdom of Spain* (Award) 5 ICSID Rep 387, 436 (ICSID, 2000, Orrego Vicuña P, Buergenthal & Wolf).

[201] *Genin, Eastern Credit Limited Inc and AS Baltoil v Republic of Estonia* (Award) 6 ICSID Rep 236 (ICSID, 2001, Fortier P, Heth & van den Berg). [202] ibid 299.

[203] *MTD* (n 7 above).

without adequately investigating the risks that the necessary zoning changes would be made to allow the planned development to proceed. The Tribunal found that the investor should bear the loss attributable to those business risks which the investor assumed.[204]

Use of powers for improper purposes

7.124   A third factor which has weighed with tribunals in the application of this standard has been whether the powers exercised by the host State administrative body have been misused for improper purposes. Thus, in *Metalclad* the Municipality had denied a construction permit for the operation of the landfill on the grounds of an environmental impact assessment which it was for the federal authorities to conduct under Mexican law. The Tribunal regarded this as improper, and as contributing to the breach of treaty.[205] *Tecmed* was also concerned with the licensing of a hazardous waste landfill in Mexico, but the impugned conduct in that case was that of the Mexican environmental agency. The Tribunal held that the investor had a fair expectation that the powers of the agency would be used for the proper purposes of the laws.[206] Instead, the agency had used its powers in order to deal with political problems arising from public opposition to the landfill.

Inconsistency

7.125   As has been seen, a decisive factor in the *MTD v Chile* case was the inconsistency of conduct vis-à-vis the investor between State agencies: encouragement and approval of the investment by the Foreign Investment Commission on the one hand, and denial of the necessary zoning permits on the other. This factor, which is closely linked to the idea of transparency, was also treated as important in *Occidental v Ecuador*.[207] The Tribunal there found that the State tax agency had materially changed the framework in which Occidental's investment had been made on the basis of an incorrect interpretation of the investment contract. The subsequent clarifications sought by the investor 'received a wholly unsatisfactory and thoroughly vague answer. The tax law was changed without providing any clarity about its meaning and extent and the practice and regulations were also inconsistent with such changes'.[208]

Coercion and harassment by State authorities

7.126   A more serious failure of investor treatment can occur when the individual is subjected to coercion and harassment by State officials. This was the nub of the arbitrators' finding on the facts in the otherwise controversial case of *Pope & Talbot*.[209]

---

[204]   *MTD* (n 7 above) 117.   [205]   *Metalclad* (n 181 above) 228.
[206]   *Tecmed* (n 171 above) 174.   [207]   *Occidental* (n 168 above).
[208]   *Occidental* (n 168 above) para 184.
[209]   *Pope & Talbot Inc v Government of Canada* (Award) 7 ICSID Rep 43 (NAFTA/UNCITRAL, 2002, Dervaird P, Greenberg & Belman).

The case concerned the imposition by Canada of an export quota on softwood lumber and the conduct of a subsequent verification review of the investor's claim that it had received a lower quota than that to which it was entitled. The Tribunal found no unfairness in the imposition of the quota system itself. It was a reasonable response to the issues as they arose, and did not single out the claimant. However, the verification review was found to breach the standard:

> ... the Tribunal found that, when the Investor instituted the claim in these proceedings, Canada's Softwood Lumber Division ('SLD') changed its previous relationship with the Investor and the Investment from one of cooperation in running the Softwood Lumber Regime to one of threats and misrepresentation. Figuring in this new attitude were assertions of non-existent policy reasons for forcing them to comply with very burdensome demands for documents, refusals to provide them with promised information, threats of reductions and even termination of the Investment's export quotas, serious misrepresentations of fact in memoranda to the Minister concerning the Investor's and the Investment's actions and even suggestions of criminal investigation of the Investment's conduct.[210]

Similarly, in *Tecmed*[211] the Tribunal found that the environmental agency's decision not to renew the landfill permit was in reality a device to coerce the investor into relocation of the landfill without compensation. Care must be taken in such cases to ensure that the hindsight afforded by the arbitral process does not construe mere bureaucratic officiousness—a decision to 'play it by the book'—as a campaign of harassment. **7.127**

Bad faith

The authorities are clear that it is not necessary to establish bad faith on the part of the host State for a claim under this head to succeed. However, if the government does act in bad faith, that will be likely to satisfy the standard. Thus, in *Waste Management II*[212] the Tribunal observed that: 'a conscious combination of various agencies of government without justification to defeat the purposes of an investment agreement—would constitute a breach of Article 1105(1). A basic obligation of the State under Article 1105(1) is to act in good faith and form, and not deliberately to set out to destroy or frustrate the investment by improper means'. **7.128**

Conversely, a good faith effort on the part of the State agencies to fulfil the requirements of host State law will be a powerful indication that the standard has been met.[213] **7.129**

Factors which may indicate standard not breached

The recent awards have also assisted in clarifying the countervailing factors which may indicate that the standard has not been breached. An overarching **7.130**

---

[210] ibid (Award on Damages) 163–164; and see further (Award on the Merits of Phase 2) 138–145.　　　[211] *Tecmed* (n 171 above) 176–178.
[212] *Waste Management II* (n 180 above) 994.　　[213] *GAMI* (n 178 above) 561.

consideration has already been mentioned—the need to preserve a legitimate scope for regulatory action in ensuring that the treatment accorded to an investor is equitable in the light of the public interest in the host State. In weighing the State's regulatory interest, tribunals have considered in particular whether there is an objective basis for the administrative decision in question; whether the impact on the foreign investor is disproportionate; and whether the alleged right asserted by the investor has a firm basis in host State or international law.

7.131 Tribunals are also concerned to ensure that the conduct is such as properly to form the subject of an international claim. Thus mere illegality under host State law will not itself give rise to a breach of the treaty standard.[214] Nor will the failure of a State agency to pay a debt, provided 'it does not amount to an outright and unjustified repudiation of the transaction and provided that some remedy is open to the creditor to address the problem'.[215]

Objective basis for decision

7.132 In *Genin*, as has been seen, the Tribunal decided that the failure of the Bank of Estonia to meet international best practice in its decision to revoke the claimant's banking licence did not breach the standard. The Tribunal was particularly influenced by its assessment that the Bank had had good cause to revoke the licence. It said that the decision must be seen in its proper context:

> ... a context comprised of serious and entirely reasonable misgivings regarding EIB's management, its operations, its investments and, ultimately, its soundness as a financial institution ...

> ... the Tribunal accepts Respondent's explanation that it took the decision to annul EIB's licence in the course of exercising its statutory obligations to regulate the Estonian banking sector. The Tribunal further accepts Respondent's explanation that the circumstances of political and economic transition prevailing in Estonia at the time justified heightened scrutiny of the banking sector. *Such regulation by a state reflects a clear and legitimate public purpose.*

> ... the Tribunal ... regards the decision by the Bank of Estonia to withdraw the licence as justified. In light of this conclusion, in order to amount to a violation of the BIT, *any procedural irregularity that may have been present would have to amount to bad faith, a wilful disregard of due process of law or an extreme insufficiency of action.* None of these are present in the case at hand. [emphasis added].[216]

7.133 The Tribunal took a similar view of the matter in *Lauder v Czech Republic*.[217] It decided, in contrast to the Tribunal seised of the parallel claim in *CME*,[218] that the Republic through its Media Council had committed no breach of treaty. The

---

[214] *ADF Group Inc v United States of America* (Award) 6 ICSID Rep 449, 532 (NAFTA/ICSID (AF), 2003, Feliciano P, de Mestral & Lamm).   [215] *Waste Management II* (n 180 above) 989.
[216] *Genin* (n 201 above) 298–299, 300–301.
[217] *Lauder v Czech Republic* (Award) 9 ICSID Rep 62 (UNCITRAL, 2001, Briner C, Cutler & Klein).   [218] *CME* (n 9 above).

arbitrators emphasized that the Media Council's conduct in bringing proceedings against Mr Lauder's company for unauthorized broadcasting was not inconsistent, since the Council had objective reasons for believing that the Media Law was being violated: 'There can not be any inconsistent conduct in a regulatory body taking the necessary actions to enforce the law, absent any specific undertaking that it will refrain from doing so.'[219]

No disproportionate impact on foreign investor

The second factor which militates against a finding that the treatment breaches **7.134** the standard is if it does not have a disproportionate impact on the foreign investor, but rather falls equally on everyone in the host State. Thus, for example, in *Pope & Talbot*[220] a principal reason why the Tribunal declined to find any aspect of the introduction of a quota regime for the export of softwood from Canada to be a breach of the standard was that it was a large-scale scheme affecting many producers, and it could not be shown that it had been implemented in a way which singled out the foreign investor. So, too, in *GAMI Investments Inc v Mexico*,[221] the Tribunal declined to find a breach of the standard simply because the Mexican authorities had failed to implement and administer the Mexican sugar programme in the way that the law intended.

Alleged right not found in host State law nor in international law

The converse of the principle that (in the absence of some specific breach of inter- **7.135** national law) the investor must take host State law as he finds it is that, if the right contended for is not recognized and protected in either host State law or international law, the failure to protect it cannot by definition constitute a breach of the standard.

This principle is well illustrated by the dismissal of the claim for breach of Article **7.136** 1105 of NAFTA at the jurisdictional stage in *UPS v Canada*.[222] The gravamen of UPS's complaint was that Canada had failed to ensure fair competition in the market for non-monopoly postal services. It was said in particular that Canada ought to have adopted measures to redress the findings of an independent Commission appointed by it. The Commission had found that Canada Post was an unregulated government monopoly engaged in unrestrained competition with the private sector in the non-monopoly postal market. Although the arbitrators allowed the claim of breach of national treatment to go to a merits hearing, the alleged breach of Article 1105 was struck out. The Tribunal found that Article 1105 encapsulates a general international law standard.[223] Thus, it was necessary

---

[219] *Lauder* (n 217 above) 108.   [220] *Pope & Talbot* (n 209 above) 130–138.
[221] *GAMI* (n 178 above).
[222] *United Parcel Service of America Inc v Government of Canada* (Award on Jurisdiction) 7 ICSID Rep 285 (NAFTA/ UNCITRAL, 2002, Keith P, Cass & Fortier).   [223] ibid 305–306.

to investigate whether a prohibition on anti-competitive behaviour could be found in customary international law—comprising both State practice and *opinio juris.*[224] However, a review of State practice indicated that there was no uniform prohibition on anti-competitive practices, and, where States had intervened to impose such a prohibition, there was no evidence that they had done so out of any sense of obligation under international law.[225] Further, no specific provision on competition could be found in a review of international law instruments.[226] Thus, the Tribunal concluded, it could not be said that a requirement to regulate anti-competitive practices formed part of customary international law, or, in turn, NAFTA.

7.137   A similar approach was taken to a claim of breach of the standard of fair and equitable treatment in the payment of State aid in *Saluka.*[227] The Tribunal held that: 'The "fair and equitable treatment" standard cannot easily be assumed to include a general prohibition of State aid. Financial assistance is a tool used by States to implement their commercial policies. Even though it tends to distort competition and to undermine the level playing field for competitors, States cannot be said to be generally bound by international law to refrain from using this tool.'

7.138   The Tribunal considered that the provision of such aid would only be likely to infringe the standard if it were provided in such a way as to breach one of the other factors considered above: in particular by being contrary to the investor's legitimate expectations or discriminatory.

7.139   The Tribunal in *ADF*[228] also reached this view with regard to domestic content and performance requirements in government procurement. Finding that such requirements were to be found in the internal legal systems or in the administrative practice of many States, the Tribunal reasoned: 'Thus, the US measures cannot be characterized as idiosyncratic or aberrant and arbitrary.'[229]

Investor conduct and duty to investigate

7.140   A final category of cases where tribunals have held the standard not breached, or have at least significantly moderated the consequences of any breach, is where the investor's own conduct has to some extent contributed to his loss. Muchlinski has given this class of cases the suggestive title '*caveat investor*'.[230] Thus, as has been seen, in *MTD v Chile*, the Tribunal found that half of the responsibility for the investor's losses lay with the investor's own failure to investigate properly the Chilean planning laws applicable to the proposed investment, and reduced the

---

[224] ibid 307.   [225] ibid 307–308.   [226] ibid 308–309.

[227] *Saluka* (n 26 above) para 445.

[228] *ADF Group Inc v United States of America* (Award) 6 ICSID Rep 449, 531 (NAFTA/ICSID (AF), 2003, Feliciano P, de Mestral & Lamm).   [229] ibid.

[230] PT Muchlinski, 'Fair and Equitable Treatment in Investment Treaty Law' British Institute of International and Comparative Law Investment Treaty Forum, 9 September 2005.

damages accordingly. Similarly, in *Maffezini v Spain*[231] the Tribunal rejected one head of claim on the ground that the investor must take responsibility himself for mistaken advice received. In *International Thunderbird* the investor had provided incomplete and misleading information to the State regulator, and knew that there was a risk that its planned investment might breach host State law.[232] The Tribunal stated: 'Bilateral Investment Treaties are not insurance policies against bad business judgments.'[233] It further insisted that the investor take responsibility for meeting in full the requirements of local law, ignorance of the law being no defence.[234]

B. Full Protection and Security

The second principal element of the non-contingent standard commonly found **7.141** in investment treaties is the requirement that investments of nationals of either contracting party shall enjoy 'full protection and security' in the territory of the other contracting party. As has been seen,[235] this provision found early expression in bilateral treaties of friendship, commerce and navigation. It was not combined with the concept of fair and equitable treatment until the modern era. But it, too, had an extensive life in the customary international law rules relating to the protection of the property of aliens through claims of State responsibility and the invocation of diplomatic protection.

In contrast to fair and equitable treatment, however, full protection and security **7.142** is typically concerned not with the process of decision-making by the organs of the State. Rather, it is concerned with failures by the State to protect the investor's property from actual damage caused by either miscreant State officials, or by the actions of others, where the State has failed to exercise due diligence. It is thus principally concerned with the exercise of police power.[236]

The possibility of State responsibility being invoked for the omission of a State to **7.143** provide protection to aliens is of course well known to international law. Such responsibility was found by the ICJ to apply to the protection of persons under a treaty of friendship and commerce in the *Tehran Hostages Case*.[237] It has figured as the principal cause of action in three main ICSID awards on this topic: *AAPL v*

---

[231] *Emilio Augustín Maffezini v Kingdom of Spain* (Award) 5 ICSID 387 (ICSID, 2000, Orrego Vicuña P, Buergenthal & Wolf). Confirmed in *Waste Management Inc v United Mexican States* (2004) 43 ILM 967, 989 (NAFTA/ICSID(AF) 2004, Crawford P, Civiletti & Gómez).

[232] See n 184 above.   [233] ibid 432.   [234] ibid 433.

[235] 7.42–7.43 above.

[236] cf the formulation in the 2004 US model BIT (Appendix 6 below) Art 5(2)(b).

[237] *Case Concerning United States Diplomatic and Consular Staff in Tehran (United States of America v Iran)* (Merits) [1980] ICJ Rep 3.

Sri Lanka;[238] *AMT v Zaire*;[239] and *Wena Hotels Ltd v Egypt*.[240] These cases concerned destruction to persons and property during internal armed conflict, riots and acts of violence, a matter typically provided for in BITs in specific provisions,[241] as well as falling within the general rubric of full protection and security. *AAPL v Sri Lanka* deserves particular attention, as the Tribunal gave careful consideration to the applicable legal test by reference to a scholarly analysis of the earlier authorities. Both *AMT* and *Wena* presented rather clearer cases of abuse of State power or flagrant neglect of the protection obligation.

AAPL v Sri Lanka

7.144 The claimants, a Hong Kong company, had entered into a joint venture with a number of Sri Lankan government agencies and private individuals to establish a Sri Lankan company (SSL), whose object was to operate a shrimp farm in Sri Lanka providing shrimp for export to the Japanese market. Unfortunately, the farm was located in a part of the country which fell under the control of the Tamil Tigers. It was subsequently destroyed during a counter-insurgency operation by Sri Lankan government security forces. The claimant's primary submission was that the Treaty established a strict liability standard, which rendered the Sri Lankan Government liable for any destruction of the investment even if caused by acts not attributable to the Government and under circumstances beyond the State's control.

7.145 The Tribunal began its analysis by observing that, as there was no common ground between the parties as to the appropriate approach to be adopted to the dispute, it would have to determine that for itself.[242] The Tribunal then recited a number of canons of construction, derived from Article 31 of the VCLT and from international jurisprudence. These factors included, after natural and ordinary meaning, integral context and object and intent, a reference to Article 31(3)(c)—the wider context of applicable international law rules.[243] The construction of the UK-Sri Lanka BIT's comprehensive system, stated the Tribunal, was of crucial importance in order to decide whether the BIT 'intended, merely, to consolidate the pre-existing rules of international law, or, on the contrary, it tended to innovate by imposing on the host state a higher standard of international responsibility'.[244]

---

[238] *Asian Agricultural Products Ltd (AAPL) v Republic of Sri Lanka* (Award) 4 ICSID Rep 245 (ICSID, 1990, El-Kosheri P, Goldman & Asante).

[239] *American Manufacturing and Trading Inc v Republic of Zaire* (Award) 5 ICSID Rep 11 (ICSID, 1997, Sucharitkul P, Golsong & Mbaye).

[240] *Wena Hotels Ltd v Arab Republic of Egypt* (Award) 6 ICSID Rep 67 (ICSID, 2000, Leigh P, Fadlallah & Wallace), upheld on annulment 6 ICSID Rep 129.

[241] Discussed 2.21–2.23 above.   [242] *AAPL v Sri Lanka* (n 238 above) 263.

[243] *AAPL v Sri Lanka* (n 238 above) 265.   [244] ibid 266.

The Tribunal found that the standard was not one of strict liability, and was in **7.146** accord with the standard in customary international law. In reaching this conclusion, it was assisted by findings to the same effect in the construction of similar language in treaties in both the *Sambiaggio Case* in 1903,[245] and in *ELSI* in 1989.[246]

It pointed out, moreover, that if the standard were one of strict liability, then the **7.147** more specific protections found in the Treaty governing destruction of property by State forces 'not caused in combat action or . . . required by the necessity of the situation'[247] would have no scope of operation. This Article contemplated a higher standard of liability and compensation for damages caused by government forces, which was 'linked with the assumption of unjustified destruction committed out of combat'.[248] The Tribunal found this Article inapplicable because: (a) it had not been sufficiently established that the damage to the farm had been caused by government forces;[249] (b) the guerilla warfare between the Tamil Tigers and the Sri Lankan Government was 'combat action'; and (c) the evidence did not enable the Tribunal to determine whether the destruction had been occasioned by the necessity of the situation.[250]

However, this did not preclude the application of the general requirements to pro- **7.148** vide compensation for losses suffered by foreign investors owing to armed conflicts[251] or to provide full protection and security. Sri Lanka accepted that these clauses could be invoked if it had failed to exercise the customary international law standard of due diligence, which it owed to protect the person or property of any alien on its territory.[252] The Tribunal relied on both jurisprudence[253] and doctrine[254] as supporting this standard. It faced great evidential difficulty in applying it to the facts. However, it finally found that Sri Lanka had breached the standard by failing to take precautionary measures, including the removal of employees from the farm, before launching the offensive.[255]

AMT v Zaire

The claimant incurred losses as a result of looting and destruction of its property **7.149** caused by Zairian soldiers during riots and acts of violence in Kinshasa. The

---

[245] *Sambiaggio Case* (1903) X RIAA 499, 512.   [246] *ELSI* (n 30 above).

[247] Agreement for the Promotion and Protection of Investments (UK-Sri Lanka) (signed 13 February 1980, entered into force 18 December 1980) 1227 UNTS 392 Art 4(2)(b).

[248] *AAPL v Sri Lanka* (n 238 above) 273.   [249] *AAPL v Sri Lanka* (n 238 above) 274.

[250] *AAPL v Sri Lanka* (n 238 above) 275.   [251] UK-Sri Lanka BIT (n 247 above) Art 4(1).

[252] *AAPL v Sri Lanka* (n 238 above) 277.

[253] Among others, *Spanish Zone of Morocco Claims (Great Britain v Spain)* (1923–4) 2 AD 157 (Note), II RIAA 615, 645 (Original French text) (Huber); *Sambiaggio Case* (n 245 above); and the decisions of the Mexico/US Claims Commission cited in *AAPL v Sri Lanka* at 280.

[254] Especially I Brownlie, *System of the Law of Nations, State Responsibility—Part I* (1983) 162; A Freeman, *Responsibility of States for Unlawful Acts of their Armed Forces* (1957); CF Amerasinghe, *State Responsibility for Injuries to Aliens* (1967).   [255] *AAPL v Sri Lanka* (n 238 above) 284–287.

Tribunal found that Zaire had taken no action whatsoever to protect the claimant's property. Accordingly, it was of little or no consequence whether the acts complained of were committed by a member of the Zairian armed forces or a common burglar, Zaire had an 'obligation of vigilance'[256] and accordingly its responsibility was invoked for a failure to provide full protection and security and for losses owing to riots or acts of violence.[257]

Wena Hotels Ltd v Egypt

7.150 The claimant, a British company, had entered into agreements with the Egyptian Hotels Company (EHC), an Egyptian State-owned company, to manage two hotels in Egypt: the Luxor and the El Nile. On 1 April 1991, the hotels were attacked by large crowds and the staff and guests were forcibly evicted. EHC, whose staff participated in the attacks, subsequently took control of the hotels, which were not returned to Wena for almost a year. The Tribunal found that Wena had not satisfied its burden of establishing that Egypt had actually participated in the seizures.[258] However, Egypt was nevertheless liable for failure to provide full protection and security. The State was aware of the seizures, but did nothing to prevent them; to protect the investment; to prevent damage to Wena's property; to sanction EHC for its role; or to compensate Wena for its losses.[259]

7.151 The reluctance of tribunals to see this standard extended beyond a due diligence obligation applicable in civil strife may be evidenced by its rejection as a ground of liability for the response of municipal authorities to protests against the investment in *Tecmed*,[260] and for the suspension or freezing of trading in shares in *Saluka*.[261] In *Tecmed* the Tribunal emphasized the burden of proof on the claimant to establish that the State had either encouraged the protests or acted unreasonably in response to them. In *Saluka* the Tribunal did not ultimately decide whether such measures could constitute a breach of this provision, which 'applies essentially when the foreign investment has been affected by civil strife and physical violence'.[262] However, it found the measures which the host State had adopted were a reasonable response to the regulatory problem, and also that the judicial system of the host State had provided a remedy.

---

[256] *AMT v Zaire* (n 239 above) 29.   [257] *AMT v Zaire* (n 239 above) 30–31.

[258] *Wena v Egypt* (n 240 above) 114 fn 198.

[259] *Wena v Egypt* (n 240 above) 112. cf the findings that the standard was not breached in the suspension and prohibition in trading in shares in *Saluka* (n 26 above) paras 482–493; or in the reaction of the municipal authorities to civil protests against the landfill in *Tecmed* (n 171 above) 180–181.

[260] *Tecmed* (n 171 above) 180–181.

[261] *Saluka* (n 26 above) paras 482–493.   [262] *Saluka* (n 26 above) para 483.

C. National Treatment

It will be recalled that customary international law does not proscribe all distinc- **7.152**
tions between aliens and nationals.[263] Accordingly, the requirement of national
treatment, found in most modern investment treaties, aims to provide a level
playing-field for foreign investors (at least post-establishment).[264]

The interpretation of the provision in investment arbitration has required close **7.153**
attention to the key comparator, which is that of the host State investor 'in like circumstances'. In *S D Myers*[265] the Tribunal had to assess the impact of an export ban
on PCB exports on Myers, an American company. It held that Myers was in similar circumstances to those of its Canadian competitors in PCB waste remediation
services. The primary indicator of a breach of the national treatment obligation
was the practical impact on the complainant, rather than the protectionist motive
of the host State.[266]

The concept of national treatment under Article 1102 of NAFTA resurfaced in **7.154**
Pope & Talbot Inc v Canada,[267] where breach of the provision was rejected by the
Tribunal. The Tribunal first held that the expression ' "no less favorable" means
equivalent to, not better or worse than, the best treatment accorded to the comparator'.[268] It further rejected an argument raised by Canada that it was necessary
to establish some disproportionate disadvantage to the foreign investor.[269] Instead
the Tribunal reformulated the test in the following terms:

> ... as a first step, the treatment accorded a foreign owned investment protected by
> Article 1102(2) should be compared with that accorded domestic investments in the
> same business or economic sector. However, that first step is not the last one.
> Differences in treatment will presumptively violate Article 1102(2), unless they have
> a reasonable nexus to rational government policies that (1) do not distinguish, on
> their face or *de facto*, between foreign-owned and domestic companies, and (2) do not
> otherwise unduly undermine the investment liberalizing objectives of NAFTA. [270]

The Tribunal's analysis of the facts focused not simply on the first element of the **7.155**
test, but also on whether any differences in treatment could be regarded as having
a reasonable nexus to rational government policies and no element of discrimination against foreign-owned producers. Assessed against this test, the Canadian
softwood lumber regime was found not to be in breach of Article 1102.

---

[263] 7.38 above.   [264] See the discussion at 7.31–7.36 above.
[265] *SD Myers Inc v Government of Canada* (Award on Liability) 8 ICSID Rep 3 (NAFTA/
UNCITRAL, 2000, Hunter P, Schwartz & Chiasson) 52–55, finding undisturbed on application
for judicial review to the Canadian Federal Court: *Attorney-General of Canada v SD Myers Inc and
United Mexican States (Intervener)* 8 ICSID Rep 194, 211.   [266] ibid 55.
[267] *Pope & Talbot* (n 209 above) 107–125.   [268] *Pope & Talbot* (n 209 above) 110.
[269] *Pope & Talbot* (n 209 above) 118.   [270] *Pope & Talbot* (n 209 above) 119–120.

7.156 The Tribunal in *Feldman v Mexico*[271] applied the same test, by a majority,[272] to find that there had been a breach of Article 1102, even where the evidence showed that there was only one local investor in the same business sector, since the record showed preferences accorded to the local investor which were not extended to the foreign investor.[273] Conversely, the claim failed in *ADF v USA*.[274] In that case, the Tribunal was concerned with the application of the national treatment standard to local content and performance requirements imposed in the context of government procurement. ADF, a Canadian company, had been sub-contracted to supply structural steel components for nine bridges in a federally-funded road project in Northern Virginia. The contract required the use of US steel. ADF had proposed to purchase US steel, but to fabricate it at its plant in Canada. The US authorities ruled that this violated federal performance conditions, requiring fabrication in the United States. The Tribunal decided that it was required to decide whether ADF's US steel was treated differently to the US steel of US investors in similar circumstances.[275] The claim failed on the basis that all of the US investors were also subjected to the 'Buy America' provisions of the legislation.[276] The Tribunal went on to note that the more specific provisions of NAFTA dealing with local content and performance requirements had a reservation for procurement by a State party.[277]

7.157 More questionable was the approach taken to this issue by the Tribunal in *Occidental v Ecuador*.[278] Finding a breach of the national treatment obligation arising from the imposition of VAT on exports of oil, the Tribunal dismissed the argument that the relevant comparator was local oil producers. It held that the comparison 'cannot be done by addressing exclusively the sector in which that particular activity is undertaken'.[279] The Tribunal rejected the WTO case law, but did not refer to the reasoning in the investment cases discussed above.[280]

---

[271] *Feldman v United Mexican States* (Award) 7 ICSID Rep 318, 388–397 (NAFTA/ICSID (AF), 2002, Kerameus P, Covarrubias Bravo & Gantz) finding undisturbed on application for judicial review to the Ontario Court: *United Mexican States v Feldman Karpa* 8 ICSID Rep 500 (Ontario Superior Court of Justice). [272] Covarrubias Bravo dissenting (ibid) 407–417.

[273] cf the curious refusal of the Tribunal in *Loewen* to entertain the national treatment claim on the basis that the only evidence of comparable treatment meted out to a local investor which had been adduced by the claimant related to the treatment accorded to the local opponent in the litigation in question: *Loewen Group Inc & anor v United States of America* (Award) 7 ICSID Rep 421, 468–469 (NAFTA/ICSID (AF), 2003, Mason P, Mikva & Mustill).

[274] *ADF Group Inc v United States of America* (Award) 6 ICSID Rep 449, 515–526 (NAFTA/ICSID (AF), 2003, Feliciano P, de Mestral & Lamm). [275] ibid 518.

[276] ibid 519.

[277] ibid 520. NAFTA (Appendix 1 below) Art 1108, paras 7(a) and 8(b).

[278] *Occidental Exploration and Production Co v Republic of Ecuador* (Award) (UNCITRAL/ LCIA, 2004, Orrego Vicuña P, Brower & Sweeney). [279] ibid para 173.

[280] The award was the subject of an unsuccessful challenge in the English courts: *Occidental Exploration and Production Co v Republic of Ecuador* [2005] EWCA 1116; [2006] 2 WLR 70; [2005]

Methanex v USA[281] is of special interest because the Tribunal heard extensive sub-   **7.158**
missions and expert evidence[282] about the applicable test, and in particular on the
extent to which the approach developed to national treatment in trade law was
applicable to the investment context. Methanex's argument, in a nutshell, was
that a ban imposed in California on the use of methanol in the reformulated gasoline market was a breach of the national treatment requirement against it, a
Canadian company. In order to construct this argument, Methanex had to submit
that the domestic producers in 'like circumstances' included US producers of
ethanol. This submission, observed the Tribunal, suffered from the fundamental
difficulty that there were also a substantial number of producers of methanol in
the United States: 'It would be a forced application of Article 1102 if a tribunal
were to ignore the identical comparator and to try to lever in an, at best, approximate (and arguably inappropriate) comparator. The fact stands—Methanex did
not receive less favourable treatment than the identical domestic comparators,
producing methanol.'[283]

In rejecting Methanex's argument, the Tribunal specifically rejected a submission   **7.159**
based on WTO jurisprudence on the meaning of the GATT term 'like products'.
The Tribunal reasoned that, if the parties to NAFTA had intended to use that
term in the Investment Chapter, they would have done so—being not only parties to the General Agreement on Tariffs and Trade (GATT), but also having used
the term with a specific cross-reference to the GATT in other parts of NAFTA.
There was no warrant for applying the technical meaning ascribed to it when construing the different concept of 'like treatment':

> The issue here is not the relevance of general international law, as the late Sir Robert
> Jennings proposed on behalf of Methanex, or the theoretical possibility of constru-
> ing a provision of NAFTA by reference to another treaty of the parties, for example
> the GATT. International law directs this Tribunal, first and foremost, to the text;
> here, the text and the drafters' intentions, which it manifests, show that trade provi-
> sions were not to be transported to investment provisions. Accordingly, the Tribunal
> holds that Article 1102 is to be read on its own terms and not as if the words 'any like,
> directly competitive or substitutable goods' appeared in it. [284]

In the result, therefore, the majority of the jurisprudence to date on national treat-   **7.160**
ment in investment treaties has preferred a relatively simple test of comparison
with the most directly comparable local investor or investors in the same business
sector. If a difference in treatment is detected through such a process, then the

---

2 Lloyd's Rep 707; *Republic of Ecuador v Occidental Exploration and Production Co* [2006] EWHC
345; [2006] 1 Lloyd's Rep 773.

[281] *Methanex* (n 192 above).
[282] Including from the late Sir Robert Jennings and Dr Claus-Dieter Ehlermann.
[283] *Methanex* (n 192 above) IV Chap B para 19.
[284] *Methanex* (n 192 above) IV Chap B para 37.

Tribunal will proceed to enquire whether the difference has a reasonable nexus to rational government policies, and is not discriminatory in its effect on foreign investors.[285]

D. Most Favoured Nation Treatment

7.161 Like national treatment, most favoured nation (MFN) treatment has an impressive lineage in both investment and trade treaties.[286] The general approach to the interpretation of such clauses has received considerable attention from international tribunals and from the International Law Commission.[287] It is not in dispute that provisions in other bilateral treaties may form the subject of comparison in the operation of an MFN clause. Indeed, in the field of investment law where most of the obligations of States have been assumed bilaterally, the inclusion of an MFN clause represents a potent ratchet by which obligations assumed or concessions made in negotiations may raise the stakes in the obligations of the host State under the BIT in question. For example, in *MTD v Chile*,[288] the Malaysian investor was, through this route, able to rely upon the more specific provisions of the Croatian and Danish BITs with Chile in relation to the observance of foreign investment contracts and the obligation to grant the necessary permits.

7.162 However, it is essential when applying an MFN clause to be satisfied that the provisions relied upon as constituting more favourable treatment in the other treaty are properly applicable, and will not have the effect of fundamentally subverting the carefully negotiated balance of the BIT in question. It is submitted that this is precisely the effect of the heretical decision of the Tribunal on objections to jurisdiction in *Maffezini v Spain*.[289] In that case, the Tribunal held that the specific provisions of the dispute resolution clause in the Argentine-Spain BIT did not constitute a bar to its jurisdiction in view of the more liberal provisions of the Chile-Spain BIT, which could be applied as a result of the MFN provision. Although this approach was followed in both *Tecmed*[290] and in *Siemens v Argentina*,[291] it was rejected in *Salini*

---

[285] At the time of writing one of the most important claims of breach of national treatment, *UPS v Canada* (n 222 above), was still pending on the merits.   [286] 7.39–7.40 above.
[287] n 58 above.
[288] *MTD Equity Sdn Bhd & anor v Republic of Chile* (Award) (2005) 44 ILM 91 (ICSID, 2004, Sureda P, Lalonde & Oreamuno Blanco).
[289] *Emilio Agustín Maffezini v Kingdom of Spain* (Jurisdiction) 5 ICSID Rep 387, 404–411 (ICSID, 2000, Orrego Vicuña P, Buergenthal & Wolf).   [290] *Tecmed* (n 171 above).
[291] *Siemens AG v Argentine Republic* (Jurisdiction) ICSID Case No ARB/02/8 (ICSID, 2004, Sureda P, Brower & Bello Janeiro). Also followed in *Suez, Sociedad General de Aguas de Barcelona SA & anor v Argentine Republic* (Jurisdiction) ICSID Case No ARB/03/17 (ICSID, 2006, Salacuse P, Kaufmann-Kohler & Nikken) para 66.

Construttori SpA v Jordan,[292] and, after a very full consideration, in *Plama Consortium Ltd v Bulgaria*.[293]

In *Maffezini*, the Argentine-Spain BIT contained a dispute settlement clause **7.163** which permitted the submission of the dispute to international arbitration only if it had first been submitted to the courts of the host State and no decision had been rendered within eighteen months.[294] The Chile-Spain BIT merely contained a cooling off period of six months, with no requirement to resort to the host State courts. The Tribunal considered the way in which MFN provisions had been dealt with by the ICJ in the *Anglo-Iranian Oil Co Case (Jurisdiction)*,[295] in the *Case Concerning the Rights of Nationals of the United States of America in Morocco*,[296] and by both the ICJ and the Arbitration Commission in the *Ambatielos Case*.[297] It observed that, as the investor could only derive its rights from the basic treaty, there was always a preliminary question as to whether the rights for which benefit was claimed by virtue of the MFN provision fell within the subject-matter scope of the basic treaty. The second question was an application of the *ejusdem generis* rule of construction. Could the dispute settlement provisions of the third-party treaty be said to be reasonably related to the requirement of fair and equitable treatment to which the MFN clause applied?

On that question, the Tribunal found that the protection of the rights of traders by **7.164** means of dispute resolution clauses was a matter which fell within the protections afforded by treaties of commerce and navigation or investment treaties. In so doing, it relied upon the finding to this effect by the Arbitration Commission in *Ambatielos*[298] (although the Commission had found on the facts in the latter case that the privileges extended in the third-party treaty were not in fact any more extensive than those in the basic treaty). Accordingly, Maffezini could take the benefit of the Chile-Spain BIT, and was not required to resort to the Spanish courts before invoking the jurisdiction of the arbitral tribunal. The Tribunal saw the only exceptions to the application of MFN clauses to the dispute settlement provisions of a BIT as being ones of public policy: where the parties to the basic treaty had

---

[292] *Salini Costruttori SpA & Italstrade SpA v Hashemite Kingdom of Jordan* (Jurisdiction) (2005) 44 ILM 573 (ICSID, 2004, Guillaume P, Cremades & Sinclair).

[293] *Plama Consortium Ltd v Republic of Bulgaria* (Jurisdiction) 20 ICSID Rev-FILJ 262 (ICSID, 2005, Salans P, van den Berg & Veeder).

[294] Acuerdo para la Promoción y la Protección Recíprocas de Inversiones ('Agreement on the Reciprocal Promotion and Protection of Investments') (Spain-Argentina) (signed 3 October 1991, entered into force 28 September 1992) 1699 UNTS 188 Art X(3)(a), reproduced in *Maffezini v Spain* (n 289 above) 399.

[295] *Anglo-Iranian Oil Co Case (United Kingdom v Iran)* (Jurisdiction) [1952] ICJ Rep 93.

[296] *Case Concerning Rights of Nationals of the United States of America in Morocco (France v United States of America)* [1952] ICJ Rep 176.

[297] *Ambatielos Case (Greece v United Kingdom)* (International Court of Justice) [1953] ICJ Rep 10; (Award) XII RIAA 82,107, (1956) 23 ILR 306, 319–320.   [298] ibid.

required the exhaustion of local remedies; made the dispute settlement provisions the subject of an irrevocable fork in the road; or specified a particular arbitral forum which one of them then sought to change by invoking the MFN clause.[299]

7.165 The correctness of this analysis was convincingly questioned in *Plama*.[300] In that case, the basic BIT, between Bulgaria and Cyprus, contained a provision for international arbitration in its dispute settlement clause, which was limited to determining the amount of compensation in a case of expropriation. The claimant sought to invoke ICSID arbitration by virtue of the more generous provisions for investor-State arbitration in other BITs to which Bulgaria was a party, including, for example, that between Bulgaria and Finland. The Tribunal rejected that submission, and, with it, the reasoning in *Maffezini*. It started with the proposition that all international arbitration must be based upon an agreement of the parties, which must be clear and unambiguous, even where reached by incorporation by reference.[301] States could provide expressly that they intended the MFN clause to apply to dispute settlement (as was the case, for example, in the UK model form BIT).[302] But the fact that the MFN clause was expressed to apply 'with respect to all matters' dealt with by the basic treaty was not sufficient to alleviate the doubt as to whether the parties had really intended it to apply to the dispute settlement clause. Could it be said that the MFN clause operated so as to replace one means of dispute settlement with another? How was a tribunal to evaluate which method of dispute settlement was in fact more favourable to the investor?

7.166 The Tribunal found that the three decisions relied upon in *Maffezini* were not authority for the proposition which it had enunciated. In fact, in both the *Morocco* and *Anglo-Iranian* cases, the ICJ had rejected the application of the MFN clause to dispute resolution. In the former case because the third-party treaties relied upon had been terminated, and could not therefore be regarded as having been incorporated permanently by reference.[303] In the latter case, the Court rejected the application of MFN to jurisdictional matters.[304] In *Ambatielos* the Arbitration Commission was concerned with the scope of the substantive protection from denial of justice, rather than with a jurisdictional provision in the basic treaty.

7.167 The Tribunal then proceeded to reject the reasoning in *Maffezini*. It found that, so far from promoting the harmonization of dispute settlement provisions, the application of an MFN approach to dispute settlement would rather produce a 'chaotic situation'.[305] Moreover, the public policy exceptions outlined in *Maffezini* were not based on authority. Rather, they were in fact reasons which fundamentally undermined the rationale for the rule which the *Maffezini* Tribunal had endorsed.[306]

---

[299] *Maffezini v Spain* (n 289 above) 410.   [300] *Plama* (n 293 above).
[301] *Plama* (n 293 above) 751–752.   [302] UK model BIT (Appendix 4 below) Art 3(3).
[303] *Morocco* (n 296 above).   [304] *Anglo-Iranian* (n 295 above) 109.
[305] *Plama* (n 293 above) 755.   [306] *Plama* (n 293 above) 755.

This analysis led the Tribunal to substitute instead a simple rule of construction to the effect that an MFN provision would not apply to dispute settlement provisions unless the parties *expressly* provided that it did.[307]

It is submitted that the reasoning of the Tribunal in *Plama* is to be strongly pre- **7.168** ferred over that in *Maffezini*. As the ICJ pointed out in *East Timor (Portugal v Australia)*,[308] the scope of application of a substantive obligation is an entirely sep- arate question to the conferral of jurisdiction upon an international tribunal. Jurisdiction in international law depends solely upon consent. This is a difficult concept in any event in investment arbitration. Given the absence of a meeting of minds between investor and host State, consent has to be constructed from the standing consent given by the State by treaty, and the subsequent consent given by the investor at the time the claim is submitted to arbitration. In those circum- stances, it is particularly important to construe the ambit of the State's consent strictly. As the discussion in Chapter 3 above has shown, the balance struck in investment treaties between the various dispute settlement options is often the subject of careful negotiation between the State parties, selecting from a range of different techniques. It is not to be presumed that this can be disrupted by an investor selecting at will from an assorted menu of other options provided in other treaties, negotiated with other State parties and in other circumstances. Moreover, it is in any event not possible to imply a hierarchy of favour to dispute settlement provisions. The clauses themselves do not do this, and it would be invidious for international tribunals to be finding (in the absence of specific evidence) that host State adjudication of treaty rights was necessarily inferior to international arbitra- tion. The same point could be made with even more force in the case of a com- parison between ICSID and other forms of arbitration which the State parties may have specified in particular investment treaties.

The result, if, as is suggested, the approach in *Plama* is preferred, will be that the **7.169** MFN clause will not apply to investment treaties' dispute settlement provisions, save where the States expressly so provide. Its domain of application will be as to the substantive rights vouchsafed to investors from third States to which special preferences have been granted.

3. An Approach to the Determination of Contested Rights

In the light of the foregoing review of both the basis and character of treatment obli- **7.170** gations in Part 1 of this Chapter, and the consideration of the modern application of the rights in investment arbitral awards in Part 2, it is now possible to summarize

---

[307] ibid.   [308] *Case Concerning East Timor (Portugal v Australia)* [1995] ICJ Rep 90.

the results of the enquiry. It is important to be clear about the function of the conclusions set out below. They are not intended to form a prescriptive set of rules. At
this stage in the development of the law in this field, that would be premature. One
must bear in mind that States have chosen to use open-textured language in their
treaty confirmations of investor protection designedly. It may be easier to reach
agreement on general language. Particular prescriptions may only serve to expose
differences between the parties and their legal systems, rather than to cement their
commonality. The extreme sensitivity over attempts to codify primary rules of custom regarding the treatment of aliens within the International Law Commission
bears witness to this. Moreover, undue particularity may operate as a straitjacket:
unnecessarily limiting the ability of the treaty guarantees to respond to the wide variety of fact patterns which may present themselves for review.

7.171 But this is not to say that no guidance can usefully be given. The standards are,
after all, as a number of tribunals have emphasized, *legal* standards. They are not
merely a warrant for unlimited arbitral discretion. It is a hallmark of legal reasoning in many legal systems that one must work with very general concepts (for
example reasonableness, good faith, and legitimate expectation) and apply them
to solve many different problems. In international law this is especially common.
But it does not make such concepts any the less law than a tax statute. Rather, the
use of very general concepts underlines a more general observation: that their
interpretation forms part of a process of legal reasoning. Thus, it is suggested that
the most important guidance which may be given in this area is to indicate an inte-
grated approach, which may usefully be followed in the determination of particular disputes. These insights are grouped into three sections: first, some observations
on the function of investor treatment obligations generally; secondly, an analysis
of the central role of the non-contingent obligations; and finally, the continuing
place of the contingent obligations.

A. General

7.172 The standards set for investor treatment in investment treaties exist on the plane
of international law. Their content is therefore determined by international law,
and not by the national legal systems of either the host State or any other State.
This has the consequence that:

(1) a breach of host State law will not necessarily give rise to a breach of the international law standard; and conversely
(2) the fact that the conduct is legal according to the law of the host State will not
necessarily mean that it conforms to the international standard.

7.173 Since the standards are found in treaties, they must be interpreted according to
the regime of interpretation provided for by Articles 31 and 32 of the VCLT.

Such a process of interpretation cannot stop at the four corners of the treaty itself. In particular:

(1) the object and purpose of investment treaties, being the intensification of the States' economic relations, calls for a balanced approach which does not over-emphasize investor protection at the risk of discouraging host States from the admission of foreign investments;

(2) subject to the next paragraph, Article 31(3)(c) and (4) mandates consider-ation of the meaning of the key operative phrases in investment treaties against the background of the broader development of these terms in international law generally.

However, the fact that the rights of investors created by investment treaties are **7.174** direct and not derivative of the States' rights has the consequence that their enjoyment should not be circumscribed by limitations necessarily imposed upon the determination and pursuit of an international delict between States arising under the customary international law of diplomatic protection and State responsibility.

The rights must be construed consistently. The protections which they afford may **7.175** be cumulative. But each must be given an independent meaning and distinctive role within the overall scheme.

B. Non-Contingent Standards

The key terms ('fair and equitable treatment' and 'full protection and security') are **7.176** expressive of 'general principles of law common to civilized nations', within the meaning of Article 38(1)(c) of the Statute of the International Court of Justice. Their acceptance in the model form BITs of many States serves to underline the extent of acceptance. These factors may also tend to support the existence of the obligation in customary international law,[309] although it may be more difficult to establish a binding obligation outside the treaty framework.

Conceived as general principles of law, the content of the non-contingent obliga- **7.177** tions must:

(1) reflect a sufficient degree of commonality as between civilized nations to jus-tify application; and
(2) be capable of evolution over time to reflect a changing consensus on expected standards.

---

[309] *Mondev International Ltd v United States of America* (Award) 6 ICSID Rep 181, 220 (NAFTA/ICSID (AF), 2002, Stephen P, Crawford & Schwebel).

Fair and equitable treatment

7.178 Fair and equitable treatment is the functional equivalent of the minimum standard of treatment at international law as applied to investments, since it affords a
basis by which international law judges the adequacy of treatment meted out to a
foreign investor by the judicial and administrative agencies of the host State. It
reflects treatment which all civilized nations should accord to their citizens as well
as to aliens. The application of the standard in investment treaties ensures that the
foreign investor receives a protection which domestic administrative law might
otherwise only vouchsafe to nationals.

7.179 As an international law standard derived from general principles of law common
to civilized nations, the standard must recognize and accept a great divergency in
legal and administrative systems in different countries.[310]

7.180 The starting-point is always that a foreign investor enters a host State voluntarily,
and must take its law as he finds it. Further, it is for the host State's own law to
define the basis for the investor's establishment, and the nature of any property
rights which he may acquire.

7.181 The standard is of its nature a broad one, and is not to be cut down or over-refined,
as this would undermine its safety-valve function as a minimum standard.[311]
However, greater guidance can be given to its content through *developments* in the
general principles of law common to civilized nations, which are capable of evolution.[312] In particular, the minimum standards of treatment found in international
human rights law relating to fair trial, the due process of law,[313] and protection
from non-discrimination[314] constitute a source by which the general test of fair
treatment may be given more specificity.

7.182 The standard is concerned with the *process* of decision-making as it affects the
rights of the investor, rather than with the protection of substantive rights (the latter being the function of the protection against expropriation and the guarantee
of full protection and security). The concept of 'fair treatment' is concerned with
the protection of fundamental rule of law values in decision-making (whether by

---

[310] eg Revised Harvard Draft (1961) 55 AJIL 545, 551 art 8(b).

[311] I Brownlie, *Principles of Public International Law* (6th edn, 2003) 503.

[312] *Mondev* (n 78 above) 221–224.

[313] Universal Declaration of Human Rights GA Res A/RES/217A (III) (10 December 1948)
Arts 8 & 10; Convention for the Protection of Human Rights and Fundamental Freedoms (signed
4 November 1950, entered into force 3 September 1953) 213 UNTS 222 ('European Convention
on Human Rights') Art 6(1).

[314] Universal Declaration (ibid) Art 7; International Covenant on Civil and Political Rights
(signed 19 December 1966, entered into force 23 March 1976) 999 UNTS 171 ('ICCPR')
Art 26.

judges or officials): predictability; accessibility; impartiality; and natural justice[315] as contrasted with arbitrary action.[316]

When applied to judicial decisions, the standard provides a protection against **7.183** denials of justice, being a failure to accord due process to the investor. This protection is concerned with the procedures applied by the host State court, and not with the substantive outcome under host State law. To constitute an international wrong sufficient to attract the protection of the treaty standard, the denial of justice must constitute a serious systemic breakdown in the host State's adjudicatory process. However, *pace Loewen*, it is submitted that it should not be necessary to exhaust local remedies (in the sense which that requirement carries in customary international law) in order to succeed in establishing this.

In assessing the adequacy of administrative decision-making, tribunals have been **7.184** primarily concerned with either (a) the protection of legitimate expectations or (b) the application of a fair decision-making process.[317]

The enquiry into legitimate expectations is itself concerned with process rather **7.185** than substance. It is concerned with ensuring consistency of treatment of an investor by the State. It starts from the proposition that the investor must take host State law as he finds it. The tribunal will attach more weight to specific representations made to a particular investor than to general policy statements. It will be concerned to leave a legitimate scope for regulatory flexibility.

In the application of the standard to the administrative decision-making process, **7.186** the following factors have been influential: discrimination against foreign investors; lack of transparency in decision-making; use of powers for improper purposes; inconsistency of treatment as between regulatory authorities; coercion and harassment by State authorities; and bad faith.

Conversely, factors which may suggest that the standard has not been breached **7.187** include: the existence of an objective basis for the State agency's decision; the lack of a disproportionate impact on the foreign investor as compared with other investors in the same industry; the fact that the right on which the investor relies is not found in either host State law or in international law; and failings in the investor's own conduct, including its failure to investigate properly the State's regulatory requirements.

---

[315] See the general discussion in B Kingsbury et al, 'Foreword: Global Governance as Administration—National and Transnational Approaches to Global Administrative Law' (2005) 68 Law & Cont Prob 1; D Dyzenhaus, 'The Rule of (Administrative) Law in International Law' (2005) 68 Law & Cont Prob 127.

[316] *Asylum Case (Colombia v Peru)* [1950] ICJ Rep 266, 284, applied in *Case concerning Elettronica Sicula SpA (ELSI) (United States of America v Italy)* [1989] ICJ Rep 15, 76.

[317] cf similar factors in international trade law: WTO, *United States—Import Prohibition of Certain Shrimp and Shrimp Products—Report of the Appellate Body* (12 October 1998) WT/DS58/AB/R, (1999) 38 ILM 121, 174–175; as to which see S Cassese, 'Global Standards for National Administrative Procedure' (2005) 68 Law & Cont Prob 109.

7.188 The concept of 'equitable treatment' adds an additional element which qualifies that of fair treatment. Equitable treatment:

(1) acts as a link with the protections of national and MFN treatment by ensuring that the national of the reciprocating State receives at least the equivalent treatment, cumulatively, to those in substantially the same position and who are nationals:

    (a) of the host State or

    (b) of another State with whom the host State has entered into bilateral treaty relations,

    and reinforcing the protection against discrimination, whether on grounds of nationality, or on any other grounds; and

(2) tempers the application of the minimum standard by enabling the tribunal to do equity to the State as well as the foreign investor, by giving due weight to the proper public purposes which the host State may wish to protect in determining whether the standard has been breached. The analogy here is with the concept of proportionality as it has been developed in administrative law, and in the application of human rights standards—as a means of balancing the private right against the State's determination of the public good. This enables the tribunal to make a determination of whether or not the impugned decision pursues some legitimate end, which might be balanced against the effect on the investor.

Full protection and security

7.189 The guarantee of full protection and security is concerned with the *substantive* protection afforded to the investor's property by the host State from damage caused to it either by host State officials, or by others acting within the host State's jurisdiction

7.190 It does not operate as an indemnity for any damage caused to the investor's property within the host State, or create a test of strict liability. Rather the enquiry is as to whether the State utilized its police powers with due diligence. It will be particularly applicable in cases of civil strife or acts of violence. Where the damage to the investment was caused by third parties rather than by State officials, the enquiry will be as to whether the State acted unreasonably in either failing to prevent the damage, or failing to take subsequent steps to prevent continuing damage or to sanction the offenders.

C. Contingent Standards

7.191 By contrast with the non-contingent standards, the contingent standards of national treatment and MFN treatment have never been regarded as forming part of customary international law, and only arise as a result of a treaty obligation voluntarily assumed. Nevertheless, the very wide use of these concepts in investment treaties has the consequence that there is a substantial common understanding as to their meaning.

The standards operate independently to the non-contingent standards in that: **7.192**

(1) the fact that a foreign investor is treated as well as a local one will not necessarily mean that the foreigner has received fair and equitable treatment or full protection and security;

(2) conversely, the conditions provided for local investors (or for those from MFNs) may exceed the standards required by fair and equitable treatment, in which case the investor is entitled to take the benefit of the higher standard;

(3) the same conduct may nevertheless give rise to a breach of both standards, since one concern of fair and equitable treatment is discrimination and the lack of even-handedness;

(4) nevertheless, the province of fair and equitable treatment is purely procedural, whereas the contingent standards are also concerned with substantive treatment.

The principal analytical tasks in the application of the contingent standards are: **7.193**

(1) the establishment of the appropriate comparator, being the relevant business or economic sector;

(2) if the measure does in fact result in a difference of treatment as between the protected investor and the like treatment accorded to the comparable group:

   (a) does the measure have a reasonable connection to a rational policy of the host State? and

   (b) does it, either expressly or in fact, discriminate against the foreign investor?

The application of MFN protection will not be justified where it subverts the **7.194** balance of rights and obligations which the parties have carefully negotiated in their investment treaty. In particular, it will not apply to the dispute settlement provisions, unless the parties expressly so provide.

8

EXPROPRIATION

A. Introduction—the Classical Claim and its Modern Elasticity

At the heart of foreign investors' claims against States prior to the 1950s was the **8.01** claim of nationalization or expropriation. The classical situation was a State's blatant seizure of the investor's assets while the State implemented a general programme of economic reform[1] or the State's highly visible acts in depriving the

---

[1] I Brownlie, *Principles of Public International Law* (6th edn, 2003) 509: 'Expropriation of one or more major national resources as part of a general programme of social and economic reform is

investor of its assets, without compensation. A small minority of investors might have had a concession contract with the host State, governed by international law, which incorporated its own contractual protections against expropriation, and allowed for international arbitration.[2] Otherwise, the investor in search of compensation or redress was usually left with the options of (a) seeking to persuade its home State to intervene through diplomatic protection (perhaps leading to international arbitration), or (b) pursuing remedies in the municipal courts of the State that had seized the assets. Neither option was particularly attractive to the aggrieved investor.

8.02 With the proliferation of investment treaties providing for direct access to international arbitral tribunals by foreign investors, and the more sophisticated efforts at domestic regulatory control undertaken by States in recent years, the classical claim has expanded. The treaty framers may have thought that they were codifying customary international law, but treaty claims on expropriation—and arbitral tribunals' interpretation of treaty provisions—have arguably overtaken customary international law and have become the focal point of the development of the international law of expropriation. Moreover, an *indirect* deprivation of a foreign investor's asset (which itself might take a variety of forms), possibly through a series of actions over time, rather than a militia storming a factory, has come to characterize modern expropriation claims. International law has thus recognized an elasticity in the nature and range of expropriatory acts, and assessing this elasticity—for example how far does it extend?[3]—has become a central issue in international investment arbitration.

B. The Absence of a Precise Definition

8.03 The concept of expropriation is reasonably clear: it is a governmental taking of property for which compensation is required. Actions 'short of direct possession

---

now generally referred to as nationalization or socialization.' Brownlie explains that, accordingly, nationalization is now understood to be a particular type of expropriation (see n 17 below for further discussion of these terms).

[2] See eg *Texaco Overseas Petroleum Co v Libyan Arab Republic* (Award) (1978) 17 ILM 3; (1979) 53 ILR 389 (Ad Hoc Arb, 1977, Dupuy); *Libyan American Oil Co [LIAMCO] v Libyan Arab Republic* (1982) 62 ILR 140 (Ad Hoc Arb, 1977, Mahmassani); *British Petroleum v Libyan Arab Republic* (1979) 53 ILR 297 (Ad Hoc Arb, 1973/1974, Lagergren); *Kuwait v Aminoil* (1984) 66 ILR 518 (Ad Hoc Arb, 1982, Reuter P, Hamed Sultan & Fitzmaurice). These awards are discussed at 8.104 and 8.116 below.

[3] An early useful statement of this modern elasticity may be found in the text of the 1967 award, *In the Matter of the Arbitration Between Valentine Petroleum & Chemical Corp and the Agency for International Development* (1970) 9 ILM 889, where the Tribunal quotes the definition of expropriatory action in the AID Contract of Guaranty, and comments that it is broad enough to include both 'constructive taking' or 'creeping expropriation', and notes that the former also comprises

of the assets may also fall within the category' of expropriation.[4] Expropriation is therefore lawful, but the compensation requirement 'makes the legality conditional'.[5] However, it is difficult to define with precision the situations covered by the concept. The definitions of expropriation appearing in investment treaties are of such a generality that they provide little guidance to parties or arbitral tribunals confronted by concrete cases.[6] In the absence of firm guidance, arbitral tribunals have fashioned a variety of tests for assessing whether States are liable for expropriation, which can create both opportunities and uncertainties for parties in circumstances where expropriation arguably has occurred. International law should not, in this respect, necessarily be viewed as less certain or variable than national law, which has had the advantage of a lengthy period of development within a narrower jurisprudential framework. As Higgins observed in the early 1980s, the 'reality is that most municipal law systems have themselves developed doctrines on the taking of property that are at best incoherent'.[7]

For example, in analysing three decades of US Supreme Court judgments in expropriation cases, a scholar referred to the 'crazy-quilt pattern of Supreme Court doctrine' on expropriation.[8] It has further been noted that although the 'process of describing general criteria to guide resolution of regulatory taking claims, begun in *Penn Central*,[9] has reduced to some extent the ad hoc character of takings law', it is 'nonetheless true that not all cases fit neatly into the categories delimited to date, and that still other cases that might be so categorized are explained in different terms by the Court'.[10] If the US position on certain significant aspects of **8.04**

'interference with the use or enjoyment of property' pursuant to the guidance provided by The American Law Institute, *Restatement (Third) Foreign Relations of the United States* (1987) Vol 1, 1987, especially Section 192.

[4] MN Shaw, *International Law* (5th edn, 2003) 740.

[5] I Brownlie, *Principles of Public International Law* (6th edn, 2003) 509–512. Brownlie adds that there are some widely recognized exceptions to the 'compensation rule', eg under particular treaty provisions; as a legitimate exercise of police power; or confiscation as a penalty for crimes.

[6] It has been said of NAFTA Art 1110(1) that its 'language is of such generality as to be difficult to apply in specific cases'. *Feldman v United Mexican States* (Award) 7 ICSID Rep 341, 366 (NAFTA/ICSID (AF), 2002, Kerameus K, Covarrubias Bravo & Gantz). Covarrubias Bravo filed a Dissenting Opinion on the issue of national treatment and discrimination.

[7] R Higgins, 'The Taking of Property by the State: Recent Developments in International Law' (1982) 176 *Recueil des Cours* 259, 268.

[8] A Dunham, '*Griggs v Allegheny County* in Perspective: Thirty Years of Supreme Court Expropriation Law' [1962] Supreme Court Review 63.

[9] *Penn Central Transportation Co v City of New York* (1978) 438 US 104 (Rehnquist and Stevens JJ, and Burger CJ dissenting).

[10] JH Killian and GA Costello (eds), *The Constitution of the United States of America: Analysis and Interpretation (Annotations of Cases Decided by the Supreme Court of the United States to June 29, 1992)* (1996) 1393. The editors add, at 1394, that the Court 'emphasizes that the taking of one "strand" or "stick" in the "bundle" of property rights does not necessarily constitute a taking as long as the property as a whole retains economic viability, but some strands are more important than others' [footnote omitted].

domestic expropriation, especially as regards the issue of regulatory or 'indirect' takings, has not crystallized into a clear formulation, it is not surprising that arbitral tribunals comprising members from many different legal backgrounds and interpreting international law have not developed a coherent doctrine of expropriation, especially as regards indirect expropriation.

8.05 Analysis of the tests as a whole fashioned by arbitral tribunals, and their application in specific cases to date, would not necessarily lead to the conclusion, at this stage of the development of the international law of expropriation, that arbitral tribunals have favoured investors at the expense of States. However, international law has undoubtedly evolved towards expanding claimants' opportunities to articulate an expropriation cause of action. This evolution can be said to reflect, in part, the increasing complexity of investment forms and methods and the concomitant sophistication of States' efforts to regulate their economic environment (while welcoming investment). It cannot be said (with persuasive evidentiary support) that there is an international law determination to lower the bar for claimants to succeed in claims of expropriation. Dolzer has commented that a teleological approach to treaty interpretation might involve multilateral and bilateral investment treaties being 'interpreted *in favorem* investor, stressing and expanding his rights so as to promote the flow of foreign investment', though such an approach would need to address 'the arguments that investment treaties are meant to benefit both investor and host state and that they are based on the recognition of the rights and obligations of both the host state and the investor'.[11]

8.06 Accordingly, an assessment of the substantive principles of the law of expropriation in the investment treaty context may usefully be undertaken by focusing more pragmatically on the ad hoc character of this growing body of law. Such an assessment also underscores the importance of knowing the writings and awards on expropriation previously produced by the individual members of the arbitral tribunal that has been constituted to resolve the investment dispute in a particular case.[12]

The lack of international uniformity, but discernible substantive principles

8.07 The difficulty of determining with precision the meaning of expropriation in international law because of the generality of language in international materials such as multilateral and bilateral investment treaties and the broad doctrinal statements that have appeared in many cases[13] is reinforced by the fact that the expropriation

---

[11] R Dolzer, 'Indirect Expropriations: New Developments?' (2002) 11 NYU Environmental Law Journal 64, 73–74.
[12] ibid 77 (US and European approaches to expropriation claims 'may not fully coincide').
[13] ibid 76.

provisions in treaties, though often similar, sometimes contain distinctions in wording. These distinctions inevitably have provoked discussion as to whether, on the one hand, a substantive difference in meaning should be recognized or, on the other hand, an emphasis on small variations in language (English language) is a misguided approach to the understanding of international law. In either event, it is nonetheless important to identify the textual definitions that have appeared in materials of major influence as well as the formulations developed by various international arbitral tribunals. In view of the vast array of sources that one might consult, it may be useful, in determining the substantive principles of expropriation law, to begin with the definitions that have appeared in the major multilateral investment treaties and to consider how certain tribunals have interpreted these definitions, before addressing the provisions on expropriation in various bilateral investment treaties.

Multilateral investment treaties

NAFTA Article 1110(1) of the North American Free Trade Agreement **8.08** (NAFTA)[14] contains the following provision:

> No Party may directly or indirectly nationalize or expropriate an investment of an investor of another Party in its territory or take a measure[15] tantamount to nationalization or expropriation of such an investment ('expropriation'), except:
>
> (a) for a public purpose;
> (b) on a non-discriminatory basis;
> (c) in accordance with due process of law and Article 1105(1);[16] and
> (d) on payment of compensation in accordance with paragraphs 2 through 6.

Additional sections of Article 1110 are also relevant to various international arbitral decisions: **8.09**

> [Article 1110(7)]
> This Article does not apply to the issuance of compulsory licences granted in relation to intellectual property rights, or to the revocation, limitation or creation of intellectual property rights, to the extent that such issuance, revocation, limitation or creation is consistent with Chapter Seventeen (Intellectual Property).

> [Article 1110(8)]
> For purposes of this Article and for greater certainty, a non-discriminatory measure of general application shall not be considered a measure tantamount to an expropriation of debt security loan covered by this Chapter solely on the ground that the measure imposes costs on the debtor that cause it to default on the debt.

---

[14] North American Free Trade Agreement (adopted 17 December 1992, entered into force 1 January 1994) CTS 1994 No 2, (1993) 32 ILM 612 ('NAFTA') (Appendix 1 below) Art 1110(1).

[15] The term 'measure' is defined in NAFTA (ibid) Art 201 to include 'any law, regulation, procedure, requirement or practice'.

[16] ibid Art 1105(1) states that treatment accorded to investors must be in accordance with international law, including fair and equitable treatment and full protection and security.

8.10 It is clear in NAFTA that 'expropriation' is explained by reference to the verbs 'expropriate' and 'nationalize', though no indication is given as to the meaning of these words.[17] Inclusion of both terms at least suggests a broad range of actions to be proscribed, as does the express inclusion of the words 'directly or indirectly' and the additional provision 'or take a measure tantamount'. However, there is no specific guidance in the instrument as to what constitutes 'direct' as opposed to 'indirect' expropriation, and how a 'measure tantamount to nationalization' differs from direct or indirect nationalization.

8.11 However, an influential arbitral tribunal's interpretation of this language has supplied some guidance on these points. The award in *Waste Management*[18] comments on the text of Article 1110 as follows:

> It may be noted that Article 1110(1) distinguishes between direct or indirect expropriation on the one hand and measures tantamount to an expropriation on the other. An indirect expropriation is still the taking of property. By contrast, where a measure tantamount to an expropriation is alleged, there may have been no actual transfer, taking or loss of property by any person or entity, but rather an effect on property which makes formal distinctions of ownership irrelevant ... Evidently the phrase 'take measures tantamount to nationalization or expropriation of such investment' in Article 1110(1) was intended to add to the meaning of the prohibition, over and above the reference to indirect expropriation. Indeed there is some indication that it was intended to have a broad meaning, otherwise it is difficult to see why Article 1110(8) was necessary. As a matter of international law a 'non-discriminatory measure of general application' in relation to a debt security or loan which imposed costs on the debtor causing it to default would not be considered expropriatory or even potentially so. It is true that paragraph (8) is stated to be 'for greater certainty', but if it was necessary even for certainty's sake to deal with such a case this suggests that the drafters entertained a broad view of what might be 'tantamount to expropriation'.[19]

8.12 The breadth afforded by the language of Article 1110 led another influential arbitral tribunal, in *Metalclad*,[20] to find that:

> ... expropriation under NAFTA includes not only open, deliberate and acknowledged takings of property, such as outright seizure or formal or obligatory transfer of

---

[17] As stated in n 1 above, a commonly understood distinction between the two terms is that nationalization consists of taking private assets into State ownership, and suggests large-scale takings, whereas expropriation would seem to have a broader scope in the sense that it does not necessarily imply that ownership has been taken by the State, but instead that a deprivation has occurred because of an action taken by the State. See also Higgins (n 7 above) 376 fn 2 (expropriation 'may affect an entire industry or individuals. Nationalization by contrast entails large-scale takings by virtue of a legislative or executive act for the purpose of transferring the interests into public-sector use').

[18] *Waste Management Inc v United Mexican States* (Award) (2004) 43 ILM 967 (NAFTA/ICSID (AF), 2004, Crawford P, Civiletti & Magallón Gómez). [19] ibid 995–996.

[20] *Metalclad Corp v United Mexican States* (Award) 5 ICSID Rep 209 (NAFTA/ICSID (AF), 2000, Lauterpacht P, Civiletti & Siqueiros).

title in favour of the host State, *but also covert or incidental interference with the use of property which has the effect of depriving the owner, in whole or in significant part, of the use or reasonably-to-be-expected economic benefit of property even if not necessarily to the obvious benefit of the host State*[21] [emphasis added].

This determination by the *Metalclad* Arbitral Tribunal is not without controversy. **8.13**
Indeed, upon judicial review in the Supreme Court of British Columbia, Tysoe J
characterized the *Metalclad* Tribunal's definition of expropriation under Article
1110 as 'extremely broad' (though this definition was not a reviewable issue)[22]
There is at least some uncertainty as to whether the *Metalclad* definition of expropriation, under either NAFTA or general principles of international law, is too
broad to be reliable, though the text of Article 1110 would appear to subject sovereign conduct to a broad scope of claims of expropriatory action.

Another point of uncertainty in Article 1110(1) of NAFTA is whether the four **8.14**
conditions mentioned under points (a) to (d) (see para 8.08 above) should be
taken into consideration in determining whether to find expropriation, and if so,
how. In *Feldman v Mexico*[23] the Arbitral Tribunal, which was troubled by NAFTA's
lack of a precise definition of expropriation, held that 'the conditions (other than
the requirement for compensation) are not of major importance in determining
expropriation'. It explained that:

> In the Tribunal's view, the essential determination is whether the actions of the . . .
> government constitute an expropriation or nationalization, or are valid governmen-
> tal activity. If there is no expropriatory action, factors a–d are of limited relevance,
> except to the extent that they have helped to differentiate between governmental acts
> that are expropriation and those that are not, or are parallel to violations of NAFTA
> Articles 1102 and 1105. If there is a finding of expropriation, compensation is
> required, even if the taking is for a public purpose, non-discriminatory and in accord-
> ance with due process of law and Article 1105(1).[24]

Although the analysis supplied by the *Feldman* Tribunal offers this clarification, **8.15**
the task of identifying 'expropriatory action' remains problematic; as the Tribunal
observes, this assessment must be made 'based on the facts of specific cases'.[25]
Moreover, there may be circumstances where it is important to determine whether
the expropriatory action is 'valid governmental activity' that has not been compensated, since expropriation is not necessarily invalid governmental activity, but
instead activity that must be accompanied by compensation. To be sure, in cases
involving investment treaties, the issue is as a practical matter whether there has

---

[21] ibid 230.
[22] Sub nom *United Mexican States v Metalclad Corp* 2001 BCSC 664; 5 ICSID Rep 236, 259
(British Colombia Supreme Court). Tysoe J observed that the Tribunal's definition 'is sufficiently
broad to include a legitimate rezoning of property by a municipality or other zoning authority'.
[23] *Feldman v Mexico* (n 6 above).   [24] *Feldman v Mexico* (n 6 above) 366.
[25] *Feldman v Mexico* (n 6 above) 367.

been an expropriation, and if so, whether the compensation (if any) for such expropriation has been 'prompt, adequate and effective'. However, Brownlie has commented that the level of compensation for expropriation that is unlawful per se (for example not for a purpose in the public interest) would include direct and consequential loss, whereas expropriation that would have been lawful if accompanied by compensation may lead to payment for direct losses only.[26]

8.16 The *Feldman* Tribunal also deemed the scope of 'indirect expropriation' and 'tantamount to expropriation' to be 'functionally equivalent'.[27] This is contrary to the analysis given by the *Waste Management* Tribunal, quoted above, which discerned an important distinction between these two concepts (ie an indirect expropriation still being a taking of property whereas a 'measure tantamount' need not involve a taking to make 'formal distinctions of ownership irrelevant'). This apparent discord between two distinguished tribunals' interpretations of the language and concepts in Article 1110 underscores the difficulties in assessing the contours of the modern claim of expropriation.

8.17 Energy Charter Treaty The uncertainty accompanying the meaning of expropriation is also raised when another definition in another recent multilateral investment treaty is considered. Article 13(1) of the Energy Charter Treaty (ECT) provides as follows:

> Investments of Investors of a Contracting Party in the Area of any other Contracting Party shall not be nationalized, expropriated or subjected to a measure or measures having effect equivalent to nationalization or expropriation (hereinafter referred to as 'Expropriation') except where such Expropriation is:
>
> (a) for a purpose which is in the public interest;
> (b) not discriminatory;
> (c) carried out under due process of law; and
> (d) accompanied by the payment of prompt, adequate and effective compensation.[28]

8.18 This wording differs from that of Article 1110(1) of NAFTA, most notably in that the ECT does not expressly refer to 'direct' or 'indirect' expropriation. Further, the ECT uses the language of measures 'having effect equivalent' to expropriation, instead of 'tantamount to' expropriation. However, Article 13(1) of the ECT has the same structure as Article 1110(1) of NAFTA—a general definition followed by four conditions—and the underlying principles would appear to be similar.

8.19 Nonetheless, on the basis of language alone the NAFTA definition of expropriation might be regarded as having a broader scope than the ECT definition, in view

---

[26] Brownlie (n 1 above) 515. Brownlie notes that the Iran-US Claims Tribunal has considered the remedial significance of this distinction in types of expropriation.

[27] *Feldman v Mexico* (n 6 above) 366.

[28] Energy Charter Treaty (signed 17 December 1994, entered into force 30 September 1999) 2080 UNTS 100 ('ECT') (Appendix 2 below).

of the express inclusion of indirect expropriation in the former.[29] There is also the possible difference between 'tantamount' and 'equivalent'. The differences in wording might permit the argument that a finding of expropriation by a NAFTA arbitral tribunal is not necessarily a suitable international law precedent for a tribunal applying the ECT standard. However, the *Pope & Talbot* and *SD Myers* Tribunals (interpreting Article 1110 of NAFTA) effectively concluded that the words 'tantamount to expropriation' meant equivalent to expropriation, and embraced the concept of 'creeping' expropriation rather than expanding the internationally accepted scope of the term expropriation. Moreover, it could be argued that as a matter of international law, 'expropriation' has come to comprise direct and indirect expropriation, and the NAFTA definition merely identifies with greater specificity of language the international law norm, which in any event is included in the 'narrower' ECT definition by the addition of the phrase on measures 'equivalent' to expropriation.

The *Nykomb Synergetics* Tribunal, in deciding an expropriation claim under the **8.20** ECT, determined that: ' "Regulatory takings" may under the circumstances amount to expropriation or the equivalent of an expropriation.'[30] The Tribunal also commented that the 'decisive factor for drawing the border line towards expropriation must primarily be the degree of possession taking or control over the enterprise that the disputed measures entail'.[31] The Tribunal assumed that 'expropriation' comprised the notion of 'indirect' or 'creeping' expropriation in the sense of a regulatory taking, though it found that the claimant failed to prove a regulatory taking. The Tribunal also appeared to make its determination while accepting the respondent's apparent concession that the issue was whether there was an expropriation 'even in the wider sense developed under recent international treaty law'.

Along these lines, focusing on the absence of the word 'indirectly' or parsing any **8.21** linguistic difference between 'equivalent' and 'tantamount' would be unhelpful. The discussion below of arbitral awards indicates the various approaches that have been taken regarding the international law norm of 'expropriation' in resolving

---

[29] *Pope & Talbot Inc v Government of Canada* (Interim Award) 7 ICSID Rep 69, 87 (NAFTA/UNCITRAL, 2000, Dervaird P, Greenberg & Belman); *SD Myers Inc v Government of Canada* (Partial Award) 8 ICSID Rep 4, 58 (NAFTA/UNCITRAL, 2000, Hunter P, Schwartz & Chiasson) (Separate Opinion by Schwartz, concurring with the Partial Award of the Tribunal except with respect to performance requirements); see also *Feldman v Mexico* (n 6 above) 367. The *Pope & Talbot* award at 87, and fn 87, notes the suggestion of Dolzer and Stevens that treaty provisions that define 'measures tantamount to expropriation' to include 'impairment ... of economic value' may 'represent the broadest scope of indirect expropriation'; however, the Tribunal stated that 'the authors' analysis does not change the basic concept at work in the treaties, NAFTA included: measures are covered only if they achieve the same results as expropriation'.

[30] *Nykomb Synergetics Technology Holding AB v Republic of Latvia* (Award) SCC Case No 118/2001 (SCC, 2003, Haug C, Schütze & Gernandt) para 4.3.1. See the discussion at 8.75 below, on the forms of 'indirect' expropriation.   [31] ibid.

investor-State disputes, and the significance to be placed on the particular wording of expropriation provisions in multilateral (and bilateral) investment treaties.

8.22 **Draft Multilateral Agreement on Investment**   The provisions on expropriation in other multilateral investment instruments provide limited assistance either in framing guidance for international arbitral tribunals on the scope of the concept or in indicating whether the differences in wording between, for example, the expropriation provisions in the NAFTA and ECT treaties, should be accorded any significance. The draft Multilateral Agreement on Investment (MAI), negotiated under the aegis of the Organization for Economic Co-operation and Development (OECD),[32] contains a provision on expropriation that is similar to that of Article 1110(1) of NAFTA in that it expressly refers to direct and indirect expropriation, but the MAI uses the word 'equivalent' instead of 'tantamount'. The version consolidated when the negotiations were discontinued in April 1998 reads as follows:

> A Contracting Party shall not expropriate or nationalise directly or indirectly an investment in its territory of an investor of another Contracting Party or take any measure or measures having equivalent effect (hereinafter referred to as 'expropriation') except: a) for a purpose which is in the public interest, b) on a non-discriminatory basis, c) in accordance with due process of law, and d) accompanied by payment of prompt, adequate and effective compensation in accordance with Articles 2.2 to 2.5 below.

8.23 **ASEAN Agreement of 15 December 1987**   The Association of Southeast Asian Nations (ASEAN) Agreement for the Promotion and Protection of Investments[33] contains a provision that is closer to Article 13(1) of the ECT in that it does not refer to direct or indirect expropriation and uses the word 'equivalent' instead of 'tantamount'. Article VI reads: 'Investments of nationals or companies of any Contracting Party shall not be subject to expropriation, nationalization or any measure equivalent thereto (in the article referred to as "expropriation"), except for public use, or public purpose, or in the public interest, and under due process of law, on a non-discriminatory basis and upon payment of adequate compensation.'

8.24 Finally, for the reasons given in earlier chapters, it should be remembered that the Washington Convention on the Settlement of Investment Disputes between States and Nationals of other States[34] (the 'ICSID Convention'), which entered into force on 14 October 1966, does *not* refer to expropriation. The ICSID Convention was intended to provide a framework for investors seeking compensation from States

---

[32] OECD, 'The MAI Negotiating Text' <http://www.oecd.org/dataoecd/46/40/1895712.pdf> accessed 20 September 2006.

[33] ASEAN Agreement for the Promotion and Protection of Investments (signed 15 December 1987) (1988) 27 ILM 612, 613 (Appendix 3 below).

[34] Convention on the Settlement of Investment Disputes between States and Nationals of other States (signed 18 March 1965, entered into force 14 October 1966) 575 UNTS 159 ('ICSID Convention') (Chapter 2, Appendix 11 below).

for a wide range of grievances, and not simply or mainly expropriation cases. Jurisdiction over investment disputes under the Washington Convention is defined by reference to the notion of investment, under Article 25.

Bilateral investment treaties

The imprecision of the definition of expropriation in multilateral investment **8.25** treaties is reinforced by the more than 2,500 bilateral investment treaties (BITs) that have been signed and ratified. It is standard for modern BITs to contain an expropriation provision, but such provisions usually do not provide any more guidance to the parties (and arbitrators) than the multilateral instruments discussed above. A review of several States' BITs over a number of years (for example those of the United States, United Kingdom, Brazil, Germany, France, Canada, the Netherlands, Australia, Singapore, and the Czech Republic) reveals a range of 'boilerplate' expropriation sections that manifest the differences in diction already seen in the multilateral instruments. A fluctuation in terminology over time defies easy identification of any trends.

Perhaps the only safe conclusion that can be drawn from such a review is that **8.26** States generally seek to incorporate in their BITs the 'customary international law standards for expropriation'.[35] Thus, States have frequently relied on the language and standards commonly thought to express the international law of expropriation that have appeared in widely cited twentieth-century materials. For example, the 1938 'Hull formula' (attributed to US Secretary of State Cordell Hull, in a note to the Mexican Government) stated that 'under every rule of law and equity, no government is entitled to expropriate private property for whatever purpose without provision for prompt, adequate and effective payment therefor.'[36] The 1961 Harvard Draft Convention on the International Responsibility of States for Injuries to Aliens provided the following wording: 'any such unreasonable interference with the use, enjoyment or disposal of property as to justify an inference that the owner thereof will not be able to use, enjoy or dispose of the property within a reasonable period of time after the inception of such interference'.[37] Article 3 of the 1967 OECD Draft Convention on the Protection of Foreign Property has also served as an important source: 'no Party shall take any measures depriving, directly or indirectly, of his property a national of another party'.[38] The

---

[35] An example of this is expressed in the Message accompanying the US-Bolivia BIT: 'Article III incorporates into the Treaty customary international law standards for expropriation.' Treaty concerning the Encouragement and Reciprocal Protection of Investment (US-Bolivia) (signed 17 April 1998, entered into force 6 June 2001) Senate Treaty Doc 106-25.

[36] (1938) 32 AJIL Supp 181; (1942) 3 Hackworth Digest of International Law 655.

[37] (1961) 55 AJIL 545, 553 (Art 10(3)a).

[38] OECD, *Draft Convention on the Protection of Foreign Property and Resolution of the Council of the OECD on the Draft Convention* (1967); see also H Abs & Shawcross, 'Draft Convention on Investments Abroad' (1960) 9 J Pub L 115, 116.

first modern BIT, that between Germany and Pakistan (1959), discussed below, also provided an early framework from which other States could draw.

8.27 The problem remains that these 'customary international law standards' are not themselves a stable or precise set of widely accepted points of law that provide adequate predictive aid to investors and States, as the discussion below of arbitral tribunal awards would suggest. Nonetheless, in a dispute proceeding under a BIT, one must commence any analysis of the expropriation standard by scrutinizing the language of the BIT itself.

8.28 **United States** Many recent BITs that the United States has entered into contain a provision such as the following, which closely resembles the provision considered above in Article 1110(1) of NAFTA:

> Neither party shall expropriate or nationalize a covered investment under this treaty either directly or indirectly through measures tantamount to expropriation or nationalization ('expropriation') except for a public purpose; in a non-discriminatory manner; upon payment of prompt, adequate and effective compensation; and in accordance with due process of law and general principles of treatment provided for in Article II, paragraph 3 [i.e. fair and equitable treatment; full protection and security; treatment no less favorable than that required by international law; no impairment by unreasonable and discriminatory measures].[39]

8.29 As described in the Letters of Submittal regarding these BITs from the US Department of State to the US President, such provisions incorporate the 'customary international law standards for expropriation' and describe 'the obligations of the Parties with respect to expropriation and nationalization of a covered investment. These obligations apply to both direct expropriation and indirect expropriation through measures "tantamount to expropriation or nationalization" and thus apply to "creeping expropriations"—a series of measures that effectively amounts to an expropriation of a covered investment without taking title.' These BITs are stated as being based on the '1994 U.S. prototype BIT'.[40]

8.30 Slightly earlier US BITs contain almost identical wording in their expropriation sections. For example, the US-Ukraine BIT,[41] based on the 1992 US prototype

---

[39] See eg US-Bolivia BIT (ibid); Treaty Concerning the Encouragement and Reciprocal Protection of Investment, with Annex and Protocol (US-Jordan) (signed 2 July 1997, entered into force 13 June 2003) Senate Treaty Doc 106-25; Treaty Concerning the Encouragement and Reciprocal Protection of Investment, with Annex and Protocol (US-Bahrain) (signed 29 September 1999, entered into force 31 May 2001) Senate Treaty Doc 106-25. The US-Bolivia BIT, Art III, also includes detailed provisions regarding the computation and payment of prompt, adequate, and effective compensation.

[40] ibid (the US 1994 model BIT is reproduced as Appendix 5 below).

[41] Treaty Concerning the Encouragement and Reciprocal Protection of Investment with Annex, and Related Exchange Letters (US-Ukraine) (signed 4 March 1994, entered into force 16 November 1996) Senate Treaty Doc 103-37. The US-Argentina expropriation provision is virtually identical, but there is no comment on expropriation in the Letter of Submittal from the US Department of State to the US President: Treaty Concerning the Reciprocal Encouragement and Protection of Investments, with Protocol (signed 14 November 1991, entered into force 20 October 1994) Senate Treaty Doc 103-02.

BIT, reads as follows: 'Investments shall not be expropriated or nationalized either directly or indirectly through measures tantamount to expropriation or nationalization ("expropriation") except: for public purpose; in a nondiscriminatory manner; upon payment of prompt, adequate and effective compensation; and in accordance with due process of law and the general principles of treatment provided for in Article II(2).'

The US-Ukraine BIT Letter of Submittal makes the same comment as noted **8.31** above that this section incorporates into the Treaty the international law standards for expropriation and compensation, and that investors are also protected from 'creeping expropriations'. There is an interesting adumbration, however, on the consequence of 'creeping expropriations', which are stated to be those 'that result in a *substantial* deprivation of the benefit of an investment without taking of the title to the investment' (emphasis added).[42] 'Substantial deprivation of the benefit' is, as we have seen, later termed 'effectively expropriate' in Letters of Submittal describing 'creeping expropriations'. It is nonetheless significant that at least the US understanding (in this BIT) is that a claim that fails to demonstrate a substantial deprivation will not succeed.

US BITs signed in the 1980s are of particular interest because, even though their **8.32** expropriation provisions vary between elaborate and terse wording, the accompanying Letters of Submittal emphasize the intention to define expropriation broadly and flexibly. In this sense, the expropriation sections of later BITs may be considered, along the curve of development of customary international law standards, to encompass such breadth and flexibility without having to continue to identify these characteristics expressly or through examples or explanations. Thus, the US-Egypt BIT[43] contains the following elaborate expropriation provision in which several instances of 'indirect' expropriation are set out:

> No investment or any part of an investment of a national or a company of either Party shall be expropriated or nationalized by the other Party or a political or administrative subdivision thereof or subjected to any other measure, direct or indirect (including, for example, the levying of taxation, the compulsory sale of all or part of such an investment, or impairment or deprivation of management, control or economic value of such an investment by the national or company concerned), if the effect of such other measure, or a series of such other measures, would be tantamount to expropriation or nationalization (all expropriations, all nationalizations and all such other measures hereinafter referred to as 'expropriation') unless the expropriation
>
> (a) is done for a public purpose;
> (b) is accomplished under due process of law;

---

[42] Similarly, the Treaty of Reciprocal Encouragement and Protection of Investments (US-Armenia) (signed 23 September 1992, entered into force 29 March 1996) Senate Treaty Doc 103-11.
[43] Treaty Concerning the Reciprocal Encouragement and Protection of Investments (US-Egypt) (signed 11 March 1986 (modified), entered into force 27 June 1992) Senate Treaty Doc 99-24.

    (c) is not discriminatory;

    (d) is accompanied by prompt and adequate compensation, freely realizable; and

    (e) does not violate any specific provision on contractual [engagement] [stability or expropriation contained in an investment agreement between the national or company concerned and the Party making the expropriation].[44]

8.33 The Letter of Submittal for the US-Egypt BIT comments that 'international law standards shall apply to the expropriation of investments and to the payment of compensation for expropriation'. It further notes that 'the meaning of "expropriation" as used in the model BIT [and incorporated in the US/Egypt BIT] is broad and flexible; it includes any measure which is "tantamount to expropriation or nationalization"'.

8.34 The US-Morocco BIT[45] was 'negotiated from a streamlined model text',[46] but was also intended to convey the broad scope of expropriation. The very brevity and simplicity of language in the US-Morocco BIT may well be regarded as effective in achieving this goal: 'Nationalization or expropriation measures, *or any other public measure having the same effect or nature*, which might be taken by either Party against investments of nationals or companies of the other Party, shall be neither discriminatory nor taken for reasons other than a public purpose. Any such measures shall only be taken under legal procedures which afford due process of law' (emphasis added).[47] The Letter of Submittal for this BIT indicates that the language covers an indirect as well as direct 'taking'. Further commentary in the Letter of Submittal states that 'the BIT's definition of expropriation is broad and flexible; essentially any measure regardless of form, which has the effect of depriving an investor of his management, control or economic value in a project may constitute an expropriation requiring compensation equal to the fair market value'.[48] The emphasis on breadth and flexibility is noteworthy, and in this Letter of Submittal the requirement for expropriation is thought to entail (at least from the US perspective) *deprivation* of management, control, or economic value, but not *substantial* deprivation, which is the US perspective concerning the later

---

[44] Sub-paragraph (e), it should be noted, constitutes a condition that is not expressly stated in many more recent BITs entered into by the US. The provision was modified in the course of various protocols; the two variants are indicated by the square brackets.

[45] Treaty Concerning the Encouragement and Reciprocal Protection of Investments, with Protocol (US-Morocco) (signed 22 July 1985, entered into force 29 May 1991) Senate Treaty Doc 99-18.

[46] Letter of Submittal; ibid.

[47] ibid. The provision continues: 'when such measures are taken, each Party shall pay promptly just and effective compensation to the nationals or companies of the other Party.'

[48] ibid. See also Treaty Concerning the Reciprocal Encouragement and Protection of Investment, with Protocol (US-Congo, Democratic Republic of (Kinshasa)) (signed 3 August 1984, entered into force 28 July 1989), containing a similar explanation in the Letter of Submittal, though the expropriation provision in the BIT uses different language: 'No investment or any part of an investment of a national or a company of either Party shall be expropriated or nationalized by the other Party or subjected to any measures, direct or indirect, tantamount to expropriation, unless . . .' This language is similar to that used in more recent US BITs, as discussed above.

US-Ukraine BIT, discussed above. It can be a far different enterprise to plead and prove *deprivation* as opposed to *substantial* deprivation.

However, it is difficult to assess whether an international arbitral tribunal would **8.35** actually set a lower barrier to recovery for the investor claimant based on the notion that the investor had only to show some deprivation as opposed to a substantial deprivation (indeed, the absence of the word substantial might suggest that a complete deprivation is actually required, so that the barrier would be higher, not lower, than substantial deprivation). Is the customary international law standard mere deprivation? This is unlikely, at present. However, the text and the parties' intentions in entering into a treaty could of course displace the customary international law standard in the case of a dispute arising out of that particular treaty. The key point here is the potential flexibility and concomitant uncertainty of the expropriatory action claim.[49]

In 2004 the US Government published an update of its 1994 model BIT. The **8.36** 2004 model US BIT[50] is a substantial forty-page document that contains a number of provisions that expressly seek to 'incorporate many of the principles from existing U.S. BITs',[51] but also reflects an acceptance, in relation to expropriation (and with certain qualifications as to 'minimum standard of treatment'), of 'customary international law' understood as the law 'that results from a general and consistent practice of States that they follow from a sense of legal obligation'.[52] Specifically, the expropriation provision of the model BIT[53] is stated to apply only to interference with 'a tangible or intangible property right or property interest in an investment', and contains a description of 'indirect expropriation' that acknowledges the need for a 'case-by-case, fact-based inquiry'.[54] Such inquiry would take

---

[49] The fair market value compensation requirement is also noteworthy in this Letter of Submittal and should be compared to the arguably lesser recovery amount set out in the first modern BIT, the 1959 Germany-Pakistan BIT (discussed at 8.43 below).   [50] 2004 US model BIT (Appendix 6 below).

[51] The Office of the United States Trade Representative notes that the update of the new US model BIT was completed in November 2004, and provides the following background: 'The new model contains provisions developed by the Administration to address the investment negotiating objectives of the Bipartisan Trade Promotion Authority Act of 2002, which incorporated many of the principles from existing U.S. BITs. The model is substantively similar to the investment chapters of the free trade agreements the United States has concluded since the 2002 Act. USTR and the State Department consulted their respective advisory committees and relevant congressional committees in the development of the new model. The United States last updated its model BIT in 1994.' Office of the United States Trade Representative, 'US Model Bilateral Investment Treaty' <http://www.ustr.gov/Trade_Sectors/Investment/Model_BIT/Section_Index.html?ht=> accessed 20 September 2006.   [52] 2004 US model BIT (Appendix 6 below) Annex A.

[53] 2004 US model BIT (Appendix 6 below) Art 6(1): 'Neither Party may expropriate or nationalize a covered investment either directly or indirectly through measures equivalent to expropriation or nationalization ('expropriation'), except: (a) for a public purpose; (b) in a non-discriminatory manner; (c) on payment of prompt, adequate, and effective compensation; and (d) in accordance with due process of law and Article 5 [Minimum Standard of Treatment] (1) through (3)' (omitting the compensation section; discussed in the following chapter).

[54] 2004 US model BIT (Appendix 6 below) Annex B.

into account, *inter alia*, the understanding that an adverse effect on the 'economic value of an investment' does not of itself establish expropriation; the interference is to be weighed against 'distinct, reasonable investment-backed expectations'; the 'character of the government action' must be taken into account; and a government's 'non-discriminatory regulatory actions' designed to protect 'legitimate public welfare objectives' do not, '[e]xcept in rare circumstances', 'constitute indirect expropriations'.[55] At the very least, then, the 2004 US model BIT serves as a useful guide to a State's approach to the incorporation of customary international law developments relating to expropriation claims in a BIT while seeking to place limits on the more expansive interpretations of expropriation that have appeared in recent investment treaty arbitral awards.

8.37 A brief review of expropriation provisions in other States' BITs, negotiated at different points in time, as set out below, provides additional perspectives on the points considered in relation to the US BITs.

8.38 **United Kingdom** A recent example of a BIT concluded by the United Kingdom is that entered into with Sierra Leone in 2000.[56] Its expropriation provision reads as follows: 'Investments of nationals or companies of either Contracting Party shall not be nationalised, expropriated or subjected to measures having effect equivalent to nationalisation or expropriation (hereinafter referred to as "expropriation") in the territory of the other Contracting Party except for a public purpose related to the internal needs of that Party on a non-discriminatory basis and against prompt, adequate and effective compensation'.

8.39 Unlike the US BITs discussed in this chapter, the UK BITs maintain a consistent use of language over time. From the outset, in the early 1970s, in developing the draft Agreement for the Promotion and Protection of Investments, UK governments sought to capture but not to 'go beyond what was thought to reflect' customary international law standards.[57] Indeed, the BIT concluded with Egypt in 1975[58] employs language in its expropriation provision that is identical to the above 2000 BIT with Sierra Leone, and there are few notable variations in this clause in examples surveyed in the intervening period or subsequently.[59] The UK BITs notably rely on the phrase 'measures having effect equivalent to nationalisation

---

[55] 2004 US model BIT (Appendix 6 below) Annex B.

[56] Agreement for the Promotion and Protection of Investments (UK-Sierra Leone) (signed 13 January 2000, entered into force 20 November 2001) 2186 UNTS 4; UKTS 17 (2002) Art 5.

[57] E Denza and S Brooks, 'Investment Protection Treaties: United Kingdom Experience' (1987) 36 ICLQ 908, 911–912; UK model BIT (Appendix 4 below) Art 5.

[58] Agreement for the Promotion and Protection of Investments (UK-Egypt) (signed 11 June 1975, entered into force 24 February 1976) 1032 UNTS 31; UKTS 97 (1976) Art 5.

[59] See eg Agreement for the Promotion and Reciprocal Protection of Investments (UK-Ukraine) (10 February 1993) 1728 UNTS 201; UKTS 24 (1993) Art 6. See also the same definition in, for instance, the Agreement for the Promotion and Protection of Investments (UK-India) (signed 14 March 1994, entered into force 6 January 1995) 1870 UNTS 213; UKTS 27 (1995) Art 5; Agreement for the Promotion and Protection of Investments (UK-Philippines) (signed 3 December 1980, entered

and expropriation' to capture forms of 'indirect' expropriation. However, the UK BITs offer no guidance as to the scope of 'indirect' expropriation, whether through examples or further elaboration. Further, there is no indication as to whether deprivations must be complete or substantial or something less than substantial.

Brazil   Examining the practice from the perspective of capital-importing States, **8.40**
one may instance two examples of BIT practice from Brazil. The Brazil-Netherlands
BIT, 1998 provides:[60]

> Neither Contracting Party shall take any measures depriving, directly or indirectly, investors of the other Contracting Party of their investments unless the following conditions are complied with:
> a) the measures are taken in the public interest and under due process of law;
> b) the measures are not discriminatory or contrary to any undertaking which the Contracting Party which takes such measures may have given.
> c) the measures are taken against just compensation.   **8.41**

A slightly different formula may be seen in the Brazil-Finland BIT, 1995:[61]
'Investments of investors of each Contracting Party shall not be nationalized, expropriated or subjected to measures having a similar effect (hereinafter referred to as "expropriation") in the territory of the other Contracting Party, unless the measures are taken in the public interest on a non discriminatory basis, under due process of law and provided that provisions have been made for effective, prompt and adequate compensation.'   **8.42**

The earlier Brazil BIT refers to 'measures having a similar effect', whereas the more recent BIT expressly uses the term 'directly or indirectly'. However, the more recent BIT does not indicate the breadth of an indirect deprivation and, again, there is no guidance as to whether a deprivation must be complete or substantial or something less than substantial.   **8.43**

Germany   The German practice is of particular interest, as Germany signed the first modern BIT: with Pakistan in 1959.[62] This contained the following expropriation provision: 'Nationals or companies of either Party shall not be subjected

---

into force 2 January 1981) 1218 UNTS 61; UKTS 7 (1981) Art 5; Agreement for the Promotion and Protection of Investments (UK-Bolivia) (signed 24 May 1988, entered into force 16 February 1990) 1640 UNTS 3; UKTS 34 (1990) Art 5; Agreement for the Promotion and Protection of Investments (UK-Vietnam) (1 August 2002) 2224 UNTS 430; UKTS 6 (2003) Art 5; Agreement for the Promotion and Protection of Investments (UK-Kenya) (13 September 1999) UKTS 8 (2000) Art 5.

[60] Agreement on the Encouragement and Reciprocal Protection of Investments (Netherlands-Brazil) (signed 25 November 1998, not yet entered into force) Tractatenblad 1998, 283 Art 6.

[61] Agreement on the Promotion and Protection of Investments (Brazil-Finland) (signed 28 March 1995, not yet entered into force) Art 5.

[62] Vertrag zwischen der Bundesrepublik Deutschland und Pakistan zur Förderung und zum Schutz von Kapitalanlagen ('Treaty for the Promotion and Protection of Investments, with Protocol and exchange notes') (Germany-Pakistan) (signed 25 November 1959, entered into force 28 April 1962) 457 UNTS 23; 1961 BGBl II 793.

to expropriation of their investments in the territory of the other Party except for public benefit against compensation, which shall represent the equivalent of the investments affected.'[63]

8.44 Two further examples show the subsequent evolution of the standard. Thus, the Germany-Jamaica BIT, 1992 states: 'Investments by nationals or companies of either Contracting Party shall not be expropriated, nationalized or subjected to any other measure the effects of which would be tantamount to expropriation or nationalization, hereinafter referred to as "comparable measure", in the territory of the other Contracting Party except for the public benefit and against compensation.'[64]

8.45 The Germany-Bosnia and Herzegovina BIT, 2001 has the formula as: 'Investments by investors of either Contracting State shall not be directly or indirectly expropriated, nationalized or subjected to any other measure the effects of which would be tantamount to expropriation or nationalization in the territory of the other Contracting State except for the public benefit and against compensation.'[65]

8.46 It is noteworthy that the 2001 Germany-Bosnia and Herzegovina BIT effectively replicates the language in Article 1110(1) of NAFTA, whereas the 1992 BIT did not include the words 'directly or indirectly'. But of greater interest is the comparison provided by the first modern BIT on record, that of Germany-Pakistan, signed in 1959. In the straightforward language of the expropriation provision of this earliest BIT, there is no term used other than 'expropriation', and nothing that would hint at the breadth or flexibility that the additional terms which are now so familiar in investment instruments—ie 'directly or indirectly', 'tantamount', 'equivalent'—would suggest. The Germany-Pakistan BIT, at least as conveyed by the stark solitariness of the word 'expropriation' (not even accompanied by the word 'nationalization'), points to an earlier stage of evolution of the customary international law standard that States have sought to incorporate in their BITs. 'Creeping' expropriation arguably was not part of the customary international law standard at the time that the Germany-Pakistan BIT was signed.

8.47 A complex cause-and-effect process may be discerned here: as the international law principle of expropriation came to be applied in broader and more flexible ways, a set of terms characterizing the widening scope came into common usage, and such terms were, to a varying extent, deemed to be needed to reflect this scope. However, arguably, now that 'expropriation' has come to comprise this broad scope, it would be difficult to argue that the word 'expropriation' used at this time and *unaccompanied*

---

[63] ibid Art 3(2).

[64] Vertrag über die gegenseitige Förderung und den Schutz von Kapitalanlagen ('Treaty concerning the Reciprocal Encouragement and Protection of Investments') (Germany-Jamaica) (signed 24 September 1992, entered into force 29 May 1996) 1996 BGBl II 58 Art 4(2).

[65] Vertrag über die Förderung und den gegenseitigen Schutz von Kapitalanlagen ('Treaty concerning the Encouragement and Reciprocal Protection of Investments') (Germany-Bosnia and Herzegovina) (signed 18 October 2001, not yet in force) 2004 BGBl II 314 Art 4(2).

by any of these terms somehow harkens back to the earlier, narrower definition. Thus, if the Germany-Pakistan BIT expropriation provision were to appear in a BIT signed in 2006, an international arbitral tribunal might nonetheless find that the parties expected the tribunal to apply the principle broadly and flexibly. An express disavowal of indirect or creeping expropriation would probably be required in order to recapture the 1959 standard. Moreover, the compensation term 'equivalent of investments affected', which in 1959 may have suggested a recovery that did not include lost profits and arguably was intended to be lower than 'fair market value', may have 'evolved' into something broader if applied today. The issue of compensation is fully discussed in Chapter 9 below.

France In English translation, a recent France BIT (the France/Mexico BIT, **8.48** 1998)[66] has the formula as follows (which, interestingly, does not use the words 'expropriate' or 'expropriation'):

> Neither Contracting Party shall take direct or indirect measures of nationalization or dispossession, or take any other measure having a similar effect, on an investment of the other Contracting Party, in its territory and in its maritime zone, except:
> (i)   in the public interest;
> (ii) provided that these measures are not discriminatory;
> (iii) in accordance with due process of law;
> (iv) on payment of a compensation in accordance with paragraphs 2 and 3 of the present Article.[67]

Older France BITs, however, use the word 'expropriation' next to 'nationalization' and 'any other measures of dispossession'. For example, Article 4 of the France/Malta BIT, 1976, reads as follows:

> 'The investments made by nationals or companies of either Contracting Party in the territory of the other Party shall not be subjected to any expropriation or nationalisation measures or any other measures of dispossession, direct or indirect, except in the public interest, non-discriminatory and against actual payment of adequate compensation'.[68]

---

[66] Accord sur l'encouragement et la Protection Réciproques des Investissements ('Agreement for the Reciprocal Promotion and Protection of Investments') (France-Mexico) (signed 12 November 1998, entered into force 12 October 2000) 2129 UNTS 176; JO 15 April 2000, 5761.

[67] Art 5(1) of the BIT reads in the original language: 'Aucune des Parties contractantes ne peut prendre de mesures, directes ou indirectes, de dépossession ou de nationalisation, ou tout autre mesure d'effect équivalent concernant un investissement de l'autre Partie, sur son territoire et dans sa zone maritime, si ce n'est:

> (i)   pour cause d'utilité publique,
> (ii) à condition que ces mesures ne soient pas discriminatoires,
> (iii) conformément à la procédure légale requise,
> (iv) moyennant le versement d'une indemnité conformément aux dispositions des paragraphes 2 et 3 du présent article.'

[68] Accord entre le Gouvernement de la République Française et le Gouvernement de la République de Matte sur l'Encouragement et la Protection Réciproques des Investissements (France-Malta) (signed 11 August 1976, entered into force 1 January 1978) 1080 UNTS 16523; JO 31 December 1977, 6361. In the original language, Art 4 of the BIT reads: 'Les investissements effectués par des ressortissants et sociétés de l'une des Parties contractantes sur le territoire de l'autre

8.49 It is apparent that the earlier France BIT's use of the term 'expropriation' was revised out by the late 1990s, when it was deemed sufficient to state 'direct measures of dispossession' and to add 'any measure having a similar effect'. Note that in French, contrary to the word 'dispossession' ('dépossession' in the French original), the word 'expropriation' used in the earlier BIT suggests a *complete* deprivation, a requirement that is not apparent in the later BIT.

8.50 **Canada**   Canada's BITs rely on the term 'effect equivalent to', which may perhaps explain in part why the Canadian Government sought to take the position (which eventually succeeded) in *Pope & Talbot*, discussed above, that 'equivalent' and 'tantamount' were synonymous and the use of tantamount in Article 1110 of NAFTA did not broaden the nature of expropriatory action.

8.51 Thus, the Canada-Costa Rica BIT, 1998 states: 'Investments of investors of either Contracting Party shall not be nationalized, expropriated or subjected to measures having an effect equivalent to nationalization or expropriation (hereinafter referred to as "expropriation") in the territory of the other Contracting Party, except for a public purpose, under due process of law, in a non-discriminatory manner and against prompt, adequate and effective compensation'.[69]

8.52 **The Netherlands**   An example of the recent Dutch practice is the Netherlands-Bosnia and Herzegovina BIT, 1998:

> Neither Contracting Party shall take any measures depriving nationals of the other Contracting Party of their investments or any measures having effect equivalent to nationalisation or expropriation unless the following conditions are complied with:
>
> a) the measures are taken in the public interest and under due process of law;
> b) the measures are not discriminatory or contrary to any undertaking which the Contracting Party which takes such measures may have given;
> c) the measures are taken against just compensation.[70]

8.53 This example is of interest because of its use of the word 'depriving' as a synonym for expropriation, with the additional protection of 'any measures having effect equivalent to nationalisation or expropriation'. 'Depriving' does not appear in

---

Partie ne seront pas l'objet de mesures d'expropriation, de nationalisation, ou de toute autre mesure de dépossession directe ou indirecte, si ce n'est à des fins d'intérêt public, de manière non discriminatoire et contre le règlement effectif d'une indemnité adéquate.'

   [69] Agreement for the Promotion and Protection of Investments (Canada-Costa Rica) (signed 18 March 1998, entered into force 29 September 1999) CTS 1999/43 Art 8. See also Agreement for the Promotion and Protection of Investments (Canada-Czech and Slovak Federal Republic) (signed 15 November 1990, entered into force 9 March 1992) CTS 1992/10 Art VI.
   [70] Agreement on Encouragement and Reciprocal Protection of Investments (Netherlands-Bosnia and Herzegovina) (signed 13 May 1998, entered into force 1 January 2002) Tractatenblad 1998, 172 Art 6.

earlier Netherlands BITs.[71] However, neither formulation indicates whether a *'substantial* deprivation' is covered.

Australia   A recent example of an Australia BIT is that of 2001, between Australia   **8.54**
and Egypt:[72]

> Neither Party shall nationalise, expropriate or subject to measures having effect
> equivalent to nationalisation or expropriation (hereinafter referred to as 'expropri-
> ation') the investments of investors of the other Party unless the following conditions
> are complied with:
> a) the expropriation is in the public interest which is related to the internal needs of
>   that Party and under due process of law;
> b) the expropriation is non-discriminatory; and
> c) the expropriation is accompanied by the payment of prompt, adequate and effect-
>   ive compensation.

There is a readily apparent consistency in the Australian practice as well as the   **8.55**
Singaporean and Czech Republic BITs set out below, in which the term 'measures
having effect equivalent to' is used in order for the parties to have the opportunity
to rely on a flexible definition of expropriation and the prevailing customary
international law standard, such as it may be.

Singapore   The formula adopted in the Singapore-Mongolia BIT, 1995 is:[73]   **8.56**

> Neither Contracting Party shall take any measure of expropriation, nationalization or
> other measures having effect equivalent to nationalization or expropriation (herein after
> referred to as 'expropriation') against the investment of nationals or companies of the
> other Contracting Party unless the measures are taken for any purpose authorised by law,
> on a non-discretionary basis, in accordance with its laws and against compensation
> which shall be effectively realisable and shall be made without unreasonable delay.

Czech Republic   A final example is taken from a treaty between two States that   **8.57**
were both formerly part of the Eastern bloc. The Czech Republic-Moldova BIT,
1999 provides:[74]

> Investments of investors of either Contracting Party shall not be nationalized, expro-
> priated or subjected to measures having effect equivalent to nationalization or

---

[71]   See eg Agreement on Encouragement and Reciprocal Protection of Investments (Netherlands-
Venezuela) (signed 22 October 1991, entered into force 1 November 1993) Tractatenblad 1993,
154 Art 6.

[72]   Agreement on the Promotion and Protection of Investments (Australia-Egypt) (5 September
2002) ATS 2002 19. This is substantially unchanged from a decade earlier. See eg Agreement on the
Reciprocal Promotion and Protection of Investments (Australia-Vietnam) (11 September 1991)
ATS 1991 36.

[73]   Agreement on the Promotion and Protection of Investments (Singapore-Mongolia) (signed
on 24 July 1994, entered into force 14 January 1996). See also Agreement on the Promotion and
Protection of Investments (Singapore-Vietnam) (signed 29 October 1992).

[74]   Agreement for the Promotion and Reciprocal Protection of Investments (Czech Republic-
Moldova) (signed 12 May 1999, entered into force 21 June 2000) 128/2000 Sb Art 5.

expropriation (herein referred to as 'expropriation') in the territory of the other Contracting Party except where for a public purpose. The expropriation shall be carried out under due process of law, on a non-discriminatory basis and shall be accompanied by provisions for the payment of prompt, adequate and effective compensation.

8.58 This review of BIT provisions among a wide range of States shows fluctuations of language over a fairly narrow range, and a marked reluctance on the part of contracting States to condescend to particulars. It is not possible to conclude that the differences in language are necessarily attributable to considerations specific to the contracting parties. Nor do they demonstrate deep doctrinal differences between States as to the extent of protection to be provided. In short, while expropriation—direct or indirect—is one of the main concerns of private investors, the increasing number of BITs has done little to assist in the determination of the actual conditions that prescribe what acts of a State would constitute expropriation under international law.[75] The frustrating generality of language commented upon by the *Feldman* Arbitral Tribunal in relation to the definition of expropriation in NAFTA could be echoed by an arbitral tribunal hearing an expropriation claim under virtually any BIT. However, there is clearly an accepted trend towards finding States potentially responsible for a broader scope of expropriatory action, while maintaining that the deprivation alleged must be very substantial, though not necessarily complete. Decisions of international arbitral tribunals are therefore crucial in clarifying and refining the nature of modern expropriation claims, and these decisions are considered more fully below.

Expropriation in the light of international law standards

8.59 In the absence of a precise definition of expropriation in investment treaties, it is usual practice for international tribunals to construe expropriation in the light 'of the whole body of state practice, treaties and judicial interpretations of that term in international law cases'.[76] Despite the generality of this reference to the sources of international law,[77] in practice tribunals have placed particular reliance on the judicial interpretations of the term in other arbitral awards, and on some codifications of the standards. They have also referred on occasion to the jurisprudence on property rights in major human rights conventions.

8.60 Judicial interpretations comprise, in particular, the awards rendered under Article 1110 of NAFTA,[78] ICSID awards, awards of other tribunals under BIT dispute

---

[75] N Gallagher & L Shore, 'Bilateral Investment Treaties' [2004] International Arbitration Law Review 49, 51.

[76] *SD Myers Inc v Government of Canada* (First Partial Award) 8 ICSID Rep 4, 58 (n 29 above).

[77] Statute of the International Court of Justice Art 38. On the approach to interpretation of treaty provisions see generally 3.51–3.83 above.

[78] Under NAFTA Art 1120(1), investors may submit their claim to arbitration under the ICSID Convention, the ICSID Additional Facility Rules, or an ad hoc arbitration under the UNCITRAL Arbitration Rules (Appendix 1 below).

provisions, decisions of other arbitral tribunals and national courts, and the decisions of the Iran-US Claims Tribunal.[79] The Iran-US Claims Tribunal has produced
a rich source of jurisprudence on expropriation, and pertinent awards will be referred
to in the course of this chapter. However, its jurisdiction is not limited to expropriation but also comprises 'other measures affecting property rights'. Iran-United
States Claims Tribunal decisions should therefore be used with particular care.[80]

A particularly influential codification, often used by international tribunals in rela- **8.61**
tion to the meaning of expropriation, is the Restatement (Third) of the Foreign
Relations Law of the United States,[81] in particular the definitions of indirect and
creeping expropriation in Section 712 (discussed below). For example, the *Pope &
Talbot* and *Saluka* Tribunals expressly relied on the Restatement (Third).[82] It
should also be remembered that the expropriation provisions in the Restatement
(Third), drawn in part from the 1961 Harvard Draft Convention prepared by
Sohn and Baxter, have by no means won universal acceptance; challenges have
come, in particular from capital-importing States (especially in relation to the
compensation provisions).[83]

Some human rights conventions also contain provisions relating to the protection **8.62**
of property, which are occasionally referred to by international tribunals when
considering the concept of expropriation. Article 21 of the American Convention
on Human Rights[84] and Article 17.2 of the Universal Declaration of Human
Rights of 1948[85] are examples of provisions relating to protection of property. The
former reads as follows: 'Rights to Property 1. Everyone has the right to the use
and enjoyment of his property. The law may subordinate such use and enjoyment
to the interest of society. 2. No one shall be deprived of his property except upon

---

[79] Declaration of the Government of the Democratic and Popular Republic of Algeria concerning
the Settlement of Claims by the Government of the United States of America and the Government
of the Islamic Republic of Iran (Claims Settlement Declaration) 19 January 1981, Art II.

[80] This point was reiterated by the Tribunal in *Pope & Talbot Inc v Government of Canada*
(Interim Award) 7 ICSID Rep 69, 87 (n 29 above): 'References to the decisions of the Iran-US
Claims Tribunal [should not] ignore the fact that that tribunal's mandate expressly extends beyond
expropriation to include "other measures affecting property rights".'

[81] American Law Institute, *Restatement (Third) Foreign Relations of the United States* (1987)
Vol 1, 1987, especially Section 712.

[82] *Pope & Talbot* (n 29 above) 86–87. This decision also relies on the *Harvard Draft Convention
on the International Responsibility of States for Injuries to Aliens* (1961), reprinted in LB Sohn and RR
Baxter, 'Responsibility of States for Injuries to the Economic Interest of Aliens' (1961) 55 AJIL 545,
576. The Tribunal in *Saluka* also relied on the 1967 OECD Draft Convention on the Protection of
Foreign Property: *Saluka Investments BV v Czech Republic* (Partial Award) Ad Hoc Arbitration
(UNCITRAL 2006, Watts A, Fortier & Behrens).

[83] American Law Institute, *Restatement (Third) Foreign Relations of the United States* (1987) Vol
1, 1987, Section 712, Reporters' Notes (Note 1—'Status of international law on expropriation').

[84] American Convention on Human Rights 'Pact of San Jose, Costa Rica' (signed 22 November
1969, entered into force 18 July 1978) 1144 UNTS 123.

[85] Adopted 10 December 1948: UNGA Res 217 A(III) (UDHR).

payment of just compensation, for reasons of public utility or social interest, and in the cases and according to the forms established by law.' The latter (Article 17(2)) states that 'No one should be arbitrarily deprived of his property'.

8.63   Article 1 of the First Protocol to the European Convention on Human Rights[86] should also be noted in this context:

> *Protection of property*
>
> Every natural or legal person is entitled to the peaceful enjoyment of his possessions. No one shall be deprived of his possessions except in the public interest and subject to the conditions provided for by law and by the general principles of international law.
>
> The preceding provisions shall not, however, in any way impair the right of a State to enforce such laws as it deems necessary to control the use of property in accordance with the general interest or to secure the payment of taxes or other contributions or penalties.

Even though the First Protocol to the European Convention on Human Rights does not contain the word 'expropriation', the European Court of Human Rights has provided guidance in its case law on whether measures taken by a State amount to expropriation. Indeed, the *Tecmed* Tribunal referred to the judgments rendered by the European Court of Human Rights in *Matos e Silva, Lda and ors v Portugal, Mellacher and ors v Austria,* and *Pressos Compania Naviera and ors v Belgium.*[87] The Tribunal explained that there 'must be a reasonable relationship of proportionality between the charge or weight imposed to the foreign investor and the aim sought to be realized by any expropriation measure'; in applying this test of proportionality the Tribunal referred to the case law developed by the Court of Strasbourg. The *Azurix* Tribunal also referred to European Court of Human Rights case law and applied the criterion of proportionality between the charge or burden to the investor and the aim sought to be realized.[88]

8.64   Thus, the decisions of the European Court of Human Rights as well as the decisions of other regional human rights courts should also be taken into consideration when seeking to understand customary international law on expropriation as well as the investment treaty elaboration of customary international law (as interpreted by arbitral tribunals).

---

[86] Protocol to the Convention for the Protection of Human Rights and the Fundamental Freedoms (European Convention on Human Rights, as amended) 213 UNTS 262 (ECHR).

[87] *Tecnicas Medioambientales Tecmed SA v United Mexican States* (2004) 43 ILM 133 (ICSID (AF), 2003, Grigera Naon P, Fernandez Rozas & Bernal Verea) 162–164: *Matos e Silva, Lda & ors v Portugal* [1996] ECHR 37; (1997) 24 EHRR 573; *Mellacher & ors v Austria* Series A No 169, (1989) 12 EHRR 391; and *Pressos Compania Naviera & ors v Belgium* (1995) Series A No 332, (1996) 21 EHRR 301.

[88] *Azurix Corp v Argentine Republic* (Award) ICSID case ARB/01/12 (ICSID, 2006, Rigo Sureda A, Lalonde & Martins).

The relationship of municipal and international law in expropriation claims

The property rights that are the subject of protection under the international **8.65** law of expropriation are created by the host State law. Thus, it is for the host State law to define the nature and extent of property rights that a foreign investor can acquire.[89] However, the fact that a 'taking' of that property by the host State may be legal under municipal law does not affect the question of whether the State's conduct is expropriatory under international law. Article 3 of the International Law Commission's Articles on the Responsibility of States for Internationally Wrongful Acts 2001 states: 'The characterization of an act of a State as internationally wrongful is governed by international law. Such characterization is not affected by the characterization of the same act as lawful by internal law.'[90]

However, the relationship of municipal and international law in an expropriation **8.66** claim can be both complex and hotly disputed. In *EnCana Corp v Republic of Ecuador*,[91] the Tribunal characterized the foreign investor's claims as follows: 'Either Ecuador has wrongfully denied rights to refunds owing to EnCana subsidiaries under Ecuadorian law, or irrespective of the legality of its measures, it has engaged in conduct having an equivalent effect to the expropriation of the investment.'[92] As a matter of indirect expropriation, it was noted that foreign investors do not have—in the absence of a commitment from the host State—any legitimate expectation that a tax regime will not change: only in an extreme case will taxation 'which is general in its incidence' be determined an expropriation.[93]

No indirect expropriation was found by the Tribunal; moreover—and here the **8.67** issue of applicable law becomes most pointed—no direct expropriation was found by the tribunal majority on the grounds that, *inter alia*, 'the denial of an incidental public law right (in an unclear, nascent domestic taxation regime) by an executive organ acting in good faith' does not amount to an expropriation of that right.[94] That is, the BIT did not convert the arbitral tribunal into an Ecuadorian tax court.[95] The Dissenting Opinion (Grigera Naon) took issue with the ruling on direct expropriation, principally on the grounds that, in his view, the ruling meant that an expropriation under a BIT was exclusively governed by the host State's local laws and had to be settled by the local courts. The divergence in the views of distinguished international lawyers in this case highlights the difficulties that future tribunals will undoubtedly confront in assessing the question of applicable law in reaching decisions on expropriation claims.

---

[89] See 3.51–3.79 above.

[90] J Crawford, *The International Law Commission's Articles on State Responsibility: Introduction, Text and Commentaries* (2002) 86–90. See also the discussion in 3.59–3.60 and 6.63–6.70 above.

[91] *EnCana Corp v Republic of Ecuador* (Award) LCIA Case UN3481 (UNCITRAL, 2006, Crawford P, Grigera Naon & Thomas).   [92] ibid para 171.

[93] ibid para 173.   [94] ibid fn 138; tribunal majority.   [95] ibid.

C. Direct and Indirect Expropriation

8.68 Expropriation can take numerous different forms. Although, as discussed above, the definitions of expropriation given by treaties are very general, they usually indicate a difference between 'direct' expropriation and 'indirect' expropriation (the latter is also sometimes referred to as de facto expropriation). These definitions also mention 'measures having effect equivalent' to expropriation or measures 'tantamount to' expropriation. In the following section, these different forms of expropriation are discussed in more detail and, in particular, as they have been considered and explicated by influential international arbitral tribunals.

Direct expropriation

8.69 'Direct expropriation' is generally understood as expropriation in its traditional meaning. Arbitral tribunals have considered direct expropriation as being relatively easy to recognize: for example, 'governmental authorities take over a mine or factory, depriving the investor of all meaningful benefits of ownership and control',[96] or there has been 'a compulsory transfer of property rights'.[97] In fact, the central element is that property must be 'taken' by State authorities or the investor must be deprived of it by State authorities.[98] Case law often refers to this as 'direct takings'.[99] This is apparent from the following descriptions:

> ... expropriation means a forcible taking by the Government of tangible or intangible property owned by private persons by means of administrative or legislative action to that effect;[100]

> In general, the term 'expropriation' carries with it the connotation of a 'taking' by a governmental-type authority of a person's 'property' with a view to transferring ownership of that property to another person, usually the authority that exercised its de jure or de facto power to do the 'taking'.[101]

> ... expropriation under NAFTA includes ... open, deliberate and acknowledged takings of property, such as outright seizure or formal or obligatory transfer of title in favour of the host State, to the obvious benefit of the host State.[102]

---

[96] *Feldman v United Mexican States* (Award) 7 ICSID Rep 341, 366–367 (n 6 above).

[97] *Amoco International Finance Corp v Government of the Islamic Republic of Iran et al* (1987) 15 Iran-USCTR 189, 220.

[98] The Tribunal in *Tippetts, Abbett, McCarthy, Stratton v TAMS-AFFA Consulting Engineers of Iran, the Government of the Islamic Republic of Iran* (1984) 6 Iran-USCTR 219, 225, stated that it 'prefers the term "deprivation" to the term "taking", although they are largely synonymous, because the latter may be understood to imply that the government has acquired something of value, which is not required'.   [99] *Feldman v Mexico* (n 6 above) 366.

[100] *Tecmed v Mexico* (n 87 above) 161.

[101] *SD Myers v Government of Canada* (Partial Award) 8 ICSID Rep 4, 58.

[102] *Metalclad Corp v United Mexican States* 5 ICSID Rep 209, 230 (n 20 above).

These descriptions are consistent with those found in leading texts, for example *Oppenheim's International Law*: 'Expropriation conveys in a general sense a deprivation of a former property owner of this property, and is equivalent to a "taking" of property'.[103]

The determination of direct expropriation by courts and tribunals does not usu- **8.70**
ally raise conceptual difficulties. However, the definition of direct expropriation is
often considered by tribunals in the context of a comparison with indirect expropriation, a concept that has posed many complexities.

Indirect expropriation

It may be helpful to attempt to grasp the sometimes slippery concept of indirect **8.71**
expropriation by first considering briefly, and in general terms, what some arbitral
tribunals have held it *not* to comprise, and then to approach it by examining in
more detail the various forms of indirect expropriation identified by tribunals.

Events not constituting indirect expropriation: effect of omissions and consent

Some arbitral tribunals have emphasized that 'omissions' are not sufficient: **8.72**

> For an expropriation to occur, there must be actions that can be considered reasonably
> appropriate for producing the effect of depriving the affected party of the property it
> owns, in such a way that whoever performs those actions will acquire, directly or indir-
> ectly, control, or at least the fruits of the expropriated property. Expropriation there-
> fore requires a teleologically driven action for it to occur; *omissions*, however egregious
> they may be, are not sufficient for it to take place [emphasis added].[104]

In this regard, the Iran-US Claims Tribunal has observed that: 'A claim founded
substantially on omissions and inaction in a situation where the evidence suggests a widespread and indiscriminate deterioration in management, disrupting
the functioning of the port of Bandar Abbas, can hardly justify a finding of
expropriation.'[105]

However, it should be kept in mind that for other arbitral tribunals a 'teleologi- **8.73**
cally driven action' of the State does not appear to have been required. These tribunals do not find a distinction between actions or inactions to be relevant; for
them the key point in defining indirect expropriation is the effect of the measure
on the investment.[106] This lack of attention to State purpose is troubling, and the

---

[103] See R Jennings & A Watts (eds), *Oppenheim's International Law* (9th edn, 1996) Vol 1, 916 fn 9. See also MN Shaw, *International Law* (5th edn, 2003) 740, quoted at n 4 above: 'Expropriation involves a taking of property, but actions short of direct possession of the assets in question may also fall within the category.'

[104] *Eudoro Armando Olguín v Republic of Paraguay* (Award) ICSID Case No ARB/98/5 (ICSID, 2001, Oreamuno Blanco P, Rezek & Alvarado).

[105] *Sea-Land Service Inc v Iran* (1984) 6 Iran-USCTR 149.

[106] See *CME Czech Republic BV v Czech Republic* (Partial Award) 9 ICSID Rep 121, 236 (UNCITRAL, 2001, Kühn, Schwebel & Hándl), discussed at 8.119 below.

Olguin 'teleologically driven' test is to be preferred: the *Olguin* test is more closely connected to the historical origins of expropriation claims; it recognizes the proposition that investment treaties do not give foreign investors a guarantee of investment success; and it further recognizes that for most tribunals an assessment of indirect expropriation in any of its forms has not somehow been disconnected from a requirement of State conduct of some sort.

8.74 Whether a State has by actions or inactions committed what might be considered an expropriatory measure, if the investor has effectively consented to such actions or inactions, a finding of indirect expropriation will generally not be made. That is, the investor must be the subject of a compulsory measure. The *Tradex* Tribunal held: 'As expropriation by definition is a "compulsory" transfer of property rights ..., an agreement reached in consent with the foreign investor and signed by it as in the Dissolution Agreement dated 21 April 1992 can hardly be seen as an act of expropriation in itself.'[107]

The different forms of indirect expropriation

8.75 Several terms, in addition to 'indirect', are used to describe indirect expropriation, for example 'de facto', 'creeping' expropriation, or measures 'tantamount to' or 'equivalent to' expropriation. Various arbitral tribunals have sought to attempt to explicate these terms and define the extent to which they should be differentiated. In a recent decision applying Article 1110 of NAFTA, the tribunal seemed to take the approach that the phrase 'indirect' expropriation comprised the above-mentioned terms:

> Generally, it is understood that the term '... equivalent to expropriation ...' or 'tantamount to expropriation' ... refers to the so-called 'indirect' expropriation' or 'creeping expropriation', as well as to the above-mentioned de facto expropriation. Although these forms of expropriation do not have a clear or unequivocal definition, it is generally understood that they materialize through actions or conduct, which do not explicitly express the purpose of depriving one of rights or assets, but actually have that effect. This type of expropriation does not necessarily take place gradually or stealthily—the term 'creeping' refers only to a type of indirect expropriation—and may be carried out through a single action, through a series of actions in a short period of time or through simultaneous actions. Therefore, a difference should be made between creeping expropriation and de facto expropriation, although they are usually included within the broader concept of 'indirect expropriation' and although both expropriation methods may take place by means of a broad number of actions that have to be examined on a case-by-case basis to conclude if one of such expropriation methods has taken place.[108]

---

[107] *Tradex Hellas SA v Albania* (Award), ICSID case ARB/94/2, (ICSID 1999, Böckstiegel P, Fielding & Giardina).

[108] *Tecmed* (n 87 above) 161. In *Feldman v Mexico* (n 6 above) 366, the Tribunal also held that creeping expropriation is a form of 'indirect expropriation', and may accordingly constitute measures 'tantamount to expropriation'.

Creeping expropriation

It is generally recognized that expropriation does not necessarily result from a sin- **8.76** gle act of the State. An investment can be taken gradually, by measures eventually resulting in expropriation. This situation, known as 'creeping' expropriation, was described by an ICSID tribunal as follows:

> As is well known, there is a wide spectrum of measures that a state may take in assert-
> ing control over property, extending from limited regulation of its use to a complete
> and formal deprivation of the owner's legal title. Likewise, the period of time involved
> in the process may vary—from an immediate and comprehensive taking to one that
> only gradually and by small steps reaches a condition in which it can be said that the
> owner has truly lost all the attributes of ownership. It is clear, however, that a measure
> or series of measures can still eventually amount to a taking, though the individual
> steps in the process do not formally purport to amount to a taking or to a transfer of
> title. What has to be identified is the extent to which the measures taken have deprived
> the owner of the normal control of his property.[109]

Arbitral tribunals have also given the following descriptions of creeping **8.77** expropriation:

> Creeping expropriation is a form of indirect expropriation with a distinctive tem-
> poral quality in the sense that it encapsulates the situation whereby a series of acts
> attributable to the State *over a period of time* culminate in the expropriatory taking of
> such property.[110]

> Under the terms of NAFTA and under general international law limitations on a
> state's right to expropriate private property include so-called 'creeping' expropriation,
> a process that has the effect of taking property through staged measures.[111]

> The conclusion that the Claimant was deprived of its property by conduct attribut-
> able to the Government of Iran, including NIOC, rests on a series of concrete actions
> rather than any particular formal decree, as the formal acts merely ratified and legit-
> imised the existing state of affairs.[112]

The Restatement (Third) of the Foreign Relations Law of the United States refers **8.78** to creeping expropriation as:

> ... actions of the government that have the effect of 'taking' the property, in whole or
> in large part, outright or in stages ... A state is responsible ... when it subjects alien
> property to taxation, regulation, or other action that is confiscatory, or that prevents,

---

[109] *Compañía del Desarrollo de Santa Elena, SA v Republic of Costa Rica* (Award) 5 ICSID Rep 153, 172 (ICSID, 2000, Fortier P, Lauterpacht & Weil).

[110] *Generation Ukraine Inc v Ukraine* (Award) ICSID case ARB/00/9 (ICSID, 2003, Paulsson J, Salpius & Voss).

[111] *Pope & Talbot Inc v Government of Canada* (Interim Award) 7 ICSID Rep 69, 82 (n 29 above) (a definition submitted by the investor).

[112] *Phillips Petroleum Co Iran v Islamic Republic of Iran, the National Iranian Oil Co* (1989) 21 Iran-USCTR 79, 116. The methods by which the Iranian Government progressively assumed con-trol over foreign enterprises after the 1979 Revolution often did not involve outright seizure. The Iran-US Claims Tribunal therefore had occasion to give elaborate consideration to situations involv-ing creeping expropriation, see the discussion and authorities cited at 8.84–8.85 below.

unreasonably interferes with, or unduly delays, effective enjoyment of an alien's property or its removal from the state's territory. Depriving an alien of control of his property, as by an order freezing his assets, might become a taking if it is long extended.[113]

The Restatement (Third) summarizes creeping expropriation as a situation where the State seeks 'to achieve the same result [as with formal expropriation] by taxation and regulatory measures designed to make continued operation of a project uneconomical so that it is abandoned'.[114]

Measures 'tantamount to' or 'equivalent to' expropriation

8.79 As discussed above, the expression 'tantamount to' expropriation can be found in Article 1110 of NAFTA as well as in many BITs (see the Germany-Bosnia and Herzegovina BIT of 2001, paras 8.45 to 8.46 above), whereas the expression 'equivalent to' expropriation is used, for example, in Article 13(1) of the Energy Charter Treaty as well as in various BITs (see the UK-Sierra Leone BIT of 2000, paras 8.38 to 8.39 above).

8.80 In *Waste Management v Mexico* the Tribunal stated that:

> An indirect expropriation is still a taking of property. By contrast where a measure tantamount to an expropriation is alleged, there may have been no actual transfer, taking or loss of property by any person or entity, but rather an effect on property which makes formal distinctions of ownership irrelevant ... Evidently the phrase 'take a measure tantamount to nationalization or expropriation of such an investment' in Article 1110(1) was intended to add to the meaning of the prohibition, over and above the reference to indirect expropriation. Indeed there is some indication that it was intended to have a broad meaning, otherwise it is difficult to see why Article 1110(8) was necessary.[115]

8.81 In *Pope & Talbot v Canada*, the investor argued that the phrase 'tantamount to expropriation' appearing in Article 1110 of NAFTA went beyond the meaning of expropriation ordinarily accepted in customary international law.[116] However, this argument was rejected by the arbitral Tribunal, which fused the two expressions 'tantamount to' and 'equivalent to' in order to limit their scope:

> ... the Tribunal does not believe that the phrase 'measure tantamount to nationalization or expropriation' in Article 1110 broadens the ordinary concept of expropriation under international law to require compensation for measures affecting property

---

[113] American Law Institute, *Restatement (Third) Foreign Relations of the United States* (1987) Vol 1, 1987, Section 712, Comment g. [114] ibid.

[115] *Waste Management Inc v United Mexican States* (2004) 43 ILM 967, 995 (n 18 above).

[116] *Pope & Talbot Inc v Government of Canada* (Interim Award) 7 ICSID Rep 69, 82 (n 29 above). The Tribunal noted that the investor argued that 'the phrase "measure tantamount to expropriation" appearing in Article 1110 comprehends a measure beyond the outright taking or creeping expropriation. It contends that the term includes "even non-discriminatory measures of general application which have the effect of substantially interfering with the investments of investors of NAFTA Parties".'

interests without regard to the magnitude or severity of that effect' ... 'Tantamount' means nothing more than equivalent. Something that is equivalent to something else cannot logically encompass more.[117]

This conclusion was approved in a later case: **8.82**

The primary meaning of the word 'tantamount' given by the Oxford English Dictionary is 'equivalent'. Both words require a Tribunal to look at the substance of what has occurred and not only at form. A Tribunal ... must look at the real interests involved and the purpose and effect of the government measure ... The Tribunal agrees with the conclusion in the Interim Award of the Pope & Talbot Arbitral Tribunal that something that is 'equivalent' to something else cannot logically encompass more. In common with the Pope & Talbot Tribunal, this Tribunal considers that the drafters of the NAFTA intended the word 'tantamount' to embrace the concept of so-called 'creeping expropriation', rather than to expand the internationally accepted scope of the term expropriation.[118]

Thus, forms of indirect expropriation are numerous and cannot readily be differ-   **8.83** entiated. Some Tribunals do not even seek to differentiate these expressions, noting that their scope should be regarded as 'functionally equivalent':[119]

The essence of any claim of expropriation is that there has been a taking of property without prompt and adequate compensation. However, many investment protection treaties and the Treaty which is the basis for the present arbitration extend the notion of a taking to include what has often been referred to as 'creeping' or 'indirect' expropriation by the State through measures which so substantially interfere with the investor's business activities that they are considered to be 'tantamount' to an expropriation.[120]

When measures are taken by a State the effect of which is to deprive the investor of the use and benefit of his investment even though he may retain nominal ownership of the respective rights being the investment, the measures are often referred to as a 'creeping' or 'indirect' expropriation or, as in the BIT, as measures 'the effect of which is tantamount to expropriation'.[121]

Such measures are sometimes referred to as 'indirect', 'creeping' or *de facto* expropriation and are frequently assimilated to formal expropriation as regards their legal consequences.[122]

For some tribunals, as indicated above, 'the form of the measures of control or   **8.84** interference is less important than the reality of their impact'[123] on the owner of

---

[117] ibid 85–87.   [118] *SD Myers v Canada* (n 29 above) 59.

[119] *Feldman v United Mexican States* 7 ICSID Rep 341, 366 (n 6 above) discusses the expressions 'indirect expropriation' and measures 'tantamount to expropriation' used in NAFTA Art 1110(1). As far as the required degree of interference with the investment is concerned, see paras 8.110–8.118 below.

[120] *Link Trading v The Republic of Moldova* (Award) Ad Hoc Arbitration (UNCITRAL, 2002, Herzfeld P, Buruiana & Zykln).

[121] *Middle East Cement Shipping and Handling Co SA v Arab Republic of Egypt* (Award) ICSID Case ARB/99/6 (ICSID, 2002, Böckstiegel P, Bernardini & Wallace).

[122] *Petrobart Ltd v The Kyrgyz Republic* (Award) SCC arb 126/2003 (SCC/ECT, 2005, Danelius P, Bring & Smets).   [123] *Tippetts, Abbett, McCarthy, Stratton v Iran* (n 98 above) 226.

the investment. Along the same lines, it has been decided that a positive act of the State may not even be necessary: ' it makes no difference whether the deprivation was caused by actions or by inactions'.[124] However, the 'sole effect doctrine' (ie the effect on the investor is the only relevant criterion) remains a highly controversial approach to indirect expropriation.[125]

A significant interference

8.85 Although the 'sole effect doctrine' is controversial, it is clear that an indirect expropriation will least in part be assessed on the basis of the effect of the measure in dispute on the investor: 'De facto expropriations or indirect expropriations measures that do not involve an overt taking but that effectively neutralize the benefit of the property of the foreign owner, are subject to expropriation claims.'[126]

8.86 Although there is not a traditional 'taking' of the investment, if the State authorities interfere to a significant degree with the enjoyment of its use or its benefit, an indirect expropriation may be found. The definition of expropriation given in the *Metalclad v Mexico* case is particularly pertinent on this point:

> Thus, expropriation under NAFTA includes not only open, deliberate and acknowledged takings of property, such as outright seizure or formal or obligatory transfer of title in favour of the host State, but also covert or incidental interference with the use of property which has the effect of depriving the owner, in whole or in significant part, of the use or reasonably-to-be-expected economic benefit of property even if not necessarily to the obvious benefit of the host State.[127]

8.87 Discussion of the concept of significant interference can also be found, for example, in *Marvin Feldman v Mexico*: 'indirect expropriations and measures "tantamount" to expropriation ... potentially encompass a variety of government regulatory activity that may significantly interfere with an investor's property rights'.[128]

8.88 Since it is the effect of the alleged expropriatory acts upon the investor's use or enjoyment of its property that is a key consideration, it is not necessary that the

---

[124] *CME Czech Republic BV v Czech Republic* (Partial Award) 9 ICSID Rep 121, 236 (UNCITRAL, 2001, Kühn P, Schwebel & Hándl).   [125] Dolzer (n 11 above) 79.

[126] *CME Czech Republic BV v Czech Republic* (Partial Award) 9 ICSID Rep 121, id. See also the award in *Seismograph Service Corp et al v National Iranian Oil Co and the Islamic Republic of Iran* (1988) 22 Iran-USCTR 3: ' On the basis of the foregoing and in the circumstances of this Case the Tribunal is not convinced, however, that this finding warrants the conclusion that CFPS thereby was deprived of the effective use, benefit and control of its Property so as to constitute an expropriation.'

[127] *Metalclad Corp v United Mexican States* (Award) 5 ICSID Rep 209, 230 (n 20 above). Although the Tribunal's findings on expropriation were subsequently set aside by the Supreme Court of British Columbia on the grounds that the Tribunal had erroneously relied on a requirement of transparency, the Court did not, as discussed above, review (though it did query) this definition, which has been relied on as authority by numerous international tribunals. *United Mexican States v Metalclad Corp* [2001] BCSC 664; 5 ICSID Rep 236, 259 [British Columbia Supreme Court].

[128] *Feldman v Mexico* (n 6 above) 366.

investor has been divested of legal title to his property. Expropriation can have occurred in cases where, although legal title to the investment may remain with the original owner, the rights that go with that title have been rendered useless:

> ... it is recognised in international law that measures taken by a State can interfere with property rights to such an extent that these rights are rendered so useless that they must be deemed to have been expropriated, even though the State does not purport to have expropriated them and the legal title to the property formally remains with the original owner.[129]

> A deprivation or taking of property may occur under international law through interference by a state in the use of that property or with the enjoyment of its benefits, even where legal title to the property is not affected.[130]

> The Tribunal agrees with the Claimant in that expropriation need not involve the transfer of title to a given property, which was the distinctive feature of traditional expropriation under international law. It may of course affect the economic value of an investment.[131]

A useful summary of the international law position on this issue may be found **8.89** in the *Revere Copper* award.[132] There the Tribunal found the host government's tax increases—which Jamaica implemented despite a stabilization clause in the concession agreement with the foreign investor—'have substantially the same impact on effective control over use and operation as if the properties were themselves conceded by a concession that was repudiated'.[133] Thus, even though the investor maintained its mining lease and was in possession of the plant and other facilities, its 'control' of the use and operation of its properties was no 'longer "effective" in view of the destruction by Government actions of its contract rights'.[134] This decision encapsulates the international law position on indirect expropriation, though, as the discussion below indicates (as well as the 2004 US model BIT considered above), a case-by-case fact-finding inquiry is at the centre of a determination on whether an action or series of actions by a State constitutes expropriation.

---

[129] *Starrett Housing Corp et al v Islamic Republic of Iran* (Interlocutory Award) (1983) 4 Iran-USCTR 122, 154.

[130] *Tippetts, Abbett, McCarthy, Stratton v TAMS-AFFA Consulting Engineers of Iran, the Government of the Islamic Republic of Iran* (1984) 6 Iran-USCTR 219, 225. See also *Foremost Tehran Inc v Islamic Republic of Iran* 10 Iran-USCTR 228, 243–244: 'It is well settled, in this Tribunal's practice as elsewhere, that property may be taken under international law through interference by a State in the use of that property or with the enjoyment of its benefits. This remains true in the absence of a formal expropriatory decree even where the formal legal title of the property is not affected'; *Sola Tiles Inc v Government of the Islamic Republic of Iran* (1987) 14 Iran-USCTR 223, 230; *Compañía del Desarrollo de Santa Elena SA v Republic of Costa Rica* (n 109 above) 172.

[131] *Occidental Exploration and Production Co v Republic of Ecuador* (Award), LCIA Case No UN3467 (UNCITRAL, 2004, Orrego Vicuña P, Brower & Barrera Sweeney).

[132] *Revere Copper & Brass Inc v Overseas Private Investment Corp* (1980) 56 ILR 258 (1978, Haight, Wetzel & Bergan). [133] ibid 291–292.

[134] ibid.

D. The Case-by-Case Approach of Tribunals

8.90 It is well settled in international law that the question of whether an expropriation has occurred is to be determined on a case-by-case basis. There are no specific rules as to which acts do or do not constitute expropriation. Arbitral tribunals conduct a balancing test in light of all the circumstances. International tribunals regularly comment on how difficult it is to draw a line between actions constituting an expropriation and those being valid governmental activities that do not require compensation. They examine different criteria, often explaining that each of them alone would be insufficient, although their combination could amount to expropriation. The outcome of disputes relating to expropriation is therefore often difficult to predict. The ensuing review seeks to foster a degree of predictability by isolating the criteria often employed by tribunals in making their expropriation determination.

Criteria considered by international tribunals

Degree of interference required

8.91 In cases of indirect expropriation, tribunals usually consider that measures are covered only if they achieve the same result as expropriation. 'The test is whether that interference is sufficiently restrictive to support the conclusion that the property has been "taken" from the owner'.[135]

8.92 This position is also reflected in the Harvard Draft Convention on the International Responsibility of States for Injuries to Aliens (1961), mentioned above, which refers to interference that would 'justify an inference that the owner ... will not be able to use, enjoy, or dispose of the property'.[136]

8.93 However, the Restatement (Third) is less restrictive, in speaking of 'action that is confiscatory, or that prevents, unreasonably interferes with, or unduly delays,

---

[135] *Pope & Talbot Inc v Government of Canada* (Interim Award) 7 ICSID Rep 69, 87 (n 29 above) relating to 'tantamount to expropriation'. See the interpretation of the *Pope & Talbot* requirement in *Gami Investment Inc v Government of the United Mexican States* (Award) (UNCITRAL/NAFTA, 2004, Reisman P, Muró & Paulsson): the 'affected property must be impaired to such an extent that it must be seen as "taken"'. See also *Otis Elevator Co v Islamic Republic of Iran and Bank Mellat* (1987) 14 Iran-USCTR 283: 'For Otis to be successful ... it is necessary for it to prove ... that its property rights had been interfered with to such an extent that its use of those rights or the enjoyment of their benefits was substantially affected'. See LY Fortier & SL Drymer, 'Indirect Expropriation in the Law of International Investment: I Know It When I See It, or *Caveat Investor*' (2004) 19 ICSID Rev-FILJ 293, especially 299–305, for a discussion of the distinction between non-compensable regulation and indirect expropriation.

[136] Harvard Draft Convention on the International Responsibility of States for Injuries to Aliens, Art 10(3)(a) of which states: 'A "taking of property" includes not only an outright taking of property but also any such unreasonable interference with the use, enjoyment, or disposal of property as to justify an inference that the owner thereof will not be able to use, enjoy, or dispose of the property within a reasonable period of time after the inception of such interference.' (1961) 55 AJIL 545, 553.

effective enjoyment or an alien's property'.[137] Again, tribunals will generally take into consideration all the circumstances of a case in order to reach their decision, and will closely examine the extent to which the State interference has affected the investment.

For example, in *Pope & Talbot v Canada* the investor claimed that Canada's Export **8.94** Control Regime constituted expropriation, as it interfered with the investor's ability to continue to export softwood lumber to the United States. The Tribunal did not accept this position. It noted that, even if the interference had, according to the investor, resulted in reduced profits on the investment, the investor nonetheless continued to export substantial quantities of softwood lumber to the United States and to earn substantial profits on those sales. Accordingly, the interference of the State was not substantial enough to amount to expropriation.[138]

The issue has also arisen of whether expropriation can consist of temporary meas- **8.95** ures. Some arbitral tribunals, such as the *Tecmed* Tribunal, refer to the requirement of a certain degree of permanence, sometimes adopting restrictive wording: 'it is understood that the measures adopted by a State, whether regulatory or not, are an indirect de facto expropriation if they are irreversible and permanent'.[139] However, in *SD Myers v Canada*, while the Tribunal agreed, as a matter of principle, that an expropriation 'usually amounts to a lasting removal of the ability of an owner to make use of its economic rights', it may be that, 'in some contexts and circumstances, it would be appropriate to view a deprivation as amounting to an expropriation, even if it were partial or temporary'.[140] The Tribunal did not find that the temporary deprivation in the case before it—a temporary closure of a border that postponed the export of hazardous waste to the investor's facilities in the United States for eighteen months—constituted an expropriation. The arbitrators held that Canada did not benefit from the measure and the evidence did not support a transfer of property or benefit directly to others; rather, an opportunity had been delayed.[141] But in *Wena Hotels*[142] a temporary deprivation was found to be sufficient to support an expropriation. The claimant had signed agreements with a company in the Egyptian public sector to lease and develop two hotels. Disputes arose concerning the terms of the lease, and the Egyptian company seized the hotels for approximately one year. Egypt argued before the Tribunal that this deprivation was merely 'ephemeral' and therefore did not constitute an expropriation. The

---

[137] American Law Institute, *Restatement (Third) Foreign Relations of the United States* (1987) Vol 1, Section 712.   [138] *Pope & Talbot* (n 29 above).

[139] *Tecmed* (n 87 above) para 116.

[140] *SD Myers v Government of Canada* (Partial Award) 8 ICSID Rep 4, 59 (n 29 above).

[141] ibid.

[142] *Wena Hotels Ltd v Arab Republic of Egypt* (Award) (2002) 41 ILM 896 (ICSID Case ARB/98/4, 2000, Leigh P, Fadlallah & Wallace). Another case where temporary measures have been considered as expropriatory is *Consortium RFCC v Kingdom of Morocco* (Award) ICSID case ARB/00/6 (ICSID, 2003, Briner P, Cremades & Fadlallah).

Tribunal held that the seizure and illegal possession for approximately one year was more than an ephemeral interference in the use of that property or in the enjoyment of its benefits.

8.96 The *SD Myers v Canada* award is also important in that it recognized the possibility for a deprivation of a 'partial' nature to support a finding of expropriation. This approach is supported by the broad definition of expropriation given in *Metalclad v Mexico*, which specifies that the investor can be deprived 'in whole or in significant part' of the use of its property.[143] Similarly, the *Iurii Bogdanov* Tribunal stated that the 'concept of indirect expropriation applies only to measures having the effect of expropriation that affect the totality or a substantial part of the investment'.[144]

8.97 The tribunal in *Waste Management v Mexico* commented that the *Metalclad* 'Tribunal held that Mexico, by tolerating and acquiescing in the action of the municipal authorities which prevented the operation of the fully constructed landfill, notwithstanding the approval and endorsement of the federal authorities, was responsible for a measure tantamount to expropriation of Metalclad's investment in breach of Article 1110 [of NAFTA]'.

8.98 Further, it held, the denial by the municipal authority of a construction permit on grounds which were not open to it and which contradicted earlier federal commitments, and the absence of a timely, orderly and substantial basis for the denial of the municipal permit amounted to an indirect expropriation. The tribunal also considered that the Ecological Decree, setting aside the area as a reserve and thus preventing the land from being used as provided for in the agreement, was an act tantamount to expropriation and a further ground for finding a breach of Article 1110 of NAFTA.[145]

8.99 The *Waste Management* Tribunal also observed that 'an enterprise is not expropriated just because its debts are not paid or other contractual obligations are breached . . . It is not the function of Article 1110 [of NAFTA] to compensate for failed business ventures, absent arbitrary intervention by the State amounting to a virtual taking or sterilising of the enterprise'.[146] The award in *Azurix* included a similar holding: 'contractual breaches by a State party or one of its instrumentalities would not normally constitute expropriation. Whether one or a series of such breaches can be considered to be measures tantamount to expropriation will depend on whether the State or its instrumentality has breached the contract in the exercise of its sovereign authority, or as a party to a contract'.[147]

---

[143] *Metalclad Corp v Mexico* (n 20 above) 230.
[144] *Iurii Bogdanov, Agurdino-Invest Ltd and Agurdino-Chimia JSC v Republic of Moldova* (Award) (SCC, 2005, Cordero Moss G).
[145] *Waste Management Inc v United Mexican States* (2004) 43 ILM 967, 997–998 (n 18 above).
[146] ibid 999.
[147] *Azurix Corp v Argentine Republic* (Award) ICSID Case ARB/01/12 (ICSID, 2006, Rigo Sureda A, Lalonde & Martins).

The *Tecmed* Tribunal, deciding a case under the provisions of the Spain-Mexico **8.100**
BIT,[148] conducted a proportionality test in order to determine whether the measure taken by the State constituted expropriation under the BIT. The Tribunal
explained that there 'must be a reasonable relationship of proportionality between
the charge or weight imposed to the foreign investor and the aim sought to be realized by any expropriatory measure'.[149] As noted above, the Tribunal relied in this
regard on case law developed by the European Court of Human Rights.

Objective impact or subjective intention?

It has been asserted by several arbitral tribunals that, when identifying expropria- **8.101**
tion, the State's intention is less important than the effects of the measure. This
does not mean that the intention of the State is not taken into account; these tribunals do not necessarily adhere to the 'sole effect doctrine'.[150] It may be that the
effect on the investment weighs more heavily in the balance than the motivation
of the State, but the motivation can nonetheless assist in assessing whether there
has been an indirect expropriation. For example, in *CCL v Republic of Kazakhstan*[151]
the claimant had concluded a concession agreement with the State for the transfer of the right to use Kazakhstan's shares in a refinery owned by the State for a
period of five years. Before the signature of the agreement, a financial analysis
performed by a consulting firm made the parties aware of the considerable debt of
the State company, including a court action brought against it by another Kazakh
company (Company X). Company X gained the right to take over the ownership of the refinery's assets in satisfaction of its claims against the Kazakh company. The claimant alleged that this amounted to an expropriation. The Tribunal
rejected the expropriation claim, stating that the claimant had not shown, and the
Tribunal had not discovered, any evidence or indication that any motivation to
expropriate lay behind any of the government's actions in connection with the
agreement.

The following dicta are instructive on this process of weighing the effect on the **8.102**
investment versus the motivation of the State:

> The intent of the government is less important than the effects of the measures on the
> owner, and the form of the measures of control or interference is less important than
> the reality of their impact.[152]

---

[148] Acuerdo para la Promocion y Proteccion reciproca de invesiones ('Agreement on the Promotion
and Reciprocal Protection of Investment') (Spain-Mexico) (signed 23 June 1995, entered into on 18
December 1996) 1965 UNTS 148.
[149] *Tecnicas Medioambientales Tecmed SA v United Mexican States* (2004) 43 ILM 133, 164 (n 18
above). A proportionality test was also applied by the *Azurix* Tribunal.   [150] See 8.84 above.
[151] (Award) SCC Case No 122/2001 (2004) (Chairman unidentified, Carter & Söderlund).
[152] *Tippetts, Abbett, McCarthy, Stratton v TAMS-AFFA Consulting Engineers of Iran, the Government
of the Islamic Republic of Iran* 6 Iran-USCTR 219, 225.

... Tribunal precedent makes clear that the key issue is the objective impact of measures affecting shareholder interests, not the subjective intention behind those measures.[153]

... The Respondent's reasons and concerns for taking control of [the company] cannot relieve it from responsibility to compensate the Claimant for the taking ... Moreover, a Government cannot avoid liability for compensation by showing that its actions were taken legitimately pursuant to its own laws.[154]

... a government's liability to compensate for expropriation of alien property does not depend on proof that the expropriation was intentional ...[155]

The motivations for the actions and omissions of Ghanaian governmental authorities are not clear. But the Tribunal need not establish those motivations to come to a conclusion in the case ...[156]

8.103 In the same way, the description given to the alleged expropriatory acts does not change their effect. The test is objective:

While the [Decree] describes the managers as 'trustees' and the administration of the factory as 'provisional', it does not indicate that they are trustees for the shareholders, and it makes clear that the factories are not to be returned to their owners unless and until debts owed to Government agencies ... are repaid out of profits.[157]

The phrase 'tantamount to expropriation' in Article 1110 [of NAFTA] does, however, require a tribunal to take a hard look at whether government conduct amounts in substance to an expropriation. The protection offered by Article 1110 does not cease to apply merely because an expropriation is dressed up in a more innocuous form, or accomplished by subtle or indirect means. The real purpose and real impact of a measure must be considered, not merely the official explanations offered by government or the technical wrapping in which the measure is cloaked.[158]

Degree of expectation of the investor

8.104 Since the *Metalclad* award, international tribunals have generally considered the 'reasonably to be expected' economic benefit of property as being one of the touchstones for an assessment of the validity of an expropriation claim. But *Metalclad* was not alone in bringing the matter of the investor's legitimate expectations to the centre of analysis. For example, the *Texaco* Tribunal in 1979 based a finding of expropriation, albeit not explicitly, on the breach by the State of the legitimate

---

[153] *Ebrahimi (Shahin Shaine) v Islamic Republic of Iran* (1994) 30 Iran-USCTR 170, 190.

[154] ibid at para 7, citing *Harold Birnbaum v Iran* (1993) 29 Iran-USCTR 260, 270.

[155] *Phillips Petroleum Co Iran v Islamic Republic of Iran, the National Iranian Oil Co* (1989) 21 Iran-USCTR 79, 115.

[156] *Antoine Biloune and Marine Drive Complex Ltd v Ghana Investments Centre and the Government of Ghana* (Awards) 95 ILR 183 (1993) (1989 and 1990, Schwebel P, Wallace & Monroe Leigh).

[157] *Phelps Dodge Corp and Overseas Private Investment Corp v Iran* (1986) 10 Iran-USCTR 121, 130.   [158] *SD Myers v Canada* (n 29 above) Separate Opinion (Schwarz) 110.

expectations of the investor.[159] Libya nationalized the property it had granted to TEXACO by means of a concession agreement (which contained a stabilization clause). The Tribunal held that:

> ... where the state has concluded with a foreign contracting party an international-ized agreement ... The state has placed itself within the international legal order in order to guarantee vis-à-vis its foreign contracting party a certain legal and economic status over a certain period of time. In consideration of this commitment, the part-ner is under the obligation to make a certain amount of investments in the country concerned and to explore and exploit at its own risk the petroleum resources which have been conceded to it ... The result is that a state cannot invoke its sovereignty to disregard commitments freely undertaken through the exercise of this same sover-eignty and cannot, though measures belonging to its internal order, make null and void the rights of the contracting party which has performed its various obligations under the contract.

More recently, the *Methanex* Tribunal[160] has also dealt with the case where the State offers specific commitments to the investor: 'as a matter of general inter-national law, a non-discriminatory regulation for a public purpose, which is enacted in accordance with due process and, which affects, inter alios, a foreign investor or investment is not deemed expropriatory and compensable unless specific com-mitments had been given by the regulating government to the then putative for-eign investor contemplating investment that the government would refrain from such regulation'.

8.105 The foreign investor's degree of expectation is commonly at issue in indirect expropriation claims, particularly in those where a State or State entity has under-taken regulatory measures that, at least arguably, are part of a lawful administrative programme. It has also been argued that in considering the legitimate expect-ations of investors, tribunals are able to focus on the legal situation in the host country, reconciling the proposition that States have the right to set their 'own rules of property which the foreigner accepts when investing' and 'the notion that expectations deserve more protection as they are increasingly backed by an invest-ment'. It also permits consideration of 'adaptations which are consistent with internationally held values and general principles of law as reflected in major domestic systems'.[161] The question is whether the foreign investor could reason-ably have expected that the economic value of its property would have been lost in

---

[159] *Texaco Overseas Petroleum Co, California Asiatic Oil Co v Government of Libyan Arab Republic*, (Award) Ad Hoc Arbitration 1977, 53 ILR 389 (1979) (Dupuy).

[160] *Methanex Corp v United States of America* (Award) (NAFTA/UNCITRAL 2005, Veeder P, Rowley & Reisman,

[161] R Dolzer, 'Indirect Expropriations: New Developments?' (2002) 11 NYU Environmental Law Journal 64, 78–79. For further discussion of the application of the doctrine of legitimate expect-ations see 7.101–7.104 above.

whole or significant part by the regulatory measures taken by the State. The Tribunal in the *International Thunderbird Gaming Corp v Mexico* case[162] held as follows:

> Having considered recent investment case law and the good faith principle of international customary law, the concept of 'legitimate expectations' relates, within the context of the NAFTA framework, to a situation where a Contracting Party's conduct creates reasonable and justifiable expectations on the part of an investor (or investment) to act in reliance on said conduct, such that a failure by the NAFTA Party to honour those expectations could cause the investor (or investment) to suffer damages. The threshold for legitimate expectations may vary depending on the nature of the violation alleged under the NAFTA and the circumstances of the case.

The expectation of economic benefit thus becomes part of the array of considerations that a tribunal must take into account in determining whether a deprivation for which the State is responsible has actually occurred.[163]

Date of expropriation

8.106   International tribunals have been relatively robust in determining for themselves, based on the facts of the case, the date of expropriation for the purposes of assessing liability. In circumstances where the 'taking' does not arguably consist of one act, tribunals will consider the relevant chain of events, and 'the taking will not necessarily be found to have occurred at the time either of the first or the last such event', but rather when the interference has deprived the claimant of fundamental rights of ownership and such deprivation is 'not merely ephemeral', or when it becomes an 'irreversible deprivation'.[164] The *Azurix* Tribunal stated: 'There is no specific time set under international law for measures constituting creeping expropriation to produce that effect. It will depend on the specific circumstances of the case. . . . When considering multiple measures, it will depend on the duration of their cumulative effect. Unfortunately, there is no mathematical formula to reach a mechanical result. How much time is needed must be judged by the specific circumstances of each case.'[165]

Governmental measures that may constitute expropriation

Organs of the State

8.107   The international law position on whether a measure has been taken by an organ of the State is expressed in Article 4 of the International Law Commission's

---

[162]   (Award) (NAFTA/UNCITRAL 2006, Van den Berg P, Ariosa & Wälde). See also *Petrobart Ltd v Kyrgyz Republic* (Award) SCC Arb 126/2003 (SCC/ECT, 2005, Danelius P, Bring & Smets); *Azurix Corp v Argentine Republic* (Award) ICSID case ARB/01/12 (ICSID, 2006, Rigo Sureda P, Lalonde & Martins); *EnCana Corp v Republic of Ecuador* (Award) LCIA Case UN3481 (UNCITRAL, 2006, Crawford P, Grigera Naón & Thomas) paras 173–177.

[163]   See LY Fortier & SL Drymer, 'Indirect Expropriation in the Law of International Investment: I Know It When I See It, or *Caveat Investor*' (2004) 19 ICSID Rev-FILJ 293, 306–308.

[164]   *Phillips Petroleum Co v Iran* (n 112 above) 116.

[165]   *Azurix Corp v Argentine Republic* (Award) ICSID case ARB/01/12 (ICSID, 2006, Rigo Sureda P, Lalonde & Martins).

Articles on the Responsibility of States for Internationally Wrongful Acts 2001:

> 1. The conduct of any State organ shall be considered an act of that State under international law, whether the organ exercises legislative, executive, judicial or any other functions, whatever position it holds in the organization of the State, and whatever its character as an organ of the central government of a territorial unit of the State.
>
> 2. An organ includes any person or entity which has that status in accordance with the internal law of the State.[166]

It is of particular note from Article 4 that judicial conduct comes within State **8.108** responsibility; Paulsson has observed that in this respect the International Law Commission Articles 'reflect the emergence of a clear consensus'.[167]

Although Article 4 may in all respects be considered as expressing the settled inter- **8.109** national law perspective on the principles by which to assess whether action has been taken (or omitted) that is attributable to the State, there nonetheless remains, in specific arbitration cases, some significant disagreement about the application of these principles to the factual matrix before the arbitral tribunal. For example, in *Eureko v Poland*[168] there was a divided tribunal on the issue of whether the disputes arising out of the contractual relations between the foreign (Dutch) investor and the State Treasury of Poland were attributable to the State. Both the majority and the dissenting positions were expressly based on Article 4. The majority stated that the 'crystal clear' text of Article 4, applied to the facts of the case, compelled the conclusion that the State Treasury constituted an organ of the Republic of Poland. However, Professor Rajska opined that the majority's conclusion was inconsistent with this text, even broadly construed. First, Professor Rajska commented that the State Treasury was exclusively liable for its obligations and was a juridical person separate from the State (ie an autonomous juridical person that could not exercise any public or regulatory functions). He further observed—and here one will note a divergence with the majority in the interpretation of the principles in Article 4 and not merely their application in the particular case—that under Article 4(2), since the State Treasury did not have the status of a State organ in accordance with Polish law, its conduct should not be considered an action of the State. Professor Rajska read sub-article 2 as limiting sub-paragraph 1, whereas other international law scholars, as Professor Crawford explains in his Commentary to Article 4,[169] would consider that sub-paragraph 2 instead explains that it is 'not sufficient to refer to internal law for the status of State organs'; 'a State cannot

---

[166] J Crawford, *The International Law Commission's Articles on State Responsibility: Introduction, Text and Commentaries* (2002) 94.

[167] J Paulsson, *Denial of Justice in International Law* (2005) 40.

[168] *Eureko BV v Republic of Poland* (Partial Award) (Ad Hoc Arb, 2005, Fortier P, Schwebel & Rajska) (Dissenting Opinion of Rajska). [169] Crawford (n 90 above) 98.

avoid responsibility for the conduct of a body which does in truth act as one of its organs merely by denying it that status under its own law'. Under this (undoubtedly majority) view, Professor Crawford observes that the use of the word 'includes' in sub-paragraph 2 is crucial; sub-paragraph 2 thus should be understood to mean 'includes but is not limited to' and therefore does not limit but rather broadly clarifies sub-paragraph 1.

The scope of State conduct under scrutiny

8.110 Arbitral tribunals have repeatedly emphasized that not every business problem experienced by a foreign investor is an expropriation; it is a fact of commercial life that individuals may be disappointed in their dealings with public authorities:[170]

> ... not all government regulatory activity that makes it difficult or impossible for an investor to carry out a particular business, change in the law or change in the application of existing laws that makes it uneconomical to continue a particular business, is an expropriation under Article 1110 [of NAFTA]. Governments, in their exercise of regulatory power, frequently change their laws and regulations in response to changing economic circumstances or changing political, economic or social considerations. Those changes may well make certain activities less profitable or even uneconomic to continue.[171]

8.111 This is asserted with particular force in the recent *Tecmed* decision: 'The principle that the State's exercise of its sovereign powers within the framework of its police power may cause economic damage to those subject to its powers as administrator without entitling them to any compensation whatsoever is undisputable.'[172]

Regulatory activity

8.112 Although certain governments have rejected the position that regulatory activity can constitute expropriation, several arbitral decisions have firmly held that regulatory activity is not, per se, outside the scope of expropriation: 'Regulations can indeed be exercised in a way that would constitute creeping expropriation. ... Indeed, much creeping expropriation could be conducted by regulation, and a

---

[170] eg *Robert Azinian and ors v United Mexican States* (Award) 5 ICSID Rep 269, 286 (NAFTA/ ICSID (AF), 1999, Paulsson P, von Wobeser & Civiletti): 'It is a fact of life everywhere that individuals may be disappointed in their dealings with public authorities ... It may be safely assumed that many Mexican parties can be found who had business dealings with governmental entities which were not to their satisfaction.'

[171] *Feldman v Mexico* 7 ICSID Rep 341, 370 (n 6 above).

[172] *Tecmed* (n 87) 163. See also *Emmanuel Too v Greater Modesto Insurance Associates and the United States of America* (1989) 23 Iran-USCTR 378, where the Tribunal held that 'a State is not responsible for loss of property or for other economic disadvantage resulting from bona fide general taxation or any other action that is commonly accepted as within the police power of States, provided it is not discriminatory and is not designed to cause the alien to abandon the property to the State or to sell it at a distress price'.

blanket exception for regulatory measures would create a gaping loophole in international protection against expropriation.'[173]

However, in responding to the widely expressed contention, notably in academic writings, that 'regulatory takings' may be incorporated in Article 1110 of NAFTA, Dr B Schwartz stated in his Separate Opinion in *SD Myers v Canada* that 'in the vast run of cases, regulatory conduct by public authorities is not remotely the subject of legitimate complaints under Article 1110'.[174] Schwartz emphasized three main differences between expropriation and regulation: first, 'expropriations tend to be severe deprivations of ownership rights; regulations tend to amount to much less interference'.[175] Secondly, 'Expropriations tend to deprive the owner and to enrich—by a corresponding amount—the public authority or the third party to whom the property is given. There is both unfair deprivation and unjust enrichment when an expropriation is carried out with compensation. By contrast, regulatory action tends to prevent an owner from using property in a way that unjustly enriches the owner.'[176] Finally, 'Expropriations without compensation tend to upset an owner's reasonable expectations concerning what belongs to him, in law and in fairness. Regulation is something that owners ought reasonably to expect. It generally does not amount to an unfair surprise.'[177]

8.113

Arbitral tribunals have also considered the criterion of reasonableness in order to distinguish between regulatory and expropriatory measures. The Tribunal in *Link Trading v Republic of Moldova*[178] held as follows: 'As a general matter, fiscal measures only become expropriatory when they are found to be an abusive taking. Abuse rises where it is demonstrated that the state has acted unfairly or inequitably towards the investment, where it has adopted measures that are arbitrary or discriminatory in character or in their manner of implementation, or where the measures taken violate an obligation undertaken by the state in regard to the investment.'

8.114

The discriminatory character of the taking has long been an influential factor in determining expropriation.[179] The Restatement (Third) of the Foreign Relations Law of the United States comments that 'a state is not responsible for loss of property or for other economic disadvantage resulting from bona fide general taxation, regulation, forfeiture for crime, or other action of the kind that is commonly accepted as within the police power of states, if is not discriminatory ... and is not designed to cause the alien to abandon the property to the state or sell it at a

8.115

---

[173] *Pope & Talbot Inc v Government of Canada* (Interim Award) 7 ICSID Rep 69, 85–86 (n 29 above), followed by *Feldman v Mexico* (n 6 above).

[174] *SD Myers v Canada* (n 29 above) Separate Opinion (Schwarz) 108–109.   [175] ibid 109.

[176] ibid.   [177] ibid.

[178] (Award) Ad Hoc Arbitration (UNCITRAL, 2002, Herzfeld P, Buruiana & Zykln).

[179] See *BP Exploration Co (Libya) Ltd v The Government of the Libyan Arab Republic* 53 ILR 297 (1973, sole arbitrator: Lagergren G); *Libyan American Oil Company (LIAMCO) v Government of the Libyan Arab Republic* 62 ILR 140 (1980) (1977, sole arbitrator: Mahmassani S).

distress price'.[180] The Restatement (Third) also points to a distinction between 'taking' and 'regulation', and observes that not every regulatory restraint can be linked to expropriation. One test that it suggests for determining whether regulation and taxation programmes are intended to achieve expropriation is whether they are applied to locally-owned enterprises as well as to alien enterprises or only to the latter. Another test relies on the degree of interference with the property interest.[181]

The taking of contractual rights may constitute expropriation

8.116 The nature of an investment is such that it carries with it certain contractual rights. They are an integral part of the investment. Consequently, a taking of these rights may amount to an expropriation of part or all of the investment. It is clear from the *LIAMCO* award in 1977[182] that contractual rights can be the subject of an expropriation. Further, in *Starrett v Iran*, where the investor, through its Iranian subsidiary, held contractual rights to develop a housing project, the Iran-US Claims Tribunal held that the introduction of legislation restricting the rights of companies to manage housing projects constituted expropriation of those contractual rights: 'The Tribunal holds that the property interest taken by the Government of Iran must be deemed to comprise the physical property as well as the right to manage the Project and to complete the construction in accordance with the Basic Project Agreement and related agreements, and to deliver the apartments and collect the proceeds of the sales as provided in the Apartment Purchase Agreements.'[183] In *Phillips Petroleum* the Iran-US Claims Tribunal further commented that 'expropriation by or attributable to a State of the property of an alien gives rise under international law to liability for compensation, and this is so whether expropriation is formal or de facto and whether the property is tangible, such as real estate or a factory, or intangible, such as the contract rights involved in the present Case'.[184]

8.117 In a case in which the State argued that expropriation did not apply to contractual and other incorporeal rights but only to real property rights, the arbitral tribunal disagreed:

> ... the Tribunal [cannot] accept the argument that the term 'expropriation' applies only to *jus in rem*. The Respondent's cancellation of the project had the effect of taking certain important rights and interests of the Claimants. What was expropriated

---

[180] American Law Institute, *Restatement (Third) Foreign Relations of the United States* (1987) Vol 1, 1987, Section 712, Comment g.

[181] ibid. See also *Pope & Talbot Inc v Canada* (n 29 above) 123–124.

[182] *Libyan American Oil Co (LIAMCO) v Government of the Libyan Arab Republic* 62 ILR 140 (1980) (1977, Mahmassani).

[183] *Starrett Housing Corp et al v Islamic Republic of Iran* (Interlocutory Award) (1983) 4 Iran-USCTR 122, 156–157.

[184] *Phillips Petroleum Co Iran v Islamic Republic of Iran, The National Iranian Oil Co* (1989) 21 Iran-USCTR 79, 106.

was not the land nor the right of usufruct, but the rights of SPP(ME), as a shareholder of ETDC, derived from EGOTH's right of usufruct, which had been 'irrevocably' transferred to ETDC by the State. Clearly, those rights and interests were of a contractual rather than *in rem* nature. However, there is considerable authority for the proposition that contract rights are entitled to the protection of international law and that the taking of such rights involves an obligation to make compensation therefor. Moreover, it has long been recognized that contractual rights may be indirectly expropriated.

The Tribunal also relied on the judgment of the Permanent Court of International Justice concerning *Certain German Interests in Polish Upper Silesia*, where the Court ruled that by taking possession of a factory, Poland had expropriated the operating company's contractual rights.[185] The Tribunal concluded that 'the duty to compensate in the event of expropriation cannot be evaded by contending that municipal regulations give a narrow meaning to the term of "expropriation" or apply the concept only to certain kinds of property'.[186]

In a notable ICSID award in 2003, the Tribunal held that any right arising out of **8.118** a contract which is considered as an investment is a right that can be the object of expropriation.[187] More generally, it has been held that expropriation 'may extend to any right which can be the object of the commercial transaction, i.e., freely sold and bought, and thus has a monetary value'.[188]

E. Conclusion

What conclusions may be drawn from this complex picture? It may be instructive **8.119** to consider how two different arbitral tribunals, reviewing the same set of facts (albeit under two different BITs), came to opposite decisions on the expropriation claims before them: in *Lauder v Czech Republic*[189] the Tribunal rejected the foreign investor's claim of expropriation; in *CME v Czech Republic*[190] the Tribunal found that the expropriation claim was justified. Even a brief outline of the claims and

---

[185] *Southern Pacific Properties (Middle East) Ltd [SPP(ME)] v Arab Republic of Egypt* (Award) 3 ICSID 189, 228 (ICSID, 1992, Jiménez de Aréchaga P, El Mahdi & Pietrowski). The PCIJ judgment that the Tribunal cited is at [1926] PCIJ Series A, No 7 at 44.

[186] ibid 229. That contractual rights can be the subject of expropriation was also endorsed by the Tribunal in *CME Czech Republic BV v Czech Republic* 9 ICSID Rep 121 (UNCITRAL, 2003, Kühn P, Schwebel and Brownlie). See 8.119–8.121 below for a discussion of the approach taken to expropriation in the *Lauder v Czech Republic* 9 ICSID 62 (UNCITRAL, 2001, Briner P, Cutler & Klein) and *CME* arbitral awards.

[187] *Consortium RFCC v Kingdom of Morocco* (Award) ICSID case ARB/00/6 (ICSID, 2003, Briner R, Cremades & Fadlallah): 'des droits issus d'un contrat peuvent être l'objet de mesure d'expropriation, à partir du moment où le dit contrat a été qualifié d'investissement par le Traité lui-même. Les créances détenues par l'investisseur font partie de cet investissement . . .'.

[188] *Amoco International Finance Corp v Government of the Islamic Republic of Iran et al* (1987) 15 Iran-USCTR 189, 220. [189] See n 186 above.

[190] See n 106 above.

holdings on expropriation in these two cases reveals current approaches and current uncertainties regarding the application of the principle of expropriation in investment treaty arbitration.

8.120   The respective claimants (Lauder, a US national, and CME, a Dutch company) were in the business of television broadcasting in the Czech Republic. Their complaints, including expropriation, arose out of the conduct of a public body, the Czech Media Council, which had issued an entity called CET 21 with a television broadcasting licence. CET 21 entered into an agreement with a subsidiary of CME, under which it agreed to form another Czech corporation and give it exclusive use of the licence. However, actions of the Media Council caused the CME subsidiary and CET 21 to revise these arrangements, and the new corporation had its use of the licence replaced with mere use of the know-how of the licence, and ceased to hold itself out as a nation-wide broadcaster. With the backing of the Media Council, CET 21 later entered into broadcasting arrangements with other parties before severing its relations altogether with the CME subsidiary.

8.121   In *Lauder v Czech Republic* the Arbitral Tribunal dismissed the claim of expropriation.[191] The Tribunal noted that BITs do not generally define the terms expropriation and nationalization (though the former is usually taken to mean coercive appropriation of private property by individual administrative measures, and the latter large-scale takings on the basis of an executive or legislative act); indirect expropriation is also not clearly defined, but involves a measure that effectively neutralizes the enjoyment of property. The Tribunal found that the CME subsidiary was not deprived to any degree of any relevant rights or economic benefits of the licence until CET 21 severed relations with the subsidiary, and that action had not been shown to be attributable to the Czech Republic. Further, any action by the Media Council had not conferred a benefit on the State or a public affiliate, and instead simply benefited CET 21. On these bases, the claimant had not demonstrated that a measure taken by the State had directly or indirectly interfered with his property or with the enjoyment of its benefits.

8.122   On the other hand, in *CME v Czech Republic*, the Arbitral Tribunal focused on the conduct of the Media Council at the stage of the revision of the arrangements and CET 21's subsequent actions, and found that such conduct and actions had resulted in the destruction of the commercial value of the foreign investor company's investment.[192] In particular, the original arrangements, which had been beneficial and effective, were found to have been replaced by worthless provisions for the 'use of the know-how' of the licence. Further, exclusivity in favour of the claimant was, pursuant to the Media Council's strategy, overridden by revisions to the arrangements and the Media Council's subsequent support of CET 21, leaving

---

[191] See n 186 above, paras 196–204.   [192] See n 106 above, paras 591–609.

no prospect of exclusivity being restored. The Tribunal accepted that deprivation of property and/or rights must be distinguished from a State's ordinary measures in properly executing the law. However, the State's actions in this case were not normal regulations in compliance with the law, and were not part of proper administrative proceedings. Thus, although the State had not taken express measures of expropriation, the Media Council had effectively neutralized the benefit of the property of the Dutch owner. Accordingly, the expropriation claim was upheld.

In short, the two arbitral tribunals applied expropriation principles that did not **8.123** diverge significantly—though the *CME* tribunal was clearly more influenced by the relatively broader approach to expropriation advanced in the *Metalclad* award, in particular the section on the significance of covert or incidental interference with use of property which has the effect of depriving the owner of its reasonably expected economic benefit, even if not to the obvious benefit of the State. However, their characterization of the key facts within the context of these broad principles was significantly different and led to opposite rulings. One can well appreciate the frustrating uncertainties facing parties arbitrating expropriation claims: two different panels of distinguished international lawyers could come to opposite conclusions by, for example, cutting into the seamless web of investment history at different times or by placing different emphases on the reasonably expected commercial value of an investment to a foreign investor and the State's obligations not to diminish that value.

However, as suggested at the beginning of this chapter, such uncertainties involv- **8.124** ing alleged 'takings' are not peculiarly the provenance of international investment arbitration. An expropriation claim may, depending on the perspectives of the individual members of the arbitral tribunal, be assessed on the grounds of some well-settled principles, albeit the application of such principles may be greatly influenced by the relative weight accorded by the tribunal to certain alternatives—for example, is the effect on the investment more important than the State's purpose or benefit; is a substantial deprivation sufficient or is a complete deprivation required; is protection of the investor's reasonably expected economic benefit a lesser public interest than the government's promotion of other public welfare objectives; is the level and nature of governmental interference consistent with the exercise of reasonable regulatory activity?

It would be unhelpful to set out a schematic chart for the assessment of an expro- **8.125** priation claim under an investment treaty in view of the vast array of potential considerations as well as the significant disagreement that has emerged in the investment treaty case law on certain points of principle. There is nevertheless, as a starting-point, a fundamental consensus that if an investor suffers a deprivation of the use or enjoyment of its investment that can in some manner be linked to conduct of the State, an expropriation claim may be viable.

8.126 In *Pope & Talbot v Canada*,[193] the Tribunal conducted a useful exercise by identifying elements that were not fulfilled in the particular case and, if they had been demonstrated, could have led to a decision by the Tribunal in favour of the expropriation claim. In so doing, the Tribunal provided a checklist of points to guide an assessment of governmental interference when expropriation is alleged. The checklist is merely that—a compilation of some of the issues that an arbitral tribunal might wish to explore further in conducting its enquiry:

(1) Does the investor remain in control of the investment?
(2) Does the investor direct the day-to-day operations of the investment?
(3) Have officers or employees of the investment been detained?
(4) Did the State supervise the work of the officers or employees of the investment?
(5) Did the State take any proceeds of the company sales (apart from taxation)?
(6) Did the State interfere with the management or shareholders' activities?
(7) Did the State prevent the investment from paying dividends to its shareholders?
(8) Did the State interfere with the appointment of the directors or management?
(9) Did the State take any other actions to oust the investor from full ownership and control of the investment?[194]

8.127 Another important factor which has emerged is the legitimate expectations of the foreign investor: 'the extent to which the government action interferes with distinct, reasonable investment-backed expectations'.[195]

8.128 The following general considerations arise from the substantive principles and authorities discussed in this chapter:

(1) Although the text of the expropriation provision in the relevant treaty must be carefully scrutinized, most tribunals are reluctant to draw sharp distinctions between the forms of expropriation that would have an impact on the sustainability of a claim.
(2) Indirect expropriation in all of its forms (for example creeping, de facto) is recognized as part of international investment law.
(3) Among the various tests applied by arbitral tribunals to assess expropriation claims are the following:
    (a) Has the investor been deprived of the use or enjoyment of its investment, at least in significant part and over a significant period, based on a reasonable expectation of economic benefit?

---

[193] *Pope & Talbot* (Interim Award) (n 29 above).
[194] ibid 86. ECT Art 13(3) expressly provides that the taking of shares is expropriation: 'For the avoidance of doubt, Expropriation shall include situations where a Contracting Party expropriates the assets of a company or enterprise in its Area in which an Investor of any other Contracting State has an Investment, including through the ownership of shares.' Energy Charter Treaty (Appendix 2 below).
[195] Annex B, para 4(a)(ii), 2004 US model BIT (Appendix 6 below).

(b) Can the deprivation be linked to State conduct of some type?
(c) What was the specific nature of the State conduct and can it be characterized as an interference with the investor's investment?
(d) What are the specific aspects of the interference?
(e) What was the underlying purpose of the interference and can the purpose be characterized as regulatory and taken in good faith, in support of reasonable public welfare objectives?
(f) If the interference can be characterized as regulatory, can it also be characterized as non-discriminatory in the sense that the particular investor was not singled out for interference?
(g) Can the claim reasonably be compared to a claim decided by an arbitral tribunal applying the same or a substantially similar expropriation provision in an investment treaty?

9

COMPENSATION

A. Introduction

The question of the amount of compensation payable for a State's breach of its **9.01** international obligations has been one of the most contentious areas of international law. Not surprisingly, this question generates much heat in the field of investment dispute arbitration, although the issues in dispute have moved on from those debated in the classical sources of public international law. The different stances taken as between investors and States are highlighted by the adversarial nature of the arbitration process.

9.02 The compensation debate in investment arbitration has proceeded from the same starting-point as the debate in public international law. This is the obligation upon the State committing the international wrong to make reparation by way of restitution or, if this is not possible, to pay monetary compensation for the loss sustained.[1]

9.03 In customary international law, the most heated areas of debate relate to (a) the appropriate standard of compensation for expropriation and (b) compensation for lost profits, in particular the applicability of the discounted cash flow (DCF) method of valuation. As the analysis in this chapter will demonstrate, for investment dispute arbitrations the question of the appropriate standard has been largely settled by the wording adopted in investment treaties and national investment laws. Similarly, it is accepted in recent tribunal awards that the appropriate way to value an income-producing asset is by using the method most applied in commercial life—the DCF method. Yet, even allowing for acceptance of the 'full' standard of compensation and (in appropriate cases) the DCF method of calculating losses, there remain many areas of current debate which can have a significant effect on the amount of compensation actually payable.

B. International Law Standards of Compensation for Expropriation

9.04 As stated in the chapter introduction, the question of compensation for expropriation has long been one of the most contentious areas of international law.[2] There has been little agreement between those advocating standards which would favour capital-exporting States, and those pressing on behalf of capital-importing States. Traditionally, the view favourable to investors has been the standard expressed by the former US Secretary of State, Cordel Hull. He declared in correspondence to the Government of Mexico in 1938 that 'under every rule of law and equity, no government is entitled to expropriate private property, for whatever purpose, without provision for prompt, adequate, and effective payment therefor.[3]

9.05 The restrictive approach is expressed by concepts such as the Calvo doctrine, formulated by the Argentinian diplomat and jurist Carlos Calvo.[4] His doctrine, which still remains part of many Latin American constitutions, provides that foreign

---

[1] *Case Concerning the Factory at Chorzów (Germany v Poland)* (Merits) PCIJ Rep Series A No 17, 47. International Law Commission, Draft Articles on State Responsibility for Internationally Wrongful Acts (2001) Arts 34–36.

[2] O Schachter, 'Compensation for Expropriation' [1984] 78 AJIL 121.

[3] The correspondence is reprinted in GH Hackworth, *Digest of International Law Volume III* (Chaps IX–XI) (1942) 655–665.

[4] *Derecho Internacional Teorica y Practico de Europa y America* (1868).

States and foreign nationals should settle claims by submitting to the jurisdiction of local courts. Diplomatic or military pressure is not to be used.

Another limiting formula is that expressed in the United Nations General Assembly **9.06** Resolution on Permanent Sovereignty over Natural Resources[5] and its Charter of Economic Rights and Duties of States.[6] These provide that the owner of nationalized or expropriated property shall be paid 'appropriate' compensation. 'Appropriate' compensation is a more subjective standard than a requirement that compensation be 'adequate and effective'.

The International Law Commission's *Draft Articles on State Responsibility* approach **9.07** the question of compensation on an objective basis, although their wording differs from that of the Hull formula. They provide that a responsible State 'is under an obligation to make *full* reparation for the injury caused by the internationally wrongful act' (emphasis added).[7] Full reparation includes 'an obligation to compensate for the damage caused thereby, insofar as such damage is not made good by restitution'.[8]

Another influential attempt at codifying the relevant principles in this area are the **9.08** *World Bank Guidelines on the Treatment of Foreign Direct Investment*.[9] These begin by talking of 'appropriate compensation'[10] but continue to state that compensation will be deemed appropriate 'if it is adequate, effective and prompt'.[11]

Given the difference between the various standards, it is not possible to say that there **9.09** is a consensus on the position in international law.[12] However, this lack of consensus does not generally pose a difficulty in modern investment disputes. Almost all bilateral investment treaties (BITs) and multilateral investment treaties contain specific provisions on the standard of compensation. Not surprisingly, given their stated aims of promoting investment, the vast majority of these treaties follow the Hull formula and require compensation to be 'prompt, adequate and effective'.

The almost universal adoption of this formula does not, however, eliminate all the **9.10** uncertainties. A wide range of compensation approaches can be characterized as

---

[5] United Nations General Assembly Resolution on Permanent Sovereignty over Natural Resources (1962) GA Res 1803.

[6] Charter of Economic Rights and Duties of States (1974) GA Res 3281.

[7] 'Responsibilities of States for Internationally Wrongful Acts: Text of the Draft Articles with Commentaries thereto' (Crawford, Special Rapporteur) in *Report of the International Law Commission on its Fifty-third Session (23 April–1 June and 2 July–10 August 2001), Official Records of the General Assembly Fifty-sixth Session*, Supplement No. 10, UN Doc A/56/10, Article 31(1).

[8] ibid Art 36(1).

[9] World Bank, 'Report to the Development Committee and Guidelines on the Treatment of Foreign Direct Investment' (1992) 31 ILM 1366 (Appendix 12 below).

[10] ibid 1382 Guideline IV, 1 (Appendix 12 below).

[11] ibid 1382 Guideline IV, 2 (Appendix 12 below).

[12] R Dolzer, 'New Foundations of the Law of Expropriation of Alien Property' [1981] 75 AJIL 553, 553. ILC (J Crawford, Special Rapporteur), 'Draft Articles on Responsibility of States for Internationally Wrongful Acts with Commentaries' in *Report of the International Law Commission of the work of its Fifty-Third Session* (23 April–1 June; 2 July–10 August 2001) UN Doc A/56/10, 244–263.

'adequate and effective'. For this reason, many BITs[13] also provide further clarification by referring to 'genuine value', 'market value' or 'fair market value'. A similar approach has been adopted in the major multilateral investment treaties. For example, Article 13(1)(d) of the Energy Charter Treaty (ECT) provides that expropriation should be 'accompanied by the payment of prompt, adequate and effective compensation' and that 'such compensation shall amount to the fair market value of the Investment expropriated . . .'[14]

9.11 Given the uniformity of treaty provisions, in almost all treaty disputes the problem of identifying a standard for compensation does not arise as a practical issue given that the treaty itself will contain provisions stating the appropriate standard. Nonetheless, the mere fact that the treaty contains a definition of the standard of compensation does not make the task of determining the amount of compensation any easier.

9.12 BITs and multilateral investment treaties often state that 'adequate and effective' compensation is to be assessed on the basis of the 'fair market' value or 'genuine' value of the asset. In the case of an asset which is regularly traded, or has recently been traded, a tribunal may determine a 'fair market' value by looking at the price at which it was recently traded. However, more often a tribunal must determine a 'fair' market value in respect of a unique asset (such as a corporation holding a valuable concession) which the seller did not want to sell and for which no willing buyer is likely to appear following an expropriation. In his Commentary on the International Law Commission's *Draft Articles*, Crawford states that tribunals valuing nationalized businesses should:

> . . . examine the assets of the business, making allowance for goodwill and profitability as appropriate. This method has the advantage of grounding compensation as much as possible in some objective assessment of value linked to the tangible asset backing of the business. The value of goodwill and other indicators of profitability may be uncertain, unless derived from information provided by recent sale or acceptable arms-length offer. Yet, for profitable business entities where the whole is greater than the sum of the parts, compensation would be incomplete without paying due regard to such factors.[15]

9.13 Many of the difficulties in this area arise when tribunals assess the likely future profitability of expropriated enterprises. Tribunals can be reluctant to award compensation for lost profits as this can oblige an often impecunious State to pay

---

[13] eg Treaty Between the United States of America and the Republic of Ecuador Concerning the Encouragement and Reciprocal Protection of Investment (US-Ecuador) (signed 27 August 1993, entered into force 11 May 1997) Senate Treaty Doc 103-15.

[14] See also North American Free Trade Agreement (adopted 17 December 1992, entered into force 1 January 1994) CTS 1994 No 2, (1993) 32 ILM 612 ('NAFTA') (Appendix 1 below) Art 1110; ASEAN Agreement for the Promotion and Protection of Investments (signed 15 December 1987) (1988) 27 ILM 612, 613 (Appendix 3 below) Art VI.

[15] J Crawford, *The International Law Commission's Articles on State Responsibility, Introduction, Text and Commentaries* (2002) 226.

a large lump sum to a wealthy foreign investor. The tensions between awarding the full measure of compensation and not wishing to award a sum that is so large it looks (even if it is not) punitive rather than compensatory lie behind many of the more contentious awards analysed in the following sections.[16]

C. Determining the Amount of Compensation

The exercise of quantifying the quantum[17] is primarily an economic exercise. The **9.14** tribunal is assessing the value of the taken property and the value in this context is its economic value. The investor will usually be seeking to recover compensation for the income the asset would have generated when used or consumed.[18]

Traditional methods of valuation

Liquidation value

Liquidation value means the amounts at which individual assets comprised in the **9.15** enterprise or the entire assets of the enterprise could be sold under conditions of liquidation to a willing buyer, less any liabilities which the enterprise has to meet.

The *World Bank Guidelines* suggest that this method is most appropriate for an **9.16** enterprise which, not being a proven going concern, demonstrates a lack of profitability.[19] This test reflects the commonsense proposition that an owner of commercial assets which cannot be put to profitable use would be acting more rationally by selling those assets.

Replacement value

Replacement value means the cash amount required to replace the individual assets **9.17** of the enterprise in their actual state as of the date of the taking.

The replacement value method is rarely applicable in the case of governmental **9.18** takings. It can only be employed when the investor can purchase replacement assets identical to the ones taken. It is rarely the case that individual discrete assets are taken by the State. In addition, the investor's assets usually possess individual unique features rendering an assessment of replacement value impossible.

---

[16] See the Tribunal's question in *Himpurna California Energy Ltd v PT (Persero) Perusahaan Listruik Negara* (1999) Mealey's International Arbitration Report 14(12) (12/99) A-55 (UNCITRAL, 1999, Paulsson P, de Fina & Setiawan), where it asks 'whether the result, in that case and often elsewhere, is not to create an illusion of scientific analysis to mask the reality of subjective approximations'.

[17] TR Stauffer, 'Valuation of Assets in International Takings' (1996) 17 Energy Law Journal 459, 460.

[18] PD Friedland & E Wong, 'Measuring Damages for the Deprivation of Income-Producing Assets: ICSID Case Studies' (1991) 6 ICSID Rev-FILJ 400, 404.

[19] World Bank, 'Report to the Development Committee and Guidelines on the Treatment of Foreign Direct Investment' (1992) 31 ILM 1366 (Appendix 12 below).

Book value

9.19 Book value is the difference between the enterprise's assets and liabilities as recorded on its financial statements or the amount at which the taken tangible assets appear on the balance sheet of the enterprise, representing their cost after deducting accumulative depreciation in accordance with generally accepted accounting principles.

9.20 Book value is sometimes seen as a means of returning the investment to the investor without allowing any sums for lost profits. It is thus sometimes justified as a way of keeping compensation awards within reasonable (from the State's point of view) bounds.[20]

9.21 However, the use of book value in quantifying compensation has been cogently criticized by various commentators.[21] The principle objections are:

(1) The value of income-producing assets depends on the cash that they are expected to generate in the future. It would thus constitute economic non-sense to distinguish between the value of the assets and the profits or revenues that the assets would have generated in the future. Book value merely measures value as recorded on a balance sheet. It has nothing to do with the value that a businessman would ascribe to an economic venture, which is related to its ability to generate profit.

(2) The book value of an enterprise cannot measure with certainty the value of that enterprise's contractual rights, know-how, goodwill, and management skills. Tribunals should not be deterred from evaluating these matters just because valuing them will be difficult.

9.22 A treaty arbitration where circumstances made it appropriate for the tribunal to adopt the book value method was *AAPL v Sri Lanka*.[22] This is an award made by an ICSID Tribunal constituted under the BIT between the United Kingdom and Sri Lanka. The State failure in this case constituted a breach of its duty to provide full protection and security to the investment. Armed insurgents destroyed a shrimp farm which was the only asset of a company in which the investor had a 48 per cent shareholding. The Tribunal refused to compensate the investor for the lost profits claimed on the basis that: 'A reasonable prospective purchaser would . . . be at least doubtful about the ability of the Company's balance sheet to cease being in the red, in the sense that the future earnings become effectively sufficient

---

[20] WM Reisman & RD Sloane, 'Indirect Expropriation and its Valuation in the BIT Generation' (2003) 74 BYIL 115, 138.

[21] n 18 above; WC Lieblich, 'Determining the Economic Value of Expropriated Income-Producing Property in International Arbitrations' (1991) 8 J Int'l Arb 59, 64–69.

[22] *Asian Agricultural Products Ltd v Republic of Sri Lanka* (Award) 4 ICSID Rep 245 (ICSID, 1990, El-Kosheri P, Goldman & Asante).

to offset the past losses as well as to service the loans which exceed in their magnitude the Company's capital assets.'[23]

Having stated its belief that there was no possibility of profits for which the investor **9.23** could be compensated, the Tribunal drew up a 'comprehensive balance sheet'[24] reflecting the company's assets and liabilities. This balance sheet was drawn up on the basis of the company's 'tangible assets'.[25] Although some commentators have suggested that the Tribunal was using the replacement value approach by looking at the company's balance sheet which would record items at the price at which they were purchased,[26] it is more likely, from its reliance on an accountant's report,[27] that the Tribunal was measuring the company's book value in accordance with standard accounting principles.

Discounted cash flow value

Discounted cash flow (DCF) value means: **9.24**

> . . . the cash receipts realistically expected from the enterprise in each future year of its economic life as reasonably projected minus that year's expected cash expenditure, after discounting this net cash flow for each year by a factor which reflects the time value of money, expected inflation, and the risk associated with such cash flow under realistic circumstances. Such discount rate may be measured by examining the rate of return available in the same market on alternative investments of comparable risk on the basis of their present value.[28]

This valuation method generates the most controversy, generally because the **9.25** sums involved can be so enormous. For example, in 2003, the Czech Republic was obliged to pay the Netherlands corporation, CME Czech Republic BV, approximately US$270 million. This sum was payable by way of compensation for the wrongful expropriation of a broadcasting licence which the Tribunal found would have generated substantial profits for a number of years after the expropriation.

The *World Bank Guidelines* identify the DCF method as a reasonable methodol- **9.26** ogy for determining the market value of a going concern with a proven record of profitability.[29]

The Report to the Development Committee which accompanies the *World Bank* **9.27** *Guidelines* emphasizes some of the problems with using the DCF valuation method: 'However, particular caution should be observed in applying this method as experience shows that investors tend to greatly exaggerate their claims of

---

[23] ibid 292.   [24] ibid 290.   [25] ibid 291.
[26] Friedland & Wong (n 21 above) 421.   [27] *AAPL v Sri Lanka* (n 22 above) 291.
[28] *World Bank Guidelines* (Appendix 12 below) 1383.
[29] *World Bank Guidelines* (Appendix 12 below) 1383.

compensation for lost future profits. Compensation under this method is not appropriate for speculative or indeterminate damage, or for alleged profits which cannot legitimately accrue under the laws and regulations of the host country.'[30]

9.28 Notwithstanding its difficulties, the DCF method is almost universally used and accepted by both the business and academic community in valuing income-producing assets.[31] The value of an income-producing capital asset can only be ascertained by valuing the cash the asset is expected to generate in the future. The DCF method is thus appropriate because it is designed to calculate the value on one specified date of cash flows that are to be received at different times.[32]

Other valuation methods

9.29 In addition to the four methods set out in the *World Bank Guidelines*, other methods have also been proposed. For example, the Tribunal in *CMS Gas Transmission Co v Argentine Republic*[33] also mentioned the 'comparable transaction' approach, which reviews comparable transactions in similar circumstances, and the 'option' approach. This studies the alternative uses which could be made of the assets in question, and their costs and benefits.[34] The Tribunal in *CME Czech Republic BV (The Netherlands) v The Czech Republic*[35] relied mainly on the 'comparable transaction' approach. Evidence of other contemporaneous valuations of a taken asset, especially those made between willing buyers and willing sellers will almost always be persuasive. However, such valuations are rarely available.

9.30 The Tribunal in *Azurix v Argentina*[36] concluded that it was appropriate to use the monetary value of the actual investments made in ascertaining fair market value to compensate for a breach of the fair and equitable treatment standard. This was perceived to be appropriate because the investment had been made by public tender and was thus 'recent and highly ascertainable'.[37] Nonetheless, the Tribunal calculated the investment value with a degree of flexibility. For example, it discounted the up-front payment made by the investor in order to win the tender from US$439 million to US$60 million because of a belief that the investor had overpaid: 'no more than a fraction of the [payment] could realistically have been recuperated under the existing Concession Agreement'.[38]

---

[30] *World Bank Guidelines* (Appendix 12 below) 1376–1377.

[31] WC Lieblich, 'Determinations by International Tribunals of the Economic Value of Expropriated Enterprises' (1990) 7 J Int'l Arb 37, 38.

[32] Lieblich (n 31 above); Friedland & Wong (n 18 above) 407.

[33] *CMS Gas Transmission Co v Argentine Republic* (Award) (2005) 44 ILM 1205 (ICSID, 2005, Orrego Vicuña P, Lalonde & Rezek).   [34] ibid 1249.

[35] *CME Czech Republic BV (The Netherlands) v Czech Republic* (Final Award) 9 ICSID Rep 264 (UNCITRAL, 2003, Kühn C, Schwebel & Brownlie).

[36] *Azurix Corp v Argentine Republic* (Award) ICSID Case No ARB/01/12 (ICSID, 2006, Sureda P, Lalonde & Martins).   [37] ibid para 425.

[38] ibid para 429.

The next section addresses the basic legal principles emerging from judicial and **9.31**
arbitral decisions on awarding lost profits by way of compensation for international wrongs committed by States.

Tribunals awarding compensation on the basis of DCF value

One of the earliest decisions regularly cited in support of tribunals awarding sums **9.32**
to compensate for lost profits is the judgment of the Permanent Court of International Justice (PCIJ) in the *Case Concerning the Factory at Chorzów*.[39] This was a
State to State claim brought by Germany against the Polish Republic for reparation
under the 1922 Convention Concerning Upper Silesia to compensate for the
Polish Government's taking over a factory to which German companies had rights.

The Court's analysis commenced with the broad observation that 'it is a principle **9.33**
of international law, and even a general conception of law, that any breach of an
engagement involves an obligation to make reparation'.[40]

Such reparation was stated to be equivalent to: 'Restitution in kind, or, if this is **9.34**
not possible, payment of a sum corresponding to the value which a restitution in
kind would bear; the award, if need be, of damages for loss sustained which would
not be covered by restitution in kind or payment in place of it—such are the principles which should serve to determine the amount of compensation due for an
act contrary to international law.'[41]

The Court then focused its attention on determining the value of the rights lost: **9.35**
'The whole damage suffered by the one or the other Company as a result of dispossession, in so far as concerns the cessation of the working and the loss of profit which
would have accrued, is determined by the value of the undertaking as such ...'[42]

In its order, the Court formulated certain questions to be addressed by a valuation **9.36**
expert. It clearly instructed the expert to assess compensation for future profits by
explaining that the purpose of its first question was, 'to determine the monetary
value, both of the object which should have been restored in kind and of the additional damage, on the basis of the estimated value of the undertaking including
stocks at the moment of taking possession by the Polish Government, together
with any probable profit that would have accrued to the undertaking between the
date of taking possession and that of the expert opinion'.[43]

The *Chorzów Factory* judgment was analysed in many of the decisions of the Iran- **9.37**
US Claims Tribunal which dealt with compensation. The earliest Iran-US Claims
Tribunal decision awarding compensation on the basis of a DCF analysis was
Starrett Housing International, Inc v Iran.[44] This claim arose out of the Iranian

---

[39] *Case Concerning the Factory at Chorzów (Germany v Poland)* (Merits) PCIJ Rep Series A No 17
(n 1 above).
[40] ibid 29.   [41] ibid 47.   [42] ibid 49.   [43] ibid 52.
[44] *Starrett Housing Corp & anor v Islamic Republic of Iran* (1987) 16 Iran-USCTR 112.

Government's expropriation of Starrett's rights in a project for the construction of apartments near Tehran. The Tribunal expressly cited *Chorzów Factory* in appointing experts to 'ascertain "the estimated value of the undertaking ..."'.[45]

9.38 The Tribunal specifically commended the DCF approach as a 'logical and appropriate'[46] method for determining fair market value. Similarly, in *Phillips Petroleum Co Iran v Iran*,[47] a case arising out of the taking of the claimant's rights under a joint structure agreement to explore and exploit petroleum reserves in the Persian Gulf, the Iran-US Claims Tribunal held that a fair market valuation would be calculated on the basis of the DCF method. The Tribunal characterized a DCF analysis not simply as 'a request to be awarded lost future profits, but rather as a relevant factor to be considered in the determination of the fair market value of its property interest at the date of taking'.[48]

9.39 However, a notable example of the Iran-US Claims Tribunal refusing to adopt the DCF approach is the judgment in *Amoco International Finance Corp v Iran*.[49] This case arose out of the expropriation of the claimants' interest in a joint venture company, called Khemco, for the production and marketing of natural gas. Khemco had been active over many years and at the time of the expropriation was a going concern. The claimant requested compensation to be assessed on a DCF basis. This was rejected by the Tribunal which, nonetheless, said that it was basing its approach on the principles set out by the PCIJ in *Chorzów Factory*. The Tribunal construed *Chorzów Factory* as separating the value of the undertaking on the date of the taking (*damnum emergens*) from the lost profits (*lucrum cessans*).

9.40 The Tribunal's approach to *Chorzów Factory* cannot be justified as a correct reading of that judgment. It is also based on flawed economic reasoning. The expected profitability of a going concern is a fundamental part of its value and the two aspects cannot be separated.[50] This was understood by the PCIJ in *Chorzów Factory*. Its instructions to the expert had asked him to estimate 'future prospects' in determining the value of the undertaking. Further, in explaining the questions addressed to the expert, the Court expressly stated that the expert should determine 'future prospects' as part of the value of the undertaking including together the lands, buildings, equipment, stocks and processes at its disposal, supply and delivery contracts, goodwill, and future prospects.[51]

---

[45] ibid 196.   [46] ibid 201.

[47] *Phillips Petroleum Co Iran v Islamic Republic of Iran, the National Iranian Oil Co* (1989) 21 Iran-USCTR 79.   [48] ibid 123.

[49] *Amoco International Finance Corp v Islamic Republic of Iran & ors* (1987) 15 Iran-USCTR 189.

[50] Lieblich (n 31 above).

[51] *Case Concerning the Factory at Chorzów* (n 1 above). See Lieblich (n 31 above) 77, for a criticism of the *Amoco* tribunal's rejection of the DCF method. Lieblich's article is a robust defence of the DCF method as the only basis on which the decisions of tribunals can 'be anything more than arbitrary

Any tribunal rejecting the DCF methodology in an appropriate case would be **9.41**
moving away from the best practice of business and economics. This was understood by the Iran-US Claims Tribunal in *Phillips Petroleum*. In finding in favour
of a DCF analysis it stated that 'a prospective buyer of the asset would almost certainly undertake such DCF analysis to help it determine the price it would be
willing to pay and that DCF calculations are, therefore, evidence the Tribunal is
justified in considering in reaching its decision on value'.[52]

The DCF method has been adopted on a number of occasions by ICSID tribunals. **9.42**
An example is *Amco Asia Corp v Republic of Indonesia*.[53] The claim arose out of a
thirty-year lease of a hotel in Indonesia which was expropriated after eleven years.
The Tribunal found that Amco was entitled to compensation for loss of the right to
manage the hotel. It applied both Indonesian and international law to determine
the amount of compensation.

In making its compensation award, the Tribunal recommended the DCF method **9.43**
as being 'one that is logically indicated by the finding that the purpose of compensation is to put Amco in the position of having received the benefits of the
contract'.[54]

It further stated that the DCF method was not speculative in its range of applic- **9.44**
ation, rather the Tribunal found merit in its flexibility: 'The method itself relies on
the application of assumptions which are necessarily judgmental. The DCF method
is at once a flexible tool, that allows for an application of factors and elements
judged as relevant. At the same time, it allows for the application of these judgmental elements to be articulated.'[55]

Substantial sums by way of compensation for lost profits were also awarded by **9.45**
ICSID Tribunals in *SOABI v Senegal*[56] and *LETCO v Liberia*.[57] *SOABI v Senegal* is
unusual because the Tribunal, albeit applying the law of Senegal rather than international law, awarded compensation for lost profits although the claimant had not
progressed to the stage of being able to demonstrate a proven record of profitability.

---

results reached under the guise of abstract legal standards' (Lieblich, 60). However, while Lieblich's
analysis is correct as a matter of economics, it fails to recognize the political and other considerations
behind many of the decisions.

[52] *Phillips Petroleum* (n 47 above) 123.

[53] *Amco Asia Corp & ors v Republic of Indonesia* (Resubmitted Case: Award) 1 ICSID Rep 377
(ICSID, 1990, Higgins P, Lalonde & Magid). See also *Benvenuti and Bonfant Srl v People's Republic of
the Congo* (Award) 1 ICSID Rep 330 (ICSID, 1980, Trolle P, Bystricky & Razafindralambo); *AGIP
SpA v People's Republic of the Congo* (Award) 1 ICSID Rep 306 (ICSID, 1979, Trolle P, Dupuy &
Rouhani).   [54] *Amco v Indonesia* (n 53 above) 617.

[55] *Amco v Indonesia* (n 53 above) 617.

[56] *Société Ouest Africaine des Bétons Industriels [SOABI] v State of Senegal* (Award) 2 ICSID Rep
164 (ICSID, 1988, Broches P, Mbaye & Schultsz).

[57] *Liberian Eastern Timber Corp [LETCO] v Government of the Republic of Liberia* (Award) 2
ICSID Rep 343 (ICSID, 1986, Cremades P, Pereira & Redfern).

9.46 The award in *CMS Gas Transmission Co v Argentine Republic*[58] is an example of a Tribunal using the DCF methodology in a treaty arbitration. (This was not an expropriation case, but a case of a State's failure to afford an investment fair and equitable treatment. Nonetheless, the Tribunal decided that it would be appropriate to use the expropriation standard of compensation due to the claimant having suffered 'important long-terms losses'.)[59] The Tribunal considered a number of different valuation approaches and concluded in favour of the DCF method: 'the tribunal . . . has no hesitation in endorsing [the DCF method] as the one which is the most appropriate in this case. [The company in which the claimant had invested] was and is a going concern; DCF techniques have been universally adopted, including by numerous arbitral tribunals, as an appropriate method for valuing business assets . . . there is adequate data to make a rational DCF valuation'.[60]

9.47 *CME Czech Republic BV v Czech Republic*[61] is a further example of a tribunal considering the DCF methodology in a treaty arbitration. In this award, the Tribunal was assessing the compensation due to a Netherlands corporation following an earlier finding that the Czech Republic had violated investment protection provisions of the Czech-Netherlands BIT.[62] The asset affected was a television broadcasting licence.

9.48 Article 5 of the BIT provided that:

> Neither Contracting Party shall take any measures depriving, directly or indirectly, investors of the other Contracting Party of their investments unless the following conditions are complied with:
>
> . . .
>
> c) the measures are accompanied by provision for the payment of just compensation. Such compensation shall represent the genuine value of the investments affected . . .

9.49 The Tribunal read the inferences to 'just compensation' and 'genuine value' in the BIT as an invocation of the Hull formula. It recited the history of the controversy over the appropriate standard for compensation in public international law but concluded that 'in the end, the international community put aside this controversy, surmounting it by the conclusion of more than 2200 bilateral (and a few multilateral) investment treaties. Today these treaties are truly universal in their reach and essential provisions. They concordantly provide for payment of "just compensation", representing the "genuine" or "fair market" value of the property taken'.[63]

---

[58] *CMS* (n 33 above).   [59] *CMS* (n 33 above) 1250.   [60] *CMS* (n 33 above) 1250.
[61] *CME* (n 35 above).
[62] Agreement on Encouragement and Reciprocal Protection of Investments (Netherlands-Czech Republic) 2242 UNTS 206 (signed 29 April 1991, entered into force 1 October 1992).
[63] *CME* (n 35 above) 369.

The Tribunal calculated the amount of compensation by reference to a previous **9.50** transaction entered into between the claimant and a third-party purchaser on the basis of arm's-length negotiations,[64] as well as by considering the DCF valuations of the parties' experts. Ultimately, the Tribunal did not decide between the opposing DCF valuations, as they could best serve as confirmation of its findings based upon the third-party transaction.

Tribunals not adopting a DCF approach

While the DCF method has been applied by many tribunals, other tribunals have **9.51** refused to apply it. In his *Commentary* to the International Law Commission's *Draft Articles on State Responsibility*, Crawford discusses some of this jurisprudence stating that:

> The discounted cash flow (DCF) method has gained some favour, especially in the context of calculations involving income over a limited duration, as in the case of wasting assets. Although developed as a tool for assessing commercial value, it can also be useful in the context of calculating value for compensation purposes. But difficulties can arise in the application of the DCF method to establish capital value in the compensation context. The method analyses a wide range of inherently speculative elements, some of which have a significant impact upon the outcome (e.g. discount rates, currency fluctuations, inflation figures, commodity prices, interest rates and other commercial risks). This has led tribunals to adopt a cautious approach to the use of the method.[65]

Recently, a number of tribunals have refused to award DCF-based compensation **9.52** to enterprises lacking a proven record of profitability (see 9.53 to 9.54). These awards do not represent any dissatisfaction with DCF methodology as a whole and are consistent with the *World Bank Guidelines*, which limit DCF awards to going concerns with a proven record of profitability.

Enterprises lacking a proven record of profitability

An example of such an award is the ICSID Additional Facility award in *Tecnicas* **9.53** *Medioambientales Tecmed SA v United Mexican States*.[66] This arbitration arose out of the expropriation by Mexico of a landfill site operated by a company controlled by Spaniards. The claim was brought under the BIT between Spain and Mexico. The Tribunal considered the DCF compensation claim submitted by the claimant but rejected the DCF approach. It noted the difference between the claimant's investment, US$4 million, and the US$52 million compensation sought. In

---

[64]   *CME* (n 35 above) 373, 384.
[65]   J Crawford (n 15 above).
[66]   *Tecnicas Medioambientales Tecmed SA v United Mexican States* (2004) 43 ILM 133 (ICSID (AF), 2003, Grigera Naon P, Fernández Rozas & Bernal Verea).

rejecting the DCF method, it stated that:

> The non-relevance of the brief history of operation of the Landfill by Cytrar—a little more than two years—and the difficulties in obtaining objective data allowing for application of the discounted cash flow method on the basis of estimates for a protracted future, not less than 15 years, together with the fact that such future cash flow also depends upon investments to be made—building of seven additional cells—in the long term, lead the Arbitral Tribunal to disregard such methodology to determine the relief to be awarded to the Claimant.[67]

9.54 A similar approach was taken by the NAFTA Tribunal in *Metalclad Corporation v United Mexican States*,[68] the ICSID Tribunal in *Wena Hotels v Egypt*[69] (a BIT case), and *Biloune v Ghana Investments Centre*[70] (an award arising out of a concession agreement).

Awarding a reasonable equitable indemnification

9.55 In *Libyan American Oil Co (LIAMCO) v Libya*[71] the sole arbitrator considered whether compensation should be paid for lost profits. The arbitration arose out of Libya's expropriation of various petroleum concession agreements in 1973–74. In reviewing the practice of various tribunals the sole arbitrator noted the many different approaches and quoted the ICJ, saying that 'the practice has been so much influenced by considerations of political expediency in the various cases, that it is not possible to discern in all this any constant and uniform usage, accepted as law, with regard to the alleged rule'.[72]

9.56 The sole arbitrator awarded a substantial sum (US$66 million) as compensation for lost profits on the basis that the claimant should receive 'a reasonable equitable indemnification'.[73] However, the sole arbitrator did not provide any explanation of the rationale leading him to award this sum.

Compensation based upon legitimate expectations

9.57 Another award in which the Tribunal rejected the DCF approach put forward by the claimants and substituted other criteria is *Kuwait v The American Independent Oil Co (AMINOIL)*.[74] This arbitration arose out of the Government of Kuwait's

---

[67] ibid 183.

[68] *Metalclad Corp v United Mexican States* (Award) 5 ICSID Rep 209 (NAFTA/ICSID (AF), 2000, Lauterpacht P, Civiletti & Siqueiros).

[69] *Wena Hotels Ltd v Arab Republic of Egypt* (Award) 6 ICSID Rep 67 (ICSID, 2000, Leigh P, Fadlallah & Wallace).

[70] *Biloune and Marine Drive Complex Ltd v Ghana Investments Centre and the Government of Ghana* (Award on Damages & Costs) (1990) 95 ILR 183 (Arb Trib, 1990, Schwebel P, Wallace & Leigh).

[71] *Libyan American Oil Co (LIAMCO) v Libyan Arab Republic* (1977) 62 ILR 140 (Mahmassani).

[72] *LIAMCO v Libya* (ibid) 209 citing *Asylum Case (Colombia v Peru)* (Merits) [1950] ICJ Rep 266, 277.　　　　[73] *LIAMCO v Libya* (n 71 above) 214.

[74] *Government of the State of Kuwait v The American Independent Oil Co (AMINOIL)* (Final Award) (1982) 21 ILM 976 (Arb Trib, 1982, Reuter P, Sultan & Fitzmaurice).

termination of an agreement between itself and AMINOIL for exploration and exploitation of petroleum and natural gas. The concession had been in place since 1948 and was due to run for many years.

As with *LIAMCO*, it is difficult to ascertain a precise methodology towards calcu- **9.58** lation from the award. The claimant asked for compensation based on two sep- arate methods, each of which would have produced a capital sum based on total anticipated profits discounted to find present value. The Tribunal agreed that both methods were 'acceptable' but introduced other criteria into its discussion of the appropriate principles. One of these was that the compensation should reflect the parties 'legitimate expectations' on the basis that:

> ... with reference to every long-term contract, especially such as involve an important investment, there must necessarily be economic calculations, and the weighing-up of rights and obligations, of chances and risks, constituting the contractual equilibrium. This equilibrium cannot be neglected—neither when it is a question of proceeding to necessary adaptations during the course of the contract, nor when it is a question of awarding compensation. It is in this fundamental equilibrium that the very essence of the contract consists.[75]

The legitimate expectation of the parties was expressed as being equivalent to a **9.59** 'reasonable rate of return'. However, the Tribunal, like the *Amoco* Tribunal some years later, also divided up the value of the going concern into, 'on the one hand of the undertaking itself, as a source of profit, and on the other of the totality of the assets, and adding together the results obtained'.[76]

In assessing its final sum the Tribunal stated that 'having regard' to all of the rea- **9.60** sons set out in its discussion of compensation, but without giving any breakdown of its valuation, it would award AMINOIL US$179,750,764.

Introducing a search for the parties' 'legitimate expectations' at the time of con- **9.61** tracting into a compensation analysis does not solve any problems. It merely moves the debate between the investor and the host State to a different area. If 'legitimate expectations' are the criteria, an investor could argue that its legitimate expect- ations were that it would be able to realize its anticipated profit over the life of the concession. In contrast, the State would argue that it did not enter into a conces- sion or a treaty to encourage and protect investments only to find that its policy- making freedom is so constrained that it must pay enormous sums by way of compensation having re-taken control over a particular area of its economy.

The issue of legitimate expectations was discussed by Brownlie in his Separate **9.62** Opinion in *CME Czech Republic BV v Czech Republic*.[77] Although Brownlie did not dissent from the Award on the basis that the sums awarded were 'on [their]

---

[75] ibid 1034.   [76] ibid 1038.
[77] *CME Czech Republic BV (The Netherlands) v Czech Republic* (Final Award, Separate Opinion of Brownlie) 9 ICSID Rep 412 (UNCITRAL, 2003, Brownlie).

own terms, moderate',[78] his Separate Opinion contains a detailed analysis of the reasons why large sums should not be awarded to compensate breaches of BITs. He based his analysis upon an assessment of the nature of a BIT stating that:

> The [BIT] is not simply a vehicle for an arbitration clause. It is an Agreement on encouragement and reciprocal protection of investments. It is not a treaty for the protection of foreign property within the territory of the Czech Republic ... In this context, it is simply unacceptable to insist that the subject-matter is exclusively 'commercial' in character or that the interests in issue are, more or less, only those of the investor ... [nor] [i]s it reasonable to suppose that, when a State like the Czech Republic, with a deregulated sector of its economy, accepts foreign investment, it is accepting the risk of national economic disaster ... The Czech Republic should have the benefit of civilised modern standards in the treatment of States. Even States which have been held responsible for wars of aggression and crimes against humanity are not subjected to economic ruin ...[79]

Award limited by abuse of rights doctrine

9.63 A novel approach to the question of DCF valuation was taken by the Tribunal in *Himpurna California Energy Ltd v PT (Persero) Perusahaan Listruik Negara (PLN)*.[80] Himpurna brought a claim against the Indonesian State Electricity Corporation following PLN's repudiation of a thirty-year Energy Sales Contract. Himpurna's DCF-based calculation of its damages amounted to US$2.3 billion.

9.64 The Tribunal refused to award such a high sum, notwithstanding that it largely arose out of a straightforward application of the contract's terms. The Tribunal would not turn the contract into 'an astonishing bargain in circumstances when performance ... would be ruinous'.[81] It took refuge in the concept of abuse of rights, stating that the doctrine must be applied 'to prevent the Claimant's undoubtedly legitimate right from being extended beyond tolerable norms'.

9.65 One Tribunal member dissented from the majority's novel use of the doctrine of abuse of rights, refusing to apply it in a situation where malicious intent or lack of good faith could not be demonstrated. It is possible that the Tribunal could have achieved the same result by resort to the flexibility inherent within the DCF approach, without resorting to abuse of rights.[82]

Other reasons not to adopt a DCF approach

9.66 As indicated above, recent awards show an increased willingness to use the DCF approach in suitable cases. In fact, tribunals do not presently tend to analyse in

---

[78] ibid 438.   [79] ibid 430–431.

[80] *Himpurna California Energy Ltd v PT (Persero) Perusahaan Listruik Negara* (1999) Mealey's International Arbitration Report 14(12) (12/99) A-1 (UNCITRAL, 1999, Paulsson P, de Fina & Setiawan).   [81] ibid A-51.

[82] H Weisburg & C Ryan, 'Means to be Made Whole: Damages in the Context of International Investment Arbitration' in R Kreindler & Y Derains (eds), *Evaluation of Damages in International Arbitration* (2006) 165, 178.

depth why they are using the DCF approach even where, as in *CMS v Argentina*,[83] the Tribunal records the respondent's arguments for the use of other valuation methods. However, it is not possible to ascertain from recent awards whether respondents have been attempting to resurrect other theories of international law to persuade tribunals to move away from valuation-based approaches in order to reduce compensation awards. Some of these theories, which continue to have academic support, are considered in the following paragraphs. Given the lack of a formal role of judicial precedent in investment arbitrations, there is no reason why respondents should not try to re-open the compensation debate on the basis of these doctrines, or the ones analysed above.

The distinction between lawful and unlawful takings

With the argument about the applicable standard of compensation being resolved **9.67** in the BIT generation, tribunals no longer seem to consider whether a taking is lawful or unlawful. This is understandable—if a claimant can receive 'full' compensation without having to overcome the extra hurdle of demonstrating that the taking was unlawful in the first place then there will be no need for claimants to attempt this extra step. It is notable that Crawford, in his *Commentary* to the International Law Commission *Draft Articles on State Responsibility*,[84] makes no distinction between lawful and unlawful takings in his analysis of the compensation payable for an internationally wrongful act. By contrast, Bowett has argued for the distinction, concluding 'that the fundamental distinction between the lawful and unlawful taking has its most important consequence. For the correct principle is believed to be that loss of future profits, whilst a legitimate head of general damages for an unlawful act, is not an appropriate head of compensation for a lawful taking'.[85]

Bowett's analysis was relied upon by Judge Seyed Khalil Khalilian, the dissenting **9.68** Iranian arbitrator in *Phillips Petroleum*.[86] In a subsequent article Judge Khalilian claimed that 'a DCF-based compensation is but a translation of a concept, namely "restitution", that has long been in disuse, if indeed it was ever in usage. Nowadays, no jurist would hesitate to state that restitution has no application where the expropriation takes place due to a lawful act of State'.[87]

Given that many expropriations are for a public purpose and non-discriminatory, **9.69** it is surprising that more respondents do not try to argue along these lines. Even Brownlie in his Separate Opinion on quantum in *CME v Czech Republic* did not. The distinction continues to be made in academic writings. For example, Reisman

---

[83] *CMS* (n 33 above) 1248.   [84] Crawford (n 15 above).
[85] DW Bowett, 'State Contracts with Aliens: Contemporary Developments on Compensation for Termination or Breach' (1988) 59 BYIL 49, 63.   [86] *Phillips* (n 47 above).
[87] SK Khalilian, 'The Place of Discounted Cash Flow in International Commercial Arbitrations: Awards by Iran-United States Claims Tribunal' (1991) 8 J Int'l Arb 31, 49–50.

and Sloane contend that in assessing compensation for an indirect expropriation (where expropriatory consequences result despite the absence of an expropriatory decree)[88] an award of lost profits would amount to a punitive award and thus one without a basis in customary international law.[89] In his textbook, Brownlie does distinguish between lawful and unlawful expropriation; and between unlawful expropriations where provision is made for compensation.[90] These are not distinctions which investment tribunals have made.

Claims settlement agreements

9.70 Another argument that would reduce compensation payable but is not featuring in recent BIT cases would be one based on claims settlement agreements. According to Bowett: 'the many post-1945 agreements disclose settlement figures ranging between ten and ninety per cent of asset value, and they disclose no support for anything like going-concern value'.[91]

9.71 The reasons why such agreements should not be binding on tribunals are obvious— they are negotiated settlements and take account of many non-judicial considerations which vary widely from case to case. It is thus hard to assert that agreements based on non-legal principles should be considered by tribunals applying strict standards of law.[92]

9.72 Nonetheless, there is nothing wrong with discerning international law from State practice, which includes such agreements. Crawford refers to certain without prejudice claims settlements as manifestations of the general international law principle of reparation in his *Commentary* to the International Law Commission *Draft Articles*.[93] The absence in recent compensation awards of tribunals even referencing a respondent's attempt to rely upon such agreements may be an indicator of the trend in investment treaty arbitrations for tribunals to be more influenced by awards of other tribunals than by any other source of international law.

Conclusion on the practical advantages of the DCF method

9.73 The view of these authors is that the DCF approach is becoming so widely accepted because it is, put simply, the best method for valuing lost profits. The critics who complain that it produces excessive levels of compensation are perhaps not paying sufficiently close attention to how the method is operated in practice. The DCF method, properly employed, reduces speculation because it forces

---

[88] WM Reisman & RD Sloane, 'Indirect Expropriation and its Valuation in the BIT Generation' (2003) 74 BYIL 115, 130. [89] ibid 138.
[90] I Brownlie, *Principles of Public International Law* (6th edn, 2003) 509–514.
[91] Bowett (n 85 above) 65.
[92] *Sedco Inc v National Iranian Oil Co & anor* (1986) 10 Iran-US CTR 180, 184–185.
[93] Crawford (n 65 above) 220. See also at 225 where he states that lump-sum compensation agreements 'provide useful principles to guide the determination of compensation'.

claimants to explain and quantify each individual area of their claim. Differences between the parties can thus be highlighted and speculative valuations can be dismissed.

It would be wrong to dismiss the method because, wrongly applied, previously 'it **9.74** has been used to justify valuations which reach beyond the "fanciful" to "wonder-land proportions"'.[94] For example, an economist has critically analysed the US$2.5 billion AMINOIL[95] claim to demonstrate, from material in the public record, how the maximum value should have been US$267 million. With the appropriate use of experts, tribunals can be put in a position to critically examine DCF claims.

Indeed, tribunals are becoming much better at these analyses. A 2001 analysis of **9.75** a number of tribunal findings arising out of DCF claims concluded that while:

> 'Baby-splitting' may be too harsh a metaphor for the valuation methods in these cases ... one must wonder how much of the tribunals' calculations in these cases was based on an analytical application of DCF or any other method of valuation. In some cases, the evidence may have been insufficient to permit anything but rough approxi-mations. In others, the result may reflect compromises between differing views of the arbitrators, views that perhaps were based on different and irreconcilable analyses.[96]

In contrast, the Tribunals' damages awards in *CME v Czech Republic* and *CMS v* **9.76** *Argentina* show the Tribunals considering the claimants' DCF valuations in a painstaking manner, and fully reasoning their decisions to adopt, or reject, various expert reports. Tribunals are assisted in this process by the adversarial nature of arbi-tration proceedings, which allows them to compare parties' opposing cases and to ask questions of the experts in order to discern the reasons for the points of differ-ence. As the *CMS* Tribunal states: 'estimates need not be arbitrary or analogous to a shot in the dark; with the appropriate methodology and the use of reasonable alternative sets of hypotheses, it is possible to arrive at figures which represent a range of values which can be rationally justified'.[97]

In *CMS v Argentina*, Argentina chose to disrupt this process by not submitting its **9.77** own valuation report. This is a common tactic for respondents in commercial arbitrations as it allows them to concentrate on attacking the claimant's valuation without having to face such an attack themselves. The fact that Argentina had not appointed valuation experts could have created difficulties for the Tribunal by pre-venting it from having someone to quantify the criticisms Argentina was making. The Tribunal overcame this difficulty by appointing its own experts.[98]

---

[94] TR Stauffer, 'Valuation of Assets in International Takings' (1996) 17 Energy Law Journal 459, 479.
[95] ibid 480–482.
[96] M Ball, 'Assessing damages in claims by investors against States' (2001) 16 ICSID Rev-FILJ 408, 426–427.
[97] *CMS Gas Transmission Co v Argentine Republic* (2005) 44 ILM 1205, 1251 (ICSID, 2005, Orrego Vicuña P, Lalonde & Rezek). [98] ibid 1250–1251.

D. Compensation for Non-Expropriatory
Breaches of International Law

9.78 Investment treaties do not generally address issues of the compensation due for breaches of their provisions, save for that which is due following a finding of expropriation. However, it does not appear that any respondent State has yet sought to argue that as a result no compensation should be payable for any breach other than an expropriation. Tribunals that have considered this issue to date have all proceeded on the basis that, as a general principle, 'a wrong committed by one state against another gives rise to a right to compensation for the economic harm sustained'.[99]

9.79 Indeed, they have taken the view that the failure of investment treaties to specify compensation for breaches other than expropriation gives tribunals considerable discretion in fashioning remedies for non-expropriatory breaches.[100]

9.80 Tribunals have attempted to construct an approach to compensation for non-expropriatory breaches on an incremental basis, building on existing principles of public international law. Yet the task is more difficult than that of assessing compensation for expropriation. When considering an expropriation, investment treaty tribunals have been able to build upon the experience of other international law tribunals over the past 100 years, such as the PCIJ, tribunals considering the energy sector nationalizations in the 1970s, and the Iran-US Claims Tribunal. There is less precedent on compensation for breaches of other treaty standards.[101]

9.81 Tribunals to date have approached the question of compensation for breaches of these provisions on two bases:

(1) breaches which do not involve the total loss or deprivation of an asset; and
(2) breaches that amount to the total loss or deprivation of an asset.

Breaches not amounting to a total loss or deprivation of an asset

9.82 The clearest position of the applicable principles is contained in the second partial award rendered by the NAFTA Tribunal in *SD Myers, Inc v Government of Canada*.[102] This case concerned breach of the NAFTA principles of fair and

---

[99] *SD Myers Inc v Government of Canada* (First Partial Award) 8 ICSID Rep 3, 63 (NAFTA, 2000, Hunter P, Schwartz & Chiasson). A similar approach was adopted in another NAFTA case, *Feldman v United Mexican States* (Award) 7 ICSID Rep 318, 397–398 (NAFTA/ICSID (AF), 2002, Kerameus P, Covarrubias Bravo & Gantz) and the BIT awards in *MTD Equity Sdn Bhd & anor v Republic of Chile* (Award) (2005) 44 ILM 91, 127 (ICSID, 2004, Sureda P, Lalonde & Oreamuno Blanco) and *CMS Gas Transmission Co v Argentine Republic* (n 97 above) 1250.

[100] *Azurix Corp v Argentine Republic* (Award) ICSID Case No ARB/01/12 (ICSID, 2006, Sureda P, Lalonde & Martins) paras 421–422.

[101] FA Mann, 'British Treaties for the Promotion and Protection of Investments' (1981) 52 BYIL 241, 243.

[102] *SD Myers Inc v Government of Canada* (Second Partial Award on Damages) 8 ICSID Rep 3 (NAFTA, 2002, Hunter P, Schwartz & Chiasson).

equitable treatment, non-discrimination, full protection and security, and international minimum standard of treatment (Articles 1102 and 1105 of NAFTA). The claimant was a US company whose business consisted of the transport of hazardous waste materials for remediation. It developed a business line consisting of transporting waste from Canada to be processed in the United States. This business was curtailed by the conduct of Canadian public authorities in issuing a measure which closed the US/Canada border to the export of the waste in question. The Tribunal determined that this measure was passed in breach of Canada's obligations under NAFTA. The claimant sought compensation for the damage caused to its business during the period in which the border was closed.

The Tribunal rejected Canada's contention that the claimant should merely be **9.83** compensated by being reimbursed for its initial expenditures: 'The Tribunal concludes that compensation should be awarded for the overall economic losses sustained by SDMI that are a proximate result of CANADA's measure, not only those that appear on the balance sheet of its investment.'[103]

In order to compensate the investor fully, the Tribunal wanted to award it dam- **9.84** ages for the opportunity that had been lost. It approached the matter by applying a common law tort standard: 'The inquiry in this case is more akin to ascertaining damages for a tort or delict. The damages recoverable are those that will put the innocent party into the position it would have been in had the interim measure not been passed. The focus is on causation, not foreseeability in the sense used in the law of contract. In contract law, foreseeability may limit the range of recoverability. That is not the case in the law of tort or delict. Remoteness is the key.'[104]

By referring to the tort standard of recovery, the Tribunal pushed questions of **9.85** causation to the forefront ('To be recoverable, a loss must be linked causally to interference with an investment located in a host State.').[105] Yet future tribunals may find it difficult to build upon this analysis as the doctrine of causation has yet to be fully developed in public international law.

Causation in international law

The International Law Commission *Draft Articles on State Responsibility* only **9.86** address the principle of causation in general terms. In describing an 'injury' for which a State is obliged to make reparation, Article 31(2) provides that injury 'includes any damage, whether material or moral, caused by the internationally wrongful act of a State'.

Deciding when an action is the cause of a loss is a difficult question, whatever legal **9.87** test is applied. The US-Yugoslavia International Claims Commission set out the generally accepted principle in the following terms in the *Dorner Claim*: 'Generally,

---

[103] ibid 140.   [104] ibid 145–146.   [105] ibid 140.

international and domestic arbitral tribunals in the determination of international claims allow compensation for indirect damages such as loss of use of property, loss of profits and the like, if such losses are reasonably certain and are ascertainable with a fair degree of accuracy. They do not allow compensation for indirect damages if they are conjectural or speculative or not reasonably certain or susceptible of accurate determination.'[106]

9.88 Graefrath in his Hague lectures listed a number of synonyms that cover the same basic principle. He speaks of ' "proximate cause", "adequate causality", "ordinary cause of events", "the cause must not be too remote or speculative", there must "be a sufficiently direct causal relationship" and also the term "foreseeability" '.[107]

9.89 It can thus be seen that a test has been defined by international scholars and tribunals. However, the real difficulty will lie in applying whatever test is taken.

9.90 However the test is defined, it will always be difficult to apply in borderline cases. Graefrath correctly alludes to the difficulty of the task in quoting with approval an observation: 'that indeed the arbitration courts declared every damage they regarded as not to be justified an indirect damage. In this way, as a result, it was ensured that direct damage only had to be compensated'.[108]

9.91 If further clarification of the applicable test is required, tribunals will have to look to definitions contained in private law. This approach would be consistent with the classic statement of the sources of public international law set out in Article 38 of the Statue of the International Court of Justice. This directs the ICJ to have regard to 'the general principles of law recognized by civilized nations'.[109]

9.92 Crawford refers to a comparative approach in his *Commentary* on the International Law Commission *Draft Articles*.[110] Similarly, Brownlie recognizes the practical need to have regard to private law solutions in stating that: 'International tribunals face the same problems as other tribunals in dealing with [albeit on a contract not a tort basis] indirect damages and deal with the issues in much the same way.'[111]

9.93 An example of an arbitral tribunal following an approach on causation derived from private law is *Sapphire International Petroleum Ltd v National Iranian Oil Co* (an award based upon breach of a concession contract).[112] Here the sole arbitrator undertook a comparative law analysis before concluding that:

> ... the object of damages is to place the party to whom they are awarded in the same pecuniary position that they would have been in if the contract had been performed

---

[106] *Dorner Claim* (1954) 21 ILR 164, 164–165.

[107] B Graefrath, 'Responsibility and Damages Caused: Relationship Between Responsibility and Damages' (1984) 185 *Recueil des Cours* 9, 95.   [108] ibid 96.

[109] *Statute of the International Court of Justice* (26 June 1945, annexed to the *Charter of the United Nations*) Art 38(1) (c).   [110] Crawford (n 15 above) 204–205, especially fn 493 and 495.

[111] Brownlie (n 90 above) 446.

[112] *Sapphire International Petroleum Ltd v National Iranian Oil Co* (1963) 35 ILR 136 (Cavin).

in the manner provided for by the parties at the time of its conclusion. They should be the natural consequence of the breach ... This rule is simply a direct deduction from the principle *pacta sunt servanda*, since its only effect is to substitute a pecuniary obligation for the obligation which was promised but not performed.[113]

In setting out this approach, the sole arbitrator was applying 'general principles of law based upon the practice common to civilized countries'[114] rather than public international law. However, these rules are part of public international law as the sole arbitrator recognized in stating that: 'These rules are enshrined in Article 38 of the Statute of the International Court of Justice as a source of law, and numerous decisions of international tribunals have made use of them and clarified them.'[115]   **9.94**

Practical examples of tribunals awarding damages

In applying its causation test, the Tribunal in *SD Myers, Inc v Canada* was prepared to award compensation for the profits lost during the time the Canadian border was closed. However, it refused to award the claimant a further sum based on the profits it would have made with the money to be earned from the business it could not carry out. Such a claim was described as 'speculative and too remote'.[116]   **9.95**

A similar approach was adopted by the Tribunal in *Pope & Talbot, Inc v Canada*.[117] Here the Tribunal held that under Article 1116 of NAFTA an investor owning a corporation, which was the applicable investment, could bring a claim for loss or damage to its interest in that investment. The investor would have to show 'that loss or damage was caused to its interest, and that it was causally connected to the breach complained of'.[118]   **9.96**

On this basis, the Tribunal awarded damages for certain out-of-pocket expenses but denied a claim for the value of management time and lost revenues from a plant shutdown, where the evidence showed that the shutdown did not cause any loss.   **9.97**

In *Maffezini v Spain*,[119] an ICSID arbitration arising out of a BIT, the Tribunal rejected a claim for damage caused by the allegedly bad information contained in a feasibility study carried out by a Spanish public body. This body had carried out an economic evaluation prior to the investor making his investment. The Tribunal held that nevertheless the investor was responsible for his losses on the basis that 'Bilateral Investment Treaties are not insurance policies against bad business judgments'.[120]   **9.98**

In the Tribunal's view, the shortcomings that existed in the evaluation did not relieve the investor of the business risks inherent in any investment. However, in   **9.99**

---

[113] ibid 185–186.   [114] ibid 173.   [115] *Sapphire* (n 112 above) 173.

[116] *SD Myers* (Second Partial Award on Damages) (n 102 above) 146.

[117] *Pope & Talbot Inc v Government of Canada* (Award on Damages) 7 ICSID Rep 43 (NAFTA/ UNCITRAL, 2002, Dervaird P, Greenberg & Belman).   [118] ibid 166.

[119] *Emilio Agustín Maffezini v Kingdom of Spain* (Award) 5 ICSID Rep 387 (ICSID, 2000, Orrego Vicuña P, Buergenthal & Wolf).   [120] ibid 432.

Maffezini the State was held not to have breached any obligations to the investor as the evaluation was not intended for third parties to rely upon. Accordingly, in this instance the quoted dicta cannot be taken as the Tribunal using the phrase to describe a break in the chain of causation, as liability was not established in any event.

9.100 The concept of causation was used at the damages assessment stage in *MTD Equity Sdn Bhd and anor v Republic of Chile*.[121] In this case, a Malaysian investor provided capital to its Chilean subsidiary to develop a real estate project in Chile. While the investment was approved by Chile, it subsequently rejected the project on the grounds that it was against Chile's urban policy. This action was held to be a breach of the obligation to afford investors fair and equitable treatment, as laid down by the Chile-Malaysia BIT. In examining the compensation payable, the Tribunal took care to distinguish between those losses caused by Chile's breach, and those which were caused to the claimant by its own actions:

> The BITs are not an insurance against business risk and the Tribunal considers that the Claimants should bear the consequences of their own actions as experienced businessmen. Their choice of partner, the acceptance of a land valuation based on future assumptions without protecting themselves contractually in case the assumptions would not materialize, including the issuance of the required development permits, are risks that the Claimants took irrespective of Chile's actions.[122]

9.101 As a result of the claimants needing to bear part of the damages suffered, the Tribunal reduced the compensation payable by 50 per cent.[123] In *Bogdanov v Moldova* the Tribunal also reduced the damages payable for a breach of the fair and equitable treatment obligation as a result of the claimant's own shortcomings.[124]

Concurrent causes and breaches in the chain of causation

9.102 The *MTD* and *Bogdanov* awards can also be categorized as concurrent cause cases, with the concurrent cause being the defaults of the investor itself, rather than those of a third party. Such cases commonly give rise to difficult questions in domestic tort systems in circumstances when responsibility for damage can be ascribed to more than one tortfeasor. Sometimes, notwithstanding the tortfeasor's breach, it is relieved of responsibility because of subsequent events which are determined to have broken the chain of causation.

9.103 Examples of these types of cases can be found in public international law. For example, it is established in public international law that a State may be fully liable to compensate for losses in a situation where it is not the sole cause of the loss.[125]

---

[121] *MTD Equity* (n 99 above).   [122] *MTD Equity* (n 99 above) 117.
[123] *MTD Equity* (n 99 above) 128.
[124] *Iurii Bogdanov, Agurino-Invest Ltd and Agurdino-Chimia JSC v Republic of Moldova* (Award) (SCC, 2005, Moss) para 5.2.
[125] n 7 above, 205–206 (paras 12 and 13 of Commentary to Art 31).

In the *Corfu Channel* case, Albania was held liable to Great Britain for all damage caused to the latter's warships as a result of mines laid by Yugoslavia.[126] The mines could not have been laid without the knowledge of the Albanian Government. Yet Yugoslavia, in not giving the warning required by international law, was also at fault.

An example of a concurrent cause case in the field of investment treaty arbitrations **9.104** is *AAPL v Sri Lanka*.[127] This was an ICSID arbitration arising out of the UK-Sri Lanka BIT. The investor's farms were destroyed by military action but neither claimant nor respondent was able to demonstrate whether the atrocities had been carried out by terrorist insurgents or by State forces. The majority of the Tribunal held that in the absence of evidence 'about what effectively caused the destruction of the farm premises', Sri Lanka would be responsible for a failure to provide adequate protection that could have stopped the destruction taking place totally or partially.[128] The Tribunal categorized the case as one where proof of facts was posing 'extreme difficulty' and was thus satisfied with 'less conclusive proof'.[129] The Dissenting Opinion pointed out the 'troublesome questions of causation' raised by this decision.[130] By holding Sri Lanka responsible for failure to take pre-cautionary measures prior to launching a counterinsurgency action, Sri Lanka was being held liable even if the damage was inflicted by third parties taking advantage of the Government's legitimate operation to commit unlawful acts. Rather than making the investor prove that Sri Lanka had caused its loss, the Tribunal was con-demning Sri Lanka for its failure to prove otherwise. Accordingly, precedent exists for tribunals ascribing all of the damage to a State in breach of an international obligation, although it is not the only party in default.

The final award in *Lauder v Czech Republic*[131] is an example of a tribunal finding **9.105** that a subsequent action breaks the chain of causation. In this ad hoc arbitration brought under the US-Czech Republic BIT, the Tribunal found that the Czech Republic had taken a discriminatory and arbitrary measure against the claimant. This consisted of having initially accepted that the claimant could invest directly in a Czech television company but subsequently requiring the investment to be channelled through a third company. Yet the Tribunal refused to award compen-sation for the breach because the matters characterized by the Tribunal as the 'last, direct act, the immediate cause' were 'so unexpected and so substantial as to have to be held to have superseded the initial cause and therefore become the main cause of the ultimate harm'.[132] Later acts, characterized as a 'typical commercial

---

[126] *Corfu Channel Case (United Kingdom v Republic of Albania)* (Merits) [1949] ICJ Rep 4.
[127] *Asian Agricultural Products Ltd v Republic of Sri Lanka* (Award) 4 ICSID Rep 245 (ICSID, 1990, El-Kosheri P, Goldman & Asante). [128] ibid 286–287.
[129] ibid 287, 273. [130] ibid 317.
[131] *Lauder v Czech Republic* 9 ICSID Rep 62 (UNCITRAL 2001, Briner C, Cutler & Klein); C Schreuer, 'Non-Pecuniary Remedies in ICSID Arbitration' (2004) 20(4) Arb Int'l 325.
[132] *Lauder v Czech Republic* 9 ICSID Rep 62, 98 (UNCITRAL, 2001, Briner C, Cutler & Klein).

dispute'[133] for which the respondent State was not responsible were found to be 'the real cause for the damage which apparently has been inflicted to the Claimant'.[134]

9.106 As noted in Chapter 8 above, a different Tribunal (*CME Czech Republic v Czech Republic*)[135] examining the same facts reached a different conclusion on the merits. This difference of opinion extended to the two Tribunals' findings on causation. The *CME* Tribunal rejected the argument that the facts amounting to the 'typical commercial dispute' absolved the Czech Republic of responsibility for the fate of the investment. The Tribunal stated that such an argument would fail 'under the accepted standards of international law'.[136] The Tribunal cited the following rule from a comparative law treatise: 'It is the very general rule that if a tortfeasor's behaviour is held to be a cause of the victim's harm, the tortfeasor is liable to pay for all of the harm so caused, notwithstanding that there was a concurrent cause of that harm and that another is responsible for that cause ... In other words, the liability of a tortfeasor is not affected vis-à-vis the victim by the consideration that another is concurrently liable.'[137]

Breaches amounting to a total loss or deprivation of an asset

9.107 This matter was addressed by the Tribunal in *CMS Gas Transmission Co v Argentine Republic*.[138] The claim arose out of Argentina's suspension of a tariff adjustment formula for gas transportation applicable to an enterprise in which the claimant was a minority shareholder. The Tribunal found that Argentina's measures breached the fair and equitable treatment standard contained in the US-Argentina BIT.[139] In considering the compensation to be paid by Argentina, the Tribunal, having explicitly dismissed an expropriation claim, nonetheless decided to use the expropriation compensation standard: 'the Tribunal is persuaded that the cumulative nature of the breaches discussed here is best dealt with by resorting to the standard of fair market value. While this standard figures prominently in respect of expropriation, it is not excluded that it might also be appropriate for breaches different from expropriation if their effect results in important long-term losses'.[140]

9.108 The exact manner in which the Tribunal applied the expropriation standard in this case is discussed at para 9.46 above.

9.109 *AAPL v Sri Lanka* is another example of a BIT award where the respondent State's breach of the BIT led to the complete loss of the investment. This was not an

---

[133] ibid 83.   [134] ibid 98.

[135] *CME Czech Republic BV (The Netherlands) v Czech Republic* (Partial Award) 9 ICSID Rep 121 (UNCITRAL, 2001, Kühn C, Schwebel and Hándl).   [136] ibid 230.

[137] ibid citing JA Weir, 'Complex Liabilities' in A Tunc (ed), *International Encyclopaedia of Comparative Law* Vol XI (1983) 41.   [138] *CMS* (n 33 above).

[139] ibid 1236.   [140] ibid 1250.

expropriation case but nonetheless the Tribunal sought to assess compensation in 'a manner that adequately reflects the full value of the investment lost'.[141]

E. Mitigation

A respondent State will not be liable to pay damages in respect of losses which **9.110** could have been mitigated by actions of the claimant. The principle of mitigation was stated by the ICJ in a case concerning the *Gabčíkovo-Nagymaros Project (Hungary/Slovakia)*[142] as being 'a principle that an injured State which has failed to take the necessary measures to limit the damage sustained would not be entitled to claim compensation for that damage which could have been avoided'.[143]

In *Middle East Cement v Egypt*[144] the Tribunal stated that a duty to mitigate loss is **9.111** one of the general principles of law which are part of international law.

F. Non-Pecuniary Remedies[145]

To date, the remedy awarded by almost all tribunals has been the payment of mon- **9.112** etary compensation. Yet this past practice should not obscure the fact that tribunals have the power to be much more flexible in their choice of remedy.

An order to a State to carry out a particular act would be seen as a far greater infringe- **9.113** ment of State sovereignty than an award of compensation. However, as investment treaty arbitrations begin to become notorious for their potential to result in big money awards against relatively poor nations, it may be time to rethink this position. Tribunals should be willing to consider preliminary orders to lift discriminatory treatments or to seek other administrative remedies that can provide full satisfaction to investors before moving to award compensation. Such an approach has been suggested by Wälde and Sabahi in a recent study.[146] The difficulty faced by tribunals wishing to adopt such an approach is the slow pace at which investment arbitrations move. By the time the tribunal addresses questions of compensation, any possibility of ordering a remedy to restore the situation as it existed prior to the infringement has usually been irrevocably lost.

---

[141] *Asian Agricultural Products Ltd v Republic of Sri Lanka* (Award) 4 ICSID Rep 245, 288 (ICSID, 1990, El-Kosheri P, Goldman & Asante).

[142] *Case Concerning the Gabčíkovo-Nagymaros Project (Hungary v Slovakia)* [1997] ICJ Rep 7.

[143] ibid 55.

[144] *Middle East Cement Shipping and Handling Co SA v Arab Republic of Egypt* (Award) 7 ICSID Rep 173, 205 (ICSID, 2002, Böckstiegel P, Bernardini & Wallace Jr).

[145] See C Schreuer, 'Non-Pecuniary Remedies in ICSID Arbitration' (2004) 20(4) Arb Int'l 325.

[146] TW Wälde & B Sabahi 'Compensation, Damages, and Valuation in International Investment Law' (ILA Committee on International Law of Foreign Investment) 45.

9.114 There is little tribunal practice to provide guidance in this area. In the only BIT arbitration to consider in depth the issue of injunctive relief, the respondent State took the traditional view of State sovereignty. In *Enron v Argentina*[147] Enron's Argentinian subsidiary had been the subject of various tax assessments. Enron sought relief pursuant to the US-Argentina BIT before the taxes had to be paid. Argentina challenged the Tribunal's jurisdiction to grant an injunction which would prevent it from collecting the taxes. It contended that, even if the tax assessments would constitute an expropriatory act, 'an ICSID tribunal cannot impede an expropriation that falls exclusively within the ambit of State sovereignty; that tribunal could only establish whether there has been an expropriation, its legality or illegality and the corresponding compensation'.[148]

9.115 Thus, Argentina would have preferred to be left alone to proceed with the expropriation, and assume the risk of monetary compensation, than be told not to enforce the tax assessment.

9.116 The Tribunal rejected Argentina's jurisdictional objection. It noted that the parties had both agreed that it had the power to issue declaratory relief but that in addition it had 'the power to order measures involving performance or injunction of certain acts'.[149]

9.117 In arriving at this conclusion, the Tribunal considered the jurisprudence of other international courts and tribunals, including the International Court of Justice. Most notably it cited the award in the *Case Concerning the Rainbow Warrior Affair*. Two French agents had arranged for an explosion on a vessel in a New Zealand harbour. In order to settle the dispute arising out of this act, France and New Zealand had agreed that the agents should be kept at a remote island. The arbitration arose out of New Zealand's attempt to seek an order for the return of the two agents whom they contended France had repatriated prematurely. The Tribunal not only confirmed its power to grant injunctive relief but also found that such powers arose inherently from its jurisdiction:

> The authority to issue an order for the cessation or discontinuance of a wrongful act or omission results from the inherent powers of a competent tribunal which is confronted with the continuous breach of an international obligation which is in force and continues to be in force. The delivery of such an order requires, therefore, two essential conditions intimately linked, namely that the wrongful act has a continuing character and that the violated rule is still in force at the time in which the order is issued.[150]

---

[147] *Enron Corp and Ponderosa Assets LP v Argentine Republic* (Jurisdiction) ICSID Case No ARB/01/3 (ICSID, 2004, Orrego Vicuña P, Espiell & Tschanz).   [148] ibid para 76.
[149] ibid para 81.
[150] *Case Concerning the Rainbow Warrior Affair (New Zealand v France)* (Award) (1990) 20 RIAA 217, 270. See also C Schreuer, 'Non-Pecuniary Remedies in ICSID Arbitration' (2004) 20(4) Arb Int'l 325.

A difficulty with the enforcement of non-pecuniary remedies is that they fall out- **9.118** side the specific ICSID enforcement framework. Article 54(1) of the ICSID Convention provides that: 'Each Contracting State shall recognize an award rendered pursuant to this Convention as binding and enforce the pecuniary obligations imposed by that award within its territories as if it were a final judgment of a court in that State.'

It is also notable that the US model BIT limits tribunals to the award of monetary **9.119** damages and restitution of property.[151]

Such potential obstacles can be overcome by a tribunal ordering a two-stage **9.120** remedy. It can order specific performance in the first place within a limited period and then provide for the payment of monetary compensation in the event that a State would not comply with the specific performance order. Such an approach, making compliance with specific performance 'voluntary', would also help to satisfy those who support maintaining the strict view of State sovereignty.[152]

A two-stage approach was adopted by the Tribunal in *Goetz v Burundi*.[153] The **9.121** Belgian claimant owned a company incorporated in Burundi which enjoyed the benefit of a free zone certificate granting tax and customs exemptions. Burundi withdrew the certificate and Goetz brought a claim under the Belgium-Burundi BIT. The Tribunal gave Burundi a choice of restoring the previous situation or paying monetary compensation:

> ... it falls to the Republic of Burundi, in order to establish the conformity with international law of the disputed decision to withdraw the certificate, to give an adequate and effective indemnity to the claimants as envisaged in Article 4 of the Belgium-Burundi investment treaty, unless it prefers to return the benefit of the free zone regime to them. The choice lies within the sovereign discretion of the Burundian government. If one of these two measures is not taken within a reasonable period, the Republic of Burundi will have committed an act contrary to international law the consequences of which it would be left to the Tribunal to ascertain.[154]

G. Interest

Article 38 of the International Law Commission *Draft Articles* provides for the **9.122** payment of interest when necessary in order to ensure full reparation. It also provides that the interest rate and mode of calculation shall be set so as to achieve that result.

---

[151] US model BIT 2004 (Appendix 6 below) Art 34(1).
[152] See Wälde & Sabahi (n 146 above).
[153] *Goetz & ors v Republic of Burundi* (Award Pt 1) 6 ICSID Rep 3 (ICSID, 1998, Weil P, Bedjaoui & Bredin). [154] ibid 44.

9.123 Crawford's *Commentary* sets out the traditional public international law position, derived from State-to-State practice, that interest should be simple, not compound. He quotes the Iran-US Claims Tribunal in *RJ Reynolds Tobacco Co v Government of the Islamic Republic of Iran* as stating that:

> 'As noted by one authority, "(t)here are few rules within the scope of the subject of damages in international law that are better settled than the one that compound interest is not allowable" ... Even though the term "all sums" could be construed to include interest and thereby to allow compound interest, the Tribunal, due to the ambiguity of the language, interprets the clause in the light of the international rule just stated, and thus excludes compound interest.'[155]

9.124 Other commentators have noted that 'arbitral tribunals (like national courts) have been nearly unanimous: compound interest (or interest on interest) is not allowed'.[156]

9.125 If the rule in State-to-State disputes is against compound interest, this is perhaps one area where investment treaty arbitration is developing its own practice. While there is no unanimity, many tribunals have been prepared to award compound interest.

9.126 In *Santa Elena v Costa Rica*[157] the Tribunal distinguished much of the State-to-State jurisprudence on interest on the grounds that it had arisen 'principally in relation to cases of injury or simple breach of contract. The same considerations do not apply to cases relating to the valuation of property or property rights. In cases such as the present, compound interest is not excluded where it is warranted by the circumstances of the case'.[158]

9.127 The Tribunal viewed entitlement to compound interest as part of the claimant's entitlement to receive the full present value of the compensation that it should have received at the time of the taking:

> ... where an owner of property has at some earlier time lost the value of his asset but has not received the monetary equivalent that then became due to him, the amount of compensation should reflect, at least in part, the additional sum that his money would have earned, had it, and the income generated by it, been reinvested each year at generally prevailing rates of interest. It is not the purpose of compound interest to attribute blame to, or to punish, anybody for the delay in the payment made to the expropriated owner; it is a mechanism to ensure that the compensation awarded the Claimant is appropriate in the circumstances.[159]

---

[155] Crawford (n 15 above) 237 quoting *RJ Reynolds Tobacco Co v Islamic Republic of Iran* (1984) 7 Iran-USCTR 181, 191–192 citing MM Whiteman, *Damages in International Law* Vol III (1943) 1997.

[156] CN Brower & JK Sharpe, 'Awards of Compound Interest in International Arbitration: the *Aminoil* Non-Precedent' in *Global Reflections on International Law, Commerce and Dispute Resolution: Liber Amicorum in Honour of Robert Briner* (2005) 155, 156.

[157] *Compañía del Desarrollo de Santa Elena SA v Republic of Costa Rica* (Award) 5 ICSID Rep 153 (ICSID, 2000, Fortier P, Lauterpacht & Weil). [158] ibid 176.

[159] ibid 178.

It would perhaps be possible to distinguish the *Santa Elena* award as having arisen **9.128** out of extreme circumstances. The expropriation took place in 1978, almost twenty-two years before the date of the award. Nonetheless, subsequent BIT tribunals have cited *Santa Elena* as authority for the principle that compound interest is payable even in cases where no such extreme circumstances exist. An example would be *Mid-East Cement v Egypt*[160] where the Tribunal concluded that 'to make the compensation "adequate and effective" pursuant to Art. 4.c) of the BIT, it is appropriate that the interest pursuant to the last sentence of Art. 4.c) of the BIT be awarded as compound interest'.[161]

The Tribunals in *CMS v Argentina*[162] and *Azurix v Argentina*[163] granted compound **9.129** interest to the claimants. The awards contain little analysis on this point but in *Azurix* the Tribunal stated that 'compound interest reflects the reality of financial transactions, and best approximates the value lost by an investor'.[164]

While most recent investment treaty tribunals have awarded compound interest, **9.130** a number have awarded simple interest. It thus can be argued that there is ample precedent on both sides of the debate. Yet on closer inspection it is possible to say that two of the simple interest awards[165] fell into the category specifically identified by the *Santa Elena* Tribunal as being suitable for simple interest, being claims for 'simple breach of contract'.[166]

This restrictive reading of the *Santa Elena* Tribunal was specifically cited in **9.131** *Autopista v Venezuela*.[167] Likewise *Occidental v Ecuador*[168] was not an expropriation claim.

While *CME v Czech Republic*[169] was an expropriation claim where the Tribunal **9.132** analysed the issue of interest in some depth, the Tribunal specifically stated that it did not need to award compound interest to compensate fully the damage sustained because of the generous interest provision it was applying by reference to a Czech statute.[170] Thus, it is submitted that a better reading of the Tribunal awards on this point will lead to the conclusion that in expropriation cases compound interest is to be preferred.[171] This is supported by the conclusion of a recent study

---

[160] *Mid-East Cement* (n 144 above).   [161] *Mid-East Cement* (n 144 above) 206.
[162] *CMS* (n 97 above).   [163] *Azurix* (n 100 above).
[164] *Azurix* (n 100 above) para 440.
[165] *Autopista Concesionada de Venezuela CA v Bolivarian Republic of Venezuela* (Award) ICSID Case No ARB/00/5 (ICSID, 2003, Kaufmann-Kohler P, Böckstiegel & Cremades); *Occidental Exploration and Production Co v Republic of Ecuador* (Award) LCIA Case No UN3467 (UNCITRAL, 2004, Orrego Vicuña P, Brower & Sweeney)   [166] *Santa Elena* (n 156 above) 176.
[167] *Autopista* (n 165 above) para 394.   [168] *Occidental* (n 165 above).
[169] *CME Czech Republic BV (The Netherlands) v Czech Republic* (Final Award) 9 ICSID Rep 264 (UNCITRAL, 2003, Kühn C, Schwebel & Brownlie).   [170] ibid 409.
[171] See, however, Brower & Sharpe (n 156 above) for a critical discussion of the tribunal jurisprudence in favour of compound interest in expropriation cases.

finding 'a growing recognition that compound interest may be necessary to fully and adequately compensate an injured investor'.[172]

9.133 The other important questions that arise in considering questions of interest are the date from which interest is payable and the rate of interest. Both of these questions are usually highly fact specific and it is difficult to offer guidance beyond that set out at Article 38(2) of the International Law Commission *Draft Articles* that: 'Interest runs from the date when the principal sum should have been paid until the date the obligation to pay is fulfilled.'

H. Costs

9.134 In commercial arbitrations it is common for the tribunal to order the losing party to pay the costs incurred by the winning party. These costs include sums paid to lawyers and the winning party's share of the arbitration expenses. In contrast, the public international law tradition is for each party to bear its own legal costs and for the tribunal costs to be shared equally.

9.135 The prevalent position in investment arbitration has been to follow the public international law tradition and avoid the 'loser pays' principle. In *Metalclad v Mexico*[173] the costs were split evenly between the parties even though the claimant was successful. Where the claimant is the losing party, tribunals have also adhered to the principle of equal allocation. For example, in *Tradex v Albania*[174] and the NAFTA case *ADF v United States*,[175] both State parties prevailed on the merits, but, in each case the losing investors were not ordered to pay the costs of the winning State. Instead, each party was ordered to bear its own legal costs and to share the costs of the arbitration.

9.136 Limited reasoning for this was provided in *ADF*, although the Tribunal considered 'the circumstances of [the] case, including the nature and complexity of the questions raised by the disputing parties'.[176] In *Tradex*, the Tribunal took into account that Tradex had prevailed on the jurisdiction challenge and that its claim could not 'be considered as frivolous in view of the many difficult aspects of fact and law involved and dealt with'.[177]

9.137 This traditional approach may, however, be changing, although it is too early to identify a definite trend. The most significant indicator of a change in tribunal

---

[172] Weisburg & Ryan (n 82 above) 182. This is also noted by Wälde & Sabahi (n 146 above).
[173] *Metalclad* (n 68 above) 235.
[174] *Tradex Hellas SA v Republic of Albania* (Award) 5 ICSID Rep 43 (ICSID, 1999, Böckstiegel P, Fielding & Giardina).
[175] *ADF Group Inc v United States of America* (Award) 6 ICSID Rep 449, 536–537 (NAFTA/ ICSID (AF), 2003, Feliciano P, de Mestral & Lamm).   [176] ibid 537.
[177] *Tradex* (174 above) 105.

practice is provided by the costs decision in a recent NAFTA case, *Thunderbird v Mexico*.[178] Here the Tribunal criticized the reasoning of previous tribunals in cases where the 'loser pays' approach had been rejected. The majority of the Tribunal said that it '[failed] to grasp the rationale' of cases in which the losing investor is not ordered to pay the costs of the Government, 'except in the case of an investor with limited financial resources where considerations of access to justice may play a role'.[179] The Tribunal argued that the same rules on costs should apply to international investment arbitration as in international commercial arbitrations.

The *Thunderbird* Tribunal considered four factors that had previously been applied **9.138** (in *Azinian v Mexico*)[180] to decide that the losing investor need not pay the costs of the State party. These were (a) the novelty of NAFTA as a dispute resolution mechanism; (b) whether the claimant presented its case in an efficient and professional manner; (c) whether the respondent may be said to some extent to have invited litigation and (d) whether the persons most accountable for the claimant's wrongful behaviour would be the least likely to be affected by an award of costs.

The Tribunal decided that factor (a) was no longer applicable because NAFTA **9.139** arbitration is now well established. Factors (c) and (d) were inapplicable to the case. Although factor (b) was satisfied, the Tribunal considered it insufficient to deviate from the general principle that the losing party should bear the costs. Accordingly, the Tribunal determined that Mexico could recover an appropriate proportion of the costs of its legal representation and of the arbitration. Given that Mexico did not prevail on the issues of jurisdiction and admissibility, the majority of the Tribunal exercised its discretion and allocated the costs between Thunderbird and Mexico on a 75:25 per cent basis. In a Separate Opinion, the third arbitrator recognized that the allocation of the bulk of the costs against the claimant was a 'significant departure from established jurisprudence'.[181]

Thunderbird is not the only case where the 'loser pays' approach has been adopted. **9.140** In *Methanex Corporation v USA*[182] the Tribunal dismissed all of Methanex's claims on the merits. The Tribunal decided that 'there is no compelling reason not to apply the general approach required by the first sentence of Article 40(1) of the UNCITRAL Rules'[183]—that the unsuccessful party should bear the costs of the arbitration. Accordingly, Methanex was ordered to pay the costs of the arbitration. With respect to the parties' legal costs, the Tribunal said that 'as a general principle

---

[178] *International Thunderbird Gaming Corp v United Mexican States* (Award) (NAFTA/UNCITRAL, 2006, van den Berg P, Wälde & Ariosa). [179] ibid para 214.
[180] *Azinian, Davitian & Baca v United Mexican States* (Award) 5 ICSID Rep 269 (NAFTA/ICSID (AF), 1998, Paulsson P, Civiletti & von Wobeser). *Thunderbird* (n 178 above) 217.
[181] *International Thunderbird Gaming Corp v United Mexican States* (Separate Opinion of Professor Wälde) (NAFTA/UNCITRAL, 2006, Wälde) para 126.
[182] *Methanex Corp v United States of America* (Final Award: Jurisdiction and Merits) (NAFTA/UNCITRAL, 2005, Veeder P, Rowley & Reisman). [183] ibid Pt V para (2)5.

the successful party should be paid its reasonable legal costs by the unsuccessful party'.[184] Given that the United States had been successful in terms of both jurisdiction and merits, the Tribunal ordered Methanex to pay the United States' reasonable legal costs of approximately US$3 million.

9.141   The principle of equal allocation of costs was also not applied in *CSOB v Slovakia*,[185] an ICSID case in which CSOB prevailed on the merits. The Tribunal ordered Slovakia to pay its own costs, as well as a US$10 million contribution (about 60 per cent) towards CSOB's costs. The decision is also notable for the fact that the Tribunal allowed the successful party to recover costs incurred by party employees on the grounds that those employees had prepared specific contributions that were caused by the arbitration and made several statements filed with the Tribunal.[186]

9.142   Unusually, in *EnCana v Ecuador*[187] the Tribunal ordered the winning party (Ecuador) to pay the arbitration costs (but not the legal costs) of the losing party. Although the Tribunal cited the general principle under Article 40(1) of the UNCITRAL Rules that the prevailing party was in principle entitled to its costs, it decided that it would be just and equitable to order Ecuador to bear the costs in view of the events giving rise to the arbitration.

9.143   A half-way principal is for the losing party to have to pay the prevailing party's costs of the arbitration with both parties being required to bear their own legal costs. This was the approach adopted by the Tribunal in *Azurix v Argentina*.[188]

I. Conclusion

9.144   In the light of the above, it is possible to state the following conclusions:

9.145   *Standard of compensation.* The standard of compensation is normally prescribed in the investment treaty out of which the dispute arises. It is usually expressed in line with the 'prompt, adequate and effective' standard, although this is formulated in a variety of wordings.

9.146   *Determining the amount of compensation.* Tribunals use a variety of different economic methods to determine the amount of compensation. These include calculating the liquidation value, the replacement value, the book value, finding a value based upon comparable transactions, or assessing the value using DCF principles. Tribunals most readily turn to discounted cash flow valuation when there is a

---

[184]   ibid Pt V para (3)10.
[185]   *Československá Obchodní Banka AS v Slovak Republic* (Award) ICSID Case No ARB/97/4 (ICSID, 2004, van Houtte P, Bernardini & Bucher).   [186]   ibid para 371.
[187]   *EnCana Corp v Republic of Ecuador* (Award) LCIA Case No UN 3481 (UNCITRAL, 2006, Crawford P, Grigera Naon & Thomas).   [188]   *Azurix* (n 100 above) para 441.

track record of profitability. This method can lead to large awards and thus its suit-ability as a valuation method has been closely examined.

Non-expropriatory breaches. Although treaties do not contain provisions setting **9.147** the standard of compensation for non-expropriatory breaches, tribunals do award compensation following a finding that a wrong has been committed. If the breach leads to the total loss or deprivation of the asset, tribunals adopt the expropriation compensation standard. If the breach does not lead to the total loss or deprivation of the asset, tribunals have used the 'tort' standard of recovery. Damages recover-able are those that would put the investor in the position it would have been in had the wrong not been committed. To be recoverable, the loss must be linked causally to the host State's interference.

Non-pecuniary compensation. Tribunals have the power to order non-pecuniary **9.148** compensation, such as injunctive relief. This power is rarely exercised.

Interest. Tribunals usually award compound, as opposed to simple, interest. This **9.149** is perceived to compensate the investor more fully. However, there are examples of tribunals awarding simple interest.

Costs. The prevalent position is for the costs of the arbitration to be shared equally. **9.150** However, some recent awards have adopted a 'loser pays' principle.

Appendices

APPENDIX 1

North American Free Trade Agreement
(Part Five: Investment, Services and Related Matters, Chapter 11: Investment)

CHAPTER 11
INVESTMENT

Section A Investment

Article 1101
Scope and Coverage

1. This Chapter applies to measures adopted or maintained by a Party relating to:
   (a) investors of another Party;
   (b) investments of investors of another Party in the territory of the Party; and
   (c) with respect to Articles 1106 and 1114, all investments in the territory of the Party.

2. A Party has the right to perform exclusively the economic activities set out in Annex III and to refuse to permit the establishment of investment in such activities.

3. This Chapter does not apply to measures adopted or maintained by a Party to the extent that they are covered by Chapter Fourteen (Financial Services).

4. Nothing in this Chapter shall be construed to prevent a Party from providing a service or performing a function such as law enforcement, correctional services, income security or insurance, social security or insurance, social welfare, public education, public training, health, and child care, in a manner that is not inconsistent with this Chapter.

Article 1102
National Treatment

1. Each Party shall accord to investors of another Party treatment no less favorable than that it accords, in like circumstances, to its own investors with respect to the establishment, acquisition, expansion, management, conduct, operation, and sale or other disposition of investments.

2. Each Party shall accord to investments of investors of another Party treatment no less favorable than that it accords, in like circumstances, to investments of its own investors with respect to the establishment, acquisition, expansion, management, conduct, operation, and sale or other disposition of investments.

3. The treatment accorded by a Party under paragraphs 1 and 2 means, with respect to a state or province, treatment no less favorable than the most favorable treatment accorded, in like circumstances, by that state or province to investors, and to investments of investors, of the Party of which it forms a part.

4. For greater certainty, no Party may:

   (a) impose on an investor of another Party a requirement that a minimum level of equity in an enterprise in the territory of the Party be held by its nationals, other than nominal qualifying shares for directors or incorporators of corporations; or
   (b) require an investor of another Party, by reason of its nationality, to sell or otherwise dispose of an investment in the territory of the Party.

Article 1103
Most-Favored-Nation Treatment

1. Each Party shall accord to investors of another Party treatment no less favorable than that it accords, in like circumstances, to investors of any other Party or of a non-Party with respect to the establishment, acquisition, expansion, management, conduct, operation, and sale or other disposition of investments.
2. Each Party shall accord to investments of investors of another Party treatment no less favorable than that it accords, in like circumstances, to investments of investors of any other Party or of a non-Party with respect to the establishment, acquisition, expansion, management, conduct, operation, and sale or other disposition of investments.

Article 1104
Standard of Treatment

Each Party shall accord to investors of another Party and to investments of investors of another Party the better of the treatment required by Articles 1102 and 1103.

Article 1105
Minimum Standard of Treatment

1. Each Party shall accord to investments of investors of another Party treatment in accordance with international law, including fair and equitable treatment and full protection and security.
2. Without prejudice to paragraph 1 and notwithstanding Article 1108(7)(b), each Party shall accord to investors of another Party, and to investments of investors of another Party, non-discriminatory treatment with respect to measures it adopts or maintains relating to losses suffered by investments in its territory owing to armed conflict or civil strife.
3. Paragraph 2 does not apply to existing measures relating to subsidies or grants that would be inconsistent with Article 1102 but for Article 1108(7)(b).

Article 1106
Performance Requirements

1. No Party may impose or enforce any of the following requirements, or enforce any commitment or undertaking, in connection with the establishment, acquisition, expansion, management, conduct or operation of an investment of an investor of a Party or of a non-Party in its territory:
   (a) to export a given level or percentage of goods or services;
   (b) to achieve a given level or percentage of domestic content;
   (c) to purchase, use or accord a preference to goods produced or services provided in its territory, or to purchase goods or services from persons in its territory;
   (d) to relate in any way the volume or value of imports to the volume or value of exports or to the amount of foreign exchange inflows associated with such investment;
   (e) to restrict sales of goods or services in its territory that such investment produces or provides by relating such sales in any way to the volume or value of its exports or foreign exchange earnings;
   (f) to transfer technology, a production process or other proprietary knowledge to a person in its territory, except when the requirement is imposed or the commitment or undertaking is enforced by a court, administrative tribunal or competition authority to remedy an alleged violation of competition laws or to act in a manner not inconsistent with other provisions of this Agreement; or
   (g) to act as the exclusive supplier of the goods it produces or services it provides to a specific region or world market.
2. A measure that requires an investment to use a technology to meet generally applicable health, safety or environmental requirements shall not be construed to be inconsistent with paragraph 1(f). For greater certainty, Articles 1102 and 1103 apply to the measure.

3. No Party may condition the receipt or continued receipt of an advantage, in connection with an investment in its territory of an investor of a Party or of a non-Party, on compliance with any of the following requirements:

   (a) to achieve a given level or percentage of domestic content;

   (b) to purchase, use or accord a preference to goods produced in its territory, or to purchase goods from producers in its territory;

   (c) to relate in any way the volume or value of imports to the volume or value of exports or to the amount of foreign exchange inflows associated with such investment; or

   (d) to restrict sales of goods or services in its territory that such investment produces or provides by relating such sales in any way to the volume or value of its exports or foreign exchange earnings.

4. Nothing in paragraph 3 shall be construed to prevent a Party from conditioning the receipt or continued receipt of an advantage, in connection with an investment in its territory of an investor of a Party or of a non-Party, on compliance with a requirement to locate production, provide a service, train or employ workers, construct or expand particular facilities, or carry out research and development, in its territory.

5. Paragraphs 1 and 3 do not apply to any requirement other than the requirements set out in those paragraphs.

6. Provided that such measures are not applied in an arbitrary or unjustifiable manner, or do not constitute a disguised restriction on international trade or investment, nothing in paragraph 1(b) or (c) or 3(a) or (b) shall be construed to prevent any Party from adopting or maintaining measures, including environmental measures:

   (a) necessary to secure compliance with laws and regulations that are not inconsistent with the provisions of this Agreement;

   (b) necessary to protect human, animal or plant life or health; or

   (c) necessary for the conservation of living or non-living exhaustible natural resources.

Article 1107
Senior Management and Boards of Directors

1. No Party may require that an enterprise of that Party that is an investment of an investor of another Party appoint to senior management positions individuals of any particular nationality.

2. A Party may require that a majority of the board of directors, or any committee thereof, of an enterprise of that Party that is an investment of an investor of another Party, be of a particular nationality, or resident in the territory of the Party, provided that the requirement does not materially impair the ability of the investor to exercise control over its investment.

Article 1108
Reservations and Exceptions

1. Articles 1102, 1103, 1106 and 1107 do not apply to:

   (a) any existing non-conforming measure that is maintained by

       (i) a Party at the federal level, as set out in its Schedule to Annex I or III,

       (ii) a state or province, for two years after the date of entry into force of this Agreement, and thereafter as set out by a Party in its Schedule to Annex I in accordance with paragraph 2, or

       (iii) a local government;

   (b) the continuation or prompt renewal of any non-conforming measure referred to in subparagraph (a); or

   (c) an amendment to any non-conforming measure referred to in subparagraph (a) to the extent that the amendment does not decrease the conformity of the measure, as it existed immediately before the amendment, with Articles 1102, 1103, 1106 and 1107.

2. Each Party may set out in its Schedule to Annex I, within two years of the date of entry into force of this Agreement, any existing nonconforming measure maintained by a state or province, not including a local government.
3. Articles 1102, 1103, 1106 and 1107 do not apply to any measure that a Party adopts or maintains with respect to sectors, subsectors or activities, as set out in its Schedule to Annex II.
4. No Party may, under any measure adopted after the date of entry into force of this Agreement and covered by its Schedule to Annex II, require an investor of another Party, by reason of its nationality, to sell or otherwise dispose of an investment existing at the time the measure becomes effective.
5. Articles 1102 and 1103 do not apply to any measure that is an exception to, or derogation from, the obligations under Article 1703 (Intellectual Property National Treatment) as specifically provided for in that Article.
6. Article 1103 does not apply to treatment accorded by a Party pursuant to agreements, or with respect to sectors, set out in its Schedule to Annex IV.
7. Articles 1102, 1103 and 1107 do not apply to:
    (a) procurement by a Party or a state enterprise; or
    (b) subsidies or grants provided by a Party or a state enterprise, including government supported loans, guarantees and insurance.
8. The provisions of:
    (a) Article 1106(1)(a), (b) and (c), and (3)(a) and (b) do not apply to qualification requirements for goods or services with respect to export promotion and foreign aid programs;
    (b) Article 1106(1)(b), (c), (f) and (g), and (3)(a) and (b) do not apply to procurement by a Party or a state enterprise; and
    (c) Article 1106(3)(a) and (b) do not apply to requirements imposed by an importing Party relating to the content of goods necessary to qualify for preferential tariffs or preferential quotas.

Article 1109
Transfers

1. Each Party shall permit all transfers relating to an investment of an investor of another Party in the territory of the Party to be made freely and without delay. Such transfers include:
    (a) profits, dividends, interest, capital gains, royalty payments, management fees, technical assistance and other fees, returns in kind and other amounts derived from the investment;
    (b) proceeds from the sale of all or any part of the investment or from the partial or complete liquidation of the investment;
    (c) payments made under a contract entered into by the investor, or its investment, including payments made pursuant to a loan agreement;
    (d) payments made pursuant to Article 1110; and
    (e) payments arising under Section B.

2. Each Party shall permit transfers to be made in a freely usable currency at the market rate of exchange prevailing on the date of transfer with respect to spot transactions in the currency to be transferred.
3. No Party may require its investors to transfer, or penalize its investors that fail to transfer, the income, earnings, profits or other amounts derived from, or attributable to, investments in the territory of another Party.
4. Notwithstanding paragraphs 1 and 2, a Party may prevent a transfer through the equitable, non-discriminatory and good faith application of its laws relating to:
    (a) bankruptcy, insolvency or the protection of the rights of creditors;
    (b) issuing, trading or dealing in securities;
    (c) criminal or penal offenses;
    (d) reports of transfers of currency or other monetary instruments; or
    (e) ensuring the satisfaction of judgments in adjudicatory proceedings.

5. Paragraph 3 shall not be construed to prevent a Party from imposing any measure through the equitable, non-discriminatory and good faith application of its laws relating to the matters set out in subparagraphs (a) through (e) of paragraph 4.

6. Notwithstanding paragraph 1, a Party may restrict transfers of returns in kind in circumstances where it could otherwise restrict such transfers under this Agreement, including as set out in paragraph 4.

Article 1110
Expropriation and Compensation

1. No Party may directly or indirectly nationalize or expropriate an investment of an investor of another Party in its territory or take a measure tantamount to nationalization or expropriation of such an investment ('expropriation'), except:
   (a) for a public purpose;
   (b) on a non-discriminatory basis;
   (c) in accordance with due process of law and Article 1105(1); and
   (d) on payment of compensation in accordance with paragraphs 2 through 6.

2. Compensation shall be equivalent to the fair market value of the expropriated investment immediately before the expropriation took place ('date of expropriation'), and shall not reflect any change in value occurring because the intended expropriation had become known earlier. Valuation criteria shall include going concern value, asset value including declared tax value of tangible property, and other criteria, as appropriate, to determine fair market value.

3. Compensation shall be paid without delay and be fully realizable.

4. If payment is made in a G7 currency, compensation shall include interest at a commercially reasonable rate for that currency from the date of expropriation until the date of actual payment.

5. If a Party elects to pay in a currency other than a G7 currency, the amount paid on the date of payment, if converted into a G7 currency at the market rate of exchange prevailing on that date, shall be no less than if the amount of compensation owed on the date of expropriation had been converted into that G7 currency at the market rate of exchange prevailing on that date, and interest had accrued at a commercially reasonable rate for that G7 currency from the date of expropriation until the date of payment.

6. On payment, compensation shall be freely transferable as provided in Article 1109.

7. This Article does not apply to the issuance of compulsory licenses granted in relation to intellectual property rights, or to the revocation, limitation or creation of intellectual property rights, to the extent that such issuance, revocation, limitation or creation is consistent with Chapter Seventeen (Intellectual Property).

8. For purposes of this Article and for greater certainty, a non-discriminatory measure of general application shall not be considered a measure tantamount to an expropriation of a debt security or loan covered by this Chapter solely on the ground that the measure imposes costs on the debtor that cause it to default on the debt.

Article 1111
Special Formalities and Information Requirements

1. Nothing in Article 1102 shall be construed to prevent a Party from adopting or maintaining a measure that prescribes special formalities in connection with the establishment of investments by investors of another Party, such as a requirement that investors be residents of the Party or that investments be legally constituted under the laws or regulations of the Party, provided that such formalities do not materially impair the protections afforded by a Party to investors of another Party and investments of investors of another Party pursuant to this Chapter.

2. Notwithstanding Articles 1102 or 1103, a Party may require an investor of another Party, or its investment in its territory, to provide routine information concerning that investment solely for informational or statistical purposes. The Party shall protect such business information that is

confidential from any disclosure that would prejudice the competitive position of the investor or the investment. Nothing in this paragraph shall be construed to prevent a Party from otherwise obtaining or disclosing information in connection with the equitable and good faith application of its law.

Article 1112
Relation to Other Chapters

1. In the event of any inconsistency between this Chapter and another Chapter, the other Chapter shall prevail to the extent of the inconsistency.
2. A requirement by a Party that a service provider of another Party post a bond or other form of financial security as a condition of providing a service into its territory does not of itself make this Chapter applicable to the provision of that cross-border service. This Chapter applies to that Party's treatment of the posted bond or financial security.

Article 1113
Denial of Benefits

1. A Party may deny the benefits of this Chapter to an investor of another Party that is an enterprise of such Party and to investments of such investor if investors of a non-Party own or control the enterprise and the denying Party:
   (a) does not maintain diplomatic relations with the non-Party; or
   (b) adopts or maintains measures with respect to the non-Party that prohibit transactions with the enterprise or that would be violated or circumvented if the benefits of this Chapter were accorded to the enterprise or to its investments.
2. Subject to prior notification and consultation in accordance with Articles 1803 (Notification and Provision of Information) and 2006 (Consultations), a Party may deny the benefits of this Chapter to an investor of another Party that is an enterprise of such Party and to investments of such investors if investors of a non-Party own or control the enterprise and the enterprise has no substantial business activities in the territory of the Party under whose law it is constituted or organized.

Article 1114
Environmental Measures

1. Nothing in this Chapter shall be construed to prevent a Party from adopting, maintaining or enforcing any measure otherwise consistent with this Chapter that it considers appropriate to ensure that investment activity in its territory is undertaken in a manner sensitive to environmental concerns.
2. The Parties recognize that it is inappropriate to encourage investment by relaxing domestic health, safety or environmental measures. Accordingly, a Party should not waive or otherwise derogate from, or offer to waive or otherwise derogate from, such measures as an encouragement for the establishment, acquisition, expansion or retention in its territory of an investment of an investor. If a Party considers that another Party has offered such an encouragement, it may request consultations with the other Party and the two Parties shall consult with a view to avoiding any such encouragement.

Section B Settlement of Disputes between a Party and an Investor of Another Party

Article 1115
Purpose

Without prejudice to the rights and obligations of the Parties under Chapter Twenty (Institutional Arrangements and Dispute Settlement Procedures), this Section establishes a mechanism for the settlement of investment disputes that assures both equal treatment among investors of the Parties in accordance with the principle of international reciprocity and due process before an impartial tribunal.

Article 1116
Claim by an Investor of a Party on Its Own Behalf

1. An investor of a Party may submit to arbitration under this Section a claim that another Party has breached an obligation under:
   (a) Section A or Article 1503(2) (State Enterprises), or
   (b) Article 1502(3)(a) (Monopolies and State Enterprises) where the monopoly has acted in a manner inconsistent with the Party's obligations under Section A, and that the investor has incurred loss or damage by reason of, or arising out of, that breach.
2. An investor may not make a claim if more than three years have elapsed from the date on which the investor first acquired, or should have first acquired, knowledge of the alleged breach and knowledge that the investor has incurred loss or damage.

Article 1117
Claim by an Investor of a Party on Behalf of an Enterprise

1. An investor of a Party, on behalf of an enterprise of another Party that is a juridical person that the investor owns or controls directly or indirectly, may submit to arbitration under this Section a claim that the other Party has breached an obligation under:
   (a) Section A or Article 1503(2) (State Enterprises), or
   (b) Article 1502(3)(a) (Monopolies and State Enterprises) where the monopoly has acted in a manner inconsistent with the Party's obligations under Section A, and that the enterprise has incurred loss or damage by reason of, or arising out of, that breach.
2. An investor may not make a claim on behalf of an enterprise described in paragraph 1 if more than three years have elapsed from the date on which the enterprise first acquired, or should have first acquired, knowledge of the alleged breach and knowledge that the enterprise has incurred loss or damage.
3. Where an investor makes a claim under this Article and the investor or a non-controlling investor in the enterprise makes a claim under Article 1116 arising out of the same events that gave rise to the claim under this Article, and two or more of the claims are submitted to arbitration under Article 1120, the claims should be heard together by a Tribunal established under Article 1126, unless the Tribunal finds that the interests of a disputing party would be prejudiced thereby.
4. An investment may not make a claim under this Section.

Article 1118
Settlement of a Claim through Consultation and Negotiation

The disputing parties should first attempt to settle a claim through consultation or negotiation.

Article 1119
Notice of Intent to Submit a Claim to Arbitration

The disputing investor shall deliver to the disputing Party written notice of its intention to submit a claim to arbitration at least 90 days before the claim is submitted, which notice shall specify:
(a) the name and address of the disputing investor and, where a claim is made under Article 1117, the name and address of the enterprise;
(b) the provisions of this Agreement alleged to have been breached and any other relevant provisions;
(c) the issues and the factual basis for the claim; and
(d) the relief sought and the approximate amount of damages claimed.

Article 1120
Submission of a Claim to Arbitration

1. Except as provided in Annex 1120.1, and provided that six months have elapsed since the events giving rise to a claim, a disputing investor may submit the claim to arbitration under:
   (a) the ICSID Convention, provided that both the disputing Party and the Party of the investor are parties to the Convention;

(b) the Additional Facility Rules of ICSID, provided that either the disputing Party or the Party of the investor, but not both, is a party to the ICSID Convention; or

(c) the UNCITRAL Arbitration Rules.

2. The applicable arbitration rules shall govern the arbitration except to the extent modified by this Section.

Article 1121
Conditions Precedent to Submission of a Claim to Arbitration

1. A disputing investor may submit a claim under Article 1116 to arbitration only if:

(a) the investor consents to arbitration in accordance with the procedures set out in this Agreement; and

(b) the investor and, where the claim is for loss or damage to an interest in an enterprise of another Party that is a juridical person that the investor owns or controls directly or indirectly, the enterprise, waive their right to initiate or continue before any administrative tribunal or court under the law of any Party, or other dispute settlement procedures, any proceedings with respect to the measure of the disputing Party that is alleged to be a breach referred to in Article 1116, except for proceedings for injunctive, declaratory or other extraordinary relief, not involving the payment of damages, before an administrative tribunal or court under the law of the disputing Party.

2. A disputing investor may submit a claim under Article 1117 to arbitration only if both the investor and the enterprise:

(a) consent to arbitration in accordance with the procedures set out in this Agreement; and

(b) waive their right to initiate or continue before any administrative tribunal or court under the law of any Party, or other dispute settlement procedures, any proceedings with respect to the measure of the disputing Party that is alleged to be a breach referred to in Article 1117, except for proceedings for injunctive, declaratory or other extraordinary relief, not involving the payment of damages, before an administrative tribunal or court under the law of the disputing Party.

3. A consent and waiver required by this Article shall be in writing, shall be delivered to the disputing Party and shall be included in the submission of a claim to arbitration.

4. Only where a disputing Party has deprived a disputing investor of control of an enterprise:

(a) a waiver from the enterprise under paragraph 1(b) or 2(b) shall not be required; and

(b) Annex 1120.1(b) shall not apply.

Article 1122
Consent to Arbitration

1. Each Party consents to the submission of a claim to arbitration in accordance with the procedures set out in this Agreement.

2. The consent given by paragraph 1 and the submission by a disputing investor of a claim to arbitration shall satisfy the requirement of:

(a) Chapter II of the ICSID Convention (Jurisdiction of the Centre) and the Additional Facility Rules for written consent of the parties;

(b) Article II of the New York Convention for an agreement in writing; and

(c) Article I of the Inter-American Convention for an agreement.

Article 1123
Number of Arbitrators and Method of Appointment

Except in respect of a Tribunal established under Article 1126, and unless the disputing parties otherwise agree, the Tribunal shall comprise three arbitrators, one arbitrator appointed by each of the disputing parties and the third, who shall be the presiding arbitrator, appointed by agreement of the disputing parties.

Article 1124
Constitution of a Tribunal When a Party Fails to Appoint an Arbitrator or the Disputing Parties Are Unable to Agree on a Presiding Arbitrator

1. The Secretary-General shall serve as appointing authority for an arbitration under this Section.
2. If a Tribunal, other than a Tribunal established under Article 1126, has not been constituted within 90 days from the date that a claim is submitted to arbitration, the Secretary-General, on the request of either disputing party, shall appoint, in his discretion, the arbitrator or arbitrators not yet appointed, except that the presiding arbitrator shall be appointed in accordance with paragraph 3.
3. The Secretary-General shall appoint the presiding arbitrator from the roster of presiding arbitrators referred to in paragraph 4, provided that the presiding arbitrator shall not be a national of the disputing Party or a national of the Party of the disputing investor. In the event that no such presiding arbitrator is available to serve, the Secretary-General shall appoint, from the ICSID Panel of Arbitrators, a presiding arbitrator who is not a national of any of the Parties.
4. On the date of entry into force of this Agreement, the Parties shall establish, and thereafter maintain, a roster of 45 presiding arbitrators meeting the qualifications of the Convention and rules referred to in Article 1120 and experienced in international law and investment matters. The roster members shall be appointed by consensus and without regard to nationality.

Article 1125
Agreement to Appointment of Arbitrators

For purposes of Article 39 of the ICSID Convention and Article 7 of Schedule C to the ICSID Additional Facility Rules, and without prejudice to an objection to an arbitrator based on Article 1124(3) or on a ground other than nationality:

(a) the disputing Party agrees to the appointment of each individual member of a Tribunal established under the ICSID Convention or the ICSID Additional Facility Rules;

(b) a disputing investor referred to in Article 1116 may submit a claim to arbitration, or continue a claim, under the ICSID Convention or the ICSID Additional Facility Rules, only on condition that the disputing investor agrees in writing to the appointment of each individual member of the Tribunal; and

(c) a disputing investor referred to in Article 1117(1) may submit a claim to arbitration, or continue a claim, under the ICSID Convention or the ICSID Additional Facility Rules, only on condition that the disputing investor and the enterprise agree in writing to the appointment of each individual member of the Tribunal.

Article 1126
Consolidation

1. A Tribunal established under this Article shall be established under the UNCITRAL Arbitration Rules and shall conduct its proceedings in accordance with those Rules, except as modified by this Section.
2. Where a Tribunal established under this Article is satisfied that claims have been submitted to arbitration under Article 1120 that have a question of law or fact in common, the Tribunal may, in the interests of fair and efficient resolution of the claims, and after hearing the disputing parties, by order:
   (a) assume jurisdiction over, and hear and determine together, all or part of the claims; or
   (b) assume jurisdiction over, and hear and determine one or more of the claims, the determination of which it believes would assist in the resolution of the others.
3. A disputing party that seeks an order under paragraph 2 shall request the Secretary-General to establish a Tribunal and shall specify in the request:
   (a) the name of the disputing Party or disputing investors against which the order is sought;
   (b) the nature of the order sought; and
   (c) the grounds on which the order is sought.

4. The disputing party shall deliver to the disputing Party or disputing investors against which the order is sought a copy of the request.
5. Within 60 days of receipt of the request, the Secretary-General shall establish a Tribunal comprising three arbitrators. The Secretary-General shall appoint the presiding arbitrator from the roster referred to in Article 1124(4). In the event that no such presiding arbitrator is available to serve, the Secretary-General shall appoint, from the ICSID Panel of Arbitrators, a presiding arbitrator who is not a national of any of the Parties. The Secretary-General shall appoint the two other members from the roster referred to in Article 1124(4), and to the extent not available from that roster, from the ICSID Panel of Arbitrators, and to the extent not available from that Panel, in the discretion of the Secretary-General. One member shall be a national of the disputing Party and one member shall be a national of a Party of the disputing investors.
6. Where a Tribunal has been established under this Article, a disputing investor that has submitted a claim to arbitration under Article 1116 or 1117 and that has not been named in a request made under paragraph 3 may make a written request to the Tribunal that it be included in an order made under paragraph 2, and shall specify in the request:
   (a) the name and address of the disputing investor;
   (b) the nature of the order sought; and
   (c) the grounds on which the order is sought.
7. A disputing investor referred to in paragraph 6 shall deliver a copy of its request to the disputing parties named in a request made under paragraph 3.
8. A Tribunal established under Article 1120 shall not have jurisdiction to decide a claim, or a part of a claim, over which a Tribunal established under this Article has assumed jurisdiction.
9. On application of a disputing party, a Tribunal established under this Article, pending its decision under paragraph 2, may order that the proceedings of a Tribunal established under Article 1120 be stayed, unless the latter Tribunal has already adjourned its proceedings.
10. A disputing Party shall deliver to the Secretariat, within 15 days of receipt by the disputing Party, a copy of:
    (a) a request for arbitration made under paragraph (1) of Article 36 of the ICSID Convention;
    (b) a notice of arbitration made under Article 2 of Schedule C of the ICSID Additional Facility Rules; or
    (c) a notice of arbitration given under the UNCITRAL Arbitration Rules.
11. A disputing Party shall deliver to the Secretariat a copy of a request made under paragraph 3:
    (a) within 15 days of receipt of the request, in the case of a request made by a disputing investor;
    (b) within 15 days of making the request, in the case of a request made by the disputing Party.
12. A disputing Party shall deliver to the Secretariat a copy of a request made under paragraph 6 within 15 days of receipt of the request.
13. The Secretariat shall maintain a public register of the documents referred to in paragraphs 10, 11 and 12.

Article 1127
Notice

A disputing Party shall deliver to the other Parties:

(a) written notice of a claim that has been submitted to arbitration no later than 30 days after the date that the claim is submitted; and
(b) copies of all pleadings filed in the arbitration.

Article 1128
Participation by a Party

On written notice to the disputing parties, a Party may make submissions to a Tribunal on a question of interpretation of this Agreement.

Article 1129
Documents

1. A Party shall be entitled to receive from the disputing Party, at the cost of the requesting Party a copy of:
   (a) the evidence that has been tendered to the Tribunal; and
   (b) the written argument of the disputing parties.

2. A Party receiving information pursuant to paragraph 1 shall treat the information as if it were a disputing Party.

Article 1130
Place of Arbitration

Unless the disputing parties agree otherwise, a Tribunal shall hold an arbitration in the territory of a Party that is a party to the New York Convention, selected in accordance with:
(a) the ICSID Additional Facility Rules if the arbitration is under those Rules or the ICSID Convention; or
(b) the UNCITRAL Arbitration Rules if the arbitration is under those Rules.

Article 1131
Governing Law

1. A Tribunal established under this Section shall decide the issues in dispute in accordance with this Agreement and applicable rules of international law.

2. An interpretation by the Commission of a provision of this Agreement shall be binding on a Tribunal established under this Section.

Article 1132
Interpretation of Annexes

1. Where a disputing Party asserts as a defense that the measure alleged to be a breach is within the scope of a reservation or exception set out in Annex I, Annex II, Annex III or Annex IV, on request of the disputing Party, the Tribunal shall request the interpretation of the Commission on the issue. The Commission, within 60 days of delivery of the request, shall submit in writing its interpretation to the Tribunal.

2. Further to Article 1131(2), a Commission interpretation submitted under paragraph 1 shall be binding on the Tribunal. If the Commission fails to submit an interpretation within 60 days, the Tribunal shall decide the issue.

Article 1133
Expert Reports

Without prejudice to the appointment of other kinds of experts where authorized by the applicable arbitration rules, a Tribunal, at the request of a disputing party or, unless the disputing parties disapprove, on its own initiative, may appoint one or more experts to report to it in writing on any factual issue concerning environmental, health, safety or other scientific matters raised by a disputing party in a proceeding, subject to such terms and conditions as the disputing parties may agree.

Article 1134
Interim Measures of Protection

A Tribunal may order an interim measure of protection to preserve the rights of a disputing party, or to ensure that the Tribunal's jurisdiction is made fully effective, including an order to preserve evidence in the possession or control of a disputing party or to protect the Tribunal's jurisdiction. A Tribunal may not order attachment or enjoin the application of the measure alleged to constitute a breach referred to in Article 1116 or 1117. For purposes of this paragraph, an order includes a recommendation.

Article 1135
Final Award

1. Where a Tribunal makes a final award against a Party, the Tribunal may award, separately or in combination, only:
   (a) monetary damages and any applicable interest;
   (b) restitution of property, in which case the award shall provide that the disputing Party may pay monetary damages and any applicable interest in lieu of restitution.
   A tribunal may also award costs in accordance with the applicable arbitration rules.
2. Subject to paragraph 1, where a claim is made under Article 1117(1):
   (a) an award of restitution of property shall provide that restitution be made to the enterprise;
   (b) an award of monetary damages and any applicable interest shall provide that the sum be paid to the enterprise; and
   (c) the award shall provide that it is made without prejudice to any right that any person may have in the relief under applicable domestic law.
3. A Tribunal may not order a Party to pay punitive damages.

Article 1136
Finality and Enforcement of an Award

1. An award made by a Tribunal shall have no binding force except between the disputing parties and in respect of the particular case.
2. Subject to paragraph 3 and the applicable review procedure for an interim award, a disputing party shall abide by and comply with an award without delay.
3. A disputing party may not seek enforcement of a final award until:
   (a) in the case of a final award made under the ICSID Convention
      (i) 120 days have elapsed from the date the award was rendered and no disputing party has requested revision or annulment of the award, or
      (ii) revision or annulment proceedings have been completed; and
   (b) in the case of a final award under the ICSID Additional Facility Rules or the UNCITRAL Arbitration Rules
      (i) three months have elapsed from the date the award was rendered and no disputing party has commenced a proceeding to revise, set aside or annul the award, or
      (ii) a court has dismissed or allowed an application to revise, set aside or annul the award and there is no further appeal.
4. Each Party shall provide for the enforcement of an award in its territory.
5. If a disputing Party fails to abide by or comply with a final award, the Commission, on delivery of a request by a Party whose investor was a party to the arbitration, shall establish a panel under Article 2008 (Request for an Arbitral Panel). The requesting Party may seek in such proceedings:
   (a) a determination that the failure to abide by or comply with the final award is inconsistent with the obligations of this Agreement; and
   (b) a recommendation that the Party abide by or comply with the final award.
6. A disputing investor may seek enforcement of an arbitration award under the ICSID Convention, the New York Convention or the InterAmerican Convention regardless of whether proceedings have been taken under paragraph 5.
7. A claim that is submitted to arbitration under this Section shall be considered to arise out of a commercial relationship or transaction for purposes of Article I of the New York Convention and Article I of the InterAmerican Convention.

Article 1137
General

Time when a Claim is Submitted to Arbitration

1. A claim is submitted to arbitration under this Section when:
   (a) the request for arbitration under paragraph (1) of Article 36 of the ICSID Convention has been received by the Secretary-General;
   (b) the notice of arbitration under Article 2 of Schedule C of the ICSID Additional Facility Rules has been received by the Secretary-General; or
   (c) the notice of arbitration given under the UNCITRAL Arbitration Rules is received by the disputing Party.

Service of Documents

2. Delivery of notice and other documents on a Party shall be made to the place named for that Party in Annex 1137.2.

Receipts under Insurance or Guarantee Contracts

3. In an arbitration under this Section, a Party shall not assert, as a defense, counterclaim, right of setoff or otherwise, that the disputing investor has received or will receive, pursuant to an insurance or guarantee contract, indemnification or other compensation for all or part of its alleged damages.

Publication of an Award

4. Annex 1137.4 applies to the Parties specified in that Annex with respect to publication of an award.

Article 1138
Exclusions

1. Without prejudice to the applicability or non-applicability of the dispute settlement provisions of this Section or of Chapter Twenty (Institutional Arrangements and Dispute Settlement Procedures) to other actions taken by a Party pursuant to Article 2102 (National Security), a decision by a Party to prohibit or restrict the acquisition of an investment in its territory by an investor of another Party, or its investment, pursuant to that Article shall not be subject to such provisions.

2. The dispute settlement provisions of this Section and of Chapter Twenty shall not apply to the matters referred to in Annex 1138.2.

Section C Definitions

Article 1139
Definitions

For purposes of this Chapter:

'disputing investor' means an investor that makes a claim under Section B;

'disputing parties' means the disputing investor and the disputing Party;

'disputing party' means the disputing investor or the disputing Party;

'disputing Party' means a Party against which a claim is made under Section B;

'enterprise' means an 'enterprise' as defined in Article 201 (Definitions of General Application), and a branch of an enterprise;

'enterprise of a Party' means an enterprise constituted or organized under the law of a Party, and a branch located in the territory of a Party and carrying out business activities there.

'equity or debt securities' includes voting and non-voting shares, bonds, convertible debentures, stock options and warrants;

'G7 Currency' means the currency of Canada, France, Germany, Italy, Japan, the United Kingdom of Great Britain and Northern Ireland or the United States;

'ICSID' means the International Centre for Settlement of Investment Disputes;

'ICSID Convention' means the *Convention on the Settlement of Investment Disputes between States and Nationals of other States*, done at Washington, March 18, 1965;

'InterAmerican Convention' means the *InterAmerican Convention on International Commercial Arbitration*, done at Panama, January 30, 1975;

'investment' means:
  (a) an enterprise;
  (b) an equity security of an enterprise;
  (c) a debt security of an enterprise
      (i)   where the enterprise is an affiliate of the investor, or
      (ii) where the original maturity of the debt security is at least three years,
          but does not include a debt security, regardless of original maturity, of a state enterprise;
  (d) a loan to an enterprise
      (i)   where the enterprise is an affiliate of the investor, or
      (ii) where the original maturity of the loan is at least three years,
          but does not include a loan, regardless of original maturity, to a state enterprise;
  (e) an interest in an enterprise that entitles the owner to share in income or profits of the enterprise;
  (f) an interest in an enterprise that entitles the owner to share in the assets of that enterprise on dissolution, other than a debt security or a loan excluded from subparagraph (c) or (d);
  (g) real estate or other property, tangible or intangible, acquired in the expectation or used for the purpose of economic benefit or other business purposes; and
  (h) interests arising from the commitment of capital or other resources in the territory of a Party to economic activity in such territory, such as under
      (i)   contracts involving the presence of an investor's property in the territory of the Party, including turnkey or construction contracts, or concessions, or
      (ii) contracts where remuneration depends substantially on the production, revenues or profits of an enterprise;
  but investment does not mean,
  (i) claims to money that arise solely from
      (i)   commercial contracts for the sale of goods or services by a national or enterprise in the territory of a Party to an enterprise in the territory of another Party, or
      (ii) the extension of credit in connection with a commercial transaction, such as trade financing, other than a loan covered by subparagraph (d); or
  (j) any other claims to money,
  that do not involve the kinds of interests set out in subparagraphs (a) through (h);

'investment of an investor of a Party' means an investment owned or controlled directly or indirectly by an investor of such Party;

'investor of a Party' means a Party or state enterprise thereof, or a national or an enterprise of such Party, that seeks to make, is making or has made an investment;

'investor of a non-Party' means an investor other than an investor of a Party, that seeks to make, is making or has made an investment;

'New York Convention' means the *United Nations Convention on the Recognition and Enforcement of Foreign Arbitral Awards*, done at New York, June 10, 1958;

'Secretary-General' means the Secretary-General of ICSID;

'transfers' means transfers and international payments;

'Tribunal' means an arbitration tribunal established under Article 1120 or 1126; and

'UNCITRAL Arbitration Rules' means the arbitration rules of the United Nations Commission on International Trade Law, approved by the United Nations General Assembly on December 15, 1976.

Annex 1120.1

Submission of a Claim to Arbitration

Mexico

With respect to the submission of a claim to arbitration:

(a) an investor of another Party may not allege that Mexico has breached an obligation under:
    (i) Section A or Article 1503(2) (State Enterprises), or
    (ii) Article 1502(3)(a) (Monopolies and State Enterprises) where the monopoly has acted in a manner inconsistent with the Party's obligations under Section A,

    both in an arbitration under this Section and in proceedings before a Mexican court or administrative tribunal; and

(b) where an enterprise of Mexico that is a juridical person that an investor of another Party owns or controls directly or indirectly alleges in proceedings before a Mexican court or administrative tribunal that Mexico has breached an obligation under:
    (i) Section A or Article 1503(2) (State Enterprises), or
    (ii) Article 1502(3)(a) (Monopolies and State Enterprises) where the monopoly has acted in a manner inconsistent with the Party's obligations under Section A,

    the investor may not allege the breach in an arbitration under this Section.

Annex 1137.2

Service of Documents on a Party Under Section B

Each Party shall set out in this Annex and publish in its official journal by January 1, 1994, the place for delivery of notice and other documents under this Section.

Annex 1137.4

Publication of an Award

Canada

Where Canada is the disputing Party, either Canada or a disputing investor that is a party to the arbitration may make an award public.

Mexico

Where Mexico is the disputing Party, the applicable arbitration rules apply to the publication of an award.

United States

Where the United States is the disputing Party, either the United States or a disputing investor that is a party to the arbitration may make an award public.

Annex 1138.2

Exclusions from Dispute Settlement

Canada

A decision by Canada following a review under the *Investment Canada Act*, with respect to whether or not to permit an acquisition that is subject to review, shall not be subject to the dispute settlement provisions of Section B or of Chapter Twenty (Institutional Arrangements and Dispute Settlement Procedures).

Mexico

A decision by the National Commission on Foreign Investment ('Comisión Nacional de Inversiones Extranjeras') following a review pursuant to Annex I, page IM4, with respect to whether or not to permit an acquisition that is subject to review, shall not be subject to the dispute settlement provisions of Section B or of Chapter Twenty (Institutional Arrangements and Dispute Settlement Procedures).

APPENDIX 2

Energy Charter Treaty (Part III: Investment Promotion and Protection, Articles 10–17)

PART III

INVESTMENT PROMOTION AND PROTECTION

Article 10

Promotion, Protection and Treatment of Investments

(1) Each Contracting Party shall, in accordance with the provisions of this Treaty, encourage and create stable, equitable, favourable and transparent conditions for Investors of other Contracting Parties to make Investments in its Area. Such conditions shall include a commitment to accord at all times to Investments of Investors of other Contracting Parties fair and equitable treatment.

Such Investments shall also enjoy the most constant protection and security and no Contracting Party shall in any way impair by unreasonable or discriminatory measures their management, maintenance, use, enjoyment or disposal. In no case shall such Investments be accorded treatment less favourable than that required by international law, including treaty obligations.

Each Contracting Party shall observe any obligations it has entered into with an Investor or an Investment of an Investor of any other Contracting Party.

(2) Each Contracting Party shall endeavour to accord to Investors of other Contracting Parties, as regards the Making of Investments in its Area, the Treatment described in paragraph(3).

(3) For the purposes of this Article, 'Treatment' means treatment accorded by a Contracting Party which is no less favourable than that which it accords to its own Investors or to Investors of any other Contracting Party or any third state, whichever is the most favourable.

(4) A supplementary treaty shall, subject to conditions to be laid down therein, oblige each party thereto to accord to Investors of other parties, as regards the Making of Investments in its Area, the Treatment described in paragraph (3). That treaty shall be open for signature by the states and Regional Economic Integration Organizations which have signed or acceded to this Treaty.

Negotiations towards the supplementary treaty shall commence not later than 1 January 1995, with a view to concluding it by 1 January 1998.

(5) Each Contracting Party shall, as regards the Making of Investments in its Area, endeavour to:

    (a) limit to the minimum the exceptions to the Treatment described in paragraph (3);

    (b) progressively remove existing restrictions affecting Investors of other Contracting Parties.

(6) (a) A Contracting Party may, as regards the Making of Investments in its Area, at any time declare voluntarily to the Charter Conference, through the Secretariat, its intention not to introduce new exceptions to the Treatment described in paragraph (3).

    (b) A Contracting Party may, furthermore, at any time make a voluntary commitment to accord to Investors of other Contracting Parties, as regards the Making of Investments in some or all Economic Activities in the Energy Sector in its Area, the Treatment described in paragraph (3).

      Such commitments shall be notified to the Secretariat and listed in Annex VC and shall be binding under this Treaty.

(7) Each Contracting Party shall accord to Investments in its Area of Investors of other Contracting Parties, and their related activities including management, maintenance, use, enjoyment or disposal, treatment no less favourable than that which it accords to Investments of its own Investors or of the Investors of any other Contracting Party or any third state and their related activities including management, maintenance, use, enjoyment or disposal, whichever is the most favourable.

(8) The modalities of application of paragraph (7) in relation to programmes under which a Contracting Party provides grants or other financial assistance, or enters into contracts, for energy technology research and development, shall be reserved for the supplementary treaty described in paragraph (4). Each Contracting Party shall through the Secretariat keep the Charter Conference informed of the modalities it applies to the programmes described in this paragraph.

(9) Each state or Regional Economic Integration Organization which signs or accedes to this Treaty shall, on the date it signs the Treaty or deposits its instrument of accession, submit to the Secretariat a report summarizing all laws, regulations or other measures relevant to:
   (a) exceptions to paragraph (2); or
   (b) the programmes referred to in paragraph (8).
   A Contracting Party shall keep its report up to date by promptly submitting amendments to the Secretariat. The Charter Conference shall review these reports periodically.
   In respect of subparagraph (a) the report may designate parts of the energy sector in which a Contracting Party accords to Investors of other Contracting Parties the Treatment described in paragraph (3).
   In respect of subparagraph (b) the review by the Charter Conference may consider the effects of such programmes on competition and Investments.

(10) Notwithstanding any other provision of this Article, the treatment described in paragraphs (3) and (7) shall not apply to the protection of Intellectual Property; instead, the treatment shall be as specified in the corresponding provisions of the applicable international agreements for the protection of Intellectual Property rights to which the respective Contracting Parties are parties.

(11) For the purposes of Article 26, the application by a Contracting Party of a trade-related investment measure as described in Article 5(1) and (2) to an Investment of an Investor of another Contracting Party existing at the time of such application shall, subject to Article 5(3) and (4), be considered a breach of an obligation of the former Contracting Party under this Part.

(12) Each Contracting Party shall ensure that its domestic law provides effective means for the assertion of claims and the enforcement of rights with respect to Investments, investment agreements, and investment authorizations.

Article 11
Key Personnel

(1) A Contracting Party shall, subject to its laws and regulations relating to the entry, stay and work of natural persons, examine in good faith requests by Investors of another Contracting Party, and key personnel who are employed by such Investors or by Investments of such Investors, to enter and remain temporarily in its Area to engage in activities connected with the making or the development, management, maintenance, use, enjoyment or disposal of relevant Investments, including the provision of advice or key technical services.

(2) A Contracting Party shall permit Investors of another Contracting Party which have Investments in its Area, and Investments of such Investors, to employ any key person of the Investor's or the Investment's choice regardless of nationality and citizenship provided that such key person has been permitted to enter, stay and work in the Area of the former Contracting Party and that the employment concerned conforms to the terms, conditions and time limits of the permission granted to such key person.

Article 12
Compensation for Losses

(1) Except where Article 13 applies, an Investor of any Contracting Party which suffers a loss with respect to any Investment in the Area of another Contracting Party owing to war or other armed conflict, state of national emergency, civil disturbance, or other similar event in that Area, shall be accorded by the latter Contracting Party, as regards restitution, indemnification, compensation or other settlement, treatment which is the most favourable of that which that Contracting Party accords to any other Investor, whether its own Investor, the Investor of any other Contracting Party, or the Investor of any third state.

(2) Without prejudice to paragraph (1), an Investor of a Contracting Party which, in any of the situations referred to in that paragraph, suffers a loss in the Area of another Contracting Party resulting from

    (a) requisitioning of its Investment or part thereof by the latter's forces or authorities; or

    (b) destruction of its Investment or part thereof by the latter's forces or authorities, which was not required by the necessity of the situation, shall be accorded restitution or compensation which in either case shall be prompt, adequate and effective.

Article 13
Expropriation

(1) Investments of Investors of a Contracting Party in the Area of any other Contracting Party shall not be nationalized, expropriated or subjected to a measure or measures having effect equivalent to nationalization or expropriation (hereinafter referred to as 'Expropriation') except where such Expropriation is:

    (a) for a purpose which is in the public interest;

    (b) not discriminatory;

    (c) carried out under due process of law; and

    (d) accompanied by the payment of prompt, adequate and effective compensation.

Such compensation shall amount to the fair market value of the Investment expropriated at the time immediately before the Expropriation or impending Expropriation became known in such a way as to affect the value of the Investment (hereinafter referred to as the 'Valuation Date').

Such fair market value shall at the request of the Investor be expressed in a Freely Convertible Currency on the basis of the market rate of exchange existing for that currency on the Valuation Date. Compensation shall also include interest at a commercial rate established on a market basis from the date of Expropriation until the date of payment.

(2) The Investor affected shall have a right to prompt review, under the law of the Contracting Party making the Expropriation, by a judicial or other competent and independent authority of that Contracting Party, of its case, of the valuation of its Investment, and of the payment of compensation, in accordance with the principles set out in paragraph (1).

(3) For the avoidance of doubt, Expropriation shall include situations where a Contracting Party expropriates the assets of a company or enterprise in its Area in which an Investor of any other Contracting Party has an Investment, including through the ownership of shares.

Article 14
Transfers Related to Investments

(1) Each Contracting Party shall with respect to Investments in its Area of Investors of any other Contracting Party guarantee the freedom of transfer into and out of its Area, including the transfer of:

    (a) The initial capital plus any additional capital for the maintenance and development of an Investment;

    (b) Returns;

(c) Payments under a contract, including amortization of principal and accrued interest payments pursuant to a loan agreement;

(d) Unspent earnings and other remuneration of personnel engaged from abroad in connection with that Investment;

(e) Proceeds from the sale or liquidation of all or any part of an Investment;

(f) Payments arising out of the settlement of a dispute;

(g) Payments of compensation pursuant to Articles 12 and 13.

(2) Transfers under paragraph (1) shall be effected without delay and (except in case of a Return in kind) in a Freely Convertible Currency.

(3) Transfers shall be made at the market rate of exchange existing on the date of transfer with respect to spot transactions in the currency to be transferred. In the absence of a market for foreign exchange, the rate to be used will be the most recent rate applied to inward investments or the most recent exchange rate for conversion of currencies into Special Drawing Rights, whichever is more favourable to the Investor.

(4) Notwithstanding paragraphs (1) to (3), a Contracting Party may protect the rights of creditors, or ensure compliance with laws on the issuing, trading and dealing in securities and the satisfaction of judgements in civil, administrative and criminal adjudicatory proceedings, through the equitable, non-discriminatory, and good faith application of its laws and regulations.

(5) Notwithstanding paragraph (2), Contracting Parties which are states that were constituent parts of the former Union of Soviet Socialist Republics may provide in agreements concluded between them that transfers of payments shall be made in the currencies of such Contracting Parties, provided that such agreements do not treat Investments in their Areas of Investors of other Contracting Parties less favourably than either Investments of Investors of the Contracting Parties which have entered into such agreements or Investments of Investors of any third state.

(6) Notwithstanding subparagraph (1)(b), a Contracting Party may restrict the transfer of a Return in kind in circumstances where the Contracting Party is permitted under Article 29(2)(a) or the GATT and Related Instruments to restrict or prohibit the exportation or the sale for export of the product constituting the Return in kind; provided that a Contracting Party shall permit transfers of Returns in kind to be effected as authorized or specified in an investment agreement, investment authorization, or other written agreement between the Contracting Party and either an Investor of another Contracting Party or its Investment.

Article 15

Subrogation

(1) If a Contracting Party or its designated agency (hereinafter referred to as the 'Indemnifying Party') makes a payment under an indemnity or guarantee given in respect of an Investment of an Investor (hereinafter referred to as the 'Party Indemnified') in the Area of another Contracting Party (hereinafter referred to as the 'Host Party'), the Host Party shall recognize:

(a) The assignment to the Indemnifying Party of all the rights and claims in respect of such Investment; and

(b) The right of the Indemnifying Party to exercise all such rights and enforce such claims by virtue of subrogation.

(2) The Indemnifying Party shall be entitled in all circumstances to:

(a) The same treatment in respect of the rights and claims acquired by it by virtue of the assignment referred to in paragraph (1); and

(b) The same payments due pursuant to those rights and claims,

as the Party Indemnified was entitled to receive by virtue of this Treaty in respect of the Investment concerned.

(3) In any proceeding under Article 26, a Contracting Party shall not assert as a defence, counter-claim, right of set-off or for any other reason, that indemnification or other compensation for all or part of the alleged damages has been received or will be received pursuant to an insurance or guarantee contract.

Article 16
Relation to other Agreements

Where two or more Contracting Parties have entered into a prior international agreement, or enter into a subsequent international agreement, whose terms in either case concern the subject matter of Part III or V of this Treaty,

(1) nothing in Part III or V of this Treaty shall be construed to derogate from any provision of such terms of the other agreement or from any right to dispute resolution with respect thereto under that agreement; and

(2) nothing in such terms of the other agreement shall be construed to derogate from any provision of Part III or V of this Treaty or from any right to dispute resolution with respect thereto under this Treaty, where any such provision is more favourable to the Investor or Investment.

Article 17
Non-Application of Part III in Certain Circumstances

Each Contracting Party reserves the right to deny the advantages of this Part to:

(1) a legal entity if citizens or nationals of a third state own or control such entity and if that entity has no substantial business activities in the Area of the Contracting Party in which it is organized; or

(2) an Investment, if the denying Contracting Party establishes that such Investment is an Investment of an Investor of a third state with or as to which the denying Contracting Party:

  (a) does not maintain a diplomatic relationship; or

  (b) adopts or maintains measures that:

    (i) prohibit transactions with Investors of that state; or

    (ii) would be violated or circumvented if the benefits of this Part were accorded to Investors of that state or to their Investments.

APPENDIX 3

ASEAN Agreement for the Promotion and Protection of Investments (15 December 1987)

AGREEMENT AMONG THE GOVERNMENT OF BRUNEI
DARUSSALAM, THE REPUBLIC OF INDONESIA, MALAYSIA,
THE REPUBLIC OF THE PHILIPPINES, THE REPUBLIC OF
SINGAPORE, AND THE KINGDOM OF THAILAND FOR
THE PROMOTION AND PROTECTION OF INVESTMENTS
MANILA, 15 DECEMBER 1987

The Governments of Brunei Darussalam, the Republic of Indonesia, Malaysia, the Republic of the Philippines, the Republic of Singapore, and the Kingdom of Thailand, hereinafter referred to as the Contracting Parties;

CONSIDERING that the Heads of Government of ASEAN agreed *inter alia* on industrial co-operation among the member states of ASEAN in the Declaration of ASEAN Concord signed at Denpansar, Bali on 24 February 1976;

FURTHER CONSIDERING that the Heads of Government of ASEAN in their Meeting in Kuala Lumpur on 4 to 5 August 1977 recognized *inter alia* that the acceleration of industrialization of the region requires the increased flow of technology and investments, and toward the attainment of this common objective, directed that measures be taken to stimulate the flow of technology, knowhow and private investments among the member states and directed, in particular, the study of a regional mechanism, and the formulation of guidelines, which would facilitate such desired flow of technology, knowhow and private investments;

DESIRING that appropriate measures be taken to carry out the foregoing intents and to create favourable conditions for investments by nationals and companies of any ASEAN member state in the territory of the other ASEAN member states and to facilitate the desired flow of private investments therein to increase prosperity in their respective territories;

RECOGNIZING that an agreement on the promotion and protection of such investments will contribute to the furtherance of the above mentioned purposes;

HAVE AGREED AS FOLLOWS:

Article I
Definition

For the purpose of this Agreement:

1. The term 'nationals' shall be as defined in the respective Constitutions and laws of each of the Contracting Parties.
2. The term 'company' of a Contracting Party shall mean a corporation, partnership or other business association, incorporated or constituted under the laws in force in the territory of any Contracting Party wherein the place of effective management is situated.
3. The term 'investment' shall mean every kind of asset and in particular shall include, though not exclusively:
   (a) movable and immovable property and any other proper rights such as mortgages, liens and pledges;

(b) shares, stocks and debentures of companies or interests in the property of such companies;

(c) claims to money or to any performed under contract having a financial value;

(d) intellectual property rights and goodwill;

(e) business concessions conferred by law or under contract, including concessions to search for, cultivate, extract, or exploit natural resources.

4. The term 'earnings' shall mean amounts yielded by an investment, particularly, though not exclusively, profits, interest, capital gains, dividends, royalties or fees.

5. The term 'freely usable currency' shall mean the United States Dollar, Pound Sterling, Deutschmark French Franc, Japanese Yen, or any other currency that is widely used to make payments for international transactions and is widely traded in the principal exchange markets.

6. The term 'host country' shall mean the Contracting Party wherein the investment is made.

Article II
Applicability or Scope

1. This Agreement shall apply only to investments brought into, derived from or directly connected with investments brought into the territory of any Contracting Party by nationals or companies of any other Contracting Party and which are specifically approved in writing and registered by the host country and upon such conditions as it deems fit for the purposes of this Agreement.

2. This Agreement shall not affect the rights and obligations of the Contracting Parties with respect to investments which, under the provisions of paragraph 1 of this Article, do not fall within the scope of the Agreement.

3. This Agreement shall also apply to investments made prior to its entry into force, provided such investments are specifically approved in writing and registered by the host country and upon such conditions as it deems fit for purpose of this Agreement subsequent in its entry into force.

Article III
General Obligations

1. Each Contracting Party shall, in a manner consistent with it national objectives, encourage and create favourable conditions in its territory for investments from the other Contracting Parties. All investments to which this Agreement relates shall, subject to this Agreement, be governed by the laws and regulations of the host country, including rules of registration and valuation of such investments.

2. Investments of nationals or companies of a[1] Party in the territory of other Contracting Parties shall at all times be accorded fair and equitable treatment and shall enjoy full protection and in the territory of the host country.

3. Each Contracting Party shall observe any obligation arising from a particular commitment it may have entered into[2] with regard to a specific investment of nationals or companies of the other Contracting Parties.

Article IV
Treatment

1. Each Contracting Party shall within its territory ensure full protection of the investments made in accordance with its legislation by investors of the other Contracting Parties and shall not impair by unjustified or discriminatory measures the management, maintenance, use, enjoyment, extension, disposition or liquidation of such investments.

2. All investments made by investors of any Contracting Party shall enjoy fair and equitable treatment in the territory of any other Contracting Party. This treatment shall be no less favourable than that granted to investor of the most-favoured-nation.

---

[1] The words 'and obligations' were deleted by the publisher.
[2] The word 'Title' was deleted by the publisher.

3. Investors of any Contracting Party who within the territory of another Contracting Party suffer damages in relation to their investment activities—in connection with their investments, owing to the outbreak of hostilities or a state of national emergency, shall be accorded treatment no less favourable than that accorded to investors of any third country, as regards restitution, compensation or other valuable consideration. Payments made under this provision shall be effectively realizable and freely transferable, subject to Article VII.

4. Any two or more of the Contracting Parties may negotiate to accord national treatment within the framework of this Agreement. Nothing herein shall entitle any other party to claim national treatment under the most-favoured-nation principle.

Article V
Exception

The Provision of this Agreement shall not apply to matters of taxation in the territory of the Contracting Parties. Such matters shall be governed by Avoidance of Double Taxation between Contracting Parties and the domestic laws of each Contracting Party.

Article VI
Expropriation and Compensation

1. Investments of nationals or companies of any Contracting Party shall not be subject to expropriation nationalisation or any measure equivalent thereto (in the article referred to as 'expropriation'), except for public use, or public purpose, or in the public interest, and under due process of law, on a non-discriminatory basis and upon payment of adequate compensation. Such compensation shall amount to the market value of the investments affected, immediately before the measure of dispossession became public knowledge and it shall be freely transferable in freely-usable currencies from the host country. The compensation shall be settled and paid without unreasonable delay. The national or company affected shall have the right, under the law of Contracting Party making the expropriation, to prompt review by a judicial body or some other independent authority of that Contracting Party in accordance with principles set out in this paragraph.

2. Where a Contracting Party expropriates the assets of a company which is incorporated or constituted under the law in force in its territory, and in which nationals or companies of another Contracting Party own shares, it shall apply the provisions of paragraph 1 of this Article so as to ensure the compensation provided for in that Paragraph to such nationals or companies to the extend of their interest in the assets Expropriated.

Article VII
Repatriation of Capital and Earnings

1. Each Contracting Party shall, subject to its laws, rules and regulations, allow without unreasonable delay the free transfer in any freely-usable currency of:
   (a) the capital, net profits, dividends, royalties, technical assistance and technical fees, interests and other income, accruing from any investments of the nationals or companies of the other Contracting Parties;
   (b) the proceeds from the total or partial liquidation of any investments made by nationals or companies of the other Contracting Parties;
   (c) funds in repayment of loans given by nationals or companies of one Contracting Party to the nationals or companies of another Contracting Party which both Contracting Parties have recognized as investments:
   (d) the earnings of nationals of the other Contracting Parties who are employed and allowed to work in connection with an investment in its territory.

2. The exchange rate applicable to such transfer shall be the rate of exchange prevailing at the time of remittance.

3. The Contracting Parties undertake to accord to transfers referred to in paragraph (1) of this Article a treatment no less favourable than that accorded to transfer originating from investments made by nationals or companies of any third State.

Article VIII
Subrogation

If any of the Contracting Parties makes payment to any of its nationals or companies under a guarantee it has granted in respect of an investment made in the territory of another Contracting Party, the latter Contracting Party shall, without prejudice to the rights of the former Contracting Party under Article IX and X, recognize the assignment of any right title or claim of such national or company to the former Contracting Party and the subrogation of the former Contracting Party to any such right, title or claim. This, however, does not necessarily imply a recognition on the part of the latter Contracting Party of the merits of any case or the amount of any claim arising therefrom.

Article IX
Dispute between The Contracting Parties

1. Any dispute between and among the Contracting Parties concerning the interpretation or application of this Agreement shall, as far as possible, be settled amicably between the parties to the dispute. Such settlement shall be reported to the ASEAN Economic Ministers (AEM).
2. If such a dispute cannot thus be settled it shall be submitted to the AEM for resolution.

Article X
Arbitration

1. Any legal dispute arising directly out of an investment between any Contracting Party and a national or company of any of the other Contracting Parties shall, as far as possible, be settled amicably between the parties to the dispute.
2. If such a dispute cannot thus be settled within six months of its being raised, then either party can elect to submit the dispute for conciliation or arbitration and such election shall be binding on the other party. The dispute may be brought before the International Centre for Settlement of Investment Disputes (ICSID), the United Nations Commission on International Trade Law (UNCITRAL), the Regional Centre for Arbitration at Kuala Lumpur or any other regional centre for arbitration in ASEAN, whichever body the parties to the dispute mutually agree to appoint for the purposes of conducting the arbitration.
3. In the event that the parties cannot agree within a period of three months on a suitable body for arbitration, an arbitral tribunal consisting of three members shall be formed. The Parties to the dispute shall appoint one member each, and these two members shall then select a national of a third Contracting Party to be the chairman of the tribunal, subject to the approval of the parties to the dispute. The appointment of the members and the chairman shall be made within two months and three months respectively, from the date a decision to form such an arbitral tribunal is made.
4. If the arbitral tribunal is not formed in the periods specified in paragraph 3 above, then either[3] party to the dispute may, in the absence of any other relevant arrangement request the President of the International Court of Justice to make the required appointments.
5. The arbitral tribunal shall reach its decisions by a majority of votes and its decisions shall be binding, The Parties involved in the dispute shall bear the cost of their respective members to the arbitral tribunal and share equally the cost of the chairman and other relevant costs. In all other respects, the arbitral tribunal shall determine its own procedures.

Article XI
Consultation

The Contracting Parties agree to consult each other at the request of any Party on any matter relating to investments covered by this Agreement, or otherwise affecting the implementation of this Agreement.

---

[3] The word 'earlier' was amended by the publisher to read 'either'.

Article XII
Amendments

All articles of this Agreement may be modified through amendments in writing to this Agreement agreed upon by consensus. All amendments shall become effective upon acceptance by all Contracting Parties.

Article XIII
Entry into Force

1. This Agreement shall enter into force on the 30th day after the deposit of the sixth Instrument of Ratification and shall thereafter remain in force for a period of the years.
2. This Agreement shall thereafter continue in force unless terminated by any Contracting Party giving not less than six months written notice through diplomatic channels. Provided however, that in respect of investments made while the Agreement was in force, its provisions shall continue in effect with respect to such investments for a period of ten years after the date of termination, and without prejudice to the application thereafter of the rules of international law.

Article XIV
Miscellaneous Provisions

1. This Agreement may not be signed with reservation nor shall reservations be admitted at the time of ratification.
2. This Agreement shall be deposited with the Secretary-General of the ASEAN Secretariat who shall promptly furnish a certified copy thereof to each Contracting Party.
3. Each Contracting Party shall deposit its instrument of Ratification with the Secretary-General of the ASEAN Secretariat who shall promptly inform each Contracting Party of such deposit.

IN WITNESS WHEREOF, the undersigned, duly authorized thereto by their respective Governments, have signed this Agreement.

DONE in Manila, Philippines this Fifteenth day of December Nineteen Hundred Eighty Seven in one original copy in the English Language.

For the Government of Brunei Darussalam:
P.G. DATO DR. HJ. ISMAIL PG. HJ. DAMIT
Minister of Development

For the Government of Malaysia:
DATIN PADUKA RAFIDAH AZIZ
Minister of Trade and Industry

For the Government of the Republic of the Philippines:
JOSE S. CONCEPCION, JR.
Secretary of Trade and Industry

For the Government of the Republic of Indonesia:
ALI WARDHANA
Minister Coordinator for Economy, Finance, Industry, and Development Supervision

For the Government of the Republic of Singapore:
RICHARD HU TSU TAO
Minister for Finance

For the Government of the Kingdom of Thailand:
DR. ARUN PANUPONG
Minister Attached to the Prime Minister's Office

Agreement between the Government of the United Kingdom of Great Britain and Northern Ireland and the Government of [Country] for the Promotion and Protection of Investments[1]

Model Text 2005 (amended Nov 06 see Article 7 and 12)

[Draft] Agreement [   ]

Between The Government of The United Kingdom of
Great Britain and Northern Ireland

and

The Government of [   ]

For the Promotion and Protection of Investments

The Government of the United Kingdom of Great Britain and Northern Ireland and the Government of   ;

Desiring to create favourable conditions for greater investment by nationals and companies of one State in the territory of the other State;

Recognising that the encouragement and reciprocal protection under international agreement of such investments will be conducive to the stimulation of individual business initiative and will increase prosperity in both States;

Have agreed as follows:

Article 1
Definitions

For the purposes of this Agreement:

(a) 'investment' means every kind of asset and in particular, though not exclusively, includes:
    (i)   movable and immovable property and any other property rights such as mortgages, liens or pledges;
    (ii) shares in and stock and debentures of a company and any other form of participation in a company;
    (iii) claims to money or to any performance under contract having a financial value;
    (iv) intellectual property rights, goodwill, technical processes and know-how;
    (v) business concessions conferred by law or under contract, including concessions to search for, cultivate, extract or exploit natural resources.

A change in the form in which assets are invested does not affect their character as investments and the term 'investment' includes all investments, whether made before or after the date of entry into force of this Agreement;

---

[1] Reproduced by kind permission of the Foreign and Commonwealth Office. This is an official government document used for internal guidance only. Therefore any use of this document by anyone other than officials representing the Foreign Office would require government approval.

(b) 'returns' means the amounts yielded by an investment and in particular, though not exclusively, includes profit, interest, capital gains, dividends, royalties and fees;

(c) 'nationals' means:

    (i) in respect of the United Kingdom: physical persons deriving their status as United Kingdom nationals from the law in force in the United Kingdom;

    (ii) in respect of   :   ;

(d) 'companies' means:

    (i) in respect of the United Kingdom: corporations, firms and associations incorporated or constituted under the law in force in any part of the United Kingdom or in any territory to which this Agreement is extended in accordance with the provisions of Article 12;

    (ii) in respect of   :   ;

(e) 'territory' means:

    (i) in respect of the United Kingdom: Great Britain and Northern Ireland, including the territorial sea and maritime area situated beyond the territorial sea of the United Kingdom which has been or might in the future be designated under the national law of the United Kingdom in accordance with international law as an area within which the United Kingdom may exercise rights with regard to the sea-bed and subsoil and the natural resources and any territory to which this Agreement is extended in accordance with the provisions of Article 12;

    (ii) in respect of   :   .

Article 2
Promotion and Protection of Investment

(1) Each Contracting Party shall encourage and create favourable conditions for nationals or companies of the other Contracting Party to invest capital in its territory, and, subject to its right to exercise powers conferred by its laws, shall admit such capital.

(2) Investments of nationals or companies of each Contracting Party shall at all times be accorded fair and equitable treatment and shall enjoy full protection and security in the territory of the other Contracting Party. Neither Contracting Party shall in any way impair by unreasonable or discriminatory measures the management, maintenance, use, enjoyment or disposal of investments in its territory of nationals or companies of the other Contracting Party. Each Contracting Party shall observe any obligation it may have entered into with regard to investments of nationals or companies of the other Contracting Party.

Article 3
National Treatment and Most-favoured-nation Provisions

(1) Neither Contracting Party shall in its territory subject investments or returns of nationals or companies of the other Contracting Party to treatment less favourable than that which it accords to investments or returns of its own nationals or companies or to investments or returns of nationals or companies of any third State.

(2) Neither Contracting Party shall in its territory subject nationals or companies of the other Contracting Party, as regards their management, maintenance, use, enjoyment or disposal of their investments, to treatment less favourable than that which it accords to its own nationals or companies or to nationals or companies of any third State.

(3) For the avoidance of doubt it is confirmed that the treatment provided for in paragraphs (1) and (2) above shall apply to the provisions of Articles 1 to 11 of this Agreement.

Article 4
Compensation for Losses

(1) Nationals or companies of one Contracting Party whose investments in the territory of the other Contracting Party suffer losses owing to war or other armed conflict, revolution, a state of national emergency, revolt, insurrection or riot in the territory of the latter Contracting Party

shall be accorded by the latter Contracting Party treatment, as regards restitution, indemnification, compensation or other settlement, no less favourable that that which the latter Contracting Party accords to its own nationals or companies or to nationals or companies of any third State. Resulting payments shall be freely transferable.

(2) Without prejudice to paragraph (1) of this Article, nationals or companies of one Contracting Party who in any of the situations referred to in that paragraph suffer losses in the territory of the other Contracting Party resulting from:

(a) requisitioning of their property by its forces or authorities, or

(b) destruction of their property by its forces or authorities, which was not caused in combat action or was not required by the necessity of the situation,

shall be accorded restitution or adequate compensation. Resulting payments shall be freely transferable.

Article 5
Expropriation

(1) Investments of nationals or companies of either Contracting Party shall not be nationalised, expropriated or subjected to measures having effect equivalent to nationalisation or expropriation (hereinafter referred to as 'expropriation') in the territory of the other Contracting Party except for a public purpose related to the internal needs of that Party on a non-discriminatory basis and against prompt, adequate and effective compensation. Such compensation shall amount to the genuine value of the investment expropriated immediately before the expropriation or before the impending expropriation became public knowledge, whichever is the earlier, shall include interest at a normal commercial rate until the date of payment, shall be made without delay, be effectively realizable and be freely transferable. The national or company affected shall have a right, under the law of the Contracting Party making the expropriation, to prompt review, by a judicial or other independent authority of that Party, of his or its case and of the valuation of his or its investment in accordance with the principles set out in this paragraph.

(2) Where a Contracting Party expropriates the assets of a company which is incorporated or constituted under the law in force in any part of its own territory, and in which nationals or companies of the other Contracting Party own shares, it shall ensure that the provisions of paragraph (1) of this Article are applied to the extent necessary to guarantee prompt, adequate and effective compensation in respect of their investment to such nationals or companies of the other Contracting Party who are owners of those shares.

Article 6
Repatriation of Investment and Returns

Each Contracting Party shall in respect of investments guarantee to nationals or companies of the other Contracting Party the unrestricted transfer of their investments and returns. Transfers shall be effected without delay in the convertible currency in which the capital was originally invested or in any other convertible currency agreed by the investor and the Contracting Party concerned. Unless otherwise agreed by the investor transfers shall be made at the rate of exchange applicable on the date of transfer pursuant to the exchange regulations in force.

Article 7
Exceptions

(1) The provisions of this Agreement relative to the grant of treatment not less favourable than that accorded to the nationals or companies of either Contracting Party or of any third State shall not be construed so as to oblige one Contracting Party to extend to the nationals or companies of the other the benefit of any treatment, preference or privilege resulting from: **Added 23 Oct 06**

(a) *any existing or future customs, economic or monetary union, a common market or a free trade area or similar international agreement to which either of the Contracting Parties is or may become a party, and includes the benefit of any treatment, preference or privilege resulting from obligations arising out of an international agreement or reciprocity arrangement of that customs, economic or monetary union, common market or free trade area; or*

(b) any international agreement or arrangement relating wholly or mainly to taxation or any domestic legislation relating wholly or mainly to taxation;

(c) *Nov 06 any requirements resulting from the United Kingdom's membership of the European Union including measures prohibiting, restricting or limiting the movement of capital to or from any third country.*

(2) Where, in exceptional circumstances, payments and capital movements between the Contracting Parties cause or threaten to cause serious difficulties for the operation of monetary policy or exchange rate policy in either Contracting Party, the Contracting Party concerned may take safeguard measures with regard to capital movements between the Contracting Parties for a period not exceeding six months if such measures are strictly necessary. The Contracting Party adopting the safeguard measures shall inform the other Contracting Party forthwith and present, as soon as possible, a time schedule for their removal.

Replacing

(a) any existing or future customs union or similar international agreement to which either of the Contracting Parties is or may become a party; or

(b) any international agreement or arrangement relating wholly or mainly to taxation or any domestic legislation relating wholly or mainly to taxation.

(c) any requirements of European Community law resulting from the United Kingdom's membership of the European Union prohibiting, restricting or limiting the movement of capital to or from any third country.

[Preferred]

Article 8
Reference to International Centre for Settlement of Investment Disputes

(1) Each Contracting Party hereby consents to submit to the International Centre for the Settlement of Investment Disputes (hereinafter referred to as 'the Centre') for settlement by conciliation or arbitration under the Convention on the Settlement of Investment Disputes between States and Nationals of Other States opened for signature at Washington DC on 18 March 1965 any legal dispute arising between that Contracting Party and a national or company of the other Contracting Party concerning an investment of the latter in the territory of the former.

(2) A company which is incorporated or constituted under the law in force in the territory of one Contracting Party and in which before such a dispute arises the majority of shares are owned by nationals or companies of the other Contracting Party shall in accordance with Article 25(2)(b) of the Convention be treated for the purposes of the Convention as a company of the other Contracting Party.

(3) If any such dispute should arise and agreement cannot be reached within three months between the parties to this dispute through pursuit of local remedies or otherwise, then, if the national or company affected also consents in writing to submit the dispute to the Centre for settlement by conciliation or arbitration under the Convention, either party may institute proceedings by addressing a request to that effect to the Secretary-General of the Centre as provided in Articles 28 and 36 of the Convention. In the event of disagreement as to whether conciliation or arbitration is the more appropriate procedure the national or company affected shall have the right to choose. The Contracting Party which is a party to the dispute shall not raise as an objection at any stage of the proceedings or enforcement of an award the fact that the national or company which is the other party to the dispute has received in pursuance of an insurance contract an indemnity in respect of some or all of his or its losses.

(4) Neither Contracting Party shall pursue through the diplomatic channel any dispute referred to the Centre unless:

    (a) the Secretary-General of the Centre, or a conciliation commission or an arbitral tribunal constituted by it, decides that the dispute is not within the jurisdiction of the Centre; or

    (b) the other Contracting Party shall fail to abide by or to comply with any award rendered by an arbitral tribunal.

[Alternative]

Article 8

Settlement of Disputes between an Investor and a Host State

(1) Disputes between a national or company of one Contracting Party and the other Contracting Party concerning an obligation of the latter under this Agreement in relation to an investment of the former which have not been amicably settled shall, after a period of three months from written notification of a claim, be submitted to international arbitration if the national or company concerned so wishes.

(2) Where the dispute is referred to international arbitration, the national or company and the Contracting Party concerned in the dispute may agree to refer the dispute either to:

    (a) the International Centre for the Settlement of Investment Disputes (having regard to the provisions, where applicable, of the Convention on the Settlement of Investment Disputes between States and Nationals of other States, opened for signature at Washington DC on 18 March 1965 and the Additional Facility for the Administration of Conciliation, Arbitration and Fact-Finding Proceedings); or

    (b) the Court of Arbitration of the International Chamber of Commerce; or

    (c) an international arbitrator or ad hoc arbitration tribunal to be appointed by a special agreement or established under the Arbitration Rules of the United Nations Commission on International Trade Law.

If after a period of three months from written notification of the claim there is no agreement to one of the above alternative procedures, the dispute shall at the request in writing of the national or company concerned be submitted to arbitration under the Arbitration Rules of the United Nations Commission on International Trade Law as then in force. The parties to the dispute may agree in writing to modify these Rules.

Article 9

Disputes between the Contracting Parties

(1) Disputes between the Contracting Parties concerning the interpretation or application of this Agreement should, if possible, be settled through the diplomatic channel.

(2) If a dispute between the Contracting Parties cannot thus be settled, it shall upon the request of either Contracting Party be submitted to an arbitral tribunal.

(3) Such an arbitral tribunal shall be constituted for each individual case in the following way. Within two months of the receipt of the request for arbitration, each Contracting Party shall appoint one member of the tribunal. Those two members shall then select a national of a third State who on approval by the two Contracting Parties shall be appointed Chairman of the tribunal. The Chairman shall be appointed within two months from the date of appointment of the other two members.

(4) If within the periods specified in paragraph (3) of this Article the necessary appointments have not been made, either Contracting Party may, in the absence of any other agreement, invite the President of the International Court of Justice to make any necessary appointments. If the President is a national of either Contracting Party or if he is otherwise prevented from discharging the said function, the Vice-President shall be invited to make the necessary appointments. If the Vice-President is a national of either Contracting Party or if he too is prevented

from discharging the said function, the Member of the International Court of Justice next in seniority who is not a national of either Contracting Party shall be invited to make the necessary appointments.

(5) The arbitral tribunal shall reach its decision by a majority of votes. Such decision shall be binding on both Contracting Parties. Each Contracting Party shall bear the cost of its own member of the tribunal and of its representation in the arbitral proceedings; the cost of the Chairman and the remaining costs shall be borne in equal parts by the Contracting Parties. The tribunal may, however, in its decision direct that a higher proportion of costs shall be borne by one of the two Contracting Parties, and this award shall be binding on both Contracting Parties. The tribunal shall determine its own procedure.

Article 10
Subrogation

(1) If one Contracting Party or its designated Agency ('the first Contracting Party') makes a payment under an indemnity given in respect of an investment in the territory of the other Contracting Party ('the second Contracting Party'), the second Contracting Party shall recognise:
  (a) the assignment to the first Contracting Party by law or by legal transaction of all the rights and claims of the party indemnified; and
  (b) that the first Contracting Party is entitled to exercise such rights and enforce such claims by virtue of subrogation, to the same extent as the party indemnified.
(2) The first Contracting Party shall be entitled in all circumstances to the same treatment in respect of:
  (a) the rights and claims acquired by it by virtue of the assignment, and
  (b) any payments received in pursuance of those rights and claims,
  as the party indemnified was entitled to receive by virtue of this Agreement in respect of the investment concerned and its related returns.
(3) Any payments received in non-convertible currency by the first Contracting Party in pursuance of the rights and claims acquired shall be freely available to the first Contracting Party for the purpose of meeting any expenditure incurred in the territory of the second Contracting Party.

Article 11
Application of other Rules

If the provisions of law of either Contracting Party or obligations under international law existing at present or established hereafter between the Contracting Parties in addition to the present Agreement contain rules, whether general or specific, entitling investments by nationals or companies of the other Contracting Party to a treatment more favourable than is provided for by the present Agreement, such rules shall to the extent that they are more favourable prevail over the present Agreement.

Article 12 (added Oct 06 from Libyan IPPA)
Scope of Application

This Agreement shall apply to all investments, whether made before or after its entry into force, but shall not apply to any dispute concerning an investment which arose, or any claim concerning an investment which was settled, before its entry into force.

Article 12
Territorial Extension

At the time of [signature] [entry into force] [ratification] of this Agreement, or at any time thereafter, the provisions of this Agreement may be extended to such territories for whose international relations the Government of the United Kingdom are responsible as may be agreed between the Contracting Parties in an Exchange of Notes.

Article 13
Entry into Force

[This Agreement shall enter into force on the day of signature.]

or

[Each Contracting Party shall notify the other in writing of the completion of the constitutional formalities required in its territory for the entry into force of this Agreement. This Agreement shall enter into force on the date of the latter of the two notifications.]

or

[The Agreement shall be ratified and shall enter into force on the exchange of Instruments of Ratification.]

Article 14
Duration and Termination

This Agreement shall remain in force for a period of ten years. Thereafter it shall continue in force until the expiration of twelve months from the date on which either Contracting Party shall have given written notice of termination to the other. Provided that in respect of investments made whilst the Agreement is in force, its provisions shall continue in effect with respect to such investments for a period of twenty years after the date of termination and without prejudice to the application thereafter of the rules of general international law.

In witness whereof the undersigned, duly authorised thereto by their respective Governments, have signed this Agreement.

Done in duplicate at . . . . this . . . . day of . . . . 200_ [in the English and . . . . languages, both texts being equally authoritative].

For the Government of   For the Government of

the United Kingdom of

Great Britain and

Northern Ireland: :

Treaty between the Government of the United States of America and the Government of [Country] Concerning the Encouragement and Reciprocal Protection of Investment (1994)

The Government of the United States of America and the Government of [Country] (hereinafter the 'Parties');

Desiring to promote greater economic cooperation between them, with respect to investment by nationals and companies of one Party in the territory of the other Party;

Recognizing that agreement upon the treatment to be accorded such investment will stimulate the flow of private capital and the economic development of the Parties;

Agreeing that a stable framework for investment will maximize effective utilization of economic resources and improve living standards;

Recognizing that the development of economic and business ties can promote respect for internationally recognized worker rights;

Agreeing that these objectives can be achieved without relaxing health, safety and environmental measures of general application; and

Having resolved to conclude a Treaty concerning the encouragement and reciprocal protection of investment;

Have agreed as follows:

Article I

For the purposes of this Treaty,
  (a) 'company' means any entity constituted or organized under applicable law, whether or not for profit, and whether privately or governmentally owned or controlled, and includes a corporation, trust, partnership, sole proprietorship, branch, joint venture, association, or other organization;
  (b) 'company of a Party' means a company constituted or organized under the laws of that Party;
  (c) 'national' of a Party means a natural person who is a national of that Party under its applicable law;
  (d) 'investment' of a national or company means every kind of investment owned or controlled directly or indirectly by that national or company, and includes investment consisting or taking the form of:
    (i)   a company;
    (ii) shares, stock, and other forms of equity participation, and bonds, debentures, and other forms of debt interests, in a company;
    (iii) contractual rights, such as under turnkey, construction or management contracts, production or revenue-sharing contracts, concessions, or other similar contracts;
    (iv) tangible property, including real property; and intangible property, including rights, such as leases, mortgages, liens and pledges;

    (v) intellectual property, including:
        copyrights and related rights,
        patents,
        rights in plant varieties,
        industrial designs,
        rights in semiconductor layout designs,
        trade secrets, including know-how and confidential business information,
        trade and service marks, and
        trade names; and
    (vi) rights conferred pursuant to law, such as licenses and permits;

(e) 'covered investment' means an investment of a national or company of a Party in the territory of the other Party;

(f) 'state enterprise' means a company owned, or controlled through ownership interests, by a Party;

(g) 'investment authorization' means an authorization granted by the foreign investment authority of a Party to a covered investment or a national or company of the other Party;

(h) 'investment agreement' means a written agreement between the national authorities of a Party and a covered investment or a national or company of the other Party that (i) grants rights with respect to natural resources or other assets controlled by the national authorities and (ii) the investment, national or company relies upon in establishing or acquiring a covered investment.

(i) 'ICSID Convention' means the Convention on the Settlement of Investment Disputes between States and Nationals of Other States, done at Washington, March 18, 1965;

(j) 'Centre' means the International Centre for Settlement of Investment Disputes Established by the ICSID Convention; and

(k) 'UNCITRAL Arbitration Rules' means the arbitration rules of the United Nations Commission on International Trade Law.

Article II

1. With respect to the establishment, acquisition, expansion, management, conduct, operation and sale or other disposition of covered investments, each Party shall accord treatment no less favorable than that it accords, in like situations, to investments in its territory of its own nationals or companies (hereinafter 'national treatment') or to investments in its territory of nationals or companies of a third country (hereinafter 'most favored nation treatment'), whichever is most favorable (hereinafter 'national and most favored nation treatment'). Each Party shall ensure that its state enterprises, in the provision of their goods or services, accord national and most favored nation treatment to covered investments.

2. (a) A Party may adopt or maintain exceptions to the obligations of paragraph 1 in the sectors or with respect to the matters specified in the Annex to this Treaty. In adopting such an exception, a Party may not require the divestment, in whole or in part, of covered investments existing at the time the exception becomes effective.

    (b) The obligations of paragraph 1 do not apply to procedures provided in multilateral agreements concluded under the auspices of the World Intellectual Property Organization relating to the acquisition or maintenance of intellectual property rights.

3. (a) Each Party shall at all times accord to covered investments fair and equitable treatment and full protection and security, and shall in no case accord treatment less favorable than that required by international law.

    (b) Neither Party shall in any way impair by unreasonable and discriminatory measures the management, conduct, operation, and sale or other disposition of covered investments.

4. Each Party shall provide effective means of asserting claims and enforcing rights with respect to covered investments.

5. Each Party shall ensure that its laws, regulations, administrative practices and procedures of general application, and adjudicatory decisions, that pertain to or affect covered investments are promptly published or otherwise made publicly available.

Article III

1. Neither Party shall expropriate or nationalize a covered investment either directly or indirectly through measures tantamount to expropriation or nationalization ('expropriation') except for a public purpose; in a non-discriminatory manner; upon payment of prompt, adequate and effective compensation; and in accordance with due process of law and the general principles of treatment provided for in Article II(3).
2. Compensation shall be paid without delay; be equivalent to the fair market value of the expropriated investment immediately before the expropriatory action was taken ('the date of expropriation'); and be fully realizable and freely transferable. The fair market value shall not reflect any change in value occurring because the expropriatory action had become known before the date of expropriation.
3. If the fair market value is denominated in a freely usable currency, the compensation paid shall be no less than the fair market value on the date of expropriation, plus interest at a commercially reasonable rate for that currency, accrued from the date of expropriation until the date of payment.
4. If the fair market value is denominated in a currency that is not freely usable, the compensation paid—converted into the currency of payment at the market rate of exchange prevailing on the date of payment—shall be no less than:
    (a) the fair market value on the date of expropriation, converted into a freely usable currency at the market rate of exchange prevailing on that date, plus
    (b) interest, at a commercially reasonable rate for that freely usable currency, accrued from the date of expropriation until the date of payment.

Article IV

1. Each Party shall accord national and most favored nation treatment to covered investments as regards any measure relating to losses that investments suffer in its territory owing to war or other armed conflict, revolution, state of national emergency, insurrection, civil disturbance, or similar events.
2. Each Party shall accord restitution, or pay compensation in accordance with paragraphs 2 through 4 of Article III, in the event that covered investments suffer losses in its territory, owing to war or other armed conflict, revolution, state of national emergency, insurrection, civil disturbance, or similar events, that result from:
    (a) requisitioning of all or part of such investments by the Party's forces or authorities, or
    (b) destruction of all or part of such investments by the Party's forces or authorities that was not required by the necessity of the situation.

Article V

1. Each Party shall permit all transfers relating to a covered investment to be made freely and without delay into and out of its territory. Such transfers include:
    (a) contributions to capital;
    (b) profits, dividends, capital gains, and proceeds from the sale of all or any part of the investment or from the partial or complete liquidation of the investment;
    (c) interest, royalty payments, management fees, and technical assistance and other fees;
    (d) payments made under a contract, including a loan agreement; and
    (e) compensation pursuant to Articles III and IV, and payments arising out of an investment dispute.
2. Each Party shall permit transfers to be made in a freely usable currency at the market rate of exchange prevailing on the date of transfer.
3. Each Party shall permit returns in kind to be made as authorized or specified in an investment authorization, investment agreement, or other written agreement between the Party and a covered investment or a national or company of the other Party.

4. Notwithstanding paragraphs 1 through 3, a Party may prevent a transfer through the equitable, non-discriminatory and good faith application of its laws relating to:
   (a) bankruptcy, insolvency or the protection of the rights of creditors;
   (b) issuing, trading or dealing in securities;
   (c) criminal or penal offenses; or
   (d) ensuring compliance with orders or judgments in adjudicatory proceedings.

Article VI

Neither Party shall mandate or enforce, as a condition for the establishment, acquisition, expansion, management, conduct or operation of a covered investment, any requirement (including any commitment or undertaking in connection with the receipt of a governmental permission or authorization):
   (a) to achieve a particular level or percentage of local content, or to purchase, use or otherwise give a preference to products or services of domestic origin or from any domestic source;
   (b) to limit imports by the investment of products or services in relation to a particular volume or value of production, exports or foreign exchange earnings;
   (c) to export a particular type, level or percentage of products or services, either generally or to a specific market region;
   (d) to limit sales by the investment of products or services in the Party's territory in relation to a particular volume or value of production, exports or foreign exchange earnings;
   (e) to transfer technology, a production process or other proprietary knowledge to a national or company in the Party's territory, except pursuant to an order, commitment or undertaking that is enforced by a court, administrative tribunal or competition authority to remedy an alleged or adjudicated violation of competition laws; or
   (f) to carry out a particular type, level or percentage of research and development in the Party's territory.
Such requirements do not include conditions for the receipt or continued receipt of an advantage.

Article VII

1. (a) Subject to its laws relating to the entry and sojourn of aliens, each Party shall permit to enter and to remain in its territory nationals of the other Party for the purpose of establishing, developing, administering or advising on the operation of an investment to which they, or a company of the other Party that employs them, have committed or are in the process of committing a substantial amount of capital or other resources.
   (b) Neither Party shall, in granting entry under paragraph 1(a), require a labor certification test or other procedures of similar effect, or apply any numerical restriction.
2. Each Party shall permit covered investments to engage top managerial personnel of their choice, regardless of nationality.

Article VIII

The Parties agree to consult promptly, on the request of either, to resolve any disputes in connection with the Treaty, or to discuss any matter relating to the interpretation or application of the Treaty or to the realization of the objectives of the Treaty.

Article IX

1. For purposes of this Treaty, an investment dispute is a dispute between a Party and a national or company of the other Party arising out of or relating to an investment authorization, an investment agreement or an alleged breach of any right conferred, created or recognized by this Treaty with respect to a covered investment.
2. A national or company that is a party to an investment dispute may submit the dispute for resolution under one of the following alternatives:
   (a) to the courts or administrative tribunals of the Party that is a party to the dispute; or
   (b) in accordance with any applicable, previously agreed dispute-settlement procedures; or
   (c) in accordance with the terms of paragraph 3.

3. (a) Provided that the national or company concerned has not submitted the dispute for resolution under paragraph 2(a) or (b), and that three months have elapsed from the date on which the dispute arose, the national or company concerned may submit the dispute for settlement by binding arbitration:

    (i) to the Centre, if the Centre is available; or

    (ii) to the Additional Facility of the Centre, if the Centre is not available; or

    (iii) in accordance with the UNCITRAL Arbitration Rules; or

    (iv) if agreed by both parties to the dispute, to any other arbitration institution or in accordance with any other arbitration rules.

  (b) a national or company, notwithstanding that it may have submitted a dispute to binding arbitration under paragraph 3(a), may seek interim injunctive relief, not involving the payment of damages, before the judicial or administrative tribunals of the Party that is a party to the dispute, prior to the institution of the arbitral proceeding or during the proceeding, for the preservation of its rights and interests.

4. Each Party hereby consents to the submission of any investment dispute for settlement by binding arbitration in accordance with the choice of the national or company under paragraph 3(a)(i), (ii), and (iii) or the mutual agreement of both parties to the dispute under paragraph 3(a)(iv). This consent and the submission of the dispute by a national or company under paragraph 3(a) shall satisfy the requirement of:

  (a) Chapter II of the ICSID Convention (Jurisdiction of the Centre) and the Additional Facility Rules for written consent of the parties to the dispute; and

  (b) Article II of the United Nations Convention on the Recognition and Enforcement of Foreign Arbitral Awards, done at New York, June 10, 1958, for an 'agreement in writing'.

5. Any arbitration under paragraph 3(a)(ii), (iii) or (iv) shall be held in a state that is a party to the United Nations Convention on the Recognition and Enforcement of Foreign Arbitral Awards, done at New York, June 10,1958.

6. Any arbitral award rendered pursuant to this Article shall be final and binding on the parties to the dispute. Each Party shall carry out without delay the provisions of any such award and provide in its territory for the enforcement of such award.

7. In any proceeding involving an investment dispute, a Party shall not assert, as a defense, counterclaim, right of set-off or for any other reason, that indemnification or other compensation for all or part of the alleged damages has been received or will be received pursuant to an insurance or guarantee contract.

8. For purposes of Article 25(2)(b) of the ICSID Convention and this Article, a company of a Party that, immediately before the occurrence of the event or events giving rise to an investment dispute, was a covered investment, shall be treated as a company of the other Party.

Article X

1. Any dispute between the Parties concerning the interpretation or application of the Treaty, that is not resolved through consultations or other diplomatic channels, shall be submitted upon the request of either Party to an arbitral tribunal for binding decision in accordance with the applicable rules of international law. In the absence of an agreement by the Parties to the contrary, the UNCITRAL Arbitration Rules shall govern, except to the extent these rules are (a) modified by the Parties or (b) modified by the arbitrators unless either Party objects to the proposed modification.

2. Within two months of receipt of a request, each Party shall appoint an arbitrator. The two arbitrators shall select a third arbitrator as chairman, who shall be a national of a third state. The UNCITRAL Arbitration Rules applicable to appointing members of three-member panels shall apply *mutatis mutandis* to the appointment of the arbitral panel except that the appointing authority referenced in those rules shall be the Secretary General of the Centre.

3. Unless otherwise agreed, all submissions shall be made and all hearings shall be completed within six months of the date of selection of the third arbitrator, and the arbitral panel shall render its

decisions within two months of the date of the final submissions or the date of the closing of the hearings, whichever is later.
4. Expenses incurred by the Chairman and other arbitrators, and other costs of the proceedings, shall be paid for equally by the Parties. However, the arbitral panel may, at its discretion, direct that a higher proportion of the costs be paid by one of the Parties.

Article XI

This Treaty shall not derogate from any of the following that entitle covered investments to treatment more favorable than that accorded by this Treaty:
   (a) laws and regulations, administrative practices or procedures, or administrative or adjudicatory decisions of a Party;
   (b) international legal obligations; or
   (c) obligations assumed by a Party, including those contained in an investment authorization or an investment agreement.

Article XII

Each Party reserves the right to deny to a company of the other Party the benefits of this Treaty if nationals of a third country own or control the company and
   (a) the denying Party does not maintain normal economic relations with the third country; or
   (b) the company has no substantial business activities in the territory of the Party under whose laws it is constituted or organized.

Article XIII

1. No provision of this Treaty shall impose obligations with respect to tax matters, except that:
   (a) Articles III, IX and X will apply with respect to expropriation; and
   (b) Article IX will apply with respect to an investment agreement or an investment authorization.
2. A national or company, that asserts in an investment dispute that a tax matter involves an expropriation, may submit that dispute to arbitration pursuant to Article IX(3) only if:
   (a) the national or company concerned has first referred to the competent tax authorities of both Parties the issue of whether the tax matter involves an expropriation; and
   (b) the competent tax authorities have not both determined, within nine months from the time the national or company referred the issue, that the matter does not involve an expropriation.

Article XIV

1. This Treaty shall not preclude a Party from applying measures necessary for the fulfillment of its obligations with respect to the maintenance or restoration of international peace or security, or the protection of its own essential security interests.
2. This Treaty shall not preclude a Party from prescribing special formalities in connection with covered investments, such as a requirement that such investments be legally constituted under the laws and regulations of that Party, or a requirement that transfers of currency or other monetary instruments be reported, provided that such formalities shall not impair the substance of any of the rights set forth in this Treaty.

Article XV

1. (a) The obligations of this Treaty shall apply to the political subdivisions of the Parties.
   (b) With respect to the treatment accorded by a State, Territory or possession of the United States of America, national treatment means treatment no less favorable than the treatment accorded thereby, in like situations, to investments of nationals of the United States of America resident in, and companies legally constituted under the laws and regulations of, other States, Territories or possessions of the United States of America.
2. A Party's obligations under this Treaty shall apply to a state enterprise in the exercise of any regulatory, administrative or other governmental authority delegated to it by that Party.

Article XVI

1. This Treaty shall enter into force thirty days after the date of exchange of instruments of ratification. It shall remain in force for a period of ten years and shall continue in force unless terminated in accordance with paragraph 2. It shall apply to covered investments existing at the time of entry into force as well as to those established or acquired thereafter.
2. A Party may terminate this treaty at the end of the initial ten year period or at any time thereafter by giving one year's written notice to the other Party.
3. For ten years from the date of termination, all other Articles shall continue to apply to covered investments established or acquired prior to the date of termination, except insofar as those Articles extend to the establishment or acquisition of covered investments.
4. The Annex [and Protocol (if any)] shall form an integral part of the Treaty.

IN WITNESS WHEREOF, the respective plenipotentiaries have signed this Treaty.

DONE in duplicate at [city] this [number] day of [month], [year], in the english and [   ] languages, each text being equally authentic.

FOR THE GOVERNMENT OF THE UNITED STATES OF AMERICA:

FOR THE GOVERNMENT OF [   ]:

ANNEX

1. The Government of the United States of America may adopt or maintain exceptions to the obligation to accord national treatment to covered investments in the sectors or with respect to the matters specified below:

   atomic energy; customhouse brokers; licenses for broadcast, common carrier, or aeronautical radio stations; COMSAT; subsidies or grants, including government-supported loans, guarantees and insurance; state and local measures exempt from Article 1102 of the North American Free Trade Agreement pursuant to Article 1108 thereof; and landing of submarine cables.

   Most favored nation treatment shall be accorded in the sectors and matters indicated above.
2. The Government of the United States of America may adopt or maintain exceptions to the obligation to accord national and most favored nation treatment to covered investments in the sectors or with respect to the matters specified below:

   fisheries; air and maritime transport, and related activities; banking* insurance* securities* and other financial services.*

   *Note: if the Treaty Partner undertakes acceptable commitments with respect to all or certain financial services, the Government of the United States of America will consider limiting these exceptions accordingly, so that, for example, particular obligations as to treatment would apply on no less favorable terms than in the North American Free Trade Agreement.

3. The Government of [   ] may adopt or maintain exceptions . . .
4. Notwithstanding paragraph 3, each Party agrees to accord national treatment to covered investments in the following sectors:

   leasing of minerals or pipeline rights-of-way on government lands.

APPENDIX 6

Treaty between the Government of the
United States of America and the
Government of [Country]
Concerning the Encouragement
and Reciprocal Protection of Investment (2004)

The Government of the United States of America and the Government of [Country] (hereinafter the 'Parties');

Desiring to promote greater economic cooperation between them with respect to investment by nationals and enterprises of one Party in the territory of the other Party;

Recognizing that agreement on the treatment to be accorded such investment will stimulate the flow of private capital and the economic development of the Parties;

Agreeing that a stable framework for investment will maximize effective utilization of economic resources and improve living standards;

Recognizing the importance of providing effective means of asserting claims and enforcing rights with respect to investment under national law as well as through international arbitration;

Desiring to achieve these objectives in a manner consistent with the protection of health, safety, and the environment, and the promotion of internationally recognized labor rights;

Having resolved to conclude a Treaty concerning the encouragement and reciprocal protection of investment;

Have agreed as follows:

Section A

Article 1
Definitions

For purposes of this Treaty:

'central level of government' means:

    (a) for the United States, the federal level of government; and
    (b) for [Country], [   ].

'Centre' means the International Centre for Settlement of Investment Disputes ('ICSID') established by the ICSID Convention.

'claimant' means an investor of a Party that is a party to an investment dispute with the other Party.

'covered investment' means, with respect to a Party, an investment in its territory of an investor of the other Party in existence as of the date of entry into force of this Treaty or established, acquired, or expanded thereafter.

'disputing parties' means the claimant and the respondent.

'disputing party' means either the claimant or the respondent.

'enterprise' means any entity constituted or organized under applicable law, whether or not for profit, and whether privately or governmentally owned or controlled, including a corporation, trust, partnership, sole proprietorship, joint venture, association, or similar organization; and a branch of an enterprise.

'enterprise of a Party' means an enterprise constituted or organized under the law of a Party, and a branch located in the territory of a Party and carrying out business activities there.

'existing' means in effect on the date of entry into force of this Treaty.

'freely usable currency' means 'freely usable currency' as determined by the International Monetary Fund under its *Articles of Agreement*.

'GATS' means the *General Agreement on Trade in Services*, contained in Annex 1B to the WTO Agreement.

'government procurement' means the process by which a government obtains the use of or acquires goods or services, or any combination thereof, for governmental purposes and not with a view to commercial sale or resale, or use in the production or supply of goods or services for commercial sale or resale.

'ICSID Additional Facility Rules' means the *Rules Governing the Additional Facility for the Administration of Proceedings by the Secretariat of the International Centre for Settlement of Investment Disputes*.

'ICSID Convention' means the *Convention on the Settlement of Investment Disputes between States and Nationals of Other States*, done at Washington, March 18, 1965.

['Inter-American Convention' means the *Inter-American Convention on International Commercial Arbitration*, done at Panama, January 30, 1975.]

'investment' means every asset that an investor owns or controls, directly or indirectly, that has the characteristics of an investment, including such characteristics as the commitment of capital or other resources, the expectation of gain or profit, or the assumption of risk. Forms that an investment may take include:

   (a) an enterprise;

   (b) shares, stock, and other forms of equity participation in an enterprise;

   (c) bonds, debentures, other debt instruments, and loans;[1]

   (d) futures, options, and other derivatives;

   (e) turnkey, construction, management, production, concession, revenue-sharing, and other similar contracts;

   (f) intellectual property rights;

   (g) licenses, authorizations, permits, and similar rights conferred pursuant to domestic law;[2,3] and

   (h) other tangible or intangible, movable or immovable property, and related property rights, such as leases, mortgages, liens, and pledges.

---

[1] Some forms of debt, such as bonds, debentures, and long-term notes, are more likely to have the characteristics of an investment, while other forms of debt, such as claims to payment that are immediately due and result from the sale of goods or services, are less likely to have such characteristics.

[2] Whether a particular type of license, authorization, permit, or similar instrument (including a concession, to the extent that it has the nature of such an instrument) has the characteristics of an investment depends on such factors as the nature and extent of the rights that the holder has under the law of the Party. Among the licenses, authorizations, permits, and similar instruments that do not have the characteristics of an investment are those that do not create any rights protected under domestic law. For greater certainty, the foregoing is without prejudice to whether any asset associated with the license, authorization, permit, or similar instrument has the characteristics of an investment.

[3] The term 'investment' does not include an order or judgment entered in a judicial or administrative action.

'investment agreement' means a written agreement[4] between a national authority[5] of a Party and a covered investment or an investor of the other Party, on which the covered investment or the investor relies in establishing or acquiring a covered investment other than the written agreement itself, that grants rights to the covered investment or investor:
  (a) with respect to natural resources that a national authority controls, such as for their exploration, extraction, refining, transportation, distribution, or sale;
  (b) to supply services to the public on behalf of the Party, such as power generation or distribution, water treatment or distribution, or telecommunications; or
  (c) to undertake infrastructure projects, such as the construction of roads, bridges, canals, dams, or pipelines, that are not for the exclusive or predominant use and benefit of the government.
'investment authorization'[6] means an authorization that the foreign investment authority of a Party grants to a covered investment or an investor of the other Party.
'investor of a non-Party' means, with respect to a Party, an investor that attempts to make, is making, or has made an investment in the territory of that Party, that is not an investor of either Party.
'investor of a Party' means a Party or state enterprise thereof, or a national or an enterprise of a Party, that attempts to make, is making, or has made an investment in the territory of the other Party; provided, however, that a natural person who is a dual national shall be deemed to be exclusively a national of the State of his or her dominant and effective nationality.
'measure' includes any law, regulation, procedure, requirement, or practice.
'national' means:
  (a) for the United States, a natural person who is a national of the United States as defined in Title III of the Immigration and Nationality Act; and
  (b) for [Country], [   ].

'New York Convention' means the *United Nations Convention on the Recognition and Enforcement of Foreign Arbitral Awards*, done at New York, June 10, 1958.
'non-disputing Party' means the Party that is not a party to an investment dispute.
'person' means a natural person or an enterprise.
'person of a Party' means a national or an enterprise of a Party.
'protected information' means confidential business information or information that is privileged or otherwise protected from disclosure under a Party's law.
'regional level of government' means:
  (a) for the United States, a state of the United States, the District of Columbia, or Puerto Rico; and
  (b) for [Country], [   ].
'respondent' means the Party that is a party to an investment dispute.
'Secretary-General' means the Secretary-General of ICSID.
'state enterprise' means an enterprise owned, or controlled through ownership interests, by a Party.
'territory' means:
  (a) with respect to the United States, [   ].
  (b) with respect to [Country,] [   ].

---

  [4] 'Written agreement' refers to an agreement in writing, executed by both parties, whether in a single instrument or in multiple instruments, that creates an exchange of rights and obligations, binding on both parties under the law applicable under Article 30[Governing Law](2). For greater certainty, (a) a unilateral act of an administrative or judicial authority, such as a permit, license, or authorization issued by a Party solely in its regulatory capacity, or a decree, order, or judgment, standing alone; and (b) an administrative or judicial consent decree or order, shall not be considered a written agreement.
  [5] For purposes of this definition, 'national authority' means (a) for the United States, an authority at the central level of government; and (b) for [Country], [   ].
  [6] For greater certainty, actions taken by a Party to enforce laws of general application, such as competition laws, are not encompassed within this definition.

'TRIPS Agreement' means *the Agreement on Trade-Related Aspects of Intellectual Property Rights,* contained in Annex 1C to the WTO Agreement.[7]

'UNCITRAL Arbitration Rules' means the arbitration rules of the United Nations Commission on International Trade Law.

'WTO Agreement' means the *Marrakesh Agreement Establishing the World Trade Organization,* done on April 15, 1994.

Article 2
Scope and Coverage

1. This Treaty applies to measures adopted or maintained by a Party relating to:
   (a) investors of the other Party;
   (b) covered investments; and
   (c) with respect to Articles 8 [Performance Requirements], 12 [Investment and Environment], and 13 [Investment and Labor], all investments in the territory of the Party.
2. A Party's obligations under Section A shall apply:
   (a) to a state enterprise or other person when it exercises any regulatory, administrative, or other governmental authority delegated to it by that Party; and
   (b) to the political subdivisions of that Party.
3. For greater certainty, this Treaty does not bind either Party in relation to any act or fact that took place or any situation that ceased to exist before the date of entry into force of this Treaty.

Article 3
National Treatment

1. Each Party shall accord to investors of the other Party treatment no less favorable than that it accords, in like circumstances, to its own investors with respect to the establishment, acquisition, expansion, management, conduct, operation, and sale or other disposition of investments in its territory.
2. Each Party shall accord to covered investments treatment no less favorable than that it accords, in like circumstances, to investments in its territory of its own investors with respect to the establishment, acquisition, expansion, management, conduct, operation, and sale or other disposition of investments.
3. The treatment to be accorded by a Party under paragraphs 1 and 2 means, with respect to a regional level of government, treatment no less favorable than the treatment accorded, in like circumstances, by that regional level of government to natural persons resident in and enterprises constituted under the laws of other regional levels of government of the Party of which it forms a part, and to their respective investments.

Article 4
Most-Favored-Nation Treatment

1. Each Party shall accord to investors of the other Party treatment no less favorable than that it accords, in like circumstances, to investors of any non-Party with respect to the establishment, acquisition, expansion, management, conduct, operation, and sale or other disposition of investments in its territory.
2. Each Party shall accord to covered investments treatment no less favorable than that it accords, in like circumstances, to investments in its territory of investors of any non-Party with respect to the establishment, acquisition, expansion, management, conduct, operation, and sale or other disposition of investments.

---

[7] For greater certainty, 'TRIPS Agreement' includes any waiver in force between the Parties of any provision of the TRIPS Agreement granted by WTO Members in accordance with the WTO Agreement.

Article 5
Minimum Standard of Treatment[8]

1. Each Party shall accord to covered investments treatment in accordance with customary international law, including fair and equitable treatment and full protection and security.
2. For greater certainty, paragraph 1 prescribes the customary international law minimum standard of treatment of aliens as the minimum standard of treatment to be afforded to covered investments. The concepts of 'fair and equitable treatment' and 'full protection and security' do not require treatment in addition to or beyond that which is required by that standard, and do not create additional substantive rights. The obligation in paragraph 1 to provide:
    (a) 'fair and equitable treatment' includes the obligation not to deny justice in criminal, civil, or administrative adjudicatory proceedings in accordance with the principle of due process embodied in the principal legal systems of the world; and
    (b) 'full protection and security' requires each Party to provide the level of police protection required under customary international law.
3. A determination that there has been a breach of another provision of this Treaty, or of a separate international agreement, does not establish that there has been a breach of this Article.
4. Notwithstanding Article 14 [Non-Conforming Measures](5)(b) [subsidies and grants], each Party shall accord to investors of the other Party, and to covered investments, non-discriminatory treatment with respect to measures it adopts or maintains relating to losses suffered by investments in its territory owing to armed conflict or civil strife.
5. Notwithstanding paragraph 4, if an investor of a Party, in the situations referred to in paragraph 4, suffers a loss in the territory of the other Party resulting from:
    (a) requisitioning of its covered investment or part thereof by the latter's forces or authorities; or
    (b) destruction of its covered investment or part thereof by the latter's forces or authorities, which was not required by the necessity of the situation,
    the latter Party shall provide the investor restitution, compensation, or both, as appropriate, for such loss. Any compensation shall be prompt, adequate, and effective in accordance with Article 6 [Expropriation and Compensation] (2) through (4), *mutatis mutandis*.
6. Paragraph 4 does not apply to existing measures relating to subsidies or grants that would be inconsistent with Article 3 [National Treatment] but for Article 14 [Non-Conforming Measures](5)(b) [subsidies and grants].

Article 6
Expropriation and Compensation[9]

1. Neither Party may expropriate or nationalize a covered investment either directly or indirectly through measures equivalent to expropriation or nationalization ('expropriation'), except:
    (a) for a public purpose;
    (b) in a non-discriminatory manner;
    (c) on payment of prompt, adequate, and effective compensation; and
    (d) in accordance with due process of law and Article 5 [Minimum Standard of Treatment](1) through (3).
2. The compensation referred to in paragraph 1(c) shall:
    (a) be paid without delay;
    (b) be equivalent to the fair market value of the expropriated investment immediately before the expropriation took place ('the date of expropriation');
    (c) not reflect any change in value occurring because the intended expropriation had become known earlier; and
    (d) be fully realizable and freely transferable.

---

[8] Article 5 [Minimum Standard of Treatment] shall be interpreted in accordance with Annex A.
[9] Article 6 [Expropriation] shall be interpreted in accordance with Annexes A and B.

3. If the fair market value is denominated in a freely usable currency, the compensation referred to in paragraph 1(c) shall be no less than the fair market value on the date of expropriation, plus interest at a commercially reasonable rate for that currency, accrued from the date of expropriation until the date of payment.

4. If the fair market value is denominated in a currency that is not freely usable, the compensation referred to in paragraph 1(c)—converted into the currency of payment at the market rate of exchange prevailing on the date of payment—shall be no less than:

    (a) the fair market value on the date of expropriation, converted into a freely usable currency at the market rate of exchange prevailing on that date, plus

    (b) interest, at a commercially reasonable rate for that freely usable currency, accrued from the date of expropriation until the date of payment.

5. This Article does not apply to the issuance of compulsory licenses granted in relation to intellectual property rights in accordance with the TRIPS Agreement, or to the revocation, limitation, or creation of intellectual property rights, to the extent that such issuance, revocation, limitation, or creation is consistent with the TRIPS Agreement.

Article 7
Transfers

1. Each Party shall permit all transfers relating to a covered investment to be made freely and without delay into and out of its territory. Such transfers include:

    (a) contributions to capital;

    (b) profits, dividends, capital gains, and proceeds from the sale of all or any part of the covered investment or from the partial or complete liquidation of the covered investment;

    (c) interest, royalty payments, management fees, and technical assistance and other fees;

    (d) payments made under a contract, including a loan agreement;

    (e) payments made pursuant to Article 5 [Minimum Standard of Treatment] (4) and (5) and Article 6 [Expropriation and Compensation]; and

    (f) payments arising out of a dispute.

2. Each Party shall permit transfers relating to a covered investment to be made in a freely usable currency at the market rate of exchange prevailing at the time of transfer.

3. Each Party shall permit returns in kind relating to a covered investment to be made as authorized or specified in a written agreement between the Party and a covered investment or an investor of the other Party.

4. Notwithstanding paragraphs 1 through 3, a Party may prevent a transfer through the equitable, non-discriminatory, and good faith application of its laws relating to:

    (a) bankruptcy, insolvency, or the protection of the rights of creditors;

    (b) issuing, trading, or dealing in securities, futures, options, or derivatives;

    (c) criminal or penal offenses;

    (d) financial reporting or record keeping of transfers when necessary to assist law enforcement or financial regulatory authorities; or

    (e) ensuring compliance with orders or judgments in judicial or administrative proceedings.

Article 8
Performance Requirements

1. Neither Party may, in connection with the establishment, acquisition, expansion, management, conduct, operation, or sale or other disposition of an investment of an investor of a Party or of a non-Party in its territory, impose or enforce any requirement or enforce any commitment or undertaking:[10]

    (a) to export a given level or percentage of goods or services;

---

[10] For greater certainty, a condition for the receipt or continued receipt of an advantage referred to in paragraph 2 does not constitute a 'commitment or undertaking' for the purposes of paragraph 1.

(b) to achieve a given level or percentage of domestic content;

(c) to purchase, use, or accord a preference to goods produced in its territory, or to purchase goods from persons in its territory;

(d) to relate in any way the volume or value of imports to the volume or value of exports or to the amount of foreign exchange inflows associated with such investment;

(e) to restrict sales of goods or services in its territory that such investment produces or supplies by relating such sales in any way to the volume or value of its exports or foreign exchange earnings;

(f) to transfer a particular technology, a production process, or other proprietary knowledge to a person in its territory; or

(g) to supply exclusively from the territory of the Party the goods that such investment produces or the services that it supplies to a specific regional market or to the world market.

2. Neither Party may condition the receipt or continued receipt of an advantage, in connection with the establishment, acquisition, expansion, management, conduct, operation, or sale or other disposition of an investment in its territory of an investor of a Party or of a non-Party, on compliance with any requirement:

(a) to achieve a given level or percentage of domestic content;

(b) to purchase, use, or accord a preference to goods produced in its territory, or to purchase goods from persons in its territory;

(c) to relate in any way the volume or value of imports to the volume or value of exports or to the amount of foreign exchange inflows associated with such investment; or

(d) to restrict sales of goods or services in its territory that such investment produces or supplies by relating such sales in any way to the volume or value of its exports or foreign exchange earnings.

3. (a) Nothing in paragraph 2 shall be construed to prevent a Party from conditioning the receipt or continued receipt of an advantage, in connection with an investment in its territory of an investor of a Party or of a non-Party, on compliance with a requirement to locate production, supply a service, train or employ workers, construct or expand particular facilities, or carry out research and development, in its territory.

(b) Paragraph 1(f) does not apply:

(i) when a Party authorizes use of an intellectual property right in accordance with Article 31 of the TRIPS Agreement, or to measures requiring the disclosure of proprietary information that fall within the scope of, and are consistent with, Article 39 of the TRIPS Agreement; or

(ii) when the requirement is imposed or the commitment or undertaking is enforced by a court, administrative tribunal, or competition authority to remedy a practice determined after judicial or administrative process to be anticompetitive under the Party's competition laws.[11]

(c) Provided that such measures are not applied in an arbitrary or unjustifiable manner, and provided that such measures do not constitute a disguised restriction on international trade or investment, paragraphs 1(b), (c), and (f), and 2(a) and (b), shall not be construed to prevent a Party from adopting or maintaining measures, including environmental measures:

(i) necessary to secure compliance with laws and regulations that are not inconsistent with this Treaty;

(ii) necessary to protect human, animal, or plant life or health; or

(iii) related to the conservation of living or non-living exhaustible natural resources.

(d) Paragraphs 1(a), (b), and (c), and 2(a) and (b), do not apply to qualification requirements for goods or services with respect to export promotion and foreign aid programs.

(e) Paragraphs 1(b), (c), (f), and (g), and 2(a) and (b), do not apply to government procurement.

---

[11] The Parties recognize that a patent does not necessarily confer market power.

(f) Paragraphs 2(a) and (b) do not apply to requirements imposed by an importing Party relating to the content of goods necessary to qualify for preferential tariffs or preferential quotas.

4. For greater certainty, paragraphs 1 and 2 do not apply to any commitment, undertaking, or requirement other than those set out in those paragraphs.

5. This Article does not preclude enforcement of any commitment, undertaking, or requirement between private parties, where a Party did not impose or require the commitment, undertaking, or requirement.

Article 9
Senior Management and Boards of Directors

1. Neither Party may require that an enterprise of that Party that is a covered investment appoint to senior management positions natural persons of any particular nationality.

2. A Party may require that a majority of the board of directors, or any committee thereof, of an enterprise of that Party that is a covered investment, be of a particular nationality, or resident in the territory of the Party, provided that the requirement does not materially impair the ability of the investor to exercise control over its investment.

Article 10
Publication of Laws and Decisions Respecting Investment

1. Each Party shall ensure that its:
   (a) laws, regulations, procedures, and administrative rulings of general application; and
   (b) adjudicatory decisions
   respecting any matter covered by this Treaty are promptly published or otherwise made publicly available.

2. For purposes of this Article, 'administrative ruling of general application' means an administrative ruling or interpretation that applies to all persons and fact situations that fall generally within its ambit and that establishes a norm of conduct but does not include:
   (a) a determination or ruling made in an administrative or quasi-judicial proceeding that applies to a particular covered investment or investor of the other Party in a specific case; or
   (b) a ruling that adjudicates with respect to a particular act or practice.

Article 11
Transparency

1. Contact Points
   (a) Each Party shall designate a contact point or points to facilitate communications between the Parties on any matter covered by this Treaty.
   (b) On the request of the other Party, the contact point(s) shall identify the office or official responsible for the matter and assist, as necessary, in facilitating communication with the requesting Party.

2. Publication
   To the extent possible, each Party shall:
   (a) publish in advance any measure referred to in Article 10(1)(a) that it proposes to adopt; and
   (b) provide interested persons and the other Party a reasonable opportunity to comment on such proposed measures.

3. Provision of Information
   (a) On request of the other Party, a Party shall promptly provide information and respond to questions pertaining to any actual or proposed measure that the requesting Party considers might materially affect the operation of this Treaty or otherwise substantially affect its interests under this Treaty.
   (b) Any request for information under this paragraph shall be provided to the other Party through the relevant contact points.

(c) Any information provided under this paragraph shall be without prejudice as to whether the measure is consistent with this Treaty.

4. Administrative Proceedings

With a view to administering in a consistent, impartial, and reasonable manner all measures referred to in Article 10(1)(a), each Party shall ensure that in its administrative proceedings applying such measures to particular covered investments or investors of the other Party in specific cases:

(a) wherever possible, covered investments or investors of the other Party that are directly affected by a proceeding are provided reasonable notice, in accordance with domestic procedures, when a proceeding is initiated, including a description of the nature of the proceeding, a statement of the legal authority under which the proceeding is initiated, and a general description of any issues in controversy;

(b) such persons are afforded a reasonable opportunity to present facts and arguments in support of their positions prior to any final administrative action, when time, the nature of the proceeding, and the public interest permit; and

(c) its procedures are in accordance with domestic law.

5. Review and Appeal

(a) Each Party shall establish or maintain judicial, quasi-judicial, or administrative tribunals or procedures for the purpose of the prompt review and, where warranted, correction of final administrative actions regarding matters covered by this Treaty. Such tribunals shall be impartial and independent of the office or authority entrusted with administrative enforcement and shall not have any substantial interest in the outcome of the matter.

(b) Each Party shall ensure that, in any such tribunals or procedures, the parties to the proceeding are provided with the right to:

(i) a reasonable opportunity to support or defend their respective positions; and

(ii) a decision based on the evidence and submissions of record or, where required by domestic law, the record compiled by the administrative authority.

(c) Each Party shall ensure, subject to appeal or further review as provided in its domestic law, that such decisions shall be implemented by, and shall govern the practice of, the offices or authorities with respect to the administrative action at issue.

Article 12
Investment and Environment

1. The Parties recognize that it is inappropriate to encourage investment by weakening or reducing the protections afforded in domestic environmental laws.[12] Accordingly, each Party shall strive to ensure that it does not waive or otherwise derogate from, or offer to waive or otherwise derogate from, such laws in a manner that weakens or reduces the protections afforded in those laws as an encouragement for the establishment, acquisition, expansion, or retention of an investment in its territory. If a Party considers that the other Party has offered such an encouragement, it may request consultations with the other Party and the two Parties shall consult with a view to avoiding any such encouragement.

2. Nothing in this Treaty shall be construed to prevent a Party from adopting, maintaining, or enforcing any measure otherwise consistent with this Treaty that it considers appropriate to ensure that investment activity in its territory is undertaken in a manner sensitive to environmental concerns.

---

[12] For the United States, 'laws' for purposes of this Article means an act of the United States Congress or regulations promulgated pursuant to an act of the United States Congress that is enforceable by action of the central level of government.

Article 13
Investment and Labor

1. The Parties recognize that it is inappropriate to encourage investment by weakening or reducing the protections afforded in domestic labor laws. Accordingly, each Party shall strive to ensure that it does not waive or otherwise derogate from, or offer to waive or otherwise derogate from, such laws in a manner that weakens or reduces adherence to the internationally recognized labor rights referred to in paragraph 2 as an encouragement for the establishment, acquisition, expansion, or retention of an investment in its territory. If a Party considers that the other Party has offered such an encouragement, it may request consultations with the other Party and the two Parties shall consult with a view to avoiding any such encouragement.

2. For purposes of this Article, 'labor laws' means each Party's statutes or regulations,[13] or provisions thereof, that are directly related to the following internationally recognized labor rights:
   (a) the right of association;
   (b) the right to organize and bargain collectively;
   (c) a prohibition on the use of any form of forced or compulsory labor;
   (d) labor protections for children and young people, including a minimum age for the employment of children and the prohibition and elimination of the worst forms of child labor; and
   (e) acceptable conditions of work with respect to minimum wages, hours of work, and occupational safety and health.

Article 14
Non-Conforming Measures

1. Articles 3 [National Treatment], 4 [Most-Favored-Nation Treatment], 8 [Performance Requirements], and 9 [Senior Management and Boards of Directors] do not apply to:
   (a) any existing non-conforming measure that is maintained by a Party at:
       (i)   the central level of government, as set out by that Party in its Schedule to Annex I or Annex III,
       (ii) a regional level of government, as set out by that Party in its Schedule to Annex I or Annex III, or
       (iii) a local level of government;
   (b) the continuation or prompt renewal of any non-conforming measure referred to in subparagraph (a); or
   (c) an amendment to any non-conforming measure referred to in subparagraph (a) to the extent that the amendment does not decrease the conformity of the measure, as it existed immediately before the amendment, with Article 3 [National Treatment], 4 [Most-Favored-Nation Treatment], 8 [Performance Requirements], or 9 [Senior Management and Boards of Directors].

2. Articles 3 [National Treatment], 4 [Most-Favored-Nation Treatment], 8 [Performance Requirements], and 9 [Senior Management and Boards of Directors] do not apply to any measure that a Party adopts or maintains with respect to sectors, subsectors, or activities, as set out in its Schedule to Annex II.

3. Neither Party may, under any measure adopted after the date of entry into force of this Treaty and covered by its Schedule to Annex II, require an investor of the other Party, by reason of its nationality, to sell or otherwise dispose of an investment existing at the time the measure becomes effective.

4. Articles 3 [National Treatment] and 4 [Most-Favored-Nation Treatment] do not apply to any measure covered by an exception to, or derogation from, the obligations under Article 3 or 4 of the TRIPS Agreement, as specifically provided in those Articles and in Article 5 of the TRIPS Agreement.

---

[13] For the United States, 'statutes or regulations' for purposes of this Article means an act of the United States Congress or regulations promulgated pursuant to an act of the United States Congress that is enforceable by action of the central level of government.

5. Articles 3 [National Treatment], 4 [Most-Favored-Nation Treatment], and 9 [Senior Management and Boards of Directors] do not apply to:
   (a) government procurement; or
   (b) subsidies or grants provided by a Party, including government-supported loans, guarantees, and insurance.

Article 15
Special Formalities and Information Requirements

1. Nothing in Article 3 [National Treatment] shall be construed to prevent a Party from adopting or maintaining a measure that prescribes special formalities in connection with covered investments, such as a requirement that investors be residents of the Party or that covered investments be legally constituted under the laws or regulations of the Party, provided that such formalities do not materially impair the protections afforded by a Party to investors of the other Party and covered investments pursuant to this Treaty.
2. Notwithstanding Articles 3 [National Treatment] and 4 [Most-Favored-Nation Treatment], a Party may require an investor of the other Party or its covered investment to provide information concerning that investment solely for informational or statistical purposes. The Party shall protect any confidential business information from any disclosure that would prejudice the competitive position of the investor or the covered investment. Nothing in this paragraph shall be construed to prevent a Party from otherwise obtaining or disclosing information in connection with the equitable and good faith application of its law.

Article 16
Non-Derogation

This Treaty shall not derogate from any of the following that entitle an investor of a Party or a covered investment to treatment more favorable than that accorded by this Treaty:
1. laws or regulations, administrative practices or procedures, or administrative or adjudicatory decisions of a Party;
2. international legal obligations of a Party; or
3. obligations assumed by a Party, including those contained in an investment authorization or an investment agreement.

Article 17
Denial of Benefits

1. A Party may deny the benefits of this Treaty to an investor of the other Party that is an enterprise of such other Party and to investments of that investor if persons of a non-Party own or control the enterprise and the denying Party:
   (a) does not maintain diplomatic relations with the non-Party; or
   (b) adopts or maintains measures with respect to the non-Party or a person of the non- Party that prohibit transactions with the enterprise or that would be violated or circumvented if the benefits of this Treaty were accorded to the enterprise or to its investments.
2. A Party may deny the benefits of this Treaty to an investor of the other Party that is an enterprise of such other Party and to investments of that investor if the enterprise has no substantial business activities in the territory of the other Party and persons of a non-Party, or of the denying Party, own or control the enterprise.

Article 18
Essential Security

Nothing in this Treaty shall be construed:
1. to require a Party to furnish or allow access to any information the disclosure of which it determines to be contrary to its essential security interests; or

2. to preclude a Party from applying measures that it considers necessary for the fulfillment of its obligations with respect to the maintenance or restoration of international peace or security, or the protection of its own essential security interests.

Article 19
Disclosure of Information

Nothing in this Treaty shall be construed to require a Party to furnish or allow access to confidential information the disclosure of which would impede law enforcement or otherwise be contrary to the public interest, or which would prejudice the legitimate commercial interests of particular enterprises, public or private.

Article 20
Financial Services

1. Notwithstanding any other provision of this Treaty, a Party shall not be prevented from adopting or maintaining measures relating to financial services for prudential reasons, including for the protection of investors, depositors, policy holders, or persons to whom a fiduciary duty is owed by a financial services supplier, or to ensure the integrity and stability of the financial system.[14] Where such measures do not conform with the provisions of this Treaty, they shall not be used as a means of avoiding the Party's commitments or obligations under this Treaty.

2. (a) Nothing in this Treaty applies to non-discriminatory measures of general application taken by any public entity in pursuit of monetary and related credit policies or exchange rate policies. This paragraph shall not affect a Party's obligations under Article 7 [Transfers] or Article 8 [Performance Requirements].[15]

   (b) For purposes of this paragraph, 'public entity' means a central bank or monetary authority of a Party.

3. Where a claimant submits a claim to arbitration under Section B [Investor-State Dispute Settlement], and the respondent invokes paragraph 1 or 2 as a defense, the following provisions shall apply:

   (a) The respondent shall, within 120 days of the date the claim is submitted to arbitration under Section B, submit in writing to the competent financial authorities[16] of both Parties a request for a joint determination on the issue of whether and to what extent paragraph 1 or 2 is a valid defense to the claim. The respondent shall promptly provide the tribunal, if constituted, a copy of such request. The arbitration may proceed with respect to the claim only as provided in subparagraph (d).

   (b) The competent financial authorities of both Parties shall make themselves available for consultations with each other and shall attempt in good faith to make a determination as described in subparagraph (a). Any such determination shall be transmitted promptly to the disputing parties and, if constituted, to the tribunal. The determination shall be binding on the tribunal.

   (c) If the competent financial authorities of both Parties, within 120 days of the date by which they have both received the respondent's written request for a joint determination under subparagraph (a), have not made a determination as described in that subparagraph, the

---

[14] It is understood that the term 'prudential reasons' includes the maintenance of the safety, soundness, integrity, or financial responsibility of individual financial institutions.

[15] For greater certainty, measures of general application taken in pursuit of monetary and related credit policies or exchange rate policies do not include measures that expressly nullify or amend contractual provisions that specify the currency of denomination or the rate of exchange of currencies.

[16] For purposes of this Article, 'competent financial authorities' means, for the United States, the Department of the Treasury for banking and other financial services, and the Office of the United States Trade Representative, in coordination with the Department of Commerce and other agencies, for insurance; and for [Country], [   ].

tribunal shall decide the issue left unresolved by the competent financial authorities. The provisions of Section B shall apply, except as modified by this subparagraph.

  (i) In the appointment of all arbitrators not yet appointed to the tribunal, each disputing party shall take appropriate steps to ensure that the tribunal has expertise or experience in financial services law or practice. The expertise of particular candidates with respect to financial services shall be taken into account in the appointment of the presiding arbitrator.

  (ii) If, before the respondent submits the request for a joint determination in conformance with subparagraph (a), the presiding arbitrator has been appointed pursuant to Article 27(3), such arbitrator shall be replaced on the request of either disputing party and the tribunal shall be reconstituted consistent with subparagraph (c)(i). If, within 30 days of the date the arbitration proceedings are resumed under subparagraph (d), the disputing parties have not agreed on the appointment of a new presiding arbitrator, the Secretary-General, on the request of a disputing party, shall appoint the presiding arbitrator consistent with subparagraph (c)(i).

  (iii) The non-disputing Party may make oral and written submissions to the tribunal regarding the issue of whether and to what extent paragraph 1 or 2 is a valid defense to the claim. Unless it makes such a submission, the non-disputing Party shall be presumed, for purposes of the arbitration, to take a position on paragraph 1 or 2 not inconsistent with that of the respondent.

  (d) The arbitration referred to in subparagraph (a) may proceed with respect to the claim:

  (i) 10 days after the date the competent financial authorities' joint determination has been received by both the disputing parties and, if constituted, the tribunal; or

  (ii) 10 days after the expiration of the 120-day period provided to the competent financial authorities in subparagraph (c).

4. Where a dispute arises under Section C and the competent financial authorities of one Party provide written notice to the competent financial authorities of the other Party that the dispute involves financial services, Section C shall apply except as modified by this paragraph and paragraph 5.

  (a) The competent financial authorities of both Parties shall make themselves available for consultations with each other regarding the dispute, and shall have 180 days from the date such notice is received to transmit a report on their consultations to the Parties. A Party may submit the dispute to arbitration under Section C only after the expiration of that 180-day period.

  (b) Either Party may make any such report available to a tribunal constituted under Section C to decide the dispute referred to in this paragraph or a similar dispute, or to a tribunal constituted under Section B to decide a claim arising out of the same events or circumstances that gave rise to the dispute under Section C.

5. Where a Party submits a dispute involving financial services to arbitration under Section C in conformance with paragraph 4, and on the request of either Party within 30 days of the date the dispute is submitted to arbitration, each Party shall, in the appointment of all arbitrators not yet appointed, take appropriate steps to ensure that the tribunal has expertise or experience in financial services law or practice. The expertise of particular candidates with respect to financial services shall be taken into account in the appointment of the presiding arbitrator.

6. Notwithstanding Article 11(2) [Transparency—Publication], each Party shall, to the extent practicable,

  (a) publish in advance any regulations of general application relating to financial services that it proposes to adopt;

  (b) provide interested persons and the other Party a reasonable opportunity to comment on such proposed regulations.

7. The terms 'financial service' or 'financial services' shall have the same meaning as in subparagraph 5(a) of the Annex on Financial Services of the GATS.

Article 21
Taxation

1. Except as provided in this Article, nothing in Section A shall impose obligations with respect to taxation measures.
2. Article 6 [Expropriation] shall apply to all taxation measures, except that a claimant that asserts that a taxation measure involves an expropriation may submit a claim to arbitration under Section B only if:
    (a) the claimant has first referred to the competent tax authorities[17] of both Parties in writing the issue of whether that taxation measure involves an expropriation; and
    (b) within 180 days after the date of such referral, the competent tax authorities of both Parties fail to agree that the taxation measure is not an expropriation.
3. Subject to paragraph 4, Article 8 [Performance Requirements](2) through (4) shall apply to all taxation measures.
4. Nothing in this Treaty shall affect the rights and obligations of either Party under any tax convention. In the event of any inconsistency between this Treaty and any such convention, that convention shall prevail to the extent of the inconsistency. In the case of a tax convention between the Parties, the competent authorities under that convention shall have sole responsibility for determining whether any inconsistency exists between this Treaty and that convention.

Article 22
Entry into Force, Duration, and Termination

1. This Treaty shall enter into force thirty days after the date the Parties exchange instruments of ratification. It shall remain in force for a period often years and shall continue in force thereafter unless terminated in accordance with paragraph 2.
2. A Party may terminate this Treaty at the end of the initial ten-year period or at any time thereafter by giving one year's written notice to the other Party.
3. For ten years from the date of termination, all other Articles shall continue to apply to covered investments established or acquired prior to the date of termination, except insofar as those Articles extend to the establishment or acquisition of covered investments.

Section B

Article 23
Consultation and Negotiation

In the event of an investment dispute, the claimant and the respondent should initially seek to resolve the dispute through consultation and negotiation, which may include the use of non- binding, third-party procedures.

Article 24
Submission of a Claim to Arbitration

1. In the event that a disputing party considers that an investment dispute cannot be settled by consultation and negotiation:
    (a) the claimant, on its own behalf, may submit to arbitration under this Section a claim
        (i) that the respondent has breached
            (A) an obligation under Articles 3 through 10,
            (B) an investment authorization, or
            (C) an investment agreement;
        and

---

[17] For the purposes of this Article, the 'competent tax authorities' means:
    (a) for the United States, the Assistant Secretary of the Treasury (Tax Policy), Department of the Treasury; and
    (b) for [Country], [   ].

       (ii) that the claimant has incurred loss or damage by reason of, or arising out of, that breach; and

  (b) the claimant, on behalf of an enterprise of the respondent that is a juridical person that the claimant owns or controls directly or indirectly, may submit to arbitration under this Section a claim

      (i) that the respondent has breached

         (A) an obligation under Articles 3 through 10,

         (B) an investment authorization, or

         (C) an investment agreement;

      and

      (ii) that the enterprise has incurred loss or damage by reason of, or arising out of, that breach,

provided that a claimant may submit pursuant to subparagraph (a)(i)(C) or (b)(i)(C) a claim for breach of an investment agreement only if the subject matter of the claim and the claimed damages directly relate to the covered investment that was established or acquired, or sought to be established or acquired, in reliance on the relevant investment agreement.

2. At least 90 days before submitting any claim to arbitration under this Section, a claimant shall deliver to the respondent a written notice of its intention to submit the claim to arbitration ('notice of intent'). The notice shall specify:

  (a) the name and address of the claimant and, where a claim is submitted on behalf of an enterprise, the name, address, and place of incorporation of the enterprise;

  (b) for each claim, the provision of this Treaty, investment authorization, or investment agreement alleged to have been breached and any other relevant provisions;

  (c) the legal and factual basis for each claim; and

  (d) the relief sought and the approximate amount of damages claimed.

3. Provided that six months have elapsed since the events giving rise to the claim, a claimant may submit a claim referred to in paragraph 1:

  (a) under the ICSID Convention and the ICSID Rules of Procedure for Arbitration Proceedings, provided that both the respondent and the non-disputing Party are parties to the ICSID Convention;

  (b) under the ICSID Additional Facility Rules, provided that either the respondent or the non-disputing Party is a party to the ICSID Convention;

  (c) under the UNCITRAL Arbitration Rules; or

  (d) if the claimant and respondent agree, to any other arbitration institution or under any other arbitration rules.

4. A claim shall be deemed submitted to arbitration under this Section when the claimant's notice of or request for arbitration ('notice of arbitration'):

  (a) referred to in paragraph 1 of Article 36 of the ICSID Convention is received by the Secretary-General;

  (b) referred to in Article 2 of Schedule C of the ICSID Additional Facility Rules is received by the Secretary-General;

  (c) referred to in Article 3 of the UNCITRAL Arbitration Rules, together with the statement of claim referred to in Article 18 of the UNCITRAL Arbitration Rules, are received by the respondent; or

  (d) referred to under any arbitral institution or arbitral rules selected under paragraph 3(d) is received by the respondent.

A claim asserted by the claimant for the first time after such notice of arbitration is submitted shall be deemed submitted to arbitration under this Section on the date of its receipt under the applicable arbitral rules.

5. The arbitration rules applicable under paragraph 3, and in effect on the date the claim or claims were submitted to arbitration under this Section, shall govern the arbitration except to the extent modified by this Treaty.

6. The claimant shall provide with the notice of arbitration:
   (a) the name of the arbitrator that the claimant appoints; or
   (b) the claimant's written consent for the Secretary-General to appoint that arbitrator.

Article 25
Consent of Each Party to Arbitration

1. Each Party consents to the submission of a claim to arbitration under this Section in accordance with this Treaty.
2. The consent under paragraph 1 and the submission of a claim to arbitration under this Section shall satisfy the requirements of:
   (a) Chapter II of the ICSID Convention (Jurisdiction of the Centre) and the ICSID Additional Facility Rules for written consent of the parties to the dispute; [and]
   (b) Article II of the New York Convention for an 'agreement in writing [.'] [;' and
   (c) Article I of the Inter-American Convention for an 'agreement.']

Article 26
Conditions and Limitations on Consent of Each Party

1. No claim may be submitted to arbitration under this Section if more than three years have elapsed from the date on which the claimant first acquired, or should have first acquired, knowledge of the breach alleged under Article 24(1) and knowledge that the claimant (for claims brought under Article 24(1)(a)) or the enterprise (for claims brought under Article 24(1)(b)) has incurred loss or damage.
2. No claim may be submitted to arbitration under this Section unless:
   (a) the claimant consents in writing to arbitration in accordance with the procedures set out in this Treaty; and
   (b) the notice of arbitration is accompanied,
       (i) for claims submitted to arbitration under Article 24(1)(a), by the claimant's written waiver, and
       (ii) for claims submitted to arbitration under Article 24(1)(b), by the claimant's and the enterprise's written waivers
   of any right to initiate or continue before any administrative tribunal or court under the law of either Party, or other dispute settlement procedures, any proceeding with respect to any measure alleged to constitute a breach referred to in Article 24.
3. Notwithstanding paragraph 2(b), the claimant (for claims brought under Article 24(1)(a)) and the claimant or the enterprise (for claims brought under Article 24(1)(b)) may initiate or continue an action that seeks interim injunctive relief and does not involve the payment of monetary damages before a judicial or administrative tribunal of the respondent, provided that the action is brought for the sole purpose of preserving the claimant's or the enterprise's rights and interests during the pendency of the arbitration.

Article 27
Selection of Arbitrators

1. Unless the disputing parties otherwise agree, the tribunal shall comprise three arbitrators, one arbitrator appointed by each of the disputing parties and the third, who shall be the presiding arbitrator, appointed by agreement of the disputing parties.
2. The Secretary-General shall serve as appointing authority for an arbitration under this Section.
3. Subject to Article 20(3), if a tribunal has not been constituted within 75 days from the date that a claim is submitted to arbitration under this Section, the Secretary-General, on the request of a disputing party, shall appoint, in his or her discretion, the arbitrator or arbitrators not yet appointed.

4. For purposes of Article 39 of the ICSID Convention and Article 7 of Schedule C to the ICSID Additional Facility Rules, and without prejudice to an objection to an arbitrator on a ground other than nationality:

    (a) the respondent agrees to the appointment of each individual member of a tribunal established under the ICSID Convention or the ICSID Additional Facility Rules;

    (b) a claimant referred to in Article 24(1)(a) may submit a claim to arbitration under this Section, or continue a claim, under the ICSID Convention or the ICSID Additional Facility Rules, only on condition that the claimant agrees in writing to the appointment of each individual member of the tribunal; and

    (c) a claimant referred to in Article 24(1)(b) may submit a claim to arbitration under this Section, or continue a claim, under the ICSID Convention or the ICSID Additional Facility Rules, only on condition that the claimant and the enterprise agree in writing to the appointment of each individual member of the tribunal.

Article 28
Conduct of the Arbitration

1. The disputing parties may agree on the legal place of any arbitration under the arbitral rules applicable under Article 24(3). If the disputing parties fail to reach agreement, the tribunal shall determine the place in accordance with the applicable arbitral rules, provided that the place shall be in the territory of a State that is a party to the New York Convention.

2. The non-disputing Party may make oral and written submissions to the tribunal regarding the interpretation of this Treaty.

3. The tribunal shall have the authority to accept and consider *amicus curiae* submissions from a person or entity that is not a disputing party.

4. Without prejudice to a tribunal's authority to address other objections as a preliminary question, a tribunal shall address and decide as a preliminary question any objection by the respondent that, as a matter of law, a claim submitted is not a claim for which an award in favor of the claimant may be made under Article 34.

    (a) Such objection shall be submitted to the tribunal as soon as possible after the tribunal is constituted, and in no event later than the date the tribunal fixes for the respondent to submit its counter-memorial (or, in the case of an amendment to the notice of arbitration, the date the tribunal fixes for the respondent to submit its response to the amendment).

    (b) On receipt of an objection under this paragraph, the tribunal shall suspend any proceedings on the merits, establish a schedule for considering the objection consistent with any schedule it has established for considering any other preliminary question, and issue a decision or award on the objection, stating the grounds therefor.

    (c) In deciding an objection under this paragraph, the tribunal shall assume to be true claimant's factual allegations in support of any claim in the notice of arbitration (or any amendment thereof) and, in disputes brought under the UNCITRAL Arbitration Rules, the statement of claim referred to in Article 18 of the UNCITRAL Arbitration Rules. The tribunal may also consider any relevant facts not in dispute.

    (d) The respondent does not waive any objection as to competence or any argument on the merits merely because the respondent did or did not raise an objection under this paragraph or make use of the expedited procedure set out in paragraph 5.

5. In the event that the respondent so requests within 45 days after the tribunal is constituted, the tribunal shall decide on an expedited basis an objection under paragraph 4 and any objection that the dispute is not within the tribunal's competence. The tribunal shall suspend any proceedings on the merits and issue a decision or award on the objection(s), stating the grounds therefor, no later than 150 days after the date of the request. However, if a disputing party requests a hearing, the tribunal may take an additional 30 days to issue the decision or award. Regardless of whether a hearing is requested, a tribunal may, on a showing of extraordinary cause, delay issuing its decision or award by an additional brief period, which may not exceed 30 days.

6. When it decides a respondent's objection under paragraph 4 or 5, the tribunal may, if warranted, award to the prevailing disputing party reasonable costs and attorney's fees incurred in submitting or opposing the objection. In determining whether such an award is warranted, the tribunal shall consider whether either the claimant's claim or the respondent's objection was frivolous, and shall provide the disputing parties a reasonable opportunity to comment.

7. A respondent may not assert as a defense, counterclaim, right of set-off, or for any other reason that the claimant has received or will receive indemnification or other compensation for all or part of the alleged damages pursuant to an insurance or guarantee contract.

8. A tribunal may order an interim measure of protection to preserve the rights of a disputing party, or to ensure that the tribunal's jurisdiction is made fully effective, including an order to preserve evidence in the possession or control of a disputing party or to protect the tribunal's jurisdiction. A tribunal may not order attachment or enjoin the application of a measure alleged to constitute a breach referred to in Article 24. For purposes of this paragraph, an order includes a recommendation.

9. (a) In any arbitration conducted under this Section, at the request of a disputing party, a tribunal shall, before issuing a decision or award on liability, transmit its proposed decision or award to the disputing parties and to the non-disputing Party. Within 60 days after the tribunal transmits its proposed decision or award, the disputing parties may submit written comments to the tribunal concerning any aspect of its proposed decision or award. The tribunal shall consider any such comments and issue its decision or award not later than 45 days after the expiration of the 60-day comment period.

   (b) Subparagraph (a) shall not apply in any arbitration conducted pursuant to this Section for which an appeal has been made available pursuant to paragraph 10 or Annex D.

10. If a separate, multilateral agreement enters into force between the Parties that establishes an appellate body for purposes of reviewing awards rendered by tribunals constituted pursuant to international trade or investment arrangements to hear investment disputes, the Parties shall strive to reach an agreement that would have such appellate body review awards rendered under Article 34 in arbitrations commenced after the multilateral agreement enters into force between the Parties.

Article 29
Transparency of Arbitral Proceedings

1. Subject to paragraphs 2 and 4, the respondent shall, after receiving the following documents, promptly transmit them to the non-disputing Party and make them available to the public:
   (a) the notice of intent;
   (b) the notice of arbitration;
   (c) pleadings, memorials, and briefs submitted to the tribunal by a disputing party and any written submissions submitted pursuant to Article 28(2) [Non-Disputing Party submissions] and (3) [*Amicus* Submissions] and Article 33 [Consolidation];
   (d) minutes or transcripts of hearings of the tribunal, where available; and
   (e) orders, awards, and decisions of the tribunal.

2. The tribunal shall conduct hearings open to the public and shall determine, in consultation with the disputing parties, the appropriate logistical arrangements. However, any disputing party that intends to use information designated as protected information in a hearing shall so advise the tribunal. The tribunal shall make appropriate arrangements to protect the information from disclosure.

3. Nothing in this Section requires a respondent to disclose protected information or to furnish or allow access to information that it may withhold in accordance with Article 18 [Essential Security Article] or Article 19 [Disclosure of Information Article].

4. Any protected information that is submitted to the tribunal shall be protected from disclosure in accordance with the following procedures:
   (a) Subject to subparagraph (d), neither the disputing parties nor the tribunal shall disclose to the non-disputing Party or to the public any protected information where the disputing party that provided the information clearly designates it in accordance with subparagraph (b);
   (b) Any disputing party claiming that certain information constitutes protected information shall clearly designate the information at the time it is submitted to the tribunal;
   (c) A disputing party shall, at the time it submits a document containing information claimed to be protected information, submit a redacted version of the document that does not contain the information. Only the redacted version shall be provided to the non-disputing Party and made public in accordance with paragraph 1; and
   (d) The tribunal shall decide any objection regarding the designation of information claimed to be protected information. If the tribunal determines that such information was not properly designated, the disputing party that submitted the information may (i) withdraw all or part of its submission containing such information, or (ii) agree to resubmit complete and redacted documents with corrected designations in accordance with the tribunal's determination and subparagraph (c). In either case, the other disputing party shall, whenever necessary, resubmit complete and redacted documents which either remove the information withdrawn under (i) by the disputing party that first submitted the information or redesignate the information consistent with the designation under (ii) of the disputing party that first submitted the information.

5. Nothing in this Section requires a respondent to withhold from the public information required to be disclosed by its laws.

Article 30
Governing Law

1. Subject to paragraph 3, when a claim is submitted under Article 24(1)(a)(i)(A) or Article 24(1)(b)(i)(A), the tribunal shall decide the issues in dispute in accordance with this Treaty and applicable rules of international law.

2. Subject to paragraph 3 and the other terms of this Section, when a claim is submitted under Article 24(1)(a)(i)(B) or (C), or Article 24(1)(b)(i)(B) or (C), the tribunal shall apply:
   (a) the rules of law specified in the pertinent investment authorization or investment agreement, or as the disputing parties may otherwise agree; or
   (b) if the rules of law have not been specified or otherwise agreed:
      (i) the law of the respondent, including its rules on the conflict of laws;[18] and
      (ii) such rules of international law as may be applicable.

3. A joint decision of the Parties, each acting through its representative designated for purposes of this Article, declaring their interpretation of a provision of this Treaty shall be binding on a tribunal, and any decision or award issued by a tribunal must be consistent with that joint decision.

Article 31
Interpretation of Annexes

1. Where a respondent asserts as a defense that the measure alleged to be a breach is within the scope of an entry set out in Annex I, II, or III, the tribunal shall, on request of the respondent, request the interpretation of the Parties on the issue. The Parties shall submit in writing any joint decision declaring their interpretation to the tribunal within 60 days of delivery of the request.

2. A joint decision issued under paragraph 1 by the Parties, each acting through its representative designated for purposes of this Article, shall be binding on the tribunal, and any decision or

---

[18] The 'law of the respondent' means the law that a domestic court or tribunal of proper jurisdiction would apply in the same case.

award issued by the tribunal must be consistent with that joint decision. If the Parties fail to issue such a decision within 60 days, the tribunal shall decide the issue.

Article 32
Expert Reports

Without prejudice to the appointment of other kinds of experts where authorized by the applicable arbitration rules, a tribunal, at the request of a disputing party or, unless the disputing parties disapprove, on its own initiative, may appoint one or more experts to report to it in writing on any factual issue concerning environmental, health, safety, or other scientific matters raised by a disputing party in a proceeding, subject to such terms and conditions as the disputing parties may agree.

Article 33
Consolidation

1. Where two or more claims have been submitted separately to arbitration under Article 24(1) and the claims have a question of law or fact in common and arise out of the same events or circumstances, any disputing party may seek a consolidation order in accordance with the agreement of all the disputing parties sought to be covered by the order or the terms of paragraphs 2 through 10.
2. A disputing party that seeks a consolidation order under this Article shall deliver, in writing, a request to the Secretary-General and to all the disputing parties sought to be covered by the order and shall specify in the request:
   (a) the names and addresses of all the disputing parties sought to be covered by the order;
   (b) the nature of the order sought; and
   (c) the grounds on which the order is sought.
3. Unless the Secretary-General finds within 30 days after receiving a request under paragraph 2 that the request is manifestly unfounded, a tribunal shall be established under this Article.
4. Unless all the disputing parties sought to be covered by the order otherwise agree, a tribunal established under this Article shall comprise three arbitrators:
   (a) one arbitrator appointed by agreement of the claimants;
   (b) one arbitrator appointed by the respondent; and
   (c) the presiding arbitrator appointed by the Secretary-General, provided, however, that the presiding arbitrator shall not be a national of either Party.
5. If, within 60 days after the Secretary-General receives a request made under paragraph 2, the respondent fails or the claimants fail to appoint an arbitrator in accordance with paragraph 4, the Secretary-General, on the request of any disputing party sought to be covered by the order, shall appoint the arbitrator or arbitrators not yet appointed. If the respondent fails to appoint an arbitrator, the Secretary-General shall appoint a national of the disputing Party, and if the claimants fail to appoint an arbitrator, the Secretary-General shall appoint a national of the non- disputing Party.
6. Where a tribunal established under this Article is satisfied that two or more claims that have been submitted to arbitration under Article 24(1) have a question of law or fact in common, and arise out of the same events or circumstances, the tribunal may, in the interest of fair and efficient resolution of the claims, and after hearing the disputing parties, by order:
   (a) assume jurisdiction over, and hear and determine together, all or part of the claims;
   (b) assume jurisdiction over, and hear and determine one or more of the claims, the determination of which it believes would assist in the resolution of the others; or
   (c) instruct a tribunal previously established under Article 27 [Selection of Arbitrators] to assume jurisdiction over, and hear and determine together, all or part of the claims, provided that
      (i) that tribunal, at the request of any claimant not previously a disputing party before that tribunal, shall be reconstituted with its original members, except that the arbitrator for the claimants shall be appointed pursuant to paragraphs 4(a) and 5; and
      (ii) that tribunal shall decide whether any prior hearing shall be repeated.

7. Where a tribunal has been established under this Article, a claimant that has submitted a claim to arbitration under Article 24(1) and that has not been named in a request made under paragraph 2 may make a written request to the tribunal that it be included in any order made under paragraph 6, and shall specify in the request:
   (a) the name and address of the claimant;
   (b) the nature of the order sought; and
   (c) the grounds on which the order is sought.
   The claimant shall deliver a copy of its request to the Secretary-General.

8. A tribunal established under this Article shall conduct its proceedings in accordance with the UNCITRAL Arbitration Rules, except as modified by this Section.

9. A tribunal established under Article 27 [Selection of Arbitrators] shall not have jurisdiction to decide a claim, or a part of a claim, over which a tribunal established or instructed under this Article has assumed jurisdiction.

10. On application of a disputing party, a tribunal established under this Article, pending its decision under paragraph 6, may order that the proceedings of a tribunal established under Article 27 [Selection of Arbitrators] be stayed, unless the latter tribunal has already adjourned its proceedings.

Article 34
Awards

1. Where a tribunal makes a final award against a respondent, the tribunal may award, separately or in combination, only:
   (a) monetary damages and any applicable interest; and
   (b) restitution of property, in which case the award shall provide that the respondent may pay monetary damages and any applicable interest in lieu of restitution.
   A tribunal may also award costs and attorney's fees in accordance with this Treaty and the applicable arbitration rules.

2. Subject to paragraph 1, where a claim is submitted to arbitration under Article 24(1)(b):
   (a) an award of restitution of property shall provide that restitution be made to the enterprise;
   (b) an award of monetary damages and any applicable interest shall provide that the sum be paid to the enterprise; and
   (c) the award shall provide that it is made without prejudice to any right that any person may have in the relief under applicable domestic law.

3. A tribunal may not award punitive damages.

4. An award made by a tribunal shall have no binding force except between the disputing parties and in respect of the particular case.

5. Subject to paragraph 6 and the applicable review procedure for an interim award, a disputing party shall abide by and comply with an award without delay.

6. A disputing party may not seek enforcement of a final award until:
   (a) in the case of a final award made under the ICSID Convention,
      (i) 120 days have elapsed from the date the award was rendered and no disputing party has requested revision or annulment of the award; or
      (ii) revision or annulment proceedings have been completed; and
   (b) in the case of a final award under the ICSID Additional Facility Rules, the UNCITRAL Arbitration Rules, or the rules selected pursuant to Article 24(3)(d),
      (i) 90 days have elapsed from the date the award was rendered and no disputing party has commenced a proceeding to revise, set aside, or annul the award; or
      (ii) a court has dismissed or allowed an application to revise, set aside, or annul the award and there is no further appeal.

7. Each Party shall provide for the enforcement of an award in its territory.

8. If the respondent fails to abide by or comply with a final award, on delivery of a request by the non-disputing Party, a tribunal shall be established under Article 37 [State-State Dispute

Settlement]. Without prejudice to other remedies available under applicable rules of international law, the requesting Party may seek in such proceedings:

(a) a determination that the failure to abide by or comply with the final award is inconsistent with the obligations of this Treaty; and

(b) a recommendation that the respondent abide by or comply with the final award.

9. A disputing party may seek enforcement of an arbitration award under the ICSID Convention or the New York Convention [or the Inter-American Convention] regardless of whether proceedings have been taken under paragraph 8.

10. A claim that is submitted to arbitration under this Section shall be considered to arise out of a commercial relationship or transaction for purposes of Article I of the New York Convention [and Article I of the Inter-American Convention].

Article 35
Annexes and Footnotes

The Annexes and footnotes shall form an integral part of this Treaty.

Article 36
Service of Documents

Delivery of notice and other documents on a Party shall be made to the place named for that Party in Annex C.

Section C

Article 37
State-State Dispute Settlement

1. Subject to paragraph 5, any dispute between the Parties concerning the interpretation or application of this Treaty, that is not resolved through consultations or other diplomatic channels, shall be submitted on the request of either Party to arbitration for a binding decision or award by a tribunal in accordance with applicable rules of international law. In the absence of an agreement by the Parties to the contrary, the UNCITRAL Arbitration Rules shall govern, except as modified by the Parties or this Treaty.

2. Unless the Parties otherwise agree, the tribunal shall comprise three arbitrators, one arbitrator appointed by each Party and the third, who shall be the presiding arbitrator, appointed by agreement of the Parties. If a tribunal has not been constituted within 75 days from the date that a claim is submitted to arbitration under this Section, the Secretary-General, on the request of either Party, shall appoint, in his or her discretion, the arbitrator or arbitrators not yet appointed.

3. Expenses incurred by the arbitrators, and other costs of the proceedings, shall be paid for equally by the Parties. However, the tribunal may, in its discretion, direct that a higher proportion of the costs be paid by one of the Parties.

4. Articles 28(3) *[Amicus Curiae* Submissions], 29 [Investor-State Transparency], 30(1) and (3) [Governing Law], and 31 [Interpretation of Annexes] shall apply *mutatis mutandis* to arbitrations under this Article.

5. Paragraphs 1 through 4 shall not apply to a matter arising under Article 12 or Article 13.

IN WITNESS WHEREOF, the respective plenipotentiaries have signed this Treaty.

DONE in duplicate at [city] this [number] day of [month, year], in the English and [foreign] languages, each text being equally authentic.

FOR THE GOVERNMENT OF   FOR THE GOVERNMENT OF
THE UNITED STATES OF AMERICA: [Country]:

ANNEX A
CUSTOMARY INTERNATIONAL LAW

The Parties confirm their shared understanding that 'customary international law' generally and as specifically referenced in Article 5 [Minimum Standard of Treatment] and Annex B [Expropriation] results from a general and consistent practice of States that they follow from a sense of legal obligation. With regard to Article 5 [Minimum Standard of Treatment], the customary international law minimum standard of treatment of aliens refers to all customary international law principles that protect the economic rights and interests of aliens.

ANNEX B
EXPROPRIATION

The Parties confirm their shared understanding that:

1. Article 6 [Expropriation and Compensation](1) is intended to reflect customary international law concerning the obligation of States with respect to expropriation.
2. An action or a series of actions by a Party cannot constitute an expropriation unless it interferes with a tangible or intangible property right or property interest in an investment.
3. Article 6 [Expropriation and Compensation](1) addresses two situations. The first is direct expropriation, where an investment is nationalized or otherwise directly expropriated through formal transfer of title or outright seizure.
4. The second situation addressed by Article 6 [Expropriation and Compensation](1) is indirect expropriation, where an action or series of actions by a Party has an effect equivalent to direct expropriation without formal transfer of title or outright seizure.
    (a) The determination of whether an action or series of actions by a Party, in a specific fact situation, constitutes an indirect expropriation, requires a case-by-case, fact-based inquiry that considers, among other factors:
        (i) the economic impact of the government action, although the fact that an action or series of actions by a Party has an adverse effect on the economic value of an investment, standing alone, does not establish that an indirect expropriation has occurred;
        (ii) the extent to which the government action interferes with distinct, reasonable investment-backed expectations; and
        (iii) the character of the government action.
    (b) Except in rare circumstances, non-discriminatory regulatory actions by a Party that are designed and applied to protect legitimate public welfare objectives, such as public health, safety, and the environment, do not constitute indirect expropriations.

ANNEX C
SERVICE OF DOCUMENTS ON A PARTY

United States

Notices and other documents shall be served on the United States by delivery to:

Executive Director (L/EX)
Office of the Legal Adviser
Department of State
Washington, D.C. 20520
United States of America

[Country]

Notices and other documents shall be served on [Country] by delivery to:
    [insert place of delivery of notices and other documents for [Country]]

Annex D
Possibility of a Bilateral Appellate Mechanism

Within three years after the date of entry into force of this Treaty, the Parties shall consider whether to establish a bilateral appellate body or similar mechanism to review awards rendered under Article 34 in arbitrations commenced after they establish the appellate body or similar mechanism.

APPENDIX 7

Treaty between the Federal Republic of Germany and [Country] Concerning the Encouragement and Reciprocal Protection of Investments

MODEL TREATY 2005

Treaty between the Federal Republic of Germany

and

[   ]

concerning the Encouragement and Reciprocal Protection of Investments

Federal Ministry of Economics and Technology

Berlin

The Federal Republic of Germany and [   ]—

desiring to intensify economic co-operation between both States,

intending to create favourable conditions for investments by investors of either State in the territory of the other State,

recognizing that the encouragement and contractual protection of such investments are apt to stimulate private business initiative and to increase the prosperity of both nations—

have agreed as follows:

Article 1

For the purposes of this Treaty

1. the term 'investments' comprises every kind of asset, in particular:
   (a) movable and immovable property as well as any other rights in rem, such as mortgages, liens and pledges;
   (b) shares of companies and other kinds of interest in companies;
   (c) claims to money which has been used to create an economic value or claims to any performance having an economic value;
   (d) intellectual property rights, in particular copyrights, patents, utility-model patents, industrial designs, trade-marks, trade-names, trade and business secrets, technical processes, know-how, and good will;
   (e) business concessions under public law, including concessions to search for, extract and exploit natural resources;
   any alteration of the form in which assets are invested shall not affect their classification as investment;
2. the term 'returns' means the amounts yielded by an investment for a definite period, such as profit, dividends, interest, royalties or fees;
3. the term 'investor' means
   (a) in respect of the Federal Republic of Germany:
       — Germans within the meaning of the Basic Law of the Federal Republic of Germany,

— any juridical person as well as any commercial or other company or association with or
without legal personality having its seat in the territory of the Federal Republic of
Germany, irrespective of whether or not its activities are directed at profit,

(b) in respect of . . . .:

— . . . .
. . . .

— . . . .
. . . .

Article 2

(1) Each Contracting State shall in its territory promote as far as possible investments by investors
of the other Contracting State and admit such investments in accordance with its legislation.

(2) Each Contracting State shall in its territory in any case accord investments by investors of the
other Contracting State fair and equitable treatment as well as full protection under the Treaty.

(3) Neither Contracting State shall in any way impair by arbitrary or discriminatory measures the
management, maintenance, use, enjoyment or disposal of investments in its territory of
investors of the other Contracting State.

Article 3

(1) Neither Contracting State shall subject investments in its territory owned or controlled
by investors of the other Contracting State to treatment less favourable than it accords to
investments of its own investors or to investments of investors of any third State.

(2) Neither Contracting State shall subject investors of the other Contracting State, as regards their
activity in connection with investments in its territory, to treatment less favourable than it
accords to its own investors or to investors of any third State.

(3) Such treatment shall not relate to privileges which either Contracting State accords to investors
of third States on account of its membership of, or association with, a customs or economic
union, a common market or a free trade area.

(4) The treatment granted under this Article shall not relate to advantages which either Contracting
State accords to investors of third States by virtue of a double taxation agreement or other
agreements regarding matters of taxation.

Article 4

(1) Investments by investors of either Contracting State shall enjoy full protection and security in
the territory of the other Contracting State.

(2) Investments by investors of either Contracting State shall not directly or indirectly be expropriated, nationalized or subjected to any other measure the effects of which would be tantamount
to expropriation or nationalization in the territory of the other Contracting State except for the
public benefit and against compensation. Such compensation shall be equivalent to the value of
the expropriated investment immediately before the date on which the actual or threatened
expropriation, nationalization or comparable measure has become publicly known. The compensation shall be paid without delay and shall carry the usual bank interest until the time of
payment; it shall be effectively realizable and freely transferable. Provision shall have been made
in an appropriate manner at or prior to the time of expropriation, nationalization or comparable measure for the determination and payment of such compensation. The legality of any
such expropriation, nationalization or comparable measure and the amount of compensation
shall be subject to review by due process of law.

(3) Investors of either Contracting State whose investments suffer losses in the territory of the other
Contracting State owing to war or other armed conflict, revolution, a state of national emergency, or revolt, shall be accorded treatment no less favourable by such other Contracting State

than that which the latter Contracting State accords to its own investors as regards restitution, indemnification, compensation or other valuable consideration. Such payments shall be freely transferable.

(4) Investors of either Contracting State shall enjoy most-favoured-nation treatment in the territory of the other Contracting State in respect of the matters provided for in this Article.

Article 5

Each Contracting State shall guarantee to investors of the other Contracting State the free transfer of payments in connection with an investment, in particular

(a) the principal and additional amounts to maintain or increase the investment;
(b) the returns;
(c) the repayment of loans;
(d) the proceeds from the liquidation or the sale of the whole or any part of the investment;
(e) the compensation provided for in Article 4.

Article 6

If either Contracting State makes a payment to any of its investors under a guarantee it has assumed in respect of an investment in the territory of the other Contracting State, the latter Contracting State shall, without prejudice to the rights of the former Contracting State under Article 10, recognize the assignment, whether under a law or pursuant to a legal transaction, of any right or claim of such investors to the former Contracting State. The latter Contracting State shall also recognize the subrogation of the former Contracting State to any such right or claim (assigned claims) which that Contracting State shall be entitled to assert to the same extent as its predecessor in title. As regards the transfer of payments made by virtue of such assigned claims, Article 4(2) and (3) as well as Article 5 shall apply mutatis mutandis.

Article 7

(1) Transfers under Article 4(2) or (3), under Article 5 or Article 6 shall be made without delay at the market rate of exchange applicable on the day of the transfer.
(2) Should there be no foreign exchange market the cross rate obtained from those rates which would be applied by the International Monetary Fund on the date of payment for conversions of the currencies concerned into Special Drawing Rights shall apply.

Article 8

(1) If the legislation of either Contracting State or obligations under international law existing at present or established hereafter between the Contracting States in addition to this Treaty contain a regulation, whether general or specific, entitling investments by investors of the other Contracting State to a treatment more favourable than is provided for by this Treaty, such regulation shall to the extent that it is more favourable prevail over this Treaty.
(2) Each Contracting State shall observe any other obligation it has assumed with regard to investments in its territory by investors of the other Contracting State.

Article 9

This Treaty shall also apply to investments made prior to its entry into force by investors of either Contracting State in the territory of the other Contracting State consistent with the latter's legislation.

Article 10

(1) Disputes between the Contracting States concerning the interpretation or application of this Treaty should as far as possible be settled by the governments of the two Contracting States.
(2) If a dispute cannot thus be settled, it shall upon the request of either Contracting State be submitted to an arbitration tribunal.
(3) Such arbitration tribunal shall be constituted ad hoc as follows: each Contracting State shall appoint one member, and these two members shall agree upon a national of a third State as their

chairman to be appointed by the governments of the two Contracting States. Such members shall be appointed within two months, and such chairman within three months from the date on which either Contracting State has informed the other Contracting State that it intends to submit the dispute to an arbitration tribunal.

(4) If the periods specified in paragraph 3 above have not been observed, either Contracting State may, in the absence of any other arrangement, invite the President of the International Court of Justice to make the necessary appointments. If the President is a national of either Contracting State or if he is otherwise prevented from discharging the said function, the Vice-President should make the necessary appointments. If the Vice-President is a national of either Contracting State or if he, too, is prevented from discharging the said function, the member of the Court next in seniority who is not a national of either Contracting State should make the necessary appointments.

(5) The arbitration tribunal shall reach its decisions by a majority of votes. Such decisions shall be binding. Each Contracting State shall bear the cost of its own member and of its representatives in the arbitration proceedings; the cost of the chairman and the remaining costs shall be borne in equal parts by the Contracting States. The arbitration tribunal may make a different regulation concerning costs. In all other respects, the arbitration tribunal shall determine its own procedure.

Model I (Membership of both Contracting States in ICSID)

Article 11

(1) Disputes concerning investments between a Contracting State and an investor of the other Contracting State should as far as possible be settled amicably between the parties in dispute.

(2) If the dispute cannot be settled within six months of the date when it has been raised by one of the parties in dispute, it shall, at the request of the investor of the other Contracting State, be submitted for arbitration. Unless the parties in dispute agree otherwise, the dispute shall be submitted for arbitration under the Convention of 18 March 1965 on the Settlement of Investment Disputes between States and Nationals of Other States.

(3) The award shall be binding and shall not be subject to any appeal or remedy other than those provided for in the said Convention. The award shall be enforced in accordance with domestic law.

(4) During arbitration proceedings or the enforcement of an award, the Contracting State involved in the dispute shall not raise the objection that the investor of the other Contracting State has received compensation under an insurance contract in respect of all or part of the damage.

Model II (Membership of only one Contracting State in ICSID)

Article 11

(1) Disputes concerning investments between a Contracting State and an investor of the other Contracting State shall as far as possible be settled amicably between the parties in dispute.

(2) If the dispute cannot be settled within six months of the date when it has been raised by one of the parties in dispute, it shall, at the request of the investor of the other Contracting State, be submitted for arbitration. Unless the parties in dispute have agreed otherwise, the provisions of Article 10(3) to (5) shall be applied mutatis mutandis on condition that the appointment of the members of the arbitration tribunal in accordance with Article 10(3) is effected by the parties in dispute and that, insofar as the periods specified in Article 10(3) are not observed, either party in dispute may, in the absence of other arrangements, invite the President of the Court of International Arbitration of the International Chamber of Commerce in Paris to make the required appointments. The award shall be enforced in accordance with domestic law.

(3) During arbitration proceedings or the enforcement of an award, the Contracting State involved in the dispute shall not raise the objection that the investor of the other Contracting State has received compensation under an insurance contract in respect of all or part of the damage.

(4) In the event of both Contracting States having become Contracting States of the Convention of 18 March 1965 on the Settlement of Investment Disputes between States and Nationals of Other States, disputes under this Article between the parties in dispute shall be submitted for arbitration under the aforementioned Convention, unless the parties in dispute agree otherwise; each Contracting State herewith declares its acceptance of such a procedure.

Article 12

This Treaty shall be in force irrespective of whether or not diplomatic or consular relations exist between the Contracting States.

Article 13

The attached Protocol shall form an integral part of this Treaty.

Article 14

(1) This Treaty shall be subject to ratification; the instruments of ratification shall be exchanged as soon as possible.

(2) This Treaty shall enter into force one month after the date of exchange of the instruments of ratification. It shall remain in force for a period of ten years and shall be extended thereafter for an unlimited period unless denounced in writing through diplomatic channels by either Contracting State twelve months before its expiration. After the expiry of the period of ten years this Treaty may be denounced at any time by either Contracting State giving twelve months' notice.

(3) In respect of investments made prior to the date of termination of this Treaty, the provisions of the preceding Articles shall continue to be effective for a further period of twenty years from the date of termination of this Treaty.

Done at   on   in duplicate in the German and
[   ] languages, both texts being equally authentic.

For the   For
Federal Republic of Germany   [   ]

Protocol to the Treaty between the Federal Republic of Germany

and

[   ]

concerning the Encouragement and Reciprocal Protection of Investments

The Federal Republic of Germany and [   ] have agreed on the following provisions to the Treaty of (date) concerning the Encouragement and Reciprocal Protection of Investments:

1. Ad Article 1
   (a) Returns from the investment and, in the event of their re-investment, the returns therefrom shall enjoy the same protection as the investment.
   (b) Without prejudice to any other method of determining nationality, in particular any person in possession of a national passport issued by the competent authorities of the Contracting State concerned shall be deemed to be a national of that Contracting State.

2. Ad Article 2.
   The Treaty shall also apply to the areas of the exclusive economic zone and the continental shelf insofar as international law permits the Contracting State concerned to exercise sovereign rights or jurisdiction in these areas.

3. Ad Article 3
   (a) The following shall more particularly, though not exclusively, be deemed 'activity' within the meaning of Article 3(2): the management, maintenance, use, enjoyment and disposal of an investment. The following shall, in particular, be deemed 'treatment less favourable' within the meaning of Article 3: unequal treatment in the case of restrictions on the purchase of raw or auxiliary materials, of energy or fuel or of means of production or operation of any kind, unequal treatment in the case of impeding the marketing of products inside or outside the country, as well as any other measures having similar effects. Measures that have to be taken for reasons of public security and order, public health or morality shall not be deemed 'treatment less favourable' within the meaning of Article 3.
   (b) The provisions of Article 3 do not oblige a Contracting State to extend to investors resident in the territory of the other Contracting State tax privileges, tax exemptions and tax reductions which according to its tax laws are granted only to investors resident in its territory.
   (c) The Contracting States shall within the framework of their national legislation give sympathetic consideration to applications for the entry and sojourn of persons of either Contracting State who wish to enter the territory of the other Contracting State in connection with an investment; the same shall apply to employed persons of either Contracting State who in connection with an investment wish to enter the territory of the other Contracting State and sojourn there to take up employment. Applications for work permits shall also be given sympathetic consideration.

4. Ad Article 7
   A transfer shall be deemed to have been made 'without delay' within the meaning of Article 7(1) if effected within such period as is normally required for the completion of transfer formalities. The said period shall commence on the day on which the relevant request has been submitted and may on no account exceed two months.

5. Whenever goods or persons connected with an investment are to be transported, each Contracting State shall neither exclude nor hinder transport enterprises of the other Contracting State and shall issue permits as required to carry out such transport. This shall include the transport of
   (a) goods directly intended for an investment within the meaning of the Treaty or acquired in the territory of either Contracting State or of any third State by or on behalf of an enterprise in which assets within the meaning of the Treaty are invested;
   (b) persons travelling in connection with an investment.

Agreement on Encouragement and Reciprocal Protection of Investments between [   ] and the Kingdom of the Netherlands

The [   ] and the Kingdom of the Netherlands,

hereinafter referred to as the Contracting Parties,

Desiring to strengthen their traditional ties of friendship and to extend and intensify the economic relations between them, particularly with respect to investments by the nationals of one Contracting Party in the territory of the other Contracting Party,

Recognising that agreement upon the treatment to be accorded to such investments will stimulate the flow of capital and technology and the economic development of the Contracting Parties and that fair and equitable treatment of investment is desirable,

Have agreed as follows:

Article 1

For the purposes of this Agreement:
(a) the term 'investments' means every kind of asset and more particularly, though not exclusively:
    (i)   movable and immovable property as well as any other rights *in rem* in respect of every kind of asset;
    (ii) rights derived from shares, bonds and other kinds of interests in companies and joint ventures;
    (iii) claims to money, to other assets or to any performance having an economic value; (iv) rights in the field of intellectual property, technical processes, goodwill and know-how;
    (v)   rights granted under public law or under contract, including rights to prospect, explore, extract and win natural resources.
(b) the term 'nationals' shall comprise with regard to either Contracting Party:
    (i)   natural persons having the nationality of that Contracting Party;
    (ii) legal persons constituted under the law of that Contracting Party;
    (iii) legal persons not constituted under the law of that Contracting Party but controlled, directly or indirectly, by natural persons as defined in (i) or by legal persons as defined in (ii).
(c) The term 'territory' means:
the territory of the Contracting Party concerned and any area adjacent to the territorial sea which, under the laws applicable in the Contracting Party concerned, and in accordance with international law, is the exclusive economic zone or continental shelf of the Contracting Party concerned, in which that Contracting Party exercises jurisdiction or sovereign rights.

Article 2

Either Contracting Party shall, within the framework of its laws and regulations, promote economic cooperation through the protection in its territory of investments of nationals of the other Contracting Party. Subject to its right to exercise powers conferred by its laws or regulations, each Contracting Party shall admit such investments.

Article 3

1. Each Contracting Party shall ensure fair and equitable treatment of the investments of nationals of the other Contracting Party and shall not impair, by unreasonable or discriminatory measures, the operation, management, maintenance, use, enjoyment or disposal thereof by those nationals. Each Contracting Party shall accord to such investments full physical security and protection.
2. More particularly, each Contracting Party shall accord to such investments treatment which in any case shall not be less favourable than that accorded either to investments of its own nationals or to investments of nationals of any third State, whichever is more favourable to the national concerned.
3. If a Contracting Party has accorded special advantages to nationals of any third State by virtue of agreements establishing customs unions, economic unions, monetary unions or similar institutions, or on the basis of interim agreements leading to such unions or institutions, that Contracting Party shall not be obliged to accord such advantages to nationals of the other Contracting Party.
4. Each Contracting Party shall observe any obligation it may have entered into with regard to investments of nationals of the other Contracting Party.
5. If the provisions of law of either Contracting Party or obligations under international law existing at present or established hereafter between the Contracting Parties in addition to the present Agreement contain a regulation, whether general or specific, entitling investments by nationals of the other Contracting Party to a treatment more favourable than is provided for by the present Agreement, such regulation shall, to the extent that it is more favourable, prevail over the present Agreement.

Article 4

With respect to taxes, fees, charges and to fiscal deductions and exemptions, each Contracting Party shall accord to nationals of the other Contracting Party who are engaged in any economic activity in its territory, treatment not less favourable than that accorded to its own nationals or to those of any third State who are in the same circumstances, whichever is more favourable to the nationals concerned. For this purpose, however, there shall not be taken into account any special fiscal advantages accorded by that Party:
(a) under an agreement for the avoidance of double taxation; or
(b) by virtue of its participation in a customs union, economic union or similar institution; or
(c) on the basis of reciprocity with a third State.

Article 5

The Contracting Parties shall guarantee that payments relating to an investment may be transferred. The transfers shall be made in a freely convertible currency, without restriction or delay. Such transfers include in particular though not exclusively:
(a) profits, interests, dividends and other current income;
(b) funds necessary:
  (i) for the acquisition of raw or auxiliary materials, semi-fabricated or finished products, or
  (ii) to replace capital assets in order to safeguard the continuity of an investment;
(c) additional funds necessary for the development of an investment;
(d) funds in repayment of loans;
(e) royalties or fees;
(f) earnings of natural persons;
(g) the proceeds of sale or liquidation of the investment;
(h) payments arising under Article 7.

Article 6

Neither Contracting Party shall take any measures depriving, directly or indirectly, nationals of the other Contracting Party of their investments unless the following conditions are complied with:

(a) the measures are taken in the public interest and under due process of law;

(b) the measures are not discriminatory or contrary to any undertaking which the Contracting Party which takes such measures may have given;

(c) the measures are taken against just compensation. Such compensation shall represent the genuine value of the investments affected, shall include interest at a normal commercial rate until the date of payment and shall, in order to be effective for the claimants, be paid and made transferable, without delay, to the country designated by the claimants concerned and in the currency of the country of which the claimants are nationals or in any freely convertible currency accepted by the claimants.

Article 7

Nationals of the one Contracting Party who suffer losses in respect of their investments in the territory of the other Contracting Party owing to war or other armed conflict, revolution, a state of national emergency, revolt, insurrection or riot shall be accorded by the latter Contracting Party treatment, as regards restitution, indemnification, compensation or other settlement, no less favourable than that which that Contracting Party accords to its own nationals or to nationals of any third State, whichever is more favourable to the nationals concerned.

Article 8

If the investments of a national of the one Contracting Party are insured against non-commercial risks or otherwise give rise to payment of indemnification in respect of such investments under a system established by law, regulation or government contract, any subrogation of the insurer or re-insurer or Agency designated by the one Contracting Party to the rights of the said national pursuant to the terms of such insurance or under any other indemnity given shall be recognised by the other Contracting Party.

Article 9

Each Contracting Party hereby consents to submit any legal dispute arising between that Contracting Party and a national of the other Contracting Party concerning an investment of that national in the territory of the former Contracting Party to the International Centre for Settlement of Investment Disputes for settlement by conciliation or arbitration under the Convention on the Settlement of Investment Disputes between States and Nationals of other States, opened for signature at Washington on 18 March 1965. A legal person which is a national of one Contracting Party and which before such a dispute arises is controlled by nationals of the other Contracting Party shall, in accordance with Article 25(2)(b) of the Convention, for the purpose of the Convention be treated as a national of the other Contracting Party.

Article 10

The provisions of this Agreement shall, from the date of entry into force thereof, also apply to investments which have been made before that date.

Article 11

Either Contracting Party may propose to the other Party that consultations be held on any matter concerning the interpretation or application of the Agreement. The other Party shall accord sympathetic consideration to the proposal and shall afford adequate opportunity for such consultations.

Article 12

1. Any dispute between the Contracting Parties concerning the interpretation or application of the present Agreement, which cannot be settled within a reasonable lapse of time by means of

diplomatic negotiations, shall, unless the Parties have otherwise agreed, be submitted, at the request of either Party, to an arbitral tribunal, composed of three members. Each Party shall appoint one arbitrator and the two arbitrators thus appointed shall together appoint a third arbitrator as their chairman who is not a national of either Party.

2. If one of the Parties fails to appoint its arbitrator and has not proceeded to do so within two months after an invitation from the other Party to make such appointment, the latter Party may invite the President of the International Court of Justice to make the necessary appointment.

3. If the two arbitrators are unable to reach agreement, in the two months following their appointment, on the choice of the third arbitrator, either Party may invite the President of the International Court of Justice to make the necessary appointment.

4. If, in the cases provided for in the paragraphs (2) and (3) of this Article, the President of the International Court of Justice is prevented from discharging the said function or is a national of either Contracting Party, the Vice-President shall be invited to make the necessary appointments. If the Vice-President is prevented from discharging the said function or is a national of either Party the most senior member of the Court available who is not a national of either Party shall be invited to make the necessary appointments.

5. The tribunal shall decide on the basis of respect for the law. Before the tribunal decides, it may at any stage of the proceedings propose to the Parties that the dispute be settled amicably. The foregoing provisions shall not prejudice settlement of the dispute *ex aequo et bono* if the Parties so agree.

6. Unless the Parties decide otherwise, the tribunal shall determine its own procedure.

7. The tribunal shall reach its decision by a majority of votes. Such decision shall be final and binding on the Parties.

Article 13

As regards the Kingdom of the Netherlands, the present Agreement shall apply to the part of the Kingdom in Europe, to the Netherlands Antilles and to Aruba, unless the notification provided for in Article 14, paragraph (1) provides otherwise.

Article 14

1. The present Agreement shall enter into force on the first day of the second month following the date on which the Contracting Parties have notified each other in writing that their constitutionally required procedures have been complied with, and shall remain in force for a period of fifteen years.

2. Unless notice of termination has been given by either Contracting Party at least six months before the date of the expiry of its validity, the present Agreement shall be extended tacitly for periods of ten years, whereby each Contracting Party reserves the right to terminate the Agreement upon notice of at least six months before the date of expiry of the current period of validity.

3. In respect of investments made before the date of the termination of the present Agreement, the foregoing Articles shall continue to be effective for a further period of fifteen years from that date.

4. Subject to the period mentioned in paragraph (2) of this Article, the Kingdom of the Netherlands shall be entitled to terminate the application of the present Agreement separately in respect of any of the parts of the Kingdom.

IN WITNESS WHEREOF, the undersigned representatives, duly authorised thereto, have signed the present Agreement.

DONE in two originals at, [   ], on [   ], in the[   ], Netherlands and English languages, the three texts being authentic. In case of difference of interpretation the English text will prevail.

For [   ] For the Kingdom of the Netherlands:

APPENDIX 9

Agreement between the Government of the Democratic Socialist Republic of Sri Lanka and the Government of [   ] for the Promotion and Protection of Investments

The Government of the Democratic Socialist Republic of Sri Lanka and the Government of [   ] (hereinafter referred to as the 'Contracting Parties');.

Desiring to create conditions favourable for greater investment by investors of one Contracting Party in the territory of the other Contracting Party;

Recognizing that the encouragement and reciprocal protection under international agreement of such investments will be conducive to the stimulation of individual business initiative and will increase prosperity in both States;

Have agreed as follows:

Article 1
Definitions

1. The term 'investment' means every kind of property or asset invested by an investor of one Contracting Party in the territory of the other Contracting Party in accordance with the laws and regulations of the Contracting Party (hereinafter referred to as the host Contracting Party) in particular though not exclusively includes:
   (a) movable and immovable property and any other rights such as mortgages liens or pledges;
   (b) shares, stocks and debentures of companies or any other similar forms of interests in such companies;
   (c) claims to money or any performance under contract, having a financial value;
   (d) industrial and intellectual property rights such as patents, utility models, industrial designs or models, trade marks and names, know-how and goodwill;
   (e) business concessions conferred by law or under contract including concessions to search for, cultivate, extract and exploit natural resources;

2. The term 'investor' with regard to either Contracting Party means the following persons who invest in the territory of the other Contracting Party:
   (a) natural persons who, having the nationality of one Contracting Party, in accordance with its laws and are not nationals of the other Contracting Party.
   (b) legal entities of either Contracting Party which are formed and incorporated under the laws of one Contracting Party and have their seat together with their substantial economic activities in the territory of that same Contracting Party.

3. The term 'nationals' means
   (a) in respect of the Republic of Sri Lanka:
   persons who are citizens of Sri Lanka according to its laws;
   (b) in respect of the Government of . . . .

4. The term 'returns' means the amounts legally yielded by an investment such as profit derived from investment, financial costs, dividends, royalties and fees.

427

5. The term 'territory' means the territory under sovereignty or jurisdiction of each Contracting Party, and also includes their relevant maritime areas.

Article 2
Promotion and Protection of Investments

1. Each Contracting Party shall, subject to its rights to exercise powers conferred by its laws, encourage and create favourable conditions for nationals and companies of the other Contracting Party to invest in its territory, and subject to the same rights, shall admit such investments.
2. Investments of nationals or companies of either Contracting Party shall at all times be accorded fair and equitable treatment and shall enjoy full protection and security in the territory of the other Contracting Party. Neither Contracting Party shall in any way impair by unreasonable or discriminatory measures the management, maintenance, use, enjoyment or disposal of investments in its territory of nationals or companies of the other Contracting Party.

Article 3
Most-Favoured-Nation Provision

1. Neither Contracting Party shall in its territory subject investments admitted in accordance with the provisions of Article 2 or returns of nationals or companies of the other Contracting Party to treatment less favourable than that which it accords to investments or returns of its own nationals or companies or to investments or returns of nationals or companies of any third State.
2. Neither Contracting Party shall in its territory subject nationals or companies of the other Contracting Party, as regards their management, use, enjoyment or disposal of their investments, to treatment less favourable than that which it accords to its own nationals or companies or to nationals or companies of any third State.

Article 4
Exceptions

The provisions of this Agreement relative to the grant of treatment not less favourable than that accorded to the nationals or companies of either Contracting Party or of any third State shall not be construed so as to oblige one Contracting Party to extend to the nationals or companies of the other Contracting Party the benefit of any treatment or preference which may be extended by the former Contracting Party by virtue of:

(a) the formation or extension of a customs or a free trade area or a common external tariff area or a monetary union or a regional association for economic co-operation; or
(b) the adoption of an agreement designed to lead to the formation or extension of such a union or area within a reasonable length of time; or
(c) any arrangement with a third State or States in the same geographical region designed to promote regional co-operation in the economic, social, labour, industrial or monetary fields within the framework of specific projects; or
(d) any international agreement or arrangement, or any domestic legislation relating wholly or mainly to taxation.

Article 5
Compensation for Losses

Investors of either Contracting Party whose investments suffer losses due to war or any armed conflict, revolution or similar state of emergency in the territory of the other Contracting Party shall be accorded by the other Contracting Party treatment no less favourable than that accorded to its own investors or to investors of any other third country whichever is the most favourable treatment as regards compensation, restitution and indemnification in relation to such losses. Resulting payments shall be freely transferable.

Article 6

Expropriation

1. Investments by nationals or companies of either Contracting Party shall enjoy full protection and security in the territory of the other Contracting Party.
2. Investments by nationals or companies of either Contracting Party shall not be expropriated, nationalized or directly or indirectly subjected to any other measure the effects of which would be tantamount to expropriation or nationalization in the territory of the other Contracting Party except for a public purpose and against prompt and effective compensation. Such compensation shall be equivalent to the value of the expropriated investment immediately before the date on which the actual or threatened expropriation, nationalization or comparable measure became publicly known and shall include interest at a normal commercial rate until the date of payment. The compensation shall be paid without delay and shall be effectively realizable and freely transferable. Provision shall have been made in an appropriate manner at or prior to the time of expropriation, nationalization or comparable measure for the determination and payment of such compensation. The national or company affected shall have a right to prompt preview by a judicial or other independent authority of the Contracting Party making the expropriation, of this or its case and of the valuation of his or its investment in accordance with the principles set out in this paragraph.
3. Nationals or companies of either Contracting Party whose investments suffer losses in the territory of the other Contracting Party owing to war or other armed conflict, revolution, a state of national emergency, or revolt, shall be accorded treatment no less favourable by such other Contracting Party than that which the latter Contracting Party accords to its own nationals or companies as regards restitution, indemnification, compensation or other valuable consideration. Such payments shall be freely transferable.
4. Nationals or companies of either Contracting Party shall enjoy most-favoured-nation treatment in the territory of the other Contracting Party in respect of the matters provided for in this Article.

Article 7

Repatriation of Investment

Each Contracting Party shall in respect of investments guarantee to nationals or companies of the other Contracting Party the free transfer of their capital and of the returns from it, subject to the right of each Contracting Party in exceptional balance of payments difficulties to exercise equitably and in good faith powers conferred by its laws; in conformity with its responsibilities and commitments as a member of the International Monetary Fund.

Article 8

Settlement of Investment Disputes Between a Contracting Party and an Investor of the Other Contracting Party

1. Any dispute between a Contracting Party and an investor of the other Contracting Party shall be notified in writing including a detailed information by the investor to the host party of the investment, and shall, if possible, be settled amicably.
2. If the dispute cannot be settled in this way within six months from the date of the written notification mentioned in paragraph 1 above, it may be submitted upon request of the investor either to:
   (a) The competent tribunal of the Contracting Party in whose territory the investment was made; or
   (b) the International Centre for the Settlement of Investment Disputes (ICSID) established by the convention [for] the settlement of investment disputes between States and Nationals of the other states opened for signature in Washington D.C. on 18th March 1965; or
   (c) the Regional Centre for International Commercial Arbitration in Cairo;
   (d) the Regional Centre for Arbitration—Kuala Lumpur;
   (e) The International Arbitration Institute of Stockholm Chamber of Commerce; or

(f) the Ad-hoc Court of Arbitration established under the arbitration rules of procedures of the United Nations Commission for International Trade Law.

3. The arbitration tribunal shall decide in accordance with:
   — The provisions of this agreement;
   — The national law of the Contracting Party in whose territory the investment was made;
   — Principles of International Law;

4. The arbitration decision shall be final and binding for the parties in the dispute. Each Contracting Party shall execute them in accordance with its laws.

Article 9
Disputes Between the Contracting Parties

1. Disputes between the Contracting Parties concerning the interpretation or application of this Agreement should, if possible, be settled through diplomatic channels.
2. If a dispute between the Contracting Parties cannot thus be settled, it shall upon the request of either Contracting Party be submitted to an arbitral tribunal.
3. Such an arbitral tribunal shall be constituted for each individual case in the following way. Within two months of the receipt of the request for arbitration, each Contracting Party shall appoint one member of the tribunal. Those two members shall then select a national of a third State who on approval by the two Contracting Parties shall be appointed Chairman of the tribunal. The Chairman shall be appointed within two months from the date of appointment of the other two members.
4. If within the periods specified in paragraph 3 of this article the necessary appointments have not been made, either contracting Party may, in the absence of any other agreement, invite the President of the International Court of Justice to make any necessary appointments. If the President is a national of either Contracting Party or if he is otherwise prevented from discharging the said function, the Vice President shall be invited to make the necessary appointments. If the Vice President is a national of either Contracting Party or if he too is prevented from discharging the said function, the member of the International Court of Justice next in seniority who is not a national of either Contracting Party shall be invited to make the necessary appointments.
5. The arbitral tribunal shall reach its decision by a majority of votes. Such decision shall be binding on both Contracting Parties. Each Contracting Party shall bear the cost of its own member of the tribunal and of its representation in the arbitral proceedings; the cost of the Chairman and the remaining costs shall be borne in equal parts by the Contracting Parties. The tribunal may however in its decision direct that a higher proportion of costs shall be borne by one of the two Contracting Parties, and this award shall be binding on both Contracting Parties. The tribunal shall determine its own procedure.

Article 10
Subrogation

If either Contracting Party or its designated agency makes a payment to its own investors under an insurance agreement or guarantee agreement against non-commercial risks it has accorded in respect of investment in the territory of the other Contracting Party, the latter Contracting Party shall recognize:

(a) the assignment, whether under the law or pursuant to a legal transaction in that country, of any right or claim from the party indemnified to the former Contracting Party or its designated Agency; and

(b) that the former Contracting Party or its designated Agency is entitled by virtue of subrogation to exercise the rights and enforce the claims of such a party, provided that such Contracting Party shall not be entitled under this paragraph to exercise any rights other than such rights as the national or company would have been entitled to exercise.

The former Contracting Party (or its designated Agency) shall accordingly if it so desires be entitled to assert any such right or claim to the same extent as its predecessor in title either before a Court or tribunal in the territory of the latter Contracting Party or in any other circumstances. If the former Contracting Party acquires amounts in the lawful currency of the other Contracting Party or credits thereof by assignment under the terms of an indemnity, the former Contracting Party shall be accorded in respect thereof treatment not less favourable than that accorded to the funds of companies or nationals of the latter Contracting Party or of any third State deriving from investment activities similar to those in which the party indemnified was engaged. Such amounts and credits shall be freely available to the former Contracting Party concerned for the purpose of meeting its expenditure in the territory of the other Contracting Party.

Article 11
Entry into Force

This Agreement shall be ratified and shall enter into force on the exchange of instruments of ratification.

Article 12
Applicability of the Agreement

This Agreement shall also apply to the investments made prior to its entry into force by nationals or companies of either Contracting Party in the territory of the other Contracting Party, consistent with the host Contracting Party's laws.

Article 13
Duration and Termination

This Agreement shall remain in force for a period of ten years. Thereafter it shall continue in force until the expiration of twelve months from the date on which either Contracting Party shall have given written notice of termination to the other. Provided that in respect of investments made whilst the Agreement is in force, its provisions shall continue in effect with respect to such investments for a period of ten years after the date of termination and without prejudice to the application thereafter of the rules of general international law.

IN WITNESS WHEREOF, the undersigned, duly authorised thereto by their respective Governments, have signed this Agreement.

Done in duplicate at [   ] this [   ] day of [   ] in the Sinhalase, [   ] and English languages, all texts being equally authentic. In the event of divergence of interpretation the English text shall prevail.

For the Government
of Democratic Socialist
Republic of Sri Lanka

For the Government
of [   ]

APPENDIX 10

Accord entre le Gouvernement de la République Française et le Gouvernement de [   ] sur l'Encouragement et la Protection Réciproques des Investissements ('France Model BIT')

APPI Modele Type FR 2006

Accord

entre le Gouvernement de la République Française et
le Gouvernement de [   ]
sur l'Encouragement et la Protection Réciproques
des Investissements

Le Gouvernement de la République française et le Gouvernement de la République de
[   ], ci-après dénommés 'les Parties contractantes',

Désireux de renforcer la coopération économique entre les deux Etats et de créer des conditions favorables pour les investissements français en [   ] et [   ] en France,

Persuadés que l'encouragement et la protection de ces investissements sont propres à stimuler les transferts de capitaux et de technologie entre les deux pays, dans l'intérêt de leur développement économique,

Sont convenus des dispositions suivantes:

Article 1
Définitions

Pour l'application du présent accord:

1. Le terme 'investissement' désigne tous les avoirs, tels que les biens, droits et intérêts de toutes natures et, plus particulièrement mais non exclusivement:
   a) les biens meubles et immeubles, ainsi que tous autres droits réels tels que les hypothèques, privilèges, usufruits, cautionnements et tous droits analogues;
   b) les actions, primes d'émission et autres formes de participation, même minoritaires ou indirectes, aux sociétés constituées sur le territoire de l'une des Parties contractantes;
   c) les obligations, créances et droits à toutes prestations ayant valeur économique;
   d) les droits de propriété intellectuelle, commerciale et industrielle tels que les droits d'auteur, les brevets d'invention, les licences, les marques déposées, les modèles et maquettes industrielles, les procédés techniques, le savoir-faire, les noms déposés et la clientèle;
   e) les concessions accordées par la loi ou en vertu d'un contrat, notamment les concessions relatives à la prospection, la culture, l'extraction ou l'exploitation de richesses naturelles, y compris celles qui se situent dans la zone maritime des Parties contractantes.

Il est entendu que lesdits avoirs doivent être ou avoir été investis conformément à la législation de la Partie contractante sur le territoire ou dans la zone maritime de laquelle l'investissement est effectué, avant ou après l'entrée en vigueur du présent accord.

Aucune modification de la forme d'investissement des avoirs n'affecte leur qualification d'investissement, à condition que cette modification ne soit pas contraire à la législation de la Partie contractante sur le territoire ou dans la zone maritime de laquelle l'investissement est réalisé.

2. Le terme d' 'investisseur' désigne:

a) Les nationaux, c'est-à-dire les personnes physiques possédant la nationalité de l'une des Parties contractantes.

b) Toute personne morale constituée sur le territoire de l'une des Parties contractantes, conformément à la législation de celle-ci et y possédant son siège social, ou contrôlée directement ou indirectement par des nationaux de l'une des Parties contractantes, ou par des personnes morales possédant leur siège social sur le territoire de l'une des Parties contractantes et constituées conformément à la législation de celle-ci.

Sont notamment considérées comme des personnes morales au sens du présent article les sociétés, d'une part, et les organisations à but non lucratif dotées de la personnalité juridique d'autre part.

3. Le terme de 'revenus' désigne toutes les sommes produites par un investissement, telles que bénéfices, redevances ou intérêts, durant une période donnée.

Les revenus de l'investissement et, en cas de réinvestissement, les revenus de leur réinvestissement jouissent de la même protection que l'investissement.

4. Le présent accord s'applique au territoire de chacune des Parties contractantes ainsi qu'à la zone maritime de chacune des Parties contractantes, ci-après définie comme la zone économique et le plateau continental qui s'étendent au-delà de la limite des eaux territoriales de chacune des Parties contractantes et sur lesquels elles ont, en conformité avec le Droit international, des droits souverains et une juridiction aux fins de prospection, d'exploitation et de préservation des ressources naturelles.

5. Aucune disposition du présent Accord ne sera interprétée comme empêchant l'une des Parties contractantes de prendre toute disposition visant à régir les investissements réalisés par des investisseurs étrangers et les conditions d'activités desdits investisseurs, dans le cadre de mesures destinées à préserver et à encourager la diversité culturelle et linguistique.

Article 2
Champ de l'accord

Pour l'application du présent Accord, il est entendu que les Parties contractantes sont responsables des actions ou omissions de leurs collectivités publiques, et notamment de leurs Etats fédérés, régions, collectivités locales ou de toute autre entité sur lesquels la Partie contractante excerce une tutelle, la représentation ou la responsabilité de ses relations internationales ou sa souveraineté.

Article 3
Encouragement et admission des investissements

Chacune des Parties contractantes encourage et admet, dans le cadre de sa législation et des dispositions du présent accord, les investissements effectués par les investisseurs de l'autre Partie sur son territoire et dans sa zone maritime.

Article 4
Traitement juste et équitable

Chacune des Parties contractantes s'engage à assurer, sur son territoire et dans sa zone maritime, un traitement juste et équitable, conformément aux principes du Droit international, aux investissements des investisseurs de l'autre Partie et à faire en sorte que l'exercice du droit ainsi reconnu ne soit entravé ni en droit, ni en fait. En particulier, bien que non exclusivement, sont considérées comme des entraves de droit ou de fait au traitement juste et équitable, toute restriction à l'achat et au transport de matières premières et de matières auxiliaires, d'énergie et de combustibles, ainsi que de moyens de production et d'exploitation de tout genre, toute entrave à la vente et au transport des produits à l'intérieur du pays et à l'étranger, ainsi que toutes autres mesures ayant un effet analogue.

Les Parties contractantes examineront avec bienveillance, dans le cadre de leur législation interne, les demandes d'entrée et d'autorisation de séjour, de travail, et de circulation introduites par des nationaux d'une Partie contractante, au titre d'un investissement réalisé sur le territoire ou dans la zone maritime de l'autre Partie contractante.

Article 5

Traitement national et traitement de la Nation la plus favorisée

Chaque Partie contractante applique, sur son territoire et dans sa zone maritime, aux investisseurs de l'autre Partie, en ce qui concerne leurs investissements et activités liées à ces investissements, un traitement non moins favorable que celui accordé à ses investisseurs, ou le traitement accordé aux investisseurs de la Nation la plus favorisée, si celui-ci est plus avantageux. A ce titre, les nationaux autorisés à travailler sur le territoire et dans la zone maritime de l'une des Parties contractantes doivent pouvoir bénéficier des facilités matérielles appropriées pour l'exercice de leurs activités professionnelles.

Ce traitement ne s'étend toutefois pas aux privilèges qu'une Partie contractante accorde aux investisseurs d'un Etat tiers, en vertu de sa participation ou de son association à une zone de libre échange, une union douanière, un marché commun ou toute autre forme d'organisation économique régionale.

Les dispositions de cet Article ne s'appliquent pas aux questions fiscales.

Article 6

Dépossession et indemnisation

1. Les investissements effectués par des investisseurs de l'une ou l'autre des Parties contractantes bénéficient, sur le territoire et dans la zone maritime de l'autre Partie contractante, d'une protection et d'une sécurité pleines et entières.

2. Les Parties contractantes ne prennent pas de mesures d'expropriation ou de nationalisation ou toutes autres mesures dont l'effet est de déposséder, directement ou indirectement, les investisseurs de l'autre Partie des investissements leur appartenant, sur leur territoire et dans leur zone maritime, si ce n'est pour cause d'utilité publique et à condition que ces mesures ne soient ni discriminatoires, ni contraires à un engagement particulier.

   Toutes les mesures de dépossession qui pourraient être prises doivent donner lieu au paiement d'une indemnité prompte et adéquate dont le montant, égal à la valeur réelle des investissements concernés, doit être évalué par rapport à une situation économique normale et antérieure à toute menace de dépossession.

   Cette indemnité, son montant et ses modalités de versement sont fixés au plus tard à la date de la dépossession. Cette indemnité est effectivement réalisable, versée sans retard et librement transférable. Elle produit, jusqu'à la date de versement, des intérêts calculés au taux d'intérêt de marché approprié.

3. Les investisseurs de l'une des Parties contractantes dont les investissements auront subi des pertes dues à la guerre ou à tout autre conflit armé, révolution, état d'urgence national ou révolte survenu sur le territoire ou dans la zone maritime de l'autre Partie contractante, bénéficieront, de la part de cette dernière, d'un traitement non moins favorable que celui accordé à ses propres investisseurs ou à ceux de la Nation la plus favorisée.

Article 7

Libre transfert

Chaque Partie contractante, sur le territoire ou dans la zone maritime de laquelle des investissements ont été effectués par des investisseurs de l'autre Partie contractante, accorde à ces investisseurs le libre transfert:

   a) des intérêts, dividendes, bénéfices et autres revenus courants;
   b) des redevances découlant des droits incorporels désignés au paragraphe 1, lettres d) et e) de l'Article 1;

434

c) des versements effectués pour le remboursement des emprunts régulièrement contractés;

d) du produit de la cession ou de la liquidation totale ou partielle de l'investissement, y compris les plus-values du capital investi;

e) des indemnités de dépossession ou de perte prévues à l'Article 6, paragraphes 2 et 3 ci-dessus.

Les nationaux de chacune des Parties contractantes qui ont été autorisés à travailler sur le territoire ou dans la zone maritime de l'autre Partie contractante, au titre d'un investissement agréé, sont également autorisés à transférer dans leur pays d'origine une quotité appropriée de leur rémunération.

Les transferts visés aux paragraphes précédents sont effectués sans retard au taux de change normal officiellement applicable à la date du transfert.

Lorsque, dans des circonstances exceptionnelles, les mouvements de capitaux en provenance ou à destination de pays tiers causent ou menacent de causer un déséquilibre grave pour la balance des paiements, chacune des Parties contractantes peut temporairement appliquer des mesures de sauvegarde relatives aux transferts, pour autant que ces mesures soient strictement nécessaires, appliquées sur une base équitable, non-discriminatoire et de bonne foi et qu'elles n'excèdent pas une période de six mois.

Les dispositions des alinéas précédents du présent article, ne s'opposent pas à l'exercice de bonne foi, par une Partie contractante, de ses obligations internationales ainsi que de ses droits et obligations au titre de sa participation ou des son association à une zone de libre échange, une union douanière, un marché commun, une union économique et monétaire ou toute autre forme de coopération ou d'intégration régionale.

Article 8
Règlement des différends entre un investisseur et une Partie contractante

Tout différend relatif aux investissements entre l'une des Parties contractantes et un investisseur de l'autre Partie contractante est réglé à l'amiable entre les deux parties concernées.

Si un tel différend n'a pas pu être réglé dans un délai de six mois à partir du moment où il a été soulevé par l'une ou l'autre des parties au différend, il est soumis à la demande de l'une ou l'autre de ces parties à l'arbitrage du Centre international pour le règlement des différends relatifs aux investissements (C.I.R.D.I.), créé par la Convention pour le règlement des différends relatifs aux investissements entre Etats et ressortissants d'autres Etats, signée à Washington le 18 mars 1965.

Dans le cas où le différend est de nature à engager la responsabilité pour les actions ou omissions de collectivités publiques ou d'organismes dépendants de l'une des deux Parties contractantes, au sens de l'article 2 du présent accord, ladite collectivité publique ou ledit organisme sont tenus de donner leur consentement de manière inconditionnelle au recours à l'arbitrage du Centre international pour le règlement des différends relatifs aux investissements (C.I.R.D.I.), au sens de l'article 25 de la Convention pour le règlement des différends relatifs aux investissements entre Etats et ressortissants d'autres Etats, signée à Washington le 18 mars 1965.

Article 9
Garantie et subrogation

1. Dans la mesure où la réglementation de l'une des Parties contractantes prévoit une garantie pour les investissements effectués à l'étranger, celle-ci peut être accordée, dans le cadre d'un examen cas par cas, à des investissements effectués par des investisseurs de cette Partie sur le territoire ou dans la zone maritime de l'autre Partie.

2. Les investissements des investisseurs de l'une des Parties contractantes sur le territoire ou dans la zone maritime de l'autre Partie ne pourront obtenir la garantie visée à l'alinéa ci-dessus que s'ils ont, au préalable, obtenu l'agrément de cette dernière Partie.

3. Si l'une des Parties contractantes, en vertu d'une garantie donnée pour un investissement réalisé sur le territoire ou dans la zone maritime de l'autre Partie, effectue des versements à l'un de ses investisseurs, elle est, de ce fait, subrogée dans les droits et actions de cet investisseur.

4. Lesdits versements n'affectent pas les droits du bénéficiaire de la garantie à recourir au C.I.R.D.I. ou à poursuivre les actions introduites devant lui jusqu'à l'aboutissement de la procédure.

Article 10
Engagement spécifique

Les investissements ayant fait l'objet d'un engagement particulier de l'une des Parties contractantes à l'égard des investisseurs de l'autre Partie contractante sont régis, sans préjudice des dispositions du présent accord, par les termes de cet engagement dans la mesure où celui-ci comporte des disposit-itions plus favorables que celles qui sont prévues par le présent accord. Les dispositions de l'article 8 du présent Accord s'appliquent même en cas d'engagement spécifique prévoyant la renonciation à l'arbitrage international ou désignant une instance arbitrale différente de celle mentionnée à l'article 8 du présent Accord.

Article 11
Règlement des différends entre Parties contractantes

1. Les différends relatifs à l'interprétation ou à l'application du présent accord, doivent être réglés, si possible, par la voie diplomatique.
2. Si dans un délai de six mois à partir du moment où il a été soulevé par l'une ou l'autre des Parties contractantes, le différend n'est pas réglé, il est soumis, à la demande de l'une ou l'autre Partie contractante, à un tribunal d'arbitrage.
3. Ledit tribunal sera constitué pour chaque cas particulier de la manière suivante: chaque Partie contractante désigne un membre, et les deux membres désignent, d'un commun accord, un ressortissant d'un Etat tiers qui est nommé Président du tribunal par les deux Parties contrac-tantes. Tous les membres doivent être nommés dans un délai de deux mois à compter de la date à laquelle une des Parties contractantes a fait part à l'autre Partie contractante de son intention de soumettre le différend à arbitrage.
4. Si les délais fixés au paragraphe 3 ci-dessus n'ont pas été observés, l'une ou l'autre Partie contrac-tante, en l'absence de tout autre accord, invite le Secrétaire général de l'Organisation des Nations-Unies à procéder aux désignations nécessaires. Si le Secrétaire général est ressortissant de l'une ou l'autre Partie contractante ou si, pour une autre raison, il est empêché d'exercer cette fonction, le Secrétaire général adjoint le plus ancien et ne possédant pas la nationalité de l'une des Parties contractantes procède aux désignations nécessaires.
5. Le tribunal d'arbitrage prend ses décisions à la majorité des voix. Ces décisions sont définitives et exécutoires de plein droit pour les Parties contractantes.

   Le tribunal fixe lui-même son règlement. Il interprète la sentence à la demande de l'une ou l'autre Partie contractante. A moins que le tribunal n'en dispose autrement, compte tenu de circon-stances particulières, les frais de la procédure arbitrale, y compris les vacations des arbitres, sont répartis également entre les Parties Contractantes.

Article 12
Entrée en vigueur et durée

Chacune des Parties notifiera à l'autre l'accomplissement des procédures internes requises pour l'entrée en vigueur du présent accord, qui prendra effet un mois après le jour de la réception de la dernière notification.

L'accord est conclu pour une durée initiale de dix ans. Il restera en vigueur après ce terme, à moins que l'une des Parties ne le dénonce par la voie diplomatique avec préavis d'un an.

A l'expiration de la période de validité du présent accord, les investissements effectués pendant qu'il était en vigueur continueront de bénéficier de la protection de ses dispositions pendant une période supplémentaire de vingt ans.

Signé à [ville (PAYS)] le [date mois année] en deux originaux, chacun en langue française et en langue
[   ], les deux textes faisant également foi [en deux originaux en langue française]

Pour le gouvernement de République française   **Pour le gouvernement de la République**
                                                  [   ]

         [Fonctions]   [Fonctions]

        [Signature]   [Signature]

     [Prénom NOM]   **[Prénom NOM]**

APPENDIX 11

Convention on the Settlement of Investment Disputes between States and Nationals of Other States (ICSID)

Chapter II
Jurisdiction of the Centre

Article 25

(1) The jurisdiction of the Centre shall extend to any legal dispute arising directly out of an investment, between a Contracting State (or any constituent subdivision or agency of a Contracting State designated to the Centre by that State) and a national of another Contracting State, which the parties to the dispute consent in writing to submit to the Centre. When the parties have given their consent, no party may withdraw its consent unilaterally.

(2) 'National of another Contracting State' means:

   (a) any natural person who had the nationality of a Contracting State other than the State party to the dispute on the date on which the parties consented to submit such dispute to conciliation or arbitration as well as on the date on which the request was registered pursuant to paragraph (3) of Article 28 or paragraph (3) of Article 36, but does not include any person who on either date also had the nationality of the Contracting State party to the dispute; and

   (b) any juridical person which had the nationality of a Contracting State other than the State party to the dispute on the date on which the parties consented to submit such dispute to conciliation or arbitration and any juridical person which had the nationality of the Contracting State party to the dispute on that date and which, because of foreign control, the parties have agreed should be treated as a national of another Contracting State for the purposes of this Convention.

(3) Consent by a constituent subdivision or agency of a Contracting State shall require the approval of that State unless that State notifies the Centre that no such approval is required.

(4) Any Contracting State may, at the time of ratification, acceptance or approval of this Convention or at any time thereafter, notify the Centre of the class or classes of disputes which it would or would not consider submitting to the jurisdiction of the Centre. The Secretary-General shall forthwith transmit such notification to all Contracting States. Such notification shall not constitute the consent required by paragraph (1).

Article 26

Consent of the parties to arbitration under this Convention shall, unless otherwise stated, be deemed consent to such arbitration to the exclusion of any other remedy. A Contracting State may require the exhaustion of local administrative or judicial remedies as a condition of its consent to arbitration under this Convention.

Article 27

(1) No Contracting State shall give diplomatic protection, or bring an international claim, in respect of a dispute which one of its nationals and another Contracting State shall have

consented to submit or shall have submitted to arbitration under this Convention, unless such other Contracting State shall have failed to abide by and comply with the award rendered in such dispute.

(2) Diplomatic protection, for the purposes of paragraph (1), shall not include informal diplomatic exchanges for the sole purpose of facilitating a settlement of the dispute.

APPENDIX 12

World Bank Guidelines on the Treatment of
Foreign Direct Investment[1]

The Development Committee

Recognizing

that a greater flow of foreign direct investment brings substantial benefits to bear on the world economy and on the economies of developing countries in particular, in terms of improving the long
term efficiency of the host country through greater competition, transfer of capital, technology and
managerial skills and enhancement of market access and in terms of the expansion of international
trade;

that the promotion of private foreign investment is a common purpose of the International Bank for
Reconstruction and Development, the International Finance Corporation and the Multilateral
Investment Guarantee Agency;

that these institutions have pursued this common objective through their operations, advisory
services and research;

that at the request of the Development Committee, a working group established by the President of
these institutions and consisting of their respective General Counsel has, after reviewing existing
legal instruments and literature, as well as best available practice identified by these institutions, prepared a set of guidelines representing a desirable overall framework which embodies essential principles meant to promote foreign direct investment in the common interest of all members;

that these guidelines, which have benefitted from a process of broad consultation inside and outside
these institutions, constitute a further step in the evolutionary process where several international
efforts aim to establish a favorable investment environment free from non-commercial risks in all
countries, and thereby foster the confidence of international investors; and

that these guidelines are not ultimate standards but an important step in the evolution of generally
acceptable international standards which complement, but do not substitute for, bilateral investment treaties,

therefore *calls the attention* of member countries to the following Guidelines as useful parameters in
the admission and treatment of private foreign investment in their territories, without prejudice to
the binding rules of international law at this stage of its development.

I

SCOPE OF APPLICATION

1. These Guidelines may be applied by members of the World Bank Group institutions to private
   foreign investment in their respective territories, as a complement to applicable bilateral and
   multilateral treaties and other international instruments, to the extent that these Guidelines
   do not conflict with such treaties and binding instruments, and as a possible source on which
   national legislation governing the treatment of private foreign investment may draw. Reference

---

[1] OUP was kindly granted permission to reproduce this document by the World Bank.

to the 'State' in these Guidelines, unless the context otherwise indicates, includes the State or any constituent subdivision, agency or instrumentality of the State and reference to 'nationals' includes natural and juridical persons who enjoy the nationality of the State.

2. The application of these Guidelines extends to existing and new investments established and operating at all times as *bona fide* private foreign investments, in full conformity with the laws and regulations of the host State.

3. These Guidelines are based on the general premise that equal treatment of investors in similar circumstances and free competition among them are prerequisites of a positive investment environment. Nothing in these Guidelines therefore suggests that foreign investors should receive a privileged treatment denied to national investors in similar circumstances.

II
ADMISSION

1. Each State will encourage nationals of other States to invest capital, technology and managerial skill in its territory and, to that end, is expected to admit such investments in accordance with the following provisions.

2. In furtherance of the foregoing principle, each State will:
   (a) facilitate the admission and establishment of investments by nationals of other States, and
   (b) avoid making unduly cumbersome or complicated procedural regulations for, or imposing unnecessary conditions on, the admission of such investments.

3. Each State maintains the right to make regulations to govern the admission of private foreign investments. In the formulation and application of such regulations, States will note that experience suggests that certain performance requirements introduced as conditions of admission are often counterproductive and that open admission, possibly subject to a restricted list of investments (which are either prohibited or require screening and licensing), is a more effective approach. Such performance requirements often discourage foreign investors from initiating investment in the State concerned or encourage evasion and corruption. Under the restricted list approach, investments in non-listed activities, which proceed without approval, remain subject to the laws and regulations applicable to investments in the State concerned.

4. Without prejudice to the general approach of free admission recommended in Section 3 above, a State may, as an exception, refuse admission to a proposed investment:
   (i) which is, in the considered opinion of the State, inconsistent with clearly defined requirements of national security; or
   (ii) which belongs to sectors reserved by the law of the State to its nationals on account of the State's economic development objectives or the strict exigencies of its national interest.

5. Restrictions applicable to national investment on account of public policy (*ordre public*), public health and the protection of the environment will equally apply to foreign investment.

6. Each State is encouraged to publish, in the form of a handbook or other medium easily accessible to other States and their investors, adequate and regularly updated information about its legislation, regulations and procedures relevant to foreign investment and other information relating to its investment policies including, *inter alia*, an indication of any classes of investment which it regards as falling under Sections 4 and 5 of this Guideline.

III
TREATMENT

1. For the promotion of international economic cooperation through the medium of private foreign investment, the establishment, operation, management, control, and exercise of rights in such an investment, as well as such other associated activities necessary therefore or incidental thereto, will be consistent with the following standards which are meant to apply simultaneously

to all States without prejudice to the provisions of applicable international instruments, and to firmly established rules of customary international law.

2. Each State will extend to investments established in its territory by nationals of any other State fair and equitable treatment according to the standards recommended in these Guidelines.

3. (a) With respect to the protection and security of their person, property rights and interests, and to the granting of permits, import and export licenses and the authorization to employ, and the issuance of the necessary entry and stay visas to their foreign personnel, and other legal matters relevant to the treatment of foreign investors as described in Section 1 above, such treatment will, subject to the requirement of fair and equitable treatment mentioned above, be as favorable as that accorded by the State to national investors in similar circumstances. In all cases, full protection and security will be accorded to the investor's rights regarding ownership, control and substantial benefits over his property, including intellectual property.

   (b) As concerns such other matters as are not relevant to national investors, treatment under the State's legislation and regulations will not discriminate among foreign investors on grounds of nationality.

4. Nothing in this Guideline will automatically entitle nationals of other States to the more favorable standards of treatment accorded to the nationals of certain States under any customs union or free trade area agreement.

5. Without restricting the generality of the foregoing, each State will:

   (a) promptly issue such licenses and permits and grant *such* concessions as may be necessary for the uninterrupted operation of the admitted investment; and

   (b) to the extent necessary for the efficient operation of the investment, authorize the employment of foreign personnel. While a State may require the foreign investor to reasonably establish his inability to recruit the required personnel locally, e.g., through local advertisement, before he resorts to the recruitment of foreign personnel, labor market flexibility in this and other areas is recognized as an important element in a positive investment environment. Of particular importance in this respect is the investor's freedom to employ top managers regardless of their nationality.

6. (1) Each State will, with respect to private investment in its territory by nationals of the other States:

   (a) freely allow regular periodic transfer of a reasonable part of the salaries and wages of foreign personnel; and, on liquidation of the investment or earlier termination of the employment, allow immediate transfer of all savings from such salaries and wages;

   (b) freely allow transfer of the net revenues realized from the investment;

   (c) allow the transfer of such sums as may be necessary for the payment of debts contracted, or the discharge of other contractual obligations incurred in connection with the investment as they fall due;

   (d) on liquidation or sale of the investment (whether covering the investment as a whole or a part thereof), allow the repatriation and transfer of the net proceeds of such liquidation or sale and all accretions thereto all at once; in the exceptional cases where the State faces foreign exchange stringencies, such transfer may as an exception be made in installments within a period *which* will be as short as possible and will not in any case exceed five years from the date of liquidation or sale, subject to interest as provided for in Section 6(3) of this Guideline;
   and

   (e) allow the transfer of any other amounts to which the investor is entitled such as those which become due under the conditions provided for in Guidelines IV and V.

   (2) Such transfer as provided for in Section 6(1) of this Guideline will be made (a) in the currency brought in by the investor where it remains convertible, in another currency designated as freely usable currency by the International Monetary Fund or in any other currency

accepted by the investor, and (b) at the applicable market rate of exchange at the time of the transfer.

(3) In the case of transfers under Section 6(1) of this Guideline, and without prejudice to Sections 7 and 8 of Guideline IV where they apply, any delay in effecting the transfers to be made through the central bank (or another authorized public authority) of the host State will be subject to interest at the normal rate applicable to the local currency involved in respect of any period intervening between the date on which such local currency has been provided to the central bank (or the other authorized public authority) for transfer and the date on which the transfer is actually effected.

(4) The provisions set forth in this Guideline with regard to the transfer of capital will also apply to the transfer of any compensation for loss due to war, armed conflict, revolution or insurrection to the extent that such compensation may be due to the investor under applicable law.

7. Each State will permit and facilitate the reinvestment in its territory of the profits realized from existing investments and the proceeds of sale or liquidation of such investments.

8. Each State will take appropriate measures for the prevention and control of corrupt business practices and the promotion of accountability and transparency in its dealings with foreign investors, and will cooperate with other States in developing international procedures and mechanisms to ensure the same.

9. Nothing in this Guideline suggests that a State should provide foreign investors with tax exemptions or other fiscal incentives. Where such incentives are deemed to be justified by the State, they may to the extent possible be automatically granted, directly linked to the type of activity to be encouraged and equally extended to national investors in similar circumstances. Competition among States in providing such incentives, especially tax exemptions, is not recommended. Reasonable and stable tax rates are deemed to provide a better incentive than exemptions followed by uncertain or excessive rates.

10. Developed and capital surplus States will not obstruct flows of investment from their territories to developing States and are encouraged to adopt appropriate measures to facilitate such flows, including taxation agreements, investment guarantees, technical assistance and the provision of information. Fiscal incentives provided by some investors' governments for the purpose of encouraging investment in developing States are recognized in particular as a possibly effective element in promoting such investment.

IV
Expropriation and Unilateral Alterations or Termination of Contracts

1. A State may not expropriate or otherwise take in whole or in part a foreign private investment in its territory, or take measures which have similar effects, except where this is done in accordance with applicable legal procedures, in pursuance in good faith of a public purpose, without discrimination on the basis of nationality and against the payment of appropriate compensation.

2. Compensation for a specific investment taken by the State will, according to the details provided below, be deemed 'appropriate' if it is adequate, effective and prompt.

3. Compensation will be deemed 'adequate' if it is based on the fair market value of the taken asset as such value is determined immediately before the time at which the taking occurred or the decision to take the asset became publicly known.

4. Determination of the 'fair market value' will be acceptable if conducted according to a method agreed by the State and the foreign investor (hereinafter referred to as the parties) or by a tribunal or another body designated by the parties.

5. In the absence of a determination on agreed by, or based on the agreement of, the parties, the fair market value will be acceptable if determined by the State according to reasonable criteria related to the market value of the investment, i.e., in an amount that a willing buyer would normally pay

to a willing seller after taking into account the nature of the investment, the circumstances in which it would operate in the future and its specific characteristics, including the period in which it has been in existence, the proportion of tangible assets in the total investment and other relevant factors pertinent to the specific circumstances of each case.

6. Without implying the exclusive validity of a single standard for the fairness by which compensation is to be determined and as an illustration of the reasonable determination by a State of the market value *of* the investment under Section 5 above, such determination will be deemed reasonable if conducted as follows:

  (i)   for a going concern with a proven record of profitability, on the basis *of* the discounted cash flow value;

  (ii) for an enterprise which, not being a proven going concern, demonstrates lack of profitability, on the basis of the liquidation value;

  (iii) for other assets, on the basis of (a) the replacement value or (b) the book value in case such value has been recently assessed or has been determined as of the date of the taking and can therefore be deemed to represent a reasonable replacement value.

For the purpose of this provision:

— a '*going concern*' means an enterprise consisting of income-producing assets which has been in operation for a sufficient period of time to generate the data required for the calculation of future income and which could have been expected with reasonable certainty, if the taking had not occurred, to continue producing legitimate income over the course of its economic life in the general circumstances following the taking by the State;

— '*discounted cash flow value*' means the cash receipts realistically expected from the enterprise in each future year of its economic life as reasonably projected minus that year's expected cash expenditure, after discounting this net cash flow for each year by a factor which reflects the time value of money, expected inflation, and the risk associated with such cash flow under realistic circumstances. Such discount rate may be measured by examining the rate of return available in the same market on alternative investments of comparable risk on the basis of their present value;

— '*liquidation value*' means the amounts at which individual assets comprising the enterprise or the entire assets of the enterprise could be sold under conditions of liquidation to a willing buyer less any liabilities which the enterprise has to meet;

— '*replacement value*' means the cash amount required to replace the individual assets of the enterprise in their actual state as of the date of the taking; and

— '*book value*' means the difference between the enterprise's assets and liabilities as recorded on its financial statements or the amount at which the taken tangible assets appear on the balance sheet of the enterprise, representing their cost after deducting accumulated depreciation in accordance with generally accepted accounting principles.

7. Compensation will be deemed 'effective' if it is paid in the currency brought in by the investor where it remains convertible, in another currency designated as freely usable by the International Monetary Fund or in any other currency accepted by the investor.

8. Compensation will be deemed to be 'prompt' in normal circumstances if paid without delay. In cases where the State faces exceptional circumstances, as reflected in an arrangement for the use of the resources of the International Monetary Fund or under similar objective circumstances of established foreign exchange stringencies, compensation in the currency designated under Section 7 above may be paid in installments within a period which will be as short as possible and which will not in any case exceed five years from the time of the taking, provided that reasonable, market-related interest applies to the deferred payments in the same currency.

9. Compensation according to the above criteria will not be due, or will be reduced in case the investment is taken by the State as a sanction against an investor who has violated the State's law and regulations which have been in force prior to the taking, as such violation is determined by a court of law. Further disputes regarding claims for compensation in such a case will be settled in accordance with the provisions of Guideline V.

10. In case of comprehensive non-discriminatory nationalizations effected in the process of large scale social reforms under exceptional circumstances of revolution, war and similar exigencies, the compensation may be determined through negotiations between the host State and the investors' home State and failing this, through international arbitration.

11. The provisions of Section I of this Guideline will apply with respect to the conditions under which a State may unilaterally terminate, amend or otherwise disclaim liability under a contract with a foreign private investor for other than commercial reasons, i.e., where the State acts as a sovereign and not as a contracting party. Compensation due to the investor in such cases will be determined in the light of the provisions of Sections 2 to 9 of this Guideline. Liability for repudiation of contract for commercial reasons, i.e., where the State acts as a contracting party, will be determined under the applicable law of the contract.

V

SETTLEMENT OF DISPUTES

1. Disputes between private foreign investors and the host State will normally be settled through negotiations between them and failing this, through national courts or through other agreed mechanisms including conciliation and binding independent arbitration.

2. Independent arbitration for the purpose of this Guideline will include any ad hoc or institutional arbitration agreed upon in writing by the State and the investor or between the State and the investor's home State where the majority of the arbitrators are not solely appointed by one party to the dispute.

3. In case of agreement on independent arbitration, each State is encouraged to accept the settlement of such disputes through arbitration under the Convention establishing the International Centre for Settlement of Investment Disputes (ICSID) if it is a party to the ICSID Convention or through the 'ICSID Additional Facility' if it is not a party to the ICSII) Convention.

SELECT BIBLIOGRAPHY

BOOKS

Aksen, G, Böckstiegel, K, Mustill, M, Patocchi, P & Whitesell, A *Global Reflections on International Law, Commerce and Dispute Resolution: Liber Amicorum in Honour of Robert Briner* (ICC Publishing, Paris 2005)

Amerasinghe, CF *State Responsibility for Injuries to Aliens* (Clarendon Press, Oxford 1967)

—— *Local Remedies in International Law* (2nd edn, Cambridge University Press, Cambridge 2004)

American Law Institute *Restatement of the Law, Third, Foreign Relations Law of the United States* (1987)

Bjorklund, A, Hannaford, J & Kinnear, M *Investment Disputes under NAFTA: An Annotated Guide to NAFTA Chapter 11* (Kluwer Law International, The Hague 2006)

Borchard, E *The Diplomatic Protection of Citizens Abroad or The Law of International Claims* (The Banks Law Publ Co, New York 1915)

Born, GB *International Commercial Arbitration: Commentary and Materials* (2nd edn, Kluwer Law International, The Hague 2001)

—— & Rutledge, PB *International Civil Litigation in United States Courts* (4th edn, Aspen Publishers, New York 2006)

Brower, CN & Brueschke, JD *The Iran-United States Claims Tribunal* (Martinus-Nijhoff, The Hague 1998)

Brownlie, I *System of the Law of Nations, State Responsibility—Part I* (Oxford University Press, Oxford 1983)

—— *Principles of Public International Law* (6th edn, Oxford University Press, Oxford 2003)

Collins, L, Morse, CG, McLean, JD, Briggs, A, Harris, J, McLachlan, C (eds) *Dicey, Morris and Collins on the Conflict of Laws* (14th edn, Sweet & Maxwell, London 2006)

Craig, WL, Park, WW & Paulsson, J *International Chamber of Commerce Arbitration* (3rd edn, Oceana Publications Inc, 2000)

Crawford, J *The International Law Commission's Articles on State Responsibility: Introduction, Text and Commentaries* (Cambridge University Press, Cambridge 2002)

Cremades, B & Lew, J (eds) *Parallel State and Arbitral Procedures in International Arbitration* (ICC Publishing, Paris 2005)

Dolzer, R & Stevens, M *Bilateral Investment Treaties* (Kluwer Law International, The Hague 1995)

Freeman, A *The International Responsibility of States for Denial of Justice* (Longmans, Green and Company, London 1938)

—— *Responsibility of States for Unlawful Acts of their Armed Forces* (AW Sijthoff, Leyden 1957)

Gaillard, E & Savage, J (eds) *Fouchard, Gaillard, Goldman on International Commercial Arbitration* (Kluwer Law International, The Hague 1999)

García Amador, F, Sohn, L & Baxter, R *Draft Articles on the Responsibility of the State for Injuries caused in its Territory to the Person or Property of Aliens* (Oceana Publications, Dobbs Ferry, New York 1974)

447

Horn, N (ed) *Arbitrating Foreign Investment Disputes* (Kluwer Law International, The Hague 2004)

Jennings, R & Watts, A (eds) *Oppenheim's International Law* (9th edn, Longman, London 1992)

Kreindler, R & Derains, Y (eds) *Evaluation of Damages in International Arbitration* (ICC Publishing, Paris 2006)

Lew, JDM, Mistelis, LA & Kröll, SM *Comparative International Commercial Arbitration* (Kluwer Law International, The Hague 2003)

Lowenfeld, AF *International Economic Law* (Clarendon Press, Oxford 2002)

Mann, FA *Further Studies in International Law* (Clarendon Press, Oxford 1990)

McNair, A *The Law of Treaties* (Clarendon Press, Oxford 1961)

Merkin, R *Arbitration Law* (Informa Business Publishing, London 2004)

Mistelis, LA & Lew, J (eds) *Pervasive Problems in International Arbitration* (Aspen Publishers, New York 2006)

Muchlinski, P *Multinational Enterprises and the Law* (Blackwell Publishers, Oxford 1995)

Mustill, MJ & Boyd, SC *Commercial Arbitration* (2nd edn, Butterworths, London 1989)

—— *Commercial Arbitration: 2001 Companion Volume* (Butterworths, London 2001)

Ortino, F, Sheppard, A & Warner, H (eds) *Investment Treaty Law: Current Issues Volume 1* (British Institute of International and Comparative Law, London 2006)

Paulsson, J *Denial of Justice in International Law* (Cambridge University Press, Cambridge 2005)

Petrochilos, G *Procedural Law in International Arbitration* (Oxford University Press, Oxford 2004)

Redfern, A & Hunter, M *Law and Practice of International Commercial Arbitration* (4th edn, Sweet & Maxwell, London 2004)

Reed, L, Paulsson, J & Blackaby, N *Guide to ICSID Arbitration* (Kluwer Law International, The Hague 2004)

Rubino-Sammartano, M *International Arbitration Law* (2nd edn, Kluwer Law International, The Hague 2001)

Schreuer, CH *The ICSID Convention: A Commentary* (Cambridge University Press, Cambridge 2001)

Schwarzenberger, G *Foreign Investments and International Law* (Stevens & Sons, London 1969)

Shany, Y *The Competing Jurisdictions of International Courts and Tribunals* (Oxford University Press, Oxford 2003)

Shaw, M *International Law* (5th edn, Cambridge University Press, Cambridge 2003)

Sornarajah, M *The International Law on Foreign Investment* (2nd edn, Cambridge University Press, Cambridge 2004)

Weiler, T (ed) *International Investment Law and Arbitration; Leading Cases from the ICSID, NAFTA, Bilateral Treaties and Customary International Law* (Cameron May, London 2005)

Whiteman, MM *Damages in International Law* (US Government Printing Office, Washington DC 1943)

Wilson, R *The International Law Standard in Treaties of the United States* (Harvard University Press, Cambridge 1953)

OFFICIAL REPORTS

International Law Commission 'Draft Articles on Most-Favoured-Nation Clauses' [1978] 2(2) YB ILC 6